SITE DETAILS

Other titles in the
ARCHITECTURAL GRAPHIC STANDARDS Series:

Charles George Ramsey and Harold Reeve Sleeper, edited by
John Ray Hoke, Jr., FAIA
ARCHITECTURAL GRAPHIC STANDARDS, EIGHTH EDITION

Charles George Ramsey and Harold Reeve Sleeper, edited by
Robert T. Packard, AIA, and Stephen A. Kliment, FAIA
ARCHITECTURAL GRAPHIC STANDARDS, STUDENT EDITION

Charles George Ramsey and Harold Reeve Sleeper, edited by
James Ambrose
**RESIDENTIAL AND LIGHT CONSTRUCTION FROM ARCHITECTURAL GRAPHIC
STANDARDS, EIGHTH EDITION**

Charles George Ramsey and Harold Reeve Sleeper, edited by
James Ambrose
**CONSTRUCTION DETAILS FROM ARCHITECTURAL GRAPHIC STANDARDS, EIGHTH
EDITION**

Charles George Ramsey and Harold Reeve Sleeper
ARCHITECTURAL GRAPHIC STANDARDS, FIRST EDITION FACSIMILE

Charles George Ramsey and Harold Reeve Sleeper, edited by
John Belle, FAIA, RIBA, John Ray Hoke, Jr., FAIA and Stephen A. Kliment, FAIA
**TRADITIONAL DETAILS FOR BUILDING RESTORATION, RENOVATION, AND
REHABILITATION**

Ramsey/Sleeper

SITE DETAILS

from
ARCHITECTURAL GRAPHIC STANDARDS
Eighth Edition

Edited by
JAMES AMBROSE

THE AMERICAN INSTITUTE OF ARCHITECTS

John Wiley & Sons, Inc.
New York / Chichester / Brisbane / Toronto / Singapore

In recognition of the importance of preserving what has been
written, it is a policy of John Wiley & Sons, Inc., to have books
of enduring value published in the United States printed on
acid-free paper, and we exert our best efforts to that end.

Library of Congress Cataloging in Publication Data:

Ramsey, Charles George, 1884–1963.
    Site details from Architectural graphic standards, eighth edition
Ramsey/Sleeper; edited by James Ambrose.
        p. cm.
    "The American Institute of Architects."
    Abridgement of 8th ed. of Architectural graphic standards designed
to provide a concise reference for site details.
    Includes bibliographical references and index.
    ISBN 0-471-57060-5
    1. Building—Details—Drawings. 2. Building sites. I. Sleeper,
Harold Reeve, 1893–1960. II. Ambrose, James E. III. Ramsey,
Charles George, 1884–1963. Architectural graphic standards.
IV. American Institute of Architects. V. Title. VI. Title:
Ramsey/Sleeper site details from Architectural graphic standards,
eighth edition.
TH2031.A84 1992
721'.022'2—dc20   91-43622
                                                            CIP

Printed and bound in the United States of America by Braun-Brumfield, Inc.

10 9 8 7 6 5 4 3 2 1

CONTENTS

1 GENERAL PLANNING
AND DESIGN DATA   1

2 SITE PLANNING   23

3 LANDSCAPING   61

4 MATERIALS AND SYSTEMS
FOR CONSTRUCTION   77

5 SITE CONSTRUCTION   115

6 SITE UTILITIES AND SERVICES   177

7 SPORTS   195

8 MISCELLANEOUS DATA   237

9 HISTORIC CONSTRUCTION   249

GENERAL REFERENCES   311

INDEX   313

PUBLISHER'S NOTE

Through eight editions spanning nearly 60 years, *Architectural Graphic Standards* has become *the* benchmark reference for the building design and construction professions. Originally the work of two authors, Charles Ramsey and Harold Sleeper, over the years *Architectural Graphic Standards* has continued to grow through the collaborative efforts of many publishing professionals both at Wiley and, since 1964, the American Institute of Architects.

This new volume on building site details is a continuation of our effort to provide the essential information from *Architectural Graphic Standards*, in the format most suitable for the user's needs. The success of the earlier abridgements, *Residential and Light Construction* and *Construction Details*, has shown us that *Architectural Graphic Standards* can continue to provide important and up-to-date information for the design community. This new volume provides basic information for the professional who specializes in design and construction for building sites.

Again the product of Wiley's long-time collaboration with the AIA, this volume is also the result of the expert editorial guidance of James Ambrose. In his 30 years as an educator, editor, and author, James Ambrose has consistently brought intelligence, insight, and clarity to the communication of complex technical information. His experience as the editor of the Parker/Ambrose series of *Simplified Design Guides,* and as author of his own books on structural design topics, makes Jim an expert in assessing the specific needs of the small-scale construction professional.

Building on the example of excellence set by Ramsey and Sleeper, John Wiley and the AIA will continue to serve the design and construction professions with the best in graphic information and design details. We trust that you will use this book with confidence.

KENNETH R. GESSER
Publisher
Professional, Reference, and Trade Group
John Wiley & Sons, Inc.

PREFACE

This abridged edition of the 8th edition of *Architectural Graphic Standards* has been developed to provide a special reference for persons with major interest in design and construction for building sites. The purpose of this book is to provide a more concise reference of somewhat limited scope, generally suitable and adequate for the work of the many people who deal primarily with issues related to the design and development of building sites. This group includes landscape architects, city planners, and civil engineers who deal with design work of various kinds related to the exterior spaces of sites. The book should also be useful for contractors and product manufacturers or suppliers who deal in this field.

Included here are all the materials in the 8th edition that may apply to site work, not only consisting of site-specific materials, but also topics such as wood, concrete, masonry, and some other basic construction materials or processes that apply to site work. To help extend the usefulness of the book, a list of available sources of information is given at the end of each chapter, concentrated on the most authoritative sources and those likely to be actually available to individuals not having major library resources at their disposal. A list of general references—relating to the general topic of the book—is provided in the Reference section at the back of the book.

Site work in developed areas frequently involves the removal, restoration, or remodeling of existing con-struction. Familiarity with construction materials and methods of the recent past is thus vital to persons engaged in design or construction work for sites. To provide some assistance in this area, selected pages from two books are provided at the back of this book. Materials included come from the 3rd edition of *Architectural Graphic Standards*, published in 1941, and from *Data Book for Civil Engineers: Design*, by Elwyn E. Seelye, published in 1945. These two books provide many details of forms of construction used extensively in the United States in the early and middle parts of this century.

This partial presentation of materials from the Ramsey and Sleeper book follows on other recent publications that have sought to extend the rich resource of this book, which has been in continuous publication since 1932, through eight editions. The 8th edition of *Architectural Graphic Standards* is an extensive and rich source of reference materials; it is well worth the investment for persons with broader scopes of concerns. Duplicating the contents of the 8th edition with a collection of other publications would assuredly cost the buyer several times over the price of the single volume. This book does not pretend to replace the 8th edition; it merely extends access to a special group of users whose interests are considerably limited.

I must acknowledge the contributions of the many individuals and organizations who contributed to the development of the 8th edition. Developers of individual book pages are listed at the bottoms of the pages, and the many organizations providing book materials are listed in the reference sections at the ends of individual chapters.

I must also acknowledge the contributions of the many generations of people—beginning with George Ramsey and Harold Sleeper—who made inputs to the development and continuation of this work over the almost 60 years of its publication. This includes the many authors, graphic artists, and editors, as well as the many people at the American Institute of Architects and John Wiley & Sons who worked on the several editions of the book.

For this book I am grateful for the contributions and support of my editor, Everett Smethurst, my publisher, Kenneth R. Gesser, and the many other editors, marketing, and production personnel at John Wiley & Sons, especially Robert J. Fletcher and Joseph Keenan.

I am also grateful for the support and direct assistance of my wife, Peggy, who did most of the work of redeveloping the extensive index—a major component of this book.

JAMES AMBROSE
Westlake Village, California
December, 1991

CHAPTER 1

GENERAL PLANNING AND DESIGN DATA

ANTHROPOMETRIC	2
THEATER DESIGN	5
LIFE CYCLE COSTING	7
SIGNS	9
SUN CONTROL	12
EARTH SHELTERS	20
PAVING AND SURFACING	21

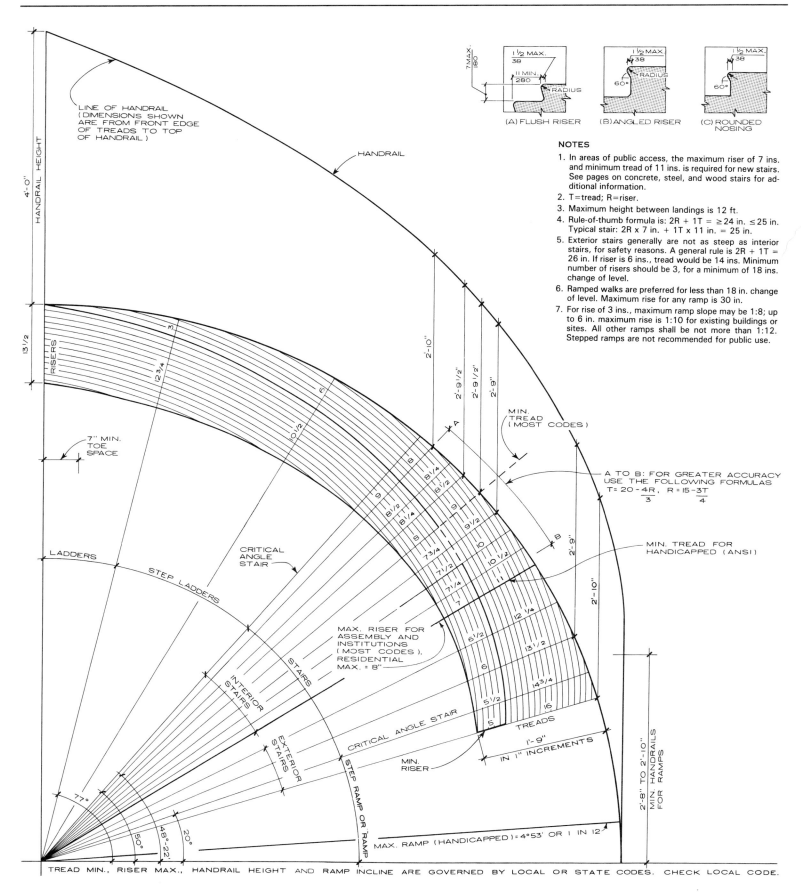

(A) FLUSH RISER   (B) ANGLED RISER   (C) ROUNDED NOSING

NOTES

1. In areas of public access, the maximum riser of 7 ins. and minimum tread of 11 ins. is required for new stairs. See pages on concrete, steel, and wood stairs for additional information.
2. T=tread; R=riser.
3. Maximum height between landings is 12 ft.
4. Rule-of-thumb formula is: 2R + 1T = ≥ 24 in. ≤ 25 in. Typical stair: 2R x 7 in. + 1T x 11 in. = 25 in.
5. Exterior stairs generally are not as steep as interior stairs, for safety reasons. A general rule is 2R + 1T = 26 in. If riser is 6 ins., tread would be 14 ins. Minimum number of risers should be 3, for a minimum of 18 ins. change of level.
6. Ramped walks are preferred for less than 18 in. change of level. Maximum rise for any ramp is 30 in.
7. For rise of 3 ins., maximum ramp slope may be 1:8; up to 6 in. maximum rise is 1:10 for existing buildings or sites. All other ramps shall be not more than 1:12. Stepped ramps are not recommended for public use.

A TO B: FOR GREATER ACCURACY USE THE FOLLOWING FORMULAS

$$T = \frac{20 - 4R}{3}, \quad R = \frac{15 - 3T}{4}$$

LINE OF HANDRAIL (DIMENSIONS SHOWN ARE FROM FRONT EDGE OF TREADS TO TOP OF HANDRAIL)

HANDRAIL

HANDRAIL HEIGHT

4'-0"

13 1/2

RISERS

7" MIN. TOE SPACE

LADDERS

STEP LADDERS

CRITICAL ANGLE STAIR

INTERIOR STAIRS

STAIRS

EXTERIOR STAIRS

CRITICAL ANGLE STAIR

MAX. RISER FOR ASSEMBLY AND INSTITUTIONS (MOST CODES). RESIDENTIAL MAX. = 8"

MIN. RISER

STEP RAMP OR RAMP

MIN. TREAD (MOST CODES)

MIN. TREAD FOR HANDICAPPED (ANSI)

TREADS

1'-9" IN 1" INCREMENTS

MIN. HANDRAILS FOR RAMPS

2'-8" TO 2'-10"

MAX. RAMP (HANDICAPPED) = 4°53' OR 1 IN 12

77°   50°   48°22'   20°

TREAD MIN., RISER MAX., HANDRAIL HEIGHT AND RAMP INCLINE ARE GOVERNED BY LOCAL OR STATE CODES. CHECK LOCAL CODE.

TREADS AND RISERS

Paul Vaughan, AIA; Charleston, West Virginia

1   **ANTHROPOMETRIC**

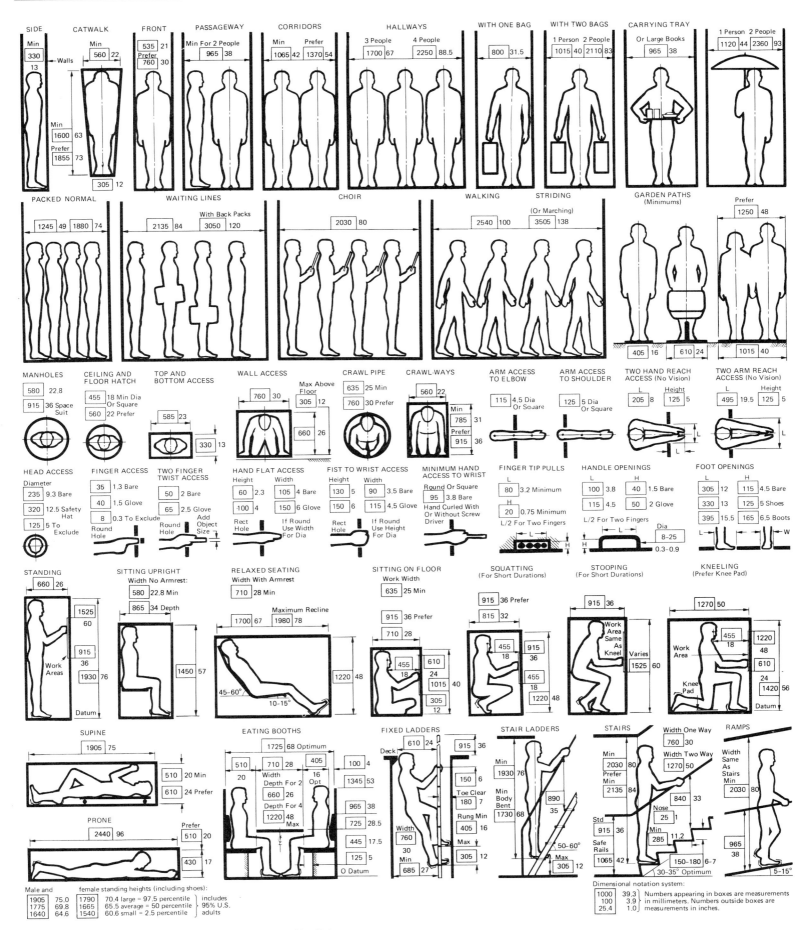

SIDE   **CATWALK**   **FRONT**   **PASSAGEWAY**   **CORRIDORS**   **HALLWAYS**   **WITH ONE BAG**   **WITH TWO BAGS**   **CARRYING TRAY** Or Large Books

Min 330 | 13 — Walls
Min 560 | 22
535 | 21
Prefer 760 | 30
Min For 2 People 965 | 38
Min 1065 | 42   Prefer 1370 | 54
3 People 1700 | 67   4 People 2250 | 88.5
800 | 31.5
1 Person 1015 | 40   2 People 2110 | 83
965 | 38
1 Person 1120 | 44   2 People 2360 | 93
Min 1600 | 63   Prefer 1855 | 73
305 | 12

PACKED NORMAL   **WAITING LINES**   **CHOIR**   **WALKING**   **STRIDING**   **GARDEN PATHS** (Minimums)

1245 | 49   1880 | 74
2135 | 84   With Back Packs 3050 | 120
2030 | 80
2540 | 100
(Or Marching) 3505 | 138
Prefer 1250 | 48
405 | 16   610 | 24   1015 | 40

MANHOLES   **CEILING AND FLOOR HATCH**   **TOP AND BOTTOM ACCESS**   **WALL ACCESS**   **CRAWL PIPE**   **CRAWL-WAYS**   **ARM ACCESS TO ELBOW**   **ARM ACCESS TO SHOULDER**   **TWO HAND REACH ACCESS (No Vision)**   **TWO ARM REACH ACCESS (No Vision)**

580 | 22.8
915 | 36 Space Suit
455 | 18 Min Dia Or Square
560 | 22 Prefer
585 | 23
330 | 13
Max Above Floor 760 | 30   305 | 12   660 | 26
635 | 25 Min
760 | 30 Prefer
560 | 22   Min 785 | 31   Prefer 915 | 36
115 | 4.5 Dia Or Square
125 | 5 Dia Or Square
L 205 | 8   Height 125 | 5
L 495 | 19.5   Height 125 | 5

HEAD ACCESS   **FINGER ACCESS**   **TWO FINGER TWIST ACCESS**   **HAND FLAT ACCESS**   **FIST TO WRIST ACCESS**   **MINIMUM HAND ACCESS TO WRIST**   **FINGER TIP PULLS**   **HANDLE OPENINGS**   **FOOT OPENINGS**

Diameter 235 | 9.3 Bare   320 | 12.5 Safety Hat   125 | 5 To Exclude
35 | 1.3 Bare   40 | 1.5 Glove   8 | 0.3 To Exclude   Round Hole
50 | 2 Bare   65 | 2.5 Glove   Round Hole   Add Object Size
Height 60 | 2.3   Width 105 | 4 Bare   100 | 4   150 | 6 Glove   Rect Hole   If Round Use Width For Dia
Height 130 | 5   Width 90 | 3.5 Bare   150 | 6   115 | 4.5 Glove   Rect Hole   If Round Use Height For Dia
Round Or Square 95 | 3.8 Bare   Hand Curled With Or Without Screw Driver
L 80 | 3.2 Minimum   L 20 | 0.75 Minimum   L/2 For Two Fingers
L 100 | 3.8   L 115 | 4.5   H 40 | 1.5 Bare   H 50 | 2 Glove   L/2 For Two Fingers   Dia 8-25 | 0.3-0.9
L 305 | 12   H 115 | 4.5 Bare   L 330 | 13   H 125 | 5 Shoes   L 395 | 15.5   H 165 | 6.5 Boots

STANDING   **SITTING UPRIGHT**   **RELAXED SEATING**   **SITTING ON FLOOR**   **SQUATTING** (For Short Durations)   **STOOPING** (For Short Durations)   **KNEELING** (Prefer Knee Pad)

660 | 26
1525 | 60   915 | 36   Work Areas   1930 | 76   Datum
Width No Armrest: 580 | 22.8 Min   865 | 34 Depth   1450 | 57
Width With Armrest 710 | 28 Min   Maximum Recline 1700 | 67   1980 | 78   1220 | 48   45-60°   10-15°
Work Width 635 | 25 Min   915 | 36 Prefer   710 | 28   455 | 18   610 | 24   1015 | 40   305 | 12
915 | 36 Prefer   815 | 32   455 | 18   915 | 36   455 | 18   1220 | 48
915 | 36   Work Area Same As Kneel   Varies 1525 | 60
1270 | 50   Work Area   455 | 18   1220 | 48   610 | 24   Knee Pad   1420 | 56   Datum

SUPINE   **EATING BOOTHS**   **FIXED LADDERS**   **STAIR LADDERS**   **STAIRS**   **RAMPS**

1905 | 75   510 | 20 Min   610 | 24 Prefer
PRONE 2440 | 96   Prefer 510 | 20   430 | 17
1725 | 68 Optimum   510 | 20   710 | 28   405 | 16   100 | 4   16 Opt   Width Depth For 2   660 | 26   Depth For 4   1220 | 48 Max   1345 | 53   965 | 38   725 | 28.5   445 | 17.5   125 | 5
Deck 610 | 24   915 | 36   150 | 6   Toe Clear 180 | 7   Rung Min 405 | 16   Width 760 | 30 Min   Max 305 | 12   O Datum   685 | 27
Min 1930 | 76   Min Body Bent 1730 | 68   890 | 35   50-60°   Max 305 | 12
Min 2030 | 80   Prefer Min 2135 | 84   Width One Way 760 | 30   Width Two Way 1270 | 50   840 | 33   Nose 25 | 1   Std 915 | 36   Min 285 | 11.2   Safe Rails 1065 | 42   150-180 | 6-7   30-35° Optimum
Width Same As Stairs Min 2030 | 80   965 | 38   5-15°

Male and female standing heights (including shoes):

1905	75.0	1790	70.4 large = 97.5 percentile	includes
1775	69.8	1665	65.5 average = 50 percentile	95% U.S.
1640	64.6	1540	60.6 small = 2.5 percentile	adults

Dimensional notation system:

1000	39.3	Numbers appearing in boxes are measurements
100	3.9	in millimeters. Numbers outside boxes are
25.4	1.0	measurements in inches.

Niels Diffrient, Alvin R. Tilley; Henry Dreyfuss Associates; New York, New York

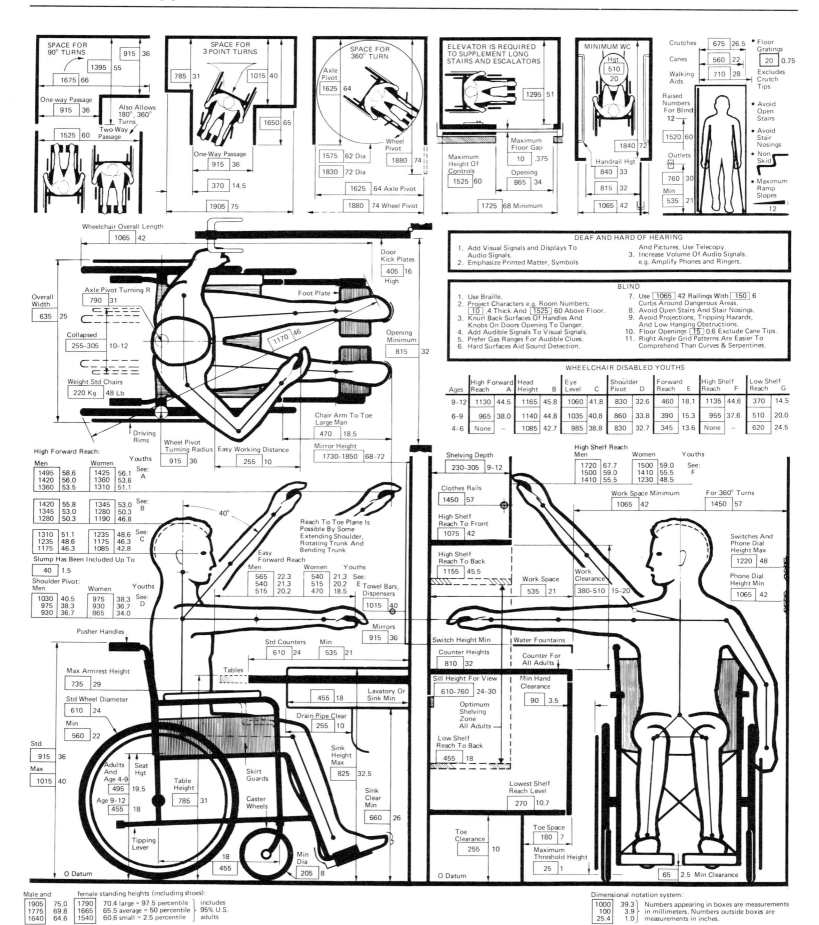

Niels Diffrient, Alvin R. Tilley; Henry Dreyfuss Associates; New York, New York

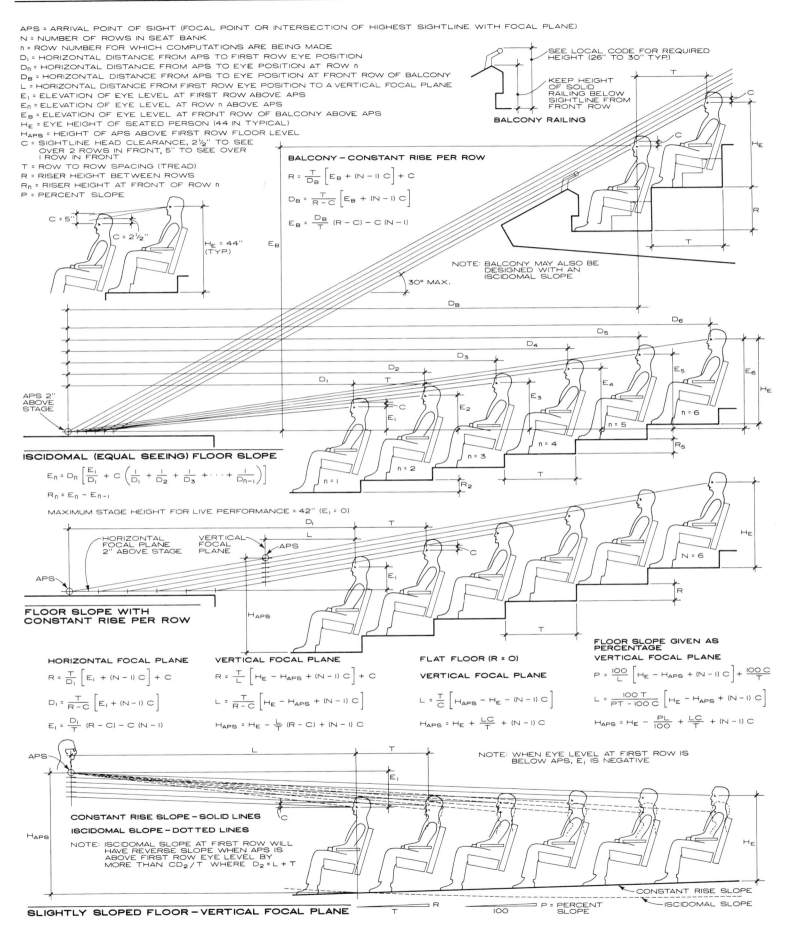

Peter H. Frink; Frink and Beuchat: Architects; Philadelphia, Pennsylvania

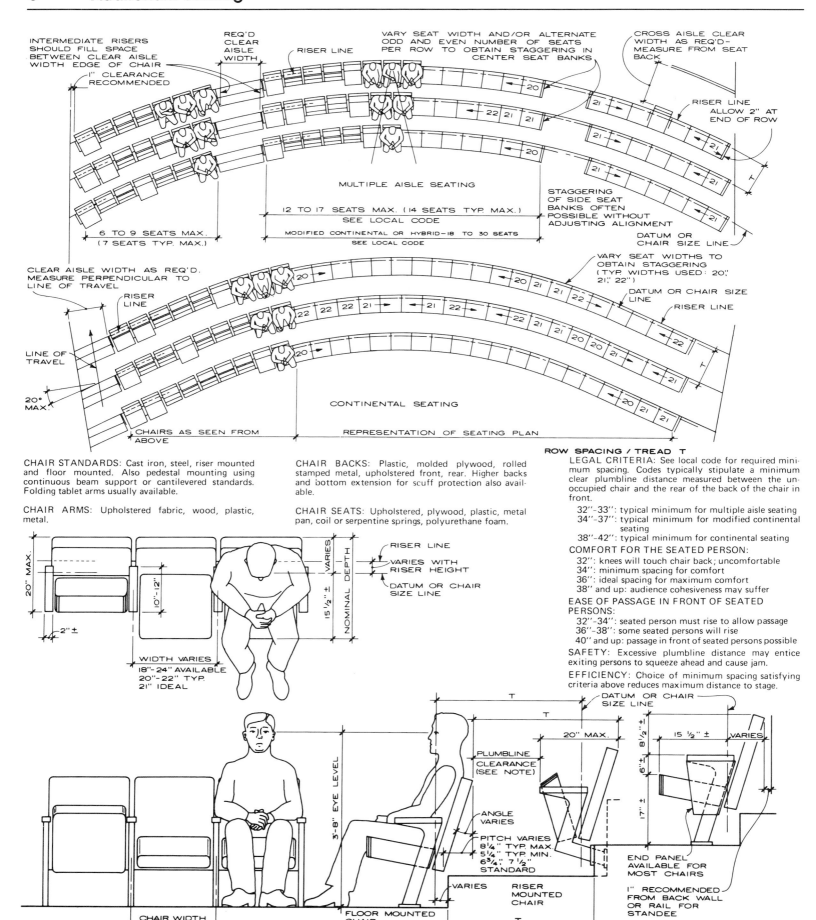

INTERMEDIATE RISERS SHOULD FILL SPACE BETWEEN CLEAR AISLE WIDTH EDGE OF CHAIR — 1" CLEARANCE RECOMMENDED

REQ'D CLEAR AISLE WIDTH

RISER LINE

VARY SEAT WIDTH AND/OR ALTERNATE ODD AND EVEN NUMBER OF SEATS PER ROW TO OBTAIN STAGGERING IN CENTER SEAT BANKS

CROSS AISLE CLEAR WIDTH AS REQ'D- MEASURE FROM SEAT BACK

RISER LINE ALLOW 2" AT END OF ROW

STAGGERING OF SIDE SEAT BANKS OFTEN POSSIBLE WITHOUT ADJUSTING ALIGNMENT

DATUM OR CHAIR SIZE LINE

MULTIPLE AISLE SEATING

12 TO 17 SEATS MAX. (14 SEATS TYP. MAX.) SEE LOCAL CODE

MODIFIED CONTINENTAL OR HYBRID–18 TO 30 SEATS SEE LOCAL CODE

6 TO 9 SEATS MAX. (7 SEATS TYP. MAX.)

CLEAR AISLE WIDTH AS REQ'D. MEASURE PERPENDICULAR TO LINE OF TRAVEL

RISER LINE

LINE OF TRAVEL

20° MAX.

CHAIRS AS SEEN FROM ABOVE

VARY SEAT WIDTHS TO OBTAIN STAGGERING (TYP. WIDTHS USED: 20", 21", 22")

DATUM OR CHAIR SIZE LINE

RISER LINE

CONTINENTAL SEATING

REPRESENTATION OF SEATING PLAN

ROW SPACING / TREAD T

CHAIR STANDARDS: Cast iron, steel, riser mounted and floor mounted. Also pedestal mounting using continuous beam support or cantilevered standards. Folding tablet arms usually available.

CHAIR ARMS: Upholstered fabric, wood, plastic, metal.

CHAIR BACKS: Plastic, molded plywood, rolled stamped metal, upholstered front, rear. Higher backs and bottom extension for scuff protection also available.

CHAIR SEATS: Upholstered, plywood, plastic, metal pan, coil or serpentine springs, polyurethane foam.

LEGAL CRITERIA: See local code for required minimum spacing. Codes typically stipulate a minimum clear plumbline distance measured between the unoccupied chair and the rear of the back of the chair in front.

32"–33": typical minimum for multiple aisle seating
34"–37": typical minimum for modified continental seating
38"–42": typical minimum for continental seating

COMFORT FOR THE SEATED PERSON:
32": knees will touch chair back; uncomfortable
34": minimum spacing for comfort
36": ideal spacing for maximum comfort
38" and up: audience cohesiveness may suffer

EASE OF PASSAGE IN FRONT OF SEATED PERSONS:
32"–34": seated person must rise to allow passage
36"–38": some seated persons will rise
40" and up: passage in front of seated persons possible

SAFETY: Excessive plumbline distance may entice exiting persons to squeeze ahead and cause jam.

EFFICIENCY: Choice of minimum spacing satisfying criteria above reduces maximum distance to stage.

20" MAX.

10"–12"

2" ±

WIDTH VARIES
18"–24" AVAILABLE
20"–22" TYP.
21" IDEAL

RISER LINE

VARIES WITH RISER HEIGHT

DATUM OR CHAIR SIZE LINE

VARIES

15½" ± NOMINAL DEPTH

3'-8" EYE LEVEL

CHAIR WIDTH

FLOOR MOUNTED CHAIR

PLUMBLINE CLEARANCE (SEE NOTE)

ANGLE VARIES

PITCH VARIES 8¼" TYP. MAX. 5¼" TYP. MIN. 6¾" 7½" STANDARD

VARIES

RISER MOUNTED CHAIR

T

T

20" MAX.

DATUM OR CHAIR SIZE LINE

8½" ±

15½" ±   VARIES

6" ±

17" ±

END PANEL AVAILABLE FOR MOST CHAIRS

1" RECOMMENDED FROM BACK WALL OR RAIL FOR STANDEE

Peter H. Frink; Frink and Beuchat: Architects; Philadelphia, Pennsylvania

1 **THEATER DESIGN**

GENERAL

Life cycle costing (LCC) is a method for evaluating all relevant costs over time of alternative building designs, systems, components, materials, or practices. The LCC method takes into account first costs, including the costs of planning, design, purchase, and installation; future costs, including costs of fuel, operation, maintenance, repair, and replacement; and any salvage value recovered during or at the end of the time period examined. These costs are displayed in the adjacent charts.

TIME ADJUSTMENTS

Adjustments to place all dollar values on a comparable time basis are necessary for valid assessment of a project's life cycle costs. The time adjustment is necessary because receiving or expending a dollar in the future is not the same as receiving or expending a dollar today. One reason for this "time value of money" is that the purchasing power of money may fall over time because of inflation. To ensure that all of a building's costs are expressed in dollars of equal purchasing power, they should be stated in "constant dollars," that is, with purely inflationary effects not included. Another reason for the "time value of money" is that money in hand may be invested productively to earn a return over time. Both inflation and the productive earning potential of resources in hand cause an investor usually to prefer to delay payments of costs or debts and to hasten receipts. The adjustment for time related earning potential can be accomplished by converting all costs to "present values," as though they were all to be incurred today, or to "annual values," as though they were all spread out over a given time in even, annual installments including the cost of money. This time adjustment, often called "discounting cash flows," is accomplished by using "discount formulas" or by multiplying dollar amounts by special "discount factors" calculated from the formulas. The most frequently used discount formulas for evaluating building projects are described below, where the following notation is used:

P = present value
F = future value
A = annual value
D = discount rate
N = number of periods
E = price escalation rate

SINGLE PRESENT WORTH

The single present worth (SPW) formula is used to find the present value of a future amount, such as the value today of a future replacement cost.

SPW (single present worth) $P = F(1 + D)^{-N}$

UNIFORM PRESENT WORTH

The uniform present worth (UPW) formula is used to find the present value of a series of uniform annual amounts, such as the value today of the costs of future yearly routine maintenance.

UPW (uniform present worth) $P = A \left[\frac{(1 + D)^N - 1}{D(1 + D)^N} \right]$

UNIFORM PRESENT WORTH— MODIFIED

A modified version of the uniform present worth formula (here designated UPW*) is used to find the present value of an initial amount escalating at a constant annual rate, such as the value today of future yearly energy costs, when energy prices are expected to escalate at a given rate.

UPW* (uniform present worth—modified)

$$P = A \left[\frac{1 + E}{D - E} \right] \left[1 - \left[\frac{1 + E}{1 + D} \right]^N \right]$$

UNIFORM SINKING FUND

The uniform sinking fund (USF) formula is used to find the annual amount that must be accumulated to yield a given future amount, such as how much money must be set aside each year at interest in order to cover expected future replacement costs.

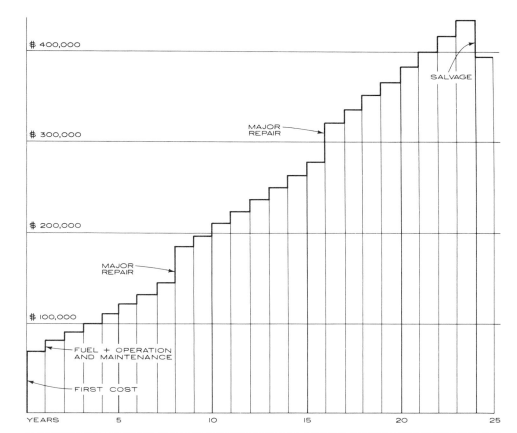

CUMULATIVE COSTS

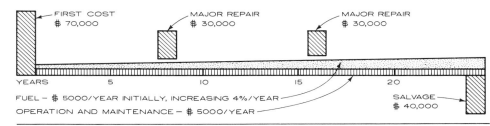

YEARLY COSTS

USF (uniform sinking fund) $A = F \left[\frac{D}{(1 + D)^N - 1} \right]$

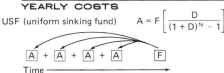

UNIFORM CAPITAL RECOVERY

The uniform capital recovery (UCR) formula is used to find the annual value of a present value amount, such as how much it would be necessary to pay each year in order to pay off a loan made today at a given rate of interest for a given period of time.

UCR (uniform capital recovery) $A = P \left[\frac{D(1 + D)^N}{(1 + D)^N - 1} \right]$

NOTE

The discount factors for each of these discounting formulas have been precalculated for a range of discount rates and time periods and put into tables to facilitate their use. These tables can be found in most engineering economics textbooks. A table of discount factors for a 10% discount rate is shown opposite.

LIFE CYCLE COST FORMULA

To find the total life cycle cost of a project, sum the present values (or, alternatively, the annual values) of each kind of cost and subtract the present values (or annual values) of any positive cash flows such as salvage values. Thus, where all dollar amounts are adjusted by discounting either present values or annual values, the following formula applies:

LCC (life cycle cost formula)

Life cycle cost = first costs + maintenance and repair
+ energy + replacement − salvage value

APPLICATIONS

Alternative projects may be compared by computing the life cycle costs for each project using the formula above and seeing which is lower.

The LCC method can be applied to many different kinds of building problems. For example, it can be used to compare the long run costs of one building design to another; to determine the expected dollar savings of retrofitting a building for energy conservation or the least expensive way of reaching a targeted energy budget for a building; to select the most economical floor coverings and furnishings; and to determine the optimal size of a solar energy system.

In addition to the life cycle formula shown above, there are other closely related ways of combining present or annual values to measure a project's economic performance over time, such as the net savings technique, savings-to-investment ratio technique, internal rate of return technique, and discounted time to payback technique.

Harold E. Marshall and Rosalie Ruegg, Economists; Porter Driscoll, AIA, Architect; Center for Building Technology, National Bureau of Standards; United States of America

SAMPLE LCC PROBLEM

Determine present value of costs occurring during the life of a component so that they can be compared with the costs of an alternative component to serve the same purpose. Cumulative and yearly costs are indicated on the charts of the preceding page.

ASSUMPTIONS

Time horizon	25 years
Discount rate	10%
Fuel price increases in excess of inflation	4%
First cost of component	$70,000
Repairs to component at 8th and 16th years	$30,000/repair
Operations and maintenance (constant dollars)	$ 5,000/year
Annual cost of fuel at onset	$ 5,000

NOTE: When financing costs and tax effects are relevant they should be incorporated into LCC analysis.

SOLUTION

1. Establish present value of equipment. Convert all equipment costs (first cost, two major repair costs, and salvage value) to present value. Since the first cost occurs in the present, no change is made to the $70,000 sum.

   The first major repair, estimated to occur 8 years in the future, is discounted at the rate of 10% back to the present using the SPW factor (see Discount Factor Chart, column 2) for 8 years at 10%, 0.4665. Therefore, PV = $30,000 x 0.4665 = $13,995. This present value is added to the $70,000 first cost as shown in the Present Value of Equipment Chart.

   The second major repair is discounted 16 years back to the present in a similar manner. The SPW factor for 16 years at 10% = 0.2176. Therefore, PV = $30,000 x 0.2176 = $6528. This amount is also added to the present value in the chart.

   The $40,000 to be realized from salvage at the end of the 25 year period is discounted back to the present in the same manner. The SPW factor for 25 years, at 10% = 0.0923. Therefore, PV = $40,000 x 0.0923 = $3692. Since this sum is income, not expense, it must be subtracted from the sum of the other present values as indicated.

   Thus the present value of equipment is determined to be $86,832.

2. Establish present value of operation and maintenance costs and fuel costs. Operation and maintenance costs are estimated to be equal amounts that occur yearly during the period and are converted to present value using the UPW factor (column 3) for 25 years at 10%, 9.0770. Therefore, PV = $5000 x 9.0770 = $45,385. This amount is added to the present value of equipment as shown in the Total Present Value Chart.

   Annual fuel costs are estimated to be $5000 based on the initial price of fuel which is projected to increase at the rate of 4% per year. These costs are converted to present value using the modified UPW* factor (column 4) for 25 years at 10%, 13.0686. Therefore, PV = $5000 x 13.0686 = $65,343.

   This amount is also added to the present values of equipment and operation and maintenance costs as shown in the Total Present Value Chart.

3. Total life cycle cost in present value is the sum of the present value of equipment, operation, and maintenance and fuel costs which equals $197,559. The equipment, operation, and maintenance and fuel costs of other components to serve the same purpose can be compared to these figures to determine the best economic value.

REFERENCES

1. Gerald W. Smith, Engineering Economy: Analysis of Capital Expenditures, Iowa State University Press, Ames, Iowa, 1973.
2. Donald Watson, ed., Energy Conservation through Building Design, "Life-cycle Costing Guide for Energy Conservation in Buildings" chapter by Harold E. Marshall and Rosalie T. Ruegg, McGraw-Hill, New York, 1979.
3. Simplified Energy Design Economics, NBS special publication 544, Center for Building Technology, National Bureau of Standards, Washington, D.C., 1980.

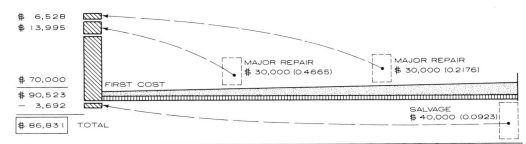

$ 6,528	
$ 13,995	
$ 70,000	FIRST COST
$ 90,523	
− 3,692	
$ 86,831	TOTAL

MAJOR REPAIR $ 30,000 (0.4665)

MAJOR REPAIR $ 30,000 (0.2176)

SALVAGE $ 40,000 (0.0923)

PRESENT VALUE OF EQUIPMENT

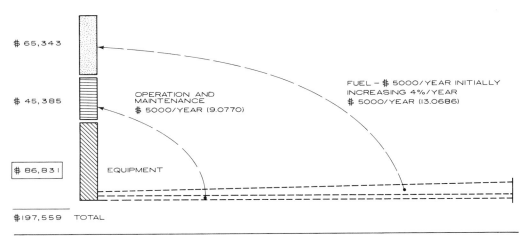

$ 65,343	
$ 45,385	
$ 86,831	EQUIPMENT

FUEL – $ 5000/YEAR INITIALLY INCREASING 4%/YEAR $ 5000/YEAR (13.0686)

OPERATION AND MAINTENANCE $ 5000/YEAR (9.0770)

$197,559	TOTAL

TOTAL PRESENT VALUE

DISCOUNT FACTORS

BASED ON 10% DISCOUNT RATE

1. YEARS	2. SPW	3. UPW	4. UPW* (4% PRICE ESCALATION)	5. USF	6. UCR
1	0.9091	0.909	0.9455	1.000 00	1.100 00
2	0.8264	1.736	1.8393	0.476 19	0.576 19
3	0.7513	2.487	2.6844	0.302 11	0.402 11
4	0.6830	3.170	3.4834	0.215 47	0.315 47
5	0.6209	3.791	4.2388	0.163 80	0.263 80
6	0.5645	4.355	4.9531	0.129 61	0.229 61
7	0.5132	4.868	5.6284	0.105 41	0.205 41
8	0.4665	5.335	6.2669	0.087 44	0.187 44
9	0.4241	5.759	6.8705	0.073 64	0.173 64
10	0.3855	6.144	7.4411	0.062 75	0.162 75
11	0.3505	6.495	7.9807	0.053 96	0.153 96
12	0.3186	6.814	8.4909	0.046 76	0.146 76
13	0.2897	7.103	8.9733	0.040 78	0.140 78
14	0.2633	7.367	9.4293	0.035 75	0.135 75
15	0.2394	7.606	9.8604	0.031 47	0.131 47
16	0.2176	7.824	10.2680	0.027 82	0.127 82
17	0.1978	8.022	10.6535	0.024 66	0.124 66
18	0.1799	8.201	11.0177	0.021 93	0.121 93
19	0.1635	8.365	11.3622	0.019 55	0.119 55
20	0.1486	8.514	11.6878	0.017 46	0.117 46
21	0.1351	8.649	11.9957	0.015 62	0.115 62
22	0.1228	8.772	12.2870	0.014 01	0.144 01
23	0.1117	8.883	12.5623	0.012 57	0.112 57
24	0.1015	8.985	12.8225	0.011 30	0.111 30
25	0.0923	9.077	13.0686	0.010 17	0.110 17

Harold E. Marshall and Rosalie Ruegg, Economists; Porter Driscoll, AIA, Architect; Center for Building Technology, National Bureau of Standards; United States of America

VEHICULAR CONSIDERATIONS

There are strong differences between the perceptual performance of the driver and that of the pedestrian. Increasing speed imposes five limitations on man:

1. MAN'S CONCENTRATION INCREASES: While stationary or walking, a person's attention may be widely dispersed. When moving in an automobile, however, he or she concentrates on those factors that are relevant to the driving experience.

2. THE POINT OF CONCENTRATION RECEDES: As speed or motion increases, a person's concentration is directed at a focal point increasingly farther away.

3. PERIPHERAL VISION DIMINISHES: As the eye concentrates on detail at a point of focus a great distance ahead, the angular field of vision shrinks. This shrinking process is a function of focusing distance, angle of vision, and distance of foreground detail.

4. FOREGROUND DETAIL FADES INCREASINGLY: While concentrating on more significant distant objects, a person perceives foreground objects to be moving and increasingly blurred.

5. SPACE PERCEPTION BECOMES IMPAIRED: As the time available for perceiving objects decreases, specific details become less noticeable, making spatial perception more difficult.

With an increasing rate of motion, it becomes more and more important that copy, including illustrations and symbols, be created specifically for out-of-doors use and not merely rescaled from other media of communication. The safety of the motorist and passengers can depend on the clarity of messages conveyed by signs.

VEHICLE SPEEDS VERSUS LETTER HEIGHT ON TRAFFIC SIGNS

INITIAL SPEED	DISTANCE TRAVELED WHILE READING	DISTANCE TRAVELED WHILE SLOWING	TOTAL DISTANCE	SIZE OF COPY AT 65 FT/IN.
30 mph	110 ft	200 ft	310 ft	4.8 in.
40 mph	147 ft	307 ft	454 ft	7.0 in.
50 mph	183 ft	360 ft	543 ft	8.4 in.
60 mph	220 ft	390 ft	610 ft	9.4 in.

NOTE: It is recommended that street name signs have 4 in. letters in area where vehicle speeds are 30–35 mph. For speeds of 40 mph and over, a 5 in. letter size is recommended.

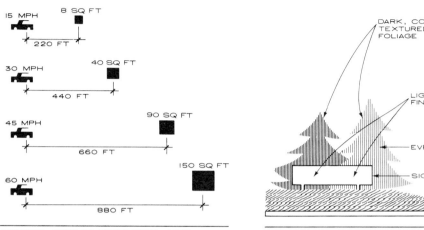

SPEED, SIGHT DISTANCE AND GRAPHIC SIZE RELATIONSHIPS

NOTE: LETTERS SHOULD CONSTITUTE APPROXIMATELY 40% OF GRAPHIC'S AREA

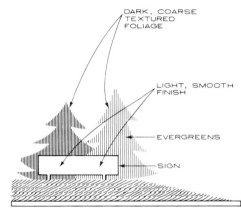

CONSIDER BACKGROUND WHEN CHOOSING COLOR AND MATERIALS

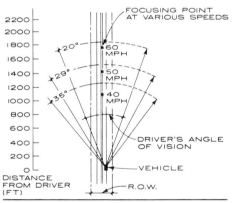

RELATIONSHIP BETWEEN DRIVER'S FOCUSING POINT AND ANGLE OF VISION DOES NOT CONSIDER EFFECT OF PRECEDING TRAFFIC

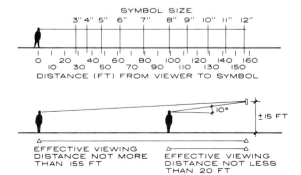

PEDESTRIAN CONSIDERATIONS

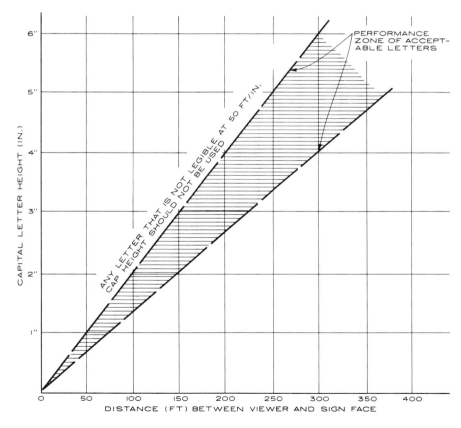

NOTE

Under normal daylight conditions, with normal vision, and an angular distortion of 0° approximately 50 ft/in. of capital height can be taken as a guideline for minimal legibility, as seen from the chart.

Johnson, Johnson & Roy, Inc.; Ann Arbor, Michigan

SYMBOLS

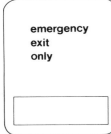
emergency
exit
only

In case of fire
do not use elevators

Use stairways

30" X 30"
RECOMMENDED SIZE

24" X 24"
RECOMMENDED SIZE

24" X 24"
RECOMMENDED SIZE

WARNING/PROHIBITORY SIGNS

PARKING
FOR
HANDICAPPED
ONLY

12" X 24"
RECOMMENDED SIZE

MEN

1
EXIT
STAIRS

12" X 12" RECOMMENDED
SIZE

12" X 18" RECOMMENDED
SIZE

HANDICAPPED

PARKING

HANDICAPPED ACCESS SIGNS

Marr Knapp Crawfis Associates, Inc.; Mansfield, Ohio
Richard J. Vitullo; Washington Grove, Maryland

 SIGNS

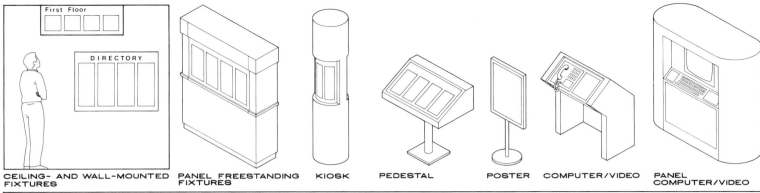

CEILING- AND WALL-MOUNTED FIXTURES **PANEL FREESTANDING FIXTURES** **KIOSK** **PEDESTAL** **POSTER** **COMPUTER/VIDEO** **PANEL COMPUTER/VIDEO**

DIRECTORIES/ORIENTATION MAPS/INFORMATION SYSTEMS

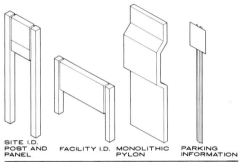

SITE I.D. POST AND PANEL   FACILITY I.D.   MONOLITHIC PYLON   PARKING INFORMATION

EXTERIOR SIGN TYPES

RIGID VINYL INSERTS   **MAGNETIC**

SLIDING   **WINDOW**

INTERIOR SIGN TYPES

GENERAL NOTES

EXTERIOR SIGNS

1. Identify entrance and exit of site and building, handicapped information, parking lot location, and facility identification.
2. Signs should be 6 ft 0 in. min. from face of curb, 7 ft 0 in. from grade to bottom of sign, and 100–200 ft from intersections.
3. Building signage materials: fabricated aluminum, illuminated plastic face, back lighted, cast aluminum, applied letter, die raised, engraved, and hot stamped.
4. Plaque and sign materials: cast bronze, cast aluminum, plastic/acrylic, stone (cornerstone), masonry, and wood.
5. For handicapped signage, designate building entrance access, identify parking areas, and direction to facilities. See ANSI 117.1 or state regulations for specific headings.

DIRECTORIES AND MAPS

1. Locate these in main entrances and/or lobbies with appropriate information for the handicapped.
2. Place directory information adjacent to "You are here" information.
3. Directories should be placed in stair/elevator lobbies of each floor.
4. Mounting choices: surface mounted, semirecessed, full recessed (flush), cantilevered, chain suspended, rigidly suspended, mechanically fastened, or track mounted.

INTERIOR SIGNS

1. Lightweight freestanding signs should not be used in high-traffic areas. Use when specific location/information maneuverability is required.
2. Electronic, computer, and videotex technologies can provide an innovative and highly flexible directory/sign display system for mapping and/or routing, information (facility and local), advertisement and messages, and management tie-in capabilities.
3. Where changeability and flexibility is a design priority, a modular system is recommended. Rigid vinyl, aluminum, and acrylic inserts as well as magnetic systems may be used.
4. For maximum ease of reading interior signs, any given line in a sign should not exceed 30 characters in width, including upper and lower case letters and spaces between words. To accommodate the visually handicapped, room numbers should be raised or accompanied with braille.
5. Choose the height and "weight" of letter styles and symbols for readability. Consider background materials and contrast when choosing a color scheme.
6. Permanent mounting:
   a. Vinyl tape/adhesive backing, usually factory applied.
   b. Silastic adhesive, usually supplied with vinyl tape strips to hold sign in place until adhesive cures.
   c. Mechanically fastened; specify hole locations.
7. Semipermanent: vinyl tape square can be used on inserts.
8. Changeable: dual-lock mating fasteners, magnets, magnetic tape, or tracks may be used.

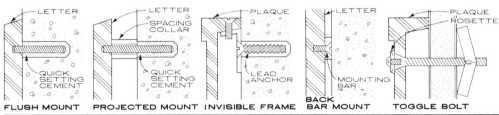

FLUSH MOUNT   **PROJECTED MOUNT**   **INVISIBLE FRAME**   **BACK BAR MOUNT**   **TOGGLE BOLT**

MOUNTING METHODS/MATERIALS

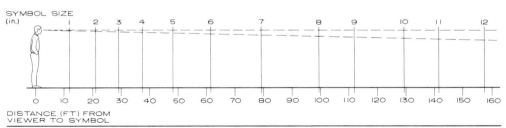

SYMBOL READABILITY

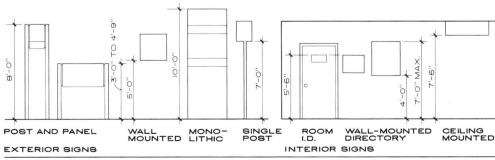

POST AND PANEL   **WALL MOUNTED**   **MONO-LITHIC**   **SINGLE POST**   **ROOM I.D.**   **WALL-MOUNTED DIRECTORY**   **CEILING MOUNTED**

EXTERIOR SIGNS   **INTERIOR SIGNS**

MOUNTING HEIGHTS

Marr Knapp Crawfis Associates, Inc.; Mansfield, Ohio
Richard J. Vitullo; Washington Grove, Maryland

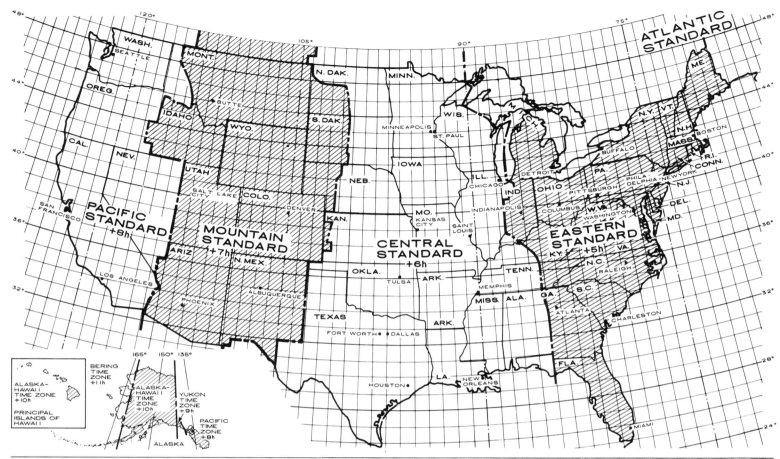

STANDARD TIME ZONES OF THE UNITED STATES
NOTE: Greenwich Standard Time is 0 h.

SOLAR TIME

Solar time generally differs from local standard or daylight saving time, and the difference can be significant, particularly when DST is in effect.

Because the sun appears to move at the rate of 360°/24 hr, its apparent motion is 4 min/1° of longitude. The procedure for finding AST (apparent solar time), explained in detail in the references cited previously, is

$$AST = LST + ET + 4(LSM - LON)$$

where ET = equation of time (min)
  LSM = local standard time meridian (degrees of arc)
  LON = local longitude, degrees of arc
  4 = minutes of time required for 1.0° rotation of earth

The longitudes of the six standard time meridians that affect the United States are: eastern ST, 75°; central ST, 90°; mountain ST, 105°; Pacific ST, 120°; Yukon ST, 135°; Alaska-Hawaii ST, 150°.

The equation of time is the measure, in minutes, of the extent by which solar time, as told by a sundial, runs faster or slower than civil or mean time, as determined by a clock running at a uniform rate. The table below gives values of the declination and the equation of time for the 21st day of each month of a typical year (other than a leap year). This date is chosen because of its significance on four particular days: (a) the winter solstice, December 21, the year's shortest day, $\delta = -23°$ 27 min; (b) the vernal and autumnal equinoxes, March 21 and September 21, when the declination is zero and the day and night are equal in length; and (c) the summer solstice, June 21, the year's longest day, $\delta = +23°$ 27 min.

EXAMPLES

Find AST at noon, local summer time, on July 21 for Washington, D.C., longitude = 77°; and for Chicago, longitude = 87.6°.

SOLUTIONS

In summer, both Washington and Chicago use daylight saving time, and noon, local summer time, is actually 11:00 a.m., local standard time. For Washington, in the eastern time zone, the local standard time meridian is 75° east of Greenwich, and for July 21, the equation of time is −6.2 min. Thus noon, Washington summer time, is actually

$$11:00 - 6.2 \text{ min} + 4 \times (75 - 77) = 10:46 \text{ a.m.}$$

For Chicago, in the central time zone, the local standard time meridian is 90°. Chicago lies 2.4° east of that line, and noon, Chicago summer time, is

$$11:00 - 6.2 \text{ min} + 4 \times 2.4 = 11:03 \text{ a.m.}$$

The hour angle, H, for these two examples would be

for Washington: $H = 0.25 \times (12:00 - 10:46)$
$= 0.25 \times 74 = 18.8°$ east

for Chicago: $H = 0.25 \times (12:00 - 11:03)$
$= 14.25°$ east

YEAR DATE, DECLINATION, AND EQUATION OF TIME FOR THE 21ST DAY OF EACH MONTH; WITH DATA* (A, B, C) USED TO CALCULATE DIRECT NORMAL RADIATION INTENSITY AT THE EARTH'S SURFACE

MONTH	JAN.	FEB.	MAR.	APR.	MAY	JUNE	JULY	AUG.	SEPT.	OCT.	NOV.	DEC.
Day of the year†	21	52	80	111	141	173	202	233	265	294	325	355
Declination, (δ) degrees	−19.9	−10.6	0.0	+11.9	+20.3	+23.45	+20.5	+12.1	0.0	−10.7	−19.9	−23.45
Equation of time (min)	−11.2	−13.9	−7.5	+1.1	+3.3	−1.4	−6.2	−2.4	+7.5	+15.4	+13.8	+1.6
Solar noon	Late			Early			Late			Early		
A: Btuh/sq ft	390	385	376	360	350	345	344	351	365	378	387	391
B: 1/m	0.142	0.144	0.156	0.180	0.196	0.205	0.207	0.201	0.177	0.160	0.149	0.142
C: dimensionless	0.058	0.060	0.071	0.097	0.121	0.134	0.136	0.122	0.092	0.073	0.063	0.057

*A is the apparent solar irradiation at air mass zero for each month; B is the atmospheric extinction coefficient; C is the ratio of the diffuse radiation on a horizontal surface to the direct normal irradiation.
†Declinations are for the year 1964.

John I. Yellott, P.E.; College of Architecture, Arizona State University; Tempe, Arizona

1   SUN CONTROL

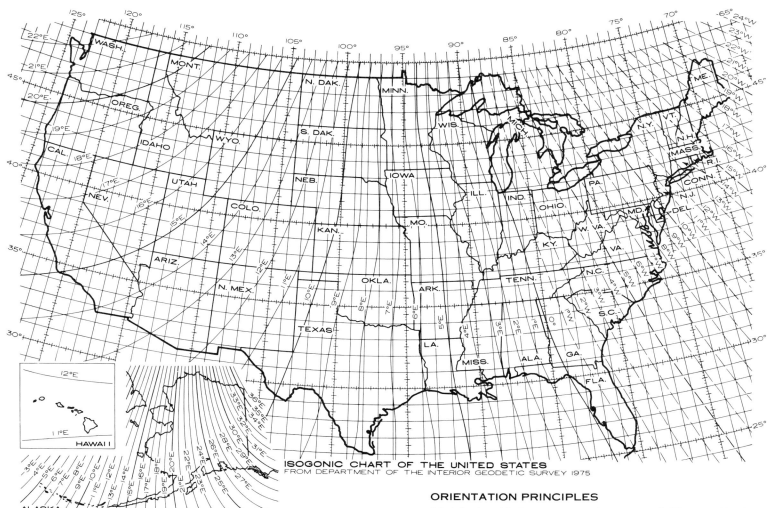

ISOGONIC CHART OF THE UNITED STATES
FROM DEPARTMENT OF THE INTERIOR GEODETIC SURVEY 1975

COMPASS ORIENTATION

The above map is the isogonic chart of the United States. The wavy lines from top to bottom show the compass variations from the true north. At the lines marked E the compass will point east of true north; at those marked W the compass will point west of true north. According to the location, correction should be done from the compass north to find the true north.

EXAMPLE: On a site in Wichita, Kansas, find the true north.

STEP 1.   Find the compass orientation on the site.

STEP 2.   Locate Wichita on the map. The nearest compass variation is the 10°E line.

STEP 3.   Adjust the orientation correction to true north.
The graphical example illustrates a building which lies 25° east with its axis from the compass orientation.

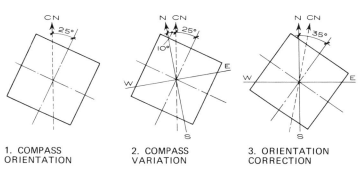

1. COMPASS ORIENTATION   2. COMPASS VARIATION   3. ORIENTATION CORRECTION

ORIENTATION PRINCIPLES

Orientation in architecture encompasses a large segment of different considerations. The expression "total orientation" refers both to the physiological and psychological aspects of the problem.

At the physiological side the factors which affect our senses and have to be taken into consideration are: the thermal impacts—the sun, wind, and temperature effects acting through our skin envelope; the visible impacts—the different illumination and brightness levels affecting our visual senses; the sonic aspects—the noise impacts and noise levels of the surroundings influencing our hearing organs. In addition, our respiratory organs are affected by the smoke, smell, and dust of the environs.

On the psychological side, the view and the privacy are aspects in orientation which quite often override the physical considerations.

Above all, as a building is only a mosaic unit in the pattern of a town organization, the spatial effects, the social intimacy, and its relation to the urban representative directions—aesthetic, political, or social—all play a part in positioning a building.

THERMAL FORCES INFLUENCING ORIENTATION

The climatic factors such as wind, solar radiation, and air temperature play the most eminent role in orientation. The position of a structure in northern latitudes, where the air temperature is generally cool, should be oriented to receive the maximum amount of sunshine without wind exposure. In southerly latitudes, however, the opposite will be desirable; the building should be turned on its axis to avoid the sun's unwanted radiation and to face the cooling breezes instead.

At right the figure shows these regional requirements diagrammatically.

Adaptation for wind orientation is not of great importance in low buildings, where the use of windbreaks and the arrangement of openings in the high and low pressure areas can help to ameliorate the airflow situation. However, for high buildings, where the surrounding terrain has little effect on the upper stories, careful consideration has to be given to wind orientation.

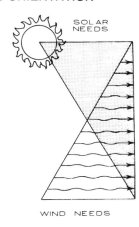

SOLAR NEEDS

WIND NEEDS

Victor Olgyay, AIA; Associate Professor; School of Architecture, Princeton University; Princeton, New Jersey

SOLAR ANGLES

The position of the sun in relation to specific geographic locations, seasons, and times of day can be determined by several methods. Model measurements, by means of solar machines or shade dials, have the advantage of direct visual observations. Tabulative and calculative methods have the advantage of exactness. However, graphic projection methods are usually preferred by architects, as they are easily understood and can be correlated to both radiant energy and shading calculations.

SOLAR PATH DIAGRAMS

A practical graphic projection is the solar path diagram method. Such diagrams depict the path of the sun within the sky vault as projected onto a horizontal plane. The horizon is represented as a circle with the observation point in the center. The sun's position at any date and hour can be determined from the diagram in terms of its altitude (β) and azimuth (ϕ). (See figure on right.) The graphs are constructed in equidistant projection. The altitude angles are represented at 10° intervals by equally spaced concentric circles; they range from 0° at the outer circle (horizon) to 90° at the center point. These intervals are graduated along the south meridian. Azimuth is represented at 10° intervals by equally spaced radii; they range from 0° at the south meridian to 180° at the north meridian. These intervals are graduated along the periphery. The solar bearing will be to the east during morning hours, and to the west during afternoon hours.

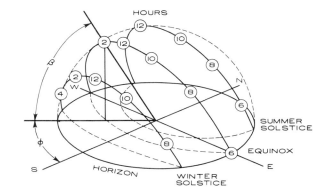

(CONTINUED
NEXT PAGE)

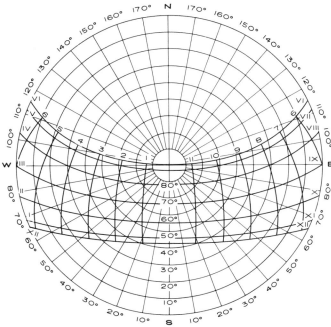

24°N LATITUDE

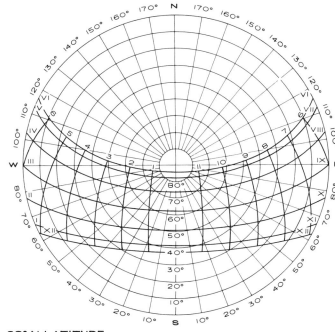

28°N LATITUDE

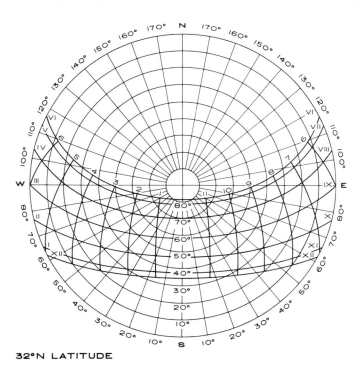

32°N LATITUDE

36°N LATITUDE

Victor Olgyay, AIA; Associate Professor; School of Architecture, Princeton University; Princeton, New Jersey

1   **SUN CONTROL**

SOLAR PATH DIAGRAMS (CONTINUED)

The earth's axis is inclined 23°27' to its orbit around the sun and rotates 15° hourly. Thus, from all points on the earth, the sun appears to move across the sky vault on various parallel circular paths with maximum declinations of ±23°27'. The declination of the sun's path changes in a cycle between the extremes of the summer solstice and winter solstice. Thus the sun follows the same path on two corresponding dates each year. Due to irregularities between the calendar year and the astronomical data, here a unified calibration is adapted. The differences, as they do not exceed 41', are negligible for architectural purposes.

DECLINATION OF THE SUN

DATE	DECLINATION	CORRESP. DATE	DECLINATION	UNIFIED CALIBR.
June 21	+23°27'			+23°27'
May 21	+20°09'	July 21	+20°31'	+20°20'
Apr. 21	+11°48'	Aug. 21	+12°12'	+12°00'
Mar. 21	+0°10'	Sep. 21	+0°47'	+0°28'
Feb. 21	−10°37'	Oct. 21	−10°38'	−10°38'
Jan. 21	−19°57'	Nov. 21	−19°53'	−19°55'
Dec. 21	−23°27'			−23°27'

The elliptical curves in the diagrams represent the horizontal projections of the sun's path. They are given on the 21st day of each month. Roman numerals designate the months. A cross grid of curves graduate the hours indicated in arabic numerals. Eight solar path diagrams are shown at 4° intervals from 24°N to 52°N latitude.

EXAMPLE

Find the sun's position in Columbus, Ohio, on February 21, 2 P.M.:

STEP 1. Locate Columbus on the map. The latitude is 40°N.
STEP 2. In the 40° sun path diagram select the February path (marked with II), and locate the 2 hr line. Where the two lines cross is the position of the sun.
STEP 3. Read the altitude on the concentric circles (32°) and the azimuth along the outer circle (35°30'W).

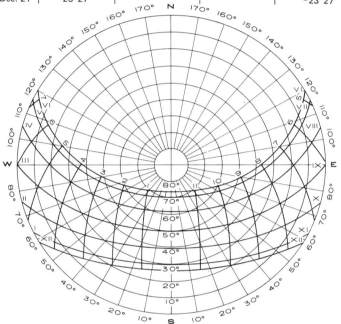

40°N LATITUDE

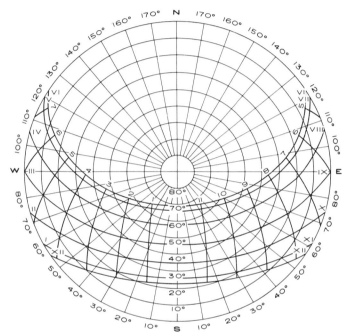

44°N LATITUDE

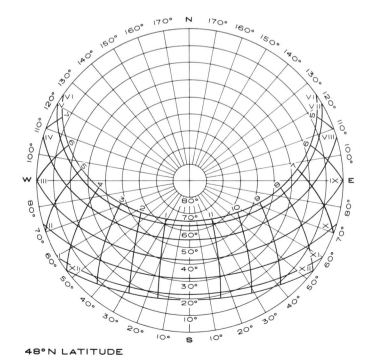

48°N LATITUDE

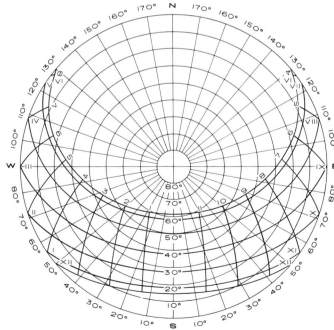

52°N LATITUDE

Victor Olgyay, AIA; Associate Professor; School of Architecture, Princeton University; Princeton, New Jersey

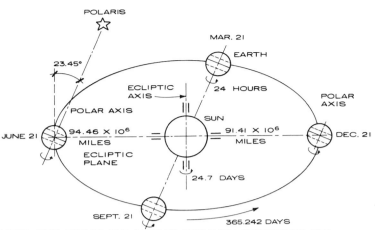

NOTE: THE TILT OF THE EARTH'S AXIS WITH RESPECT TO THE ECLIPTIC AXIS CAUSES THE CHANGING SEASONS AND THE ANNUAL VARIATIONS IN NUMBER OF HOURS OF DAYLIGHT AND DARKNESS

ANNUAL MOTION OF THE EARTH ABOUT THE SUN

NOTE: Q DESIGNATES THE SUN'S POSITION SO OQ IS THE EARTH–SUN LINE WHILE OP' IS THE NORMAL TO THE TILTED SURFACE AND OP IS PERPENDICULAR TO THE INTERSECTION, OM, BETWEEN THE TILTED SURFACE AND THE HORIZONTAL PLANE

SOLAR ANGLES WITH RESPECT TO A TILTED SURFACE

SOLAR CONSTANT

The sun is located at one focus of the earth's orbit, and we are only 147.2 million km (91.4 million miles) away from the sun in late December and early January, while the earth-sun distance on July 1 is about 152.0 million km (94.4 million miles).

Solar energy approaches the earth as electromagnetic radiation at wavelengths between 0.25 and 5.0 μm. The intensity of the incoming solar irradiance on a surface normal to the sun's rays beyond the earth's atmosphere, at the average earth-sun distance, is designated as the solar constant, I_{sc}. Although the value of I_{sc} has not yet been precisely determined by verified measurements made in outer space, the most widely used value is 429.2 Btu/sq ft · hr (1353 W/sq m) and the current ASHRAE values are based on this estimate. More recent measurements made at extremely high altitudes indicate that I_{sc} is probably close to 433.6 Btu/sq ft · hr (1367 W/sq m). The unit of radiation that is widely used by meteorologists is the langley, equivalent to one kilogram calorie/square centimeter. To convert from langleys/day to Btu/sq ft · day, multiply Ly/day by 3.67. To convert from W/sq m to Btu/sq ft · hr, multiply the electrical unit by 0.3172.

SOLAR ANGLES

At the earth's surface the amount of solar radiation received and the resulting atmospheric temperature vary widely, primarily because of the daily rotation of the earth and the fact that the rotational axis is tilted at an angle of 23.45° with respect to the orbital plane. This tilt causes the changing seasons with their varying lengths of daylight and darkness. The angle between the earth-sun line and the orbital plane, called the solar declination, d, varies throughout the year, as shown in the following table for the 21st day of each month.

JAN -19.9° APR +11.9° JUL +20.5° OCT -10.7°
FEB -10.6° MAY +20.3° AUG +12.1° NOV -19.9°
MAR   0.0°   JUN +23.5° SEP   0.0°   DEC -23.5°

Very minor changes in the declination occur from year to year, and when more precise values are needed the almanac for the year in question should be consulted.

The earth's annual orbit about the sun is slightly elliptical, and so the earth-sun distance is slightly greater in summer than in winter. The time required for each annual orbit is actually 365.242 days rather than the 365 days shown by the calendar, and this is corrected by adding a 29th day to February for each year (except century years) that is evenly divisible by 4.

To an observer standing on a particular spot on the earth's surface, with a specified longitude, LON, and latitude, L, it is the sun that appears to move around the earth in a regular daily pattern. Actually it is the earth's rotation that causes the sun's apparent motion. The position of the sun can be defined in terms of its altitude β above the horizon (angle HOQ) and its azimuth ϕ, measured as angle HOS in the horizontal plane.

At solar noon, the sun is, by definition, exactly on the meridian that contains the south-north line, and consequently the solar azimuth ϕ is 0.0°. The noon altitude β is:

$$= 90° - L + \delta$$

Because the earth's daily rotation and its annual orbit around the sun are regular and predictable, the solar altitude and azimuth may be readily calculated for any desired time of day as soon as the latitude, longitude, and date (declination) are specified.

SHADOW CONSTRUCTION WITH TRUE SUN ANGLES

Required information: angle of orientation in relation to north-south axis (C), azimuth ϕ, and altitude angle β of the sun at the desired time (Figure 1).

STEP 1. Lay out building axis, true south and azimuth ϕ of sun in plan (Figure 2).

STEP 2. Lay out altitude β upon azimuth ϕ. Construct any perpendicular to ϕ. From the intersection of this perpendicular and ϕ project a line perpendicular to elevation plane (building orientation). Measure distance x along this line from elevation plane. Connect the point at distance x from elevation plane to center to construct sun elevation β (Figure 2).

STEP 3. Use sun plan ϕ + C and sun elevation β to construct shadows in plan and elevation in conventional way (Figure 3).

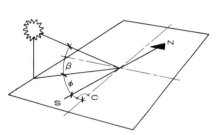

FIGURE 1

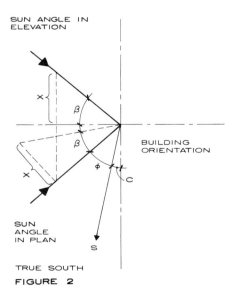

SUN ANGLE IN ELEVATION

BUILDING ORIENTATION

SUN ANGLE IN PLAN

TRUE SOUTH

FIGURE 2

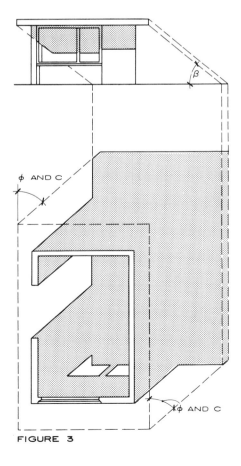

FIGURE 3

John I. Yellott, P.E.; College of Architecture, Arizona State University; Tempe, Arizona

1 SUN CONTROL

NOTES

To visualize the thermal impacts on differently exposed surfaces four locations are shown approximately at the 24°, 32°, 40° and 44° latitudes. The forces are indicated on average clear winter and summer days. The air temperature variation is indicated by the outside concentric circles. Each additional line represents a 2°F difference from the lowest daily temperature. The direction of the impact is indicated according to the sun's direction as temperatures occur. (Note the low temperatures at the east side, and the high ones in westerly directions.)

The total (direct and diffuse) radiation impact on the various sides of the building is indicated with arrows. Each arrow represents 250 Btu/sq ft · day radiation. At the bottom of the page the radiations are expressed in numerical values.

The values show that in the upper latitudes the south side of a building receives nearly twice as much radiation in winter as in summer. This effect is even more pronounced at the lower latitudes, where the ratio is about one to four. Also, in the upper latitudes, the east and west sides receive about 2½ times more radiation in summer than in winter. This ratio is not as large in the lower latitudes; but it is noteworthy that in summer these sides receive two to three times as much radiation as the south elevation. In the summer the west exposure is more disadvantageous than the east exposure, as the afternoon high temperatures combine with the radiation effects. In all latitudes the north side receives only a small amount of radiation, and this comes mainly in the summer. In the low latitudes, in the summer, the north side receives nearly twice the impact of the south side. The amount of radiation received on a horizontal roof surface exceeds all other sides.

Experimental observations were conducted on the thermal behavior of building orientation at Princeton University's Architectural Laboratory. Below are shown the summer results of structures exposed to the cardinal directions. Note the unequal heat distribution and high heat impact of the west exposure compared to the east orientation. The southern direction gives a pleasantly low heat volume, slightly higher, however, than the north exposure.

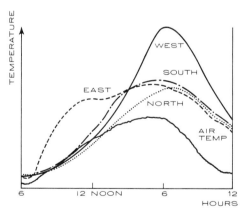

ROOM TEMPERATURE IN
DIFFERENTLY ORIENTED HOUSES

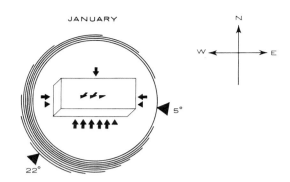

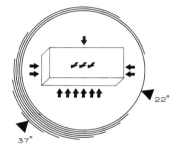

MINNEAPOLIS, MINN.

NEW YORK AREA

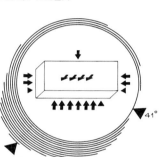

PHOENIX, ARIZ.

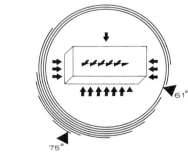

MIAMI, FLA.

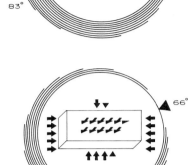

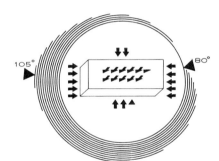

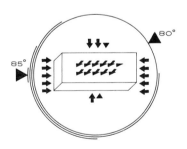

ORIENTATION: CONCLUSIONS

1. The optimum orientation will lie near the south; however, will differ in the various regions, and will depend on the daily temperature distribution.
2. In all regions an orientation eastward from south gives a better yearly performance and a more equal daily heat distribution. Westerly directions perform more poorly with unbalanced heat impacts.
3. The thermal orientation exposure has to be correlated with the local wind directions.

TOTAL DIRECT AND DIFFUSED RADIATION (BTU/SQ FT · DAY)

LATITUDE	SEASON	EAST	SOUTH	WEST	NORTH	HORIZONTAL
44° LATITUDE	WINTER	416	1374	416	83	654
	SUMMER	1314	979	1314	432	2536
40° LATITUDE	WINTER	517	1489	517	119	787
	SUMMER	1277	839	1277	430	2619
32° LATITUDE	WINTER	620	1606	620	140	954
	SUMMER	1207	563	1207	452	2596
24° LATITUDE	WINTER	734	1620	734	152	1414
	SUMMER	1193	344	1193	616	2568

Victor Olgyay, AIA; Associate Professor; School of Architecture, Princeton University; Princeton, New Jersey

SHADING DEVICES

The effect of shading devices can be plotted in the same manner as the solar path was projected. The diagrams show which part of the sky vault will be obstructed by the devices and are projections of the surface covered on the sky vault as seen from an observation point at the center of the diagram. These projections also represent those parts of the sky vault from which no sunlight will reach the observation point; if the sun passes through such an area the observation point will be shaded.

SHADING MASKS

Any building element will define a characteristic form in these projection diagrams, known as "shading masks." Masks of horizontal devices (overhangs) will create a segmental pattern; vertical intercepting elements (fins) produce a radial pattern; shading devices with horizontal and vertical members (eggcrate type) will make a combinative pattern. A shading mask can be drawn for any shading device, even for very complex ones, by geometric plotting. As the shading masks are geometric projections they are independent of latitude and exposed directions, therefore they can be used in any location and at any orientation. By overlaying a shading mask in the proper orientation on the sun-path diagram, one can read off the times when the sun rays will be intercepted. Masks can be drawn for full shade (100% mask) when the observation point is at the lowest point of the surface needing shading; or for 50% shading when the observation point is placed at the halfway mark on the surface. It is customary to design a shading device in such a way that as soon as shading is needed on a surface the masking angle should exceed 50%. Solar calculations should be used to check the specific loads. Basic shading devices are shown below, with their obstruction effect on the sky vault and with their projected shading masks.

SHADING MASK PROTRACTOR

The half of the protractor showing segmental lines is used to plot lines parallel and normal to the observed vertical surface. The half showing bearing and altitude lines is used to plot shading masks of vertical fins or any other obstruction objects. The protractor is in the same projection and scale as the sun-path diagrams (see pages on solar angles); therefore it is useful to transfer the protractor to a transparent overlay to read the obstruction effect.

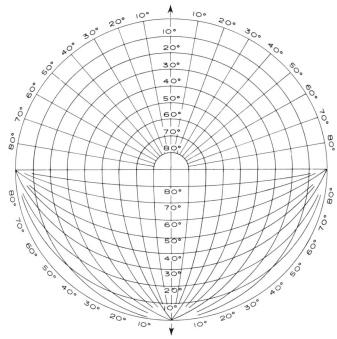

SHADING MASK PROTRACTOR

HORIZONTAL

VERTICAL

EGGCRATE

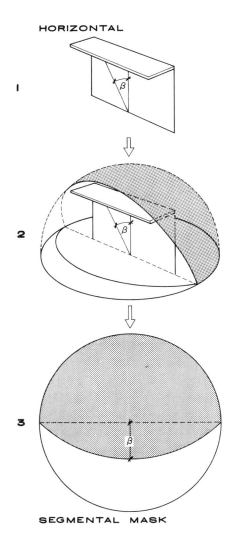

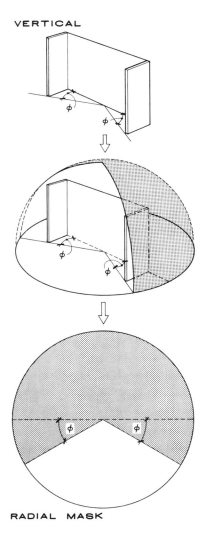

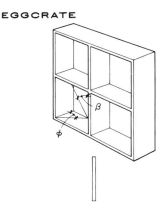

Horizontal devices produce segmental obstruction patterns, vertical fins produce radial patterns, and eggcrate devices produce combination patterns.

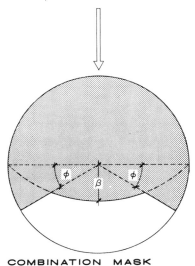

SEGMENTAL MASK

RADIAL MASK

COMBINATION MASK

Victor Olgyay, AIA; Associate Professor; School of Architecture, Princeton University; Princeton, New Jersey

1 **SUN CONTROL**

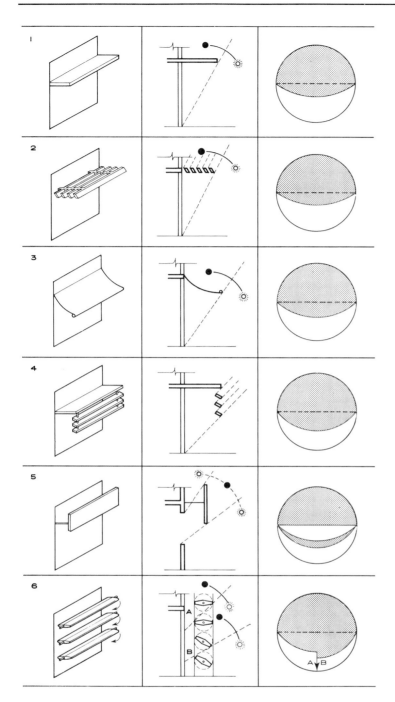

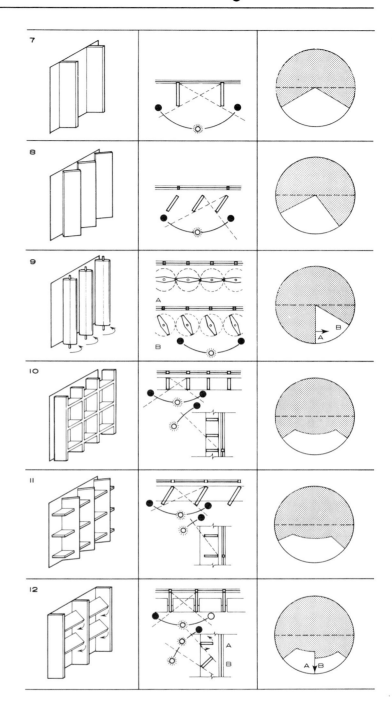

EXAMPLES OF VARIOUS TYPES OF SHADING DEVICES

The illustrations show a number of basic types of devices, classified as horizontal, vertical, and eggcrate types. The dash lines shown in the section diagram in each case indicate the sun angle at the time of 100% shading. The shading mask for each device is also shown, the extent of 100% shading being indicated by the gray area.

General rules can be deduced for the types of shading devices to be used for different orientations. Southerly orientations call for shading devices with segmental mask characteristics, and horizontal devices work in these directions efficiently. For easterly and westerly orientations vertical devices serve well, having radial shading masks. If slanted, they should incline toward the north, to give more protection from the southern positions of the sun. The eggcrate type of shading device works well on walls facing southeast, and is particularly effective for southwest orientations. Because of this type's high shading ratio and low winter head admission; its best use is in hot climate regions. For north walls, fixed vertical devices are recommended; however, their use is needed only for large glass surfaces, or in hot regions. At low latitudes on both south and north exposures eggcrate devices work efficiently.

Whether the shading devices be fixed or movable, the same recommendations apply in respect to the different orientations. The movable types can be most efficiently utilized where the sun's altitude and bearing angles change rapidly: on the east, southeast, and especially, because of the afternoon heat, on the southwest and west.

HORIZONTAL TYPES 1. Horizontal overhangs are most efficient toward south, or around southern orientations. Their mask characteristics are segmental. 2. Louvers parallel to wall have the advantage of permitting air circulation near the elevation. Slanted louvers will have the same characteristics as solid overhangs, and can be made retractable. 4. When protection is needed for low sun angles, louvers hung from solid horizontal overhangs are efficient. 5. A solid, or perforated screen strip parallel to wall cuts out the lower rays of the sun. 6. Movable horizontal louvers change their segmental mask characteristics according to their positioning.

VERTICAL TYPES 7. Vertical fins serve well toward the near east and near west orientations. Their mask characteristics are radial. 8. Vertical fins oblique to wall will result in asymmetrical mask. Separation from wall will prevent heat transmission. 9. Movable fins can shade the whole wall, or open up in different directions according to the sun's position.

EGGCRATE TYPES 10. Eggcrate types are combinations of horizontal and vertical types, and their masks are superimposed diagrams of the two masks. 11. Solid eggcrate with slanting vertical fins results in asymmetrical mask. 12. Eggcrate device with movable horizontal elements shows flexible mask shacteristics. Because of their high shading ratio, eggcrates are efficient in hot climates.

Victor Olgyay, AIA; Associate Professor; School of Architecture. Princeton University; Princeton, New Jersey

TYPES OF UNDERGROUND SPACE

Commercial underground buildings can be classified in a number of ways:

1. Cut-and-cover buildings: Buildings relatively near the surface. The structure supports earth loads from above and on the sides. The term "earth-sheltered" usually refers to cut-and-cover buildings. Also, distinctions can be made between buildings that are fully beneath existing grade and those that are bermed.
2. Mined space: Building area is created by excavating in self-supporting soil or rock.

Underground building type is determined primarily by the site, topography, and program requirements. The ability to create mined space is determined by local soils and geology. Further classification of underground buildings often is based on the surface opening. Categories include windowless chambers, atrium designs, and elevational designs (windows along a single wall).

GENERAL ADVANTAGES

Some of the many advantages associated with underground buildings are:

1. Limited visual impact of the building in natural or historical settings.
2. Preservation of surface open space above the building in dense urban or campus settings.
3. Efficient land use by extending buildings beyond normal setbacks or by building into otherwise unbuildable slopes.
4. Environmental benefits such as reducing water runoff and preserving or increasing plant and animal habitat.
5. Protection from tornadoes, storms, and fire.
6. Provision of civil defense shelters.
7. Increased security against vandalism and theft.
8. Insulation from noise and vibration, permitting some incompatible uses to be located in closer proximity.
9. Reduced exterior maintenance.
10. Reduced construction costs for exterior finishing materials and mechanical equipment.
11. Reduced life-cycle costs of the building based on reduced heating, cooling, maintenance, and insurance costs.

ENERGY-RELATED ADVANTAGES AND LIMITATIONS

In most climates underground buildings have characteristics that reduce heating and cooling loads when compared with above-ground structures. Advantages from improved energy efficiency include:

1. Reduced winter heat loss because of moderate below-grade temperatures and reduced cold infiltration.
2. Reduced summer heat gain especially when earth-bermed walls are planted with grass or ground cover. Peak cooling loads are reduced.
3. Direct cooling from earth in summer.
4. Daily and seasonal temperature fluctuations are reduced, resulting in smaller HVAC equipment sizes.
5. Large mass below-grade concrete buildings can store sun heat and off-peak electric power.

The U.S. deep-ground temperature map illustrates variations in the below-grade environment. At about 25 ft. and deeper, temperatures of undisturbed ground remain approximately constant. Ground temperatures around an in-ground building rise. Buildings nearer to the surface initially experience some temperature variations that stabilize in time.

Energy-conserving benefits are affected by climate, ground temperatures, degree of exposure, building depth, mechanical system design, and building use. Buildings requiring high levels of mechanical ventilation are less likely to benefit from below-grade placement than buildings with low to moderate ventilation requirements. Maximum energy benefits are derived from building uses such as cold storage, or precision temperature and humidity conditions control (i.e., laboratories, libraries, and special materials storage).

DISADVANTAGES

Underground building limitations present a number of disadvantages over conventional construction. Most of these can be overcome by design. Among the limitations are:

1. Limited opportunities for natural light and exterior views;
2. Limited entrance and service access;
3. Limited view of the building and its entrance;
4. Increased costs on sites that have water tables, bedrock near the surface, or adjacent buildings with shallow foundations;
5. Increased construction costs for heavier structures (especially if earth is placed on the roof), and high-quality waterproofing systems.

SPECIAL DESIGN CONCERNS

Entrance design: Entrances should be visible and clear from the exterior. Descending may occur inside or outside the building. If possible, large spaces and natural light should be provided in the entrance area. Various underground building entrance approaches are shown in drawings at the right.

Natural light and view: A primary concern in designing underground buildings is offsetting the possible negative psychological and physiological effects of windowless environments. In addition to admitting sunlight, windows provide orientation, variety, and a similarity to above-ground space. As shown in drawings at the right conventional windows, skylights, and courtyards are effective means of providing light and view in near-surface underground buildings. Where these techniques are inadequate, beamed or reflected daylighting systems may be explored.

Interior design: In underground spaces with limited opportunities for natural light and view, building interior should be organized to provide maximum exposure to light and view for the greatest number of users at each opportunity. Design techniques include large interior courtyards, high ceilings, glass walls, plants, warm colors, variety in design and lighting, and full spectrum artificial lights.

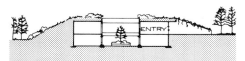

ENTRANCE INTO A BERMED STRUCTURE

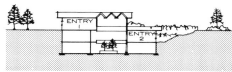

ENTRANCES AT GRADE AND SUBGRADE LEVELS

BUILDING ENTRANCE DESIGN

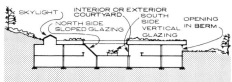

BUILDING SET INTO A SLOPING SITE

NATURAL LIGHT AND VIEW

INSULATION AND WATERPROOFING

Generally, waterproofing should be applied to all below-grade roofs and walls. When a building floor is below the water table level, waterproofing must be placed beneath the floor as well. On below-grade roofs and walls, waterproofing applied directly on the substrate (concrete, wood) is recommended. Insulation and drainage layers then can be placed over the waterproofing (see roof detail below).

When insulation is used in a below-grade application outside of the waterproofing, two characteristics are crucial:

1. Ability to resist structural loads from the earth (this limits selection to rigid board products).
2. Ability to maintain R-value and to resist degradation during constant and severe exposure to water and moisture.

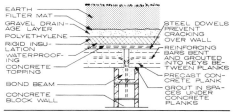

ROOF DETAIL

SUGGESTED AMOUNTS OF BELOW-GRADE INSULATION

HEATING/COOLING DEGREE DAYS (BASE; 65°F)	SUGGESTED RANGE OF BELOW-GRADE INSULATION[1]		
	ROOFS AND[2] UPPER WALL	LOWER WALL[3]	REMOTE FLOOR[4] AREAS
8,000–11,000/0–500	R-20–R-40	R-5–R-20	0–R-5
5,000–8,000/500–1,500	R-20–R-30	R-5–R-10	0–R-5
2,000–5,000/1,500–2,500	R-10–R-20	0–R-5	0
over 2,000/under 2,000	R-10–R-20	0	0

NOTES

1. This table is a general guide only and assumes an earth cover thickness in the range of 12 in. to 30 in. for the earth-covered roof.
2. Earth-covered roof with 12 in. to 30 in. of cover and walls within 8 ft of the ground surface.
3. Earth-covered wall surfaces farther than 8 ft from the ground surface.
4. Floor areas remote (i.e., more than 10 ft from the ground surface) not used as a solar storage area or for heat distribution.

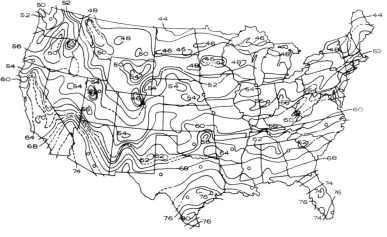

U.S. DEEP-GROUND TEMPERATURE MAP

David Eijadi, AIA, and Kyle Williams; BRW, Inc.; Minneapolis, Minnesota

1 EARTH SHELTERS

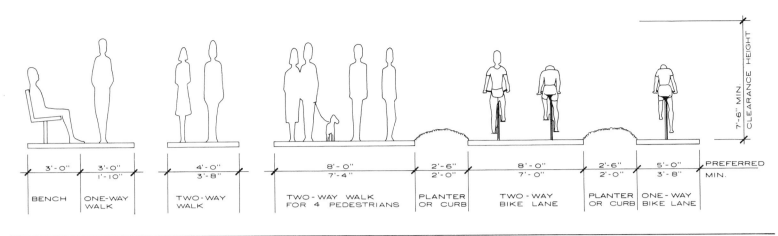

WALK AND BIKE LANE WIDTHS

BENCH	ONE-WAY WALK	TWO-WAY WALK	TWO-WAY WALK FOR 4 PEDESTRIANS	PLANTER OR CURB	TWO-WAY BIKE LANE	PLANTER OR CURB	ONE-WAY BIKE LANE	
3'-0"	3'-0" / 1'-10"	4'-0" / 3'-8"	8'-0" / 7'-4"	2'-6" / 2'-0"	8'-0" / 7'-0"	2'-6" / 2'-0"	5'-0" / 3'-8"	PREFERRED MIN.

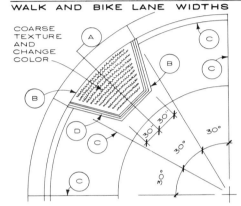

COARSE TEXTURE AND CHANGE COLOR

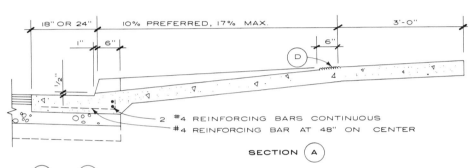

18" OR 24"   10% PREFERRED, 17% MAX.   3'-0"

2 #4 REINFORCING BARS CONTINUOUS
#4 REINFORCING BAR AT 48" ON CENTER

SECTION Ⓐ

FOR Ⓑ AND Ⓒ SEE WALK JOINTS BELOW
Ⓓ BORDER WITH ¼" GROOVES ¾" ON CENTER

WHEELCHAIR RAMP AT CURB
(ROUND CURB SHOWN IN PLAN. SECTION TYPICAL FOR ANY CURB)

AT FACE OF WALL USE EXPANSION JOINT Ⓑ

FACE OF BUILDING

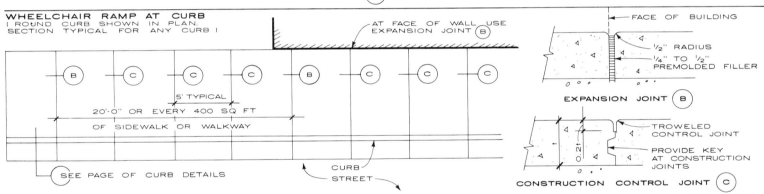

5' TYPICAL
20'-0" OR EVERY 400 SQ FT
OF SIDEWALK OR WALKWAY

SEE PAGE OF CURB DETAILS

CURB
STREET

½" RADIUS
¼" TO ½" PREMOLDED FILLER

EXPANSION JOINT Ⓑ

TROWELED CONTROL JOINT
PROVIDE KEY AT CONSTRUCTION JOINTS

CONSTRUCTION CONTROL JOINT Ⓒ

WALK AND CURB JOINTS

ROCK SALT

Spread on troweled surface and press in. Wash salt away after concrete hardens. Protect planting.

EXPOSED AGGREGATE

Seed aggregate uniformly onto surface. Embed by tamping. After setup, brush lightly and clean with spray. If using aggregate mix, trowel and expose by washing fines or use a retarder.

PRESSED OR STAMPED

Stock patterns are available. Use integral or dry shake colors. Joints may be filled with mortar.

BROOM SURFACE

Use stiff bristle for coarse texture. Use soft bristle on steel troweled surface for fine texture.

TROWELED

Use wood float for coarse texture. Use steel float for fine texture.

NONSLIP

Apply silicon carbide (sparkling) or aluminum oxide at ¼ to ½ psf; trowel lightly.

WALK SURFACES AND TEXTURES

William T. Mahan, AIA; Santa Barbara, California

REFERENCES

GENERAL REFERENCES

BOCA National Building Code, Building Officials and Code Administrators International (BOCA)

Uniform Building Code, International Conference of Building Officials (ICBO)

Southern Standard Building Code, Southern Building Code Congress (SBCC)

Fire Protection Handbook, National Fire Protection Association (NFPA)

Minimum Guidelines and Requirements for Accessible Design, Architectural and Transportation Barriers Compliance Board

DATA SOURCES: ORGANIZATIONS

American Institute of Graphic Arts, 10

American Society of Heating, Refrigerating, and Air Conditioning Engineers (ASHRAE), 12

Architectural Graphics, Inc., 10

Center for Building Technology, National Bureau of Standards, U.S. Department of Commerce (NBS), 7, 8

Geodetic Survey, U.S. Department of the Interior (USDI), 13

Mohawk Sign System, 10

Nelson–Harkins, 10

U.S. Department of Transportation (USDT), 10

DATA SOURCES: PUBLICATIONS

BOCA Basic Building Code, Building Officials and Code Administrators International (BOCA), 2

Handbook of Landscape Architectural Construction, American Society of Landscape Architects (ASLA), 21

National Building Code (NBC), American Insurance Association, 2

CHAPTER 2

SITE PLANNING

TRANSPORTATION	24
FIRE PROTECTION	43
LAND PLANNING AND SITE DEVELOPMENT	44
SITE IMPROVEMENTS	56

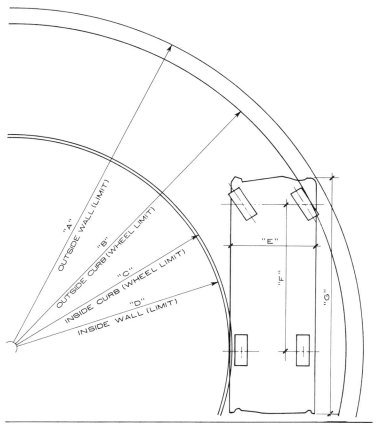

AMBULANCES AND HEARSES
DIMENSIONS AND TURNING RADII

MAKE OF CAR	A	B	C	D	E	F	G
BUICK	28'-9''	27'-3''	18'-4''	17'-10''	6'-0''	11'-7''	19'-2''
LINCOLN	30'-2''	28'-5''	18'-6''	18'-4''	6'-6''	11'-5''	19'-8''

Dimensions vary—verify with individual coach builder.

GOLF CARTS GASOLINE OR ELECTRIC POWER

3 WHEELS		4 WHEELS
46 3/4''	Overall Height	47 1/8''
10 3/4''	Floorboard Height	11 1/4''
27 3/4''	Seat Height	28 1/4''
102''	Length	102''
47''	Width	47''
68''	Wheel Base	68 3/4''
—	Front Wheel Tread	34''
34 5/8''	Rear Wheel Tread	34 5/8''
4 5/8''	Ground Clearance	4 5/8''
19'-6''	Clearance Circle	24'-0''

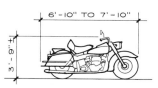

WIDTH AT HANDLEBAR 2'-7''
TO 3'-6''

When parked on stand motorcycle leans about 10° to 12°. Large vehicle requires about 3'-8'' of space.

HEAVYWEIGHTS WEIGH FROM ABOUT 400 LB TO 661 LB

HEAVYWEIGHT MOTORCYCLES

Consult manufacturers' information for width of motorcycle and sidecar.

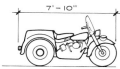

POLICE TRICYCLE
WIDTH AT BOX 4''-0''±

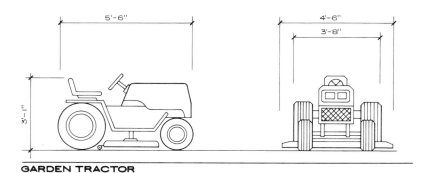

GARDEN TRACTOR

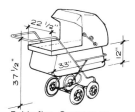

Folds flat. Converts to stroller. Body makes car bed.
BABY CARRIAGE

Handlebar width 23'' and up.
Weight about 230 lb to about 300 lb

LIGHTWEIGHT MOTORCYCLE

LAWN MOWER

IO SPEED BICYCLE

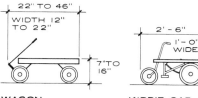

WIDTH 12'' TO 22''

WAGON

KIDDIE CAR

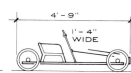

IRISH MAIL

STROLLER

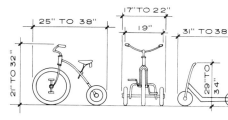

TRICYCLE

SCOOTER

Harold C. Munger, FAIA; Munger Munger + Associates Architects, Inc.; Toledo, Ohio
Foster C. Parriott; James M. Hunter & Associates; Boulder, Colorado

NOTE

Each design vehicle in Groups I, II, and III represents a composite of the critical dimensions of the real vehicles within each group below. Parking lot dimensions on the parking lot development page are based on these groups and dimensions. For parking purposes, both compact and standard size vehicles are in Group II. Turning dimensions R, R1, and C are shown on the private roads page.

DESIGN VEHICLE

GROUP I		SUBCOMPACTS
L	Length	13'–10''
W	Width	5'–5''
H	Height	4'–5''
WB	Wheelbase	8'–1''
OF	Overhang front	2'–6''
OR	Overhang rear	3'–9''
OS	Overhang sides	0'–7''
GW	Gross Weight	2100# to 2500#

GROUP II		COMPACTS
L	Length	14'–9''
W	Width	5'–8''
H	Height	4'–5''
WB	Wheelbase	8'–7''
OF	Overhang front	2'–8''
OR	Overhang rear	4'–3''
OS	Overhang sides	0'–8''
GW	Gross Weight	2300# to 2500#

GROUP III		INTERMEDIATE
L	Length	16'–8''
W	Width	6'–0''
H	Height	4'–6''
WB	Wheelbase	9'–0''
OF	Overhang front	2'–10''
OR	Overhang rear	4'–4''
OS	Overhang sides	0'–9''
GW	Gross Weight	2700# to 3200#

GROUP IV		LARGE CARS
L	Length	18'–5''
W	Width	6'–6''
H	Height	4'–9''
WB	Wheelbase	10'–2''
OF	Overhang front	2'–11''
OR	Overhang rear	4'–5''
OS	Overhang sides	0'–9''
GW	Gross Weight	3100# to 4030#

GROUP V		LARGE PICK-UP
L	Length	16'–4''
W	Width	6'–0''
H	Height	5'–8''
WB	Wheelbase	10'–5''
OF	Overhang front	2'–10''
OR	Overhang rear	4'–4''
OS	Overhang sides	0'–9''
GW	Gross Weight	3430#

LARGE VEHICLE DIMENSIONS*

VEHICLE	(L) LENGTH	(W) WIDTH	(H) HEIGHT	(OR) OVERHANG REAR
Intercity bus	45'–0''	9'–0''	9'–0''	10'–1''
City bus	40'–0''	8'–6''	8'–6''	8'–0''
School bus	39'–6''	8'–0''	8'–6''	12'–8''
Ambulance	20'–10¼''	6'–11''	10'–0''	5'–4''
Paramedic van	21'–6''	8'–0''	6'–6''	4'–0''
Hearse	22'–1''	6'–8''	9'–3''	5'–4''
Airport limousine	22'–5¾''	6'–4''	5'–0''	3'–11''
Trash truck	28'–2''	8'–0''	11'–0''	6'–0''
U.P.S. truck	26'–3''	7'–11''	10'–8''	8'–5''
Fire truck	32'–0''	8'–0''	9'–8''	10'–0''

*Exact sizes of large vehicles may vary
For truck and trailer information, see pages on truck and trailer sizes.

Harold C. Munger, FAIA; Munger Munger + Associates Architects, Inc.; Toledo, Ohio
William T. Mahan, AIA; Santa Barbara, California

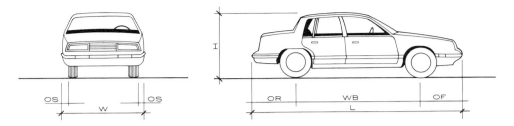

NOTE
Angles shown below may vary depending on speed, load, tire pressure, and condition of shock absorbers.

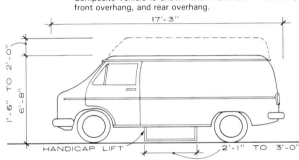

NOTE
Composite vehicle is shown with maximum wheelbase, front overhang, and rear overhang.

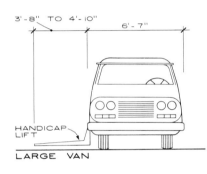

LARGE VAN

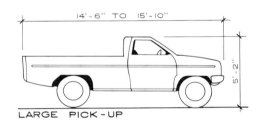

LARGE PICK-UP

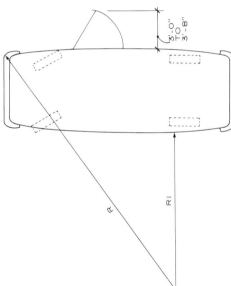

NOTE

For dimensions R and R1 see page on private roads. Typically parking for handicapped area requires 20 ft. × 12 ft.

For further parking information, see pages on parking lot development and parking garages.

See local codes and standards for parking requirements, size, and quantity of parking spaces and number of spaces required for the handicapped.

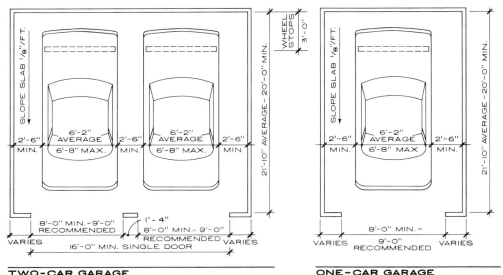

TWO-CAR GARAGE   **ONE-CAR GARAGE**

NOTES

1. Site location varies because of site constraints and design concept. Design considerations include circulation, visual safety for backing out, and visual consideration if garage is exposed to public view.
2. Garages may be enlarged to provide circulation ease by allowing spaces of 2 ft 6 in. minimum between all walls and other vehicles, and to provide space for work areas, photography laboratories, laundry room, and storage.
3. Garages may be attached directly to the house or be connected by a covered passage. Connection is preferable at or near the kitchen or utility area off the kitchen. If attached, refer to local code requirements.

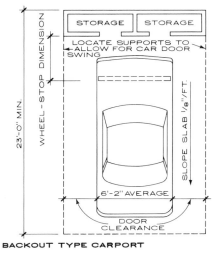

BACKOUT TYPE CARPORT

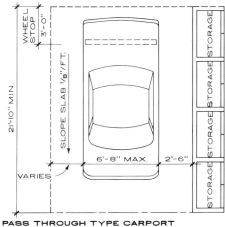

PASS THROUGH TYPE CARPORT

CARPORTS

SECTIONAL DOOR SIZES

DOOR WIDTH	NUMBER OF PANELS ACROSS
To 8'-11''	2
9'-0''–11'-11''	3
12'-0''–14'-11''	4
15'-0''–17'-11''	5

NOTE: Doors up to 8'-6'' high require 4 sections.

HINGED GARAGE DOOR WIDTHS

OPENING	TWO-DOOR	THREE-DOOR	FOUR-DOOR
8'-0''	4'-0''	2'-8''	2'-0''
8'-6''	4'-3''	2'-10''	2'-1½''
9'-0''	4'-6''	3'-0''	2'-3''

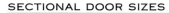

OFFSET HINGE—MULTI-LEAVE

MULTIPLE HINGED DOOR TWO OR MORE CARS

DOUBLE OR TRIPLE HINGED

NOTE

For multiple and offset hinged doors, swinging to one or both sides, hinged in or out, and used for two or more cars: 6½ to 11 in. necessary from top of opening to ceiling.

HINGED DOORS

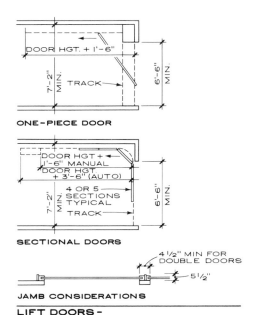

ONE-PIECE DOOR

SECTIONAL DOORS

JAMB CONSIDERATIONS

LIFT DOORS – MOST WIDELY USED – AUTOMATIC OPTIONAL
NOTE: HEIGHTS 6'-6'', 6'-10'', 7'-0'', 7'-6'' AND 8'-0''

HINGED SECTION

MULTIPLE DOORS – TWO OR MORE CARS

SINGLE DOOR

NOTE

6½ to 9 in. necessary from top of opening to ceiling (all sliding doors).

SLIDING DOORS

William T. Cannady, FAIA; Houston, Texas
DeChiara and Koppelman, see data sources

CONCRETE RUNWAYS TO GARAGE

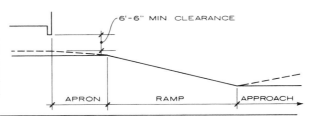

RAMP	APPROACH	APRON
4%	0% to 4%	0% to 2%
5%	0% to 3%	0% to 2%
6%	0% to 2%	0% to 2%
7%	0% to 1%	0% to 1%
8%	0%	0%

ROAD TO GARAGE RAMPS

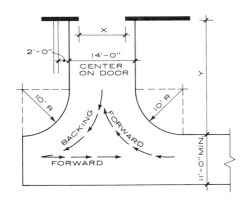

90° IN—BACK OUT (1 CAR)

X	8'-9"	9'-0"	10'-0"	11'-0"	12'-0"
Y	25'-0"	24'-6"	23'-8"	23'-0"	22'-0"

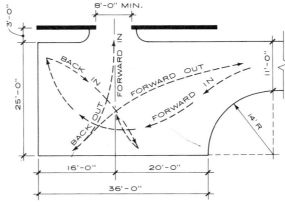

NOTE

Three maneuver entrance for single car garage. Employ only when space limitations demand use. Dimensioned for large car.

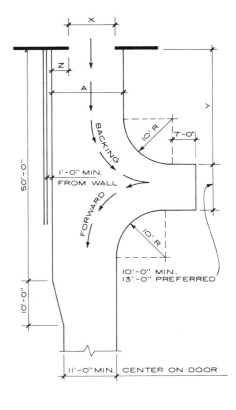

STRAIGHT IN—BACK OUT

X	9'-0"	10'-0"	12'-0"	16'-0"
Y	26'-0"	25'-0"	23'-6"	24'-0"
Z	3'-4"	3'-1"	2'-0"	3'-0"
A	14'-4"	14'-5"	14'-8"	20'-0"

PRIVATE DRIVEWAYS TO GARAGES

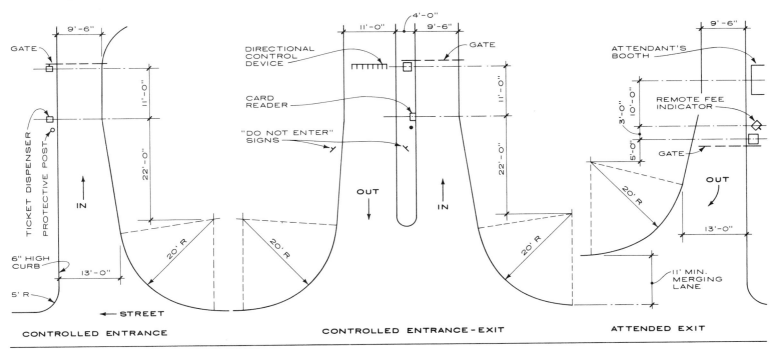

CONTROLLED ENTRANCE

CONTROLLED ENTRANCE-EXIT

ATTENDED EXIT

DRIVEWAYS FOR PARKING FACILITIES

William T. Mahan, AIA; Santa Barbara, California

GENERAL NOTES

Examples shown are for easy driving at moderate speed. See the preceding page for vehicle dimensions (L, W, and OR). The "U" drive shown below illustrates a procedure for designating any drive configuration, given the vehicle's dimensions and turning radii. The T (tangent) dimensions given here are approximate minimums only and may vary with the driver's ability and speed.

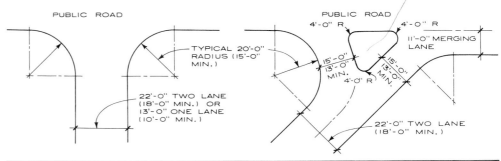

PRIVATE ROADS INTERSECTING PUBLIC ROADS

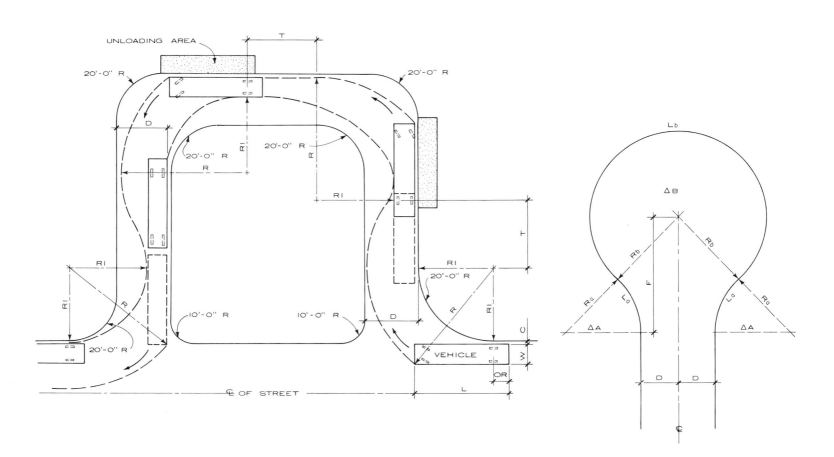

"U" DRIVE AND VEHICLE TURNING DIMENSIONS

VEHICLE	R	RI	T	D	C
Small car	19'-10''	10'-9''	12'-0''	10'-0'	6''
Compact car	21'-6''	11'-10''	15'-0''	10'-10''	7''
Standard car	22'-5''	12'-7''	15'-0''	11'-2''	8''
Large car	23'-0''	12'-7''	15'-0''	12'-0''	9''
Intercity bus*	55'-0''	33'-0''	30'-0''	22'-6''	1'-0''
City bus	53'-6''	33'-0''	30'-0''	22'-6''	1'-0''
School bus	43'-6''	26'-0''	30'-0''	19'-5''	1'-0''
Ambulance	30'-0''	18'-9''	25'-0''	13'-3''	1'-0''
Paramedic van	25'-0''	14'-0''	25'-0''	13'-0''	1'-0''
Hearse	30'-0''	18'-9''	20'-0''	13'-3''	1'-0''
Airport limousine	28'-3''	15'-1½''	20'-0''	15'-1½''	1'-0''
Trash truck†	32'-0''	18'-0''	20'-0''	16'-0''	1'-0''
U.P.S. truck	28'-0''	16'-0''	20'-0''	14'-0''	1'-0''
Fire truck	48'-0''	34'-4'	30'-0''	15'-8''	1'-0''

*Headroom = 14'.
†Headroom = 15'.

William T. Mahan, AIA; Santa Barbara, California

CUL-DE-SAC

	SMALL	LARGE
O	16'-0''	22'-0''
F	50'-11''	87'-3''
A	46.71°	35.58°
B	273.42°	251.15°
Ra	32'-0''	100'-0''
Rb	38'-0''	50'-0''
La	26'-1''	61'-8''
Lb	181'-4''	219'-2''

NOTE: R values for vehicles intended to use these culs-de-sac should not exceed Rb.

NOTE: Small car dimensions should be used only in lots designated for small cars or with entrance controls that admit only small cars. Placing small car stalls into a standard car layout is not recommended. Standard car parking dimensions will accommodate all normal passenger vehicles. Large car parking dimensions make parking easier and faster and are recommended for luxury, a high turnover, and use by the elderly. When the parking angle is 60° or less, it may be necessary to add 3 to 6 ft to the bay width to provide aisle space for pedestrians walking to and from their parked cars. Local zoning laws should be reviewed before proceeding.

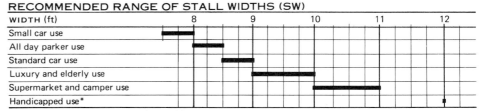

RECOMMENDED RANGE OF STALL WIDTHS (SW)

WIDTH (ft) — 8, 9, 10, 11, 12

- Small car use
- All day parker use
- Standard car use
- Luxury and elderly use
- Supermarket and camper use
- Handicapped use*

*Minimum requirements = 1 or 2 per 100 stalls or as specified by local, state, or federal law; place convenient to destination.

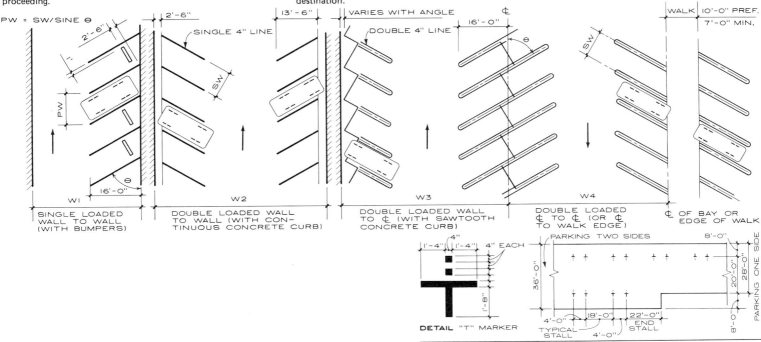

PW = SW/SINE θ

W1 — SINGLE LOADED WALL TO WALL (WITH BUMPERS)

W2 — DOUBLE LOADED WALL (WITH CONTINUOUS CONCRETE CURB)

W3 — DOUBLE LOADED WALL TO ₵ (WITH SAWTOOTH CONCRETE CURB)

W4 — DOUBLE LOADED ₵ TO ₵ (OR ₵ TO WALK EDGE)

₵ OF BAY OR EDGE OF WALK — WALK 10'-0" PREF. 7'-0" MIN.

DETAIL "T" MARKER

PARALLEL PARKING STALLS AND "T" MARKER DETAIL

PARKING DIMENSIONS IN FEET AND INCHES

	SW	W	45°	50°	55°	60°	65°	70°	75°	80°	85°	90°
Group I: small cars	8'-0"	1	25'-9"	26'-6"	27'-2"	29'-4"	31'-9"	34'-0"	36'-2"	38'-2"	40'-0"	41'-9"
		2	40'-10"	42'-0"	43'-1"	45'-8"	48'-2"	50'-6"	52'-7"	54'-4"	55'-11"	57'-2"
		3	38'-9"	40'-2"	41'-5"	44'-2"	47'-0"	49'-6"	51'-10"	53'-10"	55'-8"	57'-2"
		4	36'-8"	38'-3"	39'-9"	42'-9"	45'-9"	48'-6"	51'-1"	53'-4"	55'-5"	57'-2"
Group II: standard cars	8'-6"	1	32'-0"	32'-11"	34'-2"	36'-2"	38'-5"	41'-0"	43'-6"	45'-6"	46'-11"	48'-0"
		2	49'-10"	51'-9"	53'-10"	56'-0"	58'-4"	60'-2"	62'-0"	63'-6"	64'-9"	66'-0"
		3	47'-8"	49'-4"	51'-6"	54'-0"	56'-6"	59'-0"	61'-2"	63'-0"	64'-6"	66'-0"
		4	45'-2"	46'-10"	49'-0"	51'-8"	54'-6"	57'-10"	60'-0"	62'-6"	64'-3"	66'-0"
	9'-0"	1	32'-0"	32'-9"	34'-0"	35'-4"	37'-6"	39'-8"	42'-0"	44'-4"	46'-2"	48'-0"
		2	49'-4"	51'-0"	53'-2"	55'-6"	57'-10"	60'-0"	61'-10"	63'-4"	64'-9"	66'-0"
		3	46'-4"	48'-10"	51'-4"	53'-10"	56'-0"	58'-8"	61'-0"	63'-0"	64'-6"	66'-0"
		4	44'-8"	46'-6"	49'-0"	51'-6"	54'-0"	57'-0"	59'-8"	62'-0"	64'-2"	66'-0"
	9'-6"	1	32'-0"	32'-8"	34'-0"	35'-0"	36'-10"	38'-10"	41'-6"	43'-8"	46'-0"	48'-0"
		2	49'-2"	50'-6"	51'-10"	53'-6"	55'-4"	58'-0"	60'-6"	62'-8"	64'-6"	65'-11"
		3	47'-0"	48'-2"	49'-10"	51'-6"	53'-11"	57'-0"	59'-8"	62'-0"	64'-3"	65'-11"
		4	44'-8"	45'-10"	47'-6"	49'-10"	52'-6"	55'-9"	58'-9"	61'-6"	63'-10"	65'-11"
Group III: large cars	9'-0"	1	32'-7"	33'-0"	34'-0"	35'-11"	38'-3"	40'-11"	43'-6"	45'-5"	46'-9"	48'-0"
		2	50'-2"	51'-2"	53'-3"	55'-4"	58'-0"	60'-4"	62'-9"	64'-3"	65'-5"	66'-0"
		3	47'-9"	49'-1"	52'-3"	53'-8"	56'-2"	59'-2"	61'-11"	63'-9"	65'-2"	66'-0"
		4	45'-5"	46'-11"	49'-0"	51'-8"	54'-9"	58'-0"	61'-0"	63'-2"	64'-10"	66'-0"
	9'-6"	1	32'-4"	32'-8"	33'-10"	34'-11"	37'-2"	39'-11"	42'-5"	45'-0"	46'-6"	48'-0"
		2	49'-11"	50'-11"	52'-2"	54'-0"	56'-6"	59'-3"	61'-9"	63'-4"	64'-8"	66'-0"
		3	47'-7"	48'-9"	50'-2"	52'-4"	55'-1"	58'-4"	60'-11"	62'-10"	64'-6"	66'-0"
		4	45'-3"	46'-8"	48'-5"	50'-8"	53'-8"	57'-0"	59'-10"	62'-2"	64'-1"	66'-0"
	10'-0"	1	32'-4"	32'-8"	33'-10"	34'-11"	37'-2"	39'-11"	42'-5"	45'-0"	46'-6"	48'-0"
		2	49'-11"	50'-11"	52'-2"	54'-0"	56'-6"	59'-3"	61'-9"	63'-4"	64'-8"	66'-0"
		3	47'-7"	48'-9"	50'-2"	52'-4"	55'-1"	58'-4"	60'-11"	62'-10"	64'-6"	66'-0"
		4	45'-3"	46'-8"	48'-5"	50'-8"	53'-8"	57'-0"	59'-10"	62'-2"	64'-1"	66'-0"

θ ANGLE OF PARK

NOTE: θ angles greater than 70° have aisle widths wide enough for two-way travel.

William T. Mahan, AIA; Santa Barbara, California
Frederick J. Gaylord, AIA; McClellan/Cruz/Gaylord & Associates; Pasadena, California

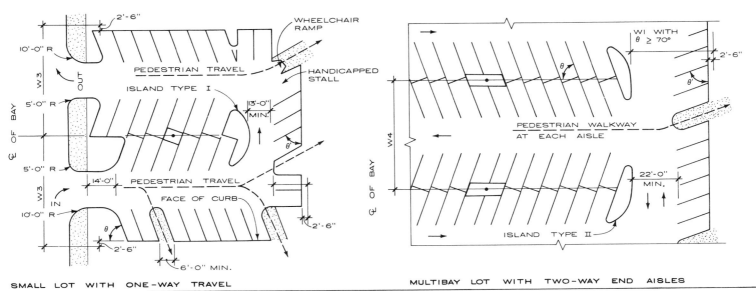

SMALL LOT WITH ONE-WAY TRAVEL

MULTIBAY LOT WITH TWO-WAY END AISLES

TYPICAL PARKING LAYOUTS

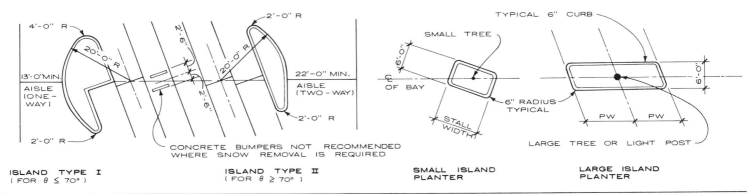

ISLAND TYPE I
(FOR θ ≤ 70°)

ISLAND TYPE II
(FOR θ ≥ 70°)

SMALL ISLAND PLANTER

LARGE ISLAND PLANTER

TYPICAL PLANTER ISLANDS

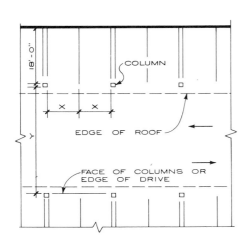

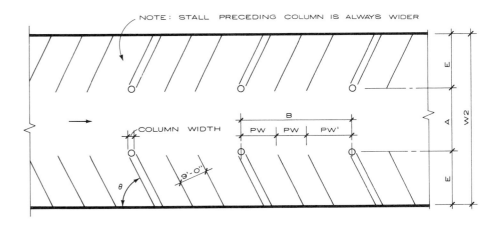

NOTE: STALL PRECEDING COLUMN IS ALWAYS WIDER

TWO STALL 90° APARTMENT CARPORTS

X	9'-0"	10'-0"	11'-0"	12'-0"
Y	35'-0"	34'-0"	33'-0"	32'-0"

ANGLE PARKING WITH 3 STALLS PER COLUMN

θ	PW	PW'	W2	E	A	B	AREA/STALL
60°	10'-5"	13'-0"	55'-0"	18'-0"	19'-0"	33'-10"	310 sq ft
70°	9'-7"	11'-1"	59'-10"	18'-0"	23'-10"	30'-3"	302 sq ft
80°	9'-1"	10'-2"	63'-4"	18'-0"	27'-4"	28'-4"	300 sq ft

PARKING LAYOUTS WITH COLUMNS

William T. Mahan, AIA; Santa Barbara, California
Frederick J. Gaylord, AIA; McClellan/Cruz/Gaylord & Associates; Pasadena, California

TRANSPORTATION

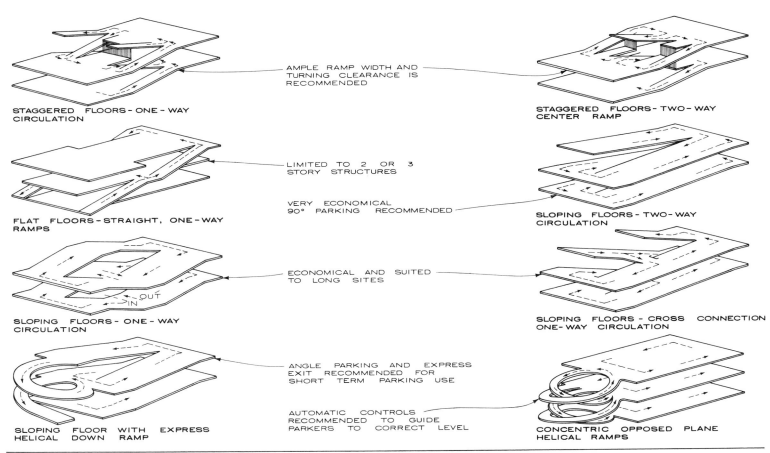

AMPLE RAMP WIDTH AND TURNING CLEARANCE IS RECOMMENDED

STAGGERED FLOORS-ONE-WAY CIRCULATION

STAGGERED FLOORS-TWO-WAY CENTER RAMP

LIMITED TO 2 OR 3 STORY STRUCTURES

VERY ECONOMICAL 90° PARKING RECOMMENDED

FLAT FLOORS-STRAIGHT, ONE-WAY RAMPS

SLOPING FLOORS-TWO-WAY CIRCULATION

ECONOMICAL AND SUITED TO LONG SITES

SLOPING FLOORS-ONE-WAY CIRCULATION

SLOPING FLOORS-CROSS CONNECTION ONE-WAY CIRCULATION

ANGLE PARKING AND EXPRESS EXIT RECOMMENDED FOR SHORT TERM PARKING USE

AUTOMATIC CONTROLS RECOMMENDED TO GUIDE PARKERS TO CORRECT LEVEL

SLOPING FLOOR WITH EXPRESS HELICAL DOWN RAMP

CONCENTRIC OPPOSED PLANE HELICAL RAMPS

TYPICAL RAMP SYSTEMS

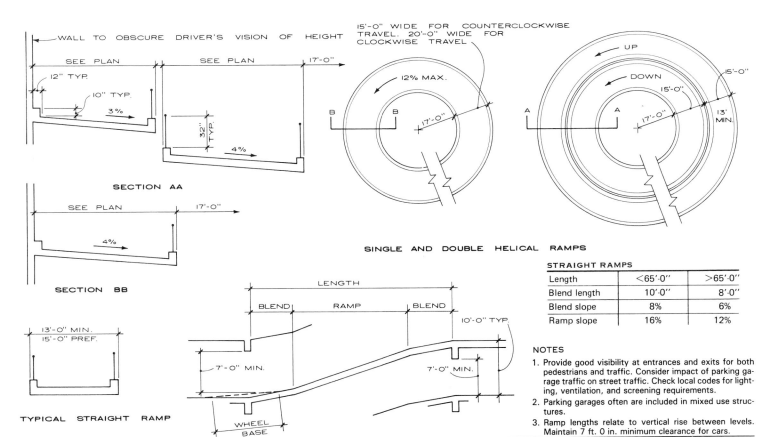

WALL TO OBSCURE DRIVER'S VISION OF HEIGHT

15'-0" WIDE FOR COUNTERCLOCKWISE TRAVEL. 20'-0" WIDE FOR CLOCKWISE TRAVEL

SECTION AA

SECTION BB

SINGLE AND DOUBLE HELICAL RAMPS

TYPICAL STRAIGHT RAMP

STRAIGHT RAMPS

	<65'-0"	>65'-0"
Length	<65'-0"	>65'-0"
Blend length	10'-0"	8'-0"
Blend slope	8%	6%
Ramp slope	16%	12%

NOTES

1. Provide good visibility at entrances and exits for both pedestrians and traffic. Consider impact of parking garage traffic on street traffic. Check local codes for lighting, ventilation, and screening requirements.
2. Parking garages often are included in mixed use structures.
3. Ramp lengths relate to vertical rise between levels. Maintain 7 ft. 0 in. minimum clearance for cars.

TYPICAL RAMP DETAILS

William T. Mahan, AIA; Santa Barbara, California

TRIPLE SEMITRAILER AND TRACTOR

MAXIMUM ALLOWABLE LENGTH
NOT PERMITTED, EXCEPT IN THOSE STATES LISTED BELOW

UNIT	STATE
90'-0"	AK
(each trailer 27'-0")	AZ
105'-0"	CO
105'-0"	ID
105'-0"	NV
105'-0"	OR
105'-0"	UT
65'-0"	IN
110'-0"	ND

DOUBLE SEMITRAILER AND TRACTOR

MAXIMUM ALLOWABLE LENGTH

UNIT	EACH TRAILER	STATE
60'-0"	28'-0"	GA, SC, VT, VA
61'-0"	—	UT
65'-0"	30'-0"	LA
65'-0"	28'-6"	MA, MN, NY, TX
65'-0"	28'-0"	DE, HI, MD, MO, NM, PA
65'-0"	—	ME, NB
70'-0"	28'-0"	CO, OK
75'-0"	28'-6"	CA, MT
75'-0"	28'-0"	ND
75'-0"	—	AK, OR
80'-0"	28'-6"	SD
85'-0"	—	WY
105'-0"	—	ID
—	30'-0"	MS
—	28'-6"	AL, AZ, IN, IA, KS, MI, TN, WI
—	28'-0"	AK, CT, DC, FL, KY, NH, NJ, NC, WV
—	27'-6"	RI
—	—	IL, NV, OH, WA

SEMITRAILER AND TRACTOR

MAXIMUM ALLOWABLE LENGTH EACH

UNIT	TRAILER	STATE
55'-0"	53'-0"	DC
55'-0"	48'-0"	MD
60'-0"	53'-0"	DE, WI
60'-0"	48'-0"	GA, NC, SC, VA, WV
60'-0"	45'-0"	MA, NY
60'-0"	—	MO, OR, VT
65'-0"	57'-0"	TX
65'-0"	53'-0"	OK
65'-0"	50'-0"	LA
65'-0"	48'-0"	HI, ME
65'-0"	—	CA, MN, NM, PA
70'-0"	48'-0"	AK
70'-0"	—	CO, NV
75'-0"	48'-0"	ID, MT
75'-0"	—	ND
80'-0"	53'-0"	SD
85'-0"	60'-0"	WY
—	53'-0"	NB, OH, IL, IN, IA, KS, KY
—	51'-0"	AZ
—	50'-0"	AL, MI, MS
—	48'-0"	AR, CT, FL, NH, NJ, RI, UT, WA
—	—	TN

STRAIGHT BODY TRUCKS

MAXIMUM ALLOWABLE LENGTH

UNIT	STATE
40'-0"	In all states, except those listed below
35'-0"	FL, KY, MA, NH, NJ, NY, NC, SC, WV
36'-0"	IN
42'-0"	IL
42'-6"	KS
45'-0"	LA, ME, SD, TX, UT
50'-0"	ND
60'-0"	CT, GA, VT, WY

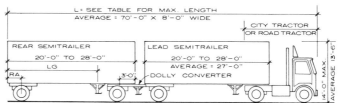

DOUBLE SEMITRAILER AND CITY TRACTOR

CITY TRACTOR

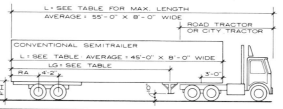

SEMITRAILER AND ROAD TRACTOR
TIRE SIZE APPROX. 41" ± DIA. X 10" ± WIDE

VEHICLE HEIGHT

MAXIMUM ALLOWABLE

TOTAL HEIGHT	STATE
13'-6"	In all states, except those listed below
13'-0"	FL
14'-0"	CA, ID, ME, NV, ND, OR, UT, WA, WY
14'-6"	CO, NB

VEHICLE WIDTH

MAXIMUM ALLOWABLE

TOTAL WIDTH	STATE
8'-6"	In all states, except those listed below
8'-0"	DE, DC, FL, IL, IA, KY, LA, MI, MO, NY, NC, PA, SC, TN, VA, WV

NOTE: Width is 8'-0" or 8'-6" according to state. Length and area restrictions vary with each state and locale. Verify exact dimensions and restrictions.

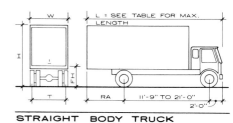

ROAD TRACTOR

STRAIGHT BODY TRUCK

AVERAGE SEMITRAILER DIMENSIONS

	LENGTH (L)			
	27'-0"	40'-0"	45'-0"	REFRIG. 40'-0"
Floor height (FH)	4'-2"	4'-2"	4'-2"	4'-9"
Rear axle (RA)	3'-0"	5'-2"	5'-10"	4'-5"
Landing gear (LG)	19'-0"	30'-0"	34'-6"	29'-5"
Cubic feet (CU)	1564±	2327±	2620±	2113±

AVERAGE DIMENSIONS OF VEHICLES

	TYPE OF VEHICLES		
	DOUBLE SEMITRAILER	CONVENTIONAL SEMITRAILER	STRAIGHT BODY TRUCK
Length (L)	70'-0"	55'-0"	17'-0" to 40'-0"
Width (W)	8'-0"	8'-0"	8'-0"
Height (H)	13'-6"	13'-6"	13'-6"
Floor Height (FH)	4'-0" to 4'-6"	4'-0" to 4'-4"	3'-0" to 4'-0"
Track (T)	6'-6"	6'-6"	5'-10"
Rear Axle (RA)	3'-0" to 4'-0"	4'-0" to 12'-0"	2'-3" to 12'-0"

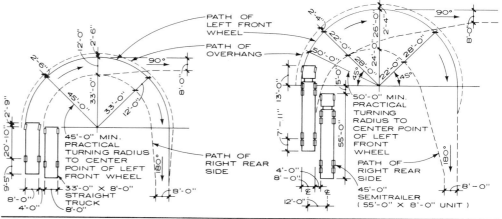

33'-0" STRAIGHT BODY TRUCK MINIMUM PRACTICAL TURNING RADIUS OF 45'-0"

55'-0" SEMITRAILER AND TRACTOR COMBINATION MINIMUM PRACTICAL TURNING RADIUS OF 50'-0"

Robert H. Lorenz, AIA; Preston Trucking Company, Inc.; Preston, Maryland
The Operations Council, American Trucking Association; Washington, D.C.

NOTES

1. Allow for off-street employee and driver parking.
2. Entrances and exits should be of reinforced concrete when excessive twisting and turning of vehicles are expected.
3. Average gate (swing or slide) 30 ft 0 in. wide for two-way traffic. People gate 5 ft 0 in. wide with concrete walkway 4 ft 0 in. to 6 ft 0 in. wide.
4. For yard security use a 6 ft 0 in. high chain link fence with barbed wire on top.
5. On-site fueling facilities are desirable for road units.
6. Provide general yard lighting from fixtures mounted on building or on 24 ft 0 in. high minimum poles at fence line. Mercury vapor or high pressure sodium preferred.
7. Tractor parking requires 12 ft 0 in. wide × 20 ft 0 in. long slot minimum. Provide motor heater outlets for diesel engines in cold climates.
8. Trailer parking requires 10 ft 0 in. wide slot minimum. Provide 10 ft 0 in. wide concrete pad for landing gear. Score concrete at 12 ft 0 in. o.c. to aid in correct spotting of trailer.
9. 4 ft 0 in. wide minimum concrete ramp from dock to grade. Slopes of 3 to 15% (10% average), score surface for traction.
10. Vehicles should circulate in a counterclockwise direction, making left hand turns, permitting driver to see rear of unit when backing into dock.
11. Double trailers are backed into dock separately.

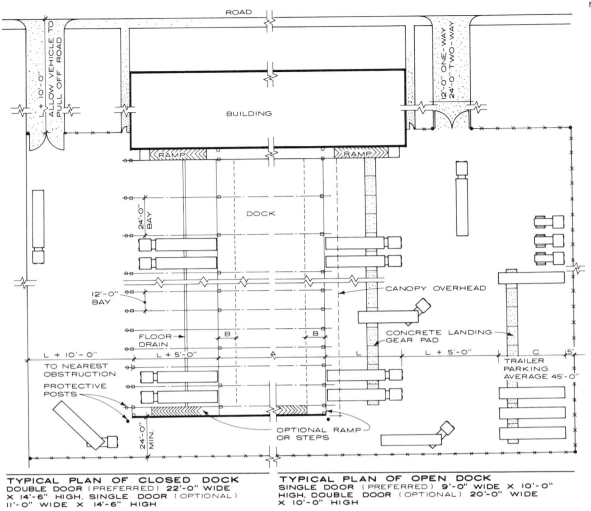

TYPICAL PLAN OF CLOSED DOCK
DOUBLE DOOR (PREFERRED) 22'-0" WIDE × 14'-6" HIGH. SINGLE DOOR (OPTIONAL) 11'-0" WIDE × 14'-6" HIGH

TYPICAL PLAN OF OPEN DOCK
SINGLE DOOR (PREFERRED) 9'-0" WIDE × 10'-0" HIGH. DOUBLE DOOR (OPTIONAL) 20'-0" WIDE × 10'-0" HIGH

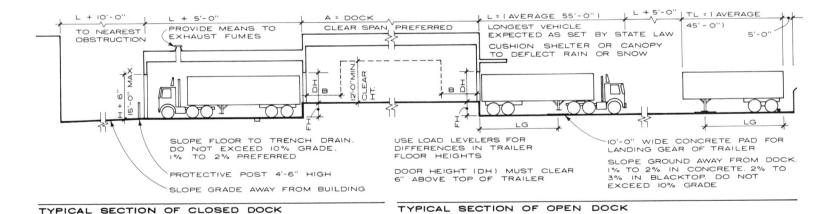

SLOPE FLOOR TO TRENCH DRAIN. DO NOT EXCEED 10% GRADE. 1% TO 2% PREFERRED

PROTECTIVE POST 4'-6" HIGH

SLOPE GRADE AWAY FROM BUILDING

USE LOAD LEVELERS FOR DIFFERENCES IN TRAILER FLOOR HEIGHTS

DOOR HEIGHT (DH) MUST CLEAR 6" ABOVE TOP OF TRAILER

10'-0" WIDE CONCRETE PAD FOR LANDING GEAR OF TRAILER

SLOPE GROUND AWAY FROM DOCK. 1% TO 2% IN CONCRETE. 2% TO 3% IN BLACKTOP. DO NOT EXCEED 10% GRADE

TYPICAL SECTION OF CLOSED DOCK

TYPICAL SECTION OF OPEN DOCK

AVERAGE VEHICLE DIMENSIONS

LENGTH OF VEHICLE (L)	FLOOR HEIGHT (FH)	VEHICLE HEIGHT (H)
60 ft tractor trailer	4'-0" to 4'-6"	14'-0"
45 ft trailer	4'-0" to 4'-2"	13'-6"
40 ft straight body	3'-8" to 4'-2"	13'-6"
18 ft van	2'-0" to 2'-8"	7'-0"

NOTE: Refer to other pages for truck and trailer sizes.

AVERAGE WIDTHS OF DOCKS

TYPE OF OPERATION	TWO-WHEEL HAND TRUCK	FOUR-WHEEL HAND TRUCK	FORKLIFT TRUCK	DRAGLINE	AUTO SPUR DRAGLINE
Dock width (A)	50'-0"	60'-0"	60'-0" to 70'-0"	80'-0"	120'-0" to 140'-0"
Work aisle (B)	6'-0"	10'-0"	15'-0"	10'-0" to 15'-0"	10'-0" to 15'-0"

Robert H. Lorenz, AIA; Preston Trucking Company, Inc.; Preston, Maryland
The Operations Council, American Trucking Association; Washington, D.C.

TRANSPORTATION 2

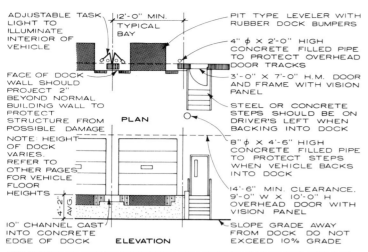

TYPICAL LOADING DOCK BAY

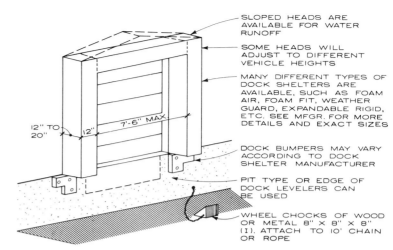

Provides positive weather seal; protects dock from wind, rain, snow, and dirt. Retains constant temperature between dock and vehicle.

CUSHIONED DOCK SHELTER

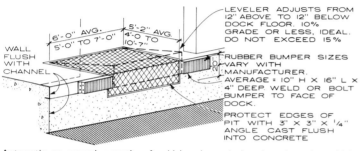

Automatic or manual operation for high volume docks where incoming vehicle heights vary widely; must be installed in a preformed concrete pit. Exact dimensions provided by manufacturer.

PIT TYPE DOCK LEVELER

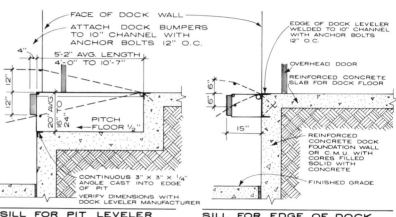

SILL FOR PIT LEVELER   **SILL FOR EDGE OF DOCK LEVELER**

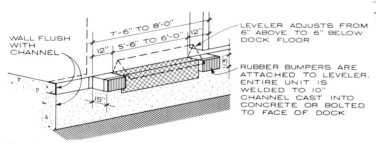

Manual operation for high or medium volume docks where pit type levelers are impractical or leased facilities are being used.

EDGE OF DOCK LEVELER

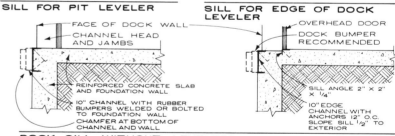

DOCK SILL WITHOUT LEVELERS

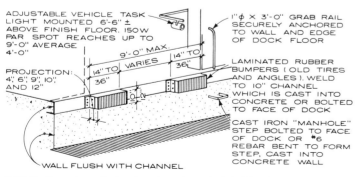

Used for low volume docks where incoming vehicle heights do not vary. Use portable type leveler such as a throw plate.

LOADING DOCK WITHOUT LEVELER

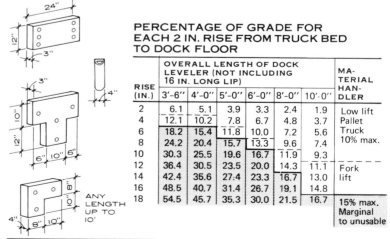

MOLDED HARD RUBBER DOCK BUMPERS

PERCENTAGE OF GRADE FOR EACH 2 IN. RISE FROM TRUCK BED TO DOCK FLOOR

RISE (IN.)	OVERALL LENGTH OF DOCK LEVELER (NOT INCLUDING 16 IN. LONG LIP)						MATERIAL HANDLER
	3'-6"	4'-0"	5'-0"	6'-0"	8'-0"	10'-0"	
2	6.1	5.1	3.9	3.3	2.4	1.9	Low lift Pallet Truck 10% max.
4	12.1	10.2	7.8	6.7	4.8	3.7	
6	18.2	15.4	11.8	10.0	7.2	5.6	
8	24.2	20.4	15.7	13.3	9.6	7.4	
10	30.3	25.5	19.6	16.7	11.9	9.3	Fork lift
12	36.4	30.5	23.5	20.0	14.3	11.1	
14	42.4	35.6	27.4	23.3	16.7	13.0	
16	48.5	40.7	31.4	26.7	19.1	14.8	
18	54.5	45.7	35.3	30.0	21.5	16.7	15% max. Marginal to unusable

Robert H. Lorenz, AIA; Preston Trucking Company, Inc.; Preston, Maryland

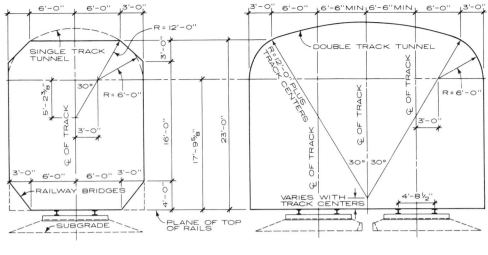

NOTES

1. Given clearances are the recommended minimums of the American Railway Engineering Association. Actual requirements vary from state to state.
2. Clearances shown are for the tangent track and new construction. Clearances for reconstruction work or for alteration are dependent on existing physical conditions and, where reasonably possible, should be improved to meet the requirements for new construction.
3. On curved track, the lateral clearances each side of track center line shall be increased 1½ in. per degree of curvature.
4. Common state requirement for lateral clearance of poles is 8 ft 6 in. (varies from 8 to 12 ft).
5. Standard American railroad gauge of 4 ft 8½ in. is measured between the inner faces of the rails.

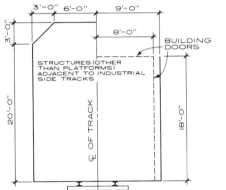

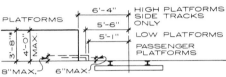

NOTE

The 6 ft 4 in. dimension will accommodate cars with either flush sliding doors or plug doors. Cars with hinged double doors require full clearance of 8 ft. Where 6 ft 4 in. platform is used, full clearance should be provided on opposite side, *except* inside buildings. (Several states allow a platform height of 4 ft 6 in. for refrigerator cars only, if the full lateral clearance of 8 ft is provided.)

RAILWAY CLEARANCES

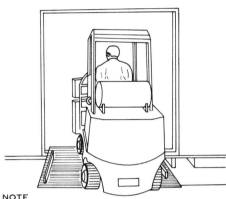

NOTE

Ramp travels laterally on rail mounted to edge of dock for positioning to rail car opening. It adjusts above and below dock level and locks to the rail when in the lowered position. Self-stores in vertical position when not in use. Available in varying lengths and widths.

RAIL DOCK RAMPS

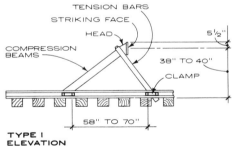

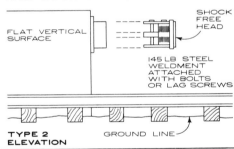

TYPICAL BUMPING POSTS

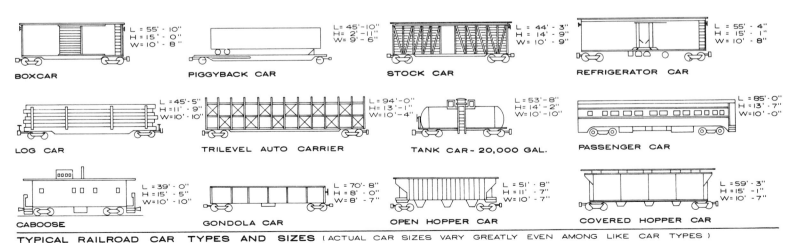

TYPICAL RAILROAD CAR TYPES AND SIZES (ACTUAL CAR SIZES VARY GREATLY EVEN AMONG LIKE CAR TYPES)

Ed Hesner; Rasmussen & Hobbs Architects; Tacoma, Washington
N. Claiborne Porter Jr., AIA; Anchorage, Alaska

MANUFACTURED HOMES

INTRODUCTION

The manufactured housing industry, formerly called mobile homes, has progressed in the past forty years: manufactured home unit widths have increased steadily from 6 to 8 ft (1950), 10 ft (1954), 12 ft (1962), 14 ft (1969), to 16 to 18 ft (1980).

The manufactured home usually has a wheeled chassis, an integral structural part of the housing unit. Manufactured home units are factory finished, interior and exterior.

ACTS AND REGULATIONS

The U.S. Congress enacted the National (then Mobile Home) Manufactured Home Construction and Safety Act of 1974, directing the Department of Housing and Urban Development (HUD) to set national construction and safety standards preempting state laws. These standards are in the Code of Federal Regulations (CFR) as follows:

24 CFR 3280 (Standards)
24 CFR 3282 (Procedural Rules)
24 CFR 3283 (Consumer Installation Manual)

Manufactured home site installation requirements usually are adopted by local and state authorities from a model code such as the one developed by the National Conference of States on Building Codes and Standards, Inc. (NCSBCS), containing ANSI 225.1 and NFPA 501 specifications.

In 1980 Congress changed the designation "Mobile Home" to "Manufactured Home."

The HUD code, which became mandatory on June 15, 1976, as Manufactured Homes Procedural and Enforcement Regulations, established three agencies: State Administrative Agency (SAA); Design Approval Primary Inspection Agency (DAPIA); In-Plant Primary Inspection Agency (IPIA).

This inspection and approval system provides for a single inspection of a home's design and plant approval. The approved home can be shipped to any state for sale without further inspections other than local set-up and foundation requirements. The HUD code includes a provision that the manufacturer remains liable for repairing certain major design or structural defects.

Restrictive zoning requirements gradually are changing. One major difference is the classification of manufactured homes on a homeowner's lot as "chattel" (personal property) instead of as "real estate." The Federal Housing Administration, FHA Title I of 1982, insured only chattel loans, which qualify for short-term, high interest bearing loans.

In 1983, HUD included manufactured housing in the FHA Title II, long-term mortgage financing programs, qualifying this form of housing for lower interest rates. Homes must comply with federal manufactured home construction and safety standards, and they must be attached to permanent site-built foundations meeting local building code requirements.

Legislation passed in 1984 allows the Veteran's Administration to guarantee mortgage financing for manufactured homes on the same basis as for site-built housing.

POST–1986 INSTALLATION INSTRUCTION MANUALS

Manufacturers are required to provide HUD-approved consumer manuals, which must include: an installation manual with instructions for setting and anchoring, and for hookup and connecting utilities, and a homeowner's manual describing maintenance procedures.

The modular home manufacturers also provide installation and homeowner manuals; however, modular homes are built in sections, or pods, and must comply with state and local standards. Foundations, anchoring, and utilities must comply with local building codes. Certification procedures for modular homes differ in each state.

HUD-code and modular homes may be constructed in the same plant and on the same assembly line.

DESIGN

Homes can be manufactured in multiple sections, in 24 to 28 ft widths, 50 to 60 ft long (up to 84 ft), with the option of adding on to. Cathedral ceilings are not uncommon, and even built-in whirlpool baths may be incorporated in the design.

FOUNDATION

The foundation system design must meet installation requirements of the manufacturer's DAPIA-approved installation manual. Soil bearing properties must be known, or analysis is required by a professional engineer. The trend is to use foundations designed by registered architects and engineers, to be approved by regulatory authorities. See NFPA 501A, Chapter 3, Manufactured Home Foundation Systems, and Appendix C, Typical Designs of Piers or Load-Bearing Supports for Manufactured Homes.

ANCHORING AND TIE-DOWN SYSTEMS

Anchors and tie-downs are used to secure the home from overturning due to wind. Systems for HUD-code homes are described in HUD-approved manuals.

Tie-downs must be weather resistant and have a minimum capacity of 3150 lb (plus a 50% overload factor) resistance to withdrawal in the direction of the tie. The same capacity applies when concrete slabs or continuous footings are used. See table below for the number of ties required for hurricane and nonhurricane resistive regions.

Over-the-roof ties are factory installed. Frame ties are furnished by the manufacturer/installer. The number of over-the-roof ties and frame ties varies by wind zone, pier height, and size of home.

The angle of the tie-down strap or cable with the horizontal or vertical plane is critical. Anchors and tie-down straps/cables should not extend outside the fascia or skirting.

BOTTOM BOARD (SKIRT), GROUND VAPOR BARRIER, CLEARANCES, RECOMMENDATIONS

The entire area under the home shall be covered with an approved ground vapor barrier, such as polyethylene film 6-mil thick, 6 in. overlap at joints. The bottom board must be equipped with nonclosing vents. The free air opening of the vents must be equal to not less than $1/300$ of the crawl space plus two times the crawl space perimeter times $1/100$.

Additional vents must be installed adjacent to air intakes, oil burners, or sealed combustion water heaters. At least 75% of the covered area underfloor should have 18 in. clearance between bottom main chassis members and ground level, and not more than 25% of the covered area may have a minimum of 12 in. clearance.

UTILITY CONNECTION, HOOK-UP TO ON-SITE SERVICES TESTING

Multiple section units require specific cross-over connections. Utility hookups must comply with local codes and ordinances. Utility systems and installations that have been equipped and factory tested must be tested on-site by qualified personnel in accordance with the manufacturer's manual and must have 12 in. minimum clearance underneath.

ACCESSORY STRUCTURES

Carports, decks, porches, utility buildings, and fences, unless designed and constructed by the manufacturer or licensed installer, must have a separate structural system and must comply with local codes and ordinances.

SITE LAYOUT

Layout of manufactured home developments does not differ from those for site-built housing developments.

Service buildings no longer are required.

The layout of manufactured home communities must take into consideration setbacks, access to community streets, community streets, walk systems, and maneuvering for the off-loading and installation of 12 to 18 ft wide units, which may be up to 84 ft in length.

See NFPA 501A, Section 2-4, Multiple Manufactured Home Site Development.

NUMBER OF TIES REQUIRED PER SIDE OF SINGLE SECTION[1] MANUFACTURED HOMES[2]
BASED ON A MINIMUM WORKING LOAD PER ANCHOR OF 3150 LB (1429 KG) WITH A 50% OVERLOAD [4725 LB TOTAL]

| LENGTH[3] (FT) | HURRICANE RESISTIVE | | | | NONHURRICANE RESISTIVE | | | |
| | | | ALTERNATE METHOD[4] | | | | ALTERNATE METHOD | |
	NO. OF VERTICAL TIES	NO. OF DIAGONAL TIES[5]	NO. OF BALING STRAPS	NO. OF DIAGONAL TIES[6]	NO. OF VERTICAL TIES	NO. OF DIAGONAL TIES[5]	NO. OF BALING STRAPS	NO. OF DIAGONAL TIES[6]
up to 40	2	4	2	5	2	3	2	3
40 to < 46	2	4	2	6	2	3	2	3
46 to < 49	2	5	2	6	2	3	2	3
49 to < 54	3	5	3	7	2	3	2	3
54 to < 58	3	5	3	7	2	4	2	4
58 to < 64	3	6	3	8	2	4	2	4
64 to < 70	3	6	3	9	2	4	2	4
70 to < 73	3	7	3	9	2	4	2	5
73 to < 84	4	7	4	10	2	5	2	5

[1] Double section manufactured homes require only the diagonal ties specified in column 3 or 7.
[2] Except when the anchoring system is designed and approved by a registered professional engineer or architect.
[3] Length of manufactured home (as used in this table) means length excluding draw bar.
[4] Alternate method. When this method is used, an approved wall reinforcement means shall be provided.
[5] Diagonal ties in this method shall deviate at least 45° from a vertical direction.
[6] Diagonal ties in this method shall be 45° ± 5° from vertical and shall be attached to the nearest main frame member.

Walter Hart Associates, AIA; White Plains, New York
Charles W. Graham, AIA; Texas A & M University; College Station, Texas

TRANSPORTATION

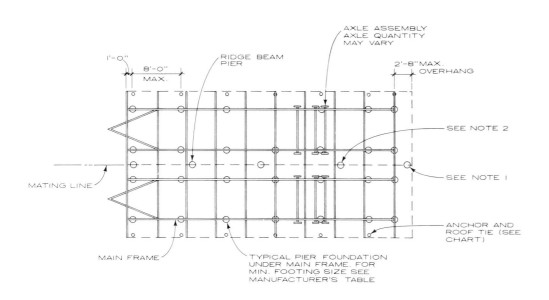

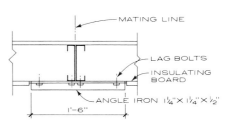

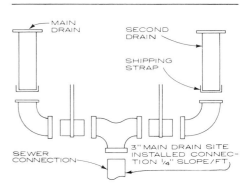

NOTES

1. Required pier capacity at each end of home equals the total distance in feet to the next ridge beam post multiplied by 165 lb/lin. ft.

2. Required pier capacity at interior ridge beam posts equals the distance between each post on each side, in feet, multiplied by 165 lb/lin. ft.

NOTE

Gutters, overflows not hooked up with the drain system shall discharge outside the home perimeter.

EXAMPLES OF FOOTING MAIN FRAME TIE-DOWN

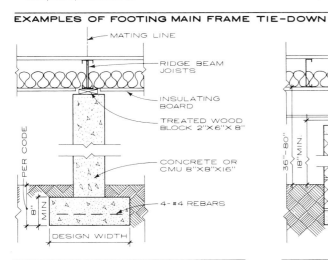

RIDGE BEAM PIER

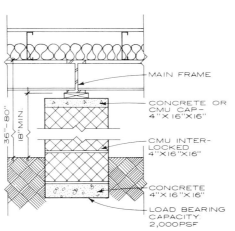

MAIN FRAME PIER

DRAIN SYSTEM HOOKUP

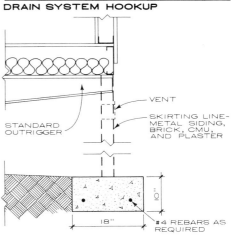

TYPICAL SIDEWALL

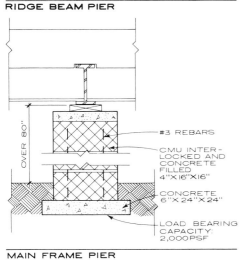

MAIN FRAME PIER

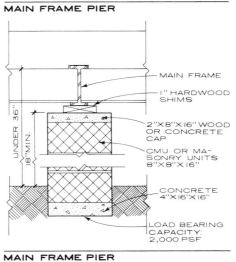

MAIN FRAME PIER

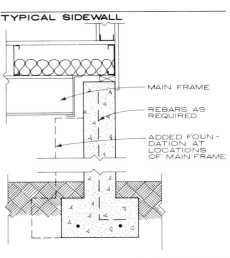

TYPICAL ENDWALL

Walter Hart Associates, AIA; White Plains, New York
Charles W. Graham, AIA; Texas A & M University; College Station, Texas

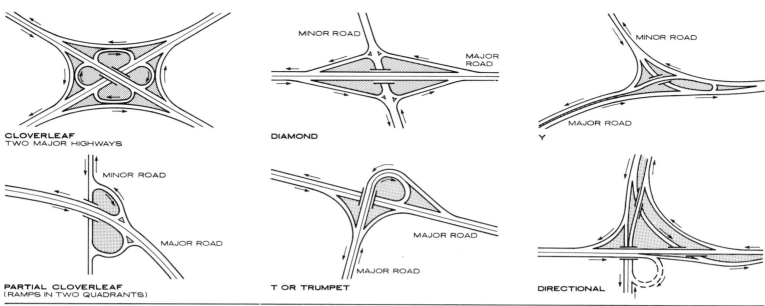

CLOVERLEAF
TWO MAJOR HIGHWAYS

DIAMOND

Y

PARTIAL CLOVERLEAF
(RAMPS IN TWO QUADRANTS)

T OR TRUMPET

DIRECTIONAL

FREEWAY GRADE SEPARATED INTERSECTIONS

"T"

4-WAY

"Y"

EXPRESSWAY / RURAL HIGHWAY
AT GRADE CHANNELIZED INTERSECTIONS

TYPE OF HIGHWAY	VEHICLE CAPABILITIES	WIDTHS		FEATURES
		ROW	PAVEMENT	

Freeway: A high-speed, controlled access highway. Connects regional or metropolitan areas.	Design Flow rate: 1500 VPH/lane
	
	Capacity: 200 VPH/lane
		200 ft.–300 ft.	Without access roads:
			
			Driving lanes: 11 ft.–12 ft. per lane
			
			Shoulders: 8 ft.–10 ft. (both sides each roadway)
			
			Median: 16 ft.–60 ft.
				Divided traffic
				Grade-separated crossings
				Continuous traffic; no stops
				
				DMG: 3%
				Extensive landscape planting
				
				Building setbacks:
				  with service road: 50 ft.
				  without service road: 75 ft.

		300 ft.–400 ft.	With access roads	
Expressway/Rural Highway: Limited-access highway providing connections between metropolitan areas and cities	Design Flow rate: 900 VPH/lane Capacity: 1500 VPH/lane	150 ft.–250 ft.	driving lanes: 11 ft.–12 ft. per lane Shoulders: 8 ft.–10 ft.	Two-way or divided traffic Channelized at grade crossings Traffic signals at major intersections DMG: 4% Landscape planting Parking prohibited Building setback: 75 ft.

VPH: Vehicles per hour   DMG: Desired maximum grade   ROW: Right-of-way

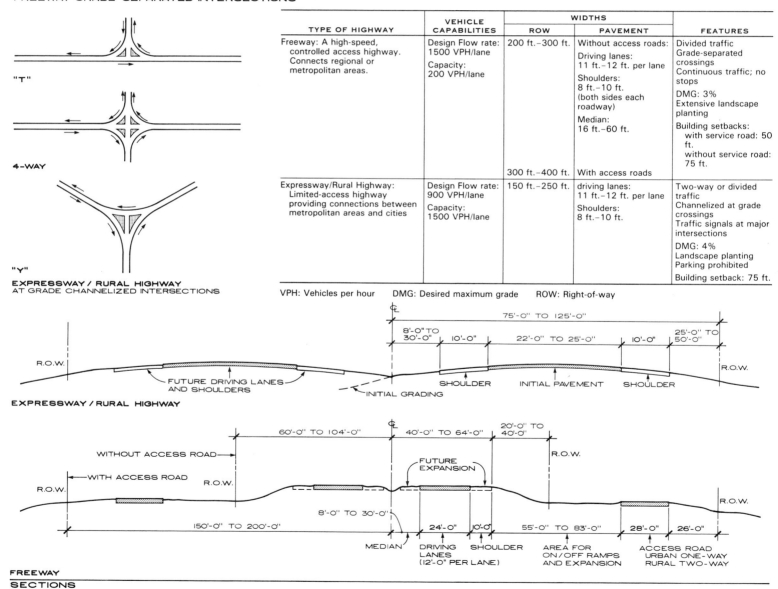

EXPRESSWAY / RURAL HIGHWAY

FREEWAY

SECTIONS

Connecticut Coastal Management Program, see data sources
William H. Evans, AIA; San Antonio, Texas

2 **TRANSPORTATION**

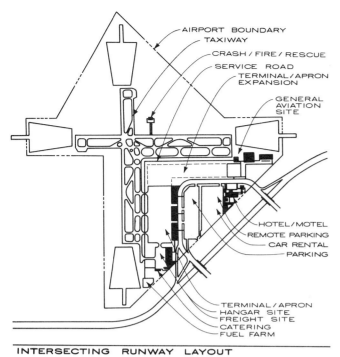

INTERSECTING RUNWAY LAYOUT

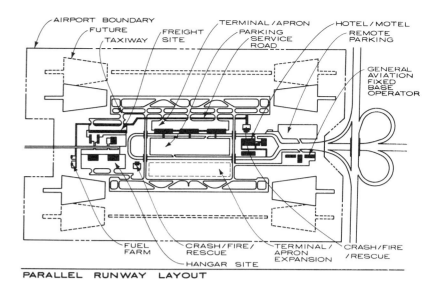

PARALLEL RUNWAY LAYOUT

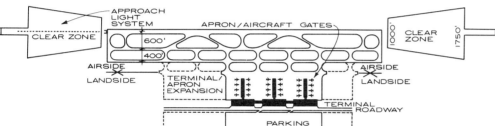

AIRPORT AIRSIDE-LANDSIDE

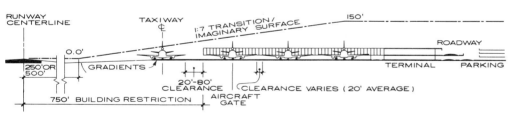

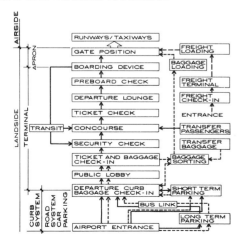

OUTBOUND—U.S. DOMESTIC AND U.S. INTERNATIONAL PASSENGER BAGGAGE AND FREIGHT FLOW FEDERAL INSPECTION SERVICES (F.I.S.) NOT REQUIRED

INBOUND—U.S. DOMESTIC AND U.S. INTERNATIONAL PASSENGER BAGGAGE AND FREIGHT FLOW FEDERAL INSPECTION SERVICES (F.I.S.) REQUIRED

Walter Hart Associates, AIA; White Plains, New York

Runway-taxiway configurations and apron terminal concepts appear in many variations, generally caused by climatic conditions, traffic characteristics, operational requirements, traffic volumes, and historical growth patterns.

Two airport plans are shown: (1) an intersecting runway configuration, total land area small to medium, the landside facilities are arranged within one quadrant, expansion capability is limited; (2) a parallel runway configuration, total land area medium to large, the landside facilities are arranged within the area between the runways, expansion capability is significant.

The airport airside consists of the runway-taxiway system, areas for clearances, and areas for navigational aides.

The airport landside consists of the passenger terminal with aircraft apron; airport ground transportation systems, roads, vehicular parking; support facilities, hangars, freight terminals, U.S. mail, catering, car rental, hotels, motels. The airside influences the location, plan development, and expansion capabilities of the landside facilities.

Requirements, recommendations, criteria, and guidelines are documented in the United States by the Department of Transportation/Federal Aviation Administration (DOT/FAA) and by the Air Transport Association of America (ATA), outside the United States by the International Civil Aviation Organization (ICAO) and the International Air Transport Association (IATA).

The following publications contain basic information on airport planning and design:

1. A Model Zoning Ordinance to Limit Height of Objects Around Airports, AC 150/5190-4, FAA, Dec. 5, 1983, Washington, D.C.
2. Utility Airports—Air Access to National Transportation, AC 150/5300-4B, FAA, June 24, 1975, incorporates Changes 1–6, Change 7, Sept. 23, 1983, Washington, D.C.
3. Airport Design Standards—Transport Airports, DOT/FAA, AC 150/5300-12, Feb. 28, 1983, Washington, D.C.
4. Planning and Design Guidelines for Airport Terminal Facilities, FAA AC 150/5360-7A, DOT/FAA, Washington, D.C.
5. Runway Capacity Criteria for Airport Planning Purposes, 5th edition, ATA, Washington, D.C.
6. Airline Aircraft Gates and Passenger Terminal Space Approximations, AD/CS Report No. 4, July 1977, ATA, Washington, D.C.
7. Aircraft Ground Support Air System Planning Guide Book, prepared for ATA, Nov. 1981, by Burns & McDonnell, Engineers, Architects, & Consultants, Kansas City, Mo.
8. Guidelines for Airport Signing and Graphics, ATA, Sept. 1984, Washington, D.C.

Small Airports:

9. Planning and Design of Airport Terminal Facilities at Non Hub Locations, AC 150/5360-9, FAA, Mar. 4, 1980.

Heliports:

10. Heliport Design Guide, AC 150/5390-1B, FAA, Aug. 1977.

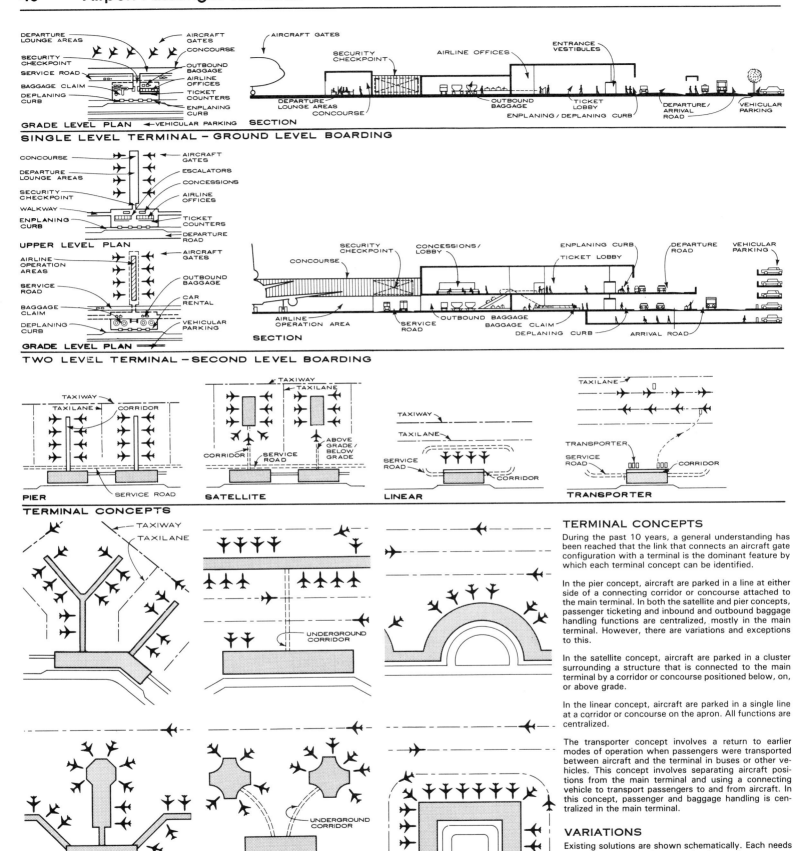

SINGLE LEVEL TERMINAL — GROUND LEVEL BOARDING

TWO LEVEL TERMINAL — SECOND LEVEL BOARDING

TERMINAL CONCEPTS

CONCEPT VARIATIONS

TERMINAL CONCEPTS

During the past 10 years, a general understanding has been reached that the link that connects an aircraft gate configuration with a terminal is the dominant feature by which each terminal concept can be identified.

In the pier concept, aircraft are parked in a line at either side of a connecting corridor or concourse attached to the main terminal. In both the satellite and pier concepts, passenger ticketing and inbound and outbound baggage handling functions are centralized, mostly in the main terminal. However, there are variations and exceptions to this.

In the satellite concept, aircraft are parked in a cluster surrounding a structure that is connected to the main terminal by a corridor or concourse positioned below, on, or above grade.

In the linear concept, aircraft are parked in a single line at a corridor or concourse on the apron. All functions are centralized.

The transporter concept involves a return to earlier modes of operation when passengers were transported between aircraft and the terminal in buses or other vehicles. This concept involves separating aircraft positions from the main terminal and using a connecting vehicle to transport passengers to and from aircraft. In this concept, passenger and baggage handling is centralized in the main terminal.

VARIATIONS

Existing solutions are shown schematically. Each needs thorough analysis before adoption in any form or combination.

Walter Hart Associates, AIA; White Plains, New York
Benito Lao, RA; Fort Worth, Texas

2 **TRANSPORTATION**

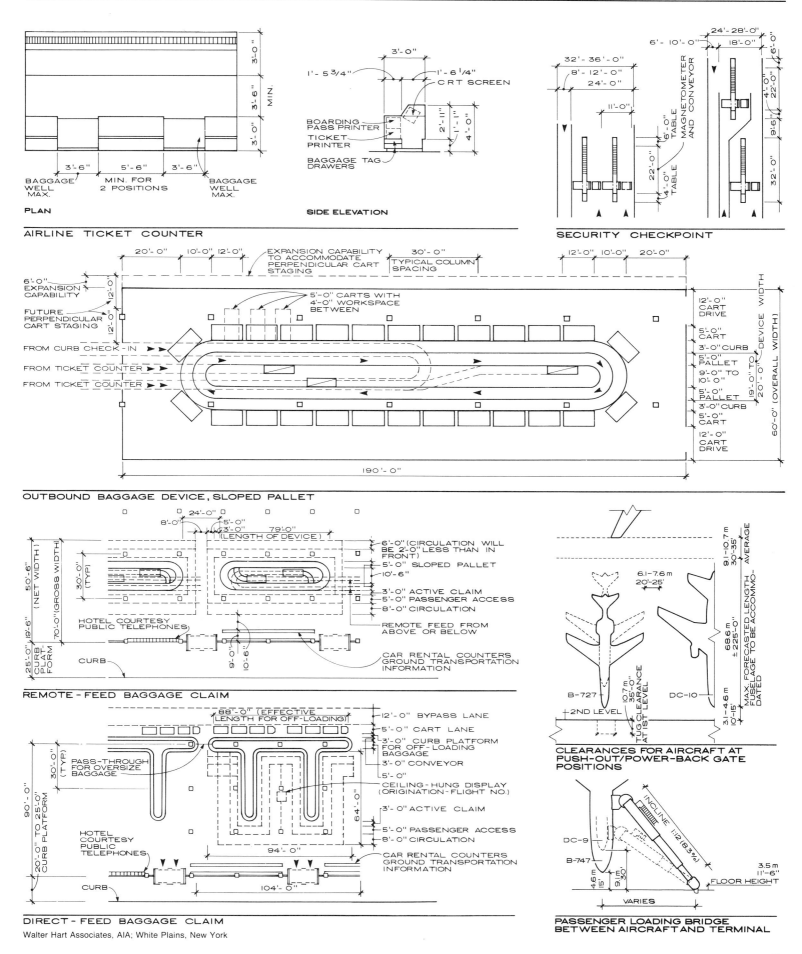

AIRLINE TICKET COUNTER

PLAN

SIDE ELEVATION

SECURITY CHECKPOINT

OUTBOUND BAGGAGE DEVICE, SLOPED PALLET

REMOTE-FEED BAGGAGE CLAIM

DIRECT-FEED BAGGAGE CLAIM

Walter Hart Associates, AIA; White Plains, New York

CLEARANCES FOR AIRCRAFT AT PUSH-OUT/POWER-BACK GATE POSITIONS

PASSENGER LOADING BRIDGE BETWEEN AIRCRAFT AND TERMINAL

GENERAL

A heliport is composed of both real and imaginary surfaces. Real surfaces are the takeoff–landing areas, which include the touchdown pad, peripheral area, taxiways, passenger service building (terminal), and maintenance and hanger facilities. Imaginary surfaces are the approach–departure paths and primary and transitional surfaces. The imaginary surfaces define the lines of flight to and from the real surfaces. Approach–departure paths are selected based on considerations of prevailing winds, the locations and heights of buildings or other objects in the area, and environmental factors. It is desirable for a heliport to have two approach–departure paths separated by an angle of at least 90°. Curved approach–departure paths are permitted and may be necessary in some cases to provide a suitable obstruction-free path.

ENVIRONMENTAL FACTORS

Establishment of a heliport should include an assessment of the following in regard to the impact on the community:
1. Public safety
2. Noise
3. Exhaust emissions
4. Land-use zoning
5. Ground traffic

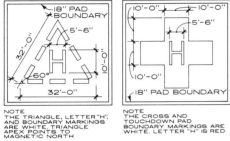

STANDARD SYMBOL **HOSPITAL SYMBOL**

NOTE
THE TRIANGLE, LETTER "H", AND BOUNDARY MARKINGS ARE WHITE. TRIANGLE APEX POINTS TO MAGNETIC NORTH

NOTE
THE CROSS AND TOUCHDOWN PAD BOUNDARY MARKINGS ARE WHITE. LETTER "H" IS RED

RECOMMENDED HELIPORT MARKINGS

CLASSIFICATIONS OF HELIPORTS

PERSONAL USE

A heliport used exclusively by the owner. Personal-use heliports are owned by individuals and corporations.

PRIVATE USE

Any heliport that restricts usage to the owner or to persons authorized by the owner. It may be owned by a public body such as a hospital or police department.

PUBLIC USE

A heliport that is open to the public and does not require permission of the owner for use. The extent of the heliport facilities may limit operations to helicopters of a specific size and weight.

FEDERAL

Heliport facilities operated by a department or nonmilitary agency of the United States government.

MILITARY

A heliport operated by one of the United States uniformed services; public use is generally prohibited.

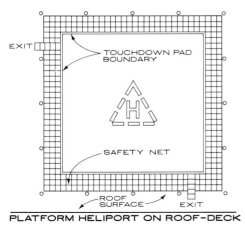

PLATFORM HELIPORT ON ROOF-DECK

Stanley N. Hall; Washington, D.C.

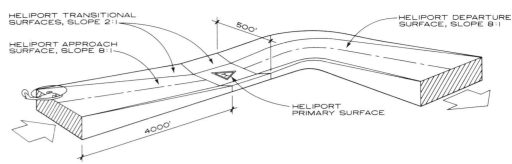

HELIPORT APPROACH/DEPARTURE PATH

HELIPORT SURFACE RELATIONSHIPS

RECOMMENDED DESIGN CRITERIA

DESIGN FEATURE	HELIPORT CLASSIFICATION	
	PUBLIC	PRIVATE
Helicopter Approach Surface		
Number of surfaces	2	
Angular separation	90° minimum, 180° preferred	
Length	4000 ft	
Inner width	1.5x helicopter overall length	
Outer width	500 ft	
Slope	8:1	
Helicopter Transitional Surface		
Length	Full length of approaches and primary surface	
Width	250 ft measured from approach and primary surface centerlines	
Slope	2:1	
Helicopter Primary Surface		
Length, width, and diameter	1.5x helicopter overall length	
Elevation	Elevation highest point of takeoff and landing area	
Takeoff and Landing Area		
Length, width, and diameter	1.5x helicopter overall length	
Touchdown Pad		
Ground level, minimum		
Length and diameter	2.0x wheelbase	1.5x wheelbase
Width	2.0x tread	1.5x tread
Elevated, minimum		
Length and diameter	1.0x rotor diameter	1.5x wheelbase
Width	1.0x rotor diameter	1.5x tread
Peripheral Area		
Recommended width	.25x helicopter overall length	
Taxiway		
Paved width	Variable, 20 ft minimum	
Parking Position		
Length, width, and diameter	1.0x helicopter overall length	
Clearances—Rotor tip to object taxiways and parking positions	10 ft minimum	
Pavement Grades		
Touchdown pad, taxiways, and parking positions	2.0% maximum	
Other Grades		
Turf shoulders, infield area, etc.	Variable, 1.5 to 3%	

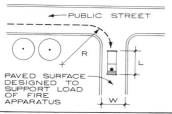

FIRE APPARATUS ACCESS

Fire apparatus (i.e., pumpers, ladder trucks, tankers) should have unobstructed access to buildings. Check with local fire department for apparatus turning radius (R), length (L), and other operating characteristics.

RESTRICTED ACCESS
Buildings constructed near cliffs or steep slopes should not restrict access by fire apparatus to only one side of the building. Grades greater than 10 percent make operation of fire apparatus difficult and dangerous.

FIRE DEPARTMENT RESPONSE TIME FACTOR
Site planning factors that determine response time are street accessibility (curbs, radii, bollards, T-turns, culs-de-sac, street and site slopes, street furniture and architectural obstructions, driveway widths), accessibility for firefighting (fire hydrant and standpipe connection layouts, outdoor lighting, identifying signs), and location (city, town, village, farm). Check with local codes, fire codes, and fire department for area regulations.

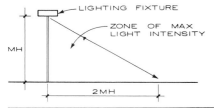

OUTDOOR LIGHTING

Streets that are properly lighted enable fire fighters to locate hydrants quickly and to position apparatus at night. Avoid layouts that place hydrants and standpipe connections in shadows. In some situations, lighting fixtures can be integrated into exterior of buildings. All buildings should have a street address number on or near the main entrance.

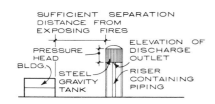

GRAVITY TANK

Gravity tanks can provide reliable source of pressure to building standpipe or sprinkler systems. Available pressure head increases by 0.434 psi/ft increase of water above tank discharge outlet. Tank capacity in gallons depends on fire hazard, water supply, and other factors. Tanks require periodic maintenance and protection against freezing during cold weather. Locations subject to seismic forces or high winds require special consideration. Gravity tanks also can be integrated within building design.

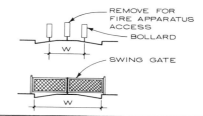

ACCESS OBSTRUCTIONS

Bollards used for traffic control and fences for security should allow sufficient open road width (W) for access by fire apparatus. Bollards and gates can be secured by standard fire department keyed locks (check with department having jurisdiction).

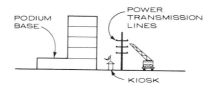

STREET FURNITURE AND ARCHITECTURAL OBSTRUCTIONS

Utility poles can obstruct use of aerial ladders for rescue and fire suppression operations. Kiosks, outdoor sculpture, fountains, newspaper boxes, and the like can also seriously impede fire fighting operations. Wide podium bases can prevent ladder access to the upper stories of buildings. Canopies and other non-structural building components can also prevent fire apparatus operations close to buildings.

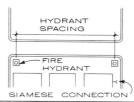

FIRE HYDRANT AND STANDPIPE CONNECTION LAYOUT

Locate fire hydrants at street intersections and at intermediate points along roads so that spacing between hydrants does not exceed about 300 ft. (Check with local authority having fire jurisdiction for specific requirements.) Hydrants should be placed 2 to 10 ft from curb lines. Siamese connections to standpipes should be visible, marked conspicuously, and be within 200 ft of hydrant to allow rapid connection by fire fighters.

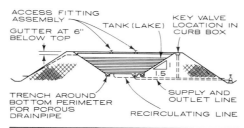

ON-SITE LAKES

Man-made and natural on-site lakes are used for private firefighting in suburbs, on farms, and at resorts. Piped supply system (suction facilities) is preferred for its quantity flexibility, better maintenance, and accessibility. Man-made lakes such as reservoir liner are berm-supported or sunk in the ground. Lakes and ponds are natural water supplies dependent on the environment. See local codes, fire codes, and fire departments for on-site lake regulations.

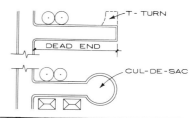

DRIVEWAY LAYOUTS

Long dead ends (greater than 150 ft) can cause time consuming, hazardous backup maneuvers. Use t-turns, culs-de-sac, and curved driveway layouts to allow unimpeded access to buildings.

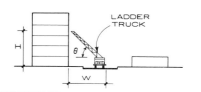

DRIVEWAY WIDTHS

For full extension of aerial ladders at a safe climbing angle (θ), sufficient driveway width (W) is required. Estimate the required width in feet by: $W = (H - 6) \cot \theta + 4$, where preferred climbing angles are 60 to 80°. Check with local fire department for aerial apparatus operating requirements.

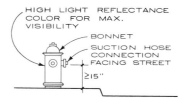

FIRE HYDRANT PLACEMENT

Fire hose connections should be at least 15″ above grade. Do not bury hydrants or locate them behind shrubs or other visual barriers. Avoid locations where runoff water and snow can accumulate. Bollards and fences used to protect hydrants from vehicular traffic must not obstruct fire fighters' access to hose connections. Suction hose connection should usually face the side of arriving fire apparatus.

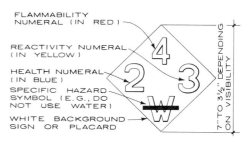

NFPA 704 DIAMOND SYMBOLS

Standard diamond symbols provide information fire fighters need to avoid injury from hazardous building contents. 0 numeral is the lowest degree of hazard, 4 is highest. Locate symbols near building entrances. Correct spatial arrangement for two kinds of diamond symbols are shown. Consider integrating symbols with overall graphics design of building. (Refer to "Identification of the Fire Hazards of Materials," NFPA No. 704, available from the National Fire Protection Association.)

M. David Egan, P.E.; College of Architecture, Clemson University; Clemson, South Carolina
Nicholas A. Phillips, AIA; Lockwood Greene; New York, New York
National Fire Protection Association, see data sources

FLOOD DAMAGE MANAGEMENT

Flood damage results from a combination of floods and non-flood-resistant construction in flood-prone areas. Floods cannot be prevented, merely diverted from one area to another. Structural flood diversion facilities such as dams and levees encourage development of high-hazard areas with consequent increases in flood damage. For example, levee overtopping or failure is involved in about one-third of all flood disasters. Floodplain management, which regulates the use of floodplains and requires flood-resistant construction, can provide more reliable protection than structural flood diversion.

The designer bears the primary responsibility for flood damage management. The designer should evaluate building sites for their intrinsic suitability for the intended use. The designer also should select suitable architectural flood-resisting measures to compensate for deficiencies in the site and in public flood damage management programs.

Successful flood damage management requires the cooperation of the designer and public bodies. Public responsibility for flood damage management is shared by local and state governments and federal agencies, such as the Federal Emergency Management Agency (FEMA), the Office of Wetlands Protection, and the Army Corps of Engineers. Local governments often regulate floodplain use and drainage design. They also may require flood-resistant construction of buildings and infrastructures. Regional, state, and federal governments may provide regional floodplain management, protect ecosystems essential for flood damage control, such as wetlands, coastal dunes, and mangrove stands, and build regional flood diversion facilities.

The National Flood Insurance Program (NFIP) is a program to reduce federal expenditures for flood disaster relief. FEMA provides subsidized flood damage insurance to induce communities to adopt floodplain management programs. NFIP minimum standards require a low level of flood damage management based on historic condition. Many communities establish higher standards. They may regulate runoff, have freeboard requirements, or may base regulatory flood elevations on projections of effects of future development. Local standards more strict than NFIP supersede NFIP standards.

FLOOD TERMS

Floodplain: The relatively flat area within which a river moves and upon which it regularly overflows.

Regulatory floodplain: That portion of the floodplain subject to floodplain regulations, usually that inundated by the base flood. Some communities regulate the 0.2% per year floodplain (500-year flood, NFIP Zone B).

Riverine flood: A great overflow of water from a river channel onto a floodplain. Riverine floods are caused by precipitation over large areas or by the melting of a winter's accumulation of snow, or both.

Flash flood: A local flood of great volume and short duration. Flash floods differ from riverine floods in their extent and duration. Flash floods generally result from a torrential rain or "cloudburst" on a relatively small drainage area. Flash floods also result from the failure of a dam or from the sudden breakup of an ice jamb.

Tidal flood: An overflow onto coastal lands bordering an ocean, an estuary, or a lake. These coastal lands, such as barrier islands, shores, and wetlands, occupy the same protective position relative to the sea that floodplains do to rivers.

Base flood (1% flood, 100-year flood): Under NFIP, the minimum size flood to be used by a community as a basis for its floodplain management regulations. It is presently required to be that flood which has a 1% chance of being equaled or exceeded in any given year.

The base flood is the still water height for riverine floods. The base flood for the Atlantic Coast and the Gulf of Mexico includes storm surge plus wave crest height because of "northeasters" and hurricanes. The base flood for the Pacific Coast includes astronomical tides plus wave runup because of tropical cyclones and tsunamis (seismic sea waves). For major lakes, the base flood includes seiche, "sloshing" because of wind, seismic activity, and storm surge.

Standard project flood: A flood that may be expected from the most severe combination of meteorological and hydrological conditions that are considered reasonably characteristic of the geographic area in which the drainage basin is located, but excluding extremely rare combinations. The peak flow for a standard project flood is generally 40–60% of the probable maximum flood for the same location. It is used in designing dams and other facilities with high damage potential.

Probable maximum flood: The most severe flood that may be expected from a combination of the most critical meteorological and hydrological conditions that are reasonably possible in a drainage basin. It is used in designing high-risk flood protection works and siting of structures and facilities that must be subject to almost no risk of flooding.

Base flood elevation (BFE): The height of the base flood in reference to mean sea level as defined by the National Geodetic Vertical Datum of 1929 (NGVD 1929).

Regulatory flood datum (RFD): The base flood plus a freeboard factor of safety established for each particular area, which tends to compensate for uncertainties that could contribute to greater flood height than that computed for a base flood.

Freeboard: A factor of safety for flood damage prevention expressed in feet above a design flood level.

Freeboard allows for hazards excluded from consideration and the uncertainties in analysis, design, and construction which cannot be fully or readily considered in an analytical fashion. Severe structural subsidence increases in floods because of obstructions in the floodplain or because of the urban runoff effect, and long-term increases in sea level and storms because of global temperature changes are often excluded from consideration. Urban conditions, low-accuracy map bases, and unplanned development are common sources of uncertainty which justify freeboard.

USE ZONES

Floodway: The channel of a watercourse and those portions of the adjoining floodplain required to provide for the passage of a specified flood with an insignificant increase in the flood levels above that of natural conditions. As used by the NFIP, floodways must be large enough to pass the 100-year flood without causing an increase in elevation of more than a specified amount (1 ft in most areas).

Uses permitted in a floodway are those having a low flood damage potential and which do not obstruct flood flows, provided they do not require structures, fill, or storage of materials or equipment. Fill is prohibited. Most structures are prohibited or strongly discouraged. The following are generally permitted uses:

Agricultural uses such as general farming, pasture, grazing, outdoor plant nurseries, horticulture, viticulture, truck farming, forestry, sod farming, and wild crop harvesting.

Incidental industrial-commercial uses such as loading areas, parking areas, and airport landing strips (except in flash flood areas).

Recreational uses such as golf courses, tennis courts, driving ranges, archery ranges, picnic grounds, boat launching ramps, swimming areas, parks, wildlife and nature preserves, game farms, fish hatcheries, shooting preserves, target ranges, trap and skeet ranges, hunting and fishing areas, and hiking and horseback riding trails.

Incidental residential uses such as lawns, gardens, parking areas, and play areas.

Floodway fringe (flood fringe): The portion of the regulatory floodplain outside of the floodway, but still subject to flooding. The flood fringe is primarily a storage area for flood waters. Where permitted, property owners on each side of the floodplain may obstruct the flood flows to an equivalent degree.

Uses permitted in the floodway fringe include those permitted in floodways and elevated or otherwise flood-proofed structures. Prohibited or strongly discouraged uses include storage of materials that are flammable or explosive in water, or toxic, and vital facilities such as hospitals and civil defense or rescue facilities, and difficult to evacuate facilities such as nursing homes and prisons.

SOURCES

Coastal Construction Manual, FEMA-55, Dames & Moore, and Bliss & Nyitray, Inc. 1986.

Elevated Residential Structures, FEMA-54, American Institute of Architects, 1984.

Elevating to the Wave Crest Level: A Benefit:Cost Analysis, FIA-6, Sheaffer & Roland, Inc., 1980.

Facing Geologic and Hydrologic Hazards: Earth-Science Considerations, W. W. Hays, ed., U.S. Geological Survey, 1981.

Floodplain Management Handbook, Flood Loss Reduction Associates, U.S. Water Resources Council, 1981.

Floodproofing Nonresidential Structures, FEMA-102, Booker Associates, Inc., 1986.

The Floodway: A Guide for Community Permit Officials, Community Assistance Series No. 4, FEMA.

The Granite Garden: Urban Nature and Human Design, Anne Whiston Spirn, Basic Books, Inc., New York, 1984.

Guidelines for Determining Flood Flow Frequency, Bulletin #17B of the Hydrology Committee, U.S. Water Resources Council, 1981.

A Levee Policy for the National Flood Insurance Program, National Research Council, National Academy Press, 1982.

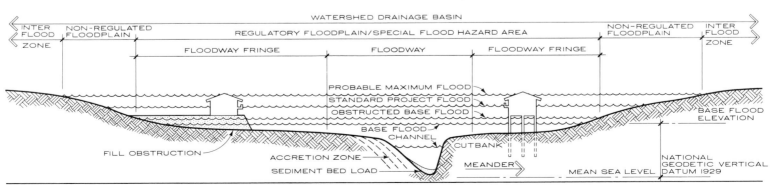

IDEALIZED RIVERINE PROFILE

Mattie Ann Fincher; Baton Rouge, Louisiana
National Research Council; Spirn; see data sources

FLOOD RISK AND FLOOD RISK FACTORS

Flood risk is the hazard or exposure to the chance of injury or loss due to floods.

Freeboard can be used to compensate for uncertainties in estimating risk. For example, some communities require up to 3 ft freeboard to compensate for low-accuracy floodplain base maps. The margin of error of base maps may be estimated as plus or minus one-half of the contour interval. Maps developed from aerial photos usually have a contour interval of 5 ft. Thus, the margin of error is ±2½ ft. Field survey maps with a contour interval of 2 ft or less are used in some communities. This reduces the uncertainty of the risk and the need for freeboard.

Flood risk factors indicate the probability that one or more floods will exceed a given magnitude within a specified period of years. The risk factor (probability of exceedance, P) is the reciprocal of the recurrence interval (T): $P = 1/T$. Thus, there is a 1% chance or risk factor that the 100-year flood will be exceeded in a given year (1% = 1/100). Actual risk may exceed the risk factor.

The risk factor chart can be used to determine the risk factor during a specified time period, and vice versa. Example: Estimate the flood risk factor for a house built at the base flood elevation (BFE) during the life of a 30-year mortgage. On the risk factor chart, (1) locate the recurrence interval, 30 years, at the bottom, (2) move up to the annual exceedance frequency curve for the base flood, 1%, and then (3) move left to interpolate the risk factor, 26%.

FLOOD RISK ZONES

Structures in flood zones must protect their interiors and contents from inundation and must resist flotation, collapse, and lateral movement. Also, they should not increase flooding in other areas. There are five major risk zones, each with special flood resistance requirements.

Interflood zone: Low-risk upland areas of a watershed above the natural floodplain.

Nonregulated floodplain: Moderate-risk floodplain between the interflood zone and the regulatory floodplain.

In the interflood zone and the nonregulated floodplain, risks are usually caused by improper design of grading and drains or moderate- to low-frequency floods. In these zones, local agencies often regulate minimum building elevations above street or sewer levels. Local regulations may also control runoff, soil erosion, and sedimentation to prevent worsening floods.

Special flood hazard areas (zone A): High-risk areas, defined by the National Flood Insurance Program (NFIP) as riverine flood-prone areas identified as susceptible to inundation by the still water base flood.

Nonvelocity coastal flood areas (zone A): High-risk areas, defined by the NFIP as coastal flood-prone areas susceptible to inundation by the base flood, including storm surges with velocity waves of less than 3 ft and a still water depth of less than 4 ft. The water may be moving at high velocities in zone A because of the residual momentum of breaking waves.

In zone A, residences must have their lowest floor, usually including basements, elevated to the BFE. Flood-resistant residential basements are permitted only in communities that meet special NFIP flood criteria and adopt special local standards for their design and construction. Commercial structures must be elevated or otherwise floodproofed to the BFE.

Coastal high hazard areas (velocity zone, zone V): Very high-risk areas, defined by the NFIP as coastal flood-prone areas identified as susceptible to inundation by the base flood, including tidal surges with velocity waves greater than 3 ft. Generally, zone V indicates the inland extent of a 3-ft breaking wave, where the still water depth during the 100-year flood decreases to less than 4 ft.

In zone V the lowest horizontal structural member of the lowest habitable floor must be elevated above the BFE. Structural requirements are most stringent in zone V. Rigid frames and semirigid frames with grade beams are used in zone V. Semirigid frames without grade beams should be used only in areas not subject to potential scour. Freestanding pole structures are unsafe for use in zone V. They develop large rotations at moment connections which induce excessive deflection of pilings under sustained lateral loads.

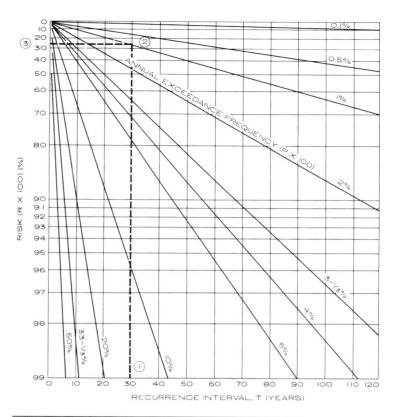

RISK FACTOR CHART

GENERAL LIMITS OF FLOODPROOFING

METHOD	DEPTH	VELOCITY	WARNING REQUIREMENTS
Levees	4-7'	<10'/sec	Advance warning required for installation of floodgates in openings
Floodwalls	4-7'	<12'/sec	
Closures (24 hr max)	4-8'	<8'/sec	5-8 hr advance warning required for installation of closures
Fill	10' +	<10'/sec	Evacuation time required unless fill connects to higher ground
Piles, piers, and columns	10-12'	<8'/sec	Adequate evacuation time required

Note: Information presented is general and warrants caution. Time available for warning may be severely limited by a flood's rate of rise.

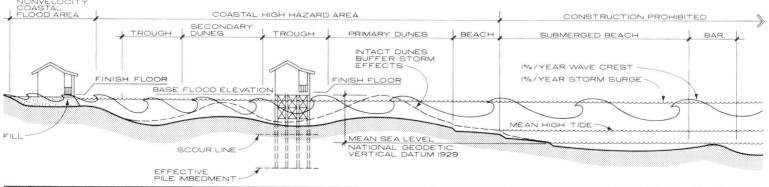

IDEALIZED COASTAL PROFILE

Mattie Ann Fincher; Baton Rouge, Louisiana

SOCIAL IMPACTS

Social impacts are simply the effects on people— the way they live, work, play, and relate to one another—caused by the decision to develop a specific site. Although social impacts can be either beneficial or harmful, it is the latter that are of most concern. Historically there has been little equity in the distribution of adverse impacts. People who have had to bear the bulk of adverse social impact are members of minority groups, the poor, the elderly and the young, all of whom for one reason or another cannot exert sufficient influence on projects to defend adequately against the negative aspects of development. Planners and all other design professionals must be sensitive to the potential social impact their work may generate along with the economic and environmental aspects.

Social impacts can occur at any time during the life of a project. There are anticipatory effects such as land speculation, which occur when a project is still in the planning stage. Later, during construction, the physical intrusion of heavy machinery accompanied by noise, dust, and fumes may assume great importance. Finally, there may be social and other environmental consequences that occur after the completion of a project, sometimes many years later. Some negative impacts are short-lived and, at worst, annoying. Others may impair seriously an individual's ability to learn or to cope effectively in society; still others may precipitate grief, depression, and occasionally, in the case of the elderly, early death.

The social impact as well as economic and environmental impacts should be addressed in all impact studies. Some key questions must be answered in assessing the social impacts of a project:

1. What problems might the project create for the people in the community?
2. How many people will be affected (who gains and who loses)?
3. For how long and how severely will people be affected?
4. What alternatives exist? What happens if another location is selected or if development does not take place?
5. What can be done to lessen the severity of an adverse impact?
6. Is it possible to compensate people adequately for any adverse consequences of the project?
7. Will it significantly alter the pattern of urban development in the area?
8. Will it alter community or neighborhood infrastructure and transportation patterns?
9. Will it generate traffic hazards to pedestrians, motor vehicles, bicyclists or equestrians?
10. Will it create or alter the need for public services in the area, including fire and police protection, and hospital services?
11. Will it have an impact on, or result in the need for new or altered utilities in the area, including water, storm drainage, waste disposal, fuel supplies, and communication systems?
12. Will it adversely affect visibility, scenic resources or viewsheds?
13. Will it change the direction or flow rate of groundwaters?
14. Will it change the quantity or quality of groundwaters, through either direct additions, withdrawals, or through interception of an aquifer by cuts or excavations?
15. Will it substantially reduce the amount of water otherwise available for public water supplies?
16. Will it increase significantly the exposure of people or property to water-related hazards such as flooding or tidal waves?
17. Will it alter the quality of air by creating objectionable odors, altered wind patterns or changes in climate?
18. Will it release air pollutants or noise pollutants?
19. Will it change the patterns of light and solar exposure for adjacent properties?
20. Will it reduce the acreage of any agricultural crop or non-renewable natural resource such as agricultural soils or open space?
21. Will it cause the destruction or impairment of a significant archeological site?
22. Will it require the destruction, removal, or alteration of a significant historical site, structure, or other important cultural resource?

All identifiable potential impacts should be addressed and considered. Potentially adverse consequences should be dealt with thoroughly by the developer or avoided if possible. A relatively straightforward method of classifying potential consequences and responses is to:

1. Identify if a significant impact potential exists for a particular facet of the project;
2. Identify measures to be taken to mitigate and minimize negative impacts; and
3. For items of significant impact, qualify each relative to the long-term productivity versus short-term gain.

Some specific environmental and social concerns may be grouped as follows:

LAND USE AND ZONING

1. Conflict with zoning or general plan designations for the property.
2. Conflict with adjacent, existing or planned land uses.
3. Induce urban growth or alter the location, distribution, density or growth rate of the human population of an area.
4. Affect existing housing or create a demand for additional housing.
5. Preclude opportunities for provision of lower income housing.

TRANSPORTATION, ACCESS AND CIRCULATION

1. Alter present patterns of circulation or movement of people and goods.
2. Alter water, rail or air traffic.
3. Generation of additional vehicular movement.
4. Effects on existing parking facilities or demand for new parking.
5. Traffic hazards to equestrians, motor vehicles, bicyclists or pedestrians.

PUBLIC SERVICES

Effect upon or result in a need for new or altered services in: education, open space and recreation, police, fire protection, hospital and ambulance.

GEOLOGY AND SOILS

1. The destruction, covering or modification of any unique geologic or physical features.
2. Exposure of people or property to earthquake hazards like surface rupture or severe ground shaking.
3. Exposure of people or property to hazards of liquefaction, ground failure or similar hazards.
4. Unstable earth conditions or changes in geologic substructures.
5. Disruptions, displacements, compaction or overcovering of the soil.
6. Destruction, covering or modification of any soils of agricultural, mineral or construction value.
7. Any increase in wind or water erosion of soils, either on or off the site.
8. Changes in deposition or erosion of beach sands, or changes in siltation, deposition or erosion which may modify the channel of a river or stream or the bed of the ocean or any bay, inlet or lake.

UTILITIES

Have an impact on, or result in need for, new or altered utilities in: water, sewer or septic tank, storm water drainage, solid waste and disposal, energy resources, or communications systems.

TOPOGRAPHY

Change in topography or ground surface relief features, which affect: slopes, visibility, scenic resources, aesthetics, or viewsheds.

HYDROLOGY

1. Changes in the currents, or the course or direction of water movements, in either marine or fresh waters.
2. Changes in absorption rates, drainage patterns, or the rate and amount of surface water runoff.
3. Alterations to the course or flow of flood waters.
4. Change in the amount of surface water in any body.
5. Discharge into surface waters, or in any alteration of surface water quality, including but not limited to temperature, dissolved oxygen or turbidity.
6. Alteration of the direction or rate or flow of groundwaters.

7. Change in the quantity or quality of groundwaters, either through direct additions or withdrawals, or through interception of an aquifer by cuts or excavations.
8. Substantial reduction in the amount of water otherwise available for public water supplies.
9. Exposure of people or property to water related hazards such as flooding or tidal waves.

AIR QUALITY

1. Increased air emissions or deterioration of ambient air quality.
2. Creation of objectionable odors.
3. Alteration of air movement, moisture or temperature, or any change in climate, either locally or regionally.
4. Exposure of persons to locally elevated levels of air pollution.

NOISE

Increase in existing noise levels.

CLIMATE

Pattern changes in winds, precipitation, temperature, or sun angles.

PLANT AND ANIMAL LIFE

1. Change in the diversity of species, or number of any species of plants or animals.
2. Reduction of the numbers of any unique, aesthetically significant, rare or endangered species of plants or animals.
3. Introduction of a new species of plants or animals into an area, or as a barrier to the normal replenishment or migration of existing species.

PALEONTOLOGIC, ARCHAEOLOGICAL, AND HISTORIC

1. Destruction, removal or alteration of a significant paleontological site.
2. Destruction, removal or alteration of a significant historical site, structure, object or building or other important cultural or scientific resource.

RANKING OF CONSTRUCTION RELATED SOCIAL IMPACTS USING A HIGHWAY CONSTRUCTION PROJECT EXAMPLE

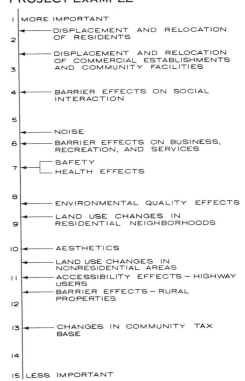

William H. Evans, AIA; San Antonio, Texas
Lynn G. Llewellyn, Ph.D., Social Psychologist; Rockville, Maryland
Connecticut Coastal Management Program, see data sources

THE SITE PLANNING PROCESS

INTRODUCTION

Site planning for any significant development project should be a sequential process, beginning with broad information-gathering and ending with specific, detailed design drawings. The process involves three basic stages: analysis, design, and implementation. The following chart indicates a planning process; however, it should be noted that the site planning process will be specific to the particular project. The following is a checklist approach to structure a project. Specifics of the site, such as physical site characteristics, urban or suburban location, and community criteria, will modify the process. The site planning process is interdisciplinary, and includes both architect and landscape architect. An integrated approach to site development and architecture helps create a quality environment.

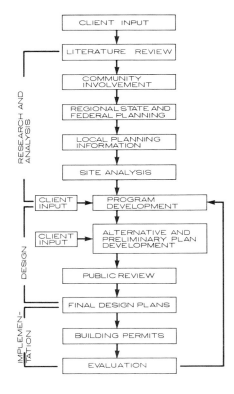

Also important, particularly in urban infill situations, is the involvement of the community in providing input to the design process. Although most site planning processes involve some form of public hearing, a less structured involvement early in the design process will be useful in designing a project that responds to existing community desires and aspirations. Certain steps in the following process may be taken simultaneously, rather than on a precise step-by-step basis.

CLIENT CONTACT AND INPUT

The first step is the contact between client and site planner. Although the site planner should be involved as early as possible in the decision-making process, the client already may have some broad objectives based on financial capabilities and market feasibility. In many cases, it may be advisable for the client to retain the site planner for assistance in selecting a site that meets the client's basic aims. It is important that the site planner obtain all client data relative to the planning of the site.

LITERATURE REVIEW

Site planning problems vary from rural and suburban sites to intensive urban sites. It often is beneficial to review literature relevant to the nature of the particular site planning problem. Current literature is available on responsibilities of designers working within an existing urban framework.

Gary Greenan, AICP; Miami, Florida
Rafael Diaz, Graphics Coordinator; Miami, Florida

COMMUNITY INVOLVEMENT

Early in the design process it is important to contact community groups that have an interest in the proposed project. Involvement of such groups may provide valuable information about their concept of the existing community and their view of possible changes. It is particularly important for infill projects when edges of the proposed project are adjacent to existing development. The compatibility of the edges—building intensity, scale, lot size and design—are typical issues that should be resolved with community participation. Also, an early cooperative effort can defray problems later at public hearing stages. Citizen contact should be maintained throughout the design process.

REGIONAL, STATE, AND FEDERAL PLANNING

In some areas of the country, regional planning agencies have been established for research and planning of intercommunity regional issues such as water management, transportation, population studies, pollution control, and other regional environmental concerns. Many communities have adopted plans that establish regional planning guidelines on land use planning. The site planner should pinpoint regional issues pertinent to the site design.

Some projects also may be affected by state and/or national criteria, although this is not a common occurrence. Adopted state plans may address broad issues applicable to large sites or impose constraints on sites involving issues of statewide concern. Also, some states require environmental impact statements for large-scale projects. At the national level, the Environmental Protection Agency, a non-permitting agency, has delegated its authority to various permitting agencies involved in the protection of air and water quality. Under the U.S. Clean Water Act, the U.S. Corps of Engineers is responsible for environmental review of proposed dredge and fill operations in navigable waters as well as wetlands. Another federal regulation that will affect many coastline projects is the Federal Flood Insurance Program, which establishes minimum elevations for potential flood areas.

LOCAL PLANNING INFORMATION

At this stage the site planner becomes involved in collecting local planning information that will influence decisions made in the site planning process. Personal contact with local planning and zoning agencies is important in order to comprehend clearly local criteria. Following is a list of information to review.

PLANNING DOCUMENTS

Many communities have adopted comprehensive plans that indicate in general terms, and in some instances in specific terms, the particular land use and intensity of the site. Also, valuable information on the availability and/or phasing of public services and utilities, environmental criteria, traffic planning information, and population trends can be found in most comprehensive plans. Some communities may require that rezoning meet the criteria provided in their comprehensive plans.

In addition to the comprehensive plan, some communities adopt neighborhood or area studies that refine the comprehensive plan as it relates to subareas. Many of these studies stipulate specific zoning categories for individual parcels of land.

URBAN DESIGN STUDIES

Many communities have adopted urban design plans that provide guidance for the coherent development of their urban areas. These documents may range from a general conceptual nature to documents that incorporate specific zoning requirements. Some documents may include compliance with specific urban design requirements. Some provide bonuses in greater land use intensities for incorporating urban amenities such as plazas and squares. These plans usually are developed with major input from the design professions.

ZONING

The intensity and type of land use that can occur is determined by the zoning on a tract of land. A zoning change is required if the planned project differs.

PUBLIC SERVICES AND UTILITIES

Although some information on public services and utilities may be provided in the comprehensive plan or neighborhood study, the critical nature of the availability of these public facilities may require additional research, especially:

1. Availability of public sewer service, access to trunk lines, capacity of the trunk lines, and available in-

creases in the flow. (If sewage lines are not immediately available, the projected phasing of these services must be determined, as well as other possible alternatives to sewage collection and treatment.)
2. Availability of potable water, with the same basic research approach as indicated for sewer service determination.
3. Local and state regulations on freshwater wells and septic tanks.
4. Access to public roads, existing and projected carrying capacity, and levels of service of the roads. (State and local road departments can provide this information.)
5. Availability and capacity of schools and other public facilities such as parks and libraries.

SITE ANALYSIS (SITE INVENTORY)

Site analysis is one of the site planner's major responsibilities. All of the on- and off-site environmental design determinants must be evaluated and synthesized during the site analysis process. The site analysis processes follow later in this section.

PROGRAM DEVELOPMENT

At the program development stage, the background research, citizen input, and the site analysis are combined with client input and synthesized into a set of site development concepts and strategies. Elements that form the basis for program development include market and financial criteria, federal, state, regional, and local planning information, development costs, and the client's basic objectives, combined with site opportunities and constraints as developed in the synthesis of environmental site determinants. Trade-offs and a balancing of the various determinants may be needed to develop an appropriate approach to site development. Consideration of dwelling unit type, density, marketing, time phasing, and other similar criteria, as well as graphic studies of the site, constitute the program. Graphic representations depicting design concepts should be developed clearly for presentation to the client and others who may have input to the process. If the program cannot be accomplished under the existing zoning, the decision to request a zoning change becomes a part of the program.

ALTERNATIVE AND PRELIMINARY PLAN PREPARATION

Once the program is established and accepted by the client, alternative design solutions that meet the program objectives, including basic zoning criteria, are developed. The accepted alternative is further developed into the preliminary plan. This plan should be relatively detailed, showing all spatial relationships, landscaping, and similar information.

PUBLIC REVIEW

If a zoning change is required to implement the plan, review by the public will be required. Some communities will require substantial data, such as impact statements and other narrative and graphic exhibits, while others may require only an application for the zoning change. Local requirements for changes can be complex, and it is imperative for the site planner or the client's attorney to be familiar with local criteria.

FINAL DESIGN PLANS

At this stage, the preliminary plan is further refined to include any modifications that may have been agreed upon at a public hearing. Final design plans, including landscape plans and all required dimensioning, must be provided in the final design.

At this stage, the preliminary plans are further refined into the final site development plans. The final site development plans include fully dimensioned drawings and all landscape plans and site details. Final development plans also include drawings such as legal plats, utilities, and street and drainage plans, prepared by the engineer or surveyor. Upon approval, final design plans are recorded in the public records in the form of plats. In addition, homeowner association agreements, deed restrictions, and other similar legal documents must be recorded, and they become binding on all owners and successive owners unless changed by legal processes. Bonding may be required for public facilities.

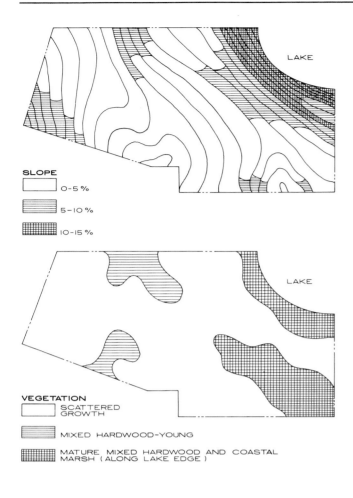

SLOPE
☐ 0-5 %
▤ 5-10 %
▦ 10-15 %

VEGETATION
☐ SCATTERED GROWTH
▤ MIXED HARDWOOD-YOUNG
▦ MATURE MIXED HARDWOOD AND COASTAL MARSH (ALONG LAKE EDGE)

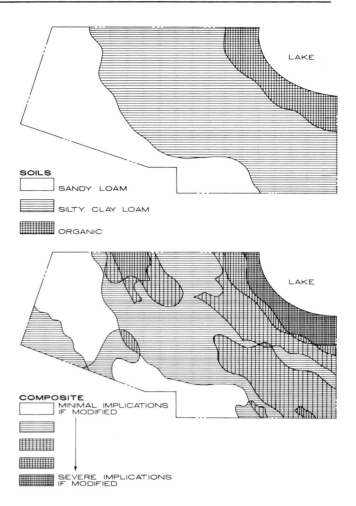

SOILS
☐ SANDY LOAM
▤ SILTY CLAY LOAM
▦ ORGANIC

COMPOSITE
☐ MINIMAL IMPLICATIONS IF MODIFIED
▤
▦
▦
▦
▦ SEVERE IMPLICATIONS IF MODIFIED

ENVIRONMENTAL SITE ANALYSIS PROCESS

If a site has numerous environmental design determinants, the site planner may analyze each environmental system individually in order to comprehend the environmental character of the site more clearly. This can be a complex process, and a site planner/landscape architect with expertise in environmental analysis should be retained to coordinate such an effort.

By preparing each analysis on transparencies, the site planner can use the overlay approach to site analysis. Values are assigned to each sheet based on impact, ranging from area of the site where change would have minimal effect to areas where change would result in severe disruption of the site. In essence, the separate sheets become abstractions with values assigned by the site planner and associated professionals. As each sheet is superimposed, a composite develops, which, when completed, constitutes the synthesis of the environmental design determinants. Lighter tones indicate areas where modification would have minimal influence, darker tones indicate areas more sensitive to change. The sketches shown simulate the overlay process. The site planner may give greater or lesser weight to certain parameters depending on the particular situation. In assigning values, the site planner should consider such factors as the value of maintaining the functioning of the individual site systems, the uniqueness of the specific site features, and the cost of modifying the site plan as an input in the site design process.

Following is a list of the environmental design determinants that, depending on the particular site, may be considered and included in an overlay format:

1. SLOPE: The slope analysis is developed on the contour map; consideration should include the percentage of slope and orientation of slope relative to the infrastructure and land uses.
2. SOIL PATTERNS: Consideration may include the analysis of soils by erosion potential, compressibility and plasticity, capability of supporting plant growth, drainage capabilities, possible sources of pollution or toxic wastes, septic tank location (if relevant), and the proposed land uses and their infrastructure.
3. VEGETATION: Consideration of indigenous species, (values of each in terms of the environmental system), size and condition, the succession of growth toward climax conditions, uniqueness, the ability of certain species to tolerate construction activities, aesthetic values, and density of undergrowth.
4. WILDLIFE: Consideration of indigenous species, their movement patterns, the degree of change that each species can tolerate, and feeding and breeding areas.
5. GEOLOGY: Consideration of underlying rock masses, the depth of different rock layers, and the suitability of different geological formations in terms of potential infrastructure and building.
6. SURFACE AND SUBSURFACE WATER: Consideration of natural drainage patterns, aquifer recharge areas, erosion potential, and flood plains.
7. CLIMATE: Consideration of microclimatic conditions including prevailing breezes (at different times of the year), wind shadows, frost pockets, and air drainage patterns.

COMPUTER APPLICATION

The above process is labor intensive when developed by hand on individual sheets of mylar; however, this particular method of environmental analysis is easily adaptable to the CAD (Computer Aided Drafting) System. Commercial drafting programs suitable for the overlay approach are readily available. Simplified, the method is as follows:

1. A map, such as a soil map, is positioned on the digitizer and the information is transferred to the processor through the use of the stylus. One major advantage to the use of a computer is that the scale of the map being recorded will be transferred to the selected scale by the processor. A hatched pattern is selected, with a less dense pattern for soil types that would have minimal influence and with more dense patterns for soil types that are more sensitive to change. Once this information is programmed into the computer, it is stored.
2. The same process is repeated for development of the next overlay; for example, vegetation. Once again any scale map may be used. This process is repeated until all overlays have been stored. At any time one or all overlays can be produced on the screen.
3. Then the individual overlays or any combination of overlays can be drawn on mylar with a plotter. If appropriate for the particular analysis, the plotter will draw in color. The resulting overlay sheets would have taken considerably longer by hand and may have been less accurate. The site also can be studied directly on the computer monitor screen. Another advantage to the use of the computer is that any part of the overlay can be enlarged for greater detail.
4. The overlay process can be recorded by video tape or by slides from the screen for use in presentations.

Gary Greenan, AICP; Miami, Florida
Rafael Diaz, Graphics Coordinator; Miami, Florida

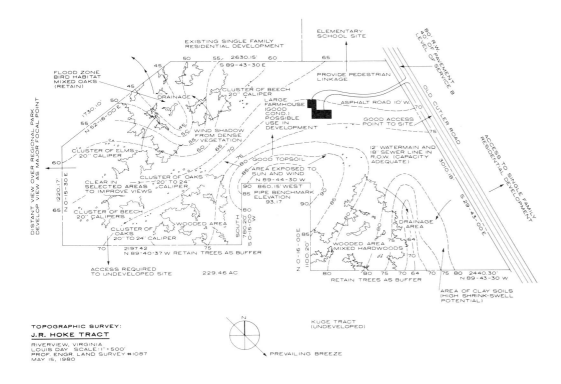

TOPOGRAPHIC SURVEY:
J.R. HOKE TRACT

RIVERVIEW, VIRGINIA
LOUIS DAY SCALE: 1" = 500'
PROF. ENGR. LAND SURVEY #1087
MAY 15, 1980

KUGE TRACT
(UNDEVELOPED)

PREVAILING BREEZE

SURVEY DATA

The first step in any site analysis is the gathering of physical site data. An aerial photograph and an accurate survey showing the following information are basic to any site analysis process:

1. Scale, north arrow, benchmark and date of survey.
2. Tract boundary lines.
3. Easements: location, width, and purpose.
4. Names and locations of existing road rights-of-way on or adjacent to the tract including bridges, curbs, gutters, and culverts.
5. Position of buildings and other structures such as foundations, walls, fences, steps, and paved areas.
6. Utilities on or adjacent to the tract, including: location of gas lines, fire hydrants, electric and telephone poles, and street lights; and direction, distance to, and size of nearest water mains and sewers and invert elevation of sewers.
7. Location of swamps, springs, streams, bodies of water, drainage ditches, water shed areas, flood plains, and other physical features.
8. Outline of wooded areas with names and condition of plant material.
9. Contour intervals of 2 ft. to 5 ft. depending on the slope gradients, and spot elevations at breaks in grade, along all drainage channels or swales, and selected points as needed.

ADDITIONAL INFORMATION

Considerable additional information may be needed, depending on design considerations and site complexities such as soil information and studies of the geological structure of the site.

SUBURBAN SITE ANALYSIS

As indicated in the previous site planning process, the site analysis is a major responsibility of the site planner. The physical analysis of the site is developed primarily from field inspections. Using the survey, the aerial photograph and, where warranted, infrared aerial photographs, the site designer, working in the field and in the office, verifies the survey and notes site design determinants. Site design determinants should include but not be limited to the following:

1. Areas of steep and moderate slopes.
2. Macro- and microclimatic conditions, including: sun angles during different seasons; prevailing breezes; wind shadows; frost pockets; and sectors where high or low points give protection from sun and wind.
3. Solar energy considerations: if solar energy appears feasible, a detailed climatic analysis must be undertaken considering such factors as: detailed sun charts; daily averages of sunlight and cloud cover; daily rain averages; areas exposed to the sun at different seasons; solar radiation patterns; and temperature patterns.
4. Areas of potential flood zones and routes of surface water runoff.
5. Possible road access to the site, including potential conflicts with existing road systems and carrying capacities of adjacent roadways. (This information usually can be obtained from local or state road departments.)
6. Natural areas that from an ecological and aesthetic standpoint should be saved; all tree masses with name and condition of tree species and understory planting.
7. Significant wildlife habitats that would be affected by site modification.
8. Soil conditions relative to supporting plant material, areas suitable for construction, erosion potential, and septic tanks, if relevant.
9. Geological considerations relative to supporting structures.
10. Exceptional views; objectionable views (use on-site photographs).
11. Adjacent existing and proposed land uses with notations on compatibility and incompatibility.
12. Potential noise sources, particularly noise generated from traffic that can be mitigated by the use of plants, berming, walls, and by extending the distance between the source and the receiver.

URBAN SITE ANALYSIS

Although much of the information presented for suburban sites may apply equally to urban sites, additional site design criteria may be necessary. The urban environment has numerous design determinants in the form of existing structures, city patterns, and microclimatic conditions.

ENVIRONMENTAL CONSIDERATIONS

1. Air movement: prevailing breezes characteristic of a region may be greatly modified by urban high rise structures. Predominant air movement patterns in a city may be along roadways and between buildings. In addition, the placement, shape, and height of existing buildings can create air turbulence caused by micro air movement patterns. These patterns may influence the location of building elements such as outdoor areas and balconies. Also, a building's design and placement can mitigate or increase local wind turbulence.
2. Sun and shadow patterns: existing structure sun and shadow patterns should be studied to determine impact on the proposed building. This is particularly important for outdoor terraces and balconies where sunlight may be desirable. Sun and shadow patterns also should be considered as sources of internal heat gain or loss. Building orientation, window sizes, and shading devices can modify internal heat gain or loss. Studies also should include daily and seasonal patterns, and the impact on existing buildings and open spaces of shadows cast by the proposed building.
3. Reflections: reflections from adjacent structures such as glass-clad buildings may be a problem. The new building should be designed to compensate for such glare, or if possible, oriented away from such glare.

URBAN CONTEXTUAL ANALYSIS

1. Building typology and hierarchy: An analysis of the particular building type (residential, commercial, public) relative to the hierarchy of the various building types in the city is useful in deciding the general design approach of a new building. For example, public buildings may be dominant in placement and design, while residential buildings are subdominant. It is important to maintain any existing hierarchy that reinforces visual order in the city. Any predominant architectural solutions and details characteristic of a building type may be useful in the new building's design to maintain a recognizable building type.
2. Regional character: An analysis of the city's regional architectural characteristics is appropriate in developing a design solution that responds to unique regional characteristics. Regional characteristics may be revealed through unique architectural types, vernacular building resulting from local climatic and cultural characteristics, and from historically significant architecture. Historical structures should be saved by modifying them for the proposed new use or by incorporating parts of the existing structure(s) into the proposed design.
3. City form: The delineation of city form created by road layout, location of major open spaces, and architecture-created forms should be analyzed. Elements that delineate city form should be reinforced by architectural development solutions for a particular place within the city. For example, a building proposed for a corner site should be designed to reinforce the corner through building form, entrance, and design details. A building proposed for mid-block may be a visually unifying element providing connection and continuity with adjacent buildings. Sites at the end of important vistas or adjacent to major city squares probably should be reserved for important public buildings.
4. Building scale and fenestrations: It is important to analyze building scale and fenestration of nearby buildings. Such detailing may be reflected, although not necessarily reproduced, in the proposed building. This can provide visual unity and continuity in the architectural character of the city. One example is the use and placement of cornice lines to define the building's lower floors in relation to adjacent buildings. Cornice lines also can define the building's relationship to pedestrians in terms of scale and use.
5. Building transition: Sometimes it may be appropriate to use arcades and porches to provide transition between the building's private interior and the public sidewalk. It may be especially worthy to include them if adjacent buildings have these elements.
6. Views: Important city views of plazas, squares, monuments, and natural features such as waterfronts and parks should be considered. They are important as views from the proposed building. It is also important to design the proposed structure to enhance and preserve such views for the public and for inhabitants of nearby buildings.

Gary Greenan, AICP; Miami, Florida
Rafael Diaz, Graphics Coordinator; Miami, Florida

INTENSITY STANDARDS FOR RESIDENTIAL DEVELOPMENT

DWELLING UNIT TYPE	DWELLING UNITS PER ACRE	COMMON OPEN SPACE AS PERCENTAGE OF TOTAL SITE	PARKING PER UNIT (1)	TREES PER ACRE OF TOTAL SITE AREA (2)	PRIVATE OPEN SPACE (3)
Single family	3 to 5 depending on lot size	Usually not provided	2.5 +/−	15+	Depends on lot size
Duplex	5 to 10 depending on lot size	Usually not provided	2+(4+ for each structure)	15+	Depends on lot size (at least 50% of lot)
Zero-lot-line (9)	4 to 8 units per acre	Usually not provided	2.25+	15+	At least 40% of lot
Single family cluster (4)	4 to 7	25% to 50%	2.25+	15 to 20 +/− for first 3 acres, 10+ for remaining acreage	Depends on lot size (at least 40% of lot)
Atrium (5)	4 to 9 units per acre	Usually not provided	2.25+	15+	25% of unit square footage
Suburban townhouse (6)	6 to 9	25% to 40%	2.25+	15 to 20 +/− for first 3 acres, 10 for remaining acreage	500 to 700 square feet per unit
Urban townhouse (7)	8 to 16	15% to 25% if provided	2.0 +/− (Some parking may be on street)	15 to 20 +/− for first 3 acres, 10 +/− for remaining acreage	400 to 600 square feet per unit
Walk-up apartment	10 to 25 (may be regulated by F.A.R.)	25% to 50%	2.0 +/− depending on number of bedrooms	15 to 20 +/− for first 3 acres, 10 +/− for remaining acreage	Usually not provided except on ground floor units
Midrise apartment up to 6 stories	15 to 35 (may be regulated by F.A.R.)	25% to 50%	2.0 +/− depending on number of bedrooms	15 to 20 +/− for first 3 acres, 10 +/− for remaining acreage	Usually not provided except on ground floor units
Highrise apartments	30 to 75 (may be 100+ in dense urban areas)	20% to 60% (may include roof terraces)	2.0 +/− depending on number of bedrooms	15 to 20 +/− for first 3 acres, 10 +/− for remaining acreage	Usually not provided
Planned unit development (8)	10 to 25 depending on type of PUD	25% to 60%	2.0 +/− depending on unit type(s)	15 to 20 +/− for first 3 acres, 10 +/− for remaining acreage	Depends on individual unit type(s)

INTRODUCTION

The standards above should be used only as a basic reference to determine spatial site functions. The final determination of intensity and dwelling type of a particular site should evolve as the end of a thorough planning process. The designer also must refer to local zoning codes and ordinances for specific criteria.

NOTES

1. PARKING PER UNIT: In determining parking requirements per unit, the site planner should consider available public transportation and the relationship of the development's location to employment centers and supporting facilities. Overestimating parking spaces to accommodate infrequent special activities can result in excess pavement. Depending on prevailing conditions, sometimes it is better to accommodate infrequent overflow parking on grassed areas, on commercial parking areas, or at community center parking lots.

2. TREES: A major unifying design element, trees also can act as climate modifiers. Extensive tree planting should be part of most site planning programs in appropriate climate areas unless the site already bears a substantial number of trees. The number of trees per acre is based more on the particular locale than on a uniform standard. Trees planted along streets at 30 ft. to 50 ft. on center provide roadway shading as well as visual unity for the development.

3. PRIVATE OPEN SPACE: Both visual and aural privacy is important in development design. Private open space for each unit may be provided by courtyards, entrance courts, porches, and rear, side, and front yards.

4. SINGLE FAMILY CLUSTER: Clusters of single-family units provide maximum open space. Units may or may not be attached.

5. ATRIUM: A single-family unit similar to early Greek and Roman structures that incorporated interior living spaces fronting on an internal court.

6. SUBURBAN TOWNHOUSE: A single-family unit attached to other single family units with a party wall. Open space usually is a major element in suburban townhouse development.

7. URBAN TOWNHOUSE: Early prototypes appear in many older cities. They are similar to suburban townhouses, although densities usually are higher and common open space usually is provided in public open space.

8. PLANNED UNIT DEVELOPMENT (PUD): All housing types included in the chart, plus associated retail support facilities and community amenities, may be found in a PUD. Emphasis is on total community design.

9. ZERO-LOT-LINE: Provides increased density over typical single-family developments by reducing individual lot sizes, and thereby reducing single-family housing costs. Zero-lot-line developments provide in-fill solutions in lower density urban areas where higher density is justified because of available urban services and higher land cost. Sketches indicate basic design considerations for zero-lot-line development.

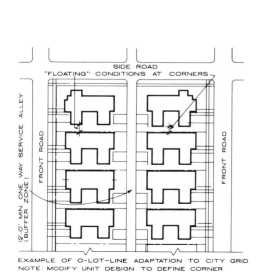

EXAMPLE OF O-LOT-LINE ADAPTATION TO CITY GRID
NOTE: MODIFY UNIT DESIGN TO DEFINE CORNER

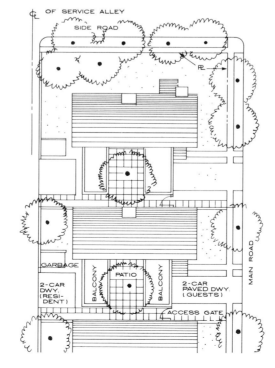

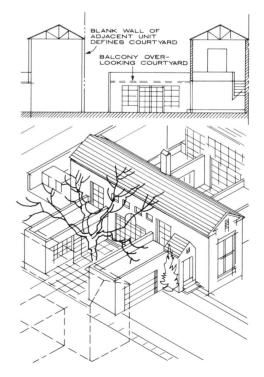

Gary Greenan, AICP; Miami, Florida
Rafael Diaz, Graphics Coordinator; Miami, Florida

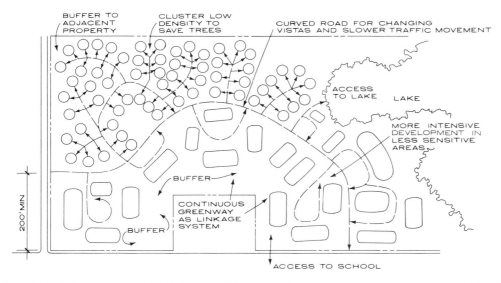

SITE ANALYSIS

CONCEPT PLANNING

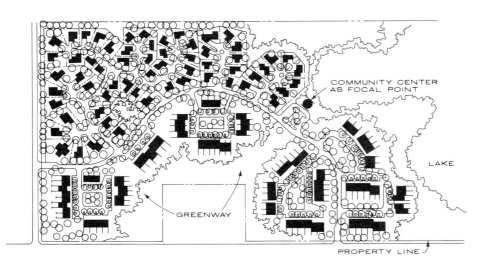

PRELIMINARY PLAN

Gary Greenan, AICP; Miami, Florida
Rafael Diaz, Graphics Coordinator; Miami, Florida

INTRODUCTION

The following steps illustrate a design process:

1. SITE ANALYSIS: A synthesis of the physical environmental design determinants and offsite influences.
2. CONCEPT PLAN: A synthesis of the site analysis, research, citizen input, and client input into design concepts. Several concept plans may be prepared.
3. PRELIMINARY PLAN: A further sophistication and detailing of the concept plan.

DESIGN SCALE

The site planner should be aware of four interdependent levels of design:

COMMUNITY

At the community, or neighborhood, scale, the site planner should be aware of elements that create design unity and give identity to the development as a whole. Major natural features, circulation systems, greenway systems, and public use spaces such as schools, shopping, and parks act as focal points or linkages in the total design of the project.

SUBCOMMUNITY

The first level down from the community scale is the subcommunity space. These spaces are created by the grouping or clustering of housing units and associated parking, paths, and landscape into a form that responds to the environmental characteristics of the site and gives identity to individual clusters.

TRANSITION

Transition spaces in the form of porches, entrance courts, patios, and yards provide a transition from the private interior spaces of a housing unit to public spaces. Consideration should be given to privacy for the individual unit and to environmental site characteristics such as breezes, sun angles, and landscape.

INTERIOR

This is the smallest scale with which the site planner is involved. Emphasis should be placed on the unit's interior design for its relationship to the exterior environment and for privacy. A close working relationship between architect and landscape architect is essential.

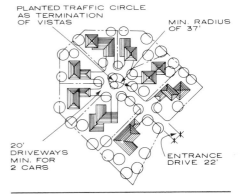

SINGLE FAMILY CLUSTER

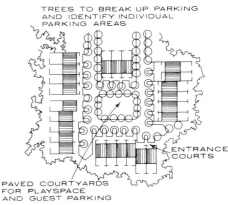

TOWN HOUSE LAYOUT

SUBDIVISION LAYOUT PROCEDURES

Residential subdivision of a tract of land requires considerable attention to design options and principles. Some of these are illustrated and described below.

REDUCE TRAFFIC HAZARD POTENTIAL BY USE OF RIGHT ANGLE INTERSECTIONS

ANGLE OF INTERSECTION

AVOID SMALL IRREGULAR BLOCKS THAT MAY BE DIFFICULT TO SERVICE AND NOT COST EFFECTIVE

BLOCK SHAPE AND SIZE

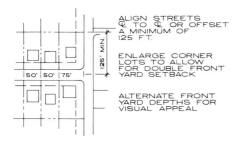

ALIGN STREETS ℄ TO ℄ OR OFFSET A MINIMUM OF 125 FT.

ENLARGE CORNER LOTS TO ALLOW FOR DOUBLE FRONT YARD SETBACK

ALTERNATE FRONT YARD DEPTHS FOR VISUAL APPEAL

INTERSECTION OFFSET, FRONT YARD SETBACK, AND CORNER LOTS

GENERAL INFORMATION

Much of the same equipment and procedures used in building layouts are used in subdivision layouts and staking. For further information, see building layout procedures page.

Usually a transit is used as the primary tool for locating and placing subdivision components. These components include, but are not limited to, streets, lots and respective lot lines, and utility systems. Horizontal and vertical control (distances and elevations) for the layout of these components usually is related to a bench mark or other monument, the location and elevation of which is more or less permanent and is recorded.

STREETS

Streets are laid out in either an open or closed traverse by a series of station points and lines established along the street's centerline. These station points typically are staked at points of grade change, intersection, horizontal and vertical curvature, and at selected intervals of 25 ft., 50 ft., or 100 ft. A point of beginning (POB) typically is established where the proposed street's centerline intersects the existing road to which it is linked. The POB is "Station 0," and it is expressed numerically as 0 + 00. Station 1 is 100 ft. along the centerline from Station 0 and is expressed numerically as 1 + 00.

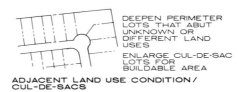

DEEPEN PERIMETER LOTS THAT ABUT UNKNOWN OR DIFFERENT LAND USES

ENLARGE CUL-DE-SAC LOTS FOR BUILDABLE AREA

ADJACENT LAND USE CONDITION / CUL-DE-SACS

AVOID DOUBLE FRONTAGE OF RESIDENTIAL LOTS

DOUBLE FRONTED LOTS

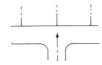

ALIGN LOT LINE WITH CENTERLINE OF STREET TO MINIMIZE NIGHTTIME GLARE OF AUTO LAMPS INTO HOUSE

LOT LINE STREET OFFSET

ADJUST STREET RIGHT OF WAY TO ACCOMMODATE EXISTING TREES OR OTHER SIGNIFICANT NATURAL FEATURES

AMENITY CONSIDERATIONS

Intermediate stations are expressed in the same manner. For example, Station 5.20 is 520 ft. along the centerline from Station 0 and is read on engineering plans as 5 + 20 (see diagram.) Proposed elevations along the street's centerline are established by setting a marked stake into the ground with its top set at the desired elevation. A road-grading machine then cuts or fills soil to the stake's marked elevation.

LOTS

Residential lots are laid out as closed traverses that have a POB, usually established at one of the lot's front corners on the street right-of-way. From the POB, lot lines are established with a series of horizontal angles (bearing/azimuths) and distance. Curved lot lines, if applicable, are laid out as circular curves with a known interior angle, tangent length, and length of curvature. They are most typically the front lot line on a curved street.

UTILITIES

Sanitary sewers also are laid out by stationing along the centerline where pipes will be installed. Manholes and sewer intersections are plotted with station points and elevations much the same as a street. Utility easements typically are recorded with horizontal bearings and distances.

CONVENTIONAL SUBDIVISION DEVELOPMENT

ELEMENTS—Lots, blocks, streets.

OBJECTIVES—Private lot ownership with public street frontage.

BENEFITS—Public street and utilities ownership or private fee, single-ownership of lots.

DENSITY—30 acres, 54 lots: density = 1.8 lots per acre (example shown).

CLUSTER DEVELOPMENT

ELEMENTS—Lots, streets, common open space, usually requires zoning or special zoning such as PUD.

OBJECTIVES—Private lot ownership combined with community ownership of common open space (requires homeowners' association to maintain open space).

BENEFITS—Opportunity to separate vehicular and pedestrian traffic. Efficient road and utility system, reduced construction and maintenance costs to community, developer, and consumer. Opportunity for controlled entry with private roads. Environmentally sensitive areas may be held for open space.

DENSITY—30 acres, 54 lots: density = 1.8 lots per acre (example shown).

ATTACHED SINGLE-FAMILY

ELEMENTS—Lots or units, private or public streets or easements, common open space (recreation facilities shown), usually requires zoning or special zoning such as PUD.

OBJECTIVES—Private ownership of lots or units, combined with community ownership of common open space (homeowners' association to maintain open space).

BENEFITS—Allows for larger, more continuous open spaces. Appeals to families or individuals who want home ownership without yard maintenance responsibilities. Cost savings mentioned in cluster development. Security, controlled access opportunities.

DENSITY—30 acres, 112 townhouses: density = 3.7 units per acre (example shown).

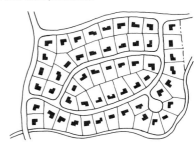

CONVENTIONAL SUBDIVISION

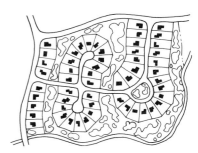

CLUSTER DEVELOPMENT

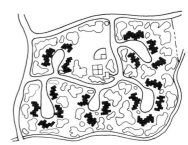

CLUSTER DEVELOPMENT - TOWNHOMES

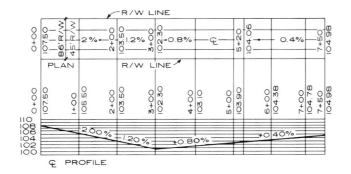

ROAD PLAN AND PROFILE

William H. Evans, AIA; San Antonio, Texas
Connecticut Coastal Management Program, see data sources
Munson, see data sources

LAND PLANNING AND SITE DEVELOPMENT

INTRODUCTION

A site designer needs a basic understanding of roadway layout to design circulation systems that function on the site and are compatible with systems off the site. Specific minimum standards that must be met are in effect for most municipalities.

HIERARCHY OF ROAD SYSTEMS

A site designer needs to know the hierarchy of road systems and the purposes of each system. At the upper end is the limited access freeway, which carries up to 1,000 or 1,300 vehicles per lane per hour at 60 mph and up to 2,000 per hour at slower speeds. Site selection is affected by accessibility to freeway systems.

Major or principal arterials and minor arterials are inter-community connectors that can carry, respectively, 600 to 800 cars per lane per hour and 400 to 500 cars per lane per hour, depending on traffic signals, on-street parking, intersections, and other physical impediments restricting traffic flow. Site selection is affected by these streets because they usually provide the direct access to a proposed development.

Collector streets are laid out by the site planner in the development to collect traffic from neighborhoods and local streets and direct it onto the arterials. They can carry efficiently 100 to 250 vehicles per lane per hour.

TRAFFIC GENERATION

In projects where traffic generation is a major factor in the road system design, it may be advisable to retain the services of a transportation engineer. Technical information on traffic generation can be found in publications produced by the Institute of Transportation Engineers. This Institute projects the following trip generation factors for residential development:

SUMMARY RATE TABLES OF DIFFERENT DWELLING UNITS

TYPE OF DWELLING UNIT	AVERAGE WEEKDAY VEHICLE TRIP ENDS PER UNIT		
	AVG.	MAX.	MIN.
Single-Family			
Detached Unit	10.0	21.9	4.3
Apartment, General	6.1	12.3	0.5
Low-Rise Apartment	6.6	9.2	5.1
High-Rise Apartment	4.0	6.4	1.2
Condominium	5.2	11.8	0.6
Mobile Home Park	4.8	7.6	2.3
Retirement Community	3.3	4.9	2.8
Planned Unit Develop.	7.8	14.4	5.8

ENVIRONMENTAL CONSIDERATIONS

A site's environmental characteristics affect the location and development of a road system. It is the responsibility of the site designer to develop systems that recognize the ecological constraints of a particular site. Following is a checklist of environmental considerations for road alignment:

1. Cause minimal disruption of existing topography by reducing cut and fill requirements, thus reducing erosion and sedimentation problems.
2. Cause minimal disruption of natural overland and subsurface water flows.
3. Cause minimal disruption to existing vegetation and animal life.
4. Avoid positive drainage along roadways into storm sewer systems where such systems directly outfall into water bodies and cause pollution. Systems of swales along the roadway help to filter nutrients from the roadway surface before entering natural water bodies, thus reducing water pollution.

NOTES

1. Bike path grades should not exceed 5 to 6 percent for short distances (200 ft. to 400 ft.) or 2 percent for long distances. Separate bike path from roadway with swales and plantings. Where possible, bike paths can be integrated into greenway systems rather than along roadway.
2. Tree species that tolerate smog and dust and with root systems that do not damage underground utilities or pavements should be selected. Where snow removal

or icy conditions occur, trees should be placed far enough from the roadway edge to prevent damage from automobiles or chemicals applied to the roadway. Tree spacing should take into consideration species and design effect; as a general rule shade trees should be 35 ft. to 50 ft. apart.

3. Street lighting. Design considerations for spacing between lights should relate to amount of illumination needed based on street type, pedestrian use, crime prevention, and similar criteria. Approximate spacing for vehicular street use is 100 ft. to 150 ft. between standards.

Gary Greenan, AICP; Miami, Florida
Rafael Diaz, Graphics Coordinator; Miami, Florida
Institute of Transportation Engineers, see data sources

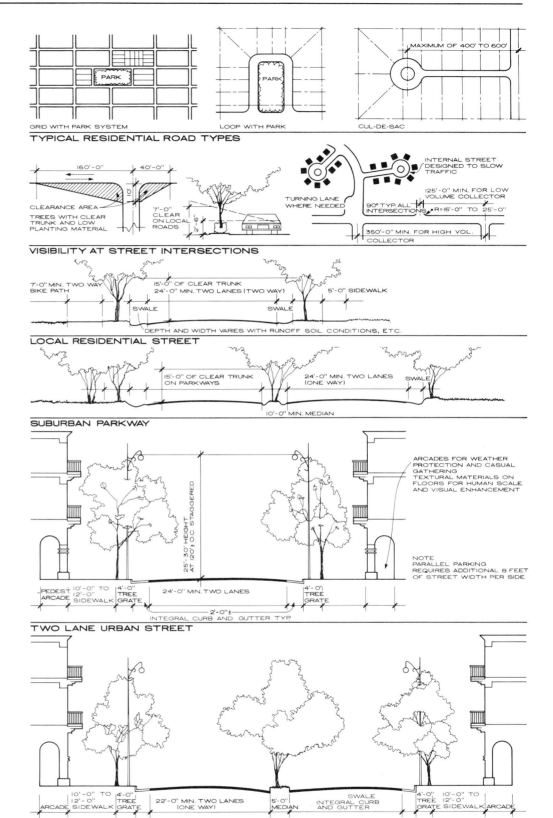

TYPICAL RESIDENTIAL ROAD TYPES

VISIBILITY AT STREET INTERSECTIONS

LOCAL RESIDENTIAL STREET

SUBURBAN PARKWAY

TWO LANE URBAN STREET

FOUR LANE URBAN STREET WITH LANDSCAPED MEDIAN

FINAL DEVELOPMENT PLANS

After all necessary approvals under the zoning process have been granted, final site development plans are initiated. The final presentation drawing, as indicated below, is prepared by the site planner as part of the presentation for the zoning and public review process or as part of the final site development plans. The technical site development plans, as listed below, usually are prepared by a registered surveyor and/or engineer. The professional preparing these plans should obtain a copy of the local subdivision code and, if available, a copy of the public works manual for specific local requirements. All drawings should show the name and location of the development, the date of preparation and any revisions, the scale, north point, datum, and approvals of local authorities. The following list of exhibits are typical requirements for most communities.

TENTATIVE OR PRELIMINARY PLAT

Platting is the process in which a piece of land, referred to as the parent tract, is subdivided into two or more parcels. A plat specifically and legally describes the layout of the development. A tentative plat is the first step in the preparation of the final drawings. It indicates the layout of the development in terms of lot layout and sizes of lots, lot frontages, road rights-of-way, setbacks, sidewalks, street offsets, and other graphic information relative to the project design. After approval of the tentative plat, the engineer can begin the utility, street paving, and drainage plans. Even if the local regulations do not require a tentative plat, it is advised that the designer prepare a sketch of the plat and meet with local authorities to avoid problems later in the final site development plan process.

STREET PAVING AND DRAINAGE PLANS

Street paving and drainage plans are final construction drawings prepared by an engineer indicating:

1. Streets and parking area plans with starting points and radii.
2. Typical cross section (some communities also may require road profiles).
3. Details and specifications of pavement base, surfacing, and curbs.
4. Indication of methods to confine storm water runoff within the right-of-way (soil tests for percolation may be required). Also, details and specifications for inlets, manholes, catch basins, and surface drainage channels.
5. Indication that roads will meet local, state, and federal flood criteria.

UTILITY PLANS

Utility plans are final drawings prepared by an engineer that indicate the location of water supply lines, sewage disposal lines, fire hydrants, and other utility functions usually located in the road right-of-way. In addition to approval by local public works departments, some communities require review of utility plans by the public health board, fire department, and departments involved in pollution control.

FINAL PLAT

The final plat is usually the last stage of the final site development process prior to the issuance of building permits. A subdivision plat, when accepted and recorded in the public land records, establishes a legal description of the streets, residential lots, and other sites in the development. If roads and other improvements are not constructed at the time of final platting, a bond, usually in excess of the estimated cost of the improvements, will be required. Following is a typical list of information that should be shown on the final plat.

1. Right-of-way lines of streets, easements, and other sites with accurate dimensions, bearings, and curve data.
2. Name and right-of-way width of each street or other right-of-way.
3. Location, dimensions, and purpose of any easements.
4. Identifying number for each lot or site.
5. Purpose for which sites, other than residential lots, are dedicated or reserved.
6. Minimum building setback line on all lots and other sites.
7. Location and description of monuments.
8. Reference to recorded subdivision plats of adjoining platted land by record, name, date, and number.
9. Certification by surveyor or engineer.
10. Statement by owner(s) dedicating streets, rights-of-way, and any sites for public use.
11. Approval by local authorities.
12. Title, scale, north arrow, and date.

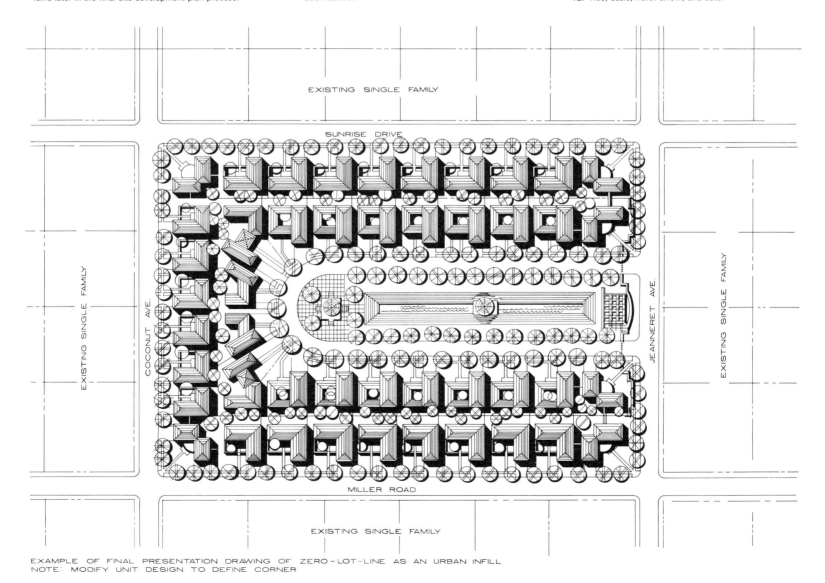

EXAMPLE OF FINAL PRESENTATION DRAWING OF ZERO-LOT-LINE AS AN URBAN INFILL
NOTE: MODIFY UNIT DESIGN TO DEFINE CORNER

Gary Greenan, AICP; Miami, Florida
Rafael Diaz, Graphics Coordinator; Miami, Florida

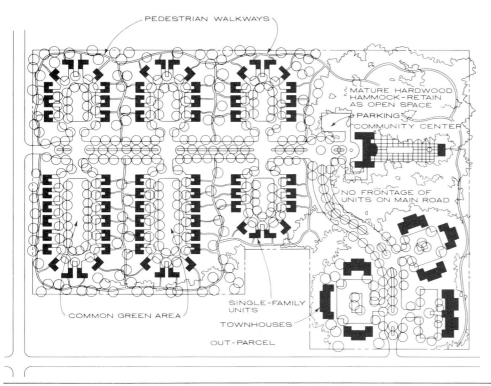

PEDESTRIAN WALKWAYS

MATURE HARDWOOD HAMMOCK—RETAIN AS OPEN SPACE

PARKING

COMMUNITY CENTER

NO FRONTAGE OF UNITS ON MAIN ROAD

SINGLE-FAMILY UNITS

TOWNHOUSES

OUT-PARCEL

COMMON GREEN AREA

PLANNED UNIT DEVELOPMENT (TWO-STORY UNITS)

The planned unit development ordinance usually incorporates standards for dwelling unit density, open space, and other spatial requirements. PUD ordinances usually place emphasis on total community design, with review of plans by local agencies and public hearing bodies as a primary requirement.

ADVANTAGES OF PLANNED UNIT DEVELOPMENT AND CLUSTER ZONING CONCEPTS

Although the lot-by-lot type of subdivision is still the prevalent development type in many suburban areas, the amenities that can be realized by the planned unit development and cluster zoning concepts are such that these approaches should be seriously considered.

In some communities the terms planned unit development (PUD) and cluster may be synonymous. Usually, however, the PUD is a more comprehensive approach than the cluster, with provisions for both single family and multifamily development and, in some instances, commercial and industrial activities. The combination of commercial and recreational development in the town or community center can be found in some PUDs. Fee simple ownership and condominium ownership usually are permitted. Often PUDs are divided into tracts and developed over a long-term period such as 10 to 20 years. The term cluster refers to the grouping of single family residences in clusters on lots smaller than permitted by the single family zoning district and compensating for the smaller lots with common open space areas of substantial and usable configurations.

Both methods offer the designer not only the flexibility of locating structures in a manner that responds to site features, but also the opportunity for developing imaginative architectural forms. A key element of these approaches is the common green space that gives design cohesiveness to the total project.

The responsibility for the maintenance of common space and associated common facilities is a major concern that must be resolved in PUD and cluster developments. The homeowners' association is the most commonly accepted approach. The association should be established by recorded agreement before the sale of the first unit by the developer. Each homeowner is automatically a member and is assessed a proportionate share of the cost in maintaining the common facilities. The developer or his attorney should evaluate the best methods of developing a homeowners' association before the initiation of site development. Many jurisdictions require a legal instrument for the association prior to final approval of the project.

The use of common open space usually allows more flexibility in effectively fitting the development to the land than does the more typical lot-by-lot approach. Following are some of the obvious advantages gained by the proper use of the planned unit development concept:

1. With smaller individual lots, excess land can be massed together to provide larger and more useful community recreational space.
2. With the use of connecting community open spaces and fewer through traffic streets, children are better protected from vehicular traffic.
3. With larger amounts of open space, the natural character of the site can be preserved.
4. With the shorter networks of streets and utilities, construction costs can be reduced.

It should be emphasized that the standard subdivision approach still retains a major part of the housing market. Where the program suggests a more typical subdivision layout, the site planner has a responsibility to respond to the same environmental design determinants of the site as for a project being developed under more flexible zoning criteria. Creative planning can be accomplished using either approach.

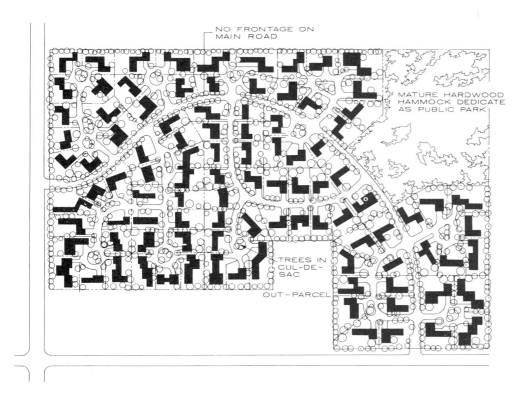

NO FRONTAGE ON MAIN ROAD

MATURE HARDWOOD HAMMOCK DEDICATE AS PUBLIC PARK

TREES IN CUL-DE-SAC

OUT-PARCEL

CONVENTIONAL SINGLE FAMILY (ONE-STORY UNITS)

CONVENTIONAL SINGLE FAMILY RESIDENTIAL ZONED DEVELOPMENT

The density determination for conventional single family residential zoning is based on minimum lot size requirements as provided by local ordinances. For planning purposes, the site planner can translate lot size to a net density figure which represents the total number of dwellings per acre within the site, after deducting for roads, parks, school sites, and other public facilities.

Gary Greenan, AICP; Miami, Florida
Rafael Diaz, Graphics Coordinator; Miami, Florida

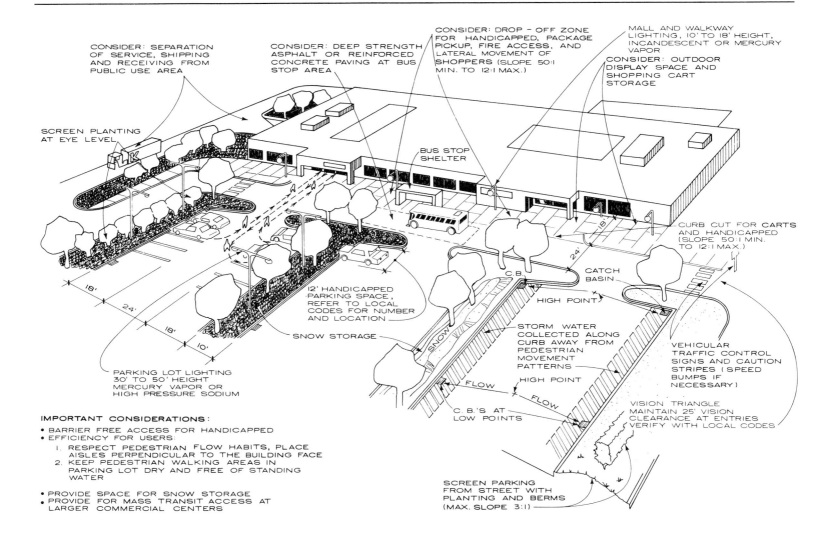

CONSIDER: SEPARATION OF SERVICE, SHIPPING AND RECEIVING FROM PUBLIC USE AREA

CONSIDER: DEEP STRENGTH ASPHALT OR REINFORCED CONCRETE PAVING AT BUS STOP AREA

CONSIDER: DROP - OFF ZONE FOR HANDICAPPED, PACKAGE PICKUP, FIRE ACCESS, AND LATERAL MOVEMENT OF SHOPPERS (SLOPE 50:1 MIN. TO 12:1 MAX.)

MALL AND WALKWAY LIGHTING, 10' TO 18' HEIGHT, INCANDESCENT OR MERCURY VAPOR

CONSIDER: OUTDOOR DISPLAY SPACE AND SHOPPING CART STORAGE

SCREEN PLANTING AT EYE LEVEL

BUS STOP SHELTER

CURB CUT FOR CARTS AND HANDICAPPED (SLOPE 50:1 MIN. TO 12:1 MAX.)

12' HANDICAPPED PARKING SPACE, REFER TO LOCAL CODES FOR NUMBER AND LOCATION

SNOW STORAGE

CATCH BASIN

HIGH POINT

STORM WATER COLLECTED ALONG CURB AWAY FROM PEDESTRIAN MOVEMENT PATTERNS

PARKING LOT LIGHTING 30' TO 50' HEIGHT MERCURY VAPOR OR HIGH PRESSURE SODIUM

FLOW

HIGH POINT

FLOW

C.B.'S AT LOW POINTS

VEHICULAR TRAFFIC CONTROL SIGNS AND CAUTION STRIPES (SPEED BUMPS IF NECESSARY)

VISION TRIANGLE MAINTAIN 25' VISION CLEARANCE AT ENTRIES VERIFY WITH LOCAL CODES

IMPORTANT CONSIDERATIONS:
- BARRIER FREE ACCESS FOR HANDICAPPED
- EFFICIENCY FOR USERS:
  1. RESPECT PEDESTRIAN FLOW HABITS, PLACE AISLES PERPENDICULAR TO THE BUILDING FACE
  2. KEEP PEDESTRIAN WALKING AREAS IN PARKING LOT DRY AND FREE OF STANDING WATER
- PROVIDE SPACE FOR SNOW STORAGE
- PROVIDE FOR MASS TRANSIT ACCESS AT LARGER COMMERCIAL CENTERS

SCREEN PARKING FROM STREET WITH PLANTING AND BERMS (MAX. SLOPE 3:1)

PLANTING CONSIDERATIONS

The distribution and placement of plants in parking areas can help to relieve the visually overwhelming scale of large parking lots. To maximize the impact of landscape materials, the screening capabilities of the plants must be considered. High branching canopy trees do not create a visual screen at eye level. When the landscaped area is concentrated in islands large enough to accommodate a diversified mixture of canopy and flowering trees, evergreen trees, and shrubs, visual screening via plants is much more effective. Planting low branching, densely foliated trees and shrubs can soften the visual impact of large parking areas. Consider the use of evergreens and avoid plants that drop fruit or sap.

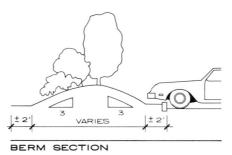

BERM SECTION

DESIGN CONSIDERATIONS

While efficiency (number of spaces per gross acres) is the major practical consideration in the development of parking areas, several other important design questions exist. Barrier free design is mandatory in most communities. Parking spaces for the handicapped should be designated near building entrances. Curb cuts for wheelchairs should be provided at entrances. The lots should not only be efficient in terms of parking spaces provided, but should also allow maximum efficiency for pedestrians once they leave their vehicles.

Pedestrians habitually walk in the aisles behind parked vehicles. This should be recognized in the orientation of the aisles to building entrances. When aisles are perpendicular to the building face, pedestrians can walk to and from the building without squeezing between parked cars with carts and packages. Pedestrian movement areas should be graded to avoid creating standing water in the paths of pedestrians. Space should be provided for snow storage within parking areas, if required.

William H. Evans, AIA; San Antonio, Texas
Johnson, Johnson & Roy, Inc.; Ann Arbor, Michigan

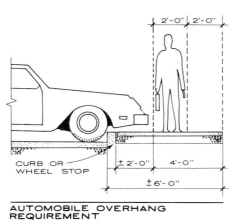

AUTOMOBILE OVERHANG REQUIREMENT

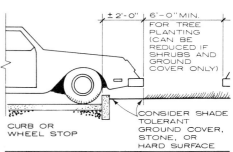

±2'-0"   6'-0" MIN. FOR TREE PLANTING (CAN BE REDUCED IF SHRUBS AND GROUND COVER ONLY)

CONSIDER SHADE TOLERANT GROUND COVER, STONE, OR HARD SURFACE

CURB OR WHEEL STOP

OVERHANGS IN PLANTING AREA

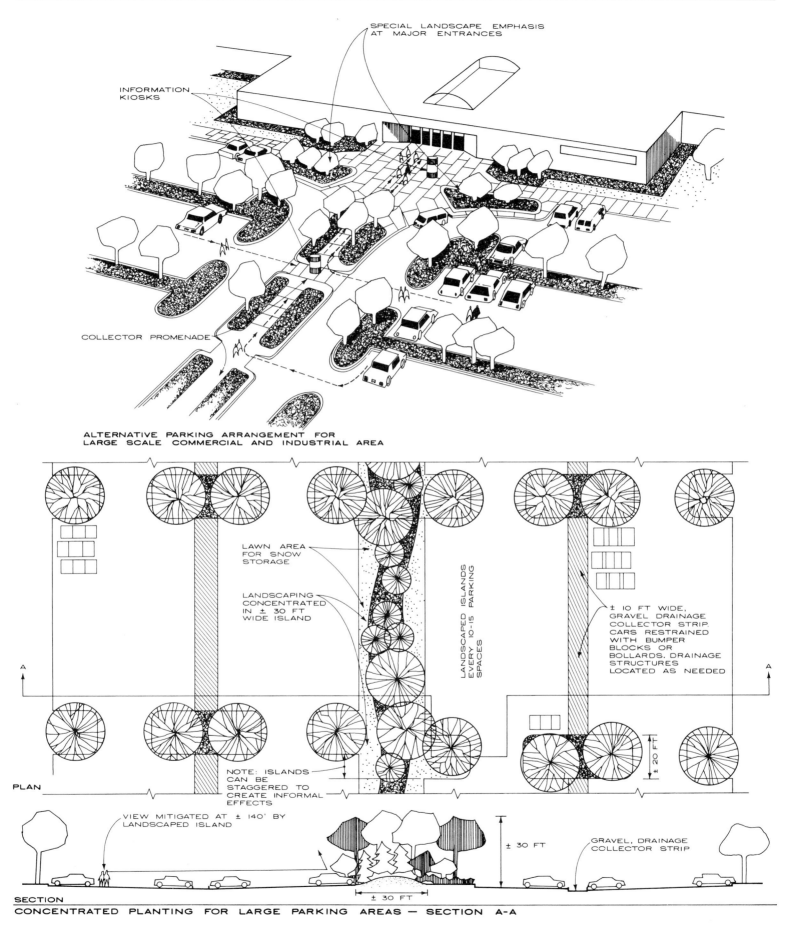

SPECIAL LANDSCAPE EMPHASIS
AT MAJOR ENTRANCES

INFORMATION
KIOSKS

COLLECTOR PROMENADE

ALTERNATIVE PARKING ARRANGEMENT FOR
LARGE SCALE COMMERCIAL AND INDUSTRIAL AREA

LAWN AREA
FOR SNOW
STORAGE

LANDSCAPING
CONCENTRATED
IN ± 30 FT
WIDE ISLAND

LANDSCAPED ISLANDS
EVERY 10-15 PARKING
SPACES

± 10 FT WIDE,
GRAVEL DRAINAGE
COLLECTOR STRIP.
CARS RESTRAINED
WITH BUMPER
BLOCKS OR
BOLLARDS, DRAINAGE
STRUCTURES
LOCATED AS NEEDED

A

A

± 20 FT

PLAN

NOTE: ISLANDS
CAN BE
STAGGERED TO
CREATE INFORMAL
EFFECTS

VIEW MITIGATED AT ± 140' BY
LANDSCAPED ISLAND

± 30 FT

GRAVEL, DRAINAGE
COLLECTOR STRIP

SECTION

± 30 FT

CONCENTRATED PLANTING FOR LARGE PARKING AREAS — SECTION A-A

Johnson, Johnson & Roy, Inc.; Ann Arbor, Michigan

BIKE PATH CLASSIFICATIONS

BIKE PATH (CLASS I BIKEWAY)

A bikeway physically separated from motorized vehicular traffic by an open space. It is located either within the roadway right-of-way or within an independent right-of-way (greenbelt).

BIKE LANE (CLASS II BIKEWAY)

A portion of a roadway that has been designated by lane stripes or traffic buttons, signs, or other pavement markings for the preferential or exclusive use of bicyclists.

BIKE ROUTE (CLASS III BIKEWAY)

A bikeway that shares the traffic right-of-way with motor vehicles and is designated only by signs. Bicycles are considered legal road vehicles, and bicyclists must obey all traffic laws. One-way bike travel only is permitted on a bike route.

CLASS I BIKEWAY

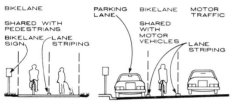

CLASS II BIKEWAY

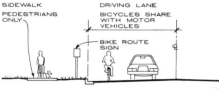

CLASS III BIKEWAY

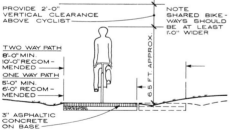

BIKEWAY CLEARANCE AND DIMENSIONS

HORIZONTAL, VERTICAL LAYOUT

Except in terrain where unavoidable, such as in mountains with numerous curves, long steep inclines should be avoided. Slopes of one percent to one-half percent have no significant effect on the use of bicycle paths by cyclists. Three percent slopes to 500 ft. are acceptable. Grades of six percent and more that are longer than 250 ft. will discourage bicycle path use except by expert cyclists using lightweight bicycles. Cyclists prefer straight or gently curving paths to circuitous, meandering paths.

PAVING SURFACE

Pavement must be smooth and durable, as 3 in. asphaltic concrete on a prepared subgrade or a minimum of 4 in. of crushed aggregate base (variable with climate and soil conditions). Concrete is satisfactory if it is well aligned. Tree root or frost heave displacement or differential settlement can create uneven paths in concrete unless doweling is provided.

TRAFFIC SAFETY

Class I Bikeways, with bicycles separated from motorized traffic, provide the most safety for cyclists. Class III Bikeways, dependent on signs, provide the least safety. They do not encourage bicycle use, but often are the only option in urban areas. On Class II and Class III Bikeways hazards can arise from suddenly opened doors of parked cars and from cross-traffic turning into driveways. Bikeways beside pedestrian walks may get interference as walkers stray onto the designated bikeway.

INTERSECTIONS

The major safety problem with bikeways is at grade intersections where motor vehicles, pedestrians, and cyclists converge or cross each other. The best solution is to provide a grade-separated intersection with an underpass or overpass planned as a part of a Class I Bikeway. Other possibilities include:

1. Provide a clearly defined mid-block crossing.
2. Merge bicycles and pedestrians a minimum of 100 ft. from four-way intersections using warning signs for both.
3. Provide warning signs for motorists approaching intersections where bikeways cross.
4. Provide and maintain adequate lighting.
5. Control planting and trimming of trees and plants to provide adequate intersection visibility.
6. Provide electronically activated signals for high traffic volume intersections.
7. At busy intersections or during peak traffic periods, restrict bicycle left turns.

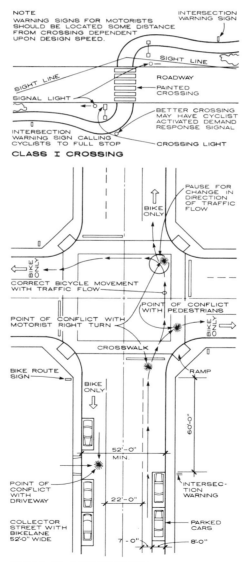

CLASS I CROSSING

CLASS II INTERSECTION

BICYCLE PARKING

Bicycle parking should be close to, but not obstructing, the main entrances to buildings. Where feasible, parking should be visible from the interior of a building or CCTV monitored. Good exterior lighting is important.

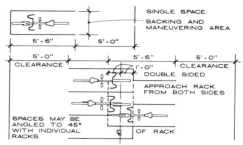

BICYCLE PARKING SPACES

Theft of bicycles, bicycle wheels, and accessories has become a significant problem. All bicycle parking devices must have provisions for locking mechanisms. Cyclists usually provide the locks. Coin-operated locks also are available on some devices. Case-hardened chains or high strength cable with heavy duty padlocks, or bar locks must be accommodated at the parking device. Parking devices shown are classified by the amount of theft protection offered.

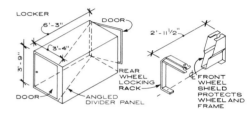

TYPE A – HIGH PROTECTION

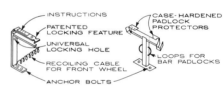

TYPE B – MEDIUM PROTECTION

All parking devices mentioned above must be constructed of hardened steel resistant to hacksaws and hammers. All must be anchored securely in concrete foundations or set with nonremovable bolts.

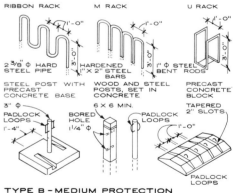

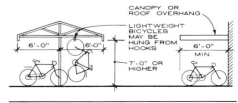

SHELTERS FOR BICYCLES

H. Thomas Wilson, AIA; Pasadena, California
Bicycle facilities designs courtesy of Rally Racks, Canterbury Designs, Brandir International, Sunshine U-Lok Corp.

SITE IMPROVEMENTS

GENERAL

Comprehensive, effective site security provides deterrents to hostile acts, barriers to unauthorized entry, access/egress control, detection of unauthorized entry or exit, and positions for security personnel. Design of the system includes:

1. Perimeter physical barriers preventing penetration by intruders and vehicles
2. Entry/exit control
3. Protective lighting
4. Standoff distance from blasts
5. Intrusion detection, alert, and notification
6. Guard posts and guard walls

Perimeter and site security are augmented by a comprehensive building security system.

SITE ACCESS

A screening facility at perimeter access points should be considered in high risk areas to detect explosives, firearms, and other weapons. A sally port detains vehicles for inspection and prevents other vehicles from gaining access by tailgating.

A protected guard booth should be located so that the guard can control entry/exit of pedestrians and vehicles. Guard booths in high risk areas should be constructed to appropriate ballistic and forced entry resistant standards. Where extensive vehicle inspection is required, a roving guard should augment guards in the booth.

PERIMETER PROTECTION

Perimeter security addresses issues of protection against forced entry by unauthorized personnel and vehicles, and against explosive blast.

PERSONNEL BARRIERS; FENCES AND WALLS

Walls and opaque fences to deter and resist intruders should be smooth-faced with no easy foot or handholds, and be a minimum 9 ft high. Open fencing should be constructed of vertical elements with 9 ft minimum between horizontal elements.

SITE SECURITY LIGHTING

A comprehensive system of security lighting should include illumination of the perimeter, structures within, and site passageways.

Continuous lighting using fixed luminaires to flood an area with overlapping cones of light is most common. Lighting across an area makes it difficult for intruders to see inside the area. Controlled lighting, which adjusts light to fit a particular strip inside and/or outside the perimeter, is less intrusive to adjacent properties.

Auxiliary standby lighting is turned on if suspicious activity is detected. Movable lighting supplements continuous or standby lighting.

EXPLOSIVE BLAST RESISTANCE

The most effective protective measure against explosive blast is to maximize the standoff distance from perimeter barriers to buildings or other assets. Blast walls are of limited effectiveness.

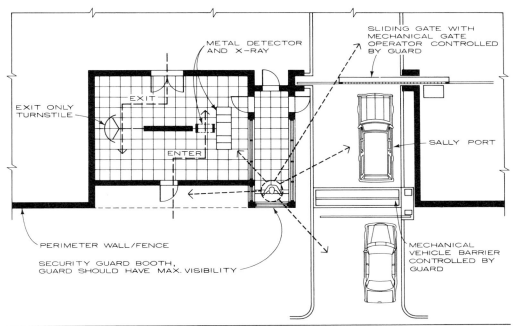

SITE ACCESS DIAGRAM

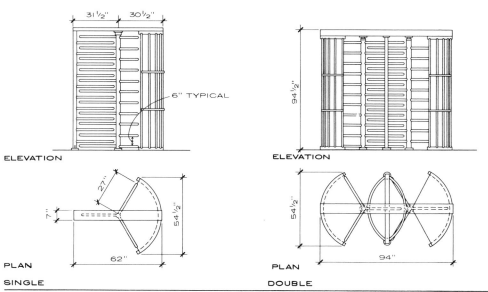

TURNSTILES

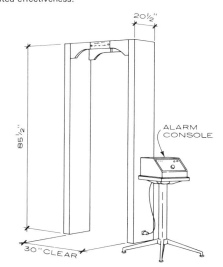

WALK THROUGH METAL DETECTOR

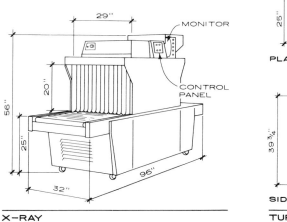

X-RAY

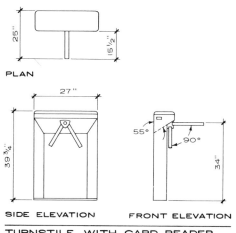

TURNSTILE WITH CARD READER

Edwin Daly, AIA; Joseph Handwerger, Architects; Washington, D.C.
William G. Miner, AIA; Washington, D.C.

SITE IMPROVEMENTS 2

60

REFERENCES

GENERAL REFERENCES

Site Planning, 3rd ed., 1988, Kevin Lynch and Gary Hack, MIT Press, Cambridge, MA

A Guide to Site and Environmental Planning, 3rd ed., 1987, Harvey M. Rubenstein, Wiley

Time-Saver Standards for Site Planning, 1984, Joseph DeCiara and Lee E. Koppleman, McGraw-Hill

Simplified Site Design, 1992, James Ambrose and Peter Brandow, Wiley

DATA SOURCES: ORGANIZATIONS

Alaska Railroad, 35

American Railway Engineering Association (AREA), 35

Brandir International, Inc., 58

Canterbury Designs, Canterbury International, Inc., 58

Computer Parking Design, 29

Federal Aviation Administration (FAA), 39, 40, 42

Federal Emergency Management Agency (FEMA), 44

International Civil Aviation Organization (ICAO), 39, 40

National Model Railroad Association (NMRA), 35

Operations Council, American Trucking Association, Inc., (ATA), 32, 33

Rally Racks, Inc., 58

Sunshine U-Lock Corporation, 58

Zamboni Corporation, 24

DATA SOURCES: PUBLICATIONS

A Levee Policy for the National Flood Insurance Program, National Research Council (NRC), Water Science and Technology Board, reprinted with permission, 44

Design for Landscape Architects, 1984, Albe E. Munsun, McGraw-Hill, 38, 46, 52, 56

Developer's Handbook, Allen Carroll, Connecticut Coastal Management Program, excerpted with permission, 38, 46, 52, 56

Fire Protection Handbook, 15th ed., 1981, National Fire Protection Agency (NFPA), reprinted with permission, 43

Identification of the Fire Hazards of Materials, National Fire Protection Association (NFPA), 43

Modern Dock Design, Kelley Company, Inc., 34

The Granite Garden: Urban Nature and Human Design, 1984, Anne Whiston Spirn, Basic Books, 44

Time-Saver Standards for Site Planning, 1966, Joseph DeChiara and Lee E. Koppleman, McGraw-Hill, 26

Trip Generation, 3rd ed., 1982, Institute of Transportation Engineers (ITE), 53

Urban Planning and Design Criteria, 1985, Joseph DeChiara and Lee E. Koppleman, Van Nostrand Reinhold, 38

CHAPTER **3**

LANDSCAPING

PLANTINGS	62
DEVELOPMENT OF PLANTING	69
PAVING AND SURFACING	72
INDOOR PLANTING	73

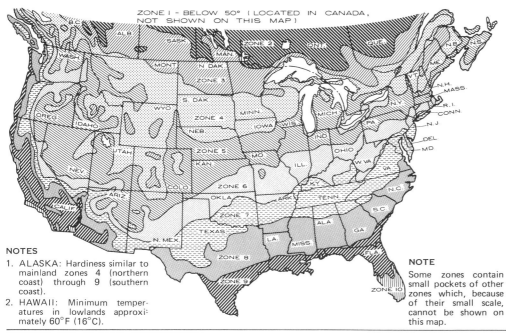

ZONE I - BELOW 50° (LOCATED IN CANADA, NOT SHOWN ON THIS MAP)

NOTE
The zone map shows in moderate detail the expected minimum temperature of most of the horticulturally important areas of the United States. Plants are listed in the coldest zone where they will grow normally, but they can be expected to grow in warmer areas.

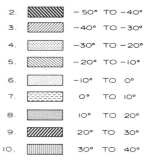

APPROXIMATE RANGE OF AVERAGE ANNUAL MINIMUM TEMPERATURES FOR EACH ZONE

2.	−50° TO −40°
3.	−40° TO −30°
4.	−30° TO −20°
5.	−20° TO −10°
6.	−10° TO 0°
7.	0° TO 10°
8.	10° TO 20°
9.	20° TO 30°
10.	30° TO 40°

NOTES
1. ALASKA: Hardiness similar to mainland zones 4 (northern coast) through 9 (southern coast).
2. HAWAII: Minimum temperatures in lowlands approximately 60°F (16°C).

NOTE
Some zones contain small pockets of other zones which, because of their small scale, cannot be shown on this map.

ZONES OF PLANT HARDINESS
(ADAPTED FROM MAP IN U.S.D.A. PUBLICATION 814)

NEEDLE EVERGREENS—30 FT AND OVER

BOTANICAL NAME	COMMON NAME	Columnar	Conical	Spreading	Slow	Medium	Fast	Urban	Seashore	Ornamental	Windbreak	Green	Light Green	Dark Green	Silver Green	Blue Green	Full Sun	Dry Soil	Moist Soil	Acid	Alkaline	Well Drained	Average	1	2	3	4	5	6	7	8	9	10
Abies concolor	White fir		•			•	•	•		•	•					•	•			•							•						
Araucaria excelsa	Norfolk Island pine		•		•			•	•					•			•		•														•
Cedrus atlantica glauca	Blue atlas cedar		•	•		•				•	•				•	•	•						•					•					
Cedrus deodara	Deodar cedar		•			•				•	•	•					•						•						•				
Cedrus libani stenocoma	Cedar of Lebanon		•	•		•				•				•			•						•					•					
Chamaecyparis lawsoniana	Lawson false cypress	•		•						•	•			•			•		•									•					
Chamaecyparis obtusa	Hinoki false cypress		•	•	•					•				•			•		•								•						
Chamaecyparis pisifera	Sawara false cypress	•	•		•					•	•	•		•			•		•								•						
Cryptomeria japonica	Cryptomeria	•	•		•			•	•					•			•		•	•								•	•			
Cunninghamia lanceolata	Common China fir			•	•					•	•	•		•			•		•				•						•			
Cupressus sempervirens 'stricta'	Italian pyramidal cypress	•			•					•	•			•			•	•					•						•			
Juniperus chinensis	Chinese juniper		•		•	•	•			•	•	•					•			•	•		•					•				
Juniperus scopulorum	Western red cedar	•			•					•	•	•			•	•	•			•	•		•					•				
Juniperus virginiana	Eastern red cedar	•	•		•			•		•	•			•			•			•	•		•	•			•					
Larix leptolepis	Japanese larch		•	•		•	•		•			•					•		•		•						•					
Libocedrus decurrens	California incense cedar	•	•			•				•	•			•			•		•									•				
Metasequoia glyptostroboides	Dawn redwood		•			•	•		•	•	•	•					•		•									•				
Picea*	Spruce											•																					
Pinus*	Pine											•																					
Podocarpus macrophyllus	Yew podocarpus	•			•					•	•			•			•													•			
Pseudolarix amabilis	Golden larch		•	•	•					•	•	•					•		•	•								•				
Pseudotsuga menziesii	Douglas fir		•	•		•	•			•	•			•			•		•								•					
Sciadopitys verticulata	Umbrella pine	•	•		•					•	•			•			•		•	•	•						•					
Sequoiadendron giganteum	Giant sequoia	•			•					•			•	•			•		•										•			
Taxodium distichum	Bald cypress	•			•			•		•		•					•		•	•			•				•					
Taxus Baccata	English yew		•	•	•					•	•			•			•			•	•		•					•				
Taxus Baccata stricta	Irish yew	•			•					•	•			•			•			•	•		•					•				
Thuja occidentalis	American arborvitae	•	•		•			•		•	•	•					•		•							•						
Thuja plicata	Giant arborvitae	•	•		•			•		•	•	•					•		•								•					
Tsuga canadensis	Canada hemlock		•	•		•	•	•		•				•			•		•	•	•						•					
Tsuga caroliniana	Carolina hemlock		•	•		•				•				•			•		•	•	•						•					

*See other references for local species and varieties.

A. E. Bye & Associates, Landscape Architects; Old Greenwich, Connecticut

PLANTINGS

BROAD LEAVED EVERGREENS

BOTANICAL NAME	COMMON NAME	Under 1 ft	1 to 3 ft	3 to 6 ft	6 to 10 ft	10 ft and over	White	Yellow-orange	Pink-red	Purple-blue	Spring	Summer	Fall	Winter	Partial sun	Full sun	Full shade	Moist soil	Dry soil	Acid soil	Alkaline soil	City	Seashore	Ornamental	Hedge	1	2	3	4	5	6	7	8	9	10
Abelia x grandiflora	Glossy abelia		•						•			•			•	•		•				•		•	•						•				
Azalea varieties*	Azalea varieties			•	•		•	•	•		•				•	•		•		•		•		•						•					
Buxus sempervirens	Common box			•											•	•		•	•						•						•				
Calliandra inaequilatera	Pink powder puff			•					•		•					•				•		•		•											•
Callistemon citrinus	Lemon bottle brush			•	•				•		•	•		•	•	•			•															•	
Calluna vulgaris	Heather		•				•		•	•		•	•			•		•		•		•								•					
Citrus sinensis	Sweet orange				•	•	•				•	•	•	•	•	•		•				•												•	•
Codiaeum variegatum	Croton			•											•	•		•						•	•										•
Cotoneaster species*	Cotoneaster species		•	•	•		•				•	•				•			•				•	•					•	•	•	•			
Daphne cneorum	Rose daphne	•							•		•				•	•		•		•	•			•						•					
Elaeagnus pungens	Thorny elaeagnus				•	•	•						•				•	•	•	•		•		•								•			
Enkianthus campanulatus	Redvein enkianthus			•				•		•				•	•		•		•				•						•					
Erica carnea	Spring heather		•				•		•		•					•		•		•		•									•				
Eriobotrya japonica	Loquat				•	•						•	•	•		•		•		•				•									•		
Euonymus japonica	Evergreen euonymus				•						•	•			•			•	•	•					•									•	
Euphorbia pulcherrima	Poinsetta		•	•					•					•		•						•													•
Fatsia japonica	Japanese fatsia				•	•							•		•		•					•	•		•								•		
Ficus benjamina	Weeping fig				•										•	•						•													•
Gardenia jasminoides	Gardenia			•			•				•	•	•		•	•			•		•		•										•		
Gaultheria shallon	Salal			•			•		•			•			•	•	•	•	•	•		•									•				
Hebe traversii	Traverse hebe			•			•					•				•	•					•		•								•		
Hibiscus rosa-sinensis	Chinese hibiscus				•		•	•			•				•		•					•		•										•	
Hypericum species*	Saint-John's-wort species	•							•		•	•			•	•						•										•		
Ilex (evergreen species)**	Holly (evergreen species)	•	•	•	•							•	•		•		•		•	•								•	•	•	•	•	•		
Ixora coccinea	Ixora				•	•			•		•	•	•	•	•	•	•		•					•	•										•
Jasminum mesnyi	Primrose jasmine				•				•		•	•			•			•	•	•		•											•	
Kalmia latifolia	Mountain laurel		•	•		•	•				•				•	•	•		•		•	•			•					•					
Laurus nobilis	Laurel			•	•						•				•		•	•	•						•							•		
Ligustrum japonicum	Japanese privet			•	•	•	•					•			•		•		•				•									•		
Mahonia aquifolia	Oregon holly-grape	•					•		•		•				•			•	•			•							•	•				
Myrtus communis 'compacta'	Compact Myrtle		•	•		•					•				•		•				•		•								•		
Nandina domestica	Nandina		•		•						•				•		•					•										•		
Nerium Oleander	Oleander			•	•	•	•	•	•	•	•				•		•		•	•		•	•									•		
Olea europarea	Common olive			•	•	•					•				•		•		•				•										•	
Osmanthus heterophyllus	Holly osmanthus			•	•	•						•			•		•					•	•								•		
Photinia serrulata	Chinese photinia			•	•	•					•				•						•											•		
Pieris floribunda	Mountain andromeda		•			•					•				•	•	•	•	•		•		•							•					
Pieris japonica	Japanese andromeda		•			•					•				•		•	•	•	•				•							•			
Pittosporum tobira	Japanese pittosporum			•		•					•				•		•		•				•	•									•	
Plumbago capensis	Cape plumbago	•								•	•	•	•	•	•	•		•				•	•										•	
Prunus laurocerasus 'schipkaenis'	Schipka cherry-laurel		•	•		•					•				•		•		•				•	•									•	•	
Pyracantha coccinea	Firethorn			•	•	•					•				•		•		•	•			•	•								•		
Rhododendron species*	Rhododendron species		•	•	•	•	•	•	•	•	•	•			•	•		•		•		•		•					•	•	•			
Schinus molle	California pepper tree				•	•	•				•				•		•		•				•											•
Skimmia japonica	Japanese skimmia		•			•					•				•		•	•					•									•		
Ulmus parvifolia pendens	Evergreen elm				•										•	•		•	•	•				•										•
Viburnum rhytidophyllum	Leatherleaf viburnum			•	•	•					•			•		•			•	•				•								•		
Xylosma senticosa	Xylosma		•		•										•		•		•				•											•	

* See other references for local species and varieties.
**Also deciduous ilex available.

A. E. Bye & Associates, Landscape Architects; Old Greenwich, Connecticut

PLANTINGS 3

DECIDUOUS TREES—20 TO 50 FT

BOTANICAL NAME	COMMON NAME	Rounded	Weeping	Spreading	Conical	Columnar	Oval	Slow	Medium	Fast	Shade Tree	Ornamental	Street Tree	Urban Tree	Seashore Tree	Flowers	Fruit	Leaf Color	Bark	Light Shade	Full Sun	Dry Soil	Moist Soil	Well Drained Soil	Acid Soil	Alkali Soil	1	2	3	4	5	6	7	8	9	10
Acer campestre	Hedge maple	●						●				●	●	●						●	●										●					
Acer ginnala	Amur maple	●								●		●	●	●		●	●	●			●	●						●									
Acer palmatum	Japanese maple	●						●				●		●				●			●	●		●	●							●					
Ailanthus altissima	Tree of heaven	●								●			●	●		●	●	●			●	●	●								●					
Albizia julibrissin	Hardy silk tree			●						●	●	●	●			●		●			●	●												●		
Amelanchier laevis	Allegany serviceberry	●								●		●		●	●	●	●	●	●	●	●	●	●	●							●					
Arbutus unedo	Strawberry tree			●				●				●				●	●	●		●		●			●										●	
Bauhinia variegata	Buddhist bauhinia	●							●	●	●	●				●				●		●		●											●
Betula populifolia	Gray birch			●		●		●				●				●	●	●	●	●	●							●	●							
Broussonetia papyrifera	Common paper mulberry	●		●						●	●	●	●		●	●		●		●	●	●										●			
Camellia japonica	Common camellia	●						●				●			●		●		●												●			
Carpinus caroliniana	American hornbeam	●						●				●	●	●				●	●	●	●							●								
Cassia fistula	Golden shower senna	●							●			●	●			●	●			●	●			●											●
Castanea mollissima	Chinese chestnut			●						●	●	●				●	●	●			●	●		●						●	●				
Cercis canadensis	Eastern redbud	●		●			●	●			●		●			●	●			●	●							●							
Chionanthus virginicus	Fringetree	●		●				●				●				●	●	●		●	●							●							
Cladastris lutea	American yellowwood	●						●		●	●	●	●		●	●	●	●		●				●			●								
Clethera barbinervis	Japanese clethera			●				●				●				●		●	●	●									●					
Cornus florida	Flowering dogwood	●	●	●				●				●		●		●	●	●	●	●	●		●					●							
Cornus kousa	Japanese dogwood			●				●				●		●		●	●	●	●	●	●		●					●							
Cornus mas	Cornelian cherry	●		●				●				●				●	●	●		●	●							●							
Crataegus species*	Hawthorne species	●		●					●	●		●	●	●	●	●	●			●	●	●		●	●			●							
Delonix regia	Royal poinciana			●					●	●	●	●				●				●	●													●
Elaeagnus angustifolia	Russian olive	●		●						●		●	●	●	●	●				●							●								
Firmiana simplex	Chinese parasol tree				●				●	●				●	●			●		●													●	
Fraxinus holotricha	Moraine ash	●			●				●	●								●											●				
Fraxinus velutina glabra	Modesto ash	●							●	●	●				●	●				●											●					
Halesia carolina	Carolina silverbell	●			●			●			●		●		●	●		●		●		●									●					
Koelreuteria paniculata	Goldenrain tree			●					●	●	●	●		●	●			●		●											●					
Laburnum watereri	Waterer laburnum					●			●		●			●				●			●										●					
Magnolia species*	Magnolia	●							●			●				●	●	●		●	●	●	●	●							●	●	●	●	●	
Malus species*	Crab apple species	●		●					●			●		●			●	●			●			●					●	●	●	●	●			
Melia azedarach	Chinaberry	●		●					●	●				●		●	●			●	●	●		●							●			
Phellodendron amurense	Amur cork tree			●					●			●	●	●		●		●	●	●	●	●	●						●					
Prunus species*	Cherries, apricots, plums, peaches	●							●		●		●	●	●	●	●				●							●	●	●	●	●	●			
Pterocarya fraxinifolia	Caucasian wing nut			●						●		●				●	●				●		●								●					
Pyrus calleryana "Bradford"	Bradford pear				●			●			●	●	●		●	●	●			●										●					
Salix babylonica	Babylon weeping willow		●						●			●						●		●	●	●												●		
Salix elegantissima	Thurlow weeping willow		●						●			●						●		●	●	●									●					
Sapium sebiferum	Chinese tallow tree			●					●	●					●	●		●	●	●														●
Sorbus alnifolia	Korean mountain ash	●		●					●	●		●	●	●	●	●		●										●					
Sorbus aucuparia	Rowan tree	●		●					●	●		●	●	●		●	●		●									●					
Stewartia koreana	Korean stewartia			●				●		●		●				●	●	●	●	●		●							●					
Styrax japonica	Japanese snowbell	●		●				●				●	●			●	●		●	●	●							●					
Syringa amurensis japonica	Japanese tree lilac			●	●			●	●			●	●	●		●					●							●					
Ulmus parvifolia	Chinese elm		●						●			●	●	●	●	●	●	●	●	●	●	●						●					
Viburnum sieboldii	Siebold viburnum	●		●				●				●		●	●	●	●	●				●						●					

*See other references for local species and varieties.

A. E. Bye & Associates, Landscape Architects; Old Greenwich, Connecticut

3   PLANTINGS

LARGE DECIDUOUS TREES—50 FT AND OVER

Botanical Name	Common Name	Rounded	Weeping	Spreading	Conical	Columnar	Oval	Slow	Medium	Fast	Shade Tree	Ornamental	Street Tree	Urban Tree	Seashore Tree	Flowers	Fruit	Leaf Color	Bark	Light Shade	Full Sun	Dry Soil	Moist Soil	Acid Soil	Alkaline Soil	Well Drained Soil	1	2	3	4	5	6	7	8	9	10
Acacia decurrens dealbata	Silver wattle			●						●		●				●					●	●				●										●
Acer platinoides and varieties	Norway maple and varieties	●			●	●			●		●	●	●	●	●	●					●					●			●							
Acer rubrum	Red or swamp maple	●					●			●	●	●	●			●	●	●			●		●						●							
Acer saccharum	Sugar maple					●		●			●	●					●			●	●	●		●		●			●							
Aesculus hippocastanum	Horse chestnut	●					●			●		●		●		●	●	●		●	●		●						●							
Betula nigra	River birch			●						●		●		●			●	●	●	●	●		●	●						●						
Betula papyrifera	Canoe or paper birch			●		●			●		●		●				●	●		●	●	●	●				●									
Betula pendula	European birch		●		●	●			●		●		●				●	●		●	●	●	●				●									
Carpinus betulus	European hornbeam	●			●		●			●		●		●	●			●	●		●											●				
Cercidiphyllum japonicum	Katsura tree	●						●	●	●		●	●			●		●	●	●	●		●							●						
Cornus controversa	Giant dogwood			●					●			●				●	●			●			●							●						
Eucalyptus species*	Eucalyptus species	●							●	●	●	●			●	●				●															●	●
Fagus grandifolia	American beech	●					●				●		●				●	●	●		●								●							
Fagus sylvatica and varieties*	European beech and varieties	●	●	●			●				●		●		●		●	●	●		●									●						
Fraxinus americana	White ash	●							●	●				●			●				●								●							
Fraxinus oregona	Oregon ash					●			●	●		●							●		●												●			
Fraxinus pennsylvanica lanceolata	Green ash	●			●				●	●							●				●						●									
Ginkgo biloba	Ginkgo			●	●	●		●				●	●				●				●	●	●					●								
Gleditsia triacanthos and varieties*	Honey locust and varieties			●					●	●		●	●	●	●			●	●		●								●							
Gordonia lasianthus	Loblolly bay gordonia				●			●			●		●			●				●	●		●										●			
Liquidambar styraciflua	Sweet gum			●					●	●		●		●				●	●	●	●		●							●						
Liriodendron tulipifera	Tulip tree				●				●	●		●		●			●	●	●		●		●							●						
Magnolia grandiflora	Southern magnolia			●				●			●		●	●		●	●	●			●			●							●					
Nyssa sylvatica	Black tupelo			●				●			●		●		●			●	●		●		●	●					●							
Pittosporum rhombifolium	Diamond leaf pittosporum	●							●			●		●	●		●				●																●
Platanus acerifolium	London plane tree	●		●					●	●	●	●	●	●	●		●		●	●	●				●				●							
Populus alba	White poplar			●		●			●		●		●			●	●			●	●						●									
Populus tremuloides	Quaking aspen			●					●	●						●	●	●	●	●	●	●			●	●										
Prunus serotina	Black cherry			●			●			●	●			●		●	●	●		●									●							
Quercus alba	White oak	●		●			●			●	●			●		●	●	●		●	●		●					●								
Quercus borealis	Red oak	●		●				●		●		●	●		●	●	●		●			●					●									
Quercus coccinea	Scarlet oak	●		●				●		●					●	●	●		●			●					●									
Quercus falcata	Southern red oak	●		●				●		●					●	●	●		●			●								●						
Quercus imbricaria	Shingle oak	●			●		●		●		●				●	●	●		●			●							●							
Quercus kelloggii	California black oak	●		●				●		●					●	●	●		●	●	●													●		
Quercus laurifolia	Laurel oak	●							●		●				●	●			●		●													●		
Quercus palustris	Pin oak				●				●		●		●	●		●			●			●							●							
Quercus phellos	Willow oak	●		●					●		●	●	●		●	●			●			●	●										●	●		
Quercus robur and varieties*	English oak and varieties	●			●		●		●		●				●				●			●						●								
Quercus shumardii	Shumard oak			●			●		●		●		●	●			●			●			●							●						
Quercus virginiana	Live oak	●					●		●		●		●		●	●			●	●														●		
Salix alba tristis	Golden weeping willow		●						●		●	●		●		●		●			●		●					●									
Sassafras albidum	Sassafras			●					●		●	●	●		●	●	●	●	●	●							●									
Sophora japonica	Japanese pagoda tree	●		●				●	●	●		●	●		●	●			●	●									●							
Tilia cordata	Little leaf linden				●		●		●	●	●	●	●		●	●			●	●								●								
Tilia euchlora	Crimean linden				●				●	●	●	●	●		●	●	●	●		●	●								●							
Tilia tomentosa	Silver linden			●		●			●	●	●	●	●	●	●	●	●		●	●	●								●							
Zelkova serrata and varieties*	Japanese zelkova and varieties*	●							●	●		●	●		●	●		●			●	●	●			●				●						

*See other references for local species and varieties.

A. E. Bye & Associates, Landscape Architects; Old Greenwich, Connecticut

DECIDUOUS SHRUBS

BOTANICAL NAME	COMMON NAME	HEIGHT 0 to 3 ft	3 to 6 ft	6 to 10 ft	10 ft and over	SPECIAL FEATURES Flowers	Fruit	Foliage Color	Good Winter Appearance	Rapid Growth	Easy Maintenance	FLOWERS COLOR White	Yellow-orange	Pink-red	Blue-purple	SEASON Spring	Summer	Fall	Winter	USES Urban	Seashore	Hedges	CULTURAL REQUIREMENTS Sun	Shade	Light Shade	Acid Soil	Alkaline Soil	Moist Soil	Dry Soil	Well drained Soil	HARDINESS ZONES 1	2	3	4	5	6	7	8	9	10
Amelanchier stolonifera	Running serviceberry		●			●	●	●			●	●				●					●		●		●	●			●	●	●				●						
Aronia species*	Chokeberry species	●	●	●	●	●	●	●	●			●	●			●				●	●	●	●		●	●	●	●	●	●					●						
Berberis species*	Barberry species	●	●	●		●	●	●	●			●		●		●				●	●	●	●		●	●	●	●	●	●					●						
Calycanthus floridus	Sweet shrub		●	●		●		●				●		●		●							●		●	●	●	●	●						●						
Caragana arborescens	Siberian pea tree			●	●	●	●						●			●				●		●	●					●	●	●			●								
Cercis chinensis	Chinese redbud		●	●		●		●				●		●	●	●								●	●					●									●		
Chaenomeles species*	Quince species	●	●			●	●					●	●	●		●				●	●	●	●		●			●	●	●					●						
Clethra alnifolia	Summer sweet		●			●		●				●		●			●				●		●	●	●	●	●		●							●					
Cornus species*	Dogwood species	●	●	●	●	●	●	●	●	●		●		●		●				●		●	●		●			●	●				●								
Corylopsis species*	Winter hazel species	●	●	●	●	●		●				●		●		●						●	●	●	●	●											●				
Cotinus species*	Smoke tree species		●	●		●		●				●		●	●	●							●					●	●	●						●					
Cotoneaster species*	Cotoneaster species	●	●	●	●	●	●	●	●					●		●				●	●	●	●					●	●						●						
Cytisus species*	Scotch broom species	●	●	●		●			●	●		●	●	●	●	●						●	●					●	●								●				
Deutzia species*	Deutzia species		●	●		●		●				●		●		●	●			●			●		●			●	●						●						
Euonymus species*	Euonymus species		●	●	●		●	●	●		●									●	●	●	●	●	●	●			●	●					●						
Exochorda species*	Pearlbush species		●	●	●	●						●				●						●			●			●	●							●					
Forsythia species*	Forsythia species	●	●	●		●			●	●			●			●				●		●		●			●	●								●					
Fothergilla species*	Fothergilla species	●	●	●		●		●				●				●						●		●		●			●							●					
Hamamelis species*	Witch hazel species		●	●	●	●	●		●			●	●			●	●	●		●		●		●			●	●								●					
Hibiscus species*	Rose of Sharon species		●	●				●				●		●	●		●	●		●	●		●		●			●		●						●					
Ilex verticillata	Winterberry		●			●	●	●	●			●										●		●	●	●		●						●							
Jasminum nudiflorum	Winter jasmine	●	●	●		●			●				●			●			●	●			●						●							●					
Kerria japonica	Kerria		●	●		●		●	●				●			●	●	●		●			●		●				●						●						
Kolkwitzia amabilis	Beauty bush		●			●	●	●	●		●			●		●						●		●			●	●								●					
Lagerstroemia indica	Crape myrtle		●	●	●	●		●	●			●		●	●		●			●		●	●			●												●			
Lespedeza species*	Bush clover species		●	●		●						●			●		●	●		●			●					●	●	●						●					
Ligustrum species*	Privet species	●	●	●	●	●			●			●				●	●	●		●	●	●	●	●	●	●			●	●	●				●						
Lindera benzoin	Spicebush		●	●	●	●	●		●			●	●			●				●			●	●	●	●			●							●					
Myrica pensylvanica	Bayberry		●	●			●		●			●								●	●		●				●			●			●								
Photinia villosa	Oriental photinia			●	●	●	●			●		●	●			●							●		●																
Plumeria rubra	Frangipani			●	●	●			●			●	●	●	●	●	●	●			●		●		●			●	●	●											●
Potentilla species*	Bush cinquefoil species		●			●						●	●	●		●	●	●		●			●					●	●			●									
Rhamnus species*	Buckthorn species			●	●		●	●												●		●	●		●			●	●			●									
Rhododendron	Azalea	●	●	●	●	●		●				●	●	●	●	●	●			●		●		●	●	●	●			●		●		●							
Rosa species*	'Shrub' rose species		●	●	●	●	●	●	●			●	●	●	●		●	●	●		●	●	●	●						●	●		●								
Spiraea species*	Spiraea species	●	●	●		●		●		●		●		●		●	●			●	●	●	●	●		●			●							●					
Stephanandra species*	Stephanandra species	●	●	●		●		●				●				●								●	●	●			●								●				
Stewartia species*	Stewartia species			●	●	●		●	●			●		●		●		●					●			●	●		●								●				
Symphoricarpos species*	Snowberry species	●	●				●		●			●					●			●		●	●		●				●	●	●		●								
Symplocos paniculata	Sapphireberry			●	●	●	●					●				●							●		●	●											●				
Syringa species*	Lilac species	●	●	●	●	●			●			●	●	●	●	●				●	●	●	●		●		●						●								
Vaccinium corymbosum	Highbush blueberry		●	●		●	●	●	●			●	●			●				●	●	●	●		●	●	●		●					●							
Viburnum species*	Viburnum species	●	●	●	●	●	●	●	●			●	●		●		●	●			●	●	●	●	●	●	●		●	●	●		●								

NOTES

*See other references for local species and varieties. Listings in this chart represent large genera of many species and varieties. Other sources need to be consulted to obtain detailed information. The hardiness zone notations indicate that most of the species within the family are hardy to that zone but there are a few that are not.

A. E. Bye & Associates, Landscape Architects; Old Greenwich, Connecticut

GROUND COVERS

Botanical Name	Common Name	Less than 6 in.	6 to 12 in.	12 to 18 in.	18 in. and over	Sun	Shade	Light Shade	Acid	Alkaline	Seashore	City	Moist Soil	Dry Soil	Well-drained Soil	Green	Dark Green	Blue Green	Gray Green	Purple Green	Flowers	Fruit	Mowable	Slopes	Rapid Growth	Easy Maintenance	1	2	3	4	5	6	7	8	9	10
DECIDUOUS																																				
Asperula odorata	Sweet woodruff		•					•	•				•			•						•				•	•			•							
Coronilla varia	Crown vetch			•	•	•		•	•	•			•	•		•						•			•	•	•		•								
Cotoneaster (spreading varieties)	Cotoneaster		•			•			•	•	•				•			•				•	•		•		•					•					
Gazania uniflora	Trailing gazania	•				•			•	•				•					•		•			•	•	•									•	
Phlox subulata	Ground pink	•				•								•	•	•	•				•				•	•	•									
Rosa wichuraiana	Memorial rose		•			•					•			•		•					•			•	•	•					•					
Trifolium repens	White clover	•				•							•			•					•		•		•	•	•									
Vaccinium angustifolium laevifolium	Low bush blueberry		•			•	•	•	•				•				•				•	•			•	•	•									
Veronica repens	Creeping speedwell	•				•	•	•					•				•				•				•	•										
Xanthorhiza simplicissima	Yellowroot			•	•	•							•				•				•				•	•			•							
BROAD LEAVED EVERGREENS																																				
Ajuga reptans	Bugleweed	•				•	•	•					•			•	•			•	•			•	•				•							
Anthemis nobilis	Chamomile	•	•			•								•			•				•		•		•			•								
Arabis albida	Wall rockcress	•				•								•				•			•				•			•								
Arctostaphylos uva-ursi	Bearberry		•			•		•	•					•			•				•	•		•		•		•								
Baccharis pilularis	Coyote bush			•	•	•			•	•	•				•		•				•			•	•	•							•		
Carissa macrocarpa 'green carpet'	Green carpet natal plum		•			•		•	•					•		•				•	•			•	•										•
Carpobrotus edulis	Hottentot fig	•				•			•				•		•				•	•	•			•	•									•
Ceanothus griseus horizontalis	Carmel creeper			•	•	•		•					•		•		•			•			•	•							•		
Ceratostigma plumbaginoides	Leadwort		•			•		•	•	•				•			•				•		•	•					•					
Cornus canadensis	Bunchberry		•				•	•	•	•			•			•				•	•			•		•					•				
Cotoneaster dammeri	Bearberry cotoneaster		•			•		•	•	•	•		•			•			•		•	•		•		•					•				
Dichondra repens	Dichondra	•				•	•	•	•	•			•			•				•			•	•										•
Drosanthemum hispidum	Rosea ice plant		•			•		•					•		•			•		•	•	•	•									•	
Euonymus fortunei coloratus	Purple-leaf wintercreeper	•				•		•	•				•		•		•		•	•			•	•				•					
Fragaria chiloensis	Wild strawberry		•			•		•	•		•		•			•			•	•	•			•				•					
Galax aphylla	Galax	•	•				•	•	•				•			•			•			•	•				•						
Hedera helix	English ivy		•				•	•	•		•	•	•			•			•			•	•				•						
Hypericum calycinum	Aaronsbeard Saint-John's-wort			•		•		•					•		•			•			•			•	•					•			
Iberis sempervirens	Evergreen candytuft		•			•			•	•	•		•			•			•			•				•				•				
Leucothoe catesbaei	Drooping leucothoe		•	•	•	•	•	•	•			•			•			•			•			•		•				•				
Lotus bertholettii	Parrot's beak, coral gem	•	•			•							•	•			•			•		•			•	•							•
Micromeria chamissonis	Yerba buena	•				•		•			•		•			•					•			•	•						•	
Pachistima canbyi	Canby pachistima		•	•		•	•	•	•			•			•			•			•			•				•				
Pachysandra terminalis	Japanese spurge		•				•	•	•			•			•			•	•			•			•				•				
Rosmarinus officinalis prostratus	Creeping rosemary			•	•	•					•			•	•		•			•			•							•	
Saxifraga stolonifera	Strawberry geranium	•					•						•			•			•	•	•		•							•	
Trachelospermum jasminoides	Star jasmine		•	•		•	•	•			•			•			•			•			•	•					•	
Vinca minor	Myrtle, periwinkle	•					•	•					•			•			•			•	•	•			•				
NEEDLE EVERGREENS																																				
Calluna vulgaris	Scotch heather	•	•	•	•	•		•	•		•		•			•					•			•			•					
Erica carnea	Spring heath		•			•		•	•	•				•			•			•			•				•				
Juniperus chinensis varieties	Varieties of Chinese juniper		•	•	•	•		•	•	•	•	•	•	•	•	•		•	•			•	•			•				
Juniperus conferta	Shore juniper		•			•		•		•				•	•		•					•	•			•				
Juniperus horizontalis douglasii	Waukegan juniper	•	•			•			•					•			•	•				•	•	•					
Juniperus horizontalis 'Bar Harbor'	Bar Harbor juniper		•			•			•	•	•		•	•		•	•	•			•	•	•					
Juniperus horizontalis 'wiltonii'	Wilton carpet juniper	•				•			•	•	•		•			•				•	•	•						
Juniperus horizontalis 'plumosa'	Andorra juniper		•			•			•	•			•			•	•			•	•			•				
Juniperus procumbens 'nana'	Japanese garden juniper	•	•			•			•	•			•			•					•	•			•				
Juniperus sabina tamariscifolia	Tamarix juniper		•			•			•	•			•	•	•	•	•			•	•	•	•		•				
Taxus baccata repandens	Spreading English yew				•	•	•	•	•				•		•		•					•				•				

A. E. Bye & Associates, Landscape Architects; Old Greenwich, Connecticut

PLANT CHARTS

The intent of the plant chart is to indicate the wide variety of plants available to the designer. There are many unusual trees, shrubs, and ground covers for every environmental and design situation. In using the charts, the designer will obtain a general perception of the plants listed. It is strongly recommended that more specific information be sought in botanic journals. The charts note the northernmost reaches of the plant listed, but some plants will not grow where winters are too warm. The southern reach of those particular plants has not been included in the charts because of conflicting and inadequate information. There are many regional variations in climate that should be considered when selecting plants. The designer is urged to consult a landscape architect to ensure the best selection for the design.

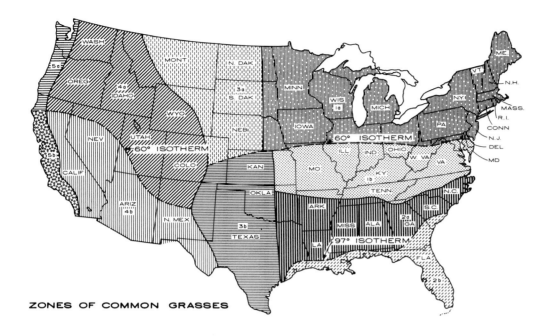

ZONES OF COMMON GRASSES

GRASSES

In selecting a type of grass for lawn development the designer must consider both environmental and use factors. The amount of available sunlight, the temperature range, rainfall, soil type, and drainage will determine the type of grass that will survive in a given location while additional consideration of tolerance to traffic and recuperative rates will ensure the best possible lawn. For example, different grasses are used for athletic fields depending on environmental factors: bluegrasses and fescues in the northern zones; Bermuda grasses and zoysias in the southern zones; and St. Augustine grass in the extreme south. All are rugged, but require different environments to grow well. Another example is bent grass. Although it requires high maintenance, it is desirable for golf courses because of its fine texture and thick growth.

Lawns can be installed by seed, sprigging, or sod at varying costs. Careful installation at the proper time of the year will ensure the health and beauty of the lawn. Proper soil preparation including aerating the soil, adding topsoil, fertilizer, lime, if necessary, good drainage, and the use of high quality certified weedfree seed is important for success. Frequently, mixtures of seeds are used, since growing conditions are rarely uniform throughout the lawn area. This practice can also mitigate the effects of lawn disease. More specific information is available from local agricultural agents.

GRASSES

BOTANICAL NAME	COMMON NAME	Sun	Shade	Light Shade	Well-drained Soil	Moist	Dry	Acid	Alkaline	Cool	Warm	Coarse	Fine	Thick	Hairy	High	Moderate	Minimal	Green	Dark Green	Light Green	Blue Green	Gray Green	Brown (hot weather)	Brown (cold weather)	1a	1b	2a	2b	3a	3b	4a	4b	5a	5b
Agropyron	Wheat	●					●		●	●	●			●				●			●		●							●	●	●			
Agrostis	Bent	●		●	●		●	●		●		●	●		●				●				●	●			●	●			*		*		●	*
Ammophila	Beach	●		●			●	●	●		●		●				●				●					●	●	●							●	*
Axonopus	Carpet	●	●		●		●			●	●				●				●					●				●	●							
Bouteloua	Blue gamma	●				●		●	●			●				●						●	●							*	●	*	●		*
Buchloë	Buffalo	●				●		●	●		●			●			●					●	●						●	●	*	*			
Cynodon	Bermuda	●		*	●		●			●		●	●		●					●				●				●	●		*		*		●	
Eremochloa	Centipede	●		●	●	*	●			●	●		●			●					●			●				●	●		*		*●		*	*
Festuca	Fescue	●	●	●	●	●	●	●		●			●			●				●						●	●	*		*		●	*	●	
Lolium	Rye	●		●	●		●	●		●			●		●				●				●				●	●	*	*		*		*	●	*
Paspalum notatum	Bahia	●		●	●	*	●			●	●			●			●			●				●				●	●							
Poa	Bluegrass	●		*	●		●	●		●			●	●		●			●				●				●	●		*		*		●		
Stenotaphrum	St. Augustine	●	●	●		●		●			●	●		●						●				●				*	●		*		*		*	
Zoysia	Zoysia	●	●	●		●			●		●			●			●				●			●	●	●	●	●		*		*	*	●	

*Will grow under special conditions: high altitude, proximity to water, or irrigation.

NOTES

1. Consult local agricultural agent, horticulturist, or nurseryman in your area for best grasses for slopes, maintenance concerns, and general planting instructions.
2. Planting slopes: (a) 3 to 1 is maximum for mowed banks. (b) 2 to 1 is maximum for unmowed banks.

A. E. Bye & Associates, Landscape Architects; Old Greenwich, Connecticut

PLANTINGS

NOTES

Several factors should be considered when designing with plants:

1. The physical environment of the site:
   - Soil conditions (acidity, porosity).
   - Available sunlight.
   - Available precipitation.
   - Seasonal temperature range.
   - Exposure of the site (wind).
2. The design needs of the project:
   - Directing movement.
   - Framing vistas.
   - Moderating the environment of the site.
   - Creating space by using plants to develop the base, vertical, and overhead planes.
3. The design character of the plants chosen:
   - Height.
   - Mass.
   - Silhouette (rounded, pyramidal, spreading).
   - Texture (fine, medium, coarse).
   - Color.
   - Seasonal interest (flowers, fruit, fall color).
   - Growth habits (fast or slow growing).

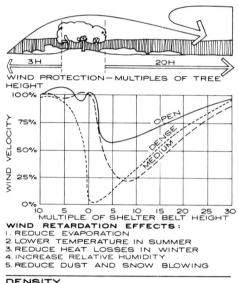

WIND RETARDATION EFFECTS:
1. REDUCE EVAPORATION
2. LOWER TEMPERATURE IN SUMMER
3. REDUCE HEAT LOSSES IN WINTER
4. INCREASE RELATIVE HUMIDITY
5. REDUCE DUST AND SNOW BLOWING

DENSITY

The density of a planted wind buffer determines the area that is protected. Height and composition are also factors in wind protection.

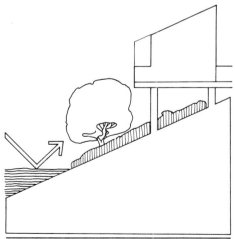

GLARE PROTECTION

The sun's vertical angle changes seasonally; therefore, the area subject to the glare of reflected sunlight varies. Plants of various heights screen glare from adjacent reflective surfaces (water, paving, glass, and building surfaces).

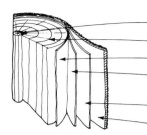

CROWN: THE HEAD OF FOLIAGE OF THE TREE LEAVES — THE FOLIAGE UNIT OF THE TREE THAT FUNCTIONS PRIMARILY IN FOOD MANUFACTURE BY PHOTOSYNTHESIS

HEARTWOOD: THE NONLIVING CENTRAL PART OF THE TREE GIVING STRENGTH AND STABILITY

ANNUAL RINGS: REVEAL AGE OF THE TREE BY SHOWING THE YEARLY GROWTH

SAPWOOD (XYLEM): CARRIES NUTRIENTS AND WATER TO THE LEAVES FROM THE ROOTS

CAMBIUM: LAYER BETWEEN THE XYLEM AND PHLOEM WHERE CELL GROWTH OCCURS, ADDING NEW SAPWOOD TO THE INSIDE AND NEW INNER BARK TO THE OUTSIDE

INNER BARK (PHLOEM): CARRIES FOOD FROM THE LEAVES TO THE BRANCHES, TRUNK, AND ROOTS

OUTER BARK: THE AGED INNER BARK THAT PROTECTS THE TREE FROM DESSICATION AND INJURY

PHYSICAL CHARACTERISTICS

SUMMER

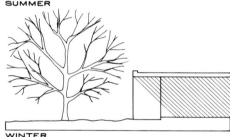

WINTER

RADIATION PROTECTION

In summer deciduous plants obstruct or filter the sun's strong radiation, thus cooling the area beneath them. In winter the sun penetrates through.

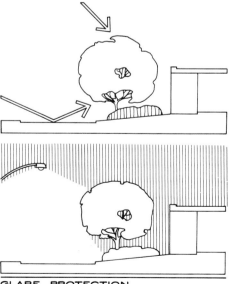

GLARE PROTECTION

Glare and reflection from sunlight and/or artificial sources can be screened or blocked by plants of various height and placement.

ROOTS: THE ROOTS ANCHOR THE TREE AND HELP HOLD THE SOIL AGAINST EROSION

ROOT HAIRS: THE TINY ROOT HAIRS ABSORB THE MINERALS FROM THE SOIL MOISTURE AND SEND THEM AS NUTRIENT SALTS IN THE SAPWOOD TO THE LEAVES

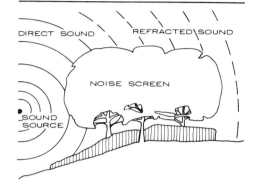

SOUND ATTENUATION

Plantings of deciduous and evergreen materials reduce sound more effectively than deciduous plants alone. Planting on earth mounds increases the attenuating effects of the buffer.

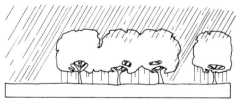

PARTICULATE MATTER TRAPPED ON THE LEAVES IS WASHED TO THE GROUND DURING A RAINFALL. GASEOUS AND OTHER POLLUTANTS ARE ASSIMILATED IN THE LEAVES

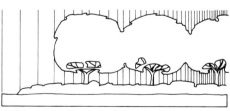

FUMES AND ODORS CAN BE MECHANICALLY MASKED BY FRAGRANT PLANTS AND CHEMICALLY METABOLIZED IN THE PHOTOSYNTHETIC PROCESS

AIR FILTRATION

Large masses of plants physically and chemically filter and deodorize the air to reduce air pollution.

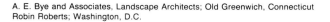

A. E. Bye and Associates, Landscape Architects; Old Greenwich, Connecticut
Robin Roberts; Washington, D.C.

DEVELOPMENT OF PLANTING 3

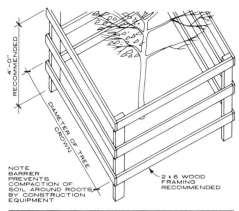

TREE PROTECTION BARRIER

NOTE BARRIER PREVENTS COMPACTION OF SOIL AROUND ROOTS BY CONSTRUCTION EQUIPMENT

2 x 6 WOOD FRAMING RECOMMENDED

4'-0" RECOMMENDED

DIAMETER OF CROWN OF TREE

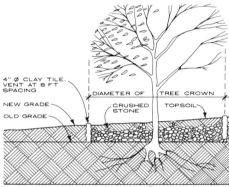

FILLING LESS THAN 30" AROUND EXISTING TREE

4" Ø CLAY TILE. VENT AT 8 FT SPACING

NEW GRADE

OLD GRADE

DIAMETER OF TREE CROWN

CRUSHED STONE

TOPSOIL

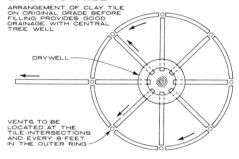

ARRANGEMENT OF CLAY TILE ON ORIGINAL GRADE BEFORE FILLING PROVIDES GOOD DRAINAGE WITH CENTRAL TREE WELL

DRYWELL

VENTS TO BE LOCATED AT THE TILE INTERSECTIONS AND EVERY 8 FEET IN THE OUTER RING

PLAN

FILLING OVER 30" AROUND EXISTING TREE

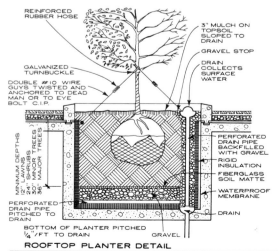

REINFORCED RUBBER HOSE

GALVANIZED TURNBUCKLE

DOUBLE #10 WIRE GUYS TWISTED AND ANCHORED TO DEAD MAN OR TO EYE BOLT C.I.P.

MINIMUM DEPTHS 12" LAWNS 24" SHRUBS 30" MINOR TREES 36" MAJOR TREES

PERFORATED DRAIN PIPE PITCHED TO DRAIN

BOTTOM OF PLANTER PITCHED ¼"/FT TO DRAIN

3" MULCH ON TOPSOIL SLOPED TO DRAIN

GRAVEL STOP

DRAIN COLLECTS SURFACE WATER

PERFORATED DRAIN PIPE BACKFILLED WITH GRAVEL

RIGID INSULATION

FIBERGLASS SOIL MATTE

WATERPROOF MEMBRANE

DRAIN

GRAVEL

ROOFTOP PLANTER DETAIL

PLANTING ON STRUCTURES

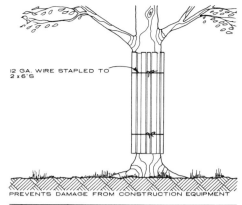

12 GA. WIRE STAPLED TO 2 x 6'S

PREVENTS DAMAGE FROM CONSTRUCTION EQUIPMENT

TREE TRUNK PROTECTION

CUTTING AROUND EXISTING TREES

Extreme care should be taken not to compact the earth within the crown of the tree. Compaction can cause severe root damage and reduce the air and water holding capacity of the soil.

If no surrounding barrier is provided, care should be taken not to operate equipment or store materials within the crown spread of the tree. If this area should be compacted, it would be necessary to aerate the soil thoroughly in the root zone immediately following construction. Certain tree species are severely affected by manipulation of the water table, and great care should be exercised to minimize this condition.

SPECIAL USE OF TREES

Trees for special uses should be branched or pruned naturally according to type. Where a form of growth is desired that is not in accordance with a natural growth habit, this form should be specified. For example:

1. BUSH FORM: Trees that start to branch close to the ground in the manner of a shrub.
2. CLUMPS: Trees with three or more main stems starting from the ground.
3. CUT BACK OR SHEARED: Trees that have been pruned back so as to multiply the branching structure and to develop a more formal effect.
4. ESPALIER: Trees pruned and trained to grow flat against a building or trellis, usually in a predetermined pattern or design.
5. PLEACHING: A technique of severe pruning, usually applied to a row or bosque of trees to produce a geometrically formal or clipped hedgelike effect.
6. POLLARDING: The technique in which annual severe pruning of certain species of trees serves to produce abundant vigorous growth the following year.
7. TOPIARY: Trees sheared or trimmed closely in a formal geometric pattern, or sculptural shapes frequently resembling animals or flowers.

SELECTING PLANTS FOR ROOFTOPS

WIND TOLERANCE

Higher elevations and exposure to wind can cause defoliation and increased transpiration rate. High parapet walls with louvers screen wind velocity and provide shelter for plants.

HIGH EVAPORATION RATE

Drying effects of wind and sun on soil around planter reduce available soil moisture rapidly. Irrigation, mulches, moisture holding soil additives (perlite, vermiculite and peat moss), and insulation assist in reducing this moisture loss.

RAPID SOIL TEMPERATURE FLUCTUATION

The conduction capacity of planter materials tends to produce a broad range of soil temperatures. Certain plant species suffer severe root damage because of cold or heat. Use of rigid insulation lining planter alleviates this condition.

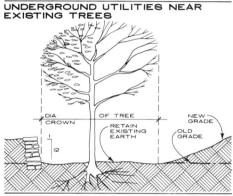

THIS   NOT THIS

FEWER ROOTS ARE SEVERED BY TUNNELING UNDER TREE THAN BY TRENCHING

UNDERGROUND UTILITIES NEAR EXISTING TREES

DIA   OF TREE
CROWN

RETAIN EXISTING EARTH

NEW GRADE

OLD GRADE

12

FILLING GRADE AROUND EXISTING TREE

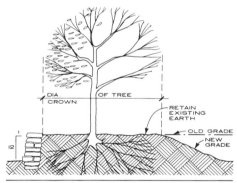

DIA   OF TREE
CROWN

RETAIN EXISTING EARTH

OLD GRADE

NEW GRADE

12

CUTTING GRADE AROUND EXISTING TREE

TOPSOIL

Topsoil in planters should be improved to provide the optimum growing condition. A general formula would add fertilizer (as per soil testing) plus 1 part peat moss or vermiculite (high water holding capacity) to 3 parts topsoil. More specific requirements for certain varieties of plants or grasses should be considered.

ROOT CAPACITY

Plant species should be carefully selected to adapt to the size of the plant bed. If species with shallow fibrous roots are used instead of species with a tap root system consult with nurseryman. Consider the ultimate maturity of the plant species in sizing planter.

Jim E. Miller and David W. Wheeler; Saratoga Associates; Saratoga Springs, New York
Erik Johnson; Lawrence Cook and Associates; Falls Church, Virginia
Connecticut Coastal Management Program, see data sources

DEVELOPMENT OF PLANTING

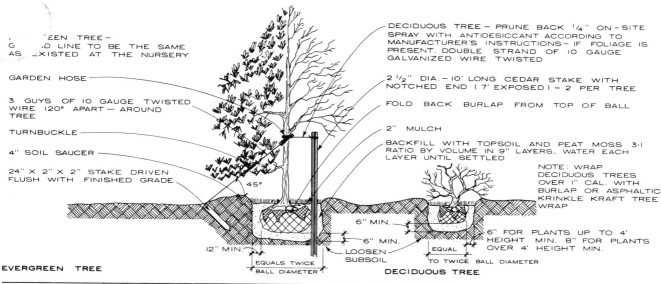

EVERGREEN TREE   **DECIDUOUS TREE**

PLANTING DETAILS — TREES AND SHRUBS

SHRUBS AND MINOR TREES BALLED AND BURLAPPED

HEIGHT RANGE (FT)	MINIMUM BALL DIAMETER (IN.)	MINIMUM BALL DEPTH (IN.)
1½–2	10	8
2–3	12	9
3–4	13	10
4–5	15	11
5–6	16	12
6–7	18	13
7–8	20	14
8–9	22	15
9–10	24	16
10–12	26	17

NOTE: Ball sizes should always be of a diameter to encompass the fibrous and feeding root system necessary for the full recovery of the plant.

STANDARD SHADE TREES—BALLED AND BURLAPPED

CALIPER* (IN.)	HEIGHT RANGE (FT)	MAXIMUM HEIGHTS (FT)	MINIMUM BALL DIAMETER (IN.)	MINIMUM BALL DEPTH (IN.)
½–¾	5–6	8	12	9
¾–1	6–8	10	14	10
1–1¼	7–9	11	16	12
1¼–1½	8–10	12	18	13
1½–1¾	10–12	14	20	14
1¾–2	10–12	14	22	15
2–2½	12–14	16	24	16
2½–3	12–14	16	28	19
3–3½	14–16	18	32	20
3½–4	14–16	18	36	22
4–5	16–18	22	44	26
5–6	18 and up	26	48	29

*Caliper indicates the diameter of the trunk taken 6 in. above the ground level up to and including 4 in. caliper size and 12 in. above the ground level for larger sizes.

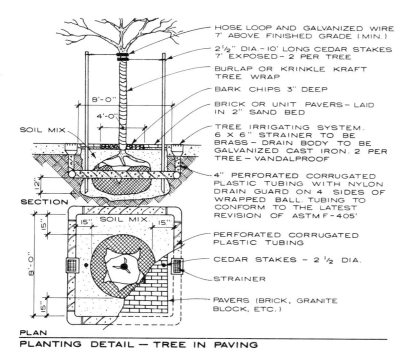

PLANTING DETAIL — TREE IN PAVING

A. E. Bye & Associates, Landscape Architects; Old Greenwich, Connecticut

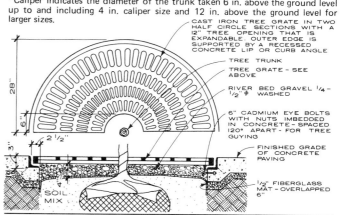

TREE GRATE DETAIL

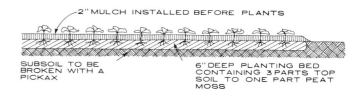

GROUND COVER PLANTING DETAIL
NOTE: GROUND COVERS SHOULD BE POT OR CONTAINER GROWN

DEVELOPMENT OF PLANTING 3

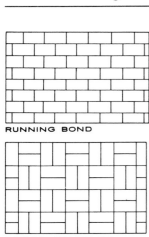
RUNNING BOND

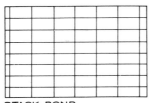
STACK BOND

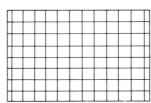
STACK BOND

TYPICAL UNIT PAVER TYPES AND NOMINAL SIZES

BRICK PAVERS: 4 in. x 4 in., 4 in. x 8 in., 4 in. x 12 in.; ½ in. to 2¼ in. thick.

PRESSED CONCRETE BRICKS: 4 in. x 8 in., 2½ in. to 3 in. thick.

PRESSED CONCRETE PAVERS: 12 in. x 12 in., 12 in. x 24 in., 18 in. x 18 in., 18 in. x 24 in., 24 in. x 24 in., 24 in. x 30 in., 24 in. x 36 in., 30 in. x 30 in., 36 in. x 36 in.; 1½ in. to 3 in. thick.

ASPHALT PAVERS: 5 in. x 12 in., 6 in. x 6 in., 6 in. x 12 in., 8 in. x 8 in., 8 in. hexagonal, 1¼ in. to 3 in. thick.

NOTES

1. Face brick, marble, and granite sometimes are used for paving.
2. See index for tile paver sizes and shapes.
3. Paving patterns shown often are rotated 45° for diagonal patterns.
4. Maximum 3 percent absorption for brick applications subject to vehicular traffic.
5. For pressed concrete and asphalt pavers subject to vehicular traffic, use 3 in. thickness.
6. Use modular size for brick paver patterns other than running and stack bond set with mortar joints. Use full size when set without mortar joints.

BASKET WEAVE OR PARQUET

HERRINGBONE

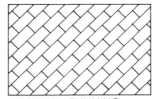
DIAGONAL RUNNING BOND

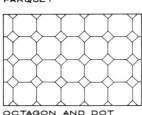
OCTAGON AND DOT

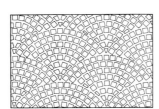
ROMAN COBBLE

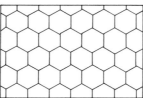
HEXAGON

UNIT PAVERS

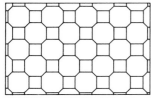
BASKET WEAVE OR PARQUET

DIAGONAL RUNNING BOND

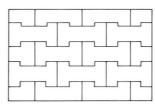
RUNNING BOND

NOTES

1. Interlocking pavers are available in concrete, hydraulically pressed concrete, asphalt, and brick, and in different weight classifications, compressive strengths, surface textures, finishes, and colors. Consult local suppliers for availability.
2. Subject to manufacturer's recommendations and local code requirements, interlocking concrete pavers may be used in areas subject to heavy vehicle loads at 30 to 40 mph speeds.
3. Continuous curb or other edge restraint is required to anchor pavers in applications subject to vehicular traffic.
4. Concrete interlocking paver sizes are based on metric dimensions. Dimensions indicated are to nearest ⅛ in.
5. Where paver shape permits, herringbone pattern is recommended for paving subject to vehicular traffic.
6. Portions have been adapted, with permission, from ASTM C 939.

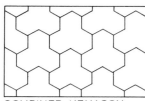
COMBINED HEXAGON

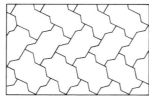
HERRINGBONE

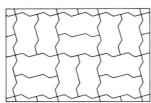
BASKET WEAVE

INTERLOCKING PAVERS

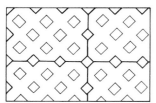
DIAGONAL SQUARES

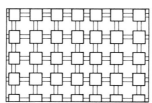
RUNNING SQUARES

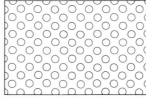
RINGS

NOTES

1. Appearance of grass pavers when voids are filled are shown by stipple to the right of the cut line. Voids may be filled with grass, a variety of ground cover, or gravel.
2. Grass pavers may be used to control erosion.
3. Herringbone pattern is recommended for concrete grass pavers subject to vehicular traffic.
4. Grass rings are available with close ring spacing for pedestrian use or wide ring spacing for vehicular use.

GRASS PAVERS

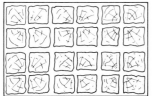
STACK BOND

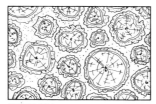
RANDOM

STACK BOND

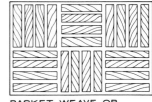
BASKET WEAVE OR PARQUET

WOOD PAVERS

Jeffrey R. Vandevoort; Talbott Wilson Associates, Inc.; Houston, Texas
John R. Hoke, Jr., AIA, Architect; Washington, D.C.

PAVING AND SURFACING

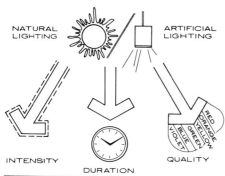

INTERIOR PLANT LIGHTING FACTORS

LIGHTING DURATION NEEDS

1. Adequate lighting is the product of intensity times duration to yield "footcandle-hours"; therefore, compensation between the two exists (e.g., 300 ft-c x 12 hr = 360 ft-c x 10 hr).
2. Recommended rule of thumb: 10-12 hr of continuous lighting on a regular basis, 7 days a week.
3. Generally, it is believed that continuous 24 hr lighting period might be detrimental to plants, but no research bears this out and many projects are under this regime with no apparent bad effects.

LIGHTING INTENSITY NEEDS

1. All plants desire good lighting, but many are tolerant and adaptable to lower light conditions.
2. Because most interior plants are native to areas with intensities of 10-14,000 ft-c, these plants must be "trained" through an acclimatization process of lowered light (2000-4000 ft-c), water and fertilizer levels for survival, and maintained appearance in the interior environment.
3. All plants have varying degrees of interior lighting intensity requirements, best understood as footcandle (lumens/square foot) requirements.
4. Lighting intensity for plants must be planned and is not simply a footcandle measurement after the building is complete (i.e., footcandle meters are "after the fact" instruments).
5. Intensity must always be above the individual light compensation point for each plant variety, for survival. (LCP is the intensity point at which the plant utilizes as much food as it produces; hence no food storage. Eventually, the plant could die with no food backup.)
6. Recommended rule of thumb: design for a MINI-MUM of 50 ft-c on the ground plane for fixed floor type of planters and 75 ft-c at desk height for movable decorative floor planters.
7. Flowering plants and flowers require extremely high intensities (above 2000 ft-c) or direct sunlight to bud, flower, or fruit, as well as lighting high in red and far-red energy.

RECOMMENDED LIGHTING SOURCES FOR PLANTS

Lighting sources are listed in order of priority, based on plant growth efficiency, color rendition preference, and energy efficiency.

CEILING HEIGHT	RECOMMENDED LIGHT SOURCE
10 ft and less	Daylight—sidewall glazing Cool white fluorescent Natural light fluorescent Incandescent Plant growth fluorescent

10-15 ft	Daylight
	  Sidewall glazing
	  Major glazing
	  Skylights
	Metal halide lamp, phosphor coated
	Mercury lamp, deluxe white
	Mercury lamp, warm deluxe white
	High pressure sodium (if color rendition not a design factor)
	Quartz halogen lamp
	Incandescent

15 ft and greater	Daylight
	  Sidewall glazing
	  Major glazing
	  Skylights
	Metal halide lamp, clear
	Metal halide lamp, phosphor coated
	Mercury lamp, deluxe white
	Mercury lamp, warm deluxe white
	High pressure sodium (if color rendition not a design factor)
	Quartz halogen lamp
	Incandescent

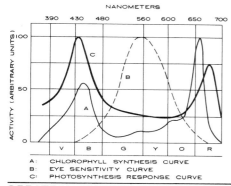

A: CHLOROPHYLL SYNTHESIS CURVE
B: EYE SENSITIVITY CURVE
C: PHOTOSYNTHESIS RESPONSE CURVE

SPECTRAL ENERGY DISTRIBUTION CURVE SHOWING OPPOSING PLANT AND HUMAN EYE RESPONSES

LIGHT QUALITY NEEDS

1. Natural lighting is about twice as efficient as cool white fluorescent lighting for plant growth, because of sunlight's broad range spectrum (i.e., 200 ft-c of CWF = 95 ft-c of natural light).
2. Chlorophyll is most responsive to blue and red wavelength energy in the production of food. The human eye is least responsive to blue and red energy and most responsive to the green-yellow region of the spectrum.
3. High blue energy emitting sources are best for overall plant maintenance (stockier growth, dark green color, little elongation).
4. High red energy emitting sources produce lighter colored foliage, elongated growth, stragglier growth.
5. Designer must be cognizant of color rendition of source, as well as light quality, if lighting is to be used for both plant lighting and illumination. (See Lamp Responses table.)
6. Ultraviolet energy is believed to be somewhat helpful to the photosynthesis process, but is not considered necessary as an integral segment of plant lighting.

LAMP RESPONSES ON INTERIOR PLANTS

BULB	ROOM APPEARANCE	COLORS STRENGTHENED	COLORS GREYED	PLANT RESPONSES
CW	Neutral to cool	Blue, yellow, orange	Red	Green foliage, stem elongates slowly, multiple side shoots, flower life long
WW	Yellow to warm	Yellow, orange	Blue, green, red	
GRO-PL	Purple to pink	Blue, red	Green, yellow	Deep green foliage, stem elongates very slowly, thick stems, multiple side shoots, late flowers on short stems
GRO-WS	Warm	Blue, yellow, red	Green	Light green foliage, stem elongates rapidly, suppressed side shoots, early flowering on long stems, plant matures and dies rapidly
AGRO	Neutral to warm	Blue, yellow, red	Green	
VITA	Neutral to warm	Blue, yellow, red	Green	
HG	Cool	Blue, green, yellow	Red	Green foliage expands, stem elongates slowly, multiple side shoots, flower life long
MH	Cool green	Blue, green, yellow	Red	
HPS	Warm	Green, yellow, orange	Blue, red	Deep green, large foliage, stem elongates very slowly, late flowers, short stems
LPS	Warm	Yellow	All except yellow	Extra deep green foliage, slow, thick stem elongation, multiple side shoots, some flowering, short stems. Some plants require supplemental sun
INC	Warm	Yellow, orange, red	Blue	Pale, thin, long foliage, stems spindly, suppressed side shoots early, short-lived flowers
INC-HG	Warm	Yellow, orange, red	Blue	

KEY

CW: cool white fluorescent.
WW: warm white fluorescent.
GRO-PL: Gro-Lux plant light.
GRO-WS: Gro-Lux wide spectrum.
AGRO: Agro-Lite.
VITA: Vita-Lite.

HG: mercury (all types).
MH: metal halide.
HPS: high pressure sodium.
LPS: low pressure sodium.
INC-HG: incandescent mercury.
INC-PL: incandescent plant light.

Richard L. Gaines, AIA; Plantscape House; Apopka, Florida

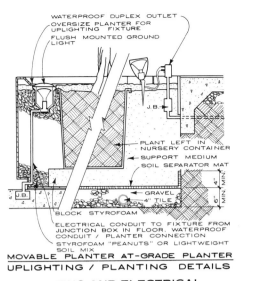

MOVABLE PLANTER AT-GRADE PLANTER
UPLIGHTING / PLANTING DETAILS

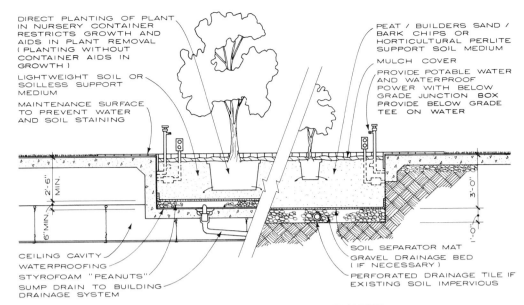

ABOVE - GRADE PLANTER   **AT - GRADE PLANTER**
FLOOR PLANTER DETAILS

UPLIGHTING AND ELECTRICAL NEEDS

1. May be of some benefit to plants, but inefficient for plant photosynthesis because of plant physiological structure. Chlorophyll is usually in upper part of leaf.
2. Uplighting should never be utilized as sole lighting source for plants.
3. Waterproof duplex outlets above soil line with a waterproof junction box below soil line are usually adequate for "atmosphere" uplighting and water fountain pumps.

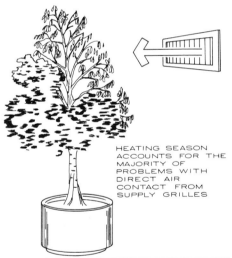

HEATING SEASON ACCOUNTS FOR THE MAJORITY OF PROBLEMS WITH DIRECT AIR CONTACT FROM SUPPLY GRILLES

FOLIAGE BURN FROM DIRECT HEAT CONTACT

HVAC EFFECT ON PLANTS

1. Air-conditioning (cooled air) is rarely detrimental to plants, even if it is "directed" at plants. The ventilation here is what counts! Good ventilation is a must with plants; otherwise oxygen and temperatures build up. Heat supply, on the other hand, when "directed" at plants, can truly be disastrous. Plan for supplies directed away from plants, but maintain adequate ventilation.
2. Extended heat or power failures of sufficient duration can damage plant health. The lower limit of temperature as a steady state is 65°F for plant survival. Brief drops to 55°F (less than 1 hr) are the lower limit before damage. Temperatures up to 85°F for only 2 days a week can usually be tolerated.
3. The relative humidity should not be allowed to fall below 30%, as plants prefer a relative humidity of 50-60%.

Richard L. Gaines, AIA; Plantscape House; Apopka, Florida

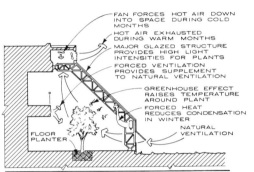

GREENHOUSE EFFECT RAISES NEED FOR ADEQUATE VENTILATION

TEMPERATURE REQUIREMENTS

1. Most plants prefer human comfort range: 70-75°F daytime temperatures and 60-65°F nighttime temperatures.
2. An absolute minimum temperature of 50°F must be observed. Plant damage will result below this figure. Rapid temperature fluctuations of 30-40°F can also be detrimental to plants.
3. "Q-10" phenomenon of respiration: for every 10°C rise in temperature, plants' respiration rate and food consumption doubles.
4. Both photosynthesis and respiration decline and stop with time, as temperatures go beyond 80°F. Beware of the greenhouse effect!

WATER SUPPLY REQUIREMENTS

1. Movable and railing planters are often watered by watering can. Provide convenient access to hot and cold potable water by hose bibbs and/or service sinks (preferably in janitor's closet) during normal working hours, with long (min. 24 in.) faucet-to-sink or floor distances. Provide for maximum of 200 ft travel on all floors.
2. At-grade floor planters are usually watered by hose and extension wand. Provide hose bibbs above soil line (for maximum travel of 50 ft) with capped "tee" stub-outs beneath soil line. If soil temperature is apt to get abnormally low in winter, provide hot and cold water by mixer-faucet type hose bibbs.
3. High concentrations of fluoride and chlorine in water supply can cause damage to plants. Provide water with low concentrations of these elements and with a pH value of 5.0-6.0. Higher or lower pH levels can result in higher plant maintenance costs.

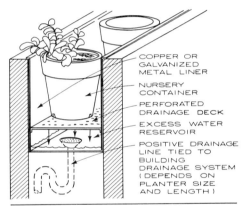

RAILING PLANTER DETAIL

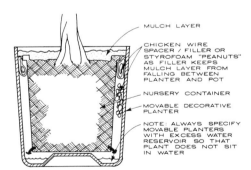

MOVABLE DECORATIVE PLANTER DETAIL

STORAGE REQUIREMENTS

Provide a secured storage space of approximately 30 sq ft for watering equipment and other maintenance materials. It may be desirable to combine water supply and janitor needs in the same storage area.

AIR POLLUTION EFFECTS ON PLANTS

Problems result from inadequate ventilation. Excessive chlorine gas from swimming pool areas can be a damaging problem, as well as excessive fumes from toxic cleaning substances for floor finishes, etc. Ventilation a must here!

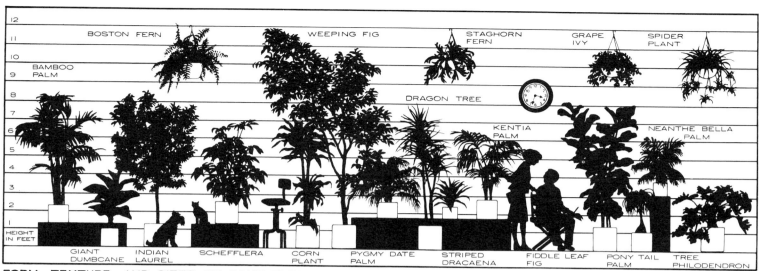

FORM, TEXTURE, AND SIZES OF SOME TYPICALLY USED INTERIOR PLANTS

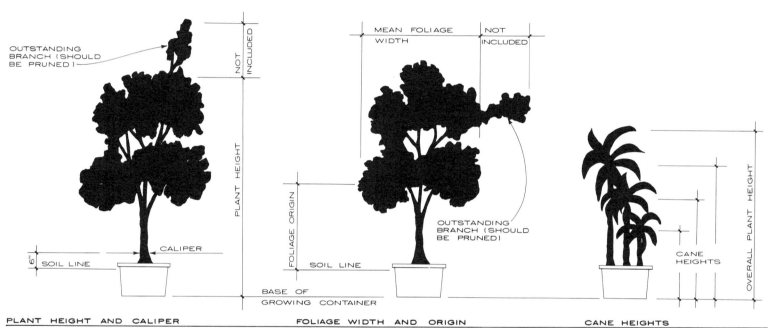

PLANT HEIGHT AND CALIPER   FOLIAGE WIDTH AND ORIGIN   CANE HEIGHTS

INTERIOR PLANT SPECIFICATIONS

NOTE

Plant height should be measured as overall height from the base of the growing container to mean foliage top. Isolated outstanding branches should not be included in height. (Since most plants are installed in movable planters, this overall height measurement should be utilized.)

NOTE

Foliage width should be measured across the nominal mean width dimension. Isolated outstanding branches should not be included in foliage width. Origin or start of foliage should be measured from the soil line.

NOTE

Many plant varieties are grown from rooted canes, with the plant being made up of one or more canes. The number of canes must be specified, if plant form is to be identified. Cane heights should always be measured from the base of the growing container.

OTHER PLANT SPECIFICATION FACTORS

1. Accurately describe plant form (e.g., multistem vs. standard tree form, clump form) and foliage spread desired. Indicate "clear trunk" measurements on trees, if desired. These measurements are from soil line to foliage origin point. Specify caliper, if significant.

2. Indicate lighting intensities designed or calculated for interior space where plants will be installed.

3. Indicate how plants will be used (i.e., in at-grade planter or in movable decorative planter). If movable decorative planters are used, indicate interior diameter and height of planter for each plant specified, since growing container sizes vary considerably.

4. Specify both botanical and common plant names.

5. Indicate any special shipping instructions or limitations.

6. Specify in-plant height column, whether plant height is measured as overall height or above-the-soil line height. Recommended height measurements:

   Interior plants: overall plant height (i.e., from bottom of growing container to mean foliage top).
   Exterior plants: above-the-soil line height.

7. Indicate whether plants are to be container grown or balled and burlapped (B & B) material.

8. Indicate location of all convenient water supply sources on all interior landscaping layouts.

Richard L. Gaines, AIA; Plantscape House; Apopka, Florida

REFERENCES

GENERAL REFERENCES

Time-Saver Standards for Landscape Architecture, 1988, Charles W. Harris and Nicholas T. Dines, McGraw-Hill

Graphic Standards for Landscape Architecture, 1986, Richard L. Austin, Thomas R. Dunbar, J. Kip Hulvershorn, and Kim W. Todd, Van Nostrand Reinhold

Landscape Design: A Practical Approach, 2nd ed., 1990, Leroy Hannebaum, Prentice Hall

The Building Site: Planning and Practice, 1983, John M. Roberts, Wiley

DATA SOURCES: ORGANIZATIONS

City Gardens, Inc., 75

Endicott Clay Products Company, 72

Florida Foliage, 75

Florist and Nursery Corps and Agriculture Engineering Laboratories, U.S. Department of Agriculture (USDA), 73

Hanover Prest-Paving Company, 72

Hastings Pavement Company, Inc., 72

Landscape Products, Inc., 72

Pavestone Company, 72

Paving Stones of Texas, 72

Pee Dee Ceramics, 72

Ritterings USA, Inc., 72

U.S. Department of Agriculture (USDA), 62

DATA SOURCES: PUBLICATIONS

Annual Book of ASTM Standards, American Society for Testing and Materials (ASTM), 72

Interior Plantscaping: Building Design for Interior Foliage Plants, Richard L. Gaines, AIA, Architectural Record Books, 73, 74

CHAPTER **4**

MATERIALS AND SYSTEMS FOR CONSTRUCTION

SUBSURFACE INVESTIGATION	78	METAL FASTENING	96
CONCRETE: GENERAL INFORMATION	79	METAL FABRICATIONS	104
CONCRETE REINFORCEMENT	81	WOOD: GENERAL INFORMATION	106
CONCRETE FORMWORK	83	WOOD TREATMENT	107
UNIT MASONRY	88	JOINT SEALER	108
MASONRY ACCESSORIES	90	TILE	111
STONE	92	PAINTING	112
METALS: GENERAL INFORMATION	94		

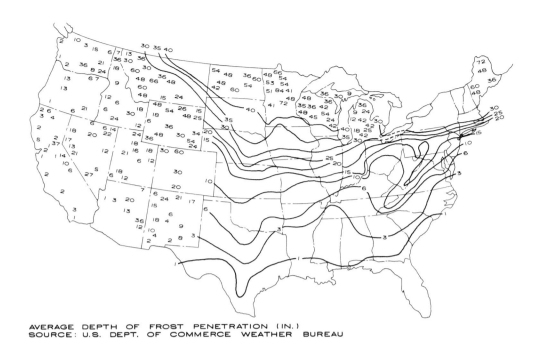

AVERAGE DEPTH OF FROST PENETRATION (IN.)
SOURCE: U.S. DEPT. OF COMMERCE WEATHER BUREAU

PRELIMINARY SUBSURFACE INFORMATION

A. Collect available information for soil, rock and water conditions, including the following:
   1. Topographic and aerial mapping.
   2. Geological survey maps and publications.
   3. Local knowledge (history of site development, experience of nearby structures, flooding, subsidence, etc.).
   4. Existing subsurface data (boreholes, well records, water soundings).
   5. Reconnaissance site survey.
   6. Previous studies.
B. Evaluate available information for site acceptability. If available data are insufficient, consult a geotechnical engineer to perform a limited subsurface investigation to gather basic information.
C. Consult geotechnical engineer for potential foundation performance at each site as part of the selection process.

DETAILED SUBSURFACE INFORMATION

After selection of a potential site a subsurface and laboratory test investigation should be carried out by a qualified geotechnical engineer before design is undertaken.

The investigation should provide an adequate understanding of the subsurface conditions and the information should be assessed to determine potential foundation behavior.

The engineer should evaluate alternative foundation methods and techniques in conjunction with the architect.

The engineer or architect should provide inspection during construction to ensure that material and construction procedures are as specified and to evaluate unexpected soil, rock, or groundwater conditions that may be exposed by excavations.

SOIL TYPES AND THEIR PROPERTIES

DIVISION	LETTER	HATCH-ING	COLOR	SOIL DESCRIPTION	VALUE AS A FOUNDATION MATERIAL	FROST ACTION	DRAINAGE
Gravel and gravelly soils	GW		Red	Well graded gravel, or gravel-sand mixture, little or no fines	Excellent	None	Excellent
	GP		Red	Poorly graded gravel, or gravel-sand mixtures, little or no fines	Good	None	Excellent
	GM		Yellow	Silty gravels, gravel-sand-silt mixtures	Good	Slight	Poor
	GC		Yellow	Clayey-gravels, gravel-clay-sand mixtures	Good	Slight	Poor
Sand and sandy soils	SW		Red	Well-graded sands, or gravelly sands, little or no fines	Good	None	Excellent
	SP		Red	Poorly graded sands, or gravelly sands, little or no fines	Fair	None	Excellent
	SM		Yellow	Silty sands, sand-silt mixtures	Fair	Slight	Fair
	SC		Yellow	Clayey sands, sand-clay mixtures	Fair	Medium	Poor
Silts and clays LL < 50	ML		Green	Inorganic silts, rock flour, silty or clayey fine sands, or clayey silts with slight plasticity	Fair	Very high	Poor
	CL		Green	Inorganic clays of low to medium plasticity, gravelly clays, silty clays, lean clays	Fair	Medium	Impervious
	OL		Green	Organic silt-clays of low plasticity	Poor	High	Impervious
Silts and clays LL > 50	MH		Blue	Inorganic silts, micaceous or diatomaceous fine sandy or silty soils, elastic silts	Poor	Very high	Poor
	CH		Blue	Inorganic clays of high plasticity, fat clays	Very poor	Medium	Impervious
	OH		Blue	Organic clays of medium to high plasticity, organic silts	Very poor	Medium	Impervious
Highly organic soils	Pt		Orange	Peat and other highly organic soils	Not suitable	Slight	Poor

NOTES
1. Consult soil engineers and local building codes for allowable soil bearing capacities.
2. LL indicates liquid limit.

Mueser, Rutledge, Johnston & DeSimone; New York, New York

 SUBSURFACE INVESTIGATION

PROPERTIES OF CONCRETE

Concrete design strength generally is stated as a minimum compressive strength at 28 days of age for concrete in various structural elements. The normal 28-day compressive strength for commercial-ready mix concrete is 3,000 psi to 4,000 psi; however, higher strengths of 5,000 psi to 7,000 psi generally are required for pre- or post-tensioned concrete. Higher strengths of 10,000 to 12,000 psi may be required for highrise concrete structures.

A typical design mix for 3,000 psi concrete would be 517 lb. of cement (5½ sacks), 1,300 lb. of sand, 1,800 lb. of gravel, and 34 gal. of water (6.2 gal. per sack), which would yield one cu. yd. of concrete, the standard unit of measure.

Compressive strength depends primarily on the type of cement, water-cement ratio, and aggregate quality; the most important is the water-cement ratio. The lower the water-cement ratio, the greater the compressive strength for workable mixes.

When cement, aggregate, and water are mixed, the water starts hydrating, a chemical reaction independent of drying. Concrete does not need air to cure. It can set under water. Concrete sets or becomes firm within hours after it has been mixed, but curing, the process of attaining strength, takes considerably longer. The majority of strength is achieved in the first days of curing. Approximately 50 percent of the total compressive strength is reached in 3 days; 70 percent is reached in 7 days. The remaining 30 percent occurs at a much slower rate in the last 21 days. The concrete's compressive strength may continue to increase beyond the designed strength, as shown in Figure 2.

CURING AND PROTECTION

Two physical conditions profoundly affect concrete's final compressive strength and curing: temperature and the rate at which water used in mixing is allowed to leave the concrete. Optimum temperature for curing concrete is 73°F (22.8°C). Any great variance from this mark reduces its compressive strength. Freezing concrete during curing affects the compressive strength and reduces its weather resistance.

Proper curing is essential to obtain design strength. Moisture, at temperatures above 50°F, must be available for hydration, and the concrete must be protected against temperatures below 40°F during early curing. The longer the water is in the concrete, the longer the reaction takes place; hence, the stronger it becomes.

Moisture conditions can be maintained by spreading wet coverings of burlap or mats, waterproof paper, or plastic sheets over concrete; by placing plastic sheets on the ground before the slab is poured; by spraying liquid curing compound on the surface of fresh concrete; and by leaving the concrete in forms longer.

HOT AND COLD WEATHER CONSTRUCTION

Additional precautions are needed in hot and cold weather to ensure proper curing of the concrete. High temperatures accelerate hardening. More water is needed to maintain the mix consistency; more cement is required to prevent reduced strength from the added water. Chilled water or ice reduces the temperature of the aggregates, and admixtures can retard the initial set. Temperatures ranging from 75°F to 90°F are hot weather construction conditions.

In cold weather the concrete must be heated to above 40°F during placing and early curing, the first 7 days. Protection against freezing may be necessary for up to 2 weeks. This is accomplished by covering the concrete with plastic sheets and heating the interior space with a portable heater. Concrete floors should be protected from carbon dioxide by using specially vented heaters that conduct the exhaust away from the concrete. The time the concrete must be protected can be reduced by using Type III and IIIA cement; a low water-cement ratio; accelerator admixtures; and steam curing. Concrete never should be placed directly on frozen ground. Fresh concrete that has frozen during curing should be removed and replaced because frozen concrete containing ice crystals has very little strength.

PROPORTION OF STRUCTURAL ELEMENTS

Rules of thumb for approximating proportions of solid rectangular beams and slabs are one inch of depth for each foot of span, and the beam width is about two-thirds the depth. The area of steel varies from 1 percent to 2 percent of cross-sectional area of the beam or slab. Columns usually have higher steel percentages than beams. The maximum for columns is 8 percent of the cross-sectional area; however, common range is 3 percent to 6 percent.

DEFLECTIONS

Deflection is affected by shrinkage, load duration, and creep. Creep is the tendency of concrete to continue to deform under sustained load. The more sustained load that a member supports, the more it creeps. The ACI-318 sets minimum length-to-depth ratios for concrete members as shown on Table 6. When members meet or exceed these minimums, deflections usually will not be a problem, and they do not need to be calculated.

FORMWORK

Forming costs can account for 30 percent to 50 percent of a concrete structure. Economy can be gained through the repetitive use of forms. Usually it is cheaper to use one column size rather than to vary column sizes.

In sizing individual floor members, usually it is more economical to use wider girders that are the same depths as the joists or beams they support than to use narrow, deeper girders. Wall pilasters, lugs, and openings should be kept to a minimum since their use increases forming costs. All members should be sized so that readily available standard forms can be used instead of custom job-built forms.

SHORING

Floor framing forms are supported by temporary columns and bracing called shoring. Concrete must be cured for a minimum time or reach a specified percentage of its design strength before shores and forms can be removed.

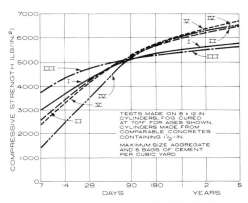

FIGURE 2. RATES OF STRENGTH DEVELOPMENT FOR CONCRETE MADE WITH VARIOUS TYPES OF CEMENT

TABLE 4. MAXIMUM WATER-CEMENT RATIOS FOR VARIOUS EXPOSURE CONDITIONS

EXPOSURE CONDITION	NORMAL WEIGHT CONCRETE, ABSOLUTE WATER-CEMENT RATIO BY WEIGHT
Concrete protected from exposure to freezing and thawing or application of deicer chemicals	Select water-cement ratio on basis of strength, workability, and finishing needs
Watertight concrete* In fresh water In seawater	0.50 0.45
Frost resistant concrete* Thin sections; any section with less than 2-in. cover over reinforcement and any concrete exposed to deicing salts All other structures	0.45 0.50
Exposure to sulfates* Moderate Severe	0.50 0.45
Placing concrete under water	Not less than 650 lb of cement per cubic yard (386 kg/m³)
Floors on grade	Select water-cement ratio for strength, plus minimum cement requirements

*Contain entrained air within the limits of Table 1.

Bob Cotton; W. E. Simpson Company Inc.; San Antonio, Texas
Quentin L. Reutershan, AIA, Architect; Potsdam, New York
Gordon B. Batson, P.E.; Potsdam, New York

TABLE 5. MAXIMUM PERMISSIBLE WATER-CEMENT RATIOS FOR CONCRETE WHEN STRENGTH DATA FROM TRIAL BATCHES OR FIELD EXPERIENCE ARE NOT AVAILABLE

SPECIFIED COMPRESSIVE STRENGTH F'c (PSI*)	MAXIMUM ABSOLUTE PERMISSIBLE WATER-CEMENT RATIO, BY WEIGHT	
	NON-AIR ENTRAINED CONCRETE	AIR ENTRAINED CONCRETE
2500	0.67	0.54
3000	0.58	0.46
3500	0.51	0.40
4000	0.44	0.35
4500	0.38	†
5000	†	†

NOTE: 1000 psi ≃ 7 MPa.
*28-day strength. With most materials, the water-cement ratios shown will provide average strengths greater than required.
†For strengths above 4500 psi (non-air entrained concrete) and 4000 psi (air entrained concrete), proportions should be established by the trial batch method.

ASTM, see data sources

TABLE 6. MINIMUM THICKNESS OF NON-PRESTRESSED BEAMS OR ONE WAY SLABS

	SIMPLY SUPPORTED	ONE END CONT.	BOTH ENDS CONT.	CANTILEVER
Solid One-Way Slabs	ℓ/20	ℓ/24	ℓ/28	ℓ/10
Beams or Ribbed One-Way Slabs	ℓ/16	ℓ/18.5	ℓ/21	ℓ/8

NOTE

Span length, l, is in inches. Values given are for members with normal weight concrete and Grade 60 reinforcement in construction not supporting or attached to partitions or other construction likely to be damaged by large deflection. For additional information, reference should be made to the American Concrete Institute Building Requirements for Reinforced Concrete (ACI 318).

CAST-IN-PLACE CONCRETE CONSTRUCTION; PRELIMINARY DATA

REINFORCED CONCRETE

Reinforced concrete consists of concrete and reinforcing steel; the concrete resists the compressive stresses and the reinforcing steel resists the tensile stresses.

Concrete is a mixture of hydraulic cement (usually portland cement), aggregate, admixtures, and water. The concrete strength develops by the hydration of the portland cement, which binds the aggregate together.

TYPES OF CEMENT

Five types of portland cement are manufactured to meet ASTM standards.

Type I is a general purpose cement for all uses. It is the most commonly used type.

Type II cement provides moderate protection from sulfate attack for concrete in drainage structures and a lower heat of hydration for concrete use in heavy retaining walls, piers, and abutments where heat buildup in the concrete can cause problems.

Type III cement provides high strengths at an early age, a week or less. Type III is used when rapid removal of forms is desired and in cold weather to reduce time of controlled curing conditions.

Type IV cement has a low heat of hydration and is used for massive concrete structures such as gravity dams.

Type V cement is sulfate-resisting cement for use where the soil and groundwater have a high sulfate content.

Pozzolans such as fly ash can be used to reduce the amount of cement in a concrete mix. Fly ash is a powdery residue resulting from combustion in coal-fired electric generating plants. It reacts chemically with calcium hydroxide produced by hydration to form cementitious compounds.

ADMIXTURES

Admixtures are various compounds, other than cement, water, and aggregates, added to a mixture to modify the fresh or hardened properties of concrete.

Air entraining admixtures disperse small air bubbles in the concrete, which improves the concrete's resistance to freezing and thawing and to scaling by deicing chemicals. Recommended total air contents are shown in Table 1 for different exposure conditions and for maximum size of aggregate.

Water reducing admixtures reduce the quantity of mixing water needed for a given consistency. Admixtures may delay the set time, and they also may entrain air.

Other mixtures are used to retard or to accelerate the set of concrete. Some accelerating admixtures contain chlorides that can cause corrosion of the reinforcing steel; therefore, they should be used with caution and only for very specific purposes. Some water reducing and accelerating admixtures may increase dry shrinkage.

Superplasticizers are high-range water reducers that can greatly affect the slump and strength of concrete. When used in concrete with normal water-cement ratios, they produce a high slump, flowable concrete that is easily placed. When used to reduce the water-cement ratio, the slump is not affected, but significantly higher than normal strengths are attained. When used to produce flowable concrete, the plasticizer's effect has a limited timespan.

AGGREGATES

The aggregate portion of a concrete mix is divided into fine and coarse aggregates. The fine aggregate generally is sand of particles less than $3/8$ in. large. The coarse aggregate is crushed rock or gravel. Concrete weighs 135 pcf to 165 pcf. Lightweight aggregate is manufactured from expanded shale, slate, clay, or slag, and the concrete weighs from 85 pcf to 115 pcf.

Normal weight aggregates must meet ASTM Specification C33. Lightweight aggregates must meet ASTM Specification C330.

The aggregate represents 60 percent to 80 percent of the concrete volume, and the gradation (range of particle sizes) affects the amount of cement and water required in the mix, the physical properties during placing and finishing, and the compressive strength. Aggregates should be clean, hard, strong, and free of surface materials.

REINFORCING STEEL

Reinforcing steel, manufactured as round rods with raised deformations for adhesion and resistance to slip in the concrete, is available in several grades (yield strengths) and diameters manufactured to ASTM standards. Commonly used reinforcing rods have a yield strength of 60,000 psi available in sizes from #3 to #18, the size being the diameter in eighths of an inch. Reinforcing rods having a yield strength of 40,000 psi also are available in the smaller bar sizes. Welded wire mesh has yield strengths of 60,000 psi to 70,000 psi, and the wire is either plain or deformed.

Table 3 summarizes the various grades of reinforcing steel, and Figure 1 shows the system of reinforcing rod identification.

SLUMP TEST

The ASTM standard slump cone test is to determine only the consistency among batches of concrete of the same mix design; it should not be used to compare mixes of greatly different mix proportions. A slump test mold is a funnel-shaped sheet metal form. The slump mold is filled from the top in three levels, each level being tamped 25 times with a $5/8$ in. diameter rod. The mold is removed slowly, allowing the concrete to slump down from its original height. The difference from the top of the mold to the top of the slumped concrete is the slump. There is no "right" slump consistency for all concrete work. It can vary from 1 in. to 6 in., depending on the specific requirements of the job. Table 2 lists typical slumps for various types of construction.

Workability is the ease or difficulty of placing, consolidating, and finishing the concrete. Concrete should be workable, but it should not segregate or bleed excessively before finishing.

CYLINDER TEST

A major problem with concrete tests is that the most important data, the compressive strength, cannot be determined until after curing has begun. This occasionally has caused the removal of deficient concrete several weeks after it was placed. A standard compression test is made in accordance with ASTM C39 by placing three layers of concrete in a cardboard cylinder 6 in. in diameter and 12 in. high. Each layer is rodded 25 times with a $5/8$ in. diameter steel rod. The cylinder should be protected from damage but placed in the same temperature and humidity environment as the concrete from which the sample was obtained. At the end of the test curing time, usually 7 to 28 days, the concrete cylinder is removed from its form and tested in compression. The load at which the cylinder fails in compression is registered on a gauge in pounds, and the strength of the concrete is calculated in pounds per square inch.

PLACING CONCRETE

Concrete should be placed as near its final position as possible, and it should not be moved horizontally in forms because segregation of the mortar from the coarser material may occur. Concrete should be placed in horizontal layers of uniform thickness, each layer being thoroughly consolidated before the next layer is positioned.

Consolidation of concrete can be achieved either by hand tamping and rodding or by mechanical internal or external vibration. The frequency and amplitude of an internal mechanical vibration should be appropriate for the plastic properties (stiffness or slump) and space in the forms to prevent segregation of the concrete during placing. External vibration can be accomplished by surface vibration for thin sections (slabs) that cannot be consolidated practically by internal vibration. Surface vibrators may be used directly on the surface of slab or with plates attached to the concrete form stiffeners. External vibration must be done for a longer time (1 to 2 min.) than for internal vibration (5 to 15 sec.) to achieve the same consolidation.

TABLE 1. RECOMMENDED AIR CONTENT PERCENTAGE

NOMINAL MAXIMUM SIZE OF COARSE AGGREGATE (IN.)	EXPOSURE	
	MILD	EXTREME
$3/8$ (10 mm)	4.5	7.5
$1/2$ (13 mm)	4.0	6.0
$3/4$ (19 mm)	3.5	6.0
1 (25 mm)	3.0	6.0
$1\frac{1}{2}$ (40 mm)	2.5	5.5
2 (50 mm)	2.0	5.0
3 (75 mm)	1.5	4.5

TABLE 2. RECOMMENDED SLUMPS FOR VARIOUS TYPES OF CONSTRUCTION

CONCRETE CONSTRUCTION	SLUMP (IN.)	
	MAXIMUM*	MINIMUM
Reinforced foundation walls and footings	3	1
Plain footings, caissons, and substructure walls	3	1
Beams and reinforced walls	4	1
Building columns	4	1
Pavements and slabs	3	1
Mass concrete	2	1

*May be increased 1 in. for consolidation by hand methods such as rodding and spading.

Quentin L. Reutershan, AIA, Architect; Potsdam, New York
Gordon B. Batson, P.E.; Potsdam, New York
Bob Cotton; W. E. Simpson Company Inc.; San Antonio, Texas

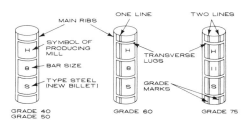

FIGURE 1. REINFORCING BAR IDENTIFICATION

MAIN RIBS / SYMBOL OF PRODUCING MILL / BAR SIZE / TYPE STEEL (NEW BILLET) / GRADE MARKS

NUMBER SYSTEM – GRADE MARKS

MAIN RIBS / ONE LINE / TWO LINES / SYMBOL OF PRODUCING MILL / BAR SIZE / TYPE STEEL (NEW BILLET) / TRANSVERSE LUGS / GRADE MARKS

GRADE 40 / GRADE 50   GRADE 60   GRADE 75

LINE SYSTEM – GRADE MARKS

TABLE 3. REINFORCING STEEL GRADES AND STRENGTHS

ASTM SPEC	YIELD STRENGTH (PSI)	ULTIMATE STRENGTH (PSI)	STEEL TYPE
New billet ASTM A–615			
Grade 40	40,000	70,000	S
Grade 60	60,000	90,000	
Rail steel ASTM A–616			
Grade 50	50,000	80,000	R
Grade 60	60,000	90,000	
Axle steel ASTM A–617			
Grade 40	40,000	70,000	A
Grade 60	60,000	90,000	
Deformed wire ASTM A–496			
Welded fabric	70,000	80,000	—
Cold drawn wire ASTM A–82			
Welded fabric			
W 1.2 Size	56,000	70,000	
W 1.2	65,000	75,000	

ASTM STANDARD REINFORCING BAR SIZES—
NOMINAL DIAMETER

BAR SIZE DESIGNATION	WEIGHT PER FOOT		DIAMETER		CROSS-SECTIONAL AREA SQUARED	
	LB	KG	IN.	CM	IN.	CM
#3	0.376	0.171	0.375	0.953	0.11	0.71
#4	0.668	0.303	0.500	1.270	0.20	1.29
#5	1.043	0.473	0.625	1.588	0.31	2.00
#6	1.502	0.681	0.750	1.905	0.44	2.84
#7	2.044	0.927	0.875	2.223	0.60	3.87
#8	2.670	1.211	1.000	2.540	0.79	5.10
#9	3.400	1.542	1.128	2.865	1.00	6.45
#10	4.303	1.952	1.270	3.226	1.27	8.19
#11	5.313	2.410	1.410	3.581	1.56	10.07
#14	7.650	3.470	1.693	4.300	2.25	14.52
#18	13.600	6.169	2.257	5.733	4.00	25.81

COMMON STOCK STYLES OF WELDED WIRE FABRIC

NEW DESIGNATION SPACING—CROSS SECTIONAL AREA (IN.)—(SQ IN./100)	OLD DESIGNATION SPACING—WIRE GAUGE (IN.)—(AS & W)	STEEL AREA PER FOOT				APPROXIMATE WEIGHT PER 100 SQ FT	
		LONGITUDINAL		TRANSVERSE			
		IN.	CM	IN.	CM	LB	KG
6 x 6—W1.4 x W1.4	6 x 6—10 x 10	0.028	0.071	0.028	0.071	21	9.53
6 x 6—W2.0 x W2.0	6 x 6—8 x 8 (1)	0.040	0.102	0.040	0.102	29	13.15
6 x 6—W2.9 x W2.9	6 x 6—6 x 6	0.058	0.147	0.058	0.147	42	19.05
6 x 6—W4.0 x W4.0	6 x 6—4 x 4	0.080	0.203	0.080	0.203	58	26.31
4 x 4—W1.4 x W1.4	4 x 4—10 x 10	0.042	0.107	0.042	0.107	31	14.06
4 x 4—W2.0 x W2.0	4 x 4—8 x 8 (1)	0.060	0.152	0.060	0.152	43	19.50
4 x 4—W2.9 x W2.9	4 x 4—6 x 6	0.087	0.221	0.087	0.221	62	28.12
4 x 4—W4.0 x W4.0	4 x 4—4 x 4	0.120	0.305	0.120	0.305	85	38.56
6 x 6—W2.9 x W2.9	6 x 6—6 x 6	0.058	0.147	0.058	0.147	42	19.05
6 x 6—W4.0 x W4.0	6 x 6—4 x 4	0.080	0.203	0.080	0.203	58	26.31
6 x 6—W5.5 x W5.5	6 x 6—2 x 2 (2)	0.110	0.279	0.110	0.279	80	36.29
4 x 4—W4.0 x W4.0	4 x 4—4 x 4	0.120	0.305	0.120	0.305	85	38.56

(Rolls: rows 1–8; Sheets: rows 9–12)

NOTES
1. Exact W-number size for 8 gauge is W2.1.
2. Exact W-number size for 2 gauge is W5.4.

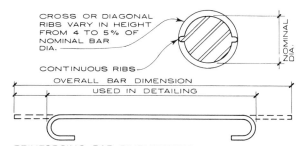

REINFORCING BAR DIMENSIONING

STANDARD STEEL WIRE SIZES AND GAUGES

A.S.&W. GAUGE	DIAMETER		AREA SQUARED		WEIGHT PER FOOT	
	IN.	CM	IN.	CM	LB	KG
00	0.3310	0.8407	0.0860	0.5549	0.2922	0.1325
0	0.3065	0.7785	0.0738	0.4762	0.2506	0.1137
1	0.2830	0.7188	0.0629	0.4058	0.2136	0.0969
2	0.2625	0.6668	0.0541	0.3491	0.1829	0.0830
— (1/4")	0.2500	0.6350	0.0491	0.3168	0.1667	0.0756
3	0.2437	0.6190	0.0466	0.3007	0.1584	0.0718
4	0.2253	0.5723	0.0397	0.2561	0.1354	0.0614
5	0.2070	0.5258	0.0337	0.2174	0.1143	0.0518
6	0.1920	0.4877	0.0290	0.1871	0.0983	0.0446
7	0.1770	0.4496	0.0246	0.1587	0.0836	0.0379
8	0.1620	0.4115	0.0206	0.1329	0.0700	0.0318
9	0.1483	0.3767	0.0173	0.1116	0.0587	0.0266
10	0.1350	0.3429	0.0143	0.0922	0.0486	0.0220
11 (1/8")	0.1250	0.3175	0.0114	0.0736	0.0387	0.0176
12	0.1055	0.2680	0.0087	0.0561	0.0297	0.0135
13	0.0915	0.2324	0.0066	0.0426	0.0223	0.0101
14	0.0800	0.2032	0.0050	0.0323	0.0171	0.0078
15	0.0720	0.1838	0.0041	0.0265	0.0138	0.0063
16 (1/16")	0.0625	0.1588	0.0031	0.0200	0.0104	0.0047

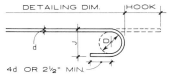

180° HOOK

d = (1) Bar Diameter
D = 6d for No. 3 to No. 8 Bars
D = 8d for No. 9 to No. 11 Bars
J = D + 2d
H = 5d + D/2 (or) 2 1/2" + d + D/2 minimum

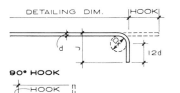

90° HOOK

d = (1) Bar Diameter
D = 6d for No. 3 to No. 8 bars
D = 8d for No. 9 to No. 11 bars
J = 13d + D/2

d = (1) Bar Diameter
D = 1 1/2" for No. 3
D = 2" for No. 4
D = 2 1/2" for No. 5
D = 6d for No. 6 to No. 8

135° HOOK STIRRUP – TIES SIMILAR

STANDARD REINFORCING BAR HOOK DETAILS

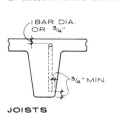

JOISTS

FLOOR SLABS

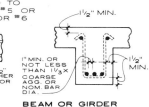

BEAM OR GIRDER

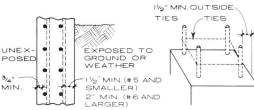

WALLS   **COLUMNS**   **FOOTINGS**

PROTECTION FOR REINFORCEMENT

LAP SPLICE REQUIREMENTS
1983 CODE IN BAR DIAMETERS

f_y' (KSI)	SPIRAL COLUMN	TIED COLUMN	LOOSE
40	15.0	16.6	20
50	18.75	20.75	25
60	22.5	24.9	30
75	32.6	36.2	43.5
80	36.0	39.9	48.0

NOTES
1. These requirements are for compression lap splices only.
2. Lap splice lengths are minimum for $f_c' \geq 3000$ psi.
3. Minimum lap is 12 in.
4. Maximum reinforcing bar size permitted in lap splice is No. 11.

TEMPERATURE REINFORCEMENT FOR STRUCTURAL FLOOR AND ROOF SLAB (ONE WAY) (IN PERCENTAGE OF CROSS-SECTIONAL AREA OF CONCRETE)

REINFORCEMENT		CONCRETE SLABS	
GRADE	TYPE		
40/50	Deformed bars	0.20%	Max. spacing five times slab thickness
—	Welded wire fabric	0.18%	
60	Deformed bars	0.18%	

Dave Keppler; Haver, Nunn and Collamer; Phoenix, Arizona

CONCRETE REINFORCEMENT   4

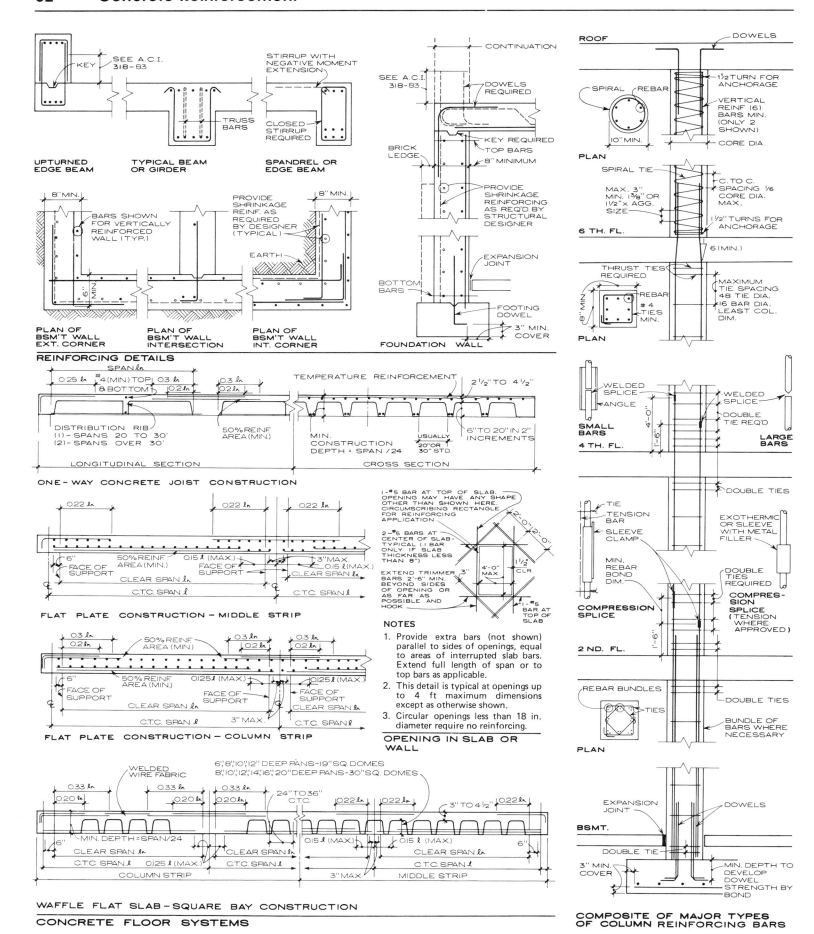

REINFORCING DETAILS

UPTURNED EDGE BEAM

TYPICAL BEAM OR GIRDER

SPANDREL OR EDGE BEAM

PLAN OF BSM'T WALL EXT. CORNER

PLAN OF BSM'T WALL INTERSECTION

PLAN OF BSM'T WALL INT. CORNER

FOUNDATION WALL

ONE-WAY CONCRETE JOIST CONSTRUCTION

FLAT PLATE CONSTRUCTION – MIDDLE STRIP

FLAT PLATE CONSTRUCTION – COLUMN STRIP

NOTES

1. Provide extra bars (not shown) parallel to sides of openings, equal to areas of interrupted slab bars. Extend full length of span or to top bars as applicable.
2. This detail is typical at openings up to 4 ft maximum dimensions except as otherwise shown.
3. Circular openings less than 18 in. diameter require no reinforcing.

OPENING IN SLAB OR WALL

WAFFLE FLAT SLAB – SQUARE BAY CONSTRUCTION

CONCRETE FLOOR SYSTEMS

COMPOSITE OF MAJOR TYPES OF COLUMN REINFORCING BARS

Thomas A. Lines; Haver, Nunn and Collamer; Phoenix, Arizona
Kenneth D. Franch, AIA, PE; Phillips Swager Associates, Inc.; Dallas, Texas

CONCRETE REINFORCEMENT

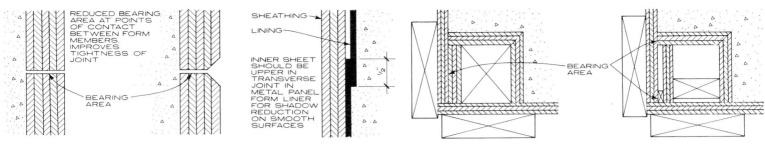

USUAL	RECOMMENDED	LINER JOINT	USUAL	RECOMMENDED

FORM JOINTS

RUBBER FORM INSERT

- 6D CASING NAIL
- CHANNEL STIFFENER CRIMPED IN PLACE
- RUBBER TO MATCH CONCRETE

WOOD FORM INSERT

- HARDWOOD STRIP–REMOVE AND CAULK JOINT
- NAILS

SHEET METAL FORM INSERT

- SHEET METAL WITH WOOD FILLER–REMOVE AND CAULK JOINT

CONTROL JOINTS

RUSTICATION (PREFERRED)

TAPED (MEDIUM LIGHT BLAST)

EPOXY ON 45° CUT

GASKETED

TONGUE AND GROOVED

SPLINED

IMPERVIOUS LINER (1/4" TO 3/8")

SHIPLAP

PLYWOOD BUTT JOINTS FOR EXPOSED AGGREGATE FINISHES

CATEGORIES OF ARCHITECTURAL CONCRETE SURFACES

CATEGORY	FINISH	COLOR	FORMS	CRITICAL DETAILS
1. As cast	Remains as is after form removal—usually board marks or wood grain	Cement first influence, fine aggregate second influence	Plastic best All others • Wire-brushed plywood • Sandblasted plywood • Exposed-grain plywood • Unfinished sheathing lumber • Ammonia sprayed wood • Tongue-and-groove bands spaced	Slump = 2½'' to 3½'' Joinery of forms Proper release agent Point form joints to avoid marks
2. Abrasive blasted surfaces A. Brush blast	Uniform scour cleaning	Cement plus fine aggregate have equal influence	All smooth	Scouring after 7 days Slump = 2½'' to 3½''
B. Light blast	Sandblast to expose fine and some coarse aggregate	Fine aggregate primary coarse aggregate plus cement secondary	All smooth	10% more coarse aggregate Slump = 2½'' to 3½'' Blasting between 7 and 45 days
C. Medium exposed aggregate	Sandblasted to expose coarse aggregate	Coarse aggregate	All smooth	Higher than normal coarse aggregate Slump = 2'' to 3'' Blast before 7 days
D. Heavy exposed aggregate	Sandblasted to expose coarse aggregate 80% viable	Coarse aggregate	All smooth	Special mix coarse aggregate Slump = 0'' to 2'' Blast within 24 hours Use high frequency vibrator
3. Chemical retardation of surface set	Chemicals expose aggregate Aggregate can be adhered to surface	Coarse aggregate and cement	All smooth, glass fiber best	Chemical Grade determines etch depth Stripping scheduled to prevent long drying between stripping and washoff
4. Mechanically fractured surfaces, scaling, bush hammering, jackhammering, tooling	Varied	Cement, fine and coarse Aggregate	Textured	Aggregate particles ⅜'' for scaling and tooling Aggregate particles
5. Combination/fluted	Striated/abrasive blasted/irregular pattern Corrugated/abrasive Vertical rusticated/abrasive blasted Reeded and bush hammered Reeded and hammered Reeded and chiseled	The shallower the surface, the more influence aggregate fines and cement have	Wood or rubber strips, corrugated sheet metal or glass fiber	Depends on type of finish desired Wood fluke kerfed and nailed loosely

D. Neil Rankins; SHWC, Inc.; Dallas, Texas

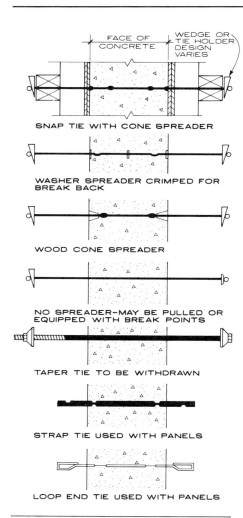

SNAP TIE WITH CONE SPREADER

WASHER SPREADER CRIMPED FOR BREAK BACK

WOOD CONE SPREADER

NO SPREADER–MAY BE PULLED OR EQUIPPED WITH BREAK POINTS

TAPER TIE TO BE WITHDRAWN

STRAP TIE USED WITH PANELS

LOOP END TIE USED WITH PANELS

TYPICAL SINGLE MEMBER TIES

CONCRETE SURFACES—GENERAL

The variety of architectural finishes is as extensive as the cost and effort expended to achieve them. There are three basic ways to improve or change the appearance of concrete:

1. Changing materials, that is, using a colored matrix and exposed aggregates.
2. Changing the mold or form by such means as a form liner.
3. By treating or tooling the concrete surface in the final stages of hardening.

The aim is to obtain maximum benefit from one of three features—color, texture, and pattern—all of which are interrelated. Color is the easiest method of changing the appearance of concrete. It should not be used on a plain concrete surface with a series of panels, since color matches are difficult to achieve. The exception is possible when white cement is used, usually as a base for the pigment to help reduce changes of color variation. Since white cement is expensive, many effects are tried with gray cement to avoid an entire plain surface. Colored concrete is most effective when it is used with an exposed aggregate finish.

FORM LINERS

1. Sandblasted Douglas fir or long leaf yellow pine dressed one side away from the concrete surface.
2. Flexible steel strip formwork adapted to curved surfaces (Schwellmer System).
3. Resin coated, striated, or sandblasted plywood.
4. Rubber mats.
5. Thermoplastic sheets with high gloss or texture laid over stone, for example.
6. Formed plastics.
7. Plaster of Paris molds for sculptured work.
8. Clay (sculpturing and staining concrete).
9. Hardboard (screen side).

D. Neil Rankins; SHWC, Inc.; Dallas, Texas

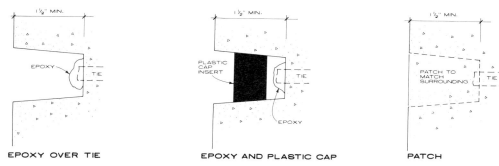

EPOXY OVER TIE   EPOXY AND PLASTIC CAP   PATCH

TIE HOLE TREATMENT OPTIONS

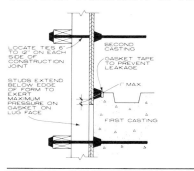

TYPICAL CONSTRUCTION JOINT

10. Standard steel forms.
11. Wood boarding and reversed battens.
12. Square-edged lumber dressed one side.
13. Resawn wood boards.

RELEASE AGENTS

1. Oils, petroleum based, used on wood, concrete, and steel forms.
2. Soft soaps.
3. Talcum.
4. Whitewash used on wood with tannin in conjunction with oils.
5. Calcium stearate powder.
6. Silicones used on steel forms.
7. Plastics used on wood forms.
8. Lacquers used on plywood and plaster forms.
9. Resins used on plywood forms.
10. Sodium silicate.
11. Membrane used over any form.
12. Grease used on plaster forms.
13. Epoxy resin plastic used on plywood.

CATEGORIES OF COMMON AGGREGATE

1. QUARTZ: Clear, white, rose.
2. MARBLE: Green, yellow, red, pink, blue, gray, white, black.
3. GRANITE: Pink, gray, black, white.
4. CERAMIC: Full range.
5. VITREOUS/GLASS: Full range.

CRITICAL FACTORS AFFECTING SURFACES

DESIGN DRAWINGS should show form details, including openings, control joints, construction joints, expansion joints, and other important specifics.

1. CEMENT: Types and brands.
2. AGGREGATES: Sources of coarse and fine aggregates.
3. TECHNIQUES: Uniformity in mixing and placing.
4. FORMS: Closure techniques or concealing joints in formwork materials.
5. SLUMP CONTROL: Ensure compliance with design.
6. CURING METHODS: Ensure compliance with design.

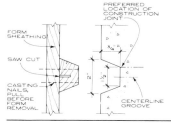

RUSTICATION AT CONSTRUCTION JOINT

TIES

A concrete tie is a tensile unit adapted to hold concrete forms secure against the lateral pressure of unhardened concrete. Two general types of concrete ties exist:

1. Continuous single member where the tensile unit is a single piece and the holding device engages the tensile unit against the exterior of the form. Standard types: working load = 2500 to 5000 lb.
2. Internal disconnecting where the tensile unit has an inner part with threaded connections to removable external members, which have suitable devices of securing them against the outside of the form. Working load = 6000 to 36,000 lb.

GUIDELINES FOR PATCHING

1. Design the patch mix to match the original, with small amount of white cement; may eliminate coarse aggregate or hand place it. Trial and error is the only reliable match method.
2. Saturate area with water and apply bonding agent to base of hole and to water of patch mix.
3. Pack patch mix to density of original.
4. Place exposed aggregate by hand.
5. Bristle brush after setup to match existing material.
6. Moist cure to prevent shrinking.
7. Use form or finish to match original.

CHECKLIST IN PLANNING FOR ARCHITECTURAL CONCRETE PLACING TECHNIQUES:

Pumping vs. bottom drop or other type of bucket.

1. FORMING SYSTEM: Evaluate whether architectural concrete forms can also be used for structural concrete.
2. SHOP DRAWINGS: Determine form quality and steel placement.
3. VIBRATORS: Verify that proper size, frequency, and power are used.
4. RELEASE AGENTS: Consider form material, color impact of agents, and possible use throughout job.
5. CURING COMPOUND: Determine how fast it wears off.
6. SAMPLES: Require approval of forms and finishes. Field mock-up is advised to evaluate appearance of panel and quality of workmanship.

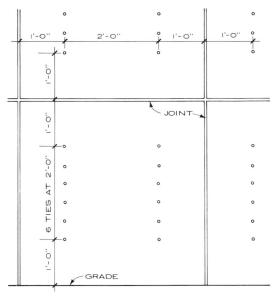

ELEVATION

**EXPOSED CONCRETE WITH
RUSTICATION STRIP** (IF DESIRED)

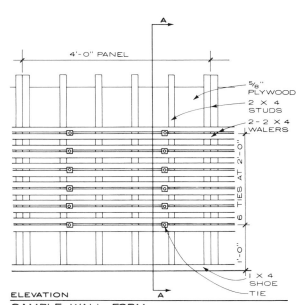

ELEVATION

SAMPLE WALL FORM

Mortar-tight forms are required for architectural exposed concrete. Consult manufacturers' literature on the proper use of metal forms or plywood forms with metal frames.

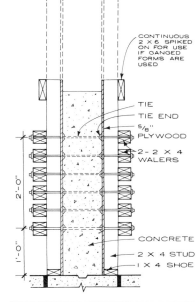

SECTION A-A

The section above will change if there are any variations in the thickness of plywood used, the type and strength of ties, or the size of studs and walers.

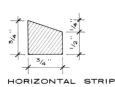

HORIZONTAL STRIP

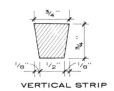

VERTICAL STRIP

RUSTICATION STRIPS

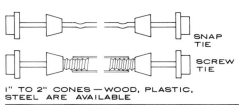

**1" TO 2" CONES — WOOD, PLASTIC,
STEEL ARE AVAILABLE**

TYPICAL TIES

**WALER AND TIE
BRACKET**

**STRONG-
BACK CAM**

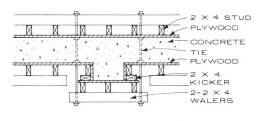

PLAN

SMALL PILASTER

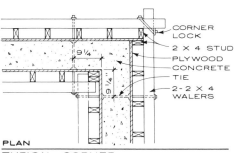

PLAN

TYPICAL CORNER

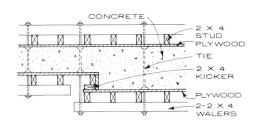

PLAN

TYPICAL WALL WITH OFFSET

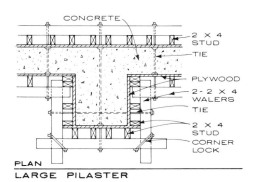

PLAN

LARGE PILASTER

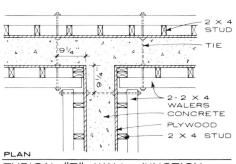

PLAN

TYPICAL "T" WALL JUNCTION

FORM DESIGN NOTES

1. Pressure depends on rate of pour (ft/hr) and concrete temperature (°F). Vibration of concrete is also a factor in form pressure.
2. Provide cleanout doors at bottom of wall forms.
3. Various types of form ties are on the market. Some are not suitable for architectural concrete work, i.e., they cannot be withdrawn from the concrete.
4. Various plastic cones 1½ in. in diameter and ½ in. deep can be used and the holes are left ungrouted to form a type of architectural feature.
5. Consult manufacturers' catalogs for form design and tie strength information.

Tucker Concrete Form Co.; Malden, Massachusetts

CONCRETE FORMWORK   4

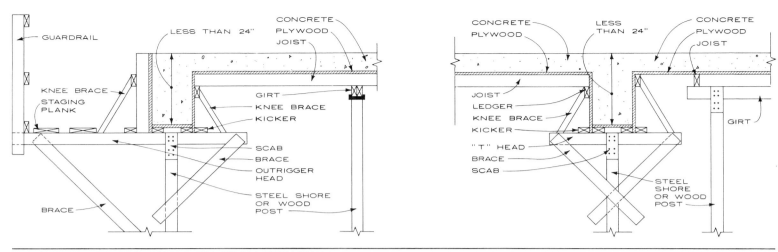

TYPICAL SLAB AND SHALLOW BEAM FORMING

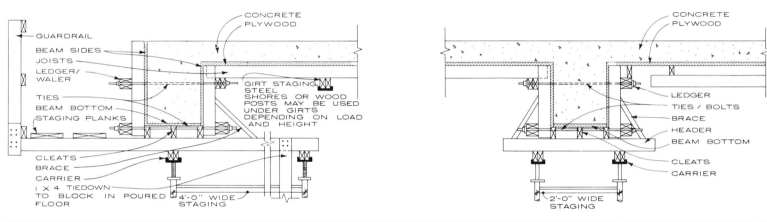

TYPICAL SLAB AND HEAVY BEAM FORMING

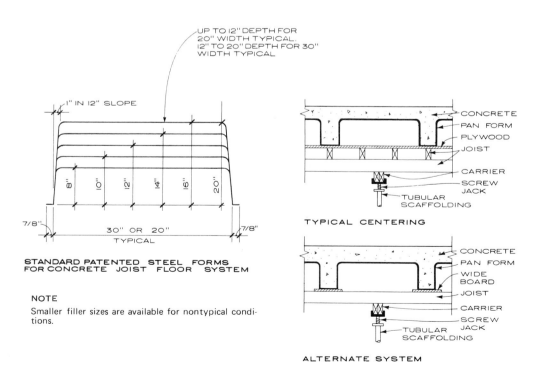

STANDARD PATENTED STEEL FORMS FOR CONCRETE JOIST FLOOR SYSTEM

NOTE

Smaller filler sizes are available for nontypical conditions.

TYPICAL CENTERING

ALTERNATE SYSTEM

NOTES

1. Staging, steel shores, or wood posts may be used under girts depending on loads and height requirements.
2. For flat slabs of flat plate forming, metal "flying forms" are commonly used.
3. Patented steel forms or fillers are also available for nontypical conditions on special order. See manufacturer's catalogs. Fiber forms, too, are on the market in similar sizes. Plywood deck is required for forming.
4. Plywood is usually $5/8''$ minimum thickness, Exposure 1.

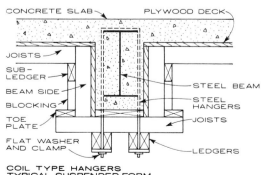

COIL TYPE HANGERS TYPICAL SUSPENDED FORM

Tucker Concrete Form Co.; Malden, Massachusetts

CONCRETE FORMWORK

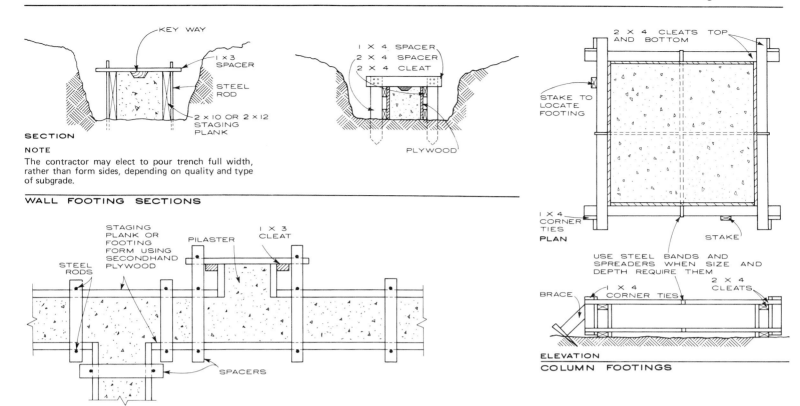

KEY WAY

1 X 3 SPACER

STEEL ROD

2 X 10 OR 2 X 12 STAGING PLANK

SECTION

NOTE

The contractor may elect to pour trench full width, rather than form sides, depending on quality and type of subgrade.

1 X 4 SPACER
2 X 4 SPACER
2 X 4 CLEAT

PLYWOOD

WALL FOOTING SECTIONS

2 X 4 CLEATS TOP AND BOTTOM

STAKE TO LOCATE FOOTING

1 X 4 CORNER TIES

PLAN

STAKE

USE STEEL BANDS AND SPREADERS WHEN SIZE AND DEPTH REQUIRE THEM

BRACE

1 X 4 CORNER TIES

2 X 4 CLEATS

ELEVATION
COLUMN FOOTINGS

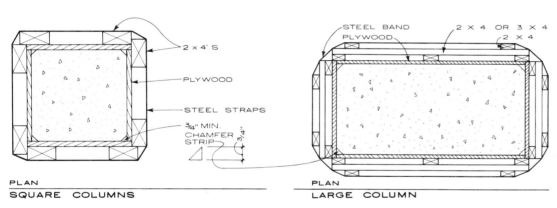

STAGING PLANK OR FOOTING FORM USING SECONDHAND PLYWOOD

PILASTER

1 X 3 CLEAT

STEEL RODS

SPACERS

PLAN OF WALL FOOTINGS

2 X 4'S

PLYWOOD

STEEL STRAPS

3/4" MIN. CHAMFER STRIP

3/4"

PLAN
SQUARE COLUMNS

STEEL BAND
PLYWOOD

2 X 4 OR 3 X 4
2 X 4

PLAN
LARGE COLUMN

NOTE

Height of column will change thickness and spaces of steel bands. Consult manufacturers' catalogs. Selection of sheathing (or plywood), type of column clamps (job built or patented metal types), and their spacing will depend on column height, rate of concrete pour (ft/hr), and concrete temperature (°F), as well as on whether the concrete is to be vibrated during pour. Consult design guides for correct selection of materials to ensure safe column forms.

It is recommended that chamfer strips be used at all outside corners to reduce damage to concrete when forms are removed.

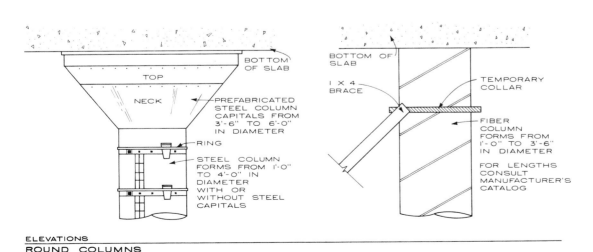

BOTTOM OF SLAB

TOP

NECK

PREFABRICATED STEEL COLUMN CAPITALS FROM 3'-6" TO 6'-0" IN DIAMETER

RING

STEEL COLUMN FORMS FROM 1'-0" TO 4'-0" IN DIAMETER WITH OR WITHOUT STEEL CAPITALS

ELEVATIONS
ROUND COLUMNS

BOTTOM OF SLAB

1 X 4 BRACE

TEMPORARY COLLAR

FIBER COLUMN FORMS FROM 1'-0" TO 3'-6" IN DIAMETER

FOR LENGTHS CONSULT MANUFACTURER'S CATALOG

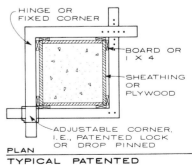

HINGE OR FIXED CORNER

BOARD OR 1 X 4

SHEATHING OR PLYWOOD

ADJUSTABLE CORNER, I.E., PATENTED LOCK OR DROP PINNED

PLAN
TYPICAL PATENTED COLUMN CLAMP

Tucker Concrete Form Co.; Malden, Massachusetts

CONCRETE FORMWORK 4

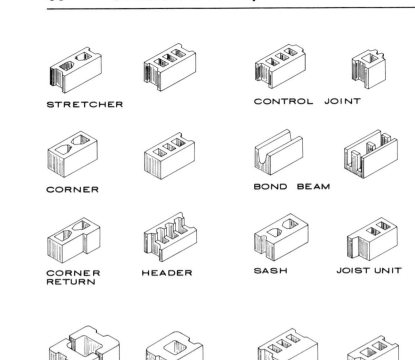

STRETCHER   **CONTROL JOINT**   **LINTEL**   **SCREEN**

CORNER   **BOND BEAM**   **SILL**   **SPLIT FACE**

CORNER RETURN   **HEADER**   **SASH**   **JOIST UNIT**   **OPEN-END UNITS**   PLUMBING STACK   VERTICAL STEEL   **RIBBED OR SCORED**   **FLUTED**

COLUMN   **GRADE**   **JAMB**   **PILASTER INSERT**   **SCREEN**   **8 X 8 SCORED FACE**   **SPLIT RIBBED**

TYPICAL CONCRETE MASONRY UNIT SHAPES

CONCRETE MASONRY UNIT SPECIFICATIONS AND FIRE RESISTANCE DATA

1. A solid (load bearing) concrete block is a unit whose cross-sectional area in every plane parallel to the bearing surface is not less than 75% of the gross cross-sectional area measured in the same plane. (ASTM C145–75.)

2. A hollow concrete block is a unit whose cross-sectional area in every plane parallel to the bearing surface is less than 75% of the gross cross-sectional area measured in the same plane. (ASTM C90–75.)

3. Actual dimension is ³⁄₈ in. less than nominal shown.

4. All shapes shown are available in all dimensions given in chart except for width (W) which may be otherwise noted.

5. Because the number of shapes and sizes for concrete masonry screen units is virtually unlimited, it is advisable for the designer to check on availability of any specific shape during early planning.

6. Screen units should be of high quality, even though they seldom are employed in load bearing construction. When tested with their hollow cells parallel to the direction of the load, screen units should have a compressive strength exceeding 1000 psi of gross area; a quality of concrete unit comparable to "Specifications for Hollow Load-Bearing Concrete Masonry Units" ASTM C90–75.

7. Building codes are quite specific in the degree of fire protection required in various areas of buildings. Local building regulations will govern the concrete masonry wall section best suited for specific applications. Fire resistance ratings of concrete masonry walls are based on fire tests made at Underwriters' Laboratories, Inc., National Bureau of Standards, Portland Cement Association, and other recognized laboratories. Methods of test are described in ASTM E119 "Standard Method of Fire Tests of Building Construction and Materials."

8. The fire resistance ratings of most concrete masonry walls are determined by heat transmission measured by temperature rise on the cold side. Fire endurance can be calculated as a function of the aggregate type used in the block unit, and the solid thickness of the wall, or the equivalent solid thickness of the wall when working with hollow units.

9. Equivalent thickness of hollow units is calculated from actual thickness and the percentage of solid materials. Both needed items of information are normally reported by the testing laboratory using standard ASTM procedures, such as ASTM C140 "Methods of Sampling and Testing Concrete Masonry Units." When walls are plastered or otherwise faced with fire resistant materials, the thickness of these materials is included in calculating the equivalent thickness effective for fire resistance. Estimated fire resistance ratings shown in the table are for fully protected construction in which all structural members are of incombustible materials. Where combustible members are framed into walls, equivalent solid thickness protecting each such member should not be less than 93% of the thicknesses shown. Plaster is effective in increasing fire resistance when combustible members are framed into masonry walls, as is filling core spaces with various fire resistant materials.

10. Walls and partitions of 1- to 4-hr ratings are governed by code requirements for actual or equivalent solid thickness computed on the percent of core area in the unit. Increasing the wall thickness or filling the cores with grout increases the rating. Units with more than 25% core area are classified as hollow, and the equivalent solid thickness must first be computed in order to determine the fire rating. Since core size and shape will vary, either manufacturer's data or laboratory test data must be used to establish exact figures. A nominal 8 in. hollow unit reported to be 55% solid would be calculated as follows: equivalent solid thickness = 0.55 x 7.625 in. (actual thickness) = 4.19 in. Lightweight aggregates such as pumice, expanded slag, clay, or shale offer greater resistance to the transfer of heat in a fire because of their increased air content. Units made with these materials require less thickness to achieve the same fire rating as a heavyweight aggregate unit.

NOMINAL DIMENSIONS OF TYPICAL CONCRETE MASONRY UNIT SHAPES

Height (H) = 4'', 8''	
Length (L) = 8'', 12'', 16'', 24''	
Width (W) = 4'', 6'', 8'', 10'', 12''	

EQUIVALENT THICKNESS FOR FIRE RATING

	1 HR	2 HR	3 HR	4 HR
Expanded slag or pumice	2.1	3.2	4.0	4.7
Expanded clay or shale	2.6	3.8	4.8	5.7
Limestone, cinders, air-cooled slag	2.7	4.0	5.0	5.9
Calcareous gravel	2.8	4.2	5.3	6.2
Siliceous gravel	3.0	4.5	5.7	6.7

R VALUE OF SINGLE WYTHE CMU, EMPTY AND WITH LOOSE-FILL INSULATION*

NOMINAL UNIT THICKNESS (IN.)	CORES	DENSITY OF CONCRETE IN CMU (PCF)				
		60	80	100	120	140
4	insul.	3.36	2.79	2.33	1.92	1.14
	empty	2.07	1.68	1.40	1.17	0.77
6	insul.	5.59	4.59	3.72	2.95	1.59
	empty	2.25	1.83	1.53	1.29	0.86
8	insul.	7.46	6.06	4.85	3.79	1.98
	empty	2.30	2.12	1.75	1.46	0.98
10	insul.	9.35	7.45	5.92	4.59	2.35
	empty	3.00	2.40	1.97	1.63	1.08
12	insul.	10.98	8.70	6.80	5.18	2.59
	empty	3.29	2.62	2.14	1.81	1.16

*Vermiculite or perlite insulation.

Robert J. Sangiamo, AIA, and Davis, Brody & Associates; New York, New York
Christine Beall, AIA, CCS; Austin, Texas

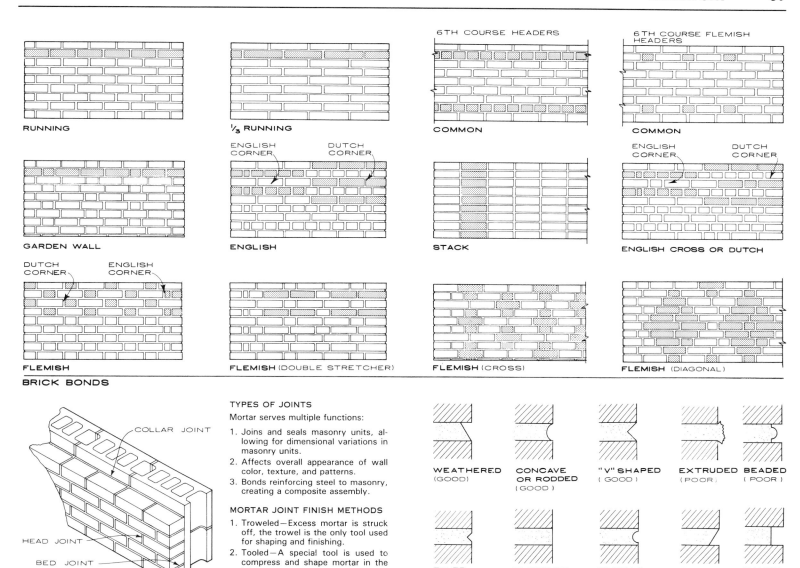

RUNNING

⅓ RUNNING

COMMON — 6TH COURSE HEADERS

COMMON — 6TH COURSE FLEMISH HEADERS

GARDEN WALL

ENGLISH — ENGLISH CORNER / DUTCH CORNER

STACK

ENGLISH CROSS OR DUTCH — ENGLISH CORNER / DUTCH CORNER

FLEMISH — DUTCH CORNER / ENGLISH CORNER

FLEMISH (DOUBLE STRETCHER)

FLEMISH (CROSS)

FLEMISH (DIAGONAL)

BRICK BONDS

COLLAR JOINT

HEAD JOINT

BED JOINT

TERMS APPLIED TO JOINTS

BRICK JOINTS

TYPES OF JOINTS

Mortar serves multiple functions:

1. Joins and seals masonry units, allowing for dimensional variations in masonry units.
2. Affects overall appearance of wall color, texture, and patterns.
3. Bonds reinforcing steel to masonry, creating a composite assembly.

MORTAR JOINT FINISH METHODS

1. Troweled—Excess mortar is struck off, the trowel is the only tool used for shaping and finishing.
2. Tooled—A special tool is used to compress and shape mortar in the joint.

WEATHERED (GOOD)

CONCAVE OR RODDED (GOOD)

"V" SHAPED (GOOD)

EXTRUDED (POOR)

BEADED (POOR)

RULED (FAIR)

FLUSH OR PLAIN CUT (FAIR)

FLUSH & RODDED (FAIR)

STRUCK (POOR)

RAKED (POOR)

TYPES OF JOINTS (WEATHERABILITY)

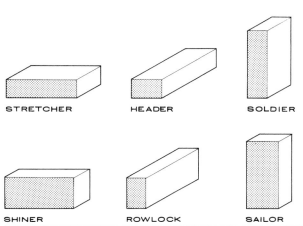

STRETCHER

HEADER

SOLDIER

SHINER

ROWLOCK

SAILOR

TERMS APPLIED TO VARIED BRICK POSITIONS

SIZES OF MODULAR BRICK

UNIT DESIGNATION	NOMINAL DIMENSIONS			
	THICKNESS	HEIGHT	LENGTH	MODULAR COURSING
MODULAR	4"	2⅔"	8"	3C = 8"
ENGINEER	4"	3⅕"	8"	5C = 16"
ECONOMY	4"	4"	8"	1C = 4"
DOUBLE	4"	5⅓"	8"	3C = 16"
ROMAN	4"	2"	12"	2C = 4"
NORMAN	4"	2⅔"	12"	3C = 8"
NORWEGIAN	4"	3⅕"	12"	5C = 16"
UTILITY[1]	4"	4"	12"	1C = 4"
TRIPLE	4"	5⅓"	12"	3C = 16"
SCR BRICK	6"	2⅔"	12"	3C = 8"
6" NORWEGIAN	6"	3⅕"	12"	5C = 16"
6" JUMBO	6"	4"	12"	1C = 4"
8" JUMBO	8"	4"	12"	1C = 4"
8" SQUARE	4"	8"	8"	1C = 8"
12" SQUARE	4"	12"	12"	1C = 12"

[1] Also called Norman Economy, General and King Norman.
* For special shapes contact local brick manufacturers.

Brick Institute of America; Reston, Virginia
Raso•Greaves An Architecture Corporation; Waco, Texas

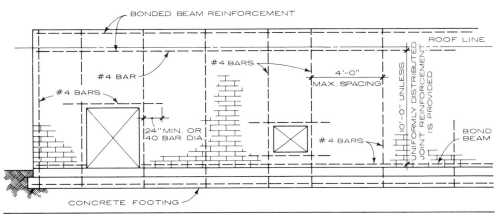

PARTIALLY REINFORCED LOAD-REINFORCED BRICK OR CMU WALL
(SEISMIC ZONES 0, 1, AND 2)

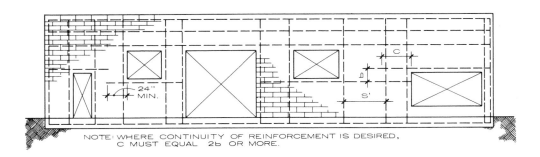

NOTE: WHERE CONTINUITY OF REINFORCEMENT IS DESIRED,
C MUST EQUAL 2b OR MORE.

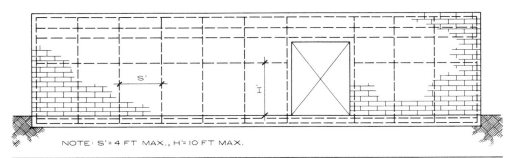

NOTE: S'= 4 FT MAX., H'= 10 FT MAX.

REINFORCED LOAD-BEARING BRICK OR CMU WALLS
(SEISMIC ZONES 3 AND 4)

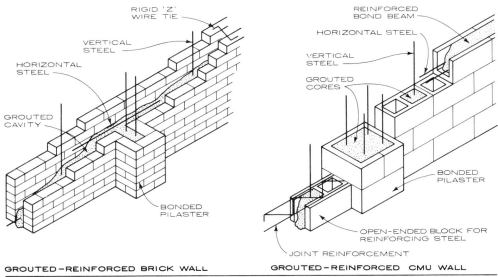

GROUTED-REINFORCED BRICK WALL   GROUTED-REINFORCED CMU WALL

METHODS OF REINFORCING

Christine Beall, AIA, CCS; Austin, Texas

LOAD-BEARING MASONRY

Engineered load-bearing masonry walls may be plain (unreinforced), partially reinforced, or reinforced. They may be single-wythe CMU or structural clay tile, multiwythe brick, or combinations of these materials. Reinforcing steel increases resistance to lateral loads and to buckling. Single-wythe brick masonry may be reinforced to function as panel wall or curtain wall systems, with relatively long spans between lateral supports.

ANCHORS AND REINFORCEMENT

Reinforced masonry uses standard deformed steel reinforcing bars, ASTM A615. Masonry wall ties should be rigid wire, minimum $3/16$ in. diameter, rectangular where open cavity occurs, rectangular or Z-ties where cavity is grouted. Do not used crimped ties with water drip, as strength is considerably reduced. Horizontal joint reinforcement is used to control shrinkage cracking in CMU construction. It may be ladder or truss type design with optional tabs for fixed or adjustable veneer anchorage. Standard widths are 2 in. less than nominal wall thickness to permit a minimum $5/8$ in. mortar cover at outside of joints. Longitudinal wires may be 10 gauge (light duty, interior only), 9 gauge (standard duty), 8 gauge (heavy duty), or $3/16$ in. diameter (extra heavy duty).

Cross wires may be a different size, generally 12 gauge minimum. For corrosion resistance, joint reinforcement and ties should be hot-dip galvanized, ASTM A153.

HORIZONTAL AND VERTICAL STEEL

Some codes permit calculation of horizontal joint reinforcement as part of the steel required for certain types of load-bearing walls. Other codes require standard deformed reinforcing bars placed horizontally in bond beam courses or grouted cavities and vertically in grouted cores or cavities.

PARTIALLY REINFORCED MASONRY (SEISMIC ZONE 2)

Partially reinforced masonry (not permitted in seismic zones 3 and 4) uses a certain minimum of code-required steel (check local requirements), plus an additional 0.2 sq in. in cross section horizontally and vertically wherever engineering design analysis indicated that tensile stress is developed. Maximum spacing of vertical steel is 4 ft 0 in. Vertical steel must also be placed at each side of window and door openings and at all corners. Bond beam courses must be provided at top of footings, bottom and top of wall openings, below roof and floor lines, and at top of parapet walls.

REINFORCED MASONRY (SEISMIC ZONES 3 AND 4)

Walls designed as reinforced masonry must have a minimum area of steel equal to 0.002 times the cross-sectional area of the wall, not more than $2/3$ of which (0.0007) may be placed in either direction. Maximum spacing principal reinforcement may not exceed 6 times the wall thickness or 48 in. o.c. Horizontal reinforcement must be provided in bond beam courses at top of footings, bottom and top of wall openings, below roof and floor lines, and at top of parapet walls. There must also be one #4 bar vertically at all window and door openings, extending at least 24 in. beyond the opening to prevent diagonal cracking at these planes of weakness. Only continuous reinforcement may be considered in computing the minimum area of steel provided.

PRECAUTIONS

Reinforcement must be lapped a minimum of 6 in. for continuity. Joint reinforcement, masonry ties, and steel wires located in mortar joints must be placed in the mortar bed and not directly on the masonry. CMU face shell bedding is acceptable except at grouted cores where cross-webs must also be bedded in mortar. Use spacers to hold vertical and horizontal reinforcement in proper alignment while grouting. Do not continue reinforcement through control or expansion joints. Do not place flashing in the same joint as reinforcement.

REFERENCES

Consult a structural engineer and local code requirements for design of grouted-reinforced masonry. For further technical information:

Masonry Design and Detailing, 2d ed. Christine Beall. New York: McGraw-Hill, 1987.
Technical Notes Series. Brick Institute of America.
TEK Series. National Concrete Masonry Association.

MASONRY ACCESSORIES

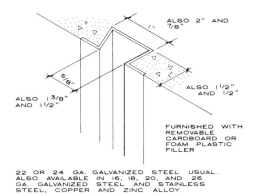

ALSO 2" AND 7/8"
1"
5/8"
ALSO 1 1/2" AND 1/2"
ALSO 1 3/8" AND 1 1/2"

FURNISHED WITH REMOVABLE CARDBOARD OR FOAM PLASTIC FILLER

22 OR 24 GA. GALVANIZED STEEL USUAL. ALSO AVAILABLE IN 16, 18, 20, AND 26 GA. GALVANIZED STEEL AND STAINLESS STEEL, COPPER AND ZINC ALLOY

DOVETAIL SLOTS

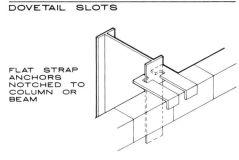

FLAT STRAP ANCHORS NOTCHED TO COLUMN OR BEAM

TWISTED TYPE COLUMN ANCHOR

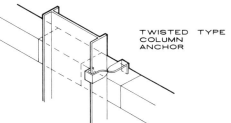

Z-TYPE ANCHOR (MASONRY TO MASONRY)

WELD-ON ANCHOR CLIP AND MASONRY TIE

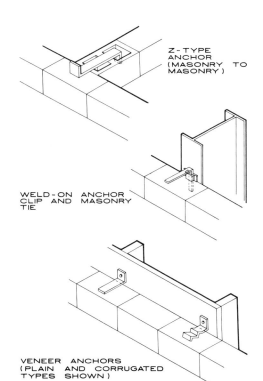

VENEER ANCHORS (PLAIN AND CORRUGATED TYPES SHOWN)

MISCELLANEOUS ANCHORS

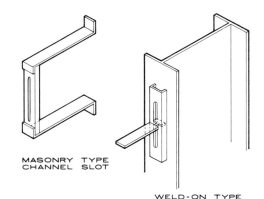

MASONRY TYPE CHANNEL SLOT

WELD-ON TYPE CHANNEL SLOT (WITH ANCHOR SHOWN)

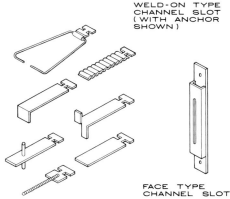

FACE TYPE CHANNEL SLOT

ANCHOR CONFIGURATIONS

CHANNEL SLOTS AND ANCHORS

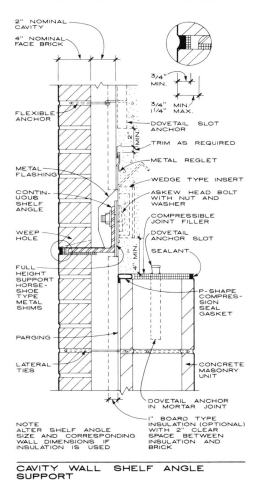

2" NOMINAL CAVITY
4" NOMINAL FACE BRICK
3/4" MIN.
3/4" MIN. 1 1/4" MAX.
FLEXIBLE ANCHOR
DOVETAIL SLOT ANCHOR
TRIM AS REQUIRED
METAL REGLET
METAL FLASHING
WEDGE TYPE INSERT
CONTINUOUS SHELF ANGLE
ASKEW HEAD BOLT WITH NUT AND WASHER
COMPRESSIBLE JOINT FILLER
WEEP HOLE
DOVETAIL ANCHOR SLOT
SEALANT
FULL HEIGHT SUPPORT HORSESHOE TYPE METAL SHIMS
P-SHAPE COMPRESSION SEAL GASKET
PARGING
LATERAL TIES
CONCRETE MASONRY UNIT
DOVETAIL ANCHOR IN MORTAR JOINT
1" BOARD TYPE INSULATION (OPTIONAL) WITH 2" CLEAR SPACE BETWEEN INSULATION AND BRICK
NOTE ALTER SHELF ANGLE SIZE AND CORRESPONDING WALL DIMENSIONS IF INSULATION IS USED

CAVITY WALL SHELF ANGLE SUPPORT

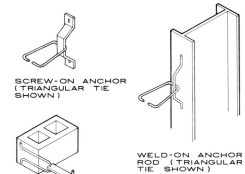

SCREW-ON ANCHOR (TRIANGULAR TIE SHOWN)

WELD-ON ANCHOR ROD (TRIANGULAR TIE SHOWN)

ADJUSTABLE U-BAR ANCHOR (FLAT TYPE PIN SHOWN)

1	Rectangular	Available with or without moisture drip in 3/16 in. or 1/4 in. mill or hot dipped galvanized steel; conforms to ASTM (A-82); space 16 in. vertically and 24 in. horizontally
2	Z	
3	Adjustable Z	
4	Mesh	1/2 in. mesh x 16 ga. hot dipped galvanized
5	Corrugated	mill or hot dipped galvanized steel 7/8 in. wide and 7 in. long; 12 to 28 ga.

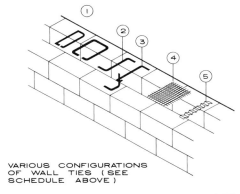

VARIOUS CONFIGURATIONS OF WALL TIES (SEE SCHEDULE ABOVE)

WIRE TIES

Masonry veneer and facing must be anchored to back-up construction. Codes usually require one anchor for 3 sq. ft. of surface area. Inserts usually are spaced 2 ft. on center horizontally, and ties usually are spaced 16 to 18 in. on center vertically. Spandrel beams over 18 in. deep require inserts and anchors for tying masonry facing to the beam. Most anchor systems permit differential movement in one or two directions. An anchoring system that allows movement only in the intended direction should be selected. See ASTM STP 778.

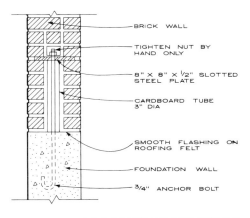

BRICK WALL
TIGHTEN NUT BY HAND ONLY
8" X 8" X 1/2" SLOTTED STEEL PLATE
CARDBOARD TUBE 3" DIA
SMOOTH FLASHING ON ROOFING FELT
FOUNDATION WALL
3/4" ANCHOR BOLT

WALL ANCHORAGE TO FOUNDATION

Narcisa P. Sanchez; Sanchez & Sanchez; Falls Church, Virginia
Metz Train Olson & Youngren, Inc.; Chicago, Illinois

MASONRY ACCESSORIES   **4**

GENERAL NOTES

Natural stone is used in building as a facing, veneer, and decoration. The major factors affecting the suitability and use of stone fall under two broad, but overlapping categories: physical and structural properties and aesthetic qualities. The three factors of building stone that most influence their selection by architects for aesthetic reasons are pattern, texture, and color. Consideration also should be given to costs, availability, weathering characteristics, physical properties, and size and thickness limitations.

Stone patterns are highly varied, and they provide special features that make building stone a unique material. Texture is varied, ranging from coarse fragments to fine grains and crystalline structures. Texture also varies with the hardness of minerals composing the stone. To accurately compare stone colors, the rock color chart published by the Geological Society of America (Boulder, CO) is recommended. Samples also may be used to establish acceptable color ranges for a particular installation.

Pattern, texture, and color all are affected by how the stone is fabricated and finished. Granites tend to hold their color and pattern, while limestone color and pattern changes with exposure. Textures may range from rough

and flamed finishes to honed or polished surfaces. The harder the stone, the better it takes and holds a polish.

The three rock classes are igneous, sedimentary, and metamorphic. Common construction stones are marketed under the names given in the table below, although specialty stones such as soapstone and serpentine also are available. Each stone has various commercial grades. Limestone grades are A, statuary; B, select; C, standard; D, rustic; E, variegated; and F, old Gothic. Marble is graded A, B, C, or D on the basis of working qualities, uniformity, and flaws and imperfections. Only grade A highest quality stone should be used for exterior applications.

The physical characteristics of a particular stone must be suitable for its intended use. It is important to determine the physical properties of the actual stone being used rather than using values from a generic table, which can be very misleading. Considerations of the physical properties of the stone being selected include modulus of rupture, shear strength, coefficient of expansion, permanent irreversible growth and change in shape, creep deflection, compressive strength, modulus of elasticity, moisture resistance, and weatherability. Epoxy and polyester adhesives, often used with stone, are affected by cleanliness of surfaces to be bonded and ambient temperature. Curing time increases with cold temperatures and decreases with warmer temperatures.

With the introduction of new systems of fabrication and installation and recent developments in the design and detailing of stone cutting, support, and anchorage, costs are better controlled. Correct design of joints, selection of mortars, and use of sealants affect the quality and durability of installation. Adequate design and detailing of the anchorage of each piece of stone are required. The size and thickness of the stone should be established based on physical properties of the stone, its method of anchorage, and the loads it must resist. Appropriate safety factors should be developed based on the variability of the stone properties as well as other considerations such as imperfect workmanship, method of support and anchorage, and degree of exposure of the cladding installation. Relieving angles for stone support and anchorage may be necessary to preclude unacceptable compressive loading of the stone. The stone should be protected from staining and breakage during shipment, delivery, and installation.

Since stone cladding design and detailing vary with type of stone and installation, the designer should consult stone suppliers, stone-setting specialty contractors, industry standards (such as ASTM), and other publications to help select and implement a stone cladding system. Resource information is available in publications such as the Indiana Limestone Institute's Indiana Limestone Handbook and the Marble Institute of America's Dimensioned Stone, Volume 3.

STONE CLASSIFIED ACCORDING TO QUALITIES AFFECTING USE

CLASS	COLOR	TEXTURE	SPECIAL FEATURES	PARTINGS	HARDNESS	CHIEF USES
Sandstone	Very light buff to light chocolate brown or brick red; may tarnish to brown	Granular, showing sand grains, cemented together	Ripple marks; oblique color bands ("cross bedding")	Bedding planes; also fractures transverse to beds	Fairly hard if well cemented	General; walls; building; flagstone
Limestone	White, light gray to light buff	Fine to crystalline; may have fossils	May show fossils	Parallel to beds; also fractures across beds	Fairly soft; steel easily scratches	All building uses
Marble	Highly varied: snow white to black; also blue-gray and light to dark olive green; also pinkish	Finely granular to very coarsely crystalline showing flat-sided crystals	May show veins of different colors or angular rock pieces or fossils	Usually not along beds but may have irregular fractures	Slightly harder than limestone	May be used for building stone but usually in decorative panels
Granite (light igneous rock)	Almost white to pink-and-white or gray-and-white	Usually coarsely crystalline; crystals may be varicolored; may be fine grained	May be banded with pink, white or gray streaks and veins	Not necessarily any regular parting but fractures irregularly	Harder than limestone and marble; keeps cut shape well	Building stone, but also in paneling if attractively colored
Dark igneous rock	Gray, dark olive green to black; Laurvikite is beautifully crystalline	Usually coarsely crystalline if quarried but may be fine grained	May be banded with lighter and darker gray bands and veins	Not necessarily any regular parting but may fracture irregularly	About like granite; retains cut shape well	Building stone but also used in panels if nicely banded or crystalline
Lavas	Varies: pink, purple, black; if usable, rarely almost white	Fine grained; may have pores locally	Note rare porosity	Not necessarily any regular parting, as a rule, but some have parallel fractures	About as strong as granite; if light colored, usually softer	Good foundation and building stone; not decorative
Quartzite	Variable: white, buff, red, brown	Dense, almost glassy ideally	Very resistant to weather and impact	Usually no special parting	Very hard if well cemented, as usually the case	Excellent for building but hard to "shape"
Slate	Grayish-green, brick red or dark brown, usually gray; may be banded	Finely crystalline; flat crystals give slaty fracture	Some slates have color-fading with age	Splits along slate surface, often crossing color bands	Softer than granite or quartzite; scratches easily	Roofing; blackboards; paving
Gneiss	Usually gray with some pink, white or light gray bands	Crystalline, like granite, often with glassy bands (veins)	Banding is decorative; some bands very weak, however	No special parting; tends to break along banding	About like granite	Used for buildings; also may be decorative if banded

PHYSICAL PROPERTIES OF REPRESENTATIVE STONES

PHYSICAL PROPERTY		IGNEOUS ROCK		SEDIMENTARY ROCK		METAMORPHIC ROCK	
		GRANITE	TRAPROCK	LIMESTONE	SANDSTONE	MARBLE	SLATE
Composition—ultimate strength	(psi)	15,000–30,000	20,000	4,000–20,000	3,000–20,000	10,000–23,000	10,000–15,000
Composition—allowable working stress	(psi)	800–1,500		500–1,000	400–700	500–900	1,000
Shear—ultimate strength	(psi)	1,800–2,700		1,000–2,000	1,200–2,500	900–1,700	
Shear—allowable working stress	(psi)	200		200	150	150	
Tension—allowable working stress	(psi)	150		125	75	125	
Weight	(psf)	156–170	180–185	147–170	135–155	165–178	170–180
Specific gravity		2.4–2.7	2.96	2.1–2.8	2.0–2.6	2.4–2.8	2.7–2.8
Absorption of water (parts by weight)		1/750		1/38	1/24	1/300	1/430
Modulus of elasticity	(psi)	6–10,000,000	12,000,000	4–14,000,000	1–7,500,000	4–13,500,000	12,000,000
Coefficient of expansion	(psf)	0.0000040		0.0000045	0.0000055	0.0000045	0.0000058

NOTE: Particular stones may vary greatly from the average properties shown in this table. A particular stone's physical properties, as well as its allowable working values, always should be developed for each particular application.

The McGuire & Shook Corporation; Indianapolis, Indiana
Christine Beall, AIA, CCS; Austin, Texas

4 **STONE**

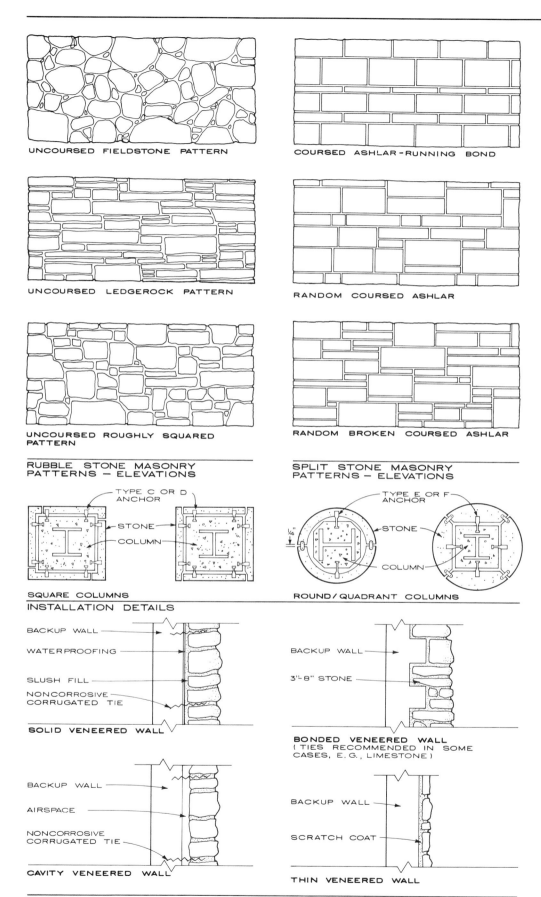

UNCOURSED FIELDSTONE PATTERN

COURSED ASHLAR-RUNNING BOND

ONE-HEIGHT PATTERN (SINGLE RISE)

UNCOURSED LEDGEROCK PATTERN

RANDOM COURSED ASHLAR

TWO-HEIGHT PATTERN (40% - 2¼";
60% - 5")

UNCOURSED ROUGHLY SQUARED
PATTERN

RANDOM BROKEN COURSED ASHLAR

THREE-HEIGHT PATTERN (15% - 2¼";
40% - 5"; 45% - 7¾")

RUBBLE STONE MASONRY
PATTERNS – ELEVATIONS

SPLIT STONE MASONRY
PATTERNS – ELEVATIONS

SPLIT STONE MASONRY HEIGHT
PATTERNS – ELEVATIONS

TYPE C OR D ANCHOR
STONE
COLUMN

TYPE E OR F ANCHOR
STONE
COLUMN

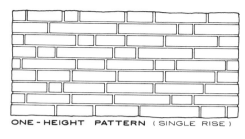

A   B   C
D   E   F

SQUARE COLUMNS

ROUND / QUADRANT COLUMNS

ANCHORS

INSTALLATION DETAILS

BACKUP WALL
WATERPROOFING
SLUSH FILL
NONCORROSIVE CORRUGATED TIE

SOLID VENEERED WALL

BACKUP WALL
3'L 8" STONE

BONDED VENEERED WALL
(TIES RECOMMENDED IN SOME
CASES, E.G., LIMESTONE)

BACKUP WALL
AIRSPACE
NONCORROSIVE CORRUGATED TIE

CAVITY VENEERED WALL

BACKUP WALL
SCRATCH COAT

THIN VENEERED WALL

TYPICAL WALL SECTIONS

NOTES

1. A course is a horizontal row of stone. Bond pattern is described by the horizontal arrangement of vertical joints. (See also Brickwork.) Structural bond refers to the physical tying together of load bearing and veneer portions of a composite wall. Structural bond can be accomplished with metal ties or with stone units set as headers into the backup.

2. Ashlar masonry is composed of squared-off building stone units of various sizes. Cut Ashlar is dressed to specific design dimensions at the mill. Ashlar is often used in random lengths and heights, with jointing worked out on the job.

3. All ties and anchors must be made of noncorrosive material. Chromium-nickel stainless steel types 302 and 304 and eraydo alloy zinc are the most resistant to corrosion and staining. Hot dipped galvanized is widely used, but is not as resistant, hence is prohibited by some building codes. Copper, brass, and bronze will stain under some conditions. Local building codes often govern the types of metal that may be used for stone anchors.

4. Nonstaining cement mortar should be used on porous and light colored stones. At all corners use extra ties and, when possible, larger stones. Joints are usually ½ to 1½ in. for rough work and ⅜ to ¾ in. for Ashlar.

Building Stone Institute; New York, New York
George M. Whiteside, III, AIA, and James D. Lloyd; Kennett Square, Pennsylvania
Alexander Keyes; Darrel Downing Rippeteau, Architect; Washington, D.C.

STONE

TYPES OF METALS

There are two general types of metals, ferrous and non-ferrous. Ferrous metals contain iron, nonferrous do not.

FERROUS METALS

Iron, which contains no trace amount of carbon, is soft, ductile, easily worked, oxidizes rapidly, but is susceptible to most acids. It is the main element in steel.

Cast iron and gray cast iron both are brittle metals with high compressive strength and capacity to absorb vibration, which makes them ideal for gratings, stair components and manhole covers. Neither should be hammered or beaten because they lack ductility. Both are relatively corrosion resistant.

Malleable iron, often used for the same purposes, is a low carbon iron that is cast, reheated and slowly cooled, or annealed, to improve its workability.

Wrought iron is soft, corrosion and fatigue resistant, and machinable. It is easily worked, making it ideal for railings, grilles, fences, screens, and various types of ornamental work. It often is cast or worked into bars, sheets or pipes. Because of its corrosion resistance, wrought iron until recently was used for below grade applications. Other metals are now preferred.

Steel is iron with low to medium amounts of carbon; carbon content is the measure used to categorize carbon steel. Greater carbon content increases strength and hardness but reduces ductility and welding capability. Its corrosion resistance is increased when a finish such as galvanizing or an organic coating is applied. Some architectural uses are as structural shapes, castings, studs, joists, fasteners, wall grilles, and ceiling suspension grids.

Steel alloys are produced when other elements are combined with carbon steel to modify steel properties. For example, high strength, low alloy steels (HSLA) improve corrosion resistance and are chosen where weight is a consideration and high strength is required. They are used infrequently in architectural applications because water runoff tends to stain adjacent materials. Below are a number of modifying alloy elements:

1. Aluminum for surface hardening.
2. Chromium for corrosion resistance.
3. Copper for resistance to atmospheric corrosion.
4. Manganese in small amounts for hardening; in larger amounts for wear resistance.
5. Molybdenum, combined with other alloying metals such as chromium and nickel, to increase corrosion resistance and to raise tensile strength without reducing ductility.
6. Nickel to increase tensile strength without reducing ductility; in high concentrations, to improve corrosion resistance.
7. Silicon to strengthen low-alloy steels and improve oxidation resistance; in larger amounts to provide hard, brittle castings resistant to corrosive chemicals.
8. Sulfur for free machining, especially in mild steels.
9. Titanium to prevent intergranular corrosion of stainless steels.
10. Tungsten, vanadium, and cobalt for hardness and abrasion resistance.

Stainless steel contains a minimum of 11.5 percent chromium. Nickel is added to boost atmospheric corrosion resistance. Where maximum corrosion resistance is required, such as resistance to pitting by sea water, molybdenum is added. Stainless steel is used in construction for flashing, coping, fasciae, wall panels, floor plates, gratings, handrails, hardware, fasteners and anchors.

NONFERROUS METALS

Nonferrous metals (those containing no iron) used in construction are:

Aluminum: High-purity aluminum is soft and ductile, highly corrosion resistant, but lacking in strength. Aluminum alloys are identified by numbers that distinguish each by its relative properties. For example, the identification number of pure aluminum is 1100. The manganese-based aluminum alloy, 3003, is used for roofing, sheet metal, siding, and conduit.

Lead: Extremely dense metal, easily worked, and corrosion resistant. Alloys are added to improve its properties

such as hardness and strength. Lead is used for waterproofing, sound and vibration isolation, and radiation shielding. It can be combined with a tin alloy to plate iron or steel, commonly called "terneplate." Care should be taken where and how lead is used because lead vapors or dust are toxic if ingested.

Zinc, although corrosion resistant in water and air, is brittle and low in strength. Its major use is in galvanizing (dipping hot iron or steel in molten zinc), but it also is used for roofing, flashing, hardware, die casting and as an alloying element.

Chromium and nickel also are used primarily as alloying elements; however, both can take a bright polish and do not tarnish in air, making them ideal for use in plating.

Monel, a nickel-copper alloy, most commonly is used to make fasteners and anchors, and is excellent where high corrosion resistance is required.

Copper is resistant to corrosion, impact and fatigue, yet it is ductile. It is used primarily in construction as electrical wiring, roofing, flashing, and piping.

Bronze originally was a copper-tin alloy; however, today copper is alloyed with various elements such as aluminum or silicon. In fact, the term "bronze" seldom is used without a modifying adjective giving the name of at least one of its alloying components, such as phosphor bronze, a copper-tin-phosphorus alloy, or leaded phosphor bronze composed of copper-lead-tin and phosphorus; aluminum bronze containing copper and aluminum; and silicon bronze, a copper-silicon alloy.

Brass is copper with zinc as its principal alloying element; however, some types of brass alloys often are called bronze even though they are not. Some nonbronze, brass alloys are: commercial bronze, 90 percent copper, 10 percent zinc; naval brass, 60 percent copper, 29 percent zinc, one percent tin; and manganese bronze, 58 percent copper, 39 percent zinc, one percent tin and iron. When a metal is identified as bronze, the alloy cannot contain zinc or nickel; if it does, it probably is brass. Architectural and commercial bronze are really brass, and are used for doors, windows, door and window frames, railings, trim and grilles and for finish hardware.

THE GALVANIC SERIES

Anode (least noble)	Magnesium, magnesium alloys
	Zinc
+	Aluminum 1100
	Cadmium
	Aluminum 2024-T4
	Steel or Iron, Cast iron
	Chromium iron (active)
	Ni-Resist
	Type 304, 316 stainless (active)
	Hastelloy "C"
electric current flows from positive (+) to negative (−)	Lead, Tin
	Nickel (Inconel) (active)
	Hastelloy "B"
	Brasses, Copper, Bronzes, Copper-Nickel alloys, Monel
	Silver solder
	Nickel (Inconel) (passive)
	Chromium iron (passive)
	Type 304, 316 stainless (passive)
−	Silver
	Titanium
Cathode (most noble)	Graphite, Gold, Platinum

CORROSION TO METALS

Galvanic action, or corrosion, occurs between dissimilar metals or metals and other materials when sufficient moisture is present to carry an electrical current. The galvanic series, a list of metals arranged in order from "least noble, most reactive to corrosion" to "most noble, least reactive to corrosion," is a good indicator of corrosion susceptibility due to galvanic action. The farther apart two metals are on the list, the greater the deterioration of the least noble one.

Metal deterioration also occurs when metals come in contact with chemically active materials, particularly when moisture is present. For example, aluminum in direct contact with concrete or mortar corrodes, or steel in contact with certain types of treated wood corrodes.

Other types of corrosion are pitting and concentration cell corrosion. Pitting corrosion occurs when particles or bubbles of gas are deposited on a metal surface. Oxygen deficiency under the deposit sets up anodic areas causing pitting. Concentration cell corrosion is similar to galvanic corrosion; the difference is in electrolytes. Concentration cell corrosion may be produced by differences in ion concentration, oxygen concentration, or foreign matter adhering to the surface.

FABRICATION ON METALS

Fabrication is a process applied to metal to obtain a shape. Following are various types of fabrication.

Rolling hot or cold metal between rollers under pressure produces most of the primary shapes available. The metal's temperature determines the properties of the end product. This method is applicable to most metals except iron.

In the extruding process metal is pushed under pressure through a die orifice producing various complex shapes limited only by the size or capability of the die. This process is applicable to all metals except iron.

Casting is a process in which molten metal is poured into molds and allowed to solidify into the shape of the mold. Casting is applicable to aluminum, copper, iron, steel, bronze, and other metals; however, surface quality and physical characteristics are affected by metal type, casting technique, and the molten metal's temperature.

In the drawing process either hot or cold metal is pulled through dies that alter or reduce its cross-sectional shape to attain three-dimensional shapes. Common extrusions are sheets, tubes, pipes, rods, bars, and wires. Drawing is applicable to all metals except iron.

Forging is a process of hammering or pressing hot or cold metal to a desired shape. It usually improves the strength and surface characteristics of the metal. Forging is applicable to aluminum, copper and steel.

Forming shapes metals by mechanical operations, excluding machining.

Bending produces curved shapes, and generally is applied to tubes, rods, and extrusions.

Brake forming, usually applied to plates or metal sheets, is a process of successive pressings to achieve specific shapes.

In the spinning process metal is shaped with tools while it is spun on an axis.

Embossing and coining are processes usually performed on flat shapes to achieve textured or raised patterns.

Blanking is shearing, sawing or cutting metal sheets with a punch press to achieve an outline.

Perforating is achieved by punching or drilling holes usually in flat shapes.

Piercing is a process that punches holes through metal without removing any of the metal.

Welding is the fusion of metals above the molten point with or without the aid of a metal filler. Gas welding is the most portable and economical. It can be used on site. The heat for fusion is provided by a torch using oxygen and acetylene gases.

Shielded metal arc welding, sometimes called manual, hand, or stick welding, can be performed in the shop or the field. An electric arc between a coated metal electrode and the components to be welded heat them both to a point where a molten pool forms on the surface of the components. As the arc is moved along the joint between the components, the pool solidifies, forming a homogeneous weld.

Gas metal arc welding also can be done on site or in a shop; however, provisions must be made on a job site to screen from any winds. This process uses an uncoated solid wire electrode and a stream of gas to provide shielding for the arc and welded metal. Several other types of welding are confined to the shop. Further information on welding is available from the American Welding Society.

FINISHES, MECHANICAL AND CHEMICAL

An as-fabricated finish is the texture and surface appearance given to a metal by the fabrication process.

A brightened finish is produced by electrolytic brightening or dipping the metal in acid solutions.

A buffed finish is produced by successive polishing and buffing operations using fine abrasives, lubricants, and soft fabric wheels.

A chemical finish produces a physical change on the metal's surface depending on the type of metal and chemical used.

Directional textured finishes have a smooth satiny sheen produced by making tiny parallel scratches on the metal surface using a belt or wheel and fine abrasive, or by hand rubbing with steel wool. Non-directional textured finishes are produced by blasting the metal under controlled conditions with sand, glass beads, or metal shot.

An etched finish produces a matte, frosted surface with varying degrees of roughness by treating the metal with an acid or alkaline solution.

Metallic finishes are created by applying one metal to another by electrolysis, hot dipping, electroplating, or other techniques.

Galvanizing is an example of metal coating where zinc is applied to steel. Zinc may be applied by electrolysis, peening, hot zinc spray, hot dip or paint. Hot dip galvanizing is used for nails, nuts and bolts, and structural members. Thickness of the zinc coating may be varied depending on the corrosive nature of the atmosphere at the place of use. Galvanized steel may be painted with special formulated coatings to substantially extend the life of the galvanized coating.

Patterned finishes, mechanically produced, are available in various textures and designs. They are produced by passing an as-fabricated sheet either between two machine matched-design rollers, embossing patterns on both sides of the sheet, or between a smooth roll and a design roll, embossing or coining on one side of the sheet only.

APPLIED COATINGS

Applied coatings are surface coverings over metal. They may be inorganic, such as porcelain enamel, or organic, like most commonly used fluorocarbons. Both can be applied over suitable primers (although not always necessary) for added corrosion resistance and to improve adhesion. Generally they are applied and baked on at the factory. Air-dry formulas usually are available for touch-ups.

Fluorocarbons generally are based on resins and are applied over primers such as epoxy-zinc chromate primers. They are available in a wide range of colors and in low to medium ranges of gloss.

Siliconized polymers, a combination of organic polymers and silicone intermediates, are applied in combination with a primer or alone. They are available in a wide range of colors and low to high gloss. The silicone extends gloss retention and improves resistance to color change and weathering. The two principal types are siliconized acrylic and siliconized polyester.

Plastisols are the top coat of a two-coat system. They require a special primer to bond to the metal surface. The top coat thickness can vary from 3 mils to 15 mils.

Conversion coatings for aluminum are amorphous chrome phosphate; for steel, a phosphate or various strong salt solutions generally is used.

Vitreous coatings are composed of inorganic glossy materials such as porcelain enamels. They are one of the hardest and most durable finishes, but they are brittle. Deformation of metal may cause cracking and spalling. These coatings are available in a wide range of colors and finishes from matte to high gloss.

Anodic finishes for coating aluminum consist of a mechanical finish, then a preanodic treatment to remove all foreign matter, and finally an oxide coating. Aluminum alloys must be suitable for anodizing. Fabrication, such as welding, can show when anodized.

REPRESENTATIVE ARCHITECTURAL USES AND COMPARATIVE PROPERTIES OF COATINGS

BINDER TYPE	TYPICAL USES	APPLICATION SHOP	FIELD	COST	OUTDOOR LIFE (YEARS)	COLOR STABLE, EXTERIOR	GLOSS RETENTION, EXTERIOR	STAIN RESISTANCE	WEATHER RESISTANCE	ABRASION AND IMPACT RESISTANCE	FLEXIBILITY	WATER REDUCIBLE AVAILABLE	CLEAR AVAILABLE	WELDABLE AS PRIMER
Acrylics— Solvent reducible	Residential siding and similar products; cabinets and implements; clear top coats	yes	no	M	10	yes	G	F	G	G	G	—	yes	yes*
Water reducible: air dried		yes	yes	M	5–10	yes	F	F	G	G	G	yes	yes	yes*
baked		yes	no	M	15–20	yes	G–E	F	G–E	G	G	yes	yes	yes*
Alkyds	Exterior primers and enamels	yes	yes	L–M	5–9	no	G	F	F	F	F–G	yes	yes	yes*
Cellulose Acetate Butyrate	Decorative high gloss finishes	yes	no	M	NA	yes	G	F	G	G	G	no	yes	no
Chlorinated rubber	Corrosion-resistant paints; swimming pool coatings; protection of dissimilar metals	yes	yes	M	10	yes	F	F	G	G	G	no	no	no
Chlorosulfonated polyethylene	Paints for piping, tanks, valves, etc.	yes	yes	VH	15	yes	NA	F	E	F–G	E	no	no	no
Epoxy	Moisture- and alkali-resistant coatings; nondecorative interior uses requiring high chemical resistance	yes	yes	H–VH	15–20	no	P	G	G–E	E	G	no	no	yes*
Fluorocarbons	High performance exterior coatings; industrial siding; curtain walls	yes	no	VH	20+	yes	E	E	E	E	G	no	no	no
Phenol formaldehyde	Chemical- and moisture-resistant coatings	yes	yes	M	10	no	F	F	G–E	G–E	G	no	yes	yes*
Polyester	Cabinets and furniture; ceiling tile; piping	yes	yes	H	15	some versions	G–E	G–E	G–E	G	G–E	yes	yes	no
Polyvinyl chloride	Residential siding; rain-carrying equipment; metal wall tile; baseboard heating covers, etc. Plastisols: industrial siding; curtain walls	yes	yes	H	15	yes	G	F	G–E	G	G–E	yes	no	yes*
Silicates (inorganic)	Corrosion-inhibitive primers; solvent-resistant coatings	yes	yes	H	NA	NA	NA	NA	NA	NA	G	G	no	no	yes
Silicone-modified polymers	High performance exterior coatings; industrial siding; curtain walls	yes	yes	H–VH	15–20	yes	G–E	G	G–E	G–E	G	yes	no	no
Urethane (aliphatic-cured)	Heavy duty coatings for stain, chemical, abrasion, and corrosion resistance	yes	yes	VH	20+	some versions	E	G–E	G–E	G–E	E	yes	yes	yes*

KEY: L = Low; M = Moderate; H = High; VH = Very High; NA = not applicable or not available; P = Poor; F = Fair; G = Good; E = Excellent   *For light welding only

NOTE: ALL WOOD SIZES ARE NOMINAL

ROUGH CARPENTRY	PENNY	INCHES	TYPE OF NAIL
1 in. thick stock	8	2½	Common nails
2 in. thick stock	16 to 20	3½ to 4	Common nails
3 in. thick stock	40 to 60	5 to 6	Common nails or spikes
Concrete forms	variable		Common or double-headed nails
Framing for general use and for large members	10, 16, 20, 60	3, 3½, 4, 6	Common nails or spikes depending on size of members
Toenailing studs, joists, etc.	10	3	Common nails
Spiking usual plates and sills	16	3½	Common nails
Toenailing rafters and plates	10	3	Common nails
Sheathing—roof and wall	8	2½	Common nails, may be zinc coated
Finished rough flooring	8	2½	Common nails, may be zinc coated

FINISH CARPENTRY			
Moldings—Sizes as required		⅞ to 1¼	Molding nails (brads)
Carpet strips, shoes	8	2½	Finishing or casing nails
Door window stops and members ¼ in. to ½ in. thick	4	1½	Finishing or casing nails
Ceiling, trim, casing, picture mold, base balusters and members ½ in. to ¾ in. thick	6	2	Finishing or casing nails
Ceiling, trim, casing, base, jambs, trim and members ¾ in. to 1 in. thick	8	2½	Finishing or casing nails
Doors and window trim, boards and other members 1 in. to 1¼ in. thick	10	3	Finishing or casing nails
Drop siding, 1 in. thick	7 or 9	2¼ or 2¾	Siding nails (7d), Casing nails (9d)
Bevel siding, ½ in. thick	6 or 8	2 or 2½	Finishing nails (6d), Siding nails (8d)

WOOD FLOORING			
See wood flooring page for nail sizes and types recommended			Cut steel, wire, finishing, wire casing, flooring brads, parquet and flooring nails

LATHING			
Wood lath	3	1¼	Blued lath nail
Gypsum lath	3	1¼	Blued common
Fiber lath			
Metal lath, interior		1	Blued lath nails, staples or offset head nails
Metal lath, exterior	3	1¼	Self-furring nails (double heads). Staple or cement coated

SHEATHING OR SIDING			
Fiber board ½ in. and 2 5/32 in.		1½ to 2	Galvanized roofing nail with 7/16 in. diameter head
Gypsum board ½ in.		1¾	Galvanized roofing nail 7/16 in. diameter head
Plywood 5/16 in. and ⅜ in. thick	6	2	Common nails
Plywood ½ in. and ⅝ in. thick	8	2½	Common nails

ROOFING & SHEET METAL			
Aluminum roofing	1	1¾ to 2½	Aluminum nail, neoprene washer optional
Asphalt shingles			Galvanized large head roofing
Copper cleats and flashing to wood			Copper wire or cut slating nails
Copper cleats and flashing to prevent joints			Barbed copper nails
Clay tile	4 to 6	1½ to 2	Copper nails
Prepared felt roofing		1 to 1¼	Zinc roofing nails or large head roofing nails (barbed preferred). Heads may be reinforced
Shingles, wood usual size for heavy butts	3 to 4 4 to 8	1¼ to 1½ 1½ to 2½	Zinc-coated, copper wire shingle, copper clad shingle, cut iron or cut steel
Slate	Use nails 1 in. larger than thickness of slate		Copper wire slating nail (large head). In dry climates zinc-coated or copper-clad nails may be used.
Tin, zinc roofing			Zinc-coated nails (roofing or slating)
Monel roofing			Monel nail
Nailing to sheet metal			Self-tapping screws, helical drive screws

TO CONCRETE OR CEMENT MORTAR			
See following pages of fastening devices			Concrete or cement nails (hardened), helical drive nails or drive bolts

NOTES

1. Thread sizes and lengths vary.
2. Hammer and powder-driven studs are intended for connections to concrete and steel. Refer to manufacturers' literature for specific applications.
3. Refer to building code provisions covering the use of powder-actuated devices. Some jurisdictions do not approve their use.
4. See ANSI A10.3 "Safety Requirements for Powder Actuated Fastening Systems" and OSHA regulations.

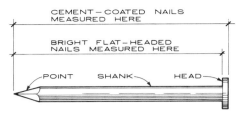

COMMON NAIL (STEEL WIRE)

COMMON NAIL (STEEL WIRE)

LENGTH	PENNY	GAUGE	DIAM. OF HEAD (IN.)	NAILS/LB.	SAFE WORKING RESISTANCE TO LATERAL SHEAR LB.
1	2	15	11/64	847	
1¼	3	14	13/64	543	
1½	4	12½	¼	296	
1¾	5	12½	¼	254	
2	6	11½	17/64	167	48
2¼	7	11½	17/64	150	
2½	8	10¼	9/32	101	64
2¾	9	10¼	9/32	92.1	
3	10	9	5/16	66	80
3¼	12	9	5/16	66.1	96
3½	16	8	11/32	47.4	128
4	20	6	13/32	29.7	160
4½	30	5	7/16	22.7	
5	40	4	15/32	17.3	
5½	50	3	½	13.5	
6	60	2	17/32	10.7	

HAMMER-DRIVEN OR POWDER-DRIVEN PIN

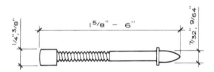

POWDER-DRIVEN UTILITY HEAD THREADED STUD

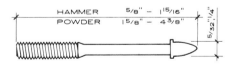

HAMMER-DRIVEN OR POWDER-DRIVEN HEADLESS THREADED STUD

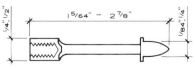

POWDER-DRIVEN INTERNALLY THREADED STUD

HAMMER- AND POWDER-DRIVEN FASTENERS

METAL FASTENING

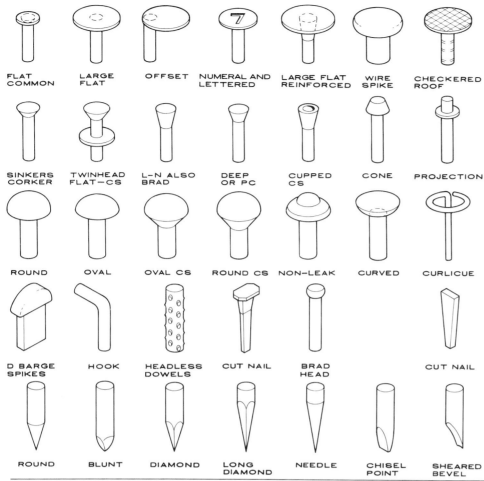

FLAT COMMON | LARGE FLAT | OFFSET | NUMERAL AND LETTERED | LARGE FLAT REINFORCED | WIRE SPIKE | CHECKERED ROOF

SINKERS CORKER | TWINHEAD FLAT—CS | L-N ALSO BRAD | DEEP OR PC | CUPPED CS | CONE | PROJECTION

ROUND | OVAL | OVAL CS | ROUND CS | NON-LEAK | CURVED | CURLICUE

D BARGE SPIKES | HOOK | HEADLESS DOWELS | CUT NAIL | BRAD HEAD | | CUT NAIL

ROUND | BLUNT | DIAMOND | LONG DIAMOND | NEEDLE | CHISEL POINT | SHEARED BEVEL

TYPES OF NAIL HEADS AND NAIL POINTS

NOTES

1. Nail diameter, length, shape and surface affect holding power (withdrawal resistance and lateral resistance). See NFPA publications.

2. Materials: Zinc, brass, monel, copper, aluminum, iron or steel, stainless steel, copper bearing steel, muntz metal.

3. Coatings: Tin, copper, cement, brass plated, zinc, nickel, chrome, cadmium, etched acid, parkerized.

4. Forms: Smooth, barbed, helical, annular-ring.

5. Colors: Blue, bright, coppered, black (annealed).

6. Gauges shown are for steel wire (Washburn and Moen).

7. Abbreviations (for the following pages of nails only):

B = blunt   F = flat   O = oval
CS = countersunk   L = long   PC = pointing cone
D = diamond   N = narrow   R = round

FASTENER FINISHES AND COATINGS

COATINGS OR FINISH	USED ON:	COMMENTS
Anodizing	Aluminum	Excellent corrosion protection
Chromate: black, clear, colored	Zinc and cadmium plated	Colors usually offer better protection than clear
Cadmiumplate	Most metals	
Copperplate	Most metals	Electroplated, fair protection
Copper, brass, bronze	Most metals	Indoor, decorative finishes
Lacquering	All metals	Some specially designed for humid conditions
Lead-tin	Steel	Applied by hot-dip. Gives good lubrication to tapping screws.
Nickel, bright and dull	Most metals	Indoor; outdoor if at least .0005 in. thick
Phosphate rust preventative	Steel	Rustproofs steel. Oils increase corrosion resistance
Phosphate paint-base preparations	Steel, aluminum zinc plate	Chemical process for painting or lacquering
Colored phosphate coatings	Steel	Superior to regular phosphated or oiled surfaces
Rust preventatives	All metals	Usually applied to phosphate and black oxide finishes
Electroplated zinc or tin; electrogalvanized zinc; hot-dip zinc or tin	All metals	Zinc or Tin
Hot-dip aluminum	Steel	Maximum corrosion protection, withstands high temperatures

Timothy B. McDonald; Washington, D.C.

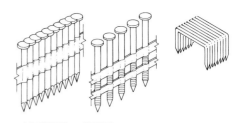

NESTED HEADED NAILS | SCREW AND RING SHANK NAILS | STAPLES

STAPLES AND NAILS FOR PNEUMATIC FASTENERS
ALLOWABLE LOADS FOR DESIGNED STRUCTURES

FAS-TENER	WIRE DIAM-ETER	WIRE GAUGE	PENE-TRA-TION INTO MAIN MEM-BER	ALLOWABLE LOAD (LBS.) (6,7)	
				LAT-ERAL (4,5)	WITH-DRAWAL
T-nail	.097	12½	1⅛	52	29
T-nail	.113	11½	1¼	63	34
T-nail	.131	10¼	1½	78	39
T-nail	.148	9	1⅝	94	44
staple	.0625	16	1	52	36
staple	.072	15	1	64	42
staple	.080	14	1	75	46
staple	.0915	13	1	92	53
staple	.1055	12	1⅛	113	62

NOTES

1. Refer to Industrial Stapling and Nailing Technical Association, HUD-FHA Bulletin No. UM-25d (1973), for complete data.

2. Crown widths range from 3/16 in. to 1 in. Leg lengths vary from 5/32 in. to 3½ in. Gauge should be chosen for shear value needed.

3. Screw shank and ring shank nails have the same allowable loads as common nails.

4. Nested nails are manufactured with a crescent-shaped piece missing in the head.

5. For wood diaphragms resisting wind or seismic loading these values may be increased 30 percent in addition to the 33⅓ percent increase permitted for duration of load.

6. The tabulated allowable lateral values are for fasteners installed in Douglas Fir-Larch or Southern Pine.

7. Allowable values shall be adjusted for duration of load in accordance with standard engineering practices. Where metal side plates are used, lateral strength values may be increased 25 percent.

8. Withdrawal values are for fasteners inserted perpendicular to the grain in pounds per linear inch of penetration into the main member based on a specific gravity of approximately 0.545.

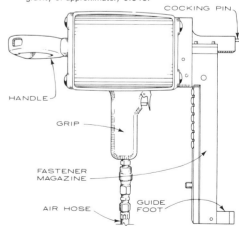

COCKING PIN
HANDLE
GRIP
FASTENER MAGAZINE
AIR HOSE
GUIDE FOOT

PNEUMATIC NAILERS AND STAPLERS

Pneumatic nailers and staplers, connected to compressors or CO_2 bottles, are capable of attaching a variety of fasteners to concrete and steel as well as wood. Consult manufacturer for special features and interchangeability of fasteners.

NAIL TYPE		SIZE		MATERIAL
F D #14 GAUGE	BARBED NAILS	1/4" TO 1½"		CEMENT COATED, BRASS, STEEL
LCSN D #14 GAUGE	CASING NAILS	2d TO 40d 6d TO 10d		BRIGHT, CEMENT COATED CUPPED HEADS AVAILABLE IN ALUMINUM
O ALSO FLAT HEAD CS D #5 TO #10 GAUGE	CEMENT NAILS ALSO CALLED CONCRETE NAILS AND HARDENED NAILS	1/2" TO 3"		SMOOTH, BRIGHT OIL QUENCHED
LNF CUP HEAD AVAILABLE #15 TO #2 GAUGE	COMMON BRAD	2d TO 60d		BRIGHT—MAY BE SECURED WITH CUPPED HEAD, CEMENT COATED—USUALLY MADE IN HEAVY GAUGES
F	CUT COMMON NAILS OR CUT COMMON SPIKE	2d TO 60d 20d TO 100d		STEEL OR IRON PLAIN OR ZINC COATED
LNF D GAUGE	COMMON NAILS (SHINGLE NAILS)	2d TO 60d		COPPER-CLAD
F D LIGHT GAUGE .095" HEAVY GAUGE .120"	COMMON BRASS WIRE NAILS	LIGHT GAUGE HEAVY GAUGE	1/2", 1" TO 3½" 3/4"—6"	BRASS, ALUMINUM
F D .109 (ABOUT 12 GAUGE)	COMMON NAILS (SHINGLE NAILS)	5/8" TO 6"		COPPER WIRE, ALUMINUM
F	STANDARD CUT NAILS (NON-FERROUS)	5/8" TO 6"		COPPER, MUNTZ METAL OR ZINC
F 2" LONG D #11½ GAUGE DOUBLE HEADED		1¾", 2", 2¼", 2½", 2¾", 3", 3½", 4", 4½"		BRIGHT, CEMENT COATED, MADE IN SEVERAL DESIGNS
CUPPED HEAD AVAILABLE D MADE IN 5 DIAMETERS	DOWEL PINS	5/8" TO 2"		BARBED – CUPPED HEAD AVAILABLE
O D MADE IN 3 GAUGES	ESCUTCHEON PINS	1/4" TO 2"		BRIGHT STEEL, BRASS PLATED, BRASS, ALSO NICKEL, SILVER, COPPER, ALUMINUM
F 6d-2" D #10 GAUGE FENCE NAILS		5d TO 20d		SMOOTH; BRIGHT, CEMENT COATED (GAUGE HEAVIER THAN COMMON)
LNF D #15 GAUGE	FINISHING NAIL, WIRE	2d TO 20d		SMOOTH; CUPPED HEADS AVAILABLE (SMALLER GAUGE THAN USUAL COMMON BRAD)
	FINISHING NAILS	STANDARD FINE	3d TO 20d 6d TO 10d	CUT IRON AND STEEL
3d-1⅛" #15 & #16 GAUGE	FINE NAILS	2d & 2d EX. FINE 3d & 3d EX. FINE		BRIGHT—SMALLER GAUGE AND HEADS THAN COMMON NAILS
PC B (ALSO WITH D. POINT) #14 GAUGE FLOORING NAILS		3d TO 20d 6d TO 20d		BRIGHT AND CEMENT COATED (DIFFERENT GAUGE) CUPPED HEADS AVAILABLE
LNCS 6d-2" D OR BLUNT D #11 GAUGE FLOORING BRAD		6d TO 20d		SMOOTH; BRIGHT AND CEMENT COATED CUPPED HEADS AVAILABLE

4   **METAL FASTENING**

NAIL TYPE		SIZE		MATERIAL
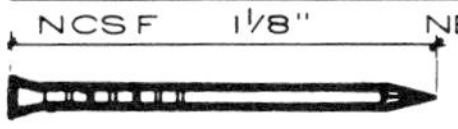 NCSF 1⅛" NEEDLE #15 GAUGE	PARQUET FLOORING NAIL OR BRAD	1", 1⅛," 1¼"		SMOOTH OR BARBED
	FLOORING NAILS	4d TO 10d		IRON OR STEEL (CUT)
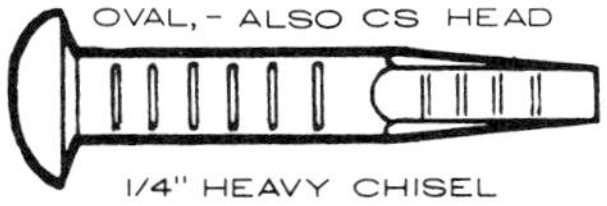 OVAL, - ALSO CS HEAD ¼" HEAVY CHISEL	HINGE NAILS	HEAVY: ¼" TO ⅜" DIA. LIGHT-3/16" TO ¼" DIA	1½"TO 4"LONG	SMOOTH, BRIGHT OR ANNEALED
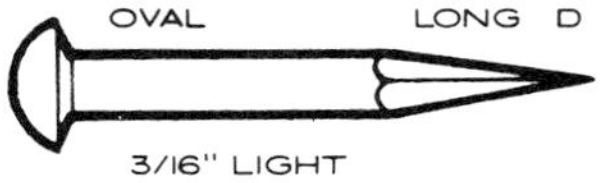 OVAL LONG D 3/16" LIGHT	HINGE NAILS	HEAVY-¼" DIA. LIGHT - 3/16" DIA.	1½"TO 3"ALSO TO 4"	SMOOTH, BRIGHT OR ANNEALED
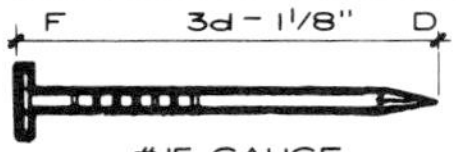 F 3d – 1⅛" D #15 GAUGE	LATH NAILS (WOOD)	2d, 2d LIGHT, 3d, 3d LIGHT, 3d HEAVY 4d.		BRIGHT (NOT RECOMMENDED), BLUED OR CEMENT COATED
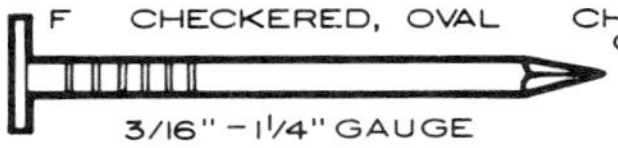 F CHECKERED, OVAL CHISEL OR D 3/16" – 1¼" GAUGE	GUTTER SPIKES	6" TO 10"		STEEL, ZINC COATED
O R #6½" GAUGE	HINGE NAILS	1½" TO 3"		STEEL, ZINC COATED
 HOOK 1⅛" #12 GAUGE	LATH NAILS (METAL)	1⅛"		BRIGHT, BLUED, ZINC COATED, ANNEALED
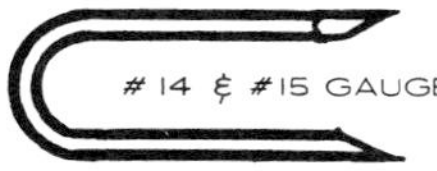 #14 & #15 GAUGE	LATH STAPLES	1" TO 1½"		BRIGHT, BLUED, ZINC COATED, ANNEALED
 OFFSET F D #10 GAUGE	LATH OFFSET HEAD NAILS FOR SELF FURRING METAL LATH	1¼" TO 1¾"		BRIGHT, ZINC COATED
 F #7 - #9 GAUGE	MASONRY NAILS USED FOR FURRING STRIPS CLEATS, PLATES	½" TO 4"		HIGH CARBON STEEL, HEATED & TEMPERED
 NCSF NEEDLE #14 GAUGE	MOLDING NAILS (BRADS)	⅞" TO 1¼"		SMOOTH, BRIGHT OR CEMENT COATED
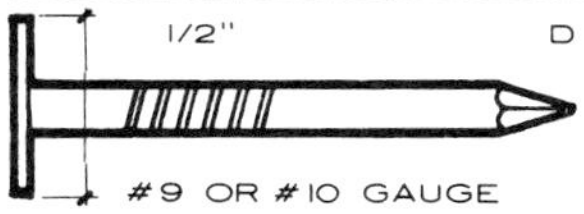 ½" D #9 OR #10 GAUGE	PLASTER-BOARD NAILS USED ALSO FOR WALL-BOARD ROCK LATH (5/16" HEAD)	1" TO 1¾" 1⅛" TO 1½"		SMOOTH, BRIGHT OR CEMENT COATED, BLUED ALUMINUM
 F D #10 GAUGE	ROOFING NAILS (STANDARD)	¾" TO 2"		BRIGHT, CEMENT COATED, ZINC COATED BARBED
 F 1" SQ. CUP REINFORCED D #12 GAUGE	ROOFING NAILS FOR BUILT-UP ROOFING	⅜" TO 2"		STEEL, ZINC COATED
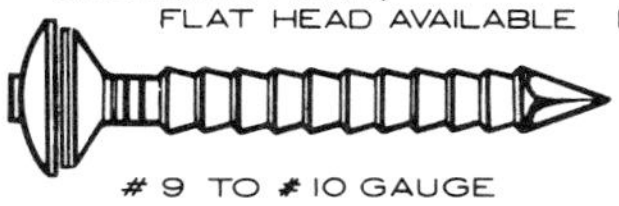 UMBRELLA HEAD, FLAT HEAD AVAILABLE D #9 TO #10 GAUGE	NEOPRENE WASHER ROOFING NAILS	1½" TO 2½"		STEEL, ZINC COATED
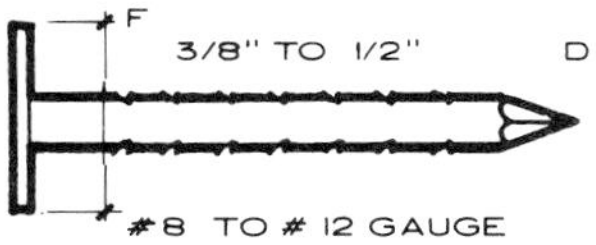 F ⅜" TO ½" D #8 TO #12 GAUGE	ROOFING NAILS LARGE HEAD	¾" TO 1¾" ALSO 2" ¾" TO 2½"		BARBED, BRIGHT OR ZINC COATED CHECKERED HEAD AVAILABLE ALUMINUM (ETCHED) NEOPRENE WASHER OPTIONAL

NAIL TYPE		SIZE		MATERIAL
F REINFORCED 5/8" DIA. 1¼" NEEDLE OR D #11 TO #12 GAUGE ALSO #10 GAUGE	ROOFING NAILS LARGE HEAD	3/4" TO 1¼"		BRIGHT OR ZINC COATED
#10 GAUGE	NON-LEAKING ROOFING NAIL	1³/4" TO 2"		ZINC COATED, ALSO WITH LEAD HEADS
	CUT SHEATHING NAILS	3/4" TO 3"		COPPER OR MUNTZ METAL
F LARGE HEAD AVAILABLE 1/4" TO 9/32" 5/16" DIA. #12 GAUGE D	SHINGLE NAILS	3d TO 6d 2d TO 6d		SMOOTH, BRIGHT, ZINC, CEMENT COATED, LIGHT AND HEAVY ALUMINUM
	CUT SHINGLE NAILS	2d TO 6d		IRON OR STEEL (CUT) PLAIN OR ZINC COATED
F D # 14 GAUGE	SIDING NAILS	2d TO 40d 6d TO 10d		SMOOTH, BRIGHT OR CEMENT COATED SMALLER DIAMETER THAN COMMON NAILS ALUMINUM
F D # 11 GAUGE	SIDING NAILS USED FOR FENCES, TANKS, GATES, ETC.	2½" TO 3"		STEEL ZINC COATED
F 5/16" TO 3/8" SEVERAL GAUGES	SLATING NAILS	3/8" HEAD SMALL HEADS COPPER WIRE	1"TO 2" 1"TO 2" 7/8"-1½"	ZINC COATED, BRIGHT, CEMENT COATED, COPPER CLAD, COPPER
	CUT SLATING NAILS, NON-FERROUS	1¼" TO 2"		COPPER, ZINC OR MUNTZ METAL
OVAL, SQUARE OR ROUND HEAD CHISEL POINT 1/4" TO 5/8" SQ. BARGE SPIKE, SQUARE		3" TO 12" ALSO 16"		PLAIN AND ZINC COATED USED FOR HARDWOOD
SQUARE OR DIAMOND HEAD 7/32" TO 1⅛" DIA. CHISEL POINT 1/4" TO 5/8" SQ. BOAT SPIKE, SQUARE		3" TO 12"		PLAIN AND ZINC COATED USED FOR HARD WOOD
1" HEAD	ROOF DECK NAILS	1" AND 1¾"		GALVANIZED – NAILS STEEL TUBE
F OR OCS D OR CHISEL POINT # 6 TO 3/8" GAUGE ROUND WIRE SPIKES		10d TO 60d & 7" TO 12" ALSO 16"		SMOOTH, BRIGHT OR ZINC COATED

4   METAL FASTENING

MACHINE BOLT ANCHORS AND SHIELDS (IN.)

BOLT DIA.	THPS PER INCH	DECIMAL EQUIV. (IN.)	SINGLE EXPANDING ANCHOR (CAULKING) A	SINGLE EXPANDING ANCHOR (CAULKING) L	SINGLE EXPANDING ANCHOR (NONCAULKING) A	SINGLE EXPANDING ANCHOR (NONCAULKING) L	MULTIPLE EXPANDING ANCHOR (PLAIN STYLE) A	MULTIPLE EXPANDING ANCHOR (PLAIN STYLE) L UNITS 2	MULTIPLE EXPANDING ANCHOR (PLAIN STYLE) L UNITS 3	MULTIPLE EXPANDING ANCHOR (THREADED STYLE) A	MULTIPLE EXPANDING ANCHOR (THREADED STYLE) L UNITS 2	MULTIPLE EXPANDING ANCHOR (THREADED STYLE) L UNITS 3	DOUBLE ACTING SHIELD A	DOUBLE ACTING SHIELD L
6	32	.138	5/16	1/2										
8	32	.164	5/16	1/2										
10	24	.190	3/8	5/8										
12	24	.216	1/2	7/8										
1/4	20	.250	1/2	7/8	1/2	1 3/8	1/2"	1 1/8		1/2	1		1/2	1 1/4
5/16	18	.312	5/8	1	5/8	1 5/8							5/8	1 1/2
3/8	16	.375	3/4	1 1/4	5/8	1 5/8	3/4	1 1/2		3/4	1 1/2		3/4	1 3/4
1/2	13	.500	7/8	1 1/2	7/8	2 1/2	1	1 3/4	2 3/8	1	1 3/4	2 1/4	7/8	2 1/4
5/8	11	.625	1 1/8	2	1	2 3/4	1 1/8	*	2 5/8	1 1/8	*	2 1/2	1	2 1/2
3/4	10	.750	1 1/4	2 1/4	1 1/4	2 7/8	1 3/8	*	3	1 3/8	*	3 1/8	1 1/4	3 1/2
7/8	9	.875					1 1/2	*	3 1/2	1 1/2	*	3 5/8	1 5/8	4"
1	8	1.00					1 5/8	*	3 7/8	1 5/8	*	3 3/4	1 3/4	4 1/4

*Use of three units in these diameters is recommended.

NOTE

1. Extension sleeve for deep setting.
2. Expansion shields and anchors shown are representative of many types, some of which may be used in single or multiple units.
3. Many are threaded for use with the head of the screw outside, some with the head inside and some types require setting tools to install.
4. In light construction plastic expansion shields are used frequently.

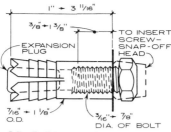

SELF-DRILLING EXPANSION ANCHOR (SNAP-OFF TYPE)

NOTE

1. Refer to manufacturers for size variations within the limits shown, and for different types of bolts.
2. The anchor is made of case hardened steel and drawn carburizing steel.

HOLLOW WALL ANCHORS

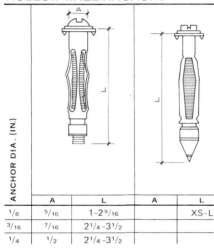

ANCHOR DIA. (IN.)	A	L	A	L
1/8	5/16	1-2 9/16		XS-L
3/16	7/16	2 1/4-3 1/2		
1/4	1/2	2 1/4-3 1/2		

SHIELDS FOR LAG BOLTS AND WOOD SCREWS (IN.)

LAG SCREW DIA. (IN.)	WOOD SCREW SIZES	DECIMAL EQUIV. (IN.)	LAG BOLT EXPANSION SHIELD A	LAG BOLT EXPANSION SHIELD L SHORT	LAG BOLT EXPANSION SHIELD L LONG	LEAD SHIELD FOR LAG BOLT OR WOOD SCREW A	LEAD SHIELD FOR LAG BOLT OR WOOD SCREW L
	6	.138				1/4	3/4-1 1/2
	8	.164				1/4	3/4-1 1/2
	10	.190				5/16	1-1 1/2
	12	.216				5/16	1-1 1/2
1/4	14	.250	1/2	1	1 1/2	5/16	1-1 1/2
	16	.268				3/8	1 1/2
	18	.294				3/8	1 1/2
5/16	20	.320	1/2	1 1/4	1 3/4	7/16	1 3/4
3/8	24	.372	5/8	1 3/4	2 1/2	7/16	1 3/4
1/2		.500	3/4	2	3		
5/8		.625	7/8	2	3 1/2		
3/4		.750	1	2	3 1/2		

ONE PIECE ANCHORS (IN.)

ANCHOR SIZE AND DRILL SIZE	DECIMAL EQUIV. (IN.)	WEDGE ANCHOR L	WEDGE ANCHOR MIN. HOLE DEPTH D	STUD ANCHOR L	STUD ANCHOR MIN. HOLE DEPTH D	SLEEVE ANCHOR L	SLEEVE ANCHOR MIN. HOLE DEPTH D	HEAD STYLE
1/4	.250	1 3/4-3 1/4	1 3/8	1 3/4-3 1/4	1 3/8	5/8-2 1/4	1/2-1 1/8	Acorn nut
5/16	.320					1 1/2-2 1/2	1 1/8	Hex nut
3/8	.375	2 1/4-5	1 3/4	2 1/4-6	1 5/8	1 7/8-3	1 1/2	''
1/2	.500	2 3/4-7	2 1/8	2 3/4-5 1/4	1 7/8	2 1/4-4	1 7/8	''
5/8	.625	3 1/2-8 1/2	2 5/8	3 3/8-7	2 3/8	2 1/4-6	2	''
3/4	.750	4 1/4-10	3 1/4	4 1/4-8 1/2	2 7/8	2 1/2-8	2 1/4-5 1/2	''
7/8	.875	6-10	3 3/4					
1	1.00	6-12	4 1/2					
1 1/4	1.25	9-12	5 1/2					

Sleeve anchors available in acorn nut, hex nut, flat head, round head, Phillips round head, and tie wire head styles.

MACHINE SCREW AND STOVE BOLT (INS.)

STOVE BOLT DIAM.	MACHINE SCREW DIAM.	ROUND HEAD	FLAT HEAD	FILLISTER HEAD	OVAL HEAD	OVEN HEAD
	2	1/8–7/8		1/8–7/8		
	3	1/8–7/8		1/8–7/8		
	4	1/8–1½	40 N.C.	1/8–1½		
	4	1/8–1½	36 N.C.	1/8–1½		1/8–3/4
1/8	5	1/8–2		1/8–2		3/8–2
	6	1/8–2		1/8–2		1/8–1
5/32	8	3/16–3		3/16–3		3/16–2
3/16	10	3/16–6		3/16–3		1/4–6
	12	1/4–3		1/4–3		
1/4	1/4	5/16–6		5/16–3		3/8–6
5/16	5/16	3/8–6		3/8–3		3/4–6
3/8	3/8	1/2–5		1/2–3		3/4–5
1/2	1/2	1–4				

Length intervals = 1/16 in. increments up to 1/2 in., 1/8 in. increments from 5/8 in. to 1¼ in., 1/4 in. increments from 1½ in. to 3 in., 1/2 in. increments from 3½ in. to 6 in.
NOTE: N.C. = Course thread

SCREW AND BOLT LENGTHS (INS.)

DIAMETER (INS.)	CAP SCREWS				BOLTS		
	BUTTON HEAD	FLAT HEAD	HEXAGON HEAD	FILLISTER HEAD	MACHINE BOLT	CARRIAGE BOLT	LAG BOLT
1/4	1/2–2¼		1/2–3½	3/4–3	1/2–8	3/4–8	1–6
5/16	1/2–2¾		1/2–3½	3/4–3¾	1/2–8	3/4–8	1–10
3/8	5/8–3		1/2–4	3/4–3½	3/4–12	3/4–12	1–12
7/16	3/4–3		3/4–4	3/4–3¾	3/4–12	1–12	1–12
1/2	3/4–4		3/4–4½	3/4–4	3/4–24	1–20	1–12
9/16	1–4		1–4½	1–4	1–30	1–20	
5/8	1–4		1–5	1¼–4½	1–30	1–20	1½–16
3/4	1–4		1¼–5	1½–4½	1–30	1–20	1½–16
7/8			2–6	1¾–5	1½–30		2–16
1			2–6	2–5	1½–30		2–16

Length intervals = 1/8 in. increments up to 1 in., 1/4 in. increments from 1¼ in. to 4 in., 1/2 in. increments from 4½ in. to 6 in.

Length intervals = 1/4 in. increments up to 6 in., 1/2 in. increments from 6½ in. to 12 in., 1 in. increments over 12 in.

Length intervals = 1/2 in. increments up to 8 in., 1 in. increments over 8 in.

ROUND FLAT OVAL PAN FILLISTER TRUSS HEX WASHER

HEAD TYPES

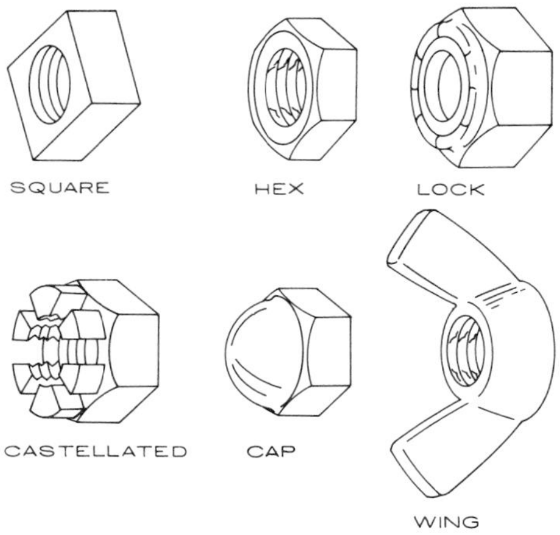

SQUARE HEX LOCK

FLAT LOCK (SPRING) COUNTERSUNK

CASTELLATED CAP

TOOTHLOCK (INTERNAL) (EXTERNAL)

WING

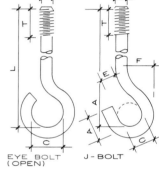

EYE BOLT (CLOSED) EYE BOLT (OPEN) J-BOLT

Self-locking nuts have a pin that acts as a rachet, sliding down the thread as the bolt is tightened, to prevent loosening from shock and vibration.

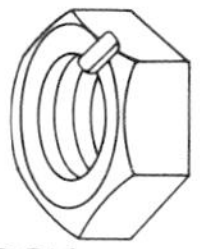

LOCK

NUTS

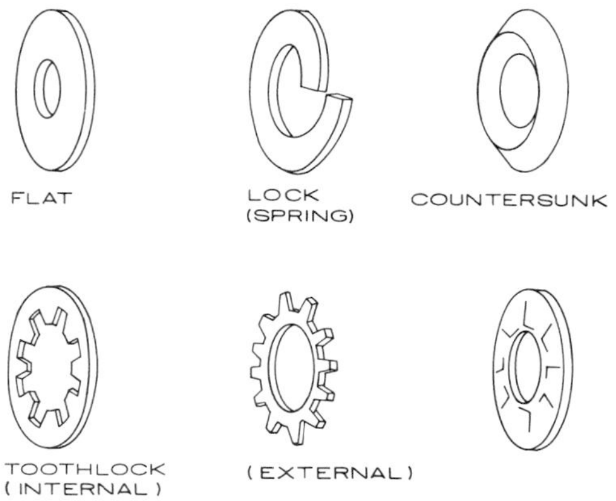

LOAD INDICATOR

WASHERS

The bolt's clamping force causes protrusions on the washer to flatten partially, closing the gap between the washer and the bolt head. Measurement of the gap indicates whether the bolt has been tightened adequately.

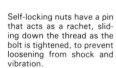

Fiberglass nuts and bolts are noncorrosive and non-conductive. Bolts are available in 3/8 in., 1/2 in., 5/8 in., 3/4 in., and 1 in. standard diameters.

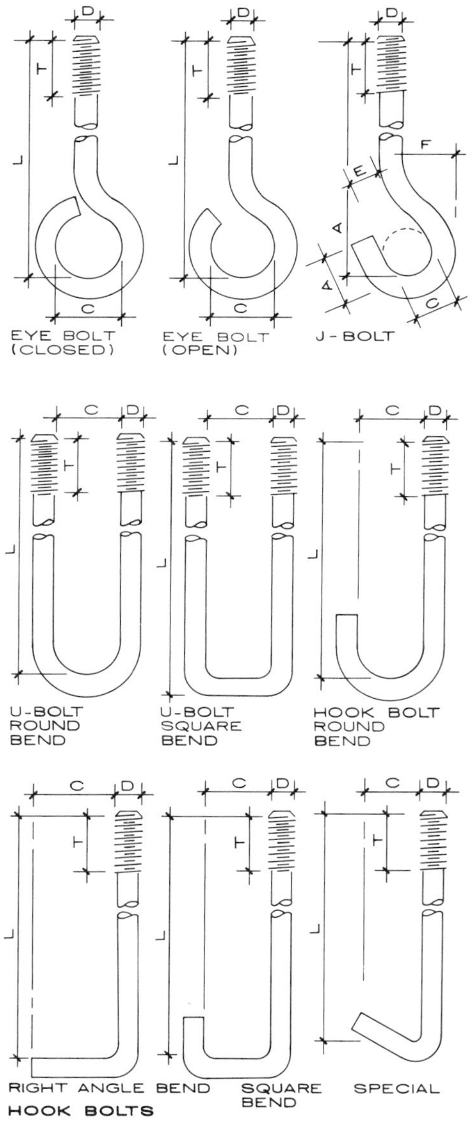

FIBERGLASS NUTS AND BOLTS

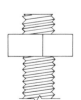

High tension, stainless steel helical inserts are held in place by spring-like pressure, and they are used to salvage damaged threads. They also eliminate thread failure due to stress conditions.

HELICAL INSERTS

U-BOLT ROUND BEND U-BOLT SQUARE BEND HOOK BOLT ROUND BEND

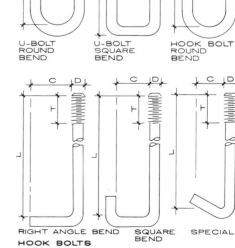

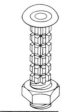

Interference body bolts are driven into reamed or drilled holes to create a joint in full bearing.

INTERFERENCE BODY BOLTS

NOTES
1. Bent bolts are specialty items made to order.
2. D = bolt diameter; C = inside opening width; T = thread length; L = inside length of bolt; A = inside depth.

RIGHT ANGLE BEND SQUARE BEND SPECIAL

HOOK BOLTS

Timothy B. McDonald; Washington, D.C.

 METAL FASTENING

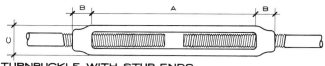

TURNBUCKLE WITH STUB ENDS

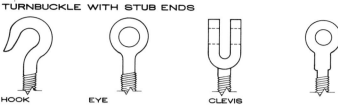

HOOK   EYE   CLEVIS

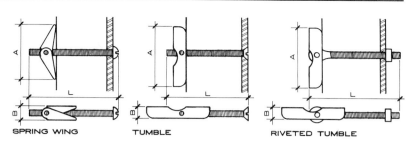

SPRING WING   TUMBLE   RIVETED TUMBLE

TURNBUCKLES (IN INCHES)

DIAMETER	1/4	5/16	3/8	1/2	5/8	3/4	7/8	1
DECI. EQUIV.	.250	.313	.375	.500	.625	.750	.875	1.00
	4	4 1/2	6"	6"	6"	6"	6"	6"
				9"	9"	9"		
A				12"	12"	12"	12"	12"
B	7/16	1/2	9/16	3/4	29/32	1 1/16	1 7/32	1 3/8
C	3/4	7/8	31/32	1 7/32	1 1/2	1 23/32	1 7/8	2 1/32

DIAMETERS OVER 1" AVAILABLE, NOT ALWAYS STOCKED.

TOGGLE BOLTS (IN INCHES)

DIAMETER		1/8	5/32	3/16	1/4	5/16	3/8	1/2
DECIMAL EQUIV.		.138	.164	.190	.250	.313	.375	.500
SPRING WING	A	1.438	1.875	1.875	2.063	2.750	2.875	4.625
	B	.375	.500	.500	.688	.875	1.000	1.250
	L	2 – 4	2 1/2 – 4	2 – 6	2 1/2 – 6	3 – 6	3 – 6	4 – 6
TUMBLE	A	1.250	2.000	2.000	2.250	2.750	2.750	
	B	.375	.500	.500	.688	.875	.875	
	L	2 – 4	2 1/2 – 4	3 – 6	3 – 6	3 – 6	3 – 6	
RIVETED TUMBLE	A		2.000	2.000	2.250	2.750	2.750	3.375
	B		.375	.375	.500	.625	.688	.875
	L		2 1/2 – 4	3 – 6	3 – 6	3 – 6	3 – 6	3 – 6

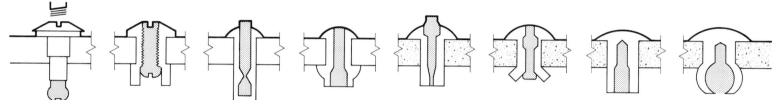

THREADED   PULL MANDREL   DRIVE PIN   CHEMICALLY EXPANDED

BLIND RIVETS FOR USE IN A JOINT THAT IS ACCESSIBLE FROM ONLY ONE SIDE

ROUND   TRUSS   FLAT   COUNTERSUNK   PAN

RIVETS
STANDARD RIVETS AVAILABLE WITH SOLID, TUBULAR AND SPLIT SHANKS OF STEEL, BRASS, COPPER, ALUMINUM, MONEL METAL AND STAINLESS STEEL; IN DIAMETERS OF 1/8" TO 7/16" AND LENGTHS OF 3/16" TO 4 IN.

OVAL HEAD

SLOTTED   ROUND HEAD

FLAT HEAD

Self-drilling fasteners: used to attach metal to metal, wood, and concrete. Consult manufacturer for sizes and drilling capabilities.

SHEET METAL GIMLET POINT

Sheet metal gimlet point: hardened, self-tapping. Used in 28 gauge to 6 gauge sheet metal; aluminum, plastic, slate, etc. Usual head types.

PHILLIPS

WOOD SCREWS (IN IN.)

DIA.	DECI. EQUIV.	LENGTH
0	.060	1/4 – 3/8
1	.073	1/4 – 1/2
2	.086	1/4 – 3/4
3	.099	1/4 – 1
4	.112	1/4 – 1 1/2
5	.125	3/8 – 1 1/2
6	.138	3/8 – 2 1/2
7	.151	3/8 – 2 1/2
8	.164	3/8 – 3
9	.177	1/2 – 3
10	.190	1/2 – 3 1/2
11	.203	5/8 – 3 1/2
12	.216	5/8 – 4
14	.242	3/4 – 5
16	.268	1 – 5
18	.294	1 1/4 – 5
20	.320	1 1/2 – 5
24	.372	3 – 5

SELF-DRILLING FASTENERS

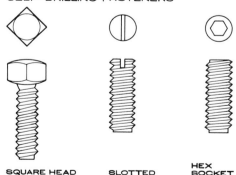

SQUARE HEAD   SLOTTED   HEX SOCKET

Set Screws: headless with socket or slotted top; made in sizes 4 in. to 1/2 in., and in lengths 1/2 in. to 5 in. Square head sizes 1/4 in. to 1 in., and lengths 1/2 in. to 5 in.

SET SCREWS

SHEET METAL BLUNT POINT

Sheet metal blunt point: hardened, self-tapping. Used in 28 to 18 gauge sheet metal. Made in sizes 4 to 14 in usual head types.

FREARSON

THREAD CUTTING- CUTTING SLOT

Thread cutting, cutting slot: hardened. Used in metals up to 1/4 in. thick in sizes 4 in. to 5/16 in. in usual head types.

SHEET METAL & THREADING SCREWS

DRIVE TYPES

Timothy B. McDonald; Washington, D.C.

METAL FASTENING   4

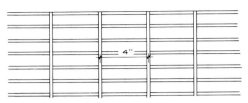

WITH SPACER BARS WELDED 4" O.C.   WITH SPACER BARS WELDED 2" O.C.

RECTANGULAR (WELDED OR PRESSURE LOCKED)

NOTES

Constructed of flat bearing bars of steel or aluminum I-bars, with spacer bars at right angles. Spacer bars may be square, rectangular, or of another shape. Spacer bars are connected to bearing bars by pressing them into prepared slots or by welding. They have open ends or perhaps ends banded with flat bars that are of about the same size as welded bearing bars. Standard bar spacings are $15/16$ and $13/16$ in.

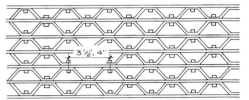

WITH SPACER BARS RIVETED APPROX. 7" O.C.
USED FOR AVERAGE INSTALLATION

WITH SPACER BARS RIVETED 3½" OR 4"
USED FOR HEAVY TRAFFIC AND WHERE
WHEELED EQUIPMENT IS USED

RETICULATED (RIVETED)

NOTES

Flat bearing bars are made of steel or aluminum, and continuous bent spacer or reticulate bars are riveted to the bearing bars. Usually they have open ends or ends that are banded with flat bars of the same size as bearing bars, welded across the ends. Normal spacing of bars: $3/4$, $1 1/8$, or $2 5/16$ in. Many bar gratings cannot be used in areas of public pedestrian traffic (crutches, canes, pogo sticks, women's shoes, etc.). Close mesh grating ($1/4$ in.) is available in steel and aluminum, for use in pedestrian traffic areas.

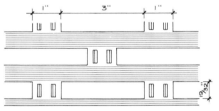

PLAN

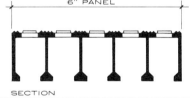

6" PANEL

SECTION

ALUMINUM PLANK

NOTES

Grating is extruded from aluminum alloy in one piece with integral I-beam ribs and can have a natural finish or be anodized. Top of surface may be solid or punched. Standard panel width is 6 in.

NOSING OF ANGLE AND ABRASIVE
STRIP AND BAR ENDS

HEAVY FRONT AND BACK BEARING
BARS AND BAR END PLATES

FLOOR PLATE NOSING, BAR END
PLATES

NOSING OF CLOSELY SPACED BARS,
ANGLE ENDS

CHECKER PLATE NOSING, BAR END
PLATES

EXTRUDED ALUMINUM CORRUGATED
NOSING, BAR END PLATES

TREADS

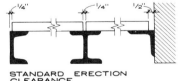

STAIR STRINGER AND TREAD CARRIER

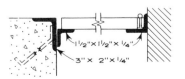

USUALLY ATTACHED BY WELDING, WHERE SUPPORT AND GRATE ARE CONSTRUCTED AS A UNIT

FIXED OR LOOSE GRATINGS

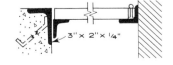

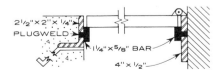

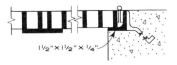

SIZES OF ANGLES SUPPORTING GRATING DEPEND ON DEPTH OF GRATING BARS

HINGED AREA GRATINGS

Vicente Cordero, AIA; Arlington, Virginia

METAL FABRICATIONS

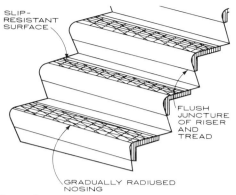

SLIP-RESISTANT SURFACE

FLUSH JUNCTURE OF RISER AND TREAD

GRADUALLY RADIUSED NOSING

"SAFE" STAIR ELEMENTS

TREAD AND RISER SIZES

Riser and tread dimensions must be uniform for the length of the stair. ANSI specifications recommend a minimum tread dimension of 11 in. nosing to nosing and a riser height of 7 in. maximum. Open risers are not permitted on stairs accessible to the handicapped.

TREAD COVERING

OSHA standards require finishes to be "reasonably slip resistant" with nosings of slip-resistant finish. Treads without nosings are acceptable provided that the tread is serrated or is of a definite slip-resistant design. Uniform color and texture are recommended for clear delineation of edges.

NOSING DESIGN

ANSI specifications recommend nosings without abrupt edges that project no more than 1½ in. beyond the edge of the riser. A safe stair uses a ½ in. radius abrasive nosing firmly anchored to the tread, with no overhangs and a clearly visible edge.

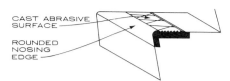

CAST ABRASIVE SURFACE

ROUNDED NOSING EDGE

PREFERRED CAST METAL ABRASIVE NOSING

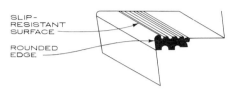

SLIP-RESISTANT SURFACE

ROUNDED EDGE

PREFERRED CAST METAL NOSING FOR CONCRETE STAIR

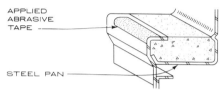

APPLIED ABRASIVE TAPE

STEEL PAN

PREFERRED ABRASIVE TAPE NOSING

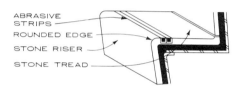

ABRASIVE STRIPS

ROUNDED EDGE

STONE RISER

STONE TREAD

PREFERRED STONE TREAD

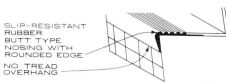

SLIP-RESISTANT RUBBER BUTT TYPE NOSING WITH ROUNDED EDGE

NO TREAD OVERHANG

PREFERRED VINYL OR RUBBER NOSING

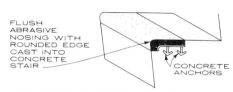

FLUSH ABRASIVE NOSING WITH ROUNDED EDGE CAST INTO CONCRETE STAIR

CONCRETE ANCHORS

PREFERRED ABRASIVE EPOXY

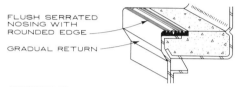

FLUSH SERRATED NOSING WITH ROUNDED EDGE

GRADUAL RETURN

PREFERRED STEEL SUBTREAD

EXTRUDED NOSING WITH ROUNDED EDGE

NO ABRUPT OVERHANG

PREFERRED ALUMINUM NOSING

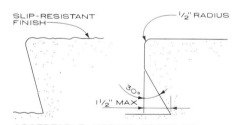

SLIP-RESISTANT FINISH

½" RADIUS

1½" MAX   30°

ACCEPTABLE NOSING PROFILES

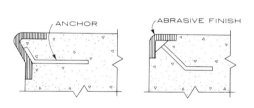

ANCHOR   ABRASIVE FINISH

PREFERRED CAST NOSINGS FOR CONCRETE

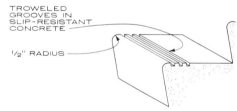

TROWELED GROOVES IN SLIP-RESISTANT CONCRETE

½" RADIUS

PREFERRED CONCRETE TREAD

DESIGN OF A "SAFE" STAIR, USABLE BY THE PHYSICALLY HANDICAPPED

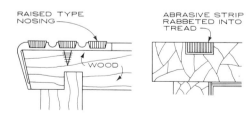

RAISED TYPE NOSING

ABRASIVE STRIP RABBETED INTO TREAD

WOOD

OTHER ALUMINUM NOSINGS WITH ABRASIVE FILLER

NOTE

Abrasive materials are used as treads, nosings, or inlay strips for new work and as surface-mounted replacement treads for old work. A homogeneous epoxy abrasive is cured on an extruded aluminum base for a smoother surface, or it is used as a filler between aluminum ribs.

NOTE

Cast nosings for concrete stairs are iron, aluminum, or bronze, custom-made to exact size. Nosings and treads come with factory-drilled countersunk holes, with riveted strap anchors, or with wing-type anchors.

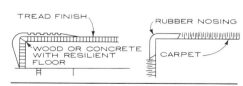

TREAD FINISH   RUBBER NOSING

WOOD OR CONCRETE WITH RESILIENT FLOOR   CARPET

OTHER SLIP-RESISTANT VINYL AND RUBBER NOSINGS

TREAD FINISH

OTHER EXTRUDED ALUMINUM NOSINGS

Olga Barmine; Darrel Downing Rippeteau, Architect; Washington, D.C.
Krommenhoek/McKeown & Associates; San Diego, California

METAL FABRICATIONS

NOMINAL AND MINIMUM DRESSED SIZES OF LUMBER PRODUCTS (IN.)
The thicknesses apply to all widths and all widths to all thicknesses.

LUMBER PRODUCT	THICKNESSES			FACE WIDTHS		
	NOMINAL	MINIMUM DRESSED DRY	MINIMUM DRESSED GREEN	NOMINAL	MINIMUM DRESSED DRY	MINIMUM DRESSED GREEN
Boards				2	$1^1/_2$	$1^9/_{16}$
				3	$2^1/_2$	$2^9/_{16}$
				4	$3^1/_2$	$3^9/_{16}$
				5	$4^1/_2$	$4^5/_8$
	1	$3/_4$	$25/_{32}$	6	$5^1/_2$	$5^5/_8$
				7	$6^1/_2$	$6^5/_8$
	$1^1/_4$	1	$1^1/_{32}$	8	$7^1/_4$	$7^1/_2$
				9	$8^1/_4$	$8^1/_2$
	$1^1/_2$	$1^1/_4$	$1^9/_{32}$	10	$9^1/_4$	$9^1/_2$
				11	$10^1/_4$	$10^1/_2$
				12	$11^1/_4$	$11^1/_2$
				14	$13^1/_4$	$13^1/_2$
				16	$15^1/_4$	$15^1/_2$
Dimension lumber				2	$1^1/_2$	$1^9/_{16}$
				3	$2^1/_2$	$2^9/_{16}$
				4	$3^1/_2$	$3^9/_{16}$
	2	$1^1/_2$	$1^9/_{16}$	5	$4^1/_2$	$4^5/_8$
	$2^1/_2$	2	$2^1/_{16}$	6	$5^1/_2$	$5^5/_8$
	3	$2^1/_2$	$2^9/_{16}$	8	$7^1/_4$	$7^1/_2$
	$3^1/_2$	3	$3^1/_{16}$	10	$9^1/_4$	$9^1/_2$
				12	$11^1/_4$	$11^1/_2$
				14	$13^1/_4$	$13^1/_2$
				16	$15^1/_4$	$15^1/_2$
				2	$1^1/_2$	$1^9/_{16}$
				3	$2^1/_2$	$2^9/_{16}$
				4	$3^1/_2$	$3^9/_{16}$
				5	$4^1/_2$	$4^5/_8$
	4	$3^1/_2$	$3^9/_{16}$	6	$5^1/_2$	$5^5/_8$
	$4^1/_2$	4	$4^1/_{16}$	8	$7^1/_4$	$7^1/_2$
				10	$9^1/_4$	$9^1/_2$
				12	$11^1/_4$	$11^1/_2$
				14		$13^1/_2$
				16		$15^1/_2$
Timbers	5 and thicker		$1/_2$ off	5 and wider		$1/_2$ off
Shiplap $3/_8$" lap				4	$3^1/_8$	$3^3/_{16}$
				6	$5^1/_8$	$5^1/_4$
				8	$6^7/_8$	$7^1/_8$
	1	$3/_4$	$25/_{32}$	10	$8^7/_8$	$9^1/_8$
				12	$10^7/_8$	$11^1/_8$
				14	$12^7/_8$	$13^1/_8$
				16	$14^7/_8$	$15^1/_8$
Shiplap $1/_2$" lap				4	3	$3^1/_{16}$
				6	5	$5^1/_8$
				8	$6^3/_4$	7
	1	$3/_4$	$25/_{32}$	10	$8^3/_4$	9
				12	$10^3/_4$	11
				14	$12^3/_4$	13
				16	$14^3/_4$	15
Centermatch $1/_4$" tongue				4	$3^1/_8$	$3^3/_{16}$
				5	$4^1/_8$	$4^1/_4$
	1	$3/_4$	$25/_{32}$	6	$5^1/_8$	$5^1/_4$
	$1^1/_4$	1	$1^1/_{32}$	8	$6^7/_8$	$7^1/_8$
	$1^1/_2$	$1^1/_4$	$1^9/_{32}$	10	$8^7/_8$	$9^1/_8$
				12	$10^7/_8$	$11^1/_8$
2" dressed and matched $3/_8$" tongue				4	3	$3^1/_{16}$
				6	5	$5^1/_8$
	2	$1^1/_2$	$1^9/_{16}$	8	$6^3/_4$	7
				10	$8^3/_4$	9
				12	$10^3/_4$	11
2" shiplap $1/_2$" lap				4	3	$3^1/_{16}$
				6	5	$5^1/_8$
	2	$1^1/_2$	$1^9/_{16}$	8	$6^3/_4$	7
				10	$8^3/_4$	9
				12	$10^3/_4$	11

NOTE: For dry lumber moisture content is 19% or less and for green lumber moisture content is in excess of 19%.

NOMINAL AND MINIMUM DRESSED DRY SIZES OF LUMBER PRODUCTS (IN.)
The thicknesses apply to all widths and all widths to all thicknesses.

LUMBER PRODUCT	THICKNESSES		FACE WIDTHS	
	NOMINAL	MINIMUM DRESSED	NOMINAL	MINIMUM DRESSED
Finish	$3/_8$	$5/_{16}$	2	$1^1/_2$
	$1/_2$	$7/_{16}$	3	$2^1/_2$
	$5/_8$	$9/_{16}$	4	$3^1/_2$
	$3/_4$	$5/_8$	5	$4^1/_2$
	1	$3/_4$	6	$5^1/_2$
	$1^1/_4$	1	7	$6^1/_2$
	$1^1/_2$	$1^1/_4$	8	$7^1/_4$
	$1^3/_4$	$1^3/_8$	9	$8^1/_4$
	2	$1^1/_2$	10	$9^1/_4$
	$2^1/_2$	2	11	$10^1/_4$
	3	$2^1/_2$	12	$11^1/_4$
	$3^1/_2$	3	14	$13^1/_4$
	4	$3^1/_2$	16	$15^1/_4$
Flooring; dimension given is face dimension excluding tongue	$3/_8$	$5/_{16}$	2	$1^1/_8$
	$1/_2$	$7/_{16}$	3	$2^1/_8$
	$5/_8$	$9/_{16}$	4	$3^1/_8$
	1	$3/_4$	5	$4^1/_8$
	$1^1/_4$	1	6	$5^1/_8$
	$1^1/_2$	$1^1/_4$		
Ceiling	$3/_8$	$5/_{16}$	3	$2^1/_8$
	$1/_2$	$7/_{16}$	4	$3^1/_8$
	$5/_8$	$9/_{16}$	5	$4^1/_8$
	$3/_4$	$11/_{16}$	6	$5^1/_8$
Partition			3	$2^1/_8$
	1	$23/_{32}$	4	$3^1/_8$
			5	$4^1/_8$
			6	$5^1/_8$
Stepping	1	$3/_4$	8	$7^1/_4$
	$1^1/_4$	1	10	$9^1/_4$
	$1^1/_2$	$1^1/_4$	12	$11^1/_4$
	2	$1^1/_2$		
Bevel siding	$1/_2$	$7/_{16}$ butt, $3/_{16}$ tip	4	$3^1/_2$
	$9/_{16}$	$15/_{32}$ butt, $3/_{16}$ tip	5	$4^1/_2$
	$5/_8$	$9/_{16}$ butt, $3/_{16}$ tip	6	$5^1/_2$
	$3/_4$	$11/_{16}$ butt, $3/_{16}$ tip	8	$7^1/_4$
	1	$3/_4$ butt, $3/_{16}$ tip	10	$9^1/_4$
			12	$11^1/_4$
Bungalow siding			8	$7^1/_4$
	$3/_4$	$11/_{16}$ butt, $3/_{16}$ tip	10	$9^1/_4$
			12	$11^1/_4$
Rustic and drop siding shiplapped $3/_8$"	$5/_8$	$9/_{16}$	4	3
	1	$23/_{32}$	5	4
			6	5
Rustic and drop siding shiplapped $1/_2$"			4	$2^7/_8$
			5	$3^7/_8$
	$5/_8$	$9/_{16}$	6	$4^7/_8$
	1	$23/_{32}$	8	$6^5/_8$
			10	$8^5/_8$
			12	$10^5/_8$
Rustic and drop siding dressed and matched			4	$3^1/_8$
	$5/_8$	$9/_{16}$	5	$4^1/_8$
	1	$23/_{32}$	6	$5^1/_8$
			8	$6^7/_8$
			10	$8^7/_8$

NOTE: Maximum moisture content is 19%.

NOTE

For additional information reference should be made to the National Bureau of Standards, Product Standard PS20-70 American Softwood Lumber Standard. Available through U.S. Government Printing Office.

NOTE

Wood is preserved by pressure treatment with an EPA registered pesticide to protect it from insect attack and decay. Treated wood should be used only where such protection is required. Exposure to preservatives may present certain hazards. Precautions should be taken in handling, using, and disposing of treated wood. Refer to local codes.

DECAY AND INSECT RESISTANT WOOD

WOLMANIZED PRESSURE TREATED WOOD AND OUTDOOR BRAND WOOD

Wolmanized wood has been pressure treated with a water solution of preservative chemicals. Has outstanding durability under any condition of exposure. Use is limited to the treatment of fully air seasoned or kiln dried material. Wolman salts, the preservative used, impart a light green, blue-green, or brownish color to the wood, depending on the species. Wolmanized wood weathers to a silver gray.

1. GENERAL USE: In the ground; in water; in contact with masonry, or when the wood will be exposed to wetting.
2. SPECIFIC USE: Decks, patios, walkways, fences, boat docks, sill plates, soffits, fascia, all weather wood foundations, pole houses, and pole buildings.
3. ADVANTAGES: Provides lasting protection against decay producing fungi and insects. Clean, oil free. Odorless. Can be painted or stained. Preservative chemicals are fiberfixed in the wood to prevent leaching. Harmless to people, plants, and animals.
4. LIMITATIONS: Air seasoning or kiln drying is required after treatment to make Wolmanized lumber paintable and to guard further against shrinkage in service. Moisture content should be 19% or less. Because undercoated steel rusts quickly, nails or bolts should be galvanized.

CELLON PRESSURE TREATED WOOD

The Cellon pressure treatment process utilizes liquefied butane gas as a solvent to carry pentachlorophenol, the preservative, deep into the wood. After treatment, the solvent is evaporated. Particularly suitable for treating hardwoods and all plywoods.

1. GENERAL USE: Ground contact, in contact with masonry, or when the wood will be exposed to wetting.
2. SPECIFIC USE: Glued laminated beams, lighting standards, pole houses and pole buildings, decking.
3. ADVANTAGES: Provides lasting protection against decay producing fungi and insects. Clean and dry to the touch. Can be painted, stained, and glued. Since neither water nor oil is used in the Cellon process, air seasoning and kiln drying are not required after treatment. Retains the wood's original texture and color. Weathers naturally.
4. LIMITATIONS: Will not protect against attack from marine organisms. Certain species such as Douglas fir, southern pine, and ponderosa pine may exude resin from knots and heartwood after treatment. Wood rich in tannin, such as redwood and oak, may develop a blue-black surface stain if the lumber has not been well seasoned prior to treatment; however, the sun's rays will bleach out the stain in several months.

PENTACHLOROPHENOL PRESSURE TREATED WOOD

Pentachlorophenol is the principal preservative in the "oil borne" category. Toxic to insects and fungi.

1. GENERAL USE: In the ground.
2. SPECIFIC USE: Industrial and farm buildings; fence posts.
3. ADVANTAGES: Protects against fungi and insect attack. Seasoned hardwoods and softwoods can be treated without fear of grain raising, checking, or splitting.
4. LIMITATIONS: Penta treated forest products may become blotchy when exposed to the weather; this condition disappears after extended service. Penta-in-oil treated wood would NOT be used as a subflooring, or in contact with materials subject to staining (plaster, wallboard). Not readily paintable; would not be used in direct contact with roofing felt, since it can cause the tar to drip. Not recommended for use in saltwater.

CREOSOTE

Creosote is the oldest commercial wood preservative currently being used. It has demonstrated, through years of actual service, outstanding durability, dependability, and general utility. Creosote contains a multitude of chemical compounds which are toxic to fungi, insects, and most marine organisms. Average life expectancy of a creosoted wood pole in the ground is 35 to 40 years, but some creosoted poles are still standing fast after more than 75 years of rugged service.

1. GENERAL USE: In the ground and in water.
2. SPECIFIC USE: Foundation piles, landscape ties, fence posts, highway guard rails, marine piling, and bulkheads.
3. ADVANTAGES: Creosote is a coal tar product that derives its effectiveness from its persistent high toxicity to wood destroying insects and fungi. Creosote effectively protects wood from the ravages of most marine organisms.
4. LIMITATIONS: Pressure creosoted lumber should NOT be used as a subflooring or in contact with materials subject to staining (plaster, wallboard). It is not readily paintable, and should not be used in direct contact with roofing felt, since it can cause the tar to drip.

CORROSION RESISTANT WOOD

KP RESIN IMPREGNATED WOOD

KP resin impregnated wood has been impregnated with a phenolic resin solution to obtain a high degree of acid resistance and excellent dimensional stability. The treatment is limited to southern pine, hard maple, cativo, and kempas. Natural wood color.

1. GENERAL USE: Where corrosion resistance or dimensional stability is required.
2. SPECIFIC USE: Filter press plates and frames, flumes, stacks, tank covers, tanks, troughs and trays, die models.
3. ADVANTAGES: High degree of acid resistance. Dimensional stability far greater than untreated wood. Can be machined. Gouging the surface does not reduce the protection.
4. LIMITATIONS: Should not be exposed to alkaline solutions, aniline, chlorine gas, strong bleaching solutions, strong oxidizing acids.

ASIDBAR IMPREGNATED WOOD

Asidbar impregnated wood has been impregnated with topped coal tar material that provides the natural structural properties of wood as well as the chemical resistant properties of coal tar composites. Color is coal-tar black. Treatment is for southern pine lumber, and southern pine and Douglas fir plywood.

1. GENERAL USE: Where corrosion resistance is required.
2. SPECIFIC USE: Beams, interior wall cladding, decking, effluent systems, platforms, roof systems, walkways.
3. ADVANTAGES: High degree of acid resistance. Gouging of surface does not reduce the protection.
4. LIMITATIONS: Tends to soften and expand in severe temperatures above 130°F. Not suitable for use with acetate solvents, benzene or benzol, ethers, trichloroethylene, xylene, or xylol.

FIRE RETARDANT TREATED WOOD

NON-COM FIRE RETARDANT TREATED WOOD

Non-Com fire retardant treated wood is used indoors where the relative humidity is normally below 80%. The wood is pressure impregnated with inorganic salts that react chemically at temperatures below the ignition point of untreated wood. This chemical reaction reduces the flammable vapors emitted by wood subjected to fire. A protective char is formed and wood underneath remains structurally sound longer than untreated and surface treated wood.

1. CLASSIFIED: Non-Com fire retardant treated lumber and plywood have an Underwriters' Laboratories designated rating of FRS, which means that the material has a fire hazard classification of 25 or less for flame spread, fuel contributed, and smoke developed, and shows no sign of progressive combustion when the 10 minute fire hazard classification test is continued for an additional 20 minutes.
2. APPROVED: The Factory Mutual Engineering Division, the Factory Insurance Association, all state insurance rating bureaus, and all branches of the Insurance Services Office frequently permit the use of Non-Com fire retardant treated wood as an alternative to materials classified as noncombustible.
3. GENERAL USE: In buildings (interior).
4. SPECIFIC USE: Studs, wall plates, and fire stops with metal lath and plaster or drywall construction of interior nonbearing walls and partitions in fire resistive buildings. Roof systems including deck, purlins, and joists.
5. ADVANTAGES: Reduces flame spread and fuel contributed. Requires no maintenance to retain its fire retardant properties. Can be installed by regular carpenter crews. Low sound transmission makes it an excellent product for remodeling as well as for new construction.
6. LIMITATIONS: If Non-Com is to be painted, sealed, or varnished, it must be kiln dried to a maximum moisture content of 12%. Not recommended for use in the ground or for exposed locations that are subject to weathering or humidity normally above 80%. At jobsite, dry lumber should be stored indoors if possible. Otherwise, it should be stored on raised platforms and covered with suitable weatherproof protective covering such as tarpaulins or polyethylene film. NOTE: NCX fire retardant treated wood is recommended for architectural appearance applications.

NCX FIRE RETARDANT TREATED WOOD

NCX fire retardant treated wood is used outside or where the relative humidity is frequently above 80%. The wood is pressure impregnated with a fire retardant monomeric resin solution. After impregnation, the wood is kiln dried to cure the chemicals in the wood. The cured chemicals in the wood are not affected by direct outdoor weather exposure and high humidity.

1. CLASSIFIED: NCX fire retardant treated lumber and plywood have an Underwriters' Laboratories designated rating of FRS, which means that the material has a fire hazard classification of 25 or less for flame spread, fuel contributed, and smoke developed, and shows no sign of progressive combustion when the 10 minute fire hazard classification test is continued for an additional 20 minutes.
2. APPROVED: The Factory Mutual Engineering Division, the Factory Insurance Association, all state insurance rating bureaus, and all branches of the Insurance Services Office frequently permit the use of NCX as an alternative to materials classified as noncombustible.
3. RECOGNIZED: For certain applications by numerous state and city building codes. Also by BOCA, ICBO, SBCC, Southern Standard, AIA, and American Insurance Association.
4. GENERAL USE: Exterior use and where humidity is frequently above 80%. Also, interior appearance applications.
5. SPECIFIC USE: Balconies and steps. Roof systems. Soffit and fascia. Architectural hardwood molding and paneling. Western red cedar shingles and shakes.
6. ADVANTAGES: Suitable for exposure to the weather or high humidity conditions. Clear architectural finishes can be applied without causing below-film blushes.
7. LIMITATIONS: Although NCX wood has excellent weathering characteristics, it is not recommended for use in the ground or in ground contact. Treatment may darken wood slightly, but basic tone or hue remains almost unchanged. Treated wood may show sticker marks after drying. Underwriters' Laboratories permits milling of some species after drying. Where marks are objectionable, milling is recommended.

Derek Martin, FAIA; Pittsburgh, Pennsylvania
Domenic F. Valente, AIA; D. F. Valente, Architect & Planner; Medford, Massachusetts

WOOD TREATMENT

MAJOR COMPONENTS

The major components of a good joint seal are the substrate, primer, joint filler, bond breaker, and sealant.

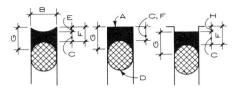

A — sealant
B — sealant width
C — sealant depth
D — joint-filler
E — tooling depth
F — joint-filler depth
G — sealant contact depth
H — sealant recess depth

TYPICAL VERTICAL APPLICATIONS, PROFILES, AND TERMINOLOGY

SUBSTRATE

The more common substrates are masonry concrete, metal, and glass. These are generally classified as porous or nonporous.

Some substrates may not be suitable for achieving a bond unless treated mechanically, chemically, or both.

When the substrate has a coating, the coating must be compatible with the sealant and its bond to the substrate and sealant must be adequate.

Proprietary treatments or protective coatings on metal and waterproofing or water-repellent treatments on concrete may inhibit bonding. Consult both substrate and sealant manufacturers for suitable joint preparation methods and the primers to be used before applying joint materials. Adhesion testing of trial applications in the field is recommended.

Surface laitance and incompatible or bond-inhibiting form release agents on concrete surfaces must be removed.

Substrates must be clean, dry, sound, and free of loose particles, contaminants, foreign matter, water-soluble material, and frost.

Joints in masonry and concrete should be sealed before cleaning exposed surfaces and applying required protective barriers.

PRIMER

The purpose of a primer is to improve the adhesion of a sealant to a substrate. Many sealants require primers on all substrates, some on only certain substrates or on none at all. Most require a primer for maximum adhesion to concrete and masonry surfaces.

JOINT FILLERS

A joint filler is used to control the depth of sealant in the joint and permit full wetting of the intended interface when tooled.

Some joint fillers may be incompatible with the substrate and sealant, causing stains on either one of them or both. Some may be factory coated with a suitable material that provides a barrier to staining. To confirm its suitability, the barrier coating should be acceptable to both the sealant and joint filler manufacturers.

Joint fillers for vertical application may be flexible, compatible, closed cell plastic foam or sponge rubber rod stock and elastomeric tubing of such materials as neoprene, butyl, and EPDM. They should resist permanent deformation before and during sealant application, be nonabsorbent to water or gas, and resist flowing upon mild heating, since this can cause bubbling of the sealant. Open cell sponge type materials such as urethane foam may be satisfactory provided that their water absorption characteristics are recognized. The sealant should be applied immediately after joint filler placement to prevent water absorption from rain. Elastomeric tubing of neoprene, butyl, or EPDM may be applied immediately as a temporary seal until the primary sealant is

put in place, after which they serve to a limited degree as a secondary water barrier. When used as temporary seals, joint fillers should be able to remain resilient at temperatures down to −15°F and have low compression set.

Joint fillers for horizontal application for floors, pavements, sidewalks, patios, and other light-traffic areas may be compatible, extruded, closed cell, high density, flexible foams, corkboard, resin-impregnated fiberboard, or elastomeric tubing or rods. These joint fillers should remain resilient down to −15°F, exhibit good recovery, not cause the sealant to bubble in the joint because of heat, and be capable of supporting the sealant in traffic areas. They should not exude liquids under compression, which could hydraulically cause sealant failure by forcing the sealant from the joint. Combinations of joint filler may be used to form a joint in concrete, and an additional joint filler material may be installed under compression across the width and to the proper depth just before the sealant is applied to provide a clean, dry, compatible backup.

BOND BREAKER

A bond breaker may be necessary to prevent adhesion of the sealant to any surface or material where such adhesion would be detrimental to the performance of the sealant.

The use of a joint filler to which the sealant will not adhere may preclude the need for a bond breaker.

The bond breaker may be a polyethylene tape with pressure-sensitive adhesive on one side or various liquid applied compounds, as recommended by the sealant manufacturer.

SEALANT

Sealants are classified as single component or multicomponent, nonsag or self-leveling, and traffic or nontraffic use, as well as according to movement capability. Characteristics of some generic types are listed in the accompanying table.

CHARACTERISTICS OF COMMON ELASTOMERIC SEALANTS

	ACRYLIC (SOLVENT RELEASES) (ONE-PART)	POLYSULFIDE		POLYURETHANE		SILICONE (ONE-PART)
		TWO-PART	ONE-PART	TWO-PART	ONE-PART	
Chief ingredients	Acrylic terpolymer, inert pigments, stabilizer, and selected fillers	Polysulfide polymers, activators, pigments, plasticizers, inert fillers, gelling, and curing agents		Polyurethane prepolymer, inert fillers, pigment, plasticizers, accelerators, activators, and extenders	Polyurethane prepolymer, inert fillers, pigment, and plasticizers	Siloxane polymer, pigment, and selected fillers
Percent solids	85–95	95–100	95–100	95–100	95–100	95–100
Curing process	Solvent release and very slow chemical cure	Chemical reaction with curing agent	Chemical reaction with moisture in the air	Chemical reaction with curing agent	Chemical reaction with moisture in air, also oxygen	Chemical reaction with moisture in air
Curing characteristics	Skins on exposed surface; interior remains soft and tacky	Cures uniformly throughout; rate affected by temperature and humidity	Skins over, cures progressively inward; final cure uniform throughout	Cures uniformly throughout; rate affected by temperature and humidity	Skins over, cures progressively inward; final cure uniform throughout	Cures progressively inward; final cure uniform throughout
Primer	Generally not required	Manufacturer's approved primer required for porous surfaces, sometimes for other surfaces		Manufacturer's approved primer required for most surfaces		Required for most surfaces
Application temperature (°F)	40–120	40–100	60–100	40–120	40–120	0–120
Tackfree time	1–7 days	6–24 hr	6–72 hr	1–24 hr	Slightly tacky until weathered	1 hr or less
Hardness, Shore A Cured 1 to 6 months Aged 5 years	0–25 45–55	15–45 30–60	25–35 40–50	20–40 35–55	25–45 30–50	20–40 35–55
Toxicity	Nontoxic	Curing agent is toxic	Contains toxic ingredients	Toxic; gloves recommended for handling		Nontoxic
Cure time (days)	14	7	14–21	3–5	14	5
Joint movement capability (max.)	±12.5%	±25%	±15%	±25%	±15%	±25% high modulus ±50% low modulus
Ultraviolet resistance (direct)	Very good	Poor to good	Good	Poor to good	Poor to good	Excellent
Dirt resistance cured	Good	Good	Good	Good	Good	Poor
Use characteristics	Excellent adhesion; poor low-temperature flexibility; not usable in traffic areas; unpleasant odor 5–12 days	Wide range of appropriate applications; curing time depends on temperature and humidity	Unpleasant odor; broad range of cured hardnesses available	Sets very fast; broad range of cured hardnesses; excellent for concrete joints and traffic areas	Excellent for concrete joints and traffic areas, but substrate must be absolutely dry; short package stability	Requires contact with air for curing; low abrasion resistance; not tough enough for use in traffic areas

Charles J. Parise, FAIA, FASTM; Smith, Hinchman & Grylls Associates, Inc.; Detroit, Michigan

JOINT DESIGN

The design geometry of a joint seal is related to numerous factors including desired appearance, spacing of joints, anticipated movement in joint, movement capability of sealant to be used, required sealant width to accommodate anticipated movement, and tooling method.

SEALANT WIDTH

The required width of the sealant relative to thermal movement is determined by the application temperature range of the sealant, the temperature extremes anticipated at the site location, the temperature at the time of sealant application, and the movement capability of the sealant to be used. in the absence of specific application temperature knowledge, an ambient application temperature from 4 to 38°C (40 to 100°F) should be assumed in determining the anticipated amount of joint movement in the design of joints. Although affected by ambient temperatures, anticipated joint movement must be determined from anticipated building material temperature extremes rather than ambient temperature extremes.

The accompanying graph provides an average working relationship of recommended joint widths for sealants with various movement capabilities based only on thermal expansion of the more common substrates. These joint widths should be considered as minimal. They do not take into consideration variations in joint dimensions encountered during construction or temperature extremes at the time of sealant application. It is advisable to consider these variables and to also incorporate a safety factor (s.f.) into the joint design by only using a percentage of the stated sealant movement capability, since sealants do not always perform at their stated maximum capabilities.

Many other factors can be involved in building joint movement including, but not limited to, material mass, color, insulation, wind loads, settlement, thermal conductivity, differential thermal stress (bowing), residual growth or shrinkage of materials, building sway, and seismic forces. Of particular importance are material and construction tolerances that can produce joints on the

job site smaller than anticipated. The design joint width should be calculated taking all possible movement and tolerance factors into consideration, as shown with the following examples:

$$J = \text{minimum joint width (inches)}$$
$$= \frac{100}{X}(M_t + M_o) + T$$

X = percentage of stated movement capability of the sealant by ASTM Test Method C719

M_t = joint movement due to thermal expansion of substrates (inches)

$$= (E_c)(\Delta_t)(L)$$

where E_c = coefficient of expansion of substrate from accompanying table (in./in./°F)

Δ_t = temperature change of substrate (°F)

L = substrate length (inches)

M_o = joint movement due to other factors (inches)

T = tolerances for construction (inches)

A sample calculation for joint width between concrete panels of 10 ft lengths, expecting a temperature change in the concrete of 120°F, construction tolerances of 0.25 in., and sealed with a sealant capable of a maximum ±25% (reduced to 20% for s.f.) movement is

$$J = \frac{100}{X}M_t + T$$
$$= \frac{100}{X}(E_c)(\Delta_t)(L) + T$$
$$= \frac{100}{20}(6 \times 10^{-6}\text{ in./in./°F})(120°F)(120\text{ in.})$$
$$+ 0.25\text{ in.}$$
$$= 0.68\text{ in.}$$

A more simplified method (but not as accurate) is to use the accompanying graph as follows:

$$J = (\text{joint width scaled}) + T$$
$$= (0.5\text{ in./in./°F})\left(\frac{120°F}{130°F}\right) + 0.25\text{ in.}$$
$$= 0.71\text{ in.}$$

SEALANT DEPTH

The sealant depth, when applied, depends on the sealant width. The following guidelines are normally accepted practice.

1. For a recommended minimum width of ¼ in., the depth should by ¼ in.

2. For joints in concrete, masonry, or stone, the depth of the sealant may be equal to the sealant width in joints up to ½ in. wide. For joints ½ to 1 in. wide, the sealant depth should be one-half the width. For joints 1 to 2 in. wide, the sealant depth should not be greater than ½ in. For widths exceeding 2 in., the depth should be determined by the sealant manufacturer.

3. For sealant widths over ¼ in. and up to ½ in. in metal, glass, and other nonporous surface joints, the minimum of ¼ in. in depth applies, and over ½ in. in width the sealant depth shold be one-half the sealant width and should in no case exceed ½ in.

When determining location of the joint filler in the joint, consideration should be given to the reduction in sealant depth with concave and recessed tooled joints, and the joint should be designed accordingly.

COEFFICIENTS OF EXPANSION

| MATERIALS | AVERAGE COEFFICIENT OF LINEAR EXPANSION (MULTIPLY BY 10^{-6}) | |
	CENTIGRADE (MM/MM/°C)	FAHRENHEIT (IN./IN./°F)
Aluminum:		
5005 or 6061 alloy	23.8	13.2
Brass:		
230 alloy	18.7	10.4
Bronze:		
220 alloy	18.4	10.2
385 alloy	20.9	11.6
Clay masonry:		
Clay or shale brick	6.5	3.6
Fire clay brick or tile	4.5	2.5
Concrete masonry:		
Dense aggregate	9.4	5.2
Lightweight aggregate	7.7	4.3
Concrete:		
Calcareous aggregate	9.0	5.0
Siliceous aggregate	10.8	6.0
Quartzite aggregate	12.6	7.0
Copper:		
110 alloy	16.9	9.4
122 alloy	16.9	9.4
Glass	8.8	4.9
Iron:		
Cast, gray	10.6	5.9
Wrought	12.1	6.7
Lead	28.6	15.9
Plastic:		
Acrylic sheet	74.0	41.0
High-impact acrylic sheet	50.0	82.0
Polycarbonate sheet	68.4	38.0
Steel, Carbon	12.1	6.7
Steel, Stainless:		
301 alloy	16.9	9.4
302 alloy	17.3	9.6
304 alloy	17.3	9.6
316 alloy	16.0	8.9
Stone:		
Granite	5.0–11.0	2.8– 6.1
Limestone	4.0–12.0	2.2– 6.7
Marble	6.7–22.1	3.7–12.3
Sandstone	8.0–12.0	4.4– 6.7
Slate	8.0–10.0	4.4– 5.6
Travertine	6.0–10.0	3.3– 5.6
Zinc	32.4	18.0

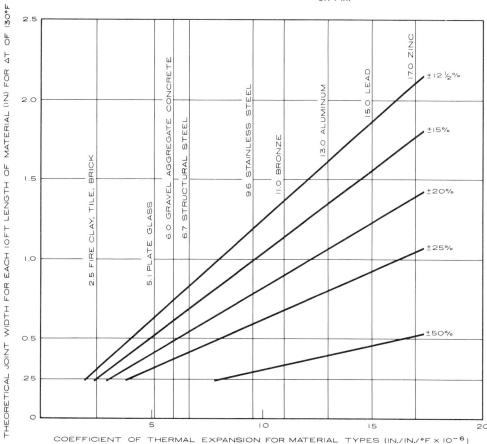

RECOMMENDED JOINT WIDTH FOR SEALANTS WITH VARIOUS MOVEMENT CAPABILITIES

Charles J. Parise, FAIA, FASTM; Smith, Hinchman & Grylls Associates, Inc.; Detroit, Michigan

APPLICATION

To obtain proper adhesion, it is essential that the sealant come in direct contact with the substrate, that the sealant wet the surface of the substrate, and that the substrate be strong enough to provide a firm anchor for the sealant. If any of these conditions is not met, poor adhesion will usually result. The sealant should be installed in such a manner as to completely fill the recess provided in the joint.

Against a porous material, the sealant must enter the pores if good adhesion is to be obtained. Sealants used for this application are thixotropic and will resist flow into the pores unless an external force is applied. Proper filling of the recess accomplishes this, in part, and proper tooling ensures it.

JOINT PREPARATION

Joints to receive sealant should be cleaned out and raked to full width and depth required for installation of joint seal materials. Thoroughly clean all joints, removing all foreign matter such as dust, paint (unless it is a permanent protective coating), oil, grease, waterproofing or water-repellent treatments, water, surface dirt, and frost. Clean porous materials such as concrete, masonry, and unglazed surfaces of ceramic tile by brushing, grinding, blast cleaning, mechanical abrading, acid washing, or a combination of these methods to provide a clean, sound substrate for optimum sealant adhesion. The surface of concrete may be cut back to remove contaminants and expose a clean surface when acceptable to the purchaser.

Remove laitance from concrete by acid washing, grinding, or mechanical abrading and remove form oils from concrete by blast cleaning. Remove loose particles originally present or resulting from grinding, abrading, or blast cleaning by blowing out joints with oil-free compressed air (or vacuuming) prior to application of primer or sealant.

Clean nonporous surfaces, such as metal, glass, porcelain enamel, and glazed surfaces of ceramic tile chemically or by other means that are not harmful to the substrate and are acceptable to the substrate manufacturer.

Remove temporary protective coatings on metallic surfaces by a solvent that leaves no residue. Apply the solvent with clean oil-free cloths or lintless paper towels. Do not dip cleaning cloths into solvent. Always pour the solvent on the cloth to eliminate the possibility of contaminating the solvent. Do not allow the solvent to air-dry without wiping. Wipe dry with a clean dry cloth or lintless paper towels. Permanent coatings that are to remain must not be removed or damaged.

MASKING TAPE

Install masking tape at joint edges when necessary to avoid undesirable sealant smears on exposed visible surfaces. Use a nonstaining, nonabsorbent, compatible type.

PRIMER AND JOINT FILLER

Install primer when and as recommended by the sealant manufacturer for optimum adhesion.

Install compatible joint filler uniformly to proper depth without twisting and braiding.

SEALANT

Install sealant in strict accordance with the manufacturer's recommendations and precautions. Completely fill the recess provided in the joint. Sealants are more safely applied at temperatures above 40°F. Joints must be dry.

TOOLING

Tooling nonsag sealants is essential to force the sealant into the joint and eliminate air pockets and should be done as soon as possible after application and before

skinning or curing begins. Tooling also ensures contact of the sealant to the sides of a joint.

Plastic or metal tools may be used. Most applicators use dry tools, but they may be surface-treated to prevent adhesion to the sealant and may be shaped as desired to produce the desired joint profile. Dipping tools in certain liquids decreases adhesion of the sealant to the tool. All liquids should first be tested and accepted for use by the manufacturer. The use of some liquids may result in surface discoloration. In using tooling liquids, care should be taken to ensure that the liquid does not contact joint surfaces prior to the sealant contacting the joint surface. If the sealant overlaps the area contaminated with the liquid, the sealant bond may be adversely affected.

Tool sealant so as to force it into the joint, eliminating air pockets and ensuring contact of the sealant with the sides of the joint. Use appropriate tool to provide a concave, flush, or recessed joint as required.

Immediately after tooling the joint, remove masking tape carefully, if used, without disturbing the sealant.

FIELD TESTING

In cases where the building joints are ready to receive sealant and the question of adhesion of the sealant to novel or untried surfaces arises, it is advisable to install the sealant in a 1.5-m (5 ft) length of joint as a test. It would be good practice to do this as a matter of standard procedure on most projects, even though unusual conditions are not suspected. Following instructions of the sealant manufacturer and using primer as and when recommended, install the sealant in the joint and examine for adhesion after cure to determine whether proper adhesion has been obtained.

Reference: ASTM C-962 "Standard Guide for Use of Elastomeric Joint Sealants." Highlights of text, graph, and figures are reprinted with permission from ASTM Committee C-24 of the American Society for Testing and Materials.

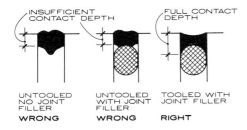

PURPOSE FOR JOINT FILLER AND TOOLING

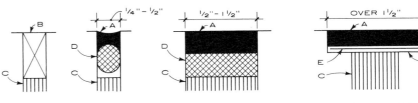

A — sealant
B — removable joint filler
C — premolded joint filler cast in concrete
D — joint filler installed under compression

E — bond breaker (use over sliding metal support in relatively wide joints)
F — concrete shoulder provides vertical support

USE OF MULTIPLE JOINT FILLERS IN HORIZONTAL APPLICATIONS IN CAST-IN-PLACE CONCRETE

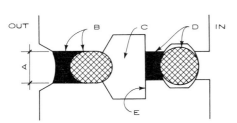

A — 1" minimum for access to interior air seal
B — sealant and joint filler preferred for rain screen; preformed compression seal also used
C — pressure equalization chamber; vent to outside, and chamber baffles at every second floor vertically and same distance horizontally
D — sealant and joint filler installed from outside to facilitate continuity of air seal; building framework hinders application of continuous air seal from interior
E — concrete shoulders required for tooling screed

TWO-STAGE PRESSURE EQUALIZED JOINT SEAL

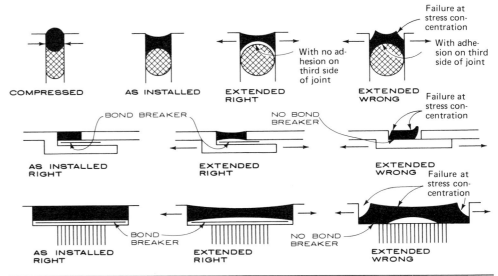

SEALANT CONFIGURATIONS WITH MOVEMENT AND EFFECT OF THREE-SIDED ADHESION

Charles J. Parise, FAIA, FASTM; Smith, Hinchman & Grylls Associates, Inc.; Detroit, Michigan

JOINT SEALER

CERAMIC MOSAIC TILE

Ceramic mosaic tile may be either natural clay or porcelain in composition. Special abrasive or slip-resistant surfaces and conductive tile are available only in 1 in. x 1 in. size. Nominal thickness is 1/4 in.

GLAZED WALL TILE

Traditional bright and matte glazed wall tile has been supplemented with tile of variegated appearance. Textured, sculptured, embossed, and engraved surface characteristics are coupled with accent designs. Imported tile has increased in availability, and it offers a wide range of variation from the native materials used in the manufacturing process as well as the process itself. Tile from Germany, France, Italy, Mexico, Switzerland, Austria, Brazil, and Spain currently are represented in manufacturer's literature. Nominal thickness is 5/16 in.

QUARRY AND PAVER TILE

Quarry and paver tile may be natural clay, shale, or porcelain in composition. These tile are characterized by their natural earth-tone coloration, high compressive strength, and slip and stain resistance. They are recommended for interior and exterior applications. Nominal thicknesses are 1/2 in. and 3/4 in. for quarry tile and 3/8 in. and 1/2 in. for paver tile.

NOTES

1. The trim diagram shows typical shapes available for portland cement mortar installations of glazed wall tile. Similar types are available for thin-set installations and for ceramic mosaic tile, quarry tile, and paver tile. See manufacturer's literature for exact shapes, colors, and glazes available.
2. Mounted tile assemblies (sometimes referred to as ready-set systems) are available for glazed tile and ceramic mosaic applications. These assemblies consist of either pregrouted sheets using flexible silicone grout or backmounted sheets that are finished with dry-set grout after installation. Both provide approximately 2 sq ft of coverage per sheet. They are designed to simplify installation and improve uniformity.
3. Ceramic bathroom accessories usually are supplied in sets that include bath and lavatory soap holders, roll-paper holder, towel post, and toothbrush tumbler holder. Designs include surface-mounted and fully recessed models. They may be used with both conventional mortar and thin-set tile installations. Colors and glazes are available to match or harmonize with glazed wall tiles.

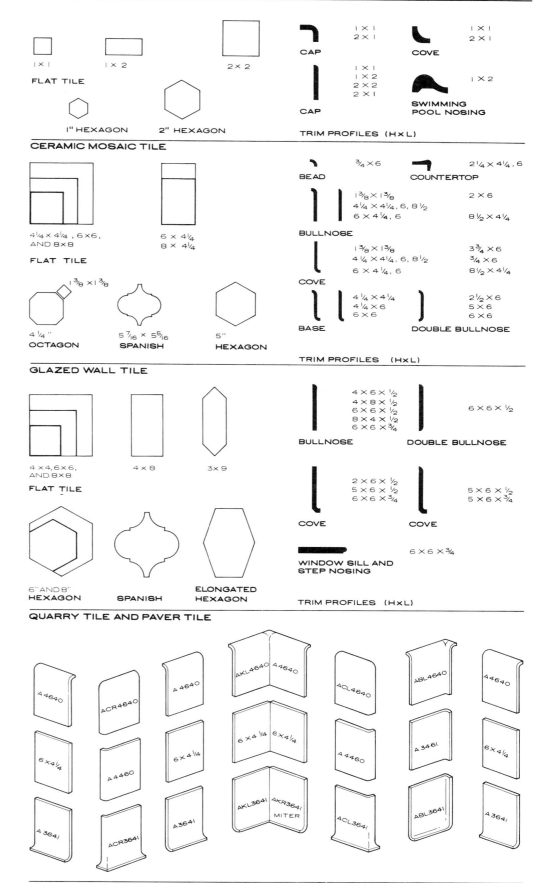

PORTLAND CEMENT MORTAR TRIM SHAPES
VERTICAL INSTALLATION 6"x4¼" GLAZED WALL TILE

Ted B. Richey, AIA; The InterDesign Group; Indianapolis, Indiana

TILE   4

COATINGS

Coatings, thin surface facings, protect components from harmful exposure. Selection of appropriate coatings is dictated by conditions under which the coating must perform: exposure to sun, rain, wind, temperature extremes, salt spray, pollution, and chemicals. Another consideration is the rate at which the coated matter deteriorates if the coating fails. Coatings consist of the surface prepared to receive the coating; the prime coat, or undercoat, when needed; and the finish coating, or topcoat. Each must be compatible from layer to layer. Incompatibilities between layers reduce adhesion and accelerate deterioration.

DESIGN CONSIDERATIONS

1. Flow: ease with which a coating can be applied.
2. Leveling: ability of a coating to smooth out after application.
3. Film thickness: amount of protection a coating provides.
4. Drying time: set-to-touch, or surface drying, when the surface resists surface contaminants. Through-dry, when drying is complete through all layers and may be recoated.
5. Permeability: moisture migration through the coating.
6. Wetting: a coating's degree of penetration to a lower level. The lower a coating's wetting ability, the more surface preparation required for adequate adhesion.
7. Adhesion: attachment between layers.
8. Flexibility: accommodation to temperature and moisture changes in the uncoated base.
9. Abrasion and impact resistance; stain resistance; and cleaning.

TYPES

Coatings, classified by composition and appearance,are liquid vehicles (alone when clear, or with pigments when opaque), consisting of a nonvolatile part (binder) and a volatile part (solvent). Pigments and binders are coating solids. Binders form the coating film. Solvents dilute the binder to facilitate application.

Solvent-based coatings contain binders in organic solvents. Water-based coatings contain binders that are soluble or dispersed in water. Clear coatings usually contain the vehicle only. They are used to preserve the base material's appearance. Semi-transparent coatings, with limited pigment in a vehicle, modify but do not change completely a base material's appearance, as in wood stains. Opaque coatings with sufficient pigment to obscure the base material's surface are used when the coating's color or texture is preferable to the base material's appearance.

Paint finishes are available in a range of gloss levels—flat, eggshell, semi-gloss, and gloss. Gloss level is determined by the pigment in the paint. More pigment provides a flatter, rougher finish. Less pigment increases gloss. Following are standard gloss ranges developed by the Consumerism Subcommittee of the NPCA Scientific Committee:

TEST METHOD

NAME	(ASTM D-523)	GLOSS RANGE
Flat	85° meter	Below 15
Eggshell	60° meter	5 to 20
Satin	60° meter	15 to 35
Semi-Gloss	60° meter	30 to 65
Gloss	60° meter	Over 65

PIGMENTS

Pigments add color to the coating film. Depending on type and concentration, they also may increase a coating's durability and protectiveness by screening out ultraviolet radiation, controlling transmission of moisture and gases, and inhibiting corrosion.

BINDERS

Binders are fundamental in film-forming coatings. They bond to the base material and incorporate special ingredients such as driers to speed up curing; plasticizers to add flexibility or moisture resistance; stabilizers to control the effects of heat and solar radiation; and thinners to facilitate application.

SOLVENT-BASED COATINGS

Solvent-based coatings may be transparent, translucent, or opaque. Binders determine clearness or opaqueness. Many binders are available in both formulations.

Binders used for clear coatings include drying oils combined with a resin, drier, and solvent. Clear coatings usually are referred to as varnishes. Clear finishes over wood exposed at length to sunlight generally will not last more than two years.

Phenolic resins have good water and weather resistance. Spar varnish with phenolic resin and tung oil is durable for exterior exposures, including marine environment, but it is a relatively dark color, and it tends to darken with age.

Shellac resin or other resins or gums dissolved in a volatile solvent are referred to as spirit varnish, a sealer for porous surfaces.

Cellulose derivations in volatile spirits are lacquers. They have limited use in building construction, but they are used as furniture finishes.

Silicon resin in a solvent solution of mineral spirits containing about five percent silicone by weight can be used as a clear coating to seal masonry and concrete walls. Life expectancy generally is five to ten years. Silicone is not applicable in all situations.

Urethane, one-component, moisture-cure, solvent-based formulations, is used as a clear floor coating when superior wear resistance is required. Some formulations yellow and chalk with age under exterior exposure.

Stains are pigmented clear coatings used over wood.

Pigmented stains are recommended for exterior exposure. Dyes are not sufficiently light-fast and allow ultraviolet radiation to pass through, degrading the wood.

OPAQUE, SOLVENT-BASED COATINGS

Opaque coatings provide the greatest property choices. Alkyds are the principal binders used in solvent-based opaque, or pigmented, coatings. They are derived from polyhydric alcohols and polybasic acids, and they are available in water dispersion as well as solvent-based.

Alkyd-oil coatings can be flat, semigloss, gloss, and clear with various properties: fast drying, hardness, flexible, durable, chalk resistant, and gloss and color retentive.

Alkyds are not resistant to strong alkali, and they are not compatible with previous coatings containing zinc or lead. Since an impermeable layer over ferrous metals is desirable, alkyd-zinc formulations are used as primers. Alkyds can be modified with other binders such as phenolics for improved resistance to water and alkali salts; vinyl-chloride acetate to improve gloss and resistance to chalking; and silicone for good color and gloss retention.

Alkyds also are used in shop-applied baked-on coatings.

Chlorinated rubber is resistant to microorganism attacks, to alkali, and to acids. It is impervious to water and water vapor and adheres to wood and concrete surfaces.

Chlorosulfonated polyethylene is used in severe corrosive conditions. It is resistant to halogens such as chlorine and bromine, and to action of hot water, oxygen, ozone, and ultraviolet radiation. It is available clear or pigmented.

Epoxy-ester is an epoxy resin reacted with drying oil. It has similar properties to alkyd resins and phenolic varnishes, except that its gloss retention is poorer and its resistance to chemical fumes and marine environment is better. Usually it can be applied over previous coatings without lifting or blistering.

Epoxy, specifically the polyamide-cured type, has excellent resistance to corrosion and chemicals such as solvents, oils, acids, and alkalies. It resists abrasion, strong detergents, and the frequent scrubbing necessary in hospitals, dairies, and chemical plants. Epoxy has excellent adhesion to concrete, wood, and metal substrates; 100% solid types will adhere and cure when applied underwater. Bitumen-epoxy, both coal tar and asphalt, is available. It generally is used for heavy-duty immersion service such as buried structural steel, underground piping, and oil storage tanks.

Oil, or oleoresinous coatings, contain pigments in drying oil, varnish, or an oleoresinous vehicle. Oil degrades by surface erosion under sunlight and water. It is permeable to water vapor and minimizes blistering over porous surfaces such as wood. It should not be used in corrosive, especially alkaline, environments. Oil is used frequently as a primer because it wets the surface and adheres well to steel.

Phenolic coatings, polymerized with formaldehyde reactant through polyamide catalysts, are used where resistance to acids, alkalies, and solvents is required. Phenolic coatings withstand continuous immersion in hot distilled water.

Polyester is available in a wide range of durability and flexibility. It also is available modified with amine and silicone. It is used more frequently in glass fiber reinforced structural plastics than as a coating.

Silicone is used mainly in heat resistant coatings where surface temperatures reach up to 1200°F. It also is used with alkyds, acrylics, polyesters, epoxies, and urethanes to improve their weathering and color retention properties. Also see clear coatings.

Vinyl is polyvinyl chloride copolymerized with polyvinyl acetate. Its adherence is poor, and special primers must be used. Vinyl-mastics, available for high-build coatings, tend to be porous. Polyvinyl chloride commonly is used in water-based coatings. Vinyls have excellent durability and resistance to acids, alkalies, salt water, oils, and fats.

WATER-BASED COATINGS

Water-based coatings first were developed as interior coatings for plaster and gypsum board surfaces, and are commonly, but incorrectly, known as latex paints. The term "latex" applies only to styrene, or styrene butadiene, the binder first used. 'Latex" generally is used only as interior coating or as primer for porous masonry surfaces. On the exterior it oxidizes, leading to yellowing and brittleness.

Other binders include acrylic, or acrylic ester resin, which is best suited for exterior exposure. Acrylic is available pigmented and clear. The clear acrylic based on methyl methacrylate has been found to offer the best protection for concrete against weathering.

Vinyl, or polyvinyl acetate, is available as homopolymer for interior application and copolymer for exterior use.

All water-based opaque coatings have high permeability to water vapor, making them suitable for use over moist porous surfaces such as concrete, masonry, or wood. They should not be used directly over chalking or previous coatings.

Cement is a water-soluble rather than a water-dispersed coating, composed of portland cement, some hydrated lime, and silica aggregate. They are mixed on-site with water for application and require moist curing like any other cement-based product that resists alkali and moisture and may be pigmented, but color retention is poor.

SPECIAL PURPOSE COATINGS

Fire-retardant insulating, or intumescent, coatings are formulated to bubble and swell on heating to form an insulating cover over the base material. The degree of protection afforded depends on the film thickness and the nature of the substrate. A heat barrier is provided for incombustible surfaces. On combustible base materials, the coating provides an additional, more fire resistant surface layer. It should not be applied over previous coatings.

Reflective coatings will absorb the ultraviolet band of solar radiation and reflect it as visible light. The life expectancy of reflective coatings is about one year when subjected to sunlight.

Bituminous coatings are water emulsions or solvent cutbacks of coal tar pitch or asphalt. They are used as low-cost coatings under corrosive and high humidity conditions, such as for buried structural steel, piping, and below-grade concrete.

PRIMERS

Primers generally are used to improve adhesion of the finish coating to a substrate. Primers also may be used to impart other desirable properties to a coating system, such as resistance to corrosion in the substrate, while the finish coating provides resistance to impact and abrasion. Primers are critical for the proper performance of a coating, especially for exterior exposure, where the substrate and the coating may be subject to heat, to chemicals, and to changes in, or high levels of, humidity. The condition of any substrate is an important consideration with any type of coating.

PRIMERS FOR WOOD BASES

Wood base material presents the following problems: it may exhibit different degrees of absorption, and it may contain water soluble dyes, such as in redwood and cedar, which may be released by moisture penetrating the substrate.

Preparation of wood base material should include the following: the wood must be dry before the coating is applied and be sanded smooth; knots and resin streaks should be sealed. Redwood and cedar must be primed with an oil primer to keep soluble dyes within them from bleeding through an opaque coating.

Primers for wood should seal the surface against moisture penetration and have controlled penetration to obtain good adhesion. Flexibility and adhesion should be sufficient to resist movement (especially across the grain) caused by variations in temperature, and the internal moisture content of the wood.

Oil-based primers are used for uncoated wooden surfaces such as vertical siding, smooth surface shingles, and trim. They provide good penetration, adhesion, and flexibility. Alkyd-oil primers are used for rough siding and shakes. The thin-bodied exterior coating is self-priming, and it also can be used as a top coat. Drying oil and/or varnish can be used as a filler for open grain wood to minimize absorption of the top coat. It can be used over stain and a shellac-type of wash coat. Shellac is used as a sealer for surface knots to prevent resin bleeding.

Timothy B. McDonald; Washington, D.C.

PRIMERS FOR CEMENT BASES

Concrete, masonry, stucco and other base materials which incorporate portland cement tend to be alkaline, especially when fresh, and they are relatively porous. Coatings used on such surfaces should be alkali-resistant and have low water sensitivity as the surfaces also may be damp.

For surface preparation, surfaces should be damp for cement-water coatings; surfaces can be damp when water-based coatings, such as acrylic, are applied, but they must be dry for application of solvent-based coatings, such as alkyd. Smooth-trowelled surfaces should be acid etched for better coating adhesion.

Salts contained in the base material also can be dissolved after the coating is applied.

Curing agents, binder breakers, and antifreeze compounds can remain on the surface or in a cement base material that impairs a coating's adhesion.

Generally, coatings for alkaline surfaces should be alkali resistant and thus self-priming. Primers are required for coatings that are not resistant to alkali when there is moisture in the base material or if there is a possibility moisture will penetrate into a dry base material.

Concrete and masonry primers usually are water-based acrylic or polyvinyl acetate, which also can be used as a top coat. Chlorinated rubber is used as a primer for high humidity or wet conditions, and also can be used as a top coat. For corrosive conditions, vinyl resin can be used as a primer and as a top coat.

Plaster should be allowed to age at least 30 days if an oil-based coating is to be applied. Water-based coatings can be applied sooner. Most conditions applicable to concrete also apply to plaster.

Gypsum board is porous. Only nonpenetrating primers or sealers should be used. Oil-based primers or coatings such as alkyd, penetrate and tend to raise the nap of the facing. Water-based primers or coatings generally are recommended.

PRIMERS FOR METAL BASES

The effects of a metallic base on coatings generally is not a factor; however, metals may have oil, grease, or chemicals remaining on their surfaces. Ferrous metals may have, in addition, rust and mill scale, and they usually require more preparation than other base metals. The degree of surface preparation required and the methods used vary for different primers and top coats from a simple manual wire brushing to remove loose rust and mill scale to extensive chemical treatments, grinding, or blast cleaning.

Primers for ferrous metal bases, which are subject to rapid corrosion in moisture, must include corrosion inhibiting pigments. Red lead is such a reactive primer. It chemically combines with some vehicles to form resistive films particularly suited for protecting surfaces that cannot be cleaned thoroughly of rust. It is used with binders such as oil and alkyd.

Basic lead–silico-chromate has excellent anticorrosive and weather resistant properties. It may be tinted to match some top coats, and the top coats also may contain the same pigment.

Zinc dust provides galvanic protection because the zinc slowly is sacrificed as a cathode in the presence of moisture, while the ferrous surface serves as the anode and remains intact. Zinc dust is used under severe conditions with organic binders such as acrylics, epoxies, alkyds, and chlorinated rubber.

Zinc chromate or zinc yellow has a low sodium content and provides inhibiting chromate ions.

Zinc dust–zinc oxide, usually 80 percent zinc dust, provides excellent rust-inhibiting properties as well as adhesion, elasticity, and abrasion resistance. Primers containing zinc dust–zinc oxide can be applied over moderately cleaned or galvanized surfaces.

Commonly used binders and vehicles for metal primers include:

Oil, which often is added to other vehicles to penetrate rust and to promote adhesion. Linseed oil, often combined with alkyd, is used with red lead. When a surface is poorly prepared, oil and straight red lead are used.

Alkyd is usable with most corrosion inhibiting pigments. It serves as a binder for primers of intermediate durability where meticulous surface preparation is not practical.

Phenolic is used with zinc chromate or basic silicon lead chromate. It provides good protection from excessive dampness or from immersion in water. It can be used with red lead also.

Epoxy has excellent adhesion to carefully prepared surfaces. It can be combined with polyamide resins and zinc dust or lead pigments for high performance primers. Epoxy esters also are used under less demanding conditions.

Chlorinated rubber has excellent resistance to water vapor transmission, acids, alkalies, and various salts.

Vinyl with zinc chromate or iron oxide provides excellent resistance to chemicals.

Silicate with zinc dust offers excellent resistance to weather, chemicals, and salt spray.

Polyesters and acrylics are used mostly with factory-applied coatings.

Nonferrous metals do not have serious corrosion problems. When coated, aluminum and other nonferrous metals (such as tin and copper) generally are pretreated with a wash primer followed by a zinc chromate primer.

APPLICATION PROPERTIES

	ALKYD	2-CAN EPOXY	ACRYLIC LATEX	LINSEED OIL	PHENOLIC	CHLORINATED RUBBER	ALIPHATIC URETHANE	VINYL
Solvents	Aliphatic or Aromatic	Lacquer	Water	Aliphatic	Aromatic	Aromatic	Lacquer	Lacquer
Min. surface preparation*	SP 3	SP 6	SP 6	SP 2	SP 6	SP 6	***	SP 6
Stability during use	EX	F	EX	EX	EX	EX	F	EX
Brushability	G	F	EX	VG	G	F	G	P
Method of cure	Oxid.	Chem.	Coal.	Oxid.	Oxid.	Evap.	Chem.	Evap.
Speed of cure								
50°F–90°F**	G	G	EX	F	G	EX	EX	EX
35°F–50°F**	F	NR	NR	P	F	G	G	G
Film build per coat	G	VG	F	G	G	G	VG	G
Use in primers	G	EX	F	EX	G	G	G	G
Use on damp surfaces	P	G	VG	P	P	P	G	G

APPEARANCE PROPERTIES

	ALKYD	2-CAN EPOXY	ACRYLIC LATEX	LINSEED OIL	PHENOLIC	CHLORINATED RUBBER	ALIPHATIC URETHANE	VINYL
Use as clear finish (varnish)	VG	F	P	NR	VG	NR	EX	NR
Use in ready mixed aluminum paint	G	F	NR	F	EX	F	F	G
Pale color	VG	G	EX	G	P	VG	EX	EX
Ability to produce high gloss	EX	EX	F	G	EX	VG	EX	F

PERFORMANCE PROPERTIES

	ALKYD	2-CAN EPOXY	ACRYLIC LATEX	LINSEED OIL	PHENOLIC	CHLORINATED RUBBER	ALIPHATIC URETHANE	VINYL
Hardness	G	VG	F	P	VG	VG	EX	G
Adhesion	G	EX	F	VG	G	VG	VG	F
Flexibility	G	G	EX	VG	F	VG	VG	EX
Resistance to:								
Abrasion	F	VG	F	P	G	VG	EX	VG
Water	G	EX	F	P	EX	EX	VG	EX
Strong Solvents	P	EX	F	P	G	P	EX	P
Acid	F	VG	F	P	EX	EX	EX	EX
Alkali	P	EX	G	P	G	EX	VG	EX
Heat—200°F	G	G	F	F	G	NR	G	NR

DURABILITY

	ALKYD	2-CAN EPOXY	ACRYLIC LATEX	LINSEED OIL	PHENOLIC	CHLORINATED RUBBER	ALIPHATIC URETHANE	VINYL
Moisture permeability	Mod	Low	High	Mod	Low	Low	Low	Low
Normal exposure	VG	VG	VG	G	VG	EX	EX	EX
Marine exposure	F	EX	F	F	G	EX	EX	EX
Corrosive exposure	F	EX	F	NR	G	VG	EX	EX
Color retention	G	P	VG	F	P	G	EX	VG
Gloss retention	G	P	EX	P	G	G	EX	VG
Chalk resistance	G	P	VG	P	G	G	EX	VG

*SSPC Surface Preparation Specifications
**Painting should not be done above 90°F or below 34°F
***Usually used in topcoats

CODES
EX—Excellent
VG—Very Good
G—Good
F—Fair
P—Poor
NR—Not Recommended

SOLVENTS
Aliphatic—Mineral spirits
Aromatic—Xylene, toluene, etc.
Lacquer—Aromatic plus kétone, ester, or ether solvents (See Solvents)

ABBREVIATIONS
Oxid.—Oxidative polymerization or oxidation
Chem.—Chemical reaction (two component)
Coal.—Coalescence (latex)
Evap.—Solvent evaporation (lacquer)
Min.—Minimum

Timothy B. McDonald; Washington, D.C.

PAINTING

REFERENCES

GENERAL REFERENCES

Fundamentals of Building Construction: Materials and Methods, 2nd ed., 1990, Edward Allen, Wiley

Construction Materials and Processes, 3rd ed., 1986, Donald Watson, McGraw-Hill

Construction Principles, Materials, and Methods, 5th ed., 1983, Harold B. Olin, John L. Schmidt, and Walter H. Lewis, Van Nostrand Reinhold

Construction Materials: Types, Uses, and Applications, 2nd ed., 1991, Caleb Hornbostel, Wiley

Building Code Requirements for Reinforced Concrete (ACI 318-88), American Concrete Institute

Simplified Design of Concrete Structures, 6th ed., 1990, Harry Parker and James Ambrose, Wiley

Building Code Requirements for Masonry Structures (ACI 530-88), and *Specifications for Masonry Structures* (ACI 530.1-88) in a single publication, American Concrete Institute

Masonry Design and Detailing, 2nd ed., 1987, Christine Beall, Prentice-Hall

Simplified Design of Masonry Structures, 1991, James Ambrose, Wiley

Manual of Steel Construction: Allowable Stress Design, 9th ed., 1989, American Institute of Steel Construction

Simplified Design of Steel Structures, 6th ed., 1990, Harry Parker and James Ambrose, Wiley

National Design Specification for Wood Construction, National Forest Products Association

Western Woods Use Book, Western Woods Products Association

Timber Construction Manual, 3rd ed., 1985, American Institute of Timber Construction, Wiley

Simplified Design of Wood Structures, 4th ed., 1988, Harry Parker and James Ambrose, Wiley

DATA SOURCES: ORGANIZATIONS

American Bolt, Nut, and Rivet Manufacturers (ABNRM), 101

American Concrete Institute (ACI), 83, 84

American Insurance Association, 107

American Society for Testing and Materials (ASTM), reprinted with permission, 79

American Society for Testing and Materials (ASTM), 80, 81

American Wood Preservers Institute (AWPI), 107

Brick Institute of America (BIA), 89

Building Stone Institute (BSI), 92, 93

Concrete Reinforcing Steel Institute (CRSI), 81, 82

Factory Mutual Engineering Division, Factory Insurance Association, 107

Forest Products Division, Koppers Company, Inc., 107

Independent Nail and Packing Company, 96, 98, 99, 100

Irving Grating, IKG Industries, Harsco Corporation, 104

National Bureau of Standards (NBS), 88

National Concrete Masonry Association (NCMA), 88

Occupational Safety and Health Administration (OSHA), U.S. Department of Labor, 105

Portland Cement Association (PCA), 79, 80, 88

Rawplug Company, 101

Red Head, ITT Phillips Drill Division, 101

Rock Color Chart, Geological Society of America, 92

Simplex Nails, Inc., 96, 98, 99, 100

Weather Bureau, U.S. Department of Commerce, 78

DATA SOURCES: PUBLICATIONS

American Softwood Lumber Standards, National Bureau of Standards (NBS), 106, 107

Annual Book of ASTM Standards, American Society for Testing and Materials (ASTM), 79

Architectural Metal Handbook, National Association of Architectural Metal Manufacturers, 104

BOCA Basic Building Code, Building Officials and Code Administrators International (BOCA), 107

Building Code Requirements for Reinforced Concrete, American Concrete Institute (ACI), 79

Landscape Architecture, 1982, Linda Jewell, American Society of Landscape Architects, Publication Board, 72

Masonry Accessories, National Wire Products Corporation, 91

Masonry Anchors and Ties, Heckman Building Products, 91

Masonry Design and Detailing, Christine Beall, McGraw-Hill, 88, 90, 92

National Design Specification for Wood Construction, National Forest Products Association, 106, 107

Shelf Angle Component Considerations in Cavity Wall Construction, C. J. Parise, American Society for Testing and Materials, 91

Southern Standard Building Code, Southern Building Code Congress (SBC), 107

Uniform Building Code, 1982 ed. and 1985 ed., International Conference of Building Officials (ICBO), reprinted with permission, 107

CHAPTER 5

SITE CONSTRUCTION

MARINE WORK	116		RAMMED EARTH	142
FOUNDATIONS	117		SITE LAYOUT	143
EARTHWORK	118		ORNAMENTAL METAL	144
PAVING AND SURFACING	120		WOOD CONSTRUCTION	146
SITE IMPROVEMENTS	122		WATERPROOFING	153
WALLS AND FENCES	127		SPECIAL DOORS	158
EXPANSION AND CONSTRUCTION JOINTS	133		TILE	160
			TERRAZZO	162
CAST-IN-PLACE CONCRETE	134		SUN CONTROL	163
UNIT MASONRY	136		EARTH SHELTERS	165
STONE	138		SPECIAL CONSTRUCTION	167
ADOBE	140			

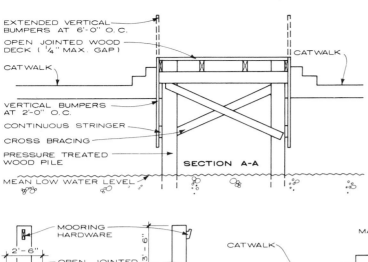

EXTENDED VERTICAL BUMPERS AT 6'-0" O.C.

OPEN JOINTED WOOD DECK (¼" MAX. GAP)

CATWALK

CATWALK

VERTICAL BUMPERS AT 2'-0" O.C.

CONTINUOUS STRINGER

CROSS BRACING

PRESSURE TREATED WOOD PILE

SECTION A-A

MEAN LOW WATER LEVEL

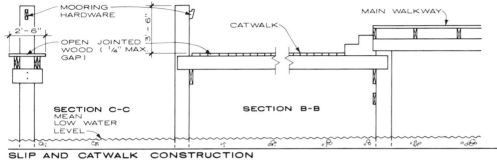

MOORING HARDWARE

2'-6"

OPEN JOINTED WOOD (¼" MAX. GAP)

CATWALK

3'-6"

MAIN WALKWAY

SECTION C-C
MEAN LOW WATER LEVEL

SECTION B-B

SLIP AND CATWALK CONSTRUCTION

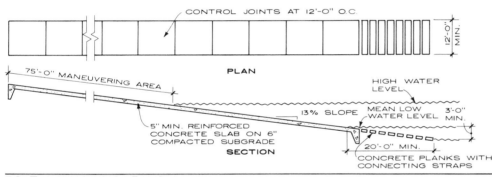

CONTROL JOINTS AT 12'-0" O.C.

12'-0" MIN.

PLAN

75'-0" MANEUVERING AREA

HIGH WATER LEVEL

13% SLOPE

MEAN LOW WATER LEVEL

3'-0" MIN.

5" MIN. REINFORCED CONCRETE SLAB ON 6" COMPACTED SUBGRADE

SECTION

20'-0" MIN.

CONCRETE PLANKS WITH CONNECTING STRAPS

BOAT LAUNCHING RAMP

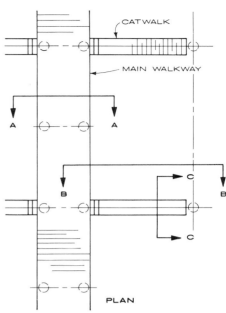

CATWALK

MAIN WALKWAY

A   A

B   C

B   C

PLAN

GENERAL NOTES

1. Wood marine construction must be pressure treated with a preservative. Wood preservatives for use in marine applications fall into two general categories, creosote and waterborne. To select a specific preservative from within these categories, the decaying agents must be identified. A preservative may then be chosen based on the recommendations of the American Wood Preservers Institute.

2. Waterborne preservatives are recommended for decks because creosote stains shoes and bare feet.

3. The preservatives selected should be approved by the Environmental Protection Agency.

4. Dock height above water is determined by average deck levels and probable water level. Maintain a 12 in. minimum dimension between water and deck. Floating docks may be required in tidal waters. Consult manufacturer for construction information.

5. Cross bracing should be minimized to avoid entanglement of swimmers.

LAUNCHING RAMPS

1. Launching ramps are for sheltered waters only.

2. A catwalk may be provided alongside the ramp.

3. Floating ramps may be required in tidal waters.

TABLE OF DIMENSIONS FOR SLIPS AND CATWALKS TO BE USED WITH PLAN DIAGRAM

LENGTH GROUP FOR BOAT	BEAM TO BE PROVIDED FOR	MIN. CLEAR WIDTH OF SLIP	GROSS SLIP WIDTH TYPE A	GROSS SLIP WIDTH TYPE B	GROSS SLIP WIDTH TYPE C	1ST CATWALK SPAN LENGTH D	2ND CATWALK SPAN LENGTH E	3RD CATWALK SPAN LENGTH F	DISTANCE G TO ANCHOR PILE
Up to 14'	6'-7"	8'-10"	10'-9"	10'-6"	11'-2"	12'-0"			17'-0"
Over 14' to 16'	7'-4"	9'-8"	11'-7"	11'-4"	12'-0"	12'-0"			19'-0"
Over 16' to 18'	8'-0"	10'-5"	12'-4"	12'-1"	12'-9"	14'-0"			21'-0"
Over 18' to 20'	8'-7"	11'-1"	13'-0"	12'-9"	13'-5"	8'-0"	8'-0"		23'-0"
Over 20' to 22'	9'-3"	11'-9"	13'-8"	13'-5"	14'-1"	10'-0"	8'-0"		25'-0"
Over 22' to 25'	10'-3"	13'-1"	15'-0"	14'-9"	15'-5"	10'-0"	8'-0"		28'-0"
Over 25' to 30'	11'-3"	14'-3"	16'-2"	15'-11"	16'-7"	10'-0"	10'-0"		33'-0"
Over 30' to 35'	12'-3"	15'-8"	17'-7"	17'-4"	18'-0"	12'-0"	10'-0"		38'-0"
Over 35' to 40'	13'-3"	16'-11"	18'-10"	18'-7"	19'-3"	12'-0"	12'-0"		43'-0"
Over 40' to 45'	14'-1"	17'-11"	19'-10"	19'-7"	20'-3"	14'-0"	12'-0"		48'-0"
Over 45' to 50'	14'-11"	19'-0"	20'-11"	20'-8"	21'-4"	9'-0"	9'-0"	10'-0"	53'-0"
Over 50' to 60'	16'-6"	21'-0"	22'-11"	22'-8"	23'-4"	11'-0"	11'-0"	12'-0"	63'-0"
Over 60' to 70'	18'-1"	23'-0"	26'-8"	24'-8"	25'-4"	11'-0"	11'-0"	12'-0"	73'-0"
Over 70' to 80'	19'-9"	24'-11"	28'-8"	26'-7"	26'-3"	11'-0"	11'-0"	12'-0"	83'-0"

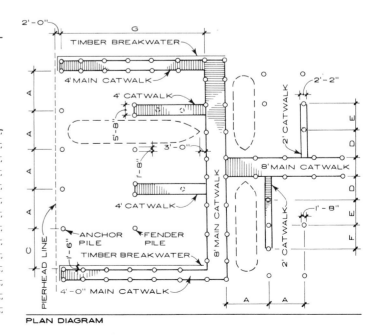

2'-0"

G

TIMBER BREAKWATER

4' MAIN CATWALK

CATWALK

2'-2"

4' CATWALK

5'-8"

3'-0"

1'-8"

2' CATWALK

E

D

8' MAIN CATWALK

4' CATWALK

8' MAIN CATWALK

2' CATWALK

D

E

1'-8"

ANCHOR PILE   FENDER PILE

1'-6"

TIMBER BREAKWATER

F

PIERHEAD LINE

4'-0" MAIN CATWALK

A   A

PLAN DIAGRAM

David E. Rose; Rossen/Neumann Associates; Southfield, Michigan

MARINE WORK

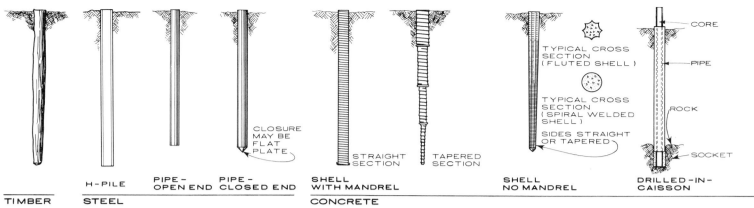

TIMBER | STEEL | CONCRETE

NOTE: A mandrel is a member inserted into a hollow pile to reinforce the pile shell while it is driven into the ground.

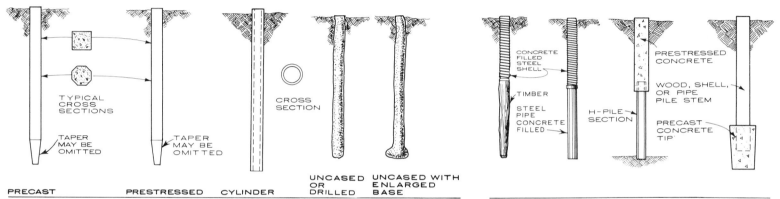

CONCRETE | COMPOSITE

GENERAL PILE DATA

PILE TYPE	MAXIMUM LENGTH (FT)	OPTIMUM LENGTH (FT)	SIZE (IN.)	MAXIMUM CAPACITY (TONS)	OPTIMUM LOAD RANGE (TONS)	USUAL SPACING
TIMBER	110	45-65	5-10 tip 12-20 butt	40	15-25	2'6'' to 3'0''
STEEL						
H-pile	250	40-150	8-14	200	50-200	2'6'' to 3'6''
Pipe—open end concrete filled	200	40-120	10-24	250	100-200	3'0'' to 4'0''
Pipe—closed end concrete filled	150	30-80	10-18	100	50-70	3'0'' to 4'0''
Shell—mandrel concrete filled straight or taper	100	40-80	8-18	75	40-60	3'0'' to 3'6''
Shell—no mandrel concrete filled	150	30-80	8-18	80	30-60	3'0'' to 3'6''
Drilled-in caisson concrete filled	250	20-120	24-48	3500	1000-2000	6'0'' to 8'0''
CONCRETE						
Precast	80	40-50	10-24	100	40-60	3'0''
Prestressed	200	60-80	10-24	200	100-150	3'0'' to 3'6''
Cylinder pile	150	60-80	36-54	500	250-400	6'0'' to 9'0''
Uncased or drilled	60	25-40	14-20	75	30-60	3'0'' to 3'6''
Uncased with enlarged base	60	25-40	14-20	150	40-100	6'0''
COMPOSITE						
Concrete—timber	150	60-100	5-10 tip 12-20 butt	40	15-25	3'0'' to 3'6''
Concrete—pipe	180	60-120	10-23	150	40-80	3'0'' to 4'0''
Prestressed concrete H-pile	200	100-150	20-24	200	120-150	3'6'' to 4'0''
Precast concrete tip	80	40	13-35	180	150	4'6''

NOTES

Timber piles must be treated with wood preservative when any portion is above permanent groundwater table.

Applicable material Specifications Concrete—ACL 318; Timber—ASTM D25: Structural Sections ASTM A36, A572 and A696.

For selection of type of pile consult foundation engineer.

Mueser, Rutledge, Johnston & DeSimone; New York, New York

Embankment stabilization is required where extremely steep slopes exist that are subject to heavy storm water runoff. The need for mechanical stabilization can be reduced by intercepting the runoff, or slowing the velocity of the runoff down the slope. Diversions are desirable at the tops of slopes to intercept the runoff. Slopes can be shelved or terraced to reduce the velocity of runoff to the point where a major erosion hazard is avoided. Use an armored channel or slope drain if concentrated runoff down a slope must be controlled.

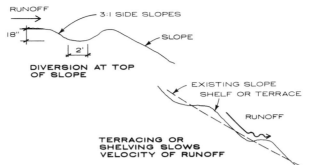

DIVERSION AT TOP OF SLOPE

TERRACING OR SHELVING SLOWS VELOCITY OF RUNOFF

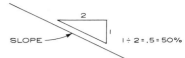

$1 \div 2 = .5 = 50\%$

SOIL	GRADIENT	RATIO
Dry sand	33%	3:1
Loam	40%	2.5:1
Compacted clay	80%	1.25:1
Saturated clay	20%	5:1

MAX. GRADIENTS FOR BARE SOILS

SLOPE STABILIZATION WITH RIPRAP

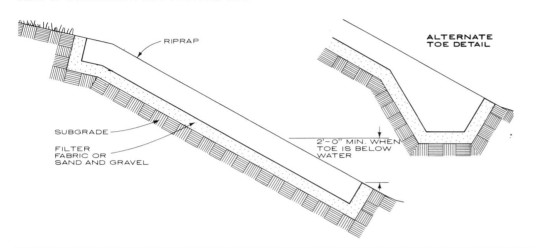

NOTE

A number of mechanical embankment stabilization materials are illustrated. Two important features all methods have in common are

1. Embedment of the toe and lateral limits to prevent undercutting and outflanking, and
2. Use of a granular or fabric filter to protect the soil beneath the protective layer from the effects of flowing water or existing groundwater.

RIPRAP EMBANKMENT WITH ALTERNATE TOE

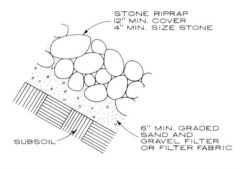

STONE

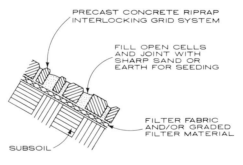

PRECAST CONCRETE

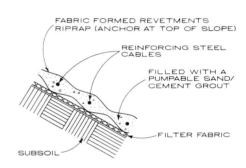

FABRIC FORMED REVETMENTS

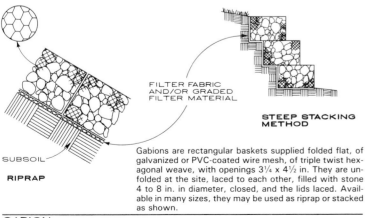

RIPRAP

Gabions are rectangular baskets supplied folded flat, of galvanized or PVC-coated wire mesh, of triple twist hexagonal weave, with openings 3¼ x 4½ in. They are unfolded at the site, laced to each other, filled with stone 4 to 8 in. in diameter, closed, and the lids laced. Available in many sizes, they may be used as riprap or stacked as shown.

GABION

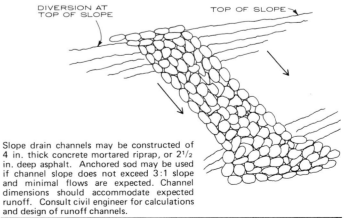

Slope drain channels may be constructed of 4 in. thick concrete mortared riprap, or 2½ in. deep asphalt. Anchored sod may be used if channel slope does not exceed 3:1 slope and minimal flows are expected. Channel dimensions should accommodate expected runoff. Consult civil engineer for calculations and design of runoff channels.

SLOPE DRAIN

Derek Martin, FAIA; Pittsburgh, Pennsylvania
John M. Beckett; Beckett, Raeder, Rankin, Inc.; Ann Arbor, Michigan
James E. Sekela, PE; United States Army Corps of Engineers, Pittsburgh, Pennsylvania

 EARTHWORK

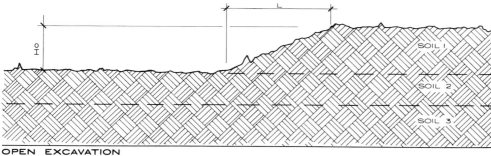

OPEN EXCAVATION

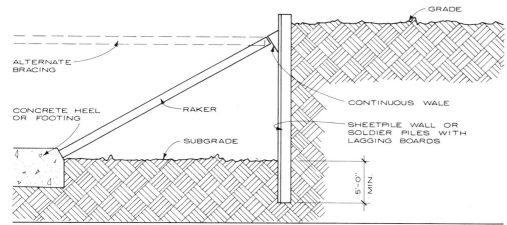

BRACED EXCAVATION USING RAKERS

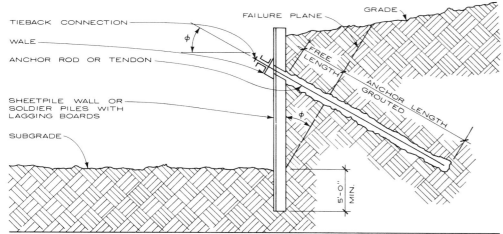

BRACED EXCAVATION USING EARTH ANCHORS

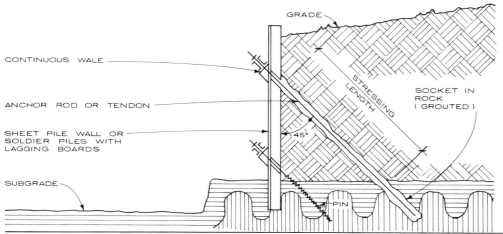

BRACED EXCAVATION USING ROCK ANCHORS

Mueser, Rutledge, Johnston & DeSimone; New York, New York

EMBANKMENT STABILITY
CONSULT FOUNDATION ENGINEER

SOIL TYPES			L/HO	REMARKS
S1	S2	S3		
Fill	Rock		>1.5	Check sliding of S1
Soft clay	Hard clay	Rock	>1.0	Check sliding of S1
Sand	Soft clay	Hard clay	>1.5	Check lateral displacement of S2
Sand	Sand	Hard clay	>1.5	
Hard clay	Soft clay	Sand	<1.0	Check lateral displacement of S2

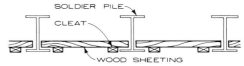

TIMBER LAGGING

TIMBER SHEETING

STEEL SHEETING

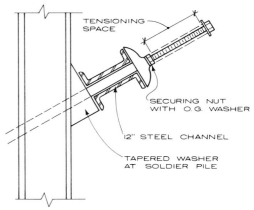

CHANNEL WALER DETAIL

NOTES
1. For shallow depths of excavation cantilever sheeting may be used, if driven to sufficient depth.
2. For deep excavations, several tiers of bracing may be necessary.
3. If subgrade of excavation is used for installation of spreadfootings or mats, proper dewatering procedures may be required to avoid disturbance of bearing level.
4. At times it may be possible to improve the bearing stratum by excavation of compressible materials and their replacement with compacted granular backfill.
5. For evaluation of problems encountered with sheeting and shoring, a foundation engineer should be consulted.
6. Local codes and OSHA regulations must be considered.
7. Proximity of utilities and other structures must be considered in design.

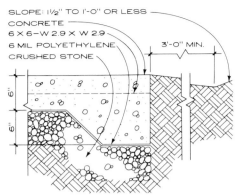

SLOPE: 1½" TO 1'-0" OR LESS
CONCRETE
6 × 6 - W 2.9 × W 2.9
6 MIL POLYETHYLENE
CRUSHED STONE
3'-0" MIN.
6"
6"

CONCRETE PAVING WITHOUT CURB

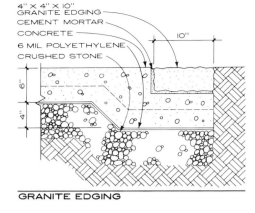

4" × 4" × 10"
GRANITE EDGING
CEMENT MORTAR
CONCRETE
6 MIL POLYETHYLENE
CRUSHED STONE
10"
6"
4"

GRANITE EDGING

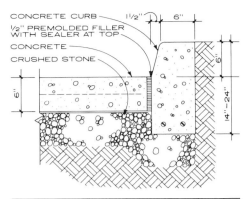

CONCRETE CURB
½" PREMOLDED FILLER
WITH SEALER AT TOP
CONCRETE
CRUSHED STONE
1½"
6"
6"
6"
14"–24"

SEPARATE CONCRETE CURB

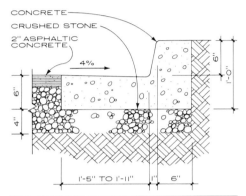

CONCRETE
CRUSHED STONE
2" ASPHALTIC
CONCRETE
4%
6"
6"
1'-0"
6"
4"
1'-5" TO 1'-11"
1"
6"

CONCRETE CURB AND GUTTER

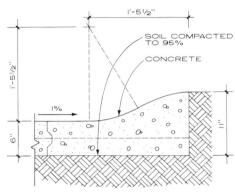

1'-5½"
SOIL COMPACTED
TO 95%
CONCRETE
1'-5½"
1%
6"
11"

MOUNTABLE CONCRETE CURB

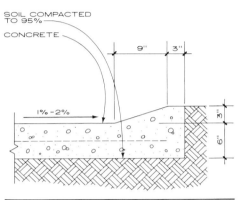

SOIL COMPACTED
TO 95%
CONCRETE
9"
3"
1%–2%
3"
6"

IOWA CONCRETE CURB

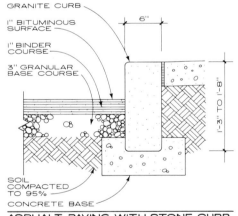

GRANITE CURB
1" BITUMINOUS
SURFACE
1" BINDER
COURSE
3" GRANULAR
BASE COURSE
6"
1'-3" TO 1'-8"
SOIL
COMPACTED
TO 95%
CONCRETE BASE

ASPHALT PAVING WITH STONE CURB

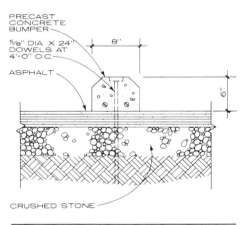

PRECAST
CONCRETE
BUMPER
⅝" DIA. × 24"
DOWELS AT
4'-0" O.C.
ASPHALT
8"
6"
CRUSHED STONE

ASPHALT PAVING WITH PRECAST CONCRETE BUMPER

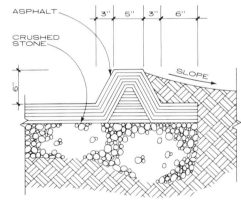

ASPHALT
CRUSHED
STONE
3"
5"
3"
6"
SLOPE
6"

NOT RECOMMENDED AS WHEEL STOP

ASPHALT CURB AND PAVING

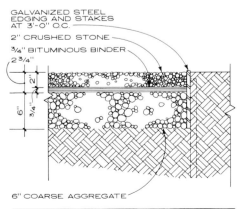

GALVANIZED STEEL
EDGING AND STAKES
AT 3'-0" O.C.
2" CRUSHED STONE
¾" BITUMINOUS BINDER
2¾"
2"
¾"
6"
6" COARSE AGGREGATE

CRUSHED STONE PAVING WITH METAL EDGE

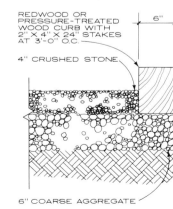

REDWOOD OR
PRESSURE-TREATED
WOOD CURB WITH
2" × 4" × 24" STAKES
AT 3'-0" O.C.
4" CRUSHED STONE
6"
4"
8"
6"
6" COARSE AGGREGATE

CRUSHED STONE PAVING WITH TIMBER CURB

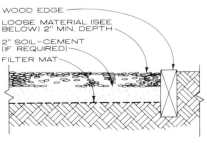

WOOD EDGE
LOOSE MATERIAL (SEE
BELOW) 2" MIN. DEPTH
2" SOIL-CEMENT
(IF REQUIRED)
FILTER MAT

LOOSE MATERIAL SIZES
WOOD CHIPS – 1" NOMINAL
SHREDDED BARK MULCH
¼" STONE CHIPS
¾" PEA GRAVEL

½" DECOMPOSED
GRANITE
¾" CRUSHED
STONE
1"–2" WASHED
STONE

NOTE: ORGANIC MATERIALS WILL DECOMPOSE

LOOSE MATERIAL PAVING WITH WOOD EDGE

Francisco J. Menendez; Washington, D.C.
Richard J. Vitullo; Washington Grove, Maryland

5 **PAVING AND SURFACING**

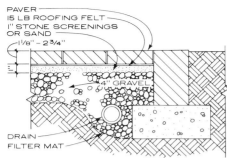

PAVER
15 LB ROOFING FELT
1" STONE SCREENINGS
OR SAND
1⅛"–2¾"

DRAIN
FILTER MAT

PAVER SIZES: 4"X 4", 4" X 8", 4" X 12",
6" X 6", 8" X 8", 12" X 12", 5¾", 8", AND 12"
HEXAGON
PAVER THICKNESS: 1⅛"–2¾"
**BRICK, CLAY TILE, OR ASPHALT BLOCK
PAVERS**

CONCRETE PAVER WITH
HANDTIGHT MORTARLESS
JOINT
2" SAND
FILTER MAT
2"–3" GRAVEL

DRAIN

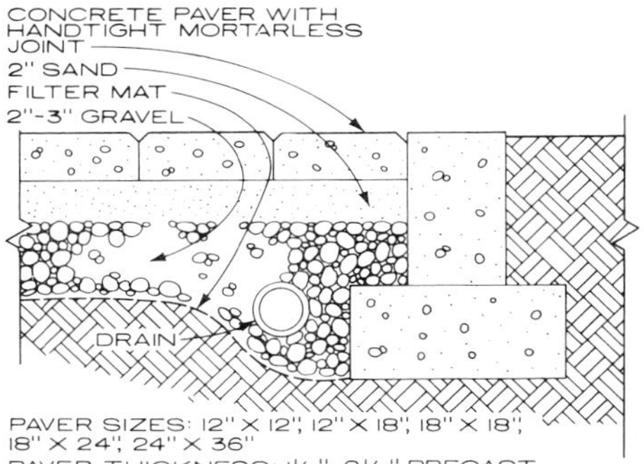

PAVER SIZES: 12"X 12", 12" X 18", 18" X 18",
18" X 24", 24" X 36"
PAVER THICKNESS: 1½"–2½" PRECAST
CONCRETE
TEXTURE: TROWEL FINISH, FLOAT
FINISH, EXPOSED AGGREGATE FINISH
CONCRETE PAVERS AND LONDON WALKS

CUT STONE WITH HANDTIGHT
MORTARLESS JOINT
2" LEVELING SAND

2" GRAVEL
DRAIN
FILTER MAT

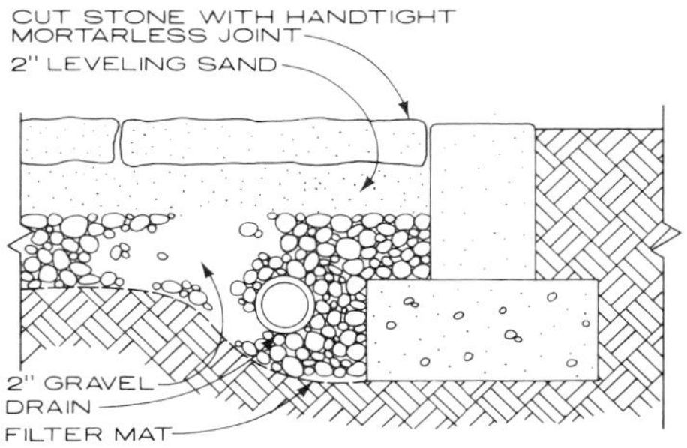

STONE SIZES: 12" X 12", 12" X 18", 18" X 18", 18" X 24",
24" X 36", OR RANDOM SHAPES
STONE THICKNESS: 1"–2" CUT STONE
TEXTURE: HONED, NATURAL CLEFT, OR
FLAME TREATED FOR NONSLIP FINISH
CUT STONE PAVERS

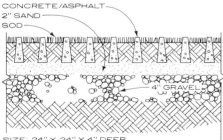

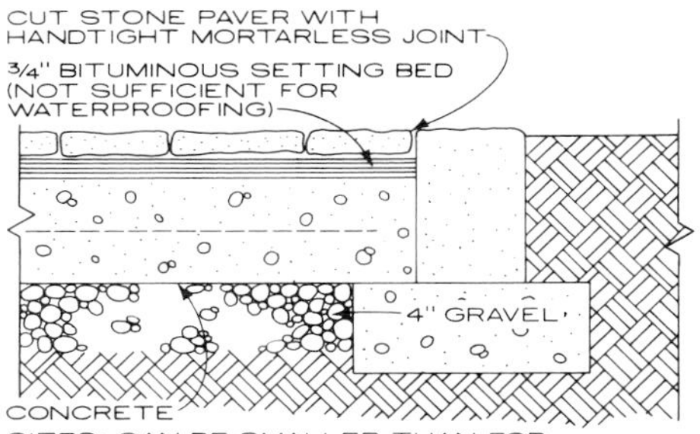

CONCRETE/ASPHALT
2" SAND
SOD

4" GRAVEL

SIZE: 24" X 24" X 4" DEEP
SURFACE TEXTURE: MODERATELY
ABRASIVE
COLOR: STANDARD GRAY OR TAN
INSTALLED WITHOUT SLAB, MORTAR, OR
GROUT. A PREFORMED LATTICE UNIT USED
FOR STORM RUNOFF CONTROL, PATHWAYS,
PARKING AREAS, AND SOIL CONSERVATION
GRID PAVING BLOCKS

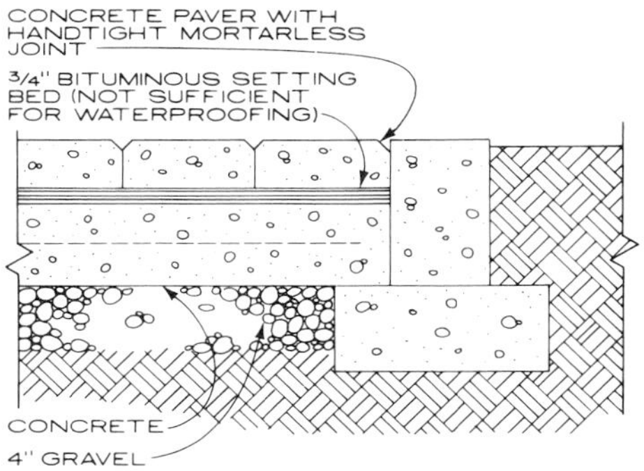

UNIT PAVERS ON FLEXIBLE BASE

GENERAL NOTES

1. Drainpipes may be omitted at well-drained areas.
2. Provide positive outflow for drainpipes.
3. Do not use unsatisfactory soil (expanding organic).
4. Satisfactory soil shall be compacted to 95%.

Charles A. Szoradi; Washington, D.C.
Richard J. Vitullo; Washington Grove, Maryland

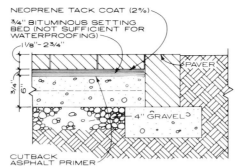

NEOPRENE TACK COAT (2%)
¾" BITUMINOUS SETTING
BED (NOT SUFFICIENT FOR
WATERPROOFING)
1⅛"–2¾"

PAVER

4" GRAVEL

CUTBACK
ASPHALT PRIMER
WHERE WEATHER PERMITS, LATEX-
MODIFIED MORTAR MAY BE USED FOR JOINTS
AND SETTING BED
**BRICK, CLAY TILE, OR ASPHALT BLOCK
PAVERS**

CONCRETE PAVER WITH
HANDTIGHT MORTARLESS
JOINT
¾" BITUMINOUS SETTING
BED (NOT SUFFICIENT
FOR WATERPROOFING)

CONCRETE
4" GRAVEL
WHERE WEATHER PERMITS, LATEX-
MODIFIED MORTAR MAY BE USED FOR JOINTS
AND SETTING BED
CONCRETE PAVERS AND LONDON WALKS

CUT STONE PAVER WITH
HANDTIGHT MORTARLESS JOINT
¾" BITUMINOUS SETTING BED
(NOT SUFFICIENT FOR
WATERPROOFING)

4" GRAVEL

CONCRETE
SIZES: CAN BE SMALLER THAN FOR
FLEXIBLE BASE WHERE WEATHER PERMITS
LATEX-MODIFIED MORTAR. MAY BE USED FOR
JOINT AND SETTING BEDS. JOINTS MAY BE
STAGGERED OR RANDOM
STONE THICKNESS: ½" SLATE OR 1"–2" CUT
STONE
CUT STONE PAVERS

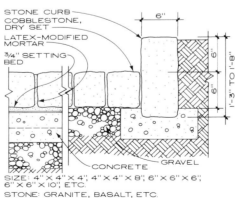

STONE CURB
COBBLESTONE,
DRY SET
LATEX-MODIFIED
MORTAR
¾" SETTING
BED

6"

6"

6"

1'-3" TO 1'-8"

CONCRETE
GRAVEL
SIZE: 4" X 4" X 4", 4" X 4" X 8", 6" X 6" X 6",
6" X 6" X 10", ETC.
STONE: GRANITE, BASALT, ETC.
COBBLESTONE PAVERS

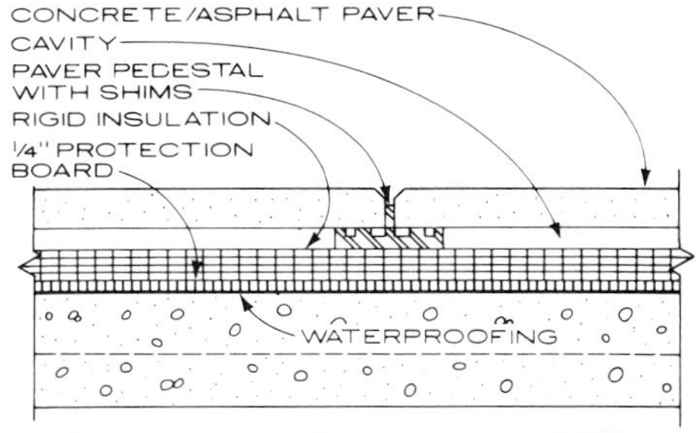

UNIT PAVERS ON RIGID BASE

5. Flexible and suspended bases shown are for light duty
only.
6. Edging width: 2, 4, 8, 12 in.; depth: 8, 12, 16, 24
in.

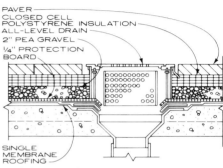

BRICK OR ASPHALT BLOCK
ALL-LEVEL DRAIN
2" PEA GRAVEL
¼" PROTECTION
BOARD
STRUCTURAL
SLAB

SINGLE
MEMBRANE
ROOFING

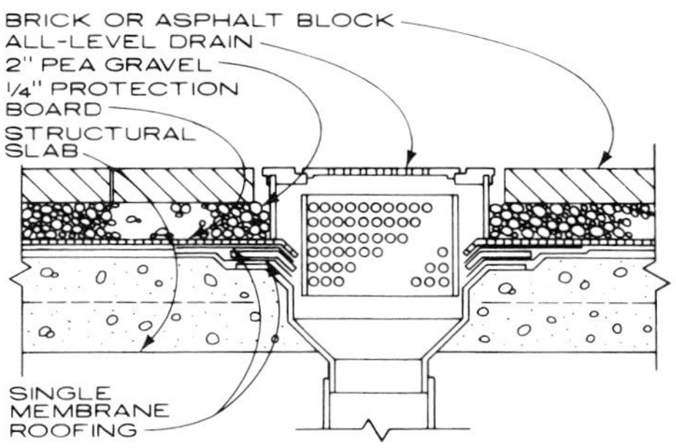

FOR HEATED SPACES UNDER STRUCTURAL
SLAB, USE CLOSED CELL INSULATION UNDER
PAVERS
**BRICK, CLAY TILE, ASPHALT BLOCK,
CONCRETE, OR STONE PAVERS OVER
UNINSULATED BASE**

PAVER
CLOSED CELL
POLYSTYRENE INSULATION
ALL-LEVEL DRAIN
2" PEA GRAVEL
¼" PROTECTION
BOARD

SINGLE
MEMBRANE
ROOFING
THIS SYSTEM SUITABLE FOR PEDESTRIAN
TRAFFIC ONLY
**BRICK, CLAY TILE, ASPHALT BLOCK,
CONCRETE, OR STONE PAVERS OVER
INSULATED BASE**

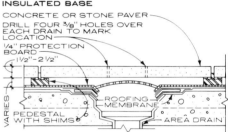

CONCRETE OR STONE PAVER
DRILL FOUR ⅜" HOLES OVER
EACH DRAIN TO MARK
LOCATION
¼" PROTECTION
BOARD
1½"–2½"

VARIES

ROOFING
MEMBRANE
PEDESTAL
WITH SHIMS
AREA DRAIN

FINISH SURFACE: LEVEL, JOINTS ACTING
AS DRAINS
DRAINAGE SURFACE: SLOPE TO DRAIN
⅛"–¼" PER FT
HEIGHT OF PEDESTALS: ½"–1½"
PEDESTAL MATERIAL: NEOPRENE,
METAL, VINYL, MORTAR
SHIMS: MULTIPLE OF ⅛"
**CONCRETE OR CUT STONE PAVER ON
PEDESTALS OVER UNINSULATED BASE**

CONCRETE/ASPHALT PAVER
CAVITY
PAVER PEDESTAL
WITH SHIMS
RIGID INSULATION
¼" PROTECTION
BOARD

WATERPROOFING

THIS SYSTEM IS SUITABLE FOR PEDESTRIAN
TRAFFIC ONLY. RIGID INSULATION SHALL BE
SUITABLE TO CARRY PEDESTRIAN LOADS
PEDESTAL MATERIAL: NEOPRENE, METAL,
VINYL, MORTAR
SHIMS: SAME AS PEDESTAL MATERIAL
**CONCRETE OR STONE PAVERS ON
PEDESTALS OVER INSULATED BASE**

UNIT PAVERS ON SUSPENDED BASE

7. Footing of edging width: 8, 12, 16, 20 in.; depth: 6,
8 in.

8. If freezing, depth is deeper than bottom of footing;
provide gravel at footing.

GROWTH AND DEVELOPMENT

As children grow their physical abilities change, as does the scale of equipment that will challenge them. Physical growth is accommodated by social development resulting in different levels and types of interaction and activity. A child's play experience must be successful as well as challenging. Therefore play equipment should be designed and selected to meet the physical and intellectual requirements of groups that will use it. The height, distance between levels, and the ability and strength required to use the equipment should be scaled to the size and level of social and intellectual development of the child.

SINGLE UNIT VS. INTEGRATED PLAY EQUIPMENT

Many types of play equipment are designed to stand alone as units. While they may often be linked to other equipment, they are generally single activity items. Where space or other conditions limit the scope of development such equipment is useful. However, since activity proceeds in a continuous flow, integrated play areas have proved to be more successful than arrangements of individual items. Linking of equipment and equipment that combines several activities on one structure increase the options available to the user and tend to increase the interest and challenge.

PLAY COMPONENTS

Several basic elements are used to create play equipment. The most commonly employed include slides (standard, spiral, tube, rail, roller, and pole), swings (standard and tire), ladders (vertical, horizontal, chain net, cables, and arch), climbers (stepped wood posts, stacks, arch, chain, rungs, tire, and rope), and miscellaneous components (decks, panels, log rollers, spring pads, balance beams, parallel bars, rings, and clatter bridges).

INTEGRATED PLAY STRUCTURES

Manufacturers offer predesigned arrangements, using a variety of play components to provide a multitude of ways to serve groups of 5 to 75 children. These systems are available in timber and powder-coated steel. Both offer modular construction, ease of installation, durability, and a variety of accessories, most of which are common to each. Plan space requirements on the number of children expected to use such a structure at one time. Allot each child about 65 to 70 sq. ft., which includes a 4 ft. safety zone around the structure.

SAFETY CONCERNS

No playground or play activity is completely safe from all potential accidents because the element of risk is inherent in most play. To design an absolutely safe playground would remove all risk and thus would be counterproductive. Children would seek challenge elsewhere, usually where risk is unmanaged. As a goal, playground equipment should provide challenging activities in the safest way possible. Structures should be solidly built. Components should have rounded edges and corners. Metal fasteners should be covered or placed in recessed holes. Above all, playground equipment always should be installed on a bed of absorbing ground cover such as granulated pine bark (12 in. deep), pea gravel (10 in. deep), or sand (10 in. deep). Asphalt, packed dirt, or exposed concrete should never be an acceptable play surface. Manufacturers recommend a minimum of 4 ft. safety zone around the play area. Adequate seating space in clear view of all play equipment should be allotted for adults supervising children.

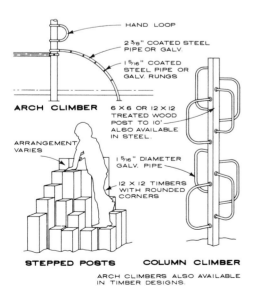

SLIDES

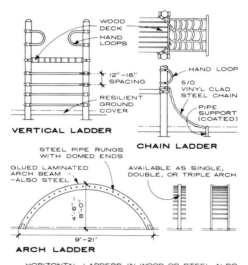

LADDERS

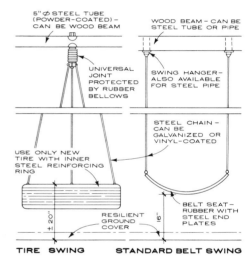

SWINGS

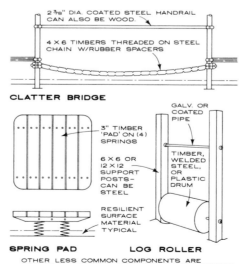

CLIMBERS

MISCELLANEOUS

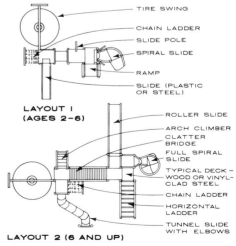

INTEGRATED PLAYSYSTEMS

Robert K. Sherrill; Wilkes, Faulkner, Jenkins & Bass; Washington, D.C.

5   SITE IMPROVEMENTS

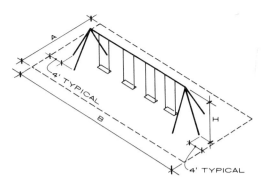

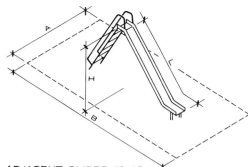

ADJACENT SLIDES: 7'-6"
(CHUTES C.TO C.) OTHERS 10' O.C.

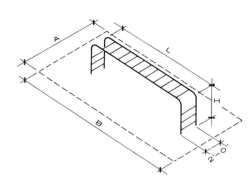

SWINGS

| SWINGS | H (FT) | SAFETY ZONE | |
		A (FT)	B (FT)
2	8	24	27
	10	28	27
	12	32	27
3	8	24	30
	10	28	30
	12	32	30
4	8	24	40
	10	28	40
	12	32	40
6	8	24	46
	10	28	46
	12	32	46
8	8	24	57
	10	28	57
	12	32	57
9	8	24	61
	10	28	61
	12	32	61

SLIDES

| H | L | SAFETY ZONE | |
		A	B
4	8	26	24
5	10	26	28
6	12	26	32
8	16	26	36

HORIZONTAL LADDER

| H (FT-IN.) | L (FT-IN.) | SAFETY ZONE | |
		A (FT)	B (FT)
6-6	12-6	14	25
7-6	16-0	14	30

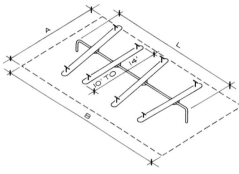

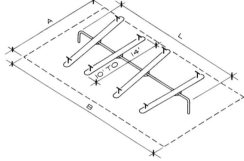

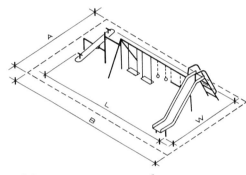

GENERAL PLANNING INFORMATION

EQUIPMENT	AREA (SQ FT)	CAPACITY (NUMBER OF CHILDREN)
Slide	450	4–6
Low swing	150	1
High swing	250	1
Horizontal ladder	375	6–8
Seesaw	100	2
Junior climbing gym	180	8–10
General climbing gym	500	15–20

SEESAWS

BOARDS	1	2	3	4	6
L	3	6	9	12	18
A	20	20	20	20	20
B	5	10	15	20	25

COMBINATION UNITS*

ENCLOSURE LIMITS
A = W + 12'-0''
B = L + 6'-0''

*Types and no. of units are variable.

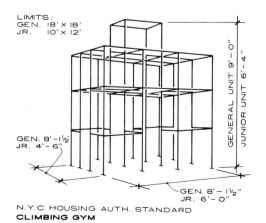

LIMITS:
GEN. 18' x 18'
JR. 10' x 12'

N.Y.C. HOUSING AUTH. STANDARD
CLIMBING GYM

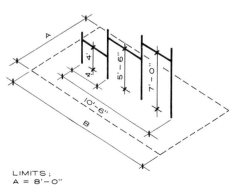

LIMITS;
A = 8'-0''
B = L +6'-0'' HEIGHTS ADJUSTABLE
HORIZONTAL BARS

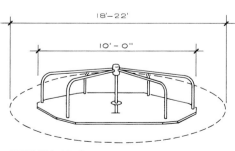

10 FT DIA. IS CONSIDERED STANDARD
OTHER DIA. = 6' AND 8'

SPIN AROUND

Robert K. Sherrill; Wilkes, Faulkner, Jenkins & Bass; Washington, D.C.
Vincent F. Nauseda; Sasaki, Dawson Associates, Inc.; Watertown, Massachusetts

SITE IMPROVEMENTS 5

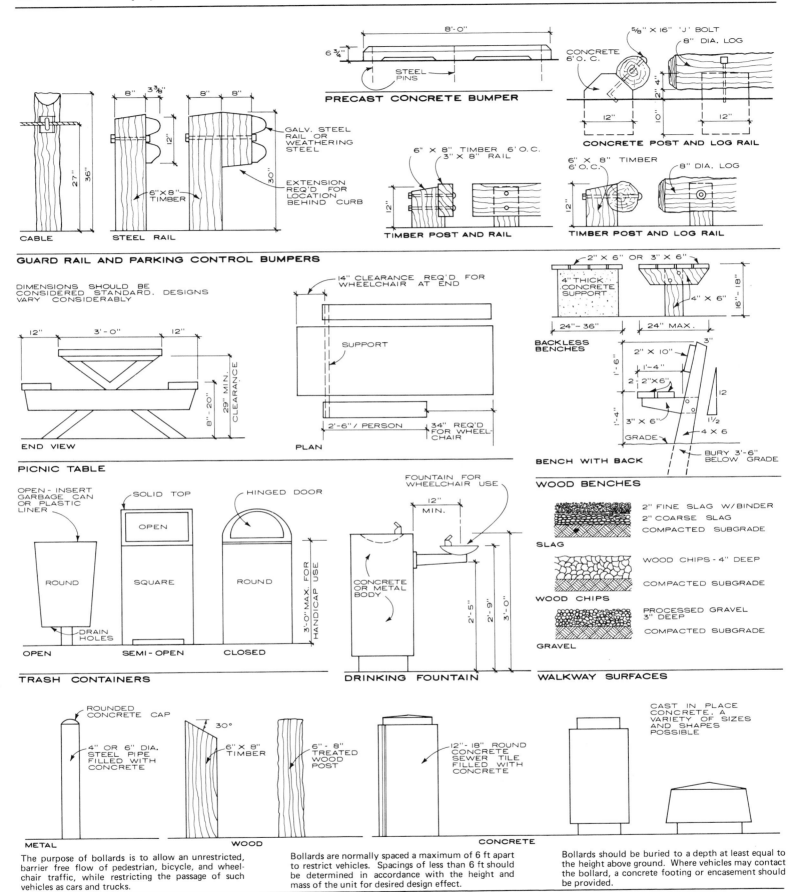

GUARD RAIL AND PARKING CONTROL BUMPERS

PRECAST CONCRETE BUMPER

CONCRETE POST AND LOG RAIL

TIMBER POST AND RAIL

TIMBER POST AND LOG RAIL

PICNIC TABLE

DIMENSIONS SHOULD BE CONSIDERED STANDARD. DESIGNS VARY CONSIDERABLY

BACKLESS BENCHES

WOOD BENCHES

BENCH WITH BACK

TRASH CONTAINERS

DRINKING FOUNTAIN

WALKWAY SURFACES

2" FINE SLAG W/BINDER
2" COARSE SLAG
COMPACTED SUBGRADE
SLAG

WOOD CHIPS - 4" DEEP
COMPACTED SUBGRADE
WOOD CHIPS

PROCESSED GRAVEL 3" DEEP
COMPACTED SUBGRADE
GRAVEL

The purpose of bollards is to allow an unrestricted, barrier free flow of pedestrian, bicycle, and wheelchair traffic, while restricting the passage of such vehicles as cars and trucks.

Bollards are normally spaced a maximum of 6 ft apart to restrict vehicles. Spacings of less than 6 ft should be determined in accordance with the height and mass of the unit for desired design effect.

Bollards should be buried to a depth at least equal to the height above ground. Where vehicles may contact the bollard, a concrete footing or encasement should be provided.

BOLLARDS

John M. Beckett; Beckett, Raeder, Rankin, Inc.; Ann Arbor, Michigan

5   **SITE IMPROVEMENTS**

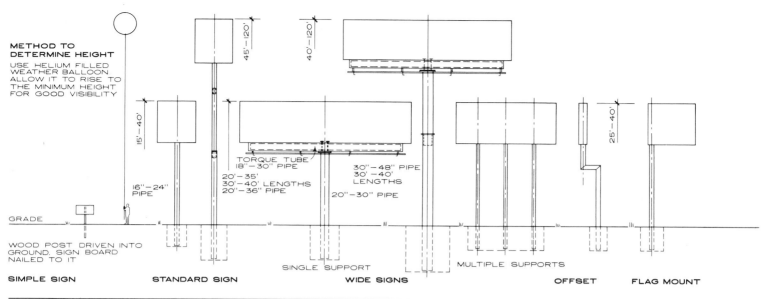

METHOD TO DETERMINE HEIGHT

USE HELIUM FILLED WEATHER BALLOON ALLOW IT TO RISE TO THE MINIMUM HEIGHT FOR GOOD VISIBILITY

16"–24" PIPE

GRADE

WOOD POST DRIVEN INTO GROUND, SIGN BOARD NAILED TO IT

45'–120'

40'–120'

15'–40'

25'–40'

TORQUE TUBE 18"–30" PIPE

20'–35' 30'–40' LENGTHS 20'–36" PIPE

30"–48" PIPE 30'–40' LENGTHS

20"–30" PIPE

SINGLE SUPPORT

MULTIPLE SUPPORTS

SIMPLE SIGN   STANDARD SIGN   WIDE SIGNS   OFFSET   FLAG MOUNT

TYPES OF SIGNS

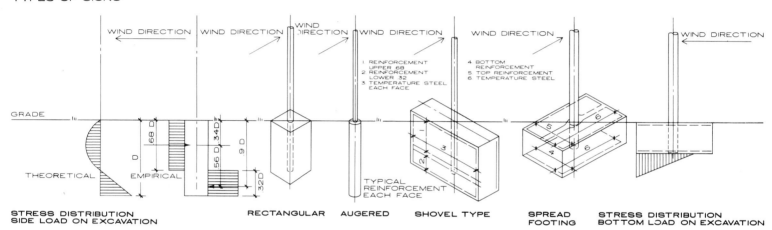

WIND DIRECTION   WIND DIRECTION   WIND DIRECTION   WIND DIRECTION   WIND DIRECTION   WIND DIRECTION

GRADE

1. REINFORCEMENT UPPER 68
2. REINFORCEMENT LOWER 32
3. TEMPERATURE STEEL EACH FACE

4. BOTTOM REINFORCEMENT
5. TOP REINFORCEMENT
6. TEMPERATURE STEEL

THEORETICAL   EMPIRICAL

68 D   34 D   9 D
56 D   32 D
D

TYPICAL REINFORCEMENT EACH FACE

STRESS DISTRIBUTION SIDE LOAD ON EXCAVATION   **RECTANGULAR   AUGERED   SHOVEL TYPE   SPREAD FOOTING   STRESS DISTRIBUTION BOTTOM LOAD ON EXCAVATION**

FOOTING TYPES

STRUCTURAL DESIGN OF SIGNS

Signs are structurally designed primarily by wind forces and secondarily by gravitational forces. Wind forces are determined by wind speed, height, location, time interval for maximum wind (100 year, 50 year, etc.), gust factor, distribution on the surface, and codes. Although the basic wind load p is computed by the formula $p = 0.00258\ V$ where V = velocity of the wind in miles per hour, the factors that modify it vary in different regions by the codes that apply. Therefore wind loads are computed differently in different parts of the country. A state code may also be modified by a local ordinance, so a designer has to make sure that code requirements are met. By following the applicable code requirements utilizing wind maps, tables, and directions, the designer is able to determine the wind load per square foot acting on the sign surface in the locality in which the sign is being erected.

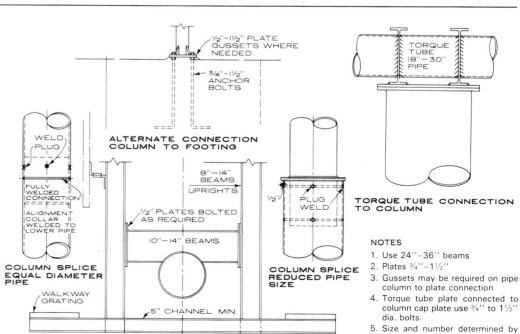

1/2"–1 1/2" PLATE GUSSETS WHERE NEEDED

3/4"–1 1/2" ANCHOR BOLTS

ALTERNATE CONNECTION COLUMN TO FOOTING

TORQUE TUBE 18"–30" PIPE

TORQUE TUBE CONNECTION TO COLUMN

WELD PLUG

FULLY WELDED CONNECTION

ALIGNMENT COLLAR WELDED TO LOWER PIPE

COLUMN SPLICE EQUAL DIAMETER PIPE

WALKWAY GRATING

8"–14" BEAMS

UPRIGHTS

1/2" PLATES BOLTED AS REQUIRED

10"–14" BEAMS

5" CHANNEL MIN.

UPRIGHT CONNECTION TO TORQUE TUBE

1/2"

PLUG WELD

COLUMN SPLICE REDUCED PIPE SIZE

NOTES

1. Use 24"–36" beams
2. Plates 3/4"–1 1/2"
3. Gussets may be required on pipe column to plate connection
4. Torque tube plate connected to column cap plate use 3/4" to 1 1/2" dia. bolts.
5. Size and number determined by design conditions

Leon Seligson, AIA; Columbus, Ohio

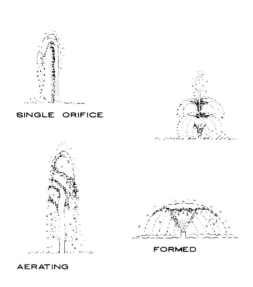

SINGLE ORIFICE

AERATING

FORMED

GENERAL JET TYPES

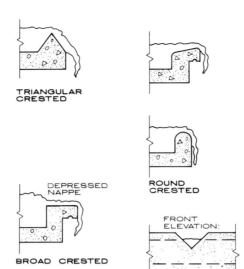

TRIANGULAR CRESTED

ROUND CRESTED

DEPRESSED NAPPE

BROAD CRESTED

FRONT ELEVATION:

'V' NOTCHED

WEIR SECTIONS

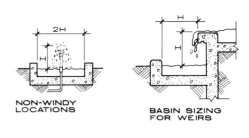

NON-WINDY LOCATIONS

BASIN SIZING FOR WEIRS

4H

BASIN SIZING FOR WINDY LOCATIONS

BASIN SIZING FOR FOUNTAINS

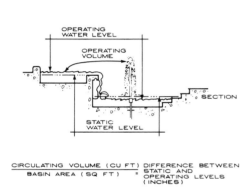

OPERATING WATER LEVEL

OPERATING VOLUME

SECTION

STATIC WATER LEVEL

$$\frac{\text{CIRCULATING VOLUME (CU FT)}}{\text{BASIN AREA (SQ FT)}} = \begin{array}{l}\text{DIFFERENCE BETWEEN}\\ \text{STATIC AND}\\ \text{OPERATING LEVELS}\\ \text{(INCHES)}\end{array}$$

STATIC AND OPERATING LEVELS OF FOUNTAINS

PURPOSE

Fountains can provide the following site considerations or program elements:

1. Recreation
2. An altered environment to increase comfort
3. Image
4. Visual focal point
5. An activities focal point
6. To frame views
7. Acoustical control

FORMS

1. Held water in pools and ponds. Form and reflectivity are design considerations.
2. Falling water. The effect depends on water velocity, water volume, container surface, or the edge over or through which the water is moving.
3. Flowing water. The visual effect of the same volume of flowing water can be changed by narrowing or widening a channel, by placing objects in its path, by changing the direction of the flow, and by changing the slope and roughness of the bottom and sides.
4. Jets. An effect derived by forcing water into the air to create a pattern. Jet types include single orifice nozzles, aerated nozzles, and formed jets.
5. Surge. An effect created by a contrast between relatively quiet water and a surge (a wave or a splash), made by quickly adding water, by raising or lowering

Barry R. Thalden, AIA; Thalden Corporation; St. Louis, Missouri

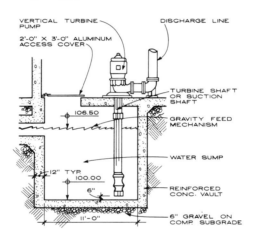

VERTICAL TURBINE PUMP

2'-0" X 3'-0" ALUMINUM ACCESS COVER

DISCHARGE LINE

TURBINE SHAFT OR SUCTION SHAFT

GRAVITY FEED MECHANISM

WATER SUMP

REINFORCED CONC. VAULT

6" GRAVEL ON COMP. SUBGRADE

106.50

12" TYP. 100.00

6"

11'-0"

VERTICAL TURBINE PUMP

an object in the water, by moving an object back and forth through the water, or by introducing strong air currents.

OVERALL DESIGN CONSIDERATIONS

1. Scale. Size of the water feature in context to the surroundings.
2. Basin sizing: Width—consider fountain height and prevailing winds. Depth—consider weight (1 cu. ft. water = 62.366 lbs.). Safety—consider children playing near or in the pool. Cover—allow space for lights, nozzles, and pumps. Local codes may classify basins of a certain depth as swimming pools. Nozzle spray may be cushioned to prevent excessive surge.
3. Bottom appearance is important when clear water is maintained. It can be enhanced by patterns, colors, materials, three-dimensional objects, or textures. Dark bottoms increase reflectivity.
4. Edges or copings. In designing the water's edge, consider the difference between the operating water level and the static water level. Loosely defined edges (as in a pond) make movement into the water possible both visually and physically. Clearly defined edges (as in a basin) use copings to delineate the water's edge.
5. Lips and weirs—A lip is an edge over which flowing water falls. A weir is a dam in the water to divert the water flow or to raise the water level. If volume and velocity are insufficient to break the surface tension, a reglet on the underside of the edge may overcome this problem.

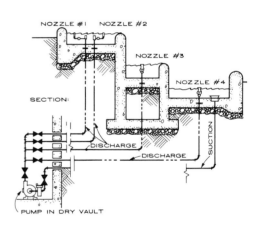

NOZZLE #1   NOZZLE #2

NOZZLE #3

NOZZLE #4

SECTION:

DISCHARGE

DISCHARGE

SUCTION

PUMP IN DRY VAULT

PIPE SCHEMATIC—DRY CENTRIFUGAL PUMP

MATERIAL SELECTION CRITERIA

1. Waterproof
2. Crack resistant
3. Weather resistant, durable
4. Stain resistant
5. Workable material appropriate for intended effect

GENERATION OF WATER PRESSURE

1. Elevated dam structures, used in early fountains, are not feasible today.
2. Submersible pumps, used for low volume fountains only, are easy to install and require short pipe runs. The pump must be covered with water to operate correctly; it may be damaged if the water level drops. Vandalism can be a problem. Motors range from $\frac{1}{20}$ to 1 horsepower.
3. Dry centrifugal pumps are used most commonly for larger water features. Motors range from $\frac{1}{4}$ to 100 horsepower. The assembly consists of a pump, electric motor, suction line, and discharge line. The pump and motor are located in an isolated dry vault.
4. Vertical turbine pumps usually are more energy efficient than pumps with suction lines because the pump uses no energy to move the water to the pump. Water flows to the pump by gravity and thus reduces the amount of work exerted by the pump. The assembly consists of a pump and motor, a water sump in the equipment vault, a gravity feed mechanism to the pump, and a discharge line.

SITE IMPROVEMENTS

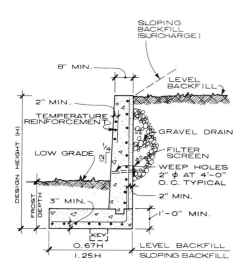

Place base below frost line. Dimensions are approximate.

L TYPE RETAINING WALLS

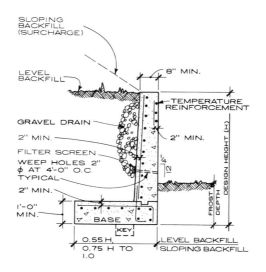

Soil pressure at toe equals 0.2 times the height in kips per square foot. Dimensions are preliminary.

GRAVITY RETAINING WALL

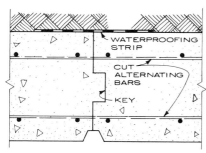

VERTICAL CONTROL JOINT

VERTICAL EXPANSION JOINT

RETAINING WALL JOINTS

NOTES

Provide control and/or construction joints in concrete retaining walls about every 25 ft and expansion joints about every fourth control and/or construction joint. Coated dowels should be used if average wall height on either side of a joint is different.

Consult with a structural engineer for final design of concrete retaining walls. An engineer's seal may be required for final design approval by local code officials.

Use temperature bars if wall is more than 10 in. thick.

Keys shown dashed may be required to prevent sliding in high walls and those on moist clay.

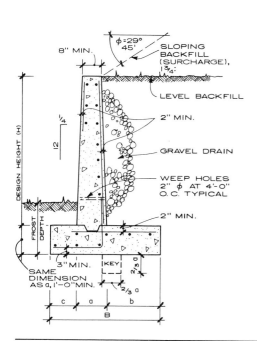

T TYPE RETAINING WALLS

PRELIMINARY DIMENSIONS

HEIGHT OF WALL H (FT)	WIDTH OF BASE B (FT)	WIDTH OF WALL a (FT)	HEEL b (FT)	TOE c (FT)
BACKFILL SLOPING ϕ = 29° 45′ (1¾:1)				
APPROXIMATE CONCRETE DIMENSIONS				
3	2′-8′′	0′-9′′	1′-5′′	0′-6′′
4	3′-5′′	0′-9′′	2′-0′′	0′-8′′
5	4′-6′′	0′-10′′	2′-6′′	1′-2′′
6	5′-4′′	0′-10′′	2′-11′′	1′-7′′
7	6′-3′′	0′-10′′	3′-5′′	2′-0′′
8	7′-0′′	1′-0′′	3′-8′′	2′-4′′
9	7′-6′′	1′-0′′	4′-2′′	2′-4′′
10	8′-6′′	1′-0′′	4′-9′′	2′-9′′
11	11′-0′′	1′-1′′	7′-2′′	2′-9′′
12	12′-0′′	1′-2′′	7′-10′′	3′-0′′
13	13′-0′′	1′-4′′	8′-5′′	3′-3′′
14	14′-0′′	1′-5′′	9′-1′′	3′-6′′
15	15′-0′′	1′-6′′	9′-9′′	3′-9′′
16	16′-0′′	1′-7′′	10′-5′′	4′-0′′
17	17′-0′′	1′-8′′	11′-1′′	4′-3′′
18	18′-0′′	1′-10′′	11′-8′′	4′-6′′
19	19′-0′′	1′-11′′	12′-4′′	4′-9′′
20	20′-0′′	2′-0′′	13′-0′′	5′-0′′
21	21′-0′′	2′-2′′	13′-7′′	5′-3′′
22	22′-0′′	2′-4′′	14′-4′′	5′-4′′

HEIGHT OF WALL H (FT)	WIDTH OF BASE B (FT)	WIDTH OF WALL a (FT)	HEEL b (FT)	TOE c (FT)
BACKFILL LEVEL—NO SURCHARGE				
APPROXIMATE CONCRETE DIMENSIONS				
3	2′-1′′	0′-8′′	1′-0′′	0′-5′′
4	2′-8′′	0′-8′′	1′-7′′	0′-5′′
5	3′-3′′	0′-8′′	2′-2′′	0′-5′′
6	3′-9′′	0′-8′′	2′-5′′	0′-8′′
7	4′-2′′	0′-8′′	2′-6′′	1′-0′′
8	4′-8′′	1′-0′′	2′-8′′	1′-0′′
9	5′-2′′	1′-0′′	3′-2′′	1′-0′′
10	5′-9′′	1′-0′′	3′-7′′	1′-2′′
11	6′-7′′	1′-1′′	4′-1′′	1′-5′′
12	7′-3′′	1′-2′′	4′-7′′	1′-6′′
13	7′-10′′	1′-2′′	5′-0′′	1′-8′′
14	8′-5′′	1′-3′′	5′-5′′	1′-9′′
15	9′-0′′	1′-4′′	5′-9′′	1′-11′′
16	9′-7′′	1′-5′′	6′-2′′	2′-0′′
17	10′-3′′	1′-6′′	6′-7′′	2′-2′′
18	10′-10′′	1′-6′′	7′-1′′	2′-3′′
19	11′-5′′	1′-7′′	7′-5′′	2′-5′′
20	12′-0′′	1′-8′′	7′-10′′	2′-6′′
21	12′-7′′	1′-9′′	8′-2′′	2′-8′′
22	13′-3′′	1′-11′′	8′-7′′	2′-9′′

Kenneth D. Franch, AIA, PE; Phillips Swager Associates, Inc.; Dallas, Texas
Neubaur · Sohn, Engineers; Washington, D.C.

WALLS AND FENCES **5**

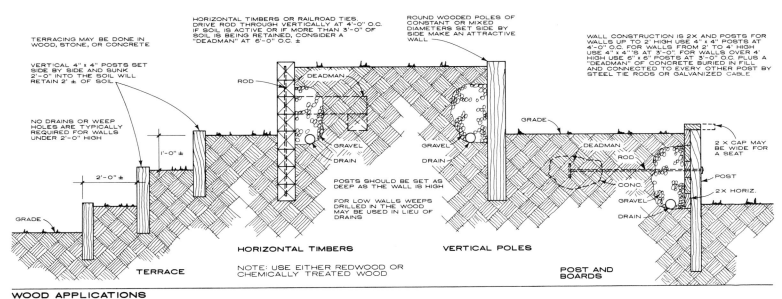

VERTICAL 4" x 4" POSTS SET SIDE BY SIDE AND SUNK 2'-0" INTO THE SOIL WILL RETAIN 2' ± OF SOIL

TERRACING MAY BE DONE IN WOOD, STONE, OR CONCRETE

NO DRAINS OR WEEP HOLES ARE TYPICALLY REQUIRED FOR WALLS UNDER 2'-0" HIGH

HORIZONTAL TIMBERS OR RAILROAD TIES. DRIVE ROD THROUGH VERTICALLY AT 4'-0" O.C. IF SOIL IS ACTIVE OR IF MORE THAN 3'-0" OF SOIL IS BEING RETAINED, CONSIDER A "DEADMAN" AT 6'-0" O.C. ±

ROUND WOODED POLES OF CONSTANT OR MIXED DIAMETERS SET SIDE BY SIDE. MAKE AN ATTRACTIVE WALL

WALL CONSTRUCTION IS 2X AND POSTS FOR WALLS UP TO 2' HIGH USE 4" x 4" POSTS AT 4'-0" O.C. FOR WALLS FROM 2' TO 4' HIGH USE 4" x 4"'S AT 3'-0". FOR WALLS OVER 4' HIGH USE 6" x 6" POSTS AT 3'-0" O.C. PLUS A "DEADMAN" OF CONCRETE BURIED IN FILL AND CONNECTED TO EVERY OTHER POST BY STEEL TIE RODS OR GALVANIZED CABLE

POSTS SHOULD BE SET AS DEEP AS THE WALL IS HIGH

FOR LOW WALLS WEEPS DRILLED IN THE WOOD MAY BE USED IN LIEU OF DRAINS

TERRACE   **HORIZONTAL TIMBERS**   **VERTICAL POLES**   **POST AND BOARDS**

NOTE: USE EITHER REDWOOD OR CHEMICALLY TREATED WOOD

WOOD APPLICATIONS

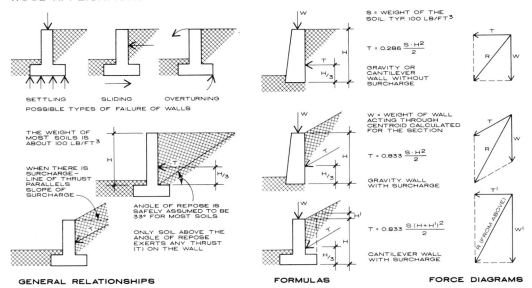

POSSIBLE TYPES OF FAILURE OF WALLS — SETTLING, SLIDING, OVERTURNING

THE WEIGHT OF MOST SOILS IS ABOUT 100 LB/FT^3

WHEN THERE IS SURCHARGE— LINE OF THRUST PARALLELS SLOPE OF SURCHARGE

ANGLE OF REPOSE IS SAFELY ASSUMED TO BE 33° FOR MOST SOILS

ONLY SOIL ABOVE THE ANGLE OF REPOSE EXERTS ANY THRUST (T) ON THE WALL

GENERAL RELATIONSHIPS

S = WEIGHT OF THE SOIL. TYP. 100 LB/FT^3

$$T = 0.286 \frac{S \cdot H^2}{2}$$

GRAVITY OR CANTILEVER WALL WITHOUT SURCHARGE

W = WEIGHT OF WALL ACTING THROUGH CENTROID CALCULATED FOR THE SECTION

$$T = 0.833 \frac{S \cdot H^2}{2}$$

GRAVITY WALL WITH SURCHARGE

$$T = 0.833 \frac{S (H + H')^2}{2}$$

CANTILEVER WALL WITH SURCHARGE

FORMULAS

FORCE DIAGRAMS

SLIDING

The thrust on the wall must be resisted. The resisting force is the weight of the wall times the coefficient of soil friction. Use a safety factor of 1.5. Therefore:

$$W(C.F.) \geq 1.5T$$

Average coefficients:

Gravel	0.6
Silt/dry clay	0.5
Sand	0.4
Wet clay	0.3

OVERTURNING

The overturning moment equals $T(H/3)$. This is resisted by the resisting moment. For symmetrical sections, resisting moment equals W times (width of base/2). Use a safety factor of 2.0. Therefore:

$$M_R \geq 2(M_0)$$

SETTLING

Soil bearing value must resist vertical force. For symmetrical sections that force is W (or W')/bearing area. Use a safety factor of 1.5. Therefore:

$$S.B. \geq 1.5(W/A)$$

STRUCTURAL DESIGN CONSIDERATIONS

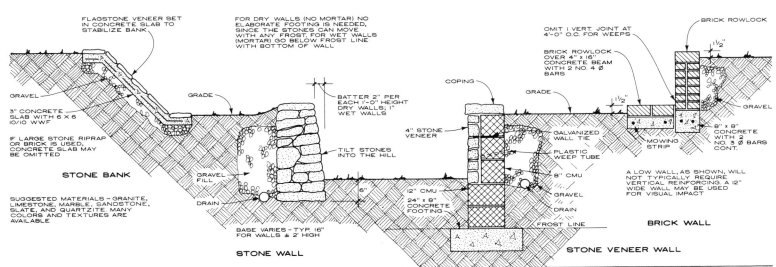

FLAGSTONE VENEER SET IN CONCRETE SLAB TO STABILIZE BANK

GRAVEL

3" CONCRETE SLAB WITH 6 x 6 10/10 WWF

IF LARGE STONE RIPRAP OR BRICK IS USED, CONCRETE SLAB MAY BE OMITTED

STONE BANK

SUGGESTED MATERIALS – GRANITE, LIMESTONE, MARBLE, SANDSTONE, SLATE, AND QUARTZITE. MANY COLORS AND TEXTURES ARE AVAILABLE

FOR DRY WALLS (NO MORTAR) NO ELABORATE FOOTING IS NEEDED, SINCE THE STONES CAN MOVE WITH ANY FROST. FOR WET WALLS (MORTAR) GO BELOW FROST LINE WITH BOTTOM OF WALL

GRADE

BATTER 2" PER EACH 1'-0" HEIGHT DRY WALLS; 1" WET WALLS

TILT STONES INTO THE HILL

GRAVEL FILL

DRAIN

STONE WALL

BASE VARIES - TYP. 16" FOR WALLS ± 2' HIGH

COPING

4" STONE VENEER

GALVANIZED WALL TIE

PLASTIC WEEP TUBE

8" CMU

12" CMU

24" x 8" CONCRETE FOOTING

FROST LINE

GRAVEL

DRAIN

STONE VENEER WALL

OMIT 1 VERT. JOINT AT 4'-0" O.C. FOR WEEPS

BRICK ROWLOCK

BRICK ROWLOCK OVER 4" x 16" CONCRETE BEAM WITH 2 NO. 4 Ø BARS

GRADE

MOWING STRIP

8" x 8" CONCRETE WITH 2 NO. 3 Ø BARS CONT.

GRAVEL

DRAIN

A LOW WALL, AS SHOWN, WILL NOT TYPICALLY REQUIRE VERTICAL REINFORCING. A 12" WIDE WALL MAY BE USED FOR VISUAL IMPACT

BRICK WALL

STONE AND MASONRY APPLICATIONS

Charles R. Heuer, AIA; Washington, D.C.

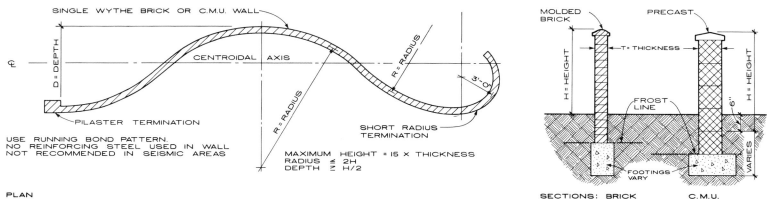

USE RUNNING BOND PATTERN.
NO REINFORCING STEEL USED IN WALL
NOT RECOMMENDED IN SEISMIC AREAS

MAXIMUM HEIGHT = 15 × THICKNESS
RADIUS ≤ 2H
DEPTH ≥ H/2

PLAN
SERPENTINE GARDEN WALLS

SECTIONS: BRICK   C.M.U.

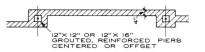

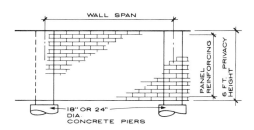

REINFORCED WALLS
PIER AND PANEL GARDEN WALLS

PANEL WALL REINFORCING STEEL

WALL SPAN (FT.)	VERTICAL SPACING* (IN.)								
	WIND LOAD 10 PSF			WIND LOAD 15 PSF			WIND LOAD 20 PSF		
	A	B	C	A	B	C	A	B	C
8	45	30	19	30	20	12	23	15	9.5
10	29	19	12	19	13	8.0	14	10	6.0
12	20	13	8.5	13	9.0	5.5	10	7.0	4.0
14	15	10	6.5	10	6.5	4.0	7.5	5.0	3.0
16	11	7.5	5.0	7.5	5.0	3.0	6.0	4.0	2.5

*A, two #2 bars; B, two 3/16 in. diameter wires; C, two 9-gauge wires.
NOTE: Wall spans between piers, no footing.

NON-REINFORCED WALLS L/T RATIO

WIND PRESSURE (P.S.F.)	MAXIMUM LENGTH/THICKNESS RATIO
5	35
10	25
15	20
20	18
25	16
30	14
35	13
40	12

NON-REINFORCED WALLS WITH CONTINUOUS FOOTINGS

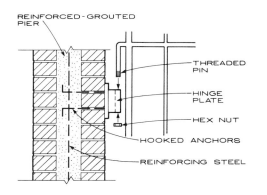

HINGE DETAIL
IRON GARDEN GATE

ANALYSIS OF SECTIONS

M_o = OVERTURNING MOMENT

M_r = RESISTING MOMENT

W = WEIGHT OF WALL AND FOOTING (LB.)

P = WIND LOAD (LB./FT.^{2}) (FROM CODE)

$M_o = PL_1$ $M_r = WL_2$

FOR STABILITY $M_r \geq M_o$;

IF NOT, REDESIGN

CANTILEVER FOOTINGS ARE OFTEN USED AT PROPERTY LINES OR TO INCREASE RESISTANCE TO OVERTURNING. BE SURE TO CHECK FOR WIND FROM EITHER DIRECTION

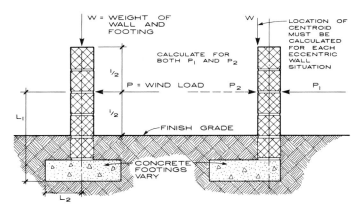

SYMMETRICAL   CANTILEVER/ECCENTRIC
HORIZONTAL LOADING - FREESTANDING WALLS

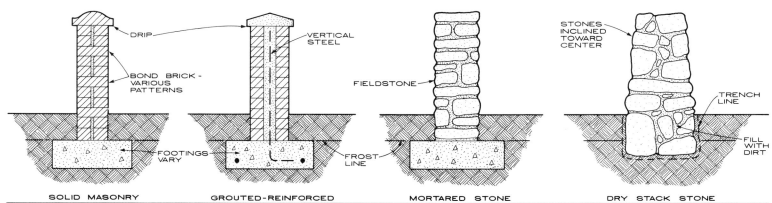

SOLID MASONRY   GROUTED-REINFORCED   MORTARED STONE   DRY STACK STONE
FREESTANDING WALL TYPES

Christine Beall, AIA, CCS; Austin, Texas
Charles R. Heuer, AIA; Washington, D.C.

WALLS AND FENCES 5

DIMENSIONS AND REINFORCEMENT

WALL	H	B	T	A	"V" BARS	"F" BARS
8"	3' 4"	2' 4"	9"	8"	#3 @ 32"	#3 @ 27"
	4' 0"	2' 9"	9"	10"	#4 @ 32"	#3 @ 27"
	4' 8"	3' 4"	10"	12"	#5 @ 32"	#3 @ 27"
	5' 4"	3' 8"	10"	14"	#4 @ 16"	#4 @ 30"
	6' 0"	4' 2"	12"	16"	#6 @ 24"	#4 @ 25"
12"	5' 4"	3' 8"	10"	14"	#4 @ 24"	#3 @ 25"
	6' 0"	4' 2"	12"	15"	#4 @ 16"	#4 @ 30"
	6' 8"	4' 6"	12"	16"	#6 @ 24"	#4 @ 22"
	7' 4"	4' 10"	12"	18"	#5 @ 16"	#5 @ 26"
	8' 0"	5' 4"	12"	20"	#7 @ 24"	#5 @ 21"
	8' 8"	5' 10"	14"	22"	#6 @ 8"	#6 @ 26"
	9' 4"	6' 2"	14"	24"	#8 @ 8"	#6 @ 21"

NOTE: See General Notes for design parameters.

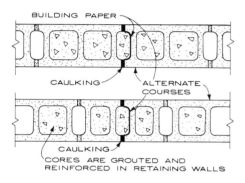

SHEAR - RESISTING CONTROL JOINT

NOTE

Long retaining walls should be broken into panels 20 ft. to 30 ft. long by vertical control joints designed to resist shear and other lateral forces while permitting longitudinal movement.

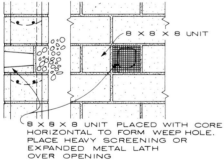

8 X 8 X 8 UNIT PLACED WITH CORE HORIZONTAL TO FORM WEEP HOLE. PLACE HEAVY SCREENING OR EXPANDED METAL LATH OVER OPENING

ALTERNATE WEEP HOLE DETAIL

NOTE

Four inch diameter weepholes located at 5 to 10 ft spacing along the base of the wall should be sufficient. Place about 1 cu ft of gravel or crushed stone around the intake of each weephole.

GENERAL NOTES

1. Materials and construction practices for concrete masonry retaining walls should comply with "Building Code Requirements for Concrete Masonry Structures (ACI 531)."
2. Use fine grout where grout space is less than 3 in. in least dimension. Use coarse grout where the least dimension of the grout space is 3 in. or more.
3. Steel reinforcement should be clean, free from harmful rust, and in compliance with applicable ASTM standards for deformed bars and steel wire.
4. Alternate vertical bars may be stopped at wall midheight. Vertical reinforcement usually is secured in

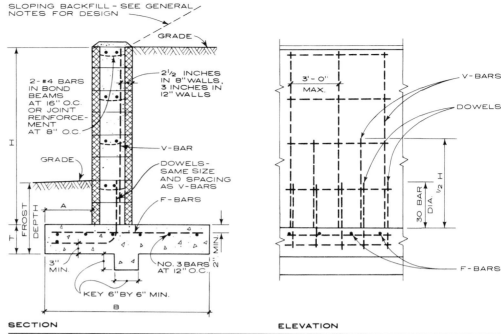

TYPICAL CANTILEVER RETAINING WALL

SECTION   **ELEVATION**

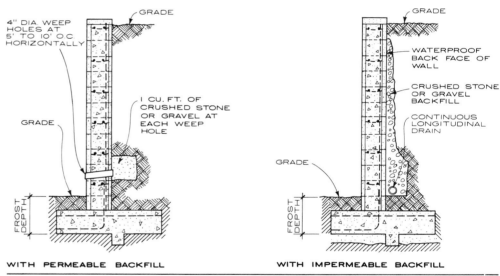

WITH PERMEABLE BACKFILL   **WITH IMPERMEABLE BACKFILL**

DRAINAGE DETAILS FOR VARYING SOIL CONDITIONS

place after the masonry work has been completed and before grouting.

5. Designs herein are based on an assumed soil weight (vertical pressure) of 100 pcf. Horizontal pressure is based on an equivalent fluid weight for the soil of 45 pcf.
6. Walls shown are designed with a safety factor against overturning of not less than 2 and a safety factor against horizontal sliding of not less than 1.5. Computations in the table for wall heights are based on level backfill. One method of providing for additional loads due to sloping backfill or surface loads is to consider them as an additional depth of soil, that is, an extra load of 300 psf can be treated as 3 ft. of extra soil weighing 100 psf.
7. Top of masonry retaining walls should be capped or otherwise protected to prevent entry of water into unfilled hollow cells and spaces. If bond beams are used, steel is placed in the beams as the wall is constructed. Horizontal joint reinforcement may be

placed in each joint (8 in. o.c.) and the bond beams omitted.

8. Allow 24 hours for masonry to set before grouting. Pour grout in 4 ft. layers, 1 hour between each pour. Break long walls into panels of 20 ft. to 30 ft. in length with vertical control joints. Allow 7 days for finished wall to set before backfilling. Prevent water from accumulating behind wall by means of 4 in. diameter weepholes at 5 ft. to 10 ft. spacing (with screen and graded stone) or by a continuous drain with felt-covered open joints combined with waterproofing.
9. Where backfill height exceeds 6 ft., provide a key under the footing base to resist the wall's tendency to slide horizontally.
10. Heavy equipment used in backfilling should not approach closer to the top of the wall than a distance equal to the height of the wall.
11. A structural engineer should be consulted for final design.

Kenneth D. Franch, AIA, PE; Phillips Swager Associates, Inc.; Dallas, Texas
Stephen J. Zipp, AIA; Wilkes and Faulkner Associates; Washington, D.C.

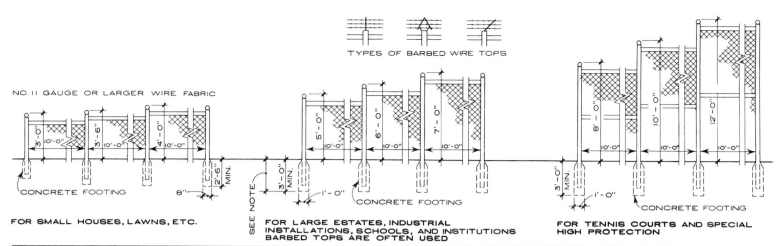

TYPES OF BARBED WIRE TOPS

NO. 11 GAUGE OR LARGER WIRE FABRIC

CONCRETE FOOTING

FOR SMALL HOUSES, LAWNS, ETC.

SEE NOTE

CONCRETE FOOTING

FOR LARGE ESTATES, INDUSTRIAL
INSTALLATIONS, SCHOOLS, AND INSTITUTIONS
BARBED TOPS ARE OFTEN USED

CONCRETE FOOTING

FOR TENNIS COURTS AND SPECIAL
HIGH PROTECTION

HEIGHTS OF FENCES FOR VARIOUS USES

See note at middle right for depth of concrete footings.

MATERIALS

SIZES GIVEN ARE NOT STANDARD BUT REPRESENT THE AVERAGE SIZES USED	
Wire gauge	Usually No. 11 or No. 9 W & M. For specially rugged use use No. 6. For tennis courts usually No. 11
Wire mesh	Usually 2″. For tennis courts usually $1^{5}/_{8}$″ or $1^{3}/_{4}$″ of chain link steel hot dip galvanized after weaving. Top and bottom salvage may be barbed or knuckled
Corner and end posts	For lawn fences usually 2″ O.D. For estate fences 2″ for low and $2^{1}/_{2}$″ for medium and 3″ O.D. for heavy or high For tennis courts 3″ O.D.
Line or intermediate posts	For lawn $1^{3}/_{8}$″ or 2″ O.D. round For estate etc. 2″, $2^{1}/_{4}$″, $2^{1}/_{2}$″ H or I sections For tennis courts $2^{1}/_{2}$″ round O.D. or $2^{1}/_{4}$″ H or I sections
Gate posts	The same or next size larger than the corner posts. Footings for gate posts 3′–6″ deep
Top rails	$1^{5}/_{8}$″ O.D. except some lawn fence may be $1^{3}/_{8}$″ O.D.
Middle rails	On 12′–0″ fence same as top rail
Gates	Single or double any width desired
Post spacing	Line posts 10′–0″ O.C., 8′–0″ O.C. may be used on heavy construction

O.D. = outside diameter.

POST SIZES FOR HEAVY DUTY GATES

A.S.A. SCHEDULE 40 PIPE SIZES	SWING GATE OPENINGS	
	SINGLE GATE	DOUBLE GATE
$2^{1}/_{2}$″	To 6′–0″	Up to 12′–0″
$3^{1}/_{2}$″	Over 6′ to 18′	Over 12′ to 26′
6″	Over 13′ to 18′	Over 26′ to 36′
8″	Over 18′ to 32′	Over 36′ to 64′

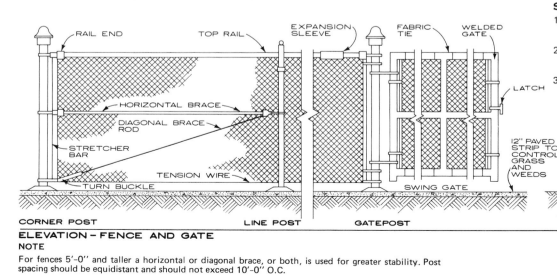

ELEVATION – FENCE AND GATE

NOTE

For fences 5′–0″ and taller a horizontal or diagonal brace, or both, is used for greater stability. Post spacing should be equidistant and should not exceed 10′–0″ O.C.

Charles Driesen; Ewing Cole Erdman & Eubank; Philadelphia, Pennsylvania

CONCRETE FOOTING

Bottom of concrete footing to be set below frost line (see local code). Concrete footing sizes shown are the recommended minimum; they should be redesigned for conditions where soil is poor.

TYPES OF WIRE FABRIC MESH

VINYL-COATED: Suitable for residential, commercial or industrial applications.
Mesh sizes: 1, $1^{1}/_{4}$, $1^{1}/_{2}$, $1^{3}/_{4}$, and 2 in.
Gauge sizes: 11, 9, 6, and 3.

REDWOOD SLATS

Used for visual privacy and appearance. Suitable for homes, swimming pools, and gardens.
Mesh size: $3^{1}/_{2}$ x 5 in.
Gauge size: 9.

1. PREGALVANIZED: Should be restricted to such residential applications as residential perimeter fencing, swimming pool enclosures, private tennis courts, dog kennels, and interior industrial storage.
   Mesh sizes: $1^{1}/_{2}$, $1^{3}/_{4}$, and 2 in. Gauge sizes: 13, 11, and 9.

2. HOT DIPPED GALVANIZED: Suitable for highway enclosures, institutional security fencing, highway bridge enclosures, exterior industrial security fences, parking lot enclosures, recreational applications, and any other environment where resistance to abuse and severe climatic conditions exist.
   Mesh sizes: $1^{1}/_{2}$, $2^{3}/_{4}$, and 2 in. Gauge sizes: 9 and 6.

COATINGS

Protective coatings used on fencing, such as zinc and aluminum. Various decorative coatings can be applied including vinyl bonded and organic coatings available from most manufacturers.

SPECIAL FENCING

1. ORNAMENTAL: Vertical struts only—no chain link fabric required. Ideal for landscape or as barrier fence.

2. ELEPHANT FENCE: This fence can actually stop an elephant, hold back a rock slide, or bring a small truck to a halt. Size: 3 gauges x 2-in. mesh.

3. SECURITY FENCE: This fabric is nonclimbable and cannot be penetrated by gun muzzles, knives, or other weapons. Suitable as security barrier for police stations, prisons, reformatories, hospitals, and mental institutions. Mesh size: $3/8$ in. for maximum security, $1/2$ in. for high security, $5/8$ in. for supersecurity, and 1 in. for standard security.

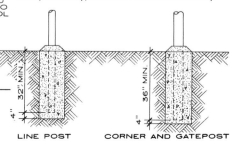

LINE POST   CORNER AND GATEPOST

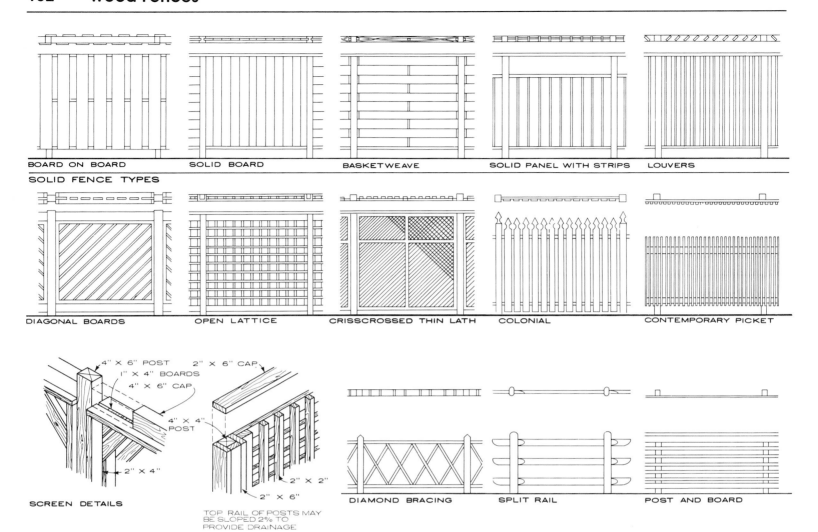

BOARD ON BOARD　　SOLID BOARD　　BASKETWEAVE　　SOLID PANEL WITH STRIPS　LOUVERS

SOLID FENCE TYPES

DIAGONAL BOARDS　　OPEN LATTICE　　CRISSCROSSED THIN LATH　COLONIAL　　CONTEMPORARY PICKET

4" X 6" POST　2" X 6" CAP.
1" X 4" BOARDS
4" X 6" CAP
4" X 4" POST
2" X 4"
2" X 2"
2" X 6"

SCREEN DETAILS

TOP RAIL OF POSTS MAY
BE SLOPED 2% TO
PROVIDE DRAINAGE

DIAMOND BRACING　　SPLIT RAIL　　POST AND BOARD

TRANSPARENT FENCES AND SCREENS

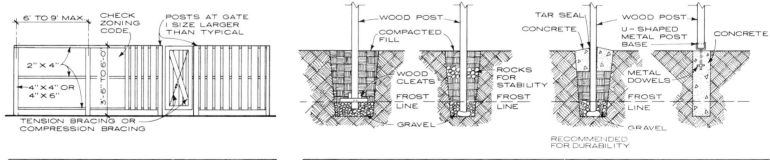

6' TO 9' MAX.　CHECK ZONING CODE　POSTS AT GATE 1 SIZE LARGER THAN TYPICAL
2" X 4"
3'-6" TO 6'-0"
4" X 4" OR 4" X 6"
TENSION BRACING OR COMPRESSION BRACING

TYPICAL FENCE DIMENSIONS

WOOD POST
COMPACTED FILL
WOOD CLEATS
FROST LINE
GRAVEL
ROCKS FOR STABILITY
FROST LINE
TAR SEAL
CONCRETE
WOOD POST
U-SHAPED METAL POST BASE
FROST LINE
GRAVEL
METAL DOWELS
CONCRETE

RECOMMENDED FOR DURABILITY

FOOTING DETAILS

NOTES

When selecting a wood fence pattern, consider:

1. Site topography and prevailing wind conditions;
2. Architectural style of surrounding buildings and adjacent land use;
3. Required fence height and size of the property to be enclosed.

PURPOSE

Wood fences are used for security, privacy, and screening of outdoor spaces. Picket fences 3 ft. or 4 ft. high keep small children or small dogs in the yard. Board-on-board fences, by standards built taller, provide greater wind and view barriers. Acoustical fences are built to keep out sound and wind, and to provide privacy. Open lattice or louvered fences, usually a minimum of 4 ft. high with self-closing gates and latches, are used for swimming pool enclosures. A semitransparent wood screen often is used to enclose an outdoor room to avoid totally obstructing the view or restricting natural ventilation. Long, open fence patterns are used best at the property line to define boundaries or limit access to a site.

FASTENERS

Fasteners should be of noncorrosive aluminum alloy or stainless steel. Top quality, hot dipped galvanized steel is acceptable. Metal flanges, cleats, bolts, and screws are better than common nails.

Pressure-treated wood commonly is used for fencing. Certain species of nontreated woods, such as cedar and redwood heart, also are suitable. Refer to pages on wood uses in Chapter 6 for further information. Natural, stain, and paint finishes may be used.

Charles R. Heuer, AIA; Washington, D.C.

 WALLS AND FENCES

GENERAL NOTES

Factors to consider in construction of all concrete slabs on grade include assurance of uniform subgrade, quality of concrete, adequacy of structural capacity, type and spacing of joints, finishing, curing, and the application of special surfaces. It is vital to design and construct the subgrade as carefully as the floor slab itself. The subgrade support must be reasonably uniform, and the upper portion of the subgrade should be of uniform material and density. A subbase, a thin layer of granular material placed on the subgrade, should be used in most cases to cushion the slab.

Wear resistance is directly related to concrete strength. A low water-cement ratio improves the surface hardness and finishability as well as internal strength of concrete. Low water-cement ratio, low slump, and well graded aggregates with coarse aggregate size as large as placing and finishing requirements will permit and enhance the quality of concrete.

Exterior concrete subjected to freeze-thaw cycles should have 6 to 8% entrained air. Reinforcement is unnecessary where frequent joint spacing is used. Where less frequent joint spacing is necessary, reinforcement is put in the top one third depth to hold together any shrinkage cracks that form. Control joint spacing of 15 to 25 ft square is recommended. Checkerboard pouring patterns allow for some shrinkage between pours, but the process is more costly and is not recommended for large areas. The total shrinkage process takes up to one year. Strip pouring, allowing for a continuous pour with control joints cut after concrete has set, is a fast economical method, recommended for large areas.

Three types of joints are recommended:

1. ISOLATION JOINTS (also called expansion joints): Allow movement between slab and fixed parts of the building such as columns, walls, and machinery bases.
2. CONTROL JOINTS: Induce cracking at preselected locations.
3. CONSTRUCTION JOINTS: Provide stopping places during floor construction. Construction joints also function as control and isolation joints.
   Sawcut control joints should be made as early as is practical after finishing the slab and should be filled in areas with wet conditions, hygienic and dust control requirements, or considerable traffic

by hard wheeled vehicles, such as forklift trucks. A semirigid filler with Shore Hardness "A" of at least 80 should be used.

Concrete floor slabs are monolithically finished by floating and troweling the concrete to a smooth dense finish. Depressions of more than $\frac{1}{8}$ in. in 10 ft or variations of more than $\frac{1}{4}$ in. from a level plane are undesirable. Special finishes are available to improve appearance. These include sprinkled (shake) finishes and high strength concrete toppings, either monolithic or separate (two-stage floor).

A vaporproof barrier should be placed under all slabs on grade where the passage of water vapor through the floor is undesirable. Permeance of vapor barrier should not exceed 0.20 perms.

Generally the controlling factor in determining the thickness of a floor on ground is the heaviest concentrated load it will carry, usually the wheel load plus impact of an industrial truck. Because of practical considerations, the minimum recommended thickness for an industrial floor is about 5 in. For Class 1, 2, and 3 floors, the minimum thickness should be 4 in.

The floor thickness required for wheel loads on relatively small areas may be obtained from the table for concrete; an allowable flexural tensile stress (psi) can be estimated from the approximate formula $f_t = 4.6 \sqrt{f_c'}$ in which f_c' is the 28-day concrete compressive strength. If f_t is not 300 psi, the table can be used by multiplying the actual total load by the ratio of 300 to the stress used and entering the chart with that value.

Assume that a 5000 psi concrete slab is to be designed for an industrial plant floor over which there will be considerable traffic—trucks with loads of 10,000 lb/wheel, each of which has a contact area of about 30 sq in. Assume that operating conditions are such that impact will be equivalent to about 25% of the load. The equivalent static load will then be 12,500 lb. The allowable flexural tensile stress for 5000 psi concrete is

$$4.6 \sqrt{5000} = 325 \text{ psi}$$

The allowable loads in the table are based on a stress of 300 psi, so that the design load must be corrected by the factor 300/325. Thus 11,500 lb on an area of 30 sq in. requires a slab about $7\frac{1}{2}$ in. thick.

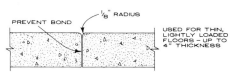

BUTT TYPE CONSTRUCTION JOINT

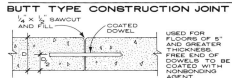

BUTT TYPE CONSTRUCTION JOINT WITH DOWELS

TONGUE AND GROOVE CONSTRUCTION JOINT

SAWED OR PREMOLDED CONTROL JOINT FOR SLABS < 4"

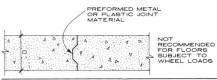

TONGUE AND GROOVE CONTROL JOINT

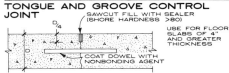

CONTROL JOINT WITH DOWELS

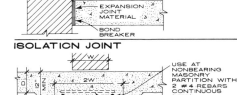

ISOLATION JOINT

THICKENED SLAB

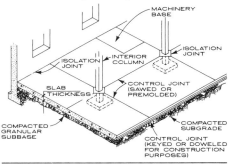

CONTROL JOINTS FOR A SLAB ON GRADE

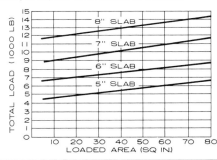

MAXIMUM WHEEL LOADS FOR INDUSTRIAL FLOORS (FLEXURAL TENSILE STRESS = 300 PSI)

CLASSIFICATION OF CONCRETE SLABS ON GRADE

CLASS	SLUMP RANGE (IN.)	MINIMUM COMPRESSIVE STRENGTH (PSI)	USUAL TRAFFIC	USE	SPECIAL CONSIDERATION	CONCRETE FINISHING TECHNIQUE
1	2-4	3500	Light foot	Residential or tile covered	Grade for drainage; plane smooth for tile	Medium steel trowel
2	2-4	3500	Foot	Offices, schools, hospitals, residential	Nonslip aggregate, mix in surface Color shake, special	Steel trowel; special finish for nonslip. Steel trowel, color exposed aggregate
3	2-4	3500	Light foot and pneumatic wheels	Drives, garage floors, sidewalks for residences	Crown; pitch joints	Float, trowel, and broom
4	1-3	4000	Foot and pneumatic wheels	Light industrial, commercial	Careful curing	Hard steel trowel and brush for nonslip
5	1-3	4500	Foot and wheels—abrasive wear	Single course industrial, integral topping	Careful curing	Special hard aggregate, float and trowel
6	2-4	3500	Foot and steel tire vehicles—severe abrasion	Bonded two-course, heavy industrial	Base: textured surface and bond Top: special aggregate	Base: surface leveled by screeding Top: special power floats
7	1-3	4000	Same as Classes 3, 4, 5, 6	Unbonded topping	Mesh reinforcing; bond breaker on old concrete surface	—

Setter, Leach & Lindstrom, Inc.; Minneapolis, Minnesota

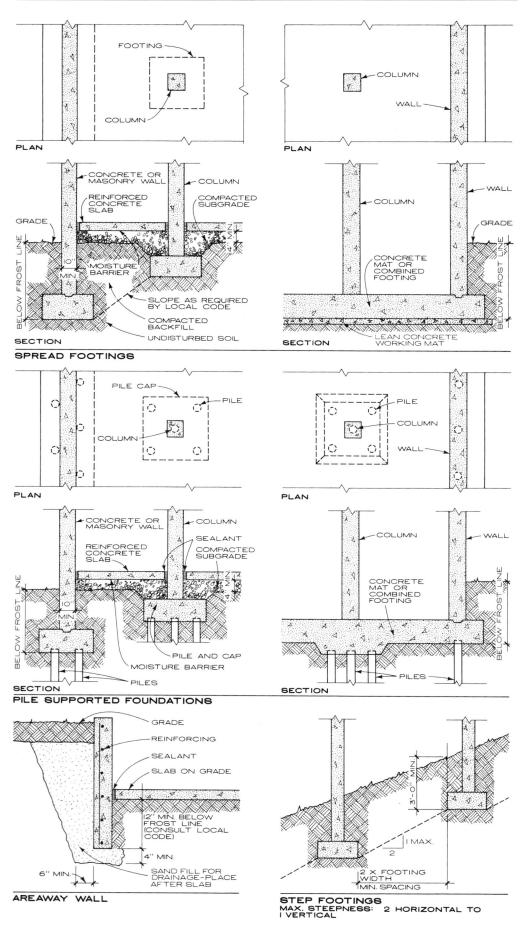

SPREAD FOOTINGS

PILE SUPPORTED FOUNDATIONS

AREAWAY WALL

STEP FOOTINGS
MAX. STEEPNESS: 2 HORIZONTAL TO
1 VERTICAL

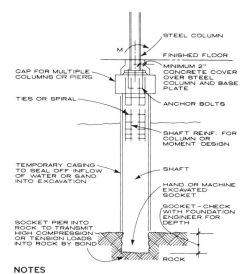

BELL PIER FOUNDATION

NOTES

1. H is a function of the passive resistance of the soil, generated by the moment applied to the pier cap.
2. Piers may be used under grade beams or concrete walls. For very heavy loads, pier foundations may be more economical than piles.

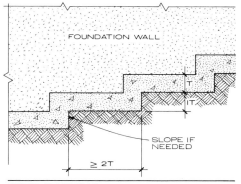

SOCKET PIER FOUNDATION

NOTES

1. Pier shaft should be poured in the dry if possible, but tremie pours can be used with appropriate control.
2. Grout bottom of shaft against artesian water or sulphur gas intrusion into the excavation.

STEP FOOTING (FOR CONTINUOUS WALL)
MAX. STEEPNESS: 2 HORIZONTAL TO
1 VERTICAL

Mueser, Rutledge, Johnston & DeSimone; New York, New York

5   **CAST-IN-PLACE CONCRETE**

NOTES

1. See page on stair dimensions for code requirements for stairs.
2. Structural designer to determine reinforcement and verify structural assumptions.

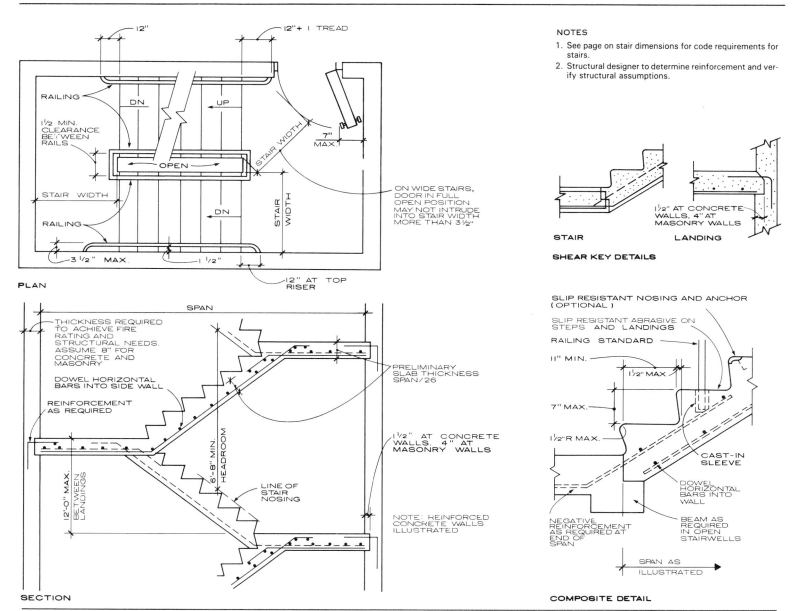

12"

12" + 1 TREAD

RAILING

DN   UP

1½ MIN. CLEARANCE BETWEEN RAILS

OPEN

7" MAX.

STAIR WIDTH

STAIR WIDTH

STAIR WIDTH

RAILING

ON WIDE STAIRS, DOOR IN FULL OPEN POSITION MAY NOT INTRUDE INTO STAIR WIDTH MORE THAN 3½"

DN

3½" MAX.

1½"

12" AT TOP RISER

PLAN

1½" AT CONCRETE WALLS. 4" AT MASONRY WALLS

STAIR   **LANDING**

SHEAR KEY DETAILS

SPAN

THICKNESS REQUIRED TO ACHIEVE FIRE RATING AND STRUCTURAL NEEDS. ASSUME 8" FOR CONCRETE AND MASONRY

DOWEL HORIZONTAL BARS INTO SIDE WALL

REINFORCEMENT AS REQUIRED

PRELIMINARY SLAB THICKNESS SPAN/26

6'-8" MIN. HEADROOM

12'-0" MAX. BETWEEN LANDINGS

LINE OF STAIR NOSING

1½" AT CONCRETE WALLS. 4" AT MASONRY WALLS

NOTE: REINFORCED CONCRETE WALLS ILLUSTRATED

SECTION

U−TYPE CONCRETE STAIRS

SLIP RESISTANT NOSING AND ANCHOR (OPTIONAL)

SLIP RESISTANT ABRASIVE ON STEPS AND LANDINGS

RAILING STANDARD

11" MIN.

1½" MAX

7" MAX.

1½"R MAX.

CAST-IN SLEEVE

DOWEL HORIZONTAL BARS INTO WALL

NEGATIVE REINFORCEMENT AS REQUIRED AT END OF SPAN

BEAM AS REQUIRED IN OPEN STAIRWELLS

SPAN AS ILLUSTRATED

COMPOSITE DETAIL

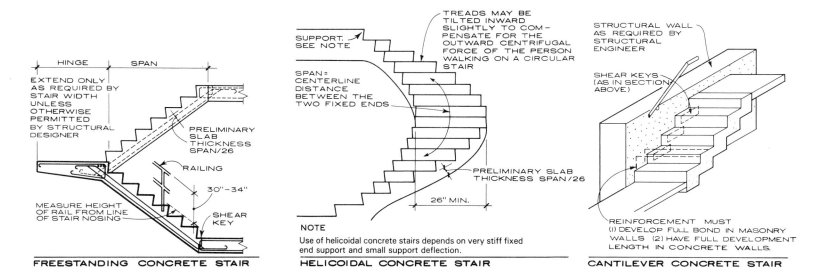

HINGE   SPAN

EXTEND ONLY AS REQUIRED BY STAIR WIDTH UNLESS OTHERWISE PERMITTED BY STRUCTURAL DESIGNER

PRELIMINARY SLAB THICKNESS SPAN/26

RAILING

30"−34"

MEASURE HEIGHT OF RAIL FROM LINE OF STAIR NOSING

SHEAR KEY

FREESTANDING CONCRETE STAIR

SUPPORT. SEE NOTE

TREADS MAY BE TILTED INWARD SLIGHTLY TO COMPENSATE FOR THE OUTWARD CENTRIFUGAL FORCE OF THE PERSON WALKING ON A CIRCULAR STAIR

SPAN = CENTERLINE DISTANCE BETWEEN THE TWO FIXED ENDS

PRELIMINARY SLAB THICKNESS SPAN/26

26" MIN.

NOTE
Use of helicoidal concrete stairs depends on very stiff fixed end support and small support deflection.

HELICOIDAL CONCRETE STAIR

STRUCTURAL WALL AS REQUIRED BY STRUCTURAL ENGINEER

SHEAR KEYS (AS IN SECTION ABOVE)

REINFORCEMENT MUST (1) DEVELOP FULL BOND IN MASONRY WALLS (2) HAVE FULL DEVELOPMENT LENGTH IN CONCRETE WALLS.

CANTILEVER CONCRETE STAIR

Krommenhoek/McKeown & Associates; San Diego, California
Karlsberger and Associates, Inc.; Columbus, Ohio

CAST-IN-PLACE CONCRETE   5

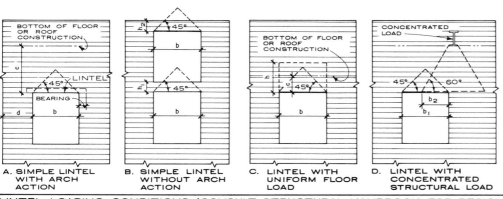

A. SIMPLE LINTEL WITH ARCH ACTION

B. SIMPLE LINTEL WITHOUT ARCH ACTION

C. LINTEL WITH UNIFORM FLOOR LOAD

D. LINTEL WITH CONCENTRATED STRUCTURAL LOAD

NOTES FOR LINTEL CONDITIONS

A. Simple lintel with arch action carries wall load only in triangle above opening:

$$c \geq b \quad \text{and} \quad d \geq b$$

B. Simple lintel without arch action carries less wall load than triangle above opening:

$$h_1 \text{ or } h_2 < 0.6b$$

C. Lintel with uniform floor load carries both wall and floor loads in rectangle above opening:

$$c < b$$

D. Lintel with concentrated load carries wall and portion of concentrated load distributed along length b_2.

LINTEL LOADING CONDITIONS (CONSULT STRUCTURAL HANDBOOK FOR DESIGN FORMULAS)

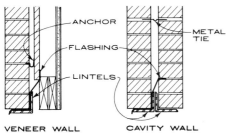

VENEER WALL **CAVITY WALL**

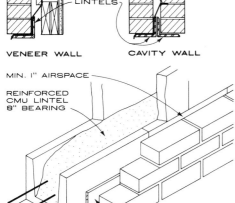

BRICK AND CMU WALL

LOOSE STEEL LINTELS FOR MASONRY WALLS

ALLOWABLE UNIFORM SUPERIMPOSED LOAD (IN LB) PER LINEAR FOOT FOR STEEL ANGLE LINTELS

HORIZONTAL LEG	ANGLE SIZE	WEIGHT PER FT. (LB)	SPAN IN FEET (CENTER TO CENTER OF REQUIRED BEARING)									
			3	4	5	6	7	8	9	10	11	12
3½	3 x 3½ x ¼	5.4	956	517	262	149	91	59				
	x ⁵⁄₁₆	6.6	1166	637	323	184	113	73				
	x ⅜	7.9	1377	756	384	218	134	87	59			
3½	3½ x 3½ x ¼	5.8	1281	718	406	232	144	94	65			
	x ⁵⁄₁₆	7.2	1589	891	507	290	179	118	80			
	x ⅜	8.5	1947	1091	589	336	208	137	93	66		
3½	4 x 3½ x ¼	6.2	1622	910	580	338	210	139	95	68		
	x ⁵⁄₁₆	7.7	2110	1184	734	421	262	173	119	85	62	
	x ⅜	9.1	2434	1365	855	490	305	201	138	98	71	
	x ⁷⁄₁₆	10.6	2760	1548	978	561	349	230	158	113	82	60
4	4 x 4 x ⁷⁄₁₆	11.3	2920	1638	1018	584	363	239	164	116	85	62
	x ½	12.8	3246	1820	1141	654	407	268	185	131	95	70
3½	5 x 3½ x ¼	7.0	2600	1460	932	636	398	264	184	132	97	73
	x ⁵⁄₁₆	8.7	3087	1733	1106	765	486	323	224	161	119	89
	x ⁷⁄₁₆	12.0	4224	2371	1513	1047	655	435	302	217	160	120
	x ½	13.6	4875	2736	1746	1177	736	488	339	244	179	134
3½	6 x 3½ x ¼	7.9	3577	2009	1283	888	650	439	306	221	164	124
	x ⁵⁄₁₆	9.8	4390	2465	1574	1090	798	538	375	271	201	151
	x ⅜	11.7	5200	2922	1865	1291	945	636	443	320	237	179
	x ½	15.3	6828	3834	2448	1695	1228	818	570	412	305	230
4	6 x 4 x ¼	8.3	3739	2099	1340	928	679	458	319	231	171	129
	x ⁵⁄₁₆	10.3	4552	2556	1632	1129	827	562	391	283	209	158
	x ⅜	12.3	5365	3012	1923	1331	974	665	463	335	248	187
	x ⁷⁄₁₆	14.3	6178	3469	2214	1533	1122	764	532	384	284	215
	x ½	16.2	6990	3925	2506	1734	1270	857	597	431	319	241

NOTE: Allowable loads to the left of the heavy line are governed by moment, and to the right by deflection. F_y = 36,000 psi. Maximum deflection ¹⁄₇₀₀. Consult structural engineer for long spans.

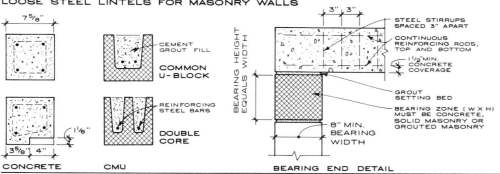

BEARING END DETAIL

NUMBER AND SIZE OF REBARS REQUIRED

Precast Concrete and Reinforced CMU Lintels (no superimposed loads)

LINTEL TYPE	CLEAR SPAN (MAX)	8" BRICK WALL (80 LB/SQ FT)	8" CMU WALL (50 LB/SQ FT)
Reinforced concrete (7⅝" square section)	4'-0"	4-#3	4-#3
	6'-0"	4-#4	4-#3
	8'-0"	4-#5	4-#4
CMU (7⅝" square section) nominal 8 x 8 x 16 unit	4'-0"	2-#4	2-#3
	6'-0"	2-#5	2-#4
	8'-0"	2-#6	2-#5

NOTE: fc' = 3000 psi concrete and grout
fy = 60,000 psi

PRECAST CONCRETE AND CMU LINTELS

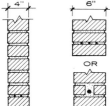
CONCRETE

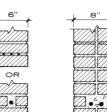
CMU

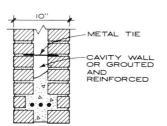

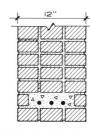

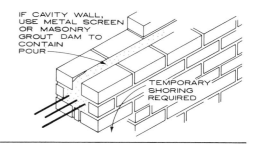

REINFORCED BRICK LINTELS

Christine Beall, AIA, CCS; Austin, Texas
Metz, Train, Olson and Youngren, Inc.; Chicago, Illinois

UNIT MASONRY

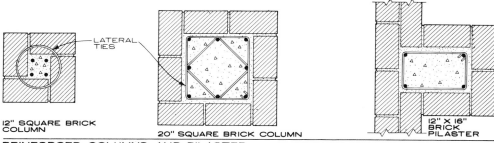

12" SQUARE BRICK COLUMN

20" SQUARE BRICK COLUMN

12" X 16" BRICK PILASTER

REINFORCED COLUMNS AND PILASTER

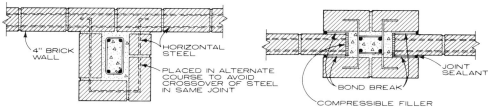

REINFORCED BRICK MASONRY COLUMN

REINFORCED BRICK MASONRY PILASTER

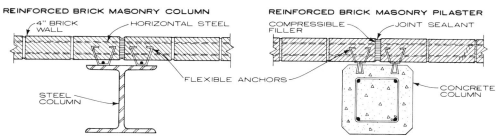

STEEL COLUMN

REINFORCED CONCRETE COLUMN

BRICK CURTAIN WALL AND PANEL WALL REINFORCEMENT AND ANCHORAGE

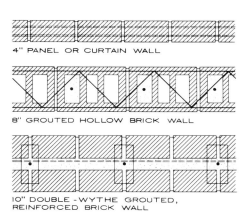

4" PANEL OR CURTAIN WALL

8" GROUTED HOLLOW BRICK WALL

10" DOUBLE-WYTHE GROUTED, REINFORCED BRICK WALL

WALL TYPES

TYPICAL RETAINING WALL DESIGN VALUES

H	B	L	D BARS	V BARS	F BARS
2'-0"	1'-9"	1'-10"	#3 @ 40"		#3 @ 40"
2'-6"	1'-9"	2'-4"	#3 @ 40"		#3 @ 40"
3'-0"	2'-0"	2'-10"	#3 @ 40"		#3 @ 40"
3'-6"	2'-0"	3'-4"	#3 @ 40"		#3 @ 40"
4'-0"	2'-4"	1'-4"	#3 @ 27" #4 @ 40"	#3 @ 27" #3 @ 40"	#3 @ 27" #3 @ 40"
4'-6"	2'-8"	1'-6"	#3 @ 19" #4 @ 35"	#3 @ 38" #3 @ 35"	#3 @ 19" #3 @ 35"
5'-0"	3'-0"	1'-8"	#3 @ 14" #4 @ 25" #5 @ 40"	#3 @ 28" #3 @ 25" #4 @ 40"	#3 @ 14" #3 @ 25" #4 @ 40"
5'-6"	3'-3"	1'-10"	#3 @ 11" #4 @ 20" #5 @ 31"	#3 @ 22" #4 @ 40" #4 @ 31"	#3 @ 11" #3 @ 20" #4 @ 31"
6'-0"	3'-6"	2'-0"	#3 @ 8" #4 @ 14" #5 @ 20"	#3 @ 16" #4 @ 28" #5 @ 40"	#3 @ 8" #3 @ 14" #4 @ 20"

NOTE: For convenience, this table was developed to aid the nondesigner in a typical application. However, materials must meet these additional minimum requirements:

1. Brick strength in excess of 6000 psi in compression.
2. Steel design tensile strength, F_s, of 20,000 psi.
3. No surcharge.

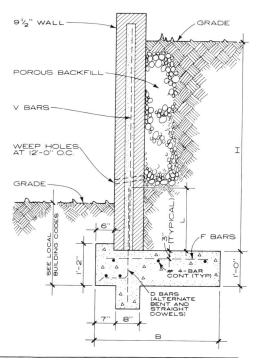

LOW BRICK MASONRY RETAINING WALL (LESS THAN 6'-0")

NOTE
Consult a qualified engineer and local code requirements for design of all grouted, reinforced masonry construction.

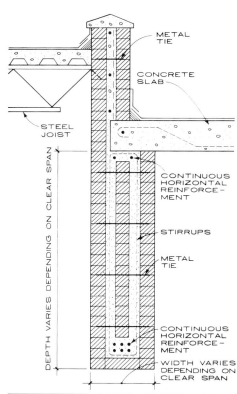

REINFORCED BRICK BEAM

The design of load-bearing masonry buildings is based on a rational analysis of the magnitude, line of action, and direction of all forces acting on the structure. Dead loads, live loads, lateral loads, and other forces such as those resulting from temperature changes, impact, and unequal settlement are considered. The combination of loads producing the greatest stresses is used to size the members. Reinforced masonry is used where compressive, flexural, and shear stresses are greater than those permitted for unreinforced or partially reinforced masonry. The minimum amount of steel reinforcing required by code is designed for seismic zones 3 and 4 where high winds or earthquake activity subject buildings to severe lateral dynamic loads. Reinforcing steel adds ductility and strength to the wall, which then bears the load with minimum deflection and maximum damping of the earthquake energy. For further technical information:

Masonry Design and Detailing, 2nd edition. Christine Beall. New York: McGraw-Hill, 1987.
Recommended Practice for Engineered Brick Masonry. Brick Institute of America. McLean, VA, 1969.
Reinforced Masonry Design. R. Schneider and W. Dickey. New York: Prentice-Hall, Inc., 1980.
Technical Notes Series. Brick Institute of America.

Christine Beall, AIA, CCS; Austin, Texas
John R. Hoke, Jr., AIA, Architect; Washington, D.C.

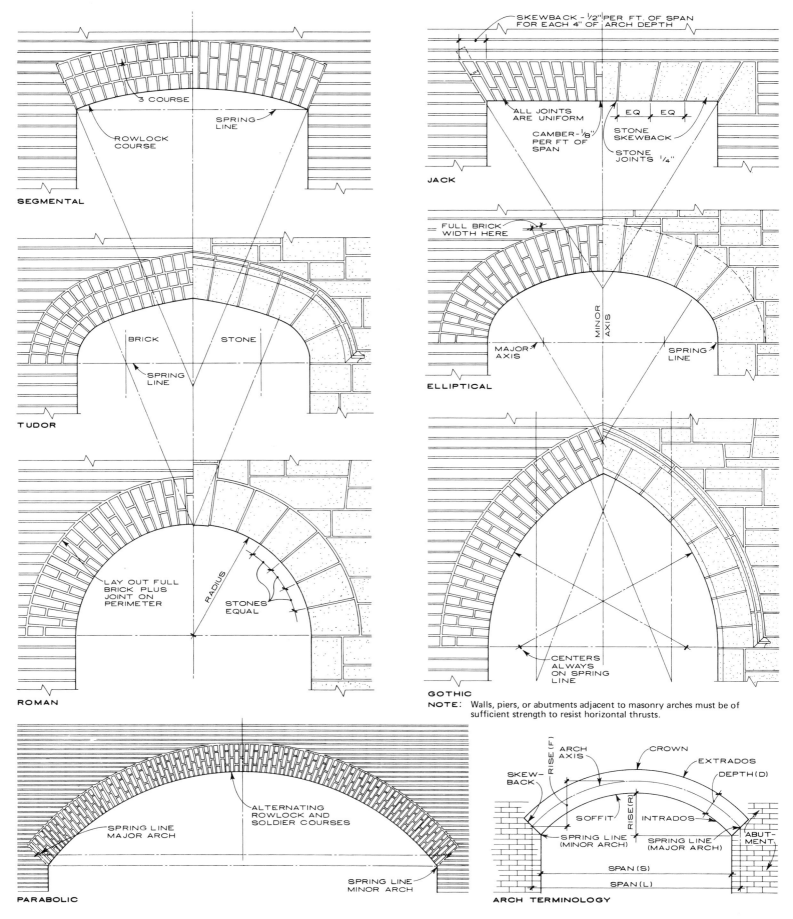

SEGMENTAL

3 COURSE

ROWLOCK COURSE

SPRING LINE

TUDOR

BRICK

STONE

SPRING LINE

ROMAN

LAY OUT FULL BRICK PLUS JOINT ON PERIMETER

RADIUS

STONES EQUAL

PARABOLIC

SPRING LINE MAJOR ARCH

ALTERNATING ROWLOCK AND SOLDIER COURSES

SPRING LINE MINOR ARCH

JACK

SKEWBACK - ½" PER FT. OF SPAN FOR EACH 4" OF ARCH DEPTH

ALL JOINTS ARE UNIFORM

CAMBER- ⅛" PER FT OF SPAN

EQ   EQ

STONE SKEWBACK

STONE JOINTS ¼"

ELLIPTICAL

FULL BRICK WIDTH HERE

MINOR AXIS

MAJOR AXIS

SPRING LINE

GOTHIC

CENTERS ALWAYS ON SPRING LINE

NOTE: Walls, piers, or abutments adjacent to masonry arches must be of sufficient strength to resist horizontal thrusts.

ARCH TERMINOLOGY

RISE (F)

ARCH AXIS

CROWN

EXTRADOS

DEPTH(D)

SKEW- BACK

SOFFIT

RISE(R)

INTRADOS

SPRING LINE (MINOR ARCH)

SPRING LINE (MAJOR ARCH)

ABUT- MENT

SPAN (S)

SPAN (L)

Brick Institute of America; Reston, Virginia

 STONE

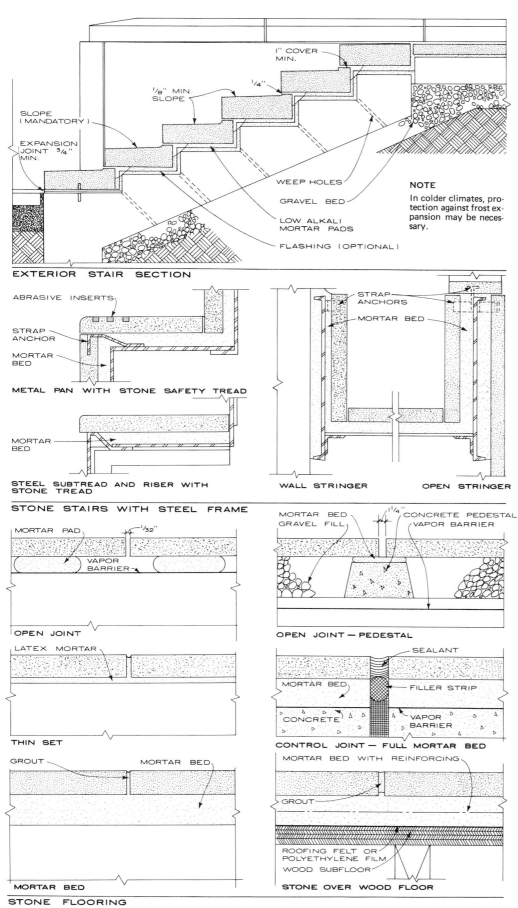

EXTERIOR STAIR SECTION

NOTE

In colder climates, protection against frost expansion may be necessary.

METAL PAN WITH STONE SAFETY TREAD

STEEL SUBTREAD AND RISER WITH STONE TREAD

STONE STAIRS WITH STEEL FRAME

WALL STRINGER   **OPEN STRINGER**

OPEN JOINT

THIN SET

MORTAR BED

STONE FLOORING

OPEN JOINT — PEDESTAL

CONTROL JOINT — FULL MORTAR BED

STONE OVER WOOD FLOOR

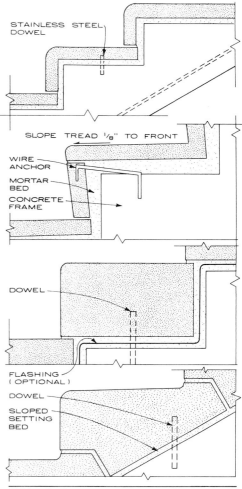

STONE STAIRS WITH CONCRETE FRAME

DESIGN FACTORS FOR STONE STAIRS

Stone used for steps should have an abrasive resistance of 10 (measured on a scale from a minimum of 6 to a maximum of 17). When different varieties of stone are used, their abrasive hardness should be similar to prevent uneven wear.

Dowels and anchoring devices should be noncorrosive.

If a safety tread is not used on stairs, a light bush hammered soft finish or nonslip finish is recommended.

To prevent future staining, dampproof the face of all concrete or concrete block, specify low alkali mortar, and provide adequate drainage (slopes and weepholes).

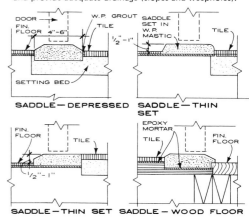

SADDLE — DEPRESSED   **SADDLE — THIN SET**

SADDLE — THIN SET   **SADDLE — WOOD FLOOR**

STONE THRESHOLDS

Building Stone Institute; New York, New York
George M. Whiteside, III, AIA, and James D. Lloyd; Kennett Square, Pennsylvania
Alexander Keyes; Darrel Downing Rippeteau, Architect; Washington, D.C.

STONE   **5**

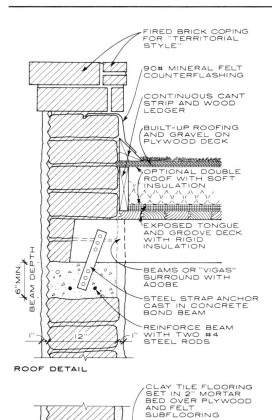

ROOF DETAIL

SECOND FLOOR DETAIL

FOUNDATION DETAIL

WALL SECTIONS (TERRITORIAL STYLE)

P. G. McHenry, Jr., AIA; Albuquerque, New Mexico

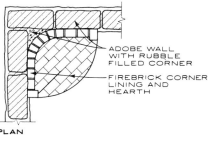
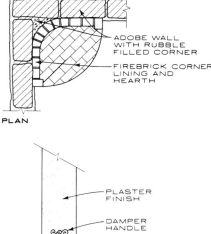

PLAN

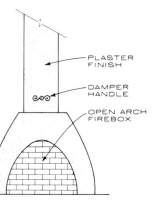

ELEVATION

"HORNO" FIREPLACES

TYPICAL SIZES OF ADOBE BRICK

HEIGHT	LENGTH	WIDTH
4''	8''	16''
4''	10''	16''
4''	9''	18''
4''	12''	18''
5''	12''	16''
5''	10''	20''
5''	12''	18''
6''	12''	24''

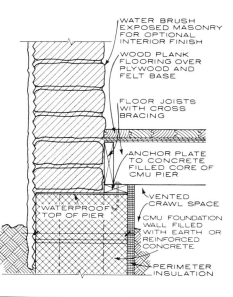

FIREPLACES

A traditional feature of most adobe homes is one or more corner "Kiva" or "Horno" fireplaces. The main masonry structure is provided by the adobe wall at a corner. If a corner is not available, sometimes a "Padercita" (little wall) is projected from another wall to provide a corner. The corner is lined with firebrick, and a masonry shell encloses the firebox and fireplace flue. A vitreous flue liner or masonry flue is projected through the roof. The curved back wall and open firebox reflect heat efficiently into the room, and the curve provides a smoke shelf. A butterfly damper in the flue or throat is controlled by a decorative wrought iron handle.

New seismic requirements in some areas require vertical steel reinforcement in the masonry of fireplaces.

SECTION

ADOBE WALL CONSTRUCTION

The strength of an adobe wall lies in its mass and homogeneous nature, using the same material, mud, for mortar. The addition of reinforcing bars or anchor bolts may weaken joints. An international use standard for adobe wall thickness-height ratio is approximately 1:10. Uniform sizes for sundried bricks vary widely with different locales. The bricks should be made near the point of use and will vary with tradition and the standards of the manufacturer. Larger sizes of great weight will increase the labor cost. Minimum bonding distance is approximately 4 in.

One story walls should be 12 in. thick in Arizona and 10 in. in New Mexico and should not exceed 12 ft in height. Two story walls should be 18 in. thick at first floor and 12 in. at second and not over 22 ft in height.

Avoidance of flowing water on mud surfaces is the most important detail consideration. Rising damp is of no consequence if the site immediately adjacent is well drained and moisture is not trapped by waterproofing materials. Unstabilized mud brick or plaster (without the addition of waterproofing compounds) bonds well to itself and to wood without the use of normal lathing reinforcement. Rain erosion of unstabilized mud surfaces will only approximate 1 in. in 20 years in rainfall areas of 10 to 25 in. per year. Monolithic slab/foundations are not desirable with mud adobe because possible concentrations of rainwater on the slab during construction may damage lower courses.

"Effective" U values for insulation are more significant than the ASHRAE "steady-state" values in common use. The "effective" values take into account the thermal mass, storage, insulation gains in various climate zones, wall compass orientation, and color.

"Burned adobe," which is merely a low fired brick, should be dealt with in the manner normal for brick masonry. Its use is not recommended in climate zones where high daily temperature fluctuations can cause severe freeze-thaw cycle damage. Mud bricks can be stabilized (waterproofed) by the addition of cement, asphalt emulsion, or other compounds. These materials often do not bond well with themselves in repeated layers and may accelerate the deterioration at the point of contact with the mud material.

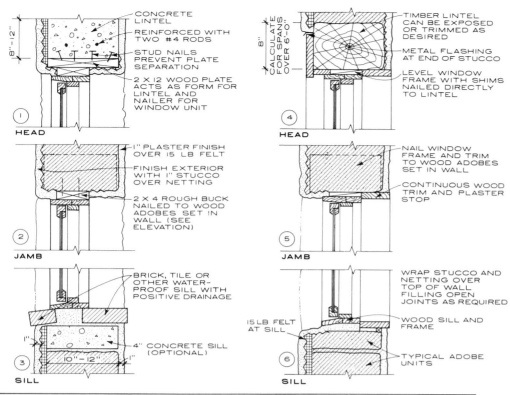

WINDOW DETAILS (SEE ELEVATION FOR ANCHORAGE OF FRAME)

Detail 1 — HEAD
- CONCRETE LINTEL
- REINFORCED WITH TWO #4 RODS
- STUD NAILS PREVENT PLATE SEPARATION
- 2 X 12 WOOD PLATE ACTS AS FORM FOR LINTEL AND NAILER FOR WINDOW UNIT
- 8"–12"

Detail 2 — JAMB
- 1" PLASTER FINISH OVER 15 LB FELT
- FINISH EXTERIOR WITH 1" STUCCO OVER NETTING
- 2 X 4 ROUGH BUCK NAILED TO WOOD ADOBES SET IN WALL (SEE ELEVATION)

Detail 3 — SILL
- BRICK, TILE OR OTHER WATER-PROOF SILL WITH POSITIVE DRAINAGE
- 4" CONCRETE SILL (OPTIONAL)
- 1"
- 10"–12"

Detail 4 — HEAD
- TIMBER LINTEL CAN BE EXPOSED OR TRIMMED AS DESIRED
- METAL FLASHING AT END OF STUCCO
- LEVEL WINDOW FRAME WITH SHIMS NAILED DIRECTLY TO LINTEL
- 8" CALCULATE FOR SPANS OVER 6'-0"

Detail 5 — JAMB
- NAIL WINDOW FRAME AND TRIM TO WOOD ADOBES SET IN WALL
- CONTINUOUS WOOD TRIM AND PLASTER STOP

Detail 6 — SILL
- WRAP STUCCO AND NETTING OVER TOP OF WALL FILLING OPEN JOINTS AS REQUIRED
- 15 LB FELT AT SILL
- WOOD SILL AND FRAME
- TYPICAL ADOBE UNITS

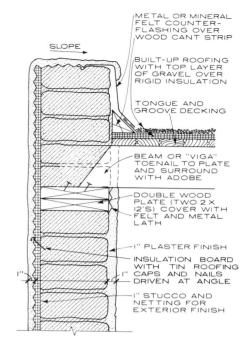

PARAPET WITH WOOD COLLAR

- METAL OR MINERAL FELT COUNTER-FLASHING OVER WOOD CANT STRIP
- SLOPE
- BUILT-UP ROOFING WITH TOP LAYER OF GRAVEL OVER RIGID INSULATION
- TONGUE AND GROOVE DECKING
- BEAM OR "VIGA" TOENAIL TO PLATE AND SURROUND WITH ADOBE
- DOUBLE WOOD PLATE (TWO 2 X 12'S) COVER WITH FELT AND METAL LATH
- 1" PLASTER FINISH
- INSULATION BOARD WITH TIN ROOFING CAPS AND NAILS DRIVEN AT ANGLE
- 1" STUCCO AND NETTING FOR EXTERIOR FINISH
- 1"

NOTES

Details deal with the use of sundried mud bricks. They may be stabilized with additives or simply made of mud. Proportions for the mud mixture of sand, silt, and clay normally are not critical. Gravel and small stones can also be present if they do not exceed 50% of the volume. Adobe is approved by local building officials in areas where adobe use is traditional or familiar to builders or construction officials. Information concerning local codes should be sought.

Nailing anchors are best provided by the use of wood adobes ("Gringo blocks"), either solid or made of scrap lumber, laid up with the wall in locations where door and window jambs may require attachment. Nails will not hold permanently when nailed into adobe bricks unless additionally secured by plaster or other material. Later attachments can be made by the use of wooden triple wedges driven into a pilot hole. Channels for wiring, pipes, and decorative features may be easily cut in the wall after it is in place.

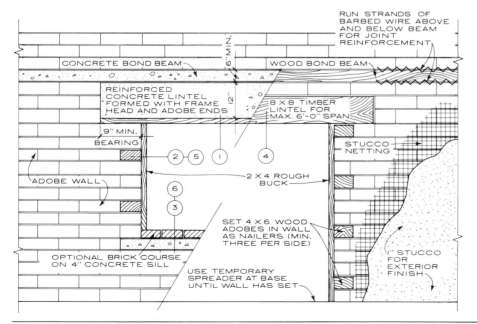

ELEVATION OF TYPICAL FRAMED OPENINGS

- RUN STRANDS OF BARBED WIRE ABOVE AND BELOW BEAM FOR JOINT REINFORCEMENT
- CONCRETE BOND BEAM
- WOOD BOND BEAM
- 6" MIN.
- REINFORCED CONCRETE LINTEL FORMED WITH FRAME HEAD AND ADOBE ENDS
- 12"
- 8 X 8 TIMBER LINTEL FOR MAX. 6'-0" SPAN
- STUCCO NETTING
- 9" MIN. BEARING
- ADOBE WALL
- 2 X 4 ROUGH BUCK
- SET 4 X 6 WOOD ADOBES IN WALL AS NAILERS (MIN. THREE PER SIDE)
- 1" STUCCO FOR EXTERIOR FINISH
- OPTIONAL BRICK COURSE ON 4" CONCRETE SILL
- USE TEMPORARY SPREADER AT BASE UNTIL WALL HAS SET

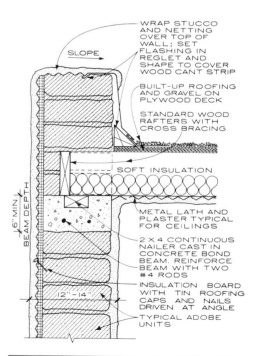

PARAPET WITH CONCRETE COLLAR

- WRAP STUCCO AND NETTING OVER TOP OF WALL; SET FLASHING IN REGLET AND SHAPE TO COVER WOOD CANT STRIP
- SLOPE
- BUILT-UP ROOFING AND GRAVEL ON PLYWOOD DECK
- STANDARD WOOD RAFTERS WITH CROSS BRACING
- SOFT INSULATION
- 6" MIN. BEAM DEPTH
- METAL LATH AND PLASTER TYPICAL FOR CEILINGS
- 2 X 4 CONTINUOUS NAILER CAST IN CONCRETE BOND BEAM. REINFORCE BEAM WITH TWO #4 RODS
- INSULATION BOARD WITH TIN ROOFING CAPS AND NAILS DRIVEN AT ANGLE
- TYPICAL ADOBE UNITS
- 12"–14"

GENERAL NOTE

Some building codes may require additional thicknesses and reinforcement of concrete bond beams. The anchorage of pitched roof structures may be done by normal attachment to the bond beams shown.

P. G. McHenry, Jr., AIA; Albuquerque, New Mexico

ADOBE **5**

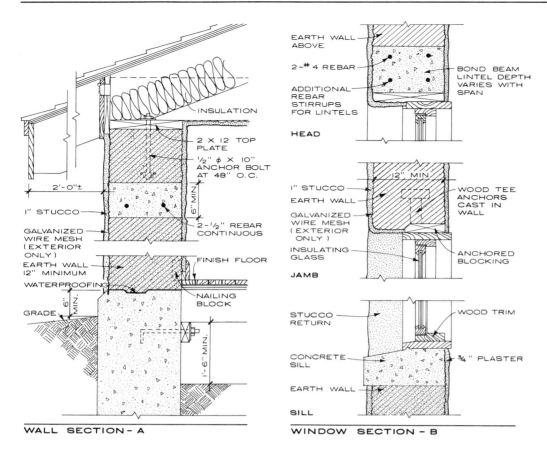

WALL SECTION - A

- INSULATION
- 2 X 12 TOP PLATE
- ½" φ X 10" ANCHOR BOLT AT 48" O.C.
- 1" STUCCO
- GALVANIZED WIRE MESH (EXTERIOR ONLY)
- 2-½" REBAR CONTINUOUS
- FINISH FLOOR
- NAILING BLOCK
- EARTH WALL 12" MINIMUM
- WATERPROOFING
- GRADE
- 2'-0"±
- 6" MIN.
- 6" MIN.
- 1'-6" MIN.

WINDOW SECTION - B

HEAD
- EARTH WALL ABOVE
- 2-# 4 REBAR
- ADDITIONAL REBAR STIRRUPS FOR LINTELS
- BOND BEAM LINTEL DEPTH VARIES WITH SPAN

JAMB
- 1" STUCCO
- EARTH WALL
- GALVANIZED WIRE MESH (EXTERIOR ONLY)
- INSULATING GLASS
- 12" MIN
- WOOD TEE ANCHORS CAST IN WALL
- ANCHORED BLOCKING

SILL
- STUCCO RETURN
- CONCRETE SILL
- EARTH WALL
- WOOD TRIM
- ¾" PLASTER

NOTES

1. Rammed earth wall construction is an old technique used effectively in many parts of the world. The basic material is earth, with allowable proportions of clay, silt, and aggregate, commonly found almost everywhere. The soil in most locations has naturally usable proportions that do not require further tempering. The ideal soil mixture will have less than 50% clay and silt, and a maximum aggregate size of ¼ in. The solid is dampened to a moisture content of approximately 10% by weight, of dry soil. Saltwater should not be used under any circumstances.

2. The walls are constructed by the use of slip forms, (24 to 36 in. high x 8 to 12 ft long) placed level and secure. The forms are filled with damp (not wet) earth in 4 in. lifts. Each lift is rammed with a tamper until full compaction is reached. The tamp should be flat, approximately 6 x 6 in., weighing 18 to 25 lb, tamped by hand or mechanically. Full compaction can be determined by a ringing sound when the tamp compacts the fill. When the form is full and compacted, it is moved to a new location and secured and the process is repeated. The corners should be placed first, with special corner forms. When the full circumference is completed, the next course is started. The form heights (courses) are best coordinated with heights of window and door lintels. Form replacement can begin as soon as compaction is reached, without further drying.

3. Exterior wall thickness should be a minimum of 12 in. for one story, 18 in. to support a second story, and interior walls of not less than 9 in. Wall thickness can be increased as appropriate to the design. Basic rammed earth walls have many of the same characteristics of sundried adobe. The insulation value of the walls is not as great as more efficient insulating materials, but will provide thermal mass for heat storage, sound control, and other benefits.

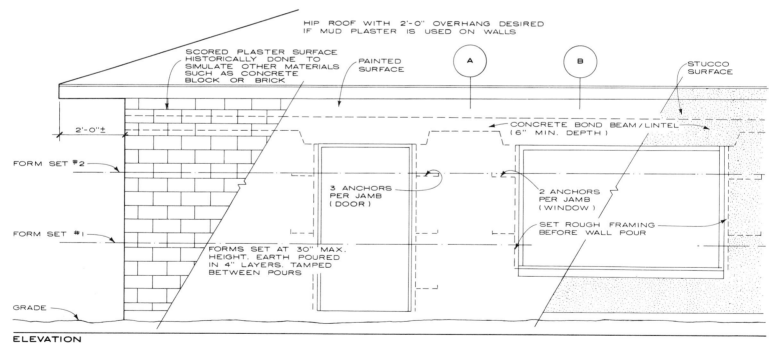

ELEVATION

- HIP ROOF WITH 2'-0" OVERHANG DESIRED IF MUD PLASTER IS USED ON WALLS
- SCORED PLASTER SURFACE HISTORICALLY DONE TO SIMULATE OTHER MATERIALS SUCH AS CONCRETE BLOCK OR BRICK
- PAINTED SURFACE
- A
- B
- STUCCO SURFACE
- 2'-0"±
- FORM SET #2
- FORM SET #1
- CONCRETE BOND BEAM / LINTEL (6" MIN. DEPTH)
- 3 ANCHORS PER JAMB (DOOR)
- 2 ANCHORS PER JAMB (WINDOW)
- SET ROUGH FRAMING BEFORE WALL POUR
- FORMS SET AT 30" MAX. HEIGHT. EARTH POURED IN 4" LAYERS. TAMPED BETWEEN POURS
- GRADE

NOTES

1. Foundations are normally conventional spread footings of sufficient width to support the heavy (3000 # per lin ft) walls. The foundation wall should be of a waterproof material, topped with a vapor barrier to prevent capillary moisture rise. Attachment anchors in the form of wood tees or plugs are placed in the wall as it is erected, in the positions required to secure window and door frames. A continuous steel reinforced concrete beam (6 in. thick) is placed as a continuous lintel beam to support walls above the openings.

2. A top plate of wood is secured by means of anchor bolts cast in the top of the walls. The plate provides load distribution and an attachment point for the roof structure. Interior and exterior walls can be finished by the application of conventional stucco or plaster. Simpler treatment can be achieved by smoothing or texturing the earth wall with a sponge rubber float, wet burlap, or sheepskin, and painting it. Sealing and preparation of the surface before painting is the same as for plaster. If waterproof stucco is not used, roof overhangs should be of sufficient width to protect the walls from rain erosion.

P. G. McHenry, Jr., AIA; Albuquerque, New Mexico

GENERAL INFORMATION AND TERMINOLOGY

Building layout requires a site plan that has been accurately drawn to a specific scale (e.g., 1 in. = 20 ft), showing all relevant information regarding: building outline (footprint) dimensioned location from the property lines, existing and new streets and curbs, above and below ground utilities, easements, all site improvements (other than the building footprint) such as driveways, retaining walls, and patios, and other features unique to the site. Existing and new contour lines, spot grade elevations, and bench marks should be shown on a site plan if there is not a separate grading plan. All information, especially building location, should be verified to conform to local codes and zoning ordinance requirements prior to layout.

1. Angles: The difference in direction of two intersecting lines.
2. Azimuths: Angles measured clockwise from any meridian, usually north; however, the National Geodetic Survey uses south.
3. Bearings: The acute angle between the meridian and a line, measured from north or south, toward east or west to give a reading of less than 90° (e.g., S 31° 13' E).
4. Transit: A precise general-purpose surveying instrument primarily used for measuring horizontal (azimuth and bearing) angles, vertical (altitude) angles, and to run level lines. It can also be used to measure distances directly by subtense and stadia measurement.
5. Taping: Tape lengths are not guaranteed accurate. Certified tapes are those having their lengths verified at the National Bureau of Standards, checked at a temperature of 68°F at both 10 lb pull (fully supported) and 12 lb pull (ends supported). To obtain accurate measurements, the measured distance must be corrected for temperature differences. The coefficient of thermal expansion for steel tapes is 0.0000065/unit of length/°F. Invar tapes, made of special nickel steel alloy, do not need temperature corrections. A spring balance is used to measure standard pull. The tape must be horizontal and in true alignment.
6. Stadia measurement: A rapid, efficient method of measuring distances accurately enough for locating topographic details. The transit has two horizontal cross hairs, spaced equidistant from the center cross hair. The interval between hairs gives a vertical intercept of 1 ft on the rod for every 100 ft of distance to the rod; thus the distance to a point can be read directly by counting the number of hundredths of a foot between stadia hairs.
7. Subtense bar: The angle between targets is determined by using a transit reading to an accuracy of 1 sec of an arc or less. The horizontal distance from the transit to the bar is computed mathematically or read from a table.
8. Bench mark (BM): An established elevation point, used as a reference for survey purposes. Mean sea level is the national reference elevation. Local datum may exist in many areas.
9. Leveling: The process of finding the difference in elevations between points. The transit is set up approximately one-half the distance between the BM and the point to be determined. A back sight (BS) is taken on the BM and the height of instrument (HI) determined by reading the rod at the center cross hair (rod reading + BM + HI). The rod is then placed on the new point. A foresight is taken and the rod reading subtracted from HI to determine the elevation of the point (HI − rod reading = elevation in ft).
10. Leveling rods: Tall rods, usually wood, graduated in feet, tenths, and hundredths of a foot; or in metric using meters, centimeters, and millimeters.
11. Cadastral surveys: Surveys that are made to establish property boundary lines. Deed descriptions are essential parts of any document denoting ownership or conveyance of land. The basic rule of property lines and corners is that they shall remain in their original positions as established on the ground. This basic rule is important because most land surveys are resurveys. The original description may be followed, but this description is merely an aid to the discovery of the originally established lines and corners. Substantial discrepancies are frequently found. In some states, surveys are conducted on the metes and bounds principle, and in others, the basic subdivisions are rectangular. If boundaries to be described an irregular line (a winding stream), the line can be located by a series of closely spaced perpendicular offsets from an auxiliary straight line.

John J. Hare, AIA; Haddonfield, New Jersey
Walter H. Sobel, FAIA, and Associates; Chicago, Illinois

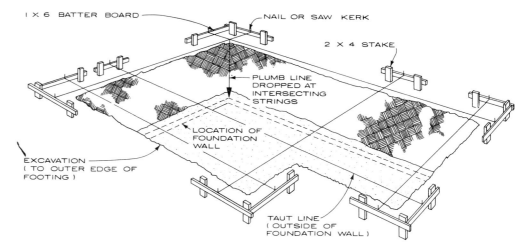

NOTES

First locate the building in its correct relationship to the property lines. Set stakes at the building corners, using a transit to reestablish correct angles and steel tapes for distance measurements. Mark exact corner locations on the stake heads with finishing nails. Set offset stakes or batter boards 3 to 5 ft outside the corners to allow room for construction operations. Set batter boards at a predetermined elevation. Then project the location of the building corners to the tops of the batter boards and set nails. Stretch strings taut between nails to define the corners and outside wall lines. For small buildings, the elevation of the top of the footings can be located by measuring down from the strings. Strings sag over long distances and with changes in humidity, so for large buildings stakes indicating top of footings are set with the transit.

BUILDING LAYOUT PROCEDURES

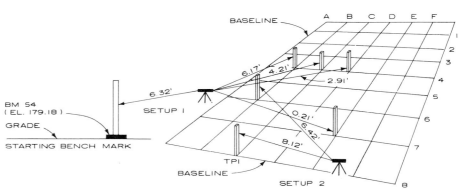

NOTES

A grid system can be used for identifying those points whose elevation is required. The transit is set where both the BM and the points on the grid can be observed. Sighting on the BM determines HI. Elevations of grid points can then be found by sighting the rod held at each point. The rod reading is subtracted from the HI to obtain the elevation of the point sighted (HI − rod reading = elevation point). Resight the BM periodically to assure the instrument has not moved. Contour lines are then sketched between elevation points by interpolation.

TOPOGRAPHIC SURVEY—GRID SYSTEM

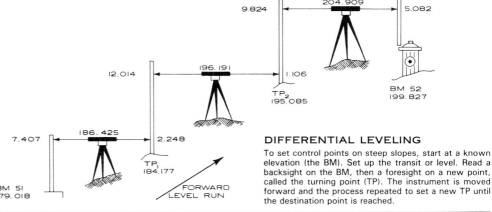

DIFFERENTIAL LEVELING

To set control points on steep slopes, start at a known elevation (the BM). Set up the transit or level. Read a backsight on the BM, then a foresight on a new point, called the turning point (TP). The instrument is moved forward and the process repeated to set a new TP until the destination point is reached.

DIFFERENTIAL LEVELING

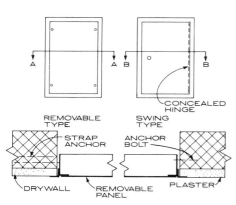

SECTION A-A

NOTES

1. Frames usually are set into building construction; doors are constructed to fit later. Doors may be hinged, set in with clips, or fastened with screws. Hinges may be butt or pivot, separate or continuous, surface or concealed. Assorted stock sizes range from 8 in. x 8 in. to 24 in. x 36 in.
2. Access panels should have a fire rating similar to the wall in which they occur. Access panels of more than 144 sq. ins. require automatic closers.
3. Minimum size for attic and crawl space access often is specified by building code.

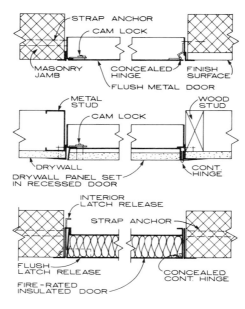

SECTION B-B

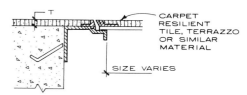

PLASTER

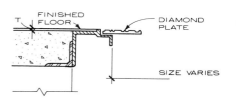

ACOUSTICAL PLASTER

ACOUSTICAL TILE

NOTES

1. Spring-operated, swingdown panels and swingup panels frequently are used for ceiling access.
2. Standard sizes range from 12 in. x 12 in. to 24 in. x 36 in.
3. Other finish ceiling panels are detailed similar to acoustical tiles.

ACCESS DOORS

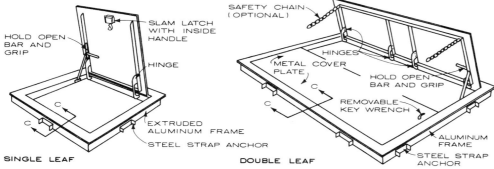

SINGLE LEAF

1. MATERIAL: Steel or aluminum.
2. SIZES: Single leaf—2 ft. x 2 ft., 2 ft. 6 in. x 2 ft. 6 in., 2 ft. 6 in. x 3 ft., 3 ft. x 3 ft. Double leaf—3 ft. 6 in. x 3 ft. 6 in., 4 ft. x 4 ft., 4 ft. x 6 ft., 5 ft. x 5 ft.

DOUBLE LEAF

Thickness "T" varies from 1/8 in. for resilient flooring to 3/16 in. for carpet; some manufacturers offer 3/4 in. for terrazzo and tile floor.

Double-leaf floor hatch is recommended for areas where there is danger a person could fall into the opening. Safety codes require that floor openings be protected. Check local codes for special requirements.

CEILING ACCESS PANELS

FLOOR HATCH – SECTION C-C

FLOOR HATCH – SECTION C-C

LIGHT-DUTY TRENCH COVERS

1. MATERIAL: Extruded aluminum.
2. SIZE: 2 in. to 36 in. wide. Side frames are available in cut length of 20 ft. stocks that can be spliced to any length. Recessed cover plates are available in 20 ft. stock; other covers are available in 10 ft. and 12 ft. stock.
3. Side frames normally are cast in concrete around trough form.

HEAVY-DUTY TRENCH COVERS

1. MATERIAL: Cast iron or ductile iron.
2. SIZES: Heavy duty cast iron trench covers should be planned carefully to use standard stock length to avoid cutting, or special length casting should be ordered.
3. STOCK COVER SIZE: To 48 in. wide and 24 in. long. Frames are manufactured in standard lengths of 24 in. or 36 in. depending on size and manufacturer. Cast iron troughs are 8 in. deep, 6 in. to 24 in. wide, and 48 in. in stock lengths.
4. Minimum grating size in walkways is specified in ANSI A117.1-1986.

FLOOR HATCHES

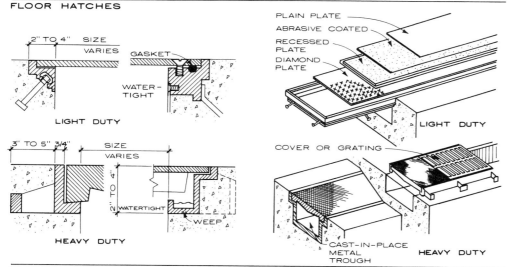

TRENCH COVERS

Cohen, Karydas & Associates, Chartered; Washington, D.C.
Harold C. Munger, FAIA; Munger Munger + Associates Architects, Inc.; Toledo, Ohio

ORNAMENTAL METAL

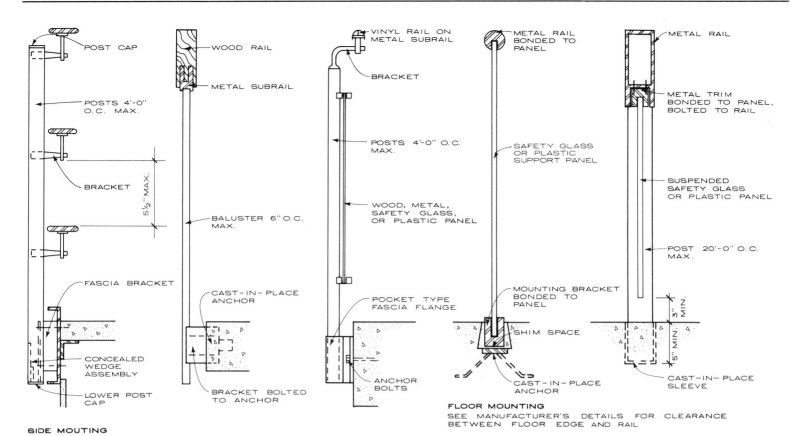

SIDE MOUTING

POST CAP

POSTS 4'-0" O.C. MAX.

BRACKET

FASCIA BRACKET

CONCEALED WEDGE ASSEMBLY

LOWER POST CAP

5½" MAX.

WOOD RAIL

METAL SUBRAIL

BALUSTER 6" O.C. MAX.

CAST-IN-PLACE ANCHOR

BRACKET BOLTED TO ANCHOR

VINYL RAIL ON METAL SUBRAIL

BRACKET

POSTS 4'-0" O.C. MAX.

WOOD, METAL, SAFETY GLASS, OR PLASTIC PANEL

POCKET TYPE FASCIA FLANGE

ANCHOR BOLTS

METAL RAIL BONDED TO PANEL

SAFETY GLASS OR PLASTIC SUPPORT PANEL

MOUNTING BRACKET BONDED TO PANEL

SHIM SPACE

CAST-IN-PLACE ANCHOR

METAL RAIL

METAL TRIM BONDED TO PANEL, BOLTED TO RAIL

SUSPENDED SAFETY GLASS OR PLASTIC PANEL

POST 20'-0" O.C. MAX.

3" MIN.

5" MIN.

CAST-IN-PLACE SLEEVE

FLOOR MOUNTING
SEE MANUFACTURER'S DETAILS FOR CLEARANCE BETWEEN FLOOR EDGE AND RAIL

CONSULT CODE FOR RAILING HEIGHT, POST RAIL, AND BALUSTER SPACING, AND LOADING REQUIREMENTS

TYPICAL POST AND RAIL DETAILS

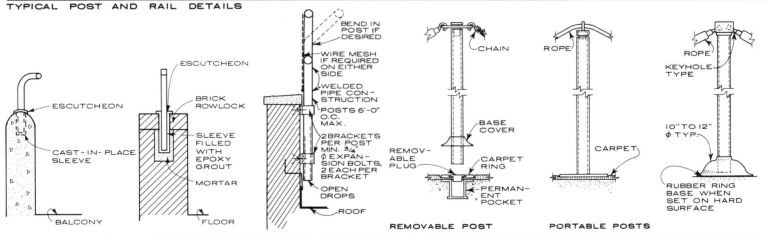

ESCUTCHEON

ESCUTCHEON

CAST-IN-PLACE SLEEVE

BALCONY

ESCUTCHEON

BRICK ROWLOCK

SLEEVE FILLED WITH EPOXY GROUT

MORTAR

FLOOR

BEND IN POST IF DESIRED

WIRE MESH IF REQUIRED ON EITHER SIDE

WELDED PIPE CONSTRUCTION

POSTS 6'-0" O.C. MAX.

2 BRACKETS PER POST MIN. ¾" Φ EXPANSION BOLTS, 2 EACH PER BRACKET

OPEN DROPS

ROOF

CHAIN

BASE COVER

REMOVABLE PLUG

CARPET RING

PERMANENT POCKET

ROPE

CARPET

ROPE

KEYHOLE TYPE

10" TO 12" Φ TYP.

RUBBER RING BASE WHEN SET ON HARD SURFACE

TYPICAL RAILING ON LOW WALLS

REMOVABLE POST   **PORTABLE POSTS**

CONTROL POSTS

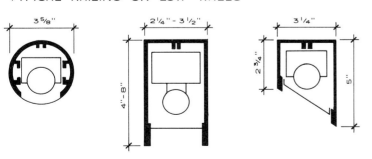

3⅝"

2¼" – 3½"

4" – 8"

3¼"

2¾"

5"

FLUORESCENT FIXTURES AND PLASTIC DIFFUSERS, SMALLER HANDRAILS AVAILABLE WITH INCANDESCENT FIXTURES

LIGHTED HANDRAILS

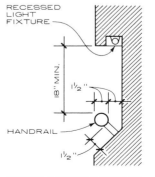

RECESSED LIGHT FIXTURE

HANDRAIL

18" MIN.

1½"

1½"

RECESSED HANDRAIL

GUIDELINES

Factors to consider for railing design include:

1. Follow all local code requirements, especially as they relate to handicap requirements, ramps, rail diameter, and rail clearances.
2. Verify allowable design stresses of rails, posts, and panels.
3. Verify the structural value of fasteners and anchorage to building structure for both vertical and lateral (horizontal) forces.
4. Requirements for uniform loading may vary from 100 to 200 lb/linear foot.
5. Requirements for concentrated loads, at any point along the rail, may vary from 200 to 300 lb.
6. Horizontal guardrail or rail at ramps is 42 in. above floor surface.
7. Guardrails and rails at stairs should be designed to prevent passage of a 6 in. diameter sphere, at any opening, in areas accessible to the public.
8. Refer to ASTM E-985 for additional information.

John McCartney, AIA; Washington, D.C.

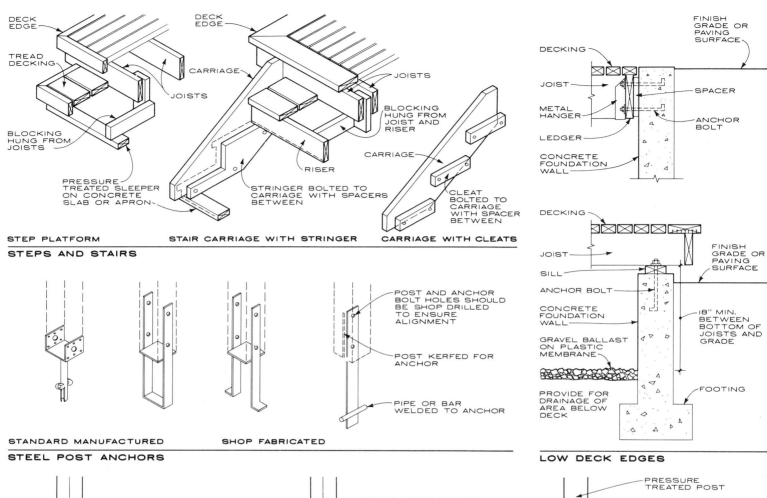

STEP PLATFORM   STAIR CARRIAGE WITH STRINGER   CARRIAGE WITH CLEATS

STEPS AND STAIRS

LOW DECK EDGES

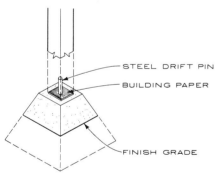

STANDARD MANUFACTURED   SHOP FABRICATED

STEEL POST ANCHORS

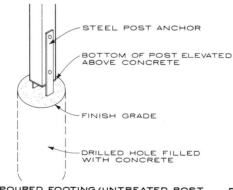

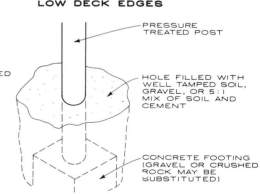

PRECAST CONCRETE PLINTH/UNTREATED POST   POURED FOOTING/UNTREATED POST   POURED OR PRECAST FOOTING/TREATED POST

POSTS AND FOOTINGS

FASTENERS

1. Smooth shank nails lose holding strength after repeated wet/dry cycles. Ring or spiral grooved shank nails are preferable.
2. Use galvanized or plated fasteners to avoid corrosion and staining.
3. To reduce board splitting by nailing: blunt nail points; predrill (3/4 of nail diameter); stagger nailing; place nails no closer to edge than one half of board thickness.
4. Avoid end grain nailing and toenailing if possible.
5. Use flat washers under heads of lag screws and bolts, and under nuts.

MOISTURE PROTECTION

1. All wood members should be protected from weather by pressure treatment or field application of preservatives, stains, or paints.
2. All wood in direct contact with soil must be pressure treated.
3. Bottoms of posts on piers should be 6 in. above grade.
4. Sterilize or cover soil with membrane to keep plant growth away from wood members so as to minimize moisture exchange.
5. Treat all ends, cuts, holes, and so on with preservative prior to placement.
6. Decking and flat trim boards, 2 x 6 and wider, should be kerfed on the underside with 3/4 in. deep saw cuts at 1 in. on center to prevent cupping.
7. Avoid horizontal exposure of endgrain or provide adequate protection by flashing or sealing. Avoid or minimize joint situations where moisture may be trapped by using spacers and/or flashing, caulking, sealant, plastic roofing cement.

CONSTRUCTION

1. WOOD SELECTION: Usual requirements are good decay resistance, nonsplintering, fair stiffness, strength, hardness, and warp resistance. Selection varies according to local climate and exposure.
2. BRACING: On large decks, or decks where post heights exceed 5 ft, lateral stability should be achieved with horizontal bracing (metal or wood diagonal ties on top or bottom of joists, or diagonal application of decking) in combination with vertical bracing (rigid bolted or gusseted connections at top of posts, knee bracing, or "X" bracing between posts), and/or connection to a braced building wall. Lateral stability should be checked by a structural engineer.

The Bumgardner Partnership/Architects; Seattle, Washington

5   **WOOD CONSTRUCTION**

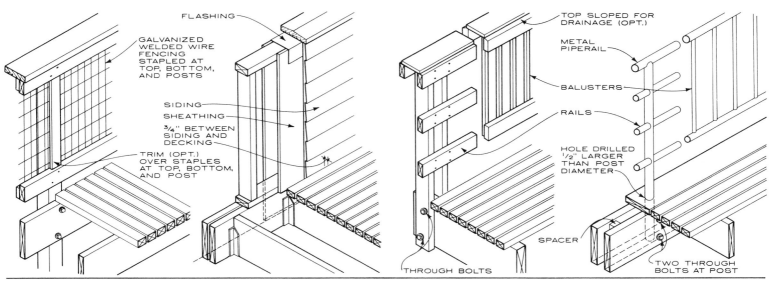

RAILINGS

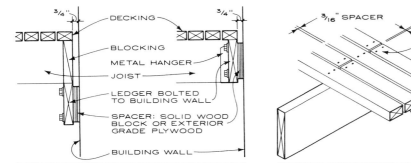

CONNECTIONS AT BUILDING WALL

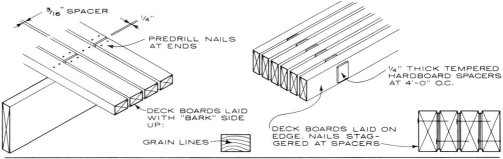

DECKING APPLICATIONS

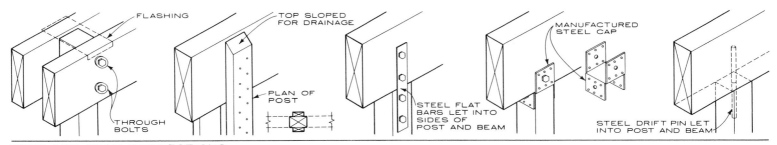

POST AND BEAM CONNECTIONS

RELATIVE COMPARISON OF VARIOUS QUALITIES OF WOOD USED IN DECK CONSTRUCTION

	DOUGLAS FIR—LARCH	SOUTHERN PINE	HEMLOCK FIR*	SOFT PINES†	WESTERN RED CEDAR	REDWOOD	SPRUCE	CYPRESS
Hardness	Fair	Fair	Poor	Poor	Poor	Fair	Poor	Fair
Warp resistance	Fair	Fair	Fair	Good	Good	Good	Fair	Fair
Ease of working	Poor	Fair	Fair	Good	Good	Fair	Fair	Fair
Paint holding	Poor	Poor	Poor	Good	Good	Good	Fair	Good
Stain acceptance†	Fair	Fair	Fair	Fair	Good	Good	Fair	Fair
Nail holding	Good	Good	Poor	Poor	Poor	Fair	Fair	Fair
Heartwood decay resistance	Fair	Fair	Poor	Poor	Good	Good	Poor	Good
Proportion of heartwood	Good	Poor	Poor	Fair	Good	Good	Poor	Good
Bending strength	Good	Good	Fair	Poor	Poor	Fair	Fair	Fair
Stiffness	Good	Good	Good	Poor	Poor	Fair	Fair	Fair
Strength as a post	Good	Good	Fair	Poor	Fair	Good	Fair	Fair
Freedom from pitch	Fair	Poor	Good	Fair	Good	Good	Good	Good

*Includes West Coast and eastern hemlocks.
†Includes western and northeastern pines.
‡Categories refer to semitransparent oil base stain.

The Bumgardner Partnership/Architects; Seattle, Washington

MAXIMUM SPAN OF DECK BOARDS

	FLAT		ON EDGE	
	1 x 4	2 x 2 (x3)(x4)	2 x 3	2 x 4
Douglas fir, larch, and southern pine	1'-4''	5'-0''	7'-6''	12'-0''
Hemlock-fir, Douglas-fir, southern	1'-2''	4'-0''	6'-6''	10'-0''
Western pines and cedars, redwoods, spruce	1'-0''	3'-6''	5'-6''	9'-0''

NOTES

Size and spacing of joists, posts, and beams may be selected according to other pages in chapter.

WOOD CONSTRUCTION **5**

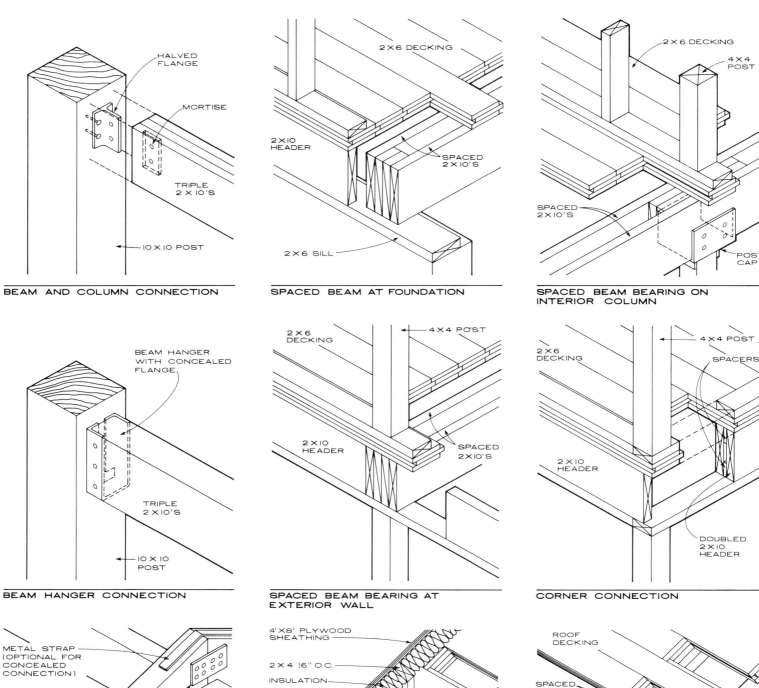

BEAM AND COLUMN CONNECTION

SPACED BEAM AT FOUNDATION

SPACED BEAM BEARING ON INTERIOR COLUMN

BEAM HANGER CONNECTION

SPACED BEAM BEARING AT EXTERIOR WALL

CORNER CONNECTION

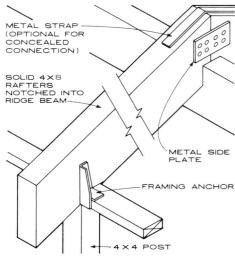

ROOF BEAM AT COLUMN AND RIDGE

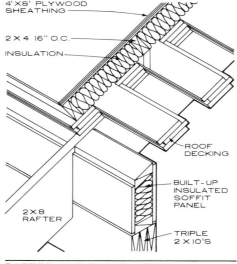

RAFTER AND PLATE DETAIL

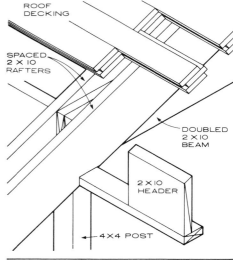

SPACED ROOF BEAM AT EXTERIOR COLUMN

Timothy B. McDonald; Washington, D.C.

 WOOD CONSTRUCTION

NOTES

1. Pole embedment depth depends on soil, slope and seismic zone.
2. Cross-bracing between poles may be required to resist lateral loads if shallow embedment. Treat all exposed surfaces with approved pressure treatment.
3. Pole notching for major beams can help align beams and walls that otherwise would be out of plumb due to pole warp. Notching improves bearing of major beams but weakens poles.
4. Roofs, walls and floors should be insulated to suit local climatic conditions. Wall and soffit insulation should meet continuously at the joint. Penetration of insulation should be minimal.
5. Various siding types can be used.
6. Dapping is a U.S. carpentry term for cutting wood to receive timber connectors.

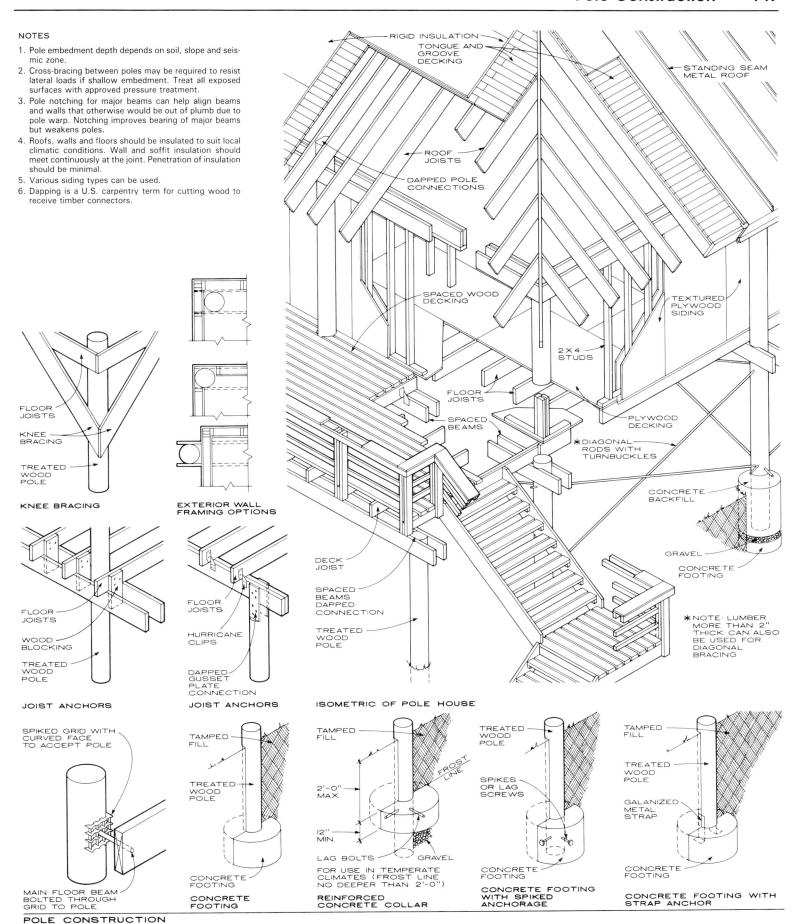

KNEE BRACING

EXTERIOR WALL FRAMING OPTIONS

JOIST ANCHORS

JOIST ANCHORS

ISOMETRIC OF POLE HOUSE

POLE CONSTRUCTION

CONCRETE FOOTING

REINFORCED CONCRETE COLLAR

CONCRETE FOOTING WITH SPIKED ANCHORAGE

CONCRETE FOOTING WITH STRAP ANCHOR

Timothy B. McDonald; Washington, D.C.

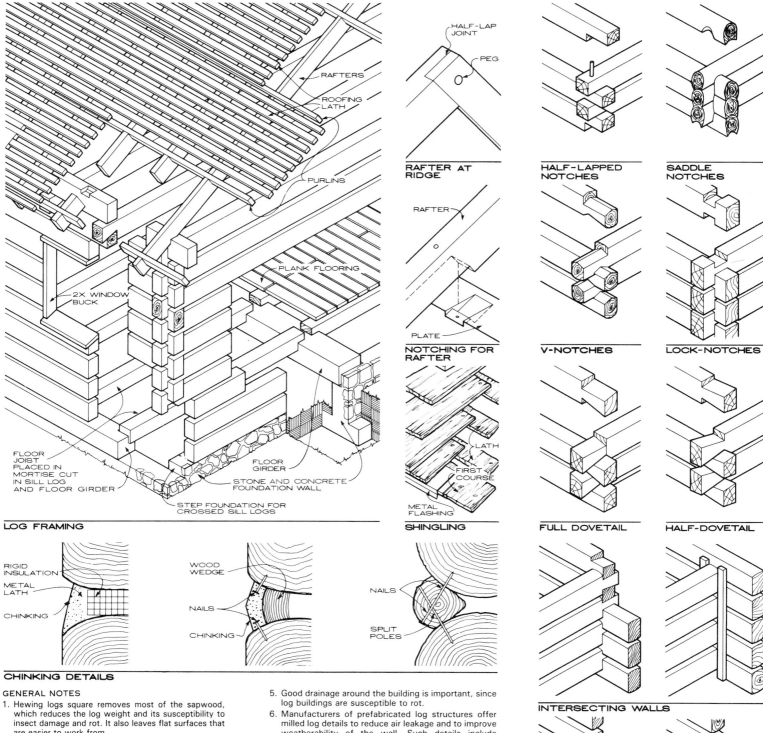

LOG FRAMING

RAFTERS
ROOFING LATH
PURLINS
2X WINDOW BUCK
PLANK FLOORING
FLOOR JOIST PLACED IN MORTISE CUT IN SILL LOG AND FLOOR GIRDER
FLOOR GIRDER
STONE AND CONCRETE FOUNDATION WALL
STEP FOUNDATION FOR CROSSED SILL LOGS

CHINKING DETAILS

RIGID INSULATION
METAL LATH
CHINKING
WOOD WEDGE
NAILS
CHINKING
NAILS
SPLIT POLES

HALF-LAP JOINT
PEG
RAFTER AT RIDGE

RAFTER
PLATE
NOTCHING FOR RAFTER

LATH
FIRST COURSE
METAL FLASHING
SHINGLING

HALF-LAPPED NOTCHES
SADDLE NOTCHES
V-NOTCHES
LOCK-NOTCHES
FULL DOVETAIL
HALF-DOVETAIL

INTERSECTING WALLS

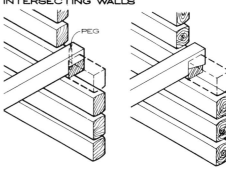

PEG
SECOND FLOOR JOISTS

GENERAL NOTES

1. Hewing logs square removes most of the sapwood, which reduces the log weight and its susceptibility to insect damage and rot. It also leaves flat surfaces that are easier to work from.

2. Damage from rot (fungi decay) can be prevented or controlled in several ways: removing sapwood, which is high in cellulose and lignum on which fungi feed; reducing the log's moisture content to 20 percent or less by air or kiln drying; and by providing proper air circulation under floors and around foundations. Generous roof overhangs and properly maintained gutters help keep water off the sides of the building.

3. Insect damage from termites, beetles, and carpenter ants can be prevented by properly seasoning the wood (kiln or air drying), and by providing continuous vapor barriers under ground floors. Also, good air circulation can help prevent infestations.

4. Exposed interior logs must be coordinated carefully with placement of plumbing, electrical wiring, and mechanical equipment.

5. Good drainage around the building is important, since log buildings are susceptible to rot.

6. Manufacturers of prefabricated log structures offer milled log details to reduce air leakage and to improve weatherability of the wall. Such details include tongue-and-groove joints, dovetailing use of steel splines, and butyl gaskets.

7. Spaces between individual logs (chink area) are filled with chinking, which varies from $\frac{1}{2}$ to 10 in. thick.

COMMON CHINKING FORMULAS

Chinking formulas that use large amounts of cement are not porous enough to let moisture trapped between the logs migrate to the surface. High-lime formulas are more porous, allowing the surface to dry more quickly. They are more elastic.

1. 1 part portland cement, 4–8 parts lime, 7–10 parts sand.

2. $\frac{1}{4}$ part cement, 11 parts lime, 4 parts sand, $\frac{1}{8}$ part dry color, excelsior.

3. 1 part cement, 4 parts lime, 6 parts sand.

Timothy B. McDonald; Washington, D.C.

5 **WOOD CONSTRUCTION**

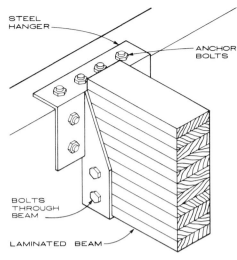

STEEL HANGER

ANCHOR BOLTS

BOLTS THROUGH BEAM

LAMINATED BEAM

BEAM HANGER

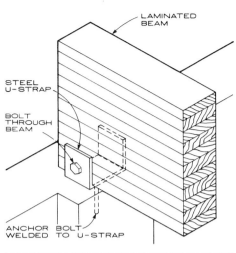

LAMINATED BEAM

STEEL U-STRAP

BOLT THROUGH BEAM

ANCHOR BOLT WELDED TO U-STRAP

BEAM ANCHOR

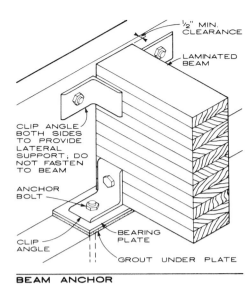

½" MIN. CLEARANCE

LAMINATED BEAM

CLIP ANGLE BOTH SIDES TO PROVIDE LATERAL SUPPORT; DO NOT FASTEN TO BEAM

ANCHOR BOLT

CLIP ANGLE

BEARING PLATE

GROUT UNDER PLATE

BEAM ANCHOR

LAMINATED BEAM

ANCHOR BOLTS

CONCRETE BASE

PROVIDE WEEP HOLES

FIXED ARCH ANCHORAGE

LAMINATED BEAM

CONCRETE BASE

BRIDGE PIN

ANCHOR BOLTS

STEEL SHOE

PROVIDE WEEP HOLES

TRUE HINGE ANCHORAGE FOR ARCHES

SLOPE > 4:12

SLOPE < 3:12

ARCH PEAK CONNECTION

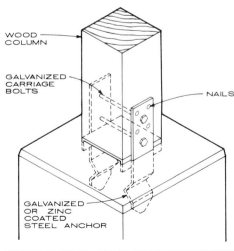

WOOD COLUMN

GALVANIZED CARRIAGE BOLTS

NAILS

ANCHOR BOLTS

GALVANIZED OR ZINC COATED STEEL ANCHOR

WET POST ANCHORAGE TO CONCRETE BASE

WOOD COLUMN

GALVANIZED CARRIAGE BOLTS

WELDED STEEL BASEPLATE

CONCRETE BASE

ANCHOR BOLTS

PROVIDE WEEP HOLES

GROUT LEVELING BED

WOOD COLUMN ANCHORED WITH STEEL BASEPLATE

WOOD COLUMN

BOLTS

BEARING PLATE

CEMENT WASH

STEEL U-STRAP

CONCRETE BASE

U-STRAP COLUMN ANCHORAGE TO CONCRETE BASE

This detail is recommended for heavy duty use where moisture protection is desired. Anchor is set and leveled in wet concrete after screeding.

This detail is recommended for industrial buildings and warehouses to resist both horizontal forces and uplift. Moisture barrier is recommended. It may be used with shear plates.

Timothy B. McDonald; Washington, D.C.

WOOD CONSTRUCTION 5

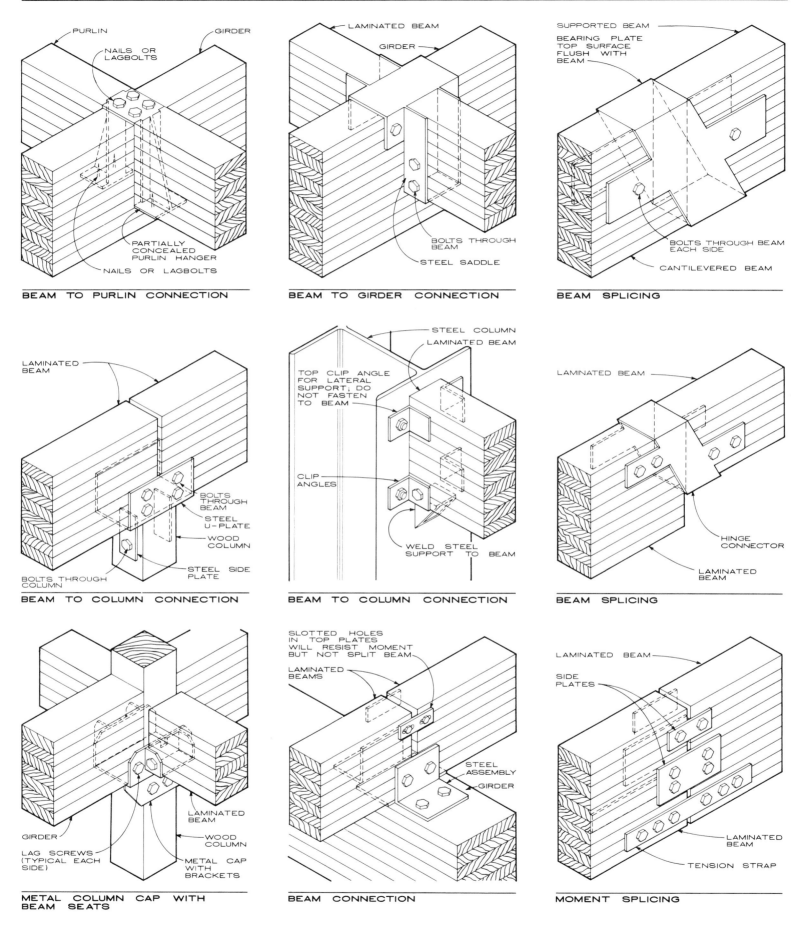

PURLIN
GIRDER
NAILS OR LAGBOLTS
PARTIALLY CONCEALED PURLIN HANGER
NAILS OR LAGBOLTS

BEAM TO PURLIN CONNECTION

LAMINATED BEAM
GIRDER
BOLTS THROUGH BEAM
STEEL SADDLE

BEAM TO GIRDER CONNECTION

SUPPORTED BEAM
BEARING PLATE TOP SURFACE FLUSH WITH BEAM
BOLTS THROUGH BEAM EACH SIDE
CANTILEVERED BEAM

BEAM SPLICING

LAMINATED BEAM
BOLTS THROUGH BEAM
STEEL U-PLATE
WOOD COLUMN
STEEL SIDE PLATE
BOLTS THROUGH COLUMN

BEAM TO COLUMN CONNECTION

STEEL COLUMN
LAMINATED BEAM
TOP CLIP ANGLE FOR LATERAL SUPPORT; DO NOT FASTEN TO BEAM
CLIP ANGLES
WELD STEEL SUPPORT TO BEAM

BEAM TO COLUMN CONNECTION

LAMINATED BEAM
HINGE CONNECTOR
LAMINATED BEAM

BEAM SPLICING

GIRDER
LAG SCREWS (TYPICAL EACH SIDE)
LAMINATED BEAM
WOOD COLUMN
METAL CAP WITH BRACKETS

METAL COLUMN CAP WITH BEAM SEATS

SLOTTED HOLES IN TOP PLATES WILL RESIST MOMENT BUT NOT SPLIT BEAM
LAMINATED BEAMS
STEEL ASSEMBLY
GIRDER

BEAM CONNECTION

LAMINATED BEAM
SIDE PLATES
LAMINATED BEAM
TENSION STRAP

MOMENT SPLICING

Timothy B. McDonald; Washington, D.C.

5 WOOD CONSTRUCTION

NOTES

1. Consult a soils engineer to determine soil types and groundwater levels and their effect on selection of drainage and waterproofing methods.
2. Most membranes require a stable, rigid, and level substrate for their application. Generally a subslab (mudslab) is used when the membrane is below the structural slab. When placed on the structural slab, a protective cover, such as another concrete slab, is required.
3. Bentonite panels may be placed over level, well-compacted fill. Cover them with polyethylene film to prevent premature expansion from wet concrete placed over them. Note: Bentonite forms an impermeable barrier when confined by foundation backfill or by lagging or sheet piling. The material may swell, exerting pressure on adjacent construction. Consult with structural engineer and manufacturer to assure appropriate use and structural adequacy.
4. Protect the water-resistant membrane during construction and backfill operations by covering it with a protection course of parging or solid sheets of protection boards.
5. Some drainage membranes or composites may also serve as the protection course.
6. Footing drains recommended when groundwater level may rise above top of floor slab or when subject to hydrostatic pressure after heavy rain. The drainage composite conveys water to the drain, thus reducing hydrostatic pressure.
7. Water-resistant membrane of interior face of foundation wall only recommended when outside is not accessible.

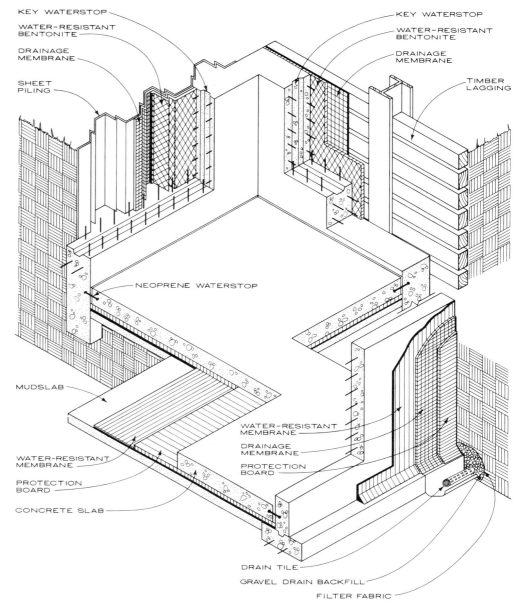

FOUNDATION CONDITIONS

WATER RESISTANCE APPLICATIONS

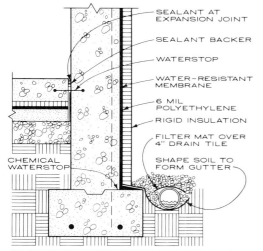

FOOTING WATER RESISTANCE – TYPE 1

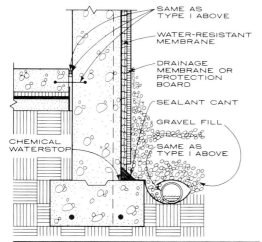

FOOTING WATER RESISTANCE – TYPE 2

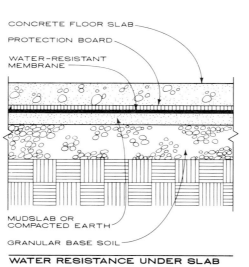

WATER RESISTANCE UNDER SLAB

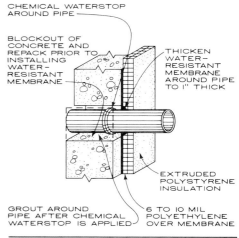

PIPE PENETRATION AT WALL

Krommenhoek/McKeown & Associates; San Diego, California

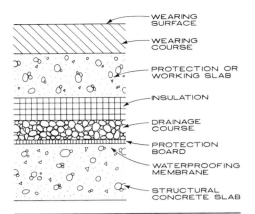

BASIC COMPONENTS OF WATERPROOFING SYSTEMS

GENERAL

The basic components, subsystems, and features for a building deck waterproofing system are the structural building deck or substrate to be waterproofed, waterproofing membrane, protection of membrane, drainage, insulation, and wearing course. See following pages for generic membrane applications.

SUBSTRATE

The substrate referred to is reinforced cast-in-place structural concrete. Precast concrete slabs pose more technical problems than cast-in-place concrete and the probability of lasting watertightness is greatly diminished and difficult to achieve because of the multitude of joints which have the capability of movement and must be treated accordingly.

The concrete used for the substrate should have a minimum density of 1762 kg/m³ (110 lb/ft³) and have a maximum moisture content of 8% when cured.

SLOPE FOR DRAINAGE

A monolithic concrete substrate slope of a minimum 11 mm/m (⅛ in./ft) should be maintained. Slope is best achieved with a monolithic structural slab and not with a separate concrete fill layer.

MEMBRANE

Detection of leakage can be a significant problem when the membrane is not bonded to the structural slab or when additional layers of materials separate it from the structural slab. Therefore, only membranes that can be bonded to the substrate should be used.

The membrane should be applied under dry, frost-free conditions on the surface as well as throughout the depth of the concrete slab.

When the membrane is turned up on a wall, it is preferable to terminate it above the wearing surface to eliminate the possibility of ponded surface water penetrating the wall above the membrane and running down behind it into the building.

Penetrations should be avoided wherever possible. For protection at such critical locations, pipe sleeves should be cast into the structural slab against which the membrane can be terminated.

Treatment at reinforced and nonreinforced joints depends on the membrane used. See following pages.

There are basically two concepts that could be considered in the detailing of expansion joints at the membrane level. These are the positive seal concept directly at the membrane level and the watershed concept with the seal at a higher lever than the membrane. Where additional safeguards are desired, a drainage gutter under the joint could be considered. Flexible support of the membrane is required in each case. Expansion joint details should be considered and used in accordance with their movement capability.

The positive seal concept entails a greater risk than the watershed concept, since it relies fully on positive seal joinery of materials at the membrane level, where the membrane is most vulnerable to water penetration. Since the precision required is not always attainable, this concept is best avoided.

The watershed concept, although requiring a greater height and more costly concrete forming, is superior in safeguarding against leakage, having the advantage of providing a water dam at the membrane level. However, if a head of water rises to the height of the materials joinery, this concept becomes almost as vulnerable as the positive seal concept. Therefore, drainage is recommended at the membrane level.

PROTECTION BOARD

The membrane should be protected from damage prior to and during the remainder of construction. Protection board should be applied after the membrane is installed. The proper timing of application after placement of the membrane is important and could vary with the type of membrane used. The manufacturer's printed instructions should be followed.

DRAINAGE SYSTEM

Drainage should be considered as a total system from the wearing surface down to the membrane, including use of multilevel drains.

Drainage at the wearing surface is generally accomplished in one of two ways:

1. By an open joint and pedestal system permitting most of the rainwater to penetrate rapidly down to the membrane level and subsurface drainage system, and

2. By a closed-joint system designed to remove most of the rainwater rapidly by slope to surface drains and to allow a minor portion to infiltrate to membrane.

A drainage course of washed, round gravel should be provided above the protection board, over the membrane. This permits water to filter to the drain and provides a place where it can collect and freeze without potential damage to the wearing course.

INSULATION

When required, insulation should be located above the membrane, but not in direct contact with it.

PROTECTION OR WORKING SLAB

A concrete slab could be placed soon after the membrane, protection board, drainage course, and insulation, if required, have been installed. It would serve as protection for the permanent waterproofing materials and insulation below, provide a working platform for construction traffic and storage of materials (within weight limits), and provide a substantial substrate for the placement of the finish wearing course materials near the completion of the project.

WEARING COURSE

The major requirements for the wearing course are a stable support of sufficient strength, resistance against lateral thrust, adequate drainage to avoid ponding of water, and proper treatment of joints.

Joints in which movement is anticipated should be treated as expansion joints.

Various proprietary compression seals are available that can be inserted into a formed joint under compression. Most of these, however, are not flush at the top surface and could fill up with sand or dirt.

Wet sealants are the materials most commonly used in moving joints at the wearing surface level. Dimension A is the design width dimension or the dimension at which the joint will be formed. The criterion normally used for determining this dimension with sealants capable of ±25% movement is to multiply the maximum expected movement in one direction by 4. Generally, this is expected to be about three-fourths of the total anticipated joint movement, but if there is any doubt, multiply the total anticipated joint movement by 4. It is better to have the joint too wide than too narrow. Dimension B (sealant depth) is related to dimension A and is best established by the sealant manufacturer. Generally, B is equal to A for widths up to 13 mm (½ in.), 15 mm (⁹⁄₁₆ in.) for a 16 mm (⅝ in.) width, and 16 mm (⅝ in.) for 19 mm (¾ in.) and greater widths. This allows some tolerance for self-leveling sealants.

Reference: ASTM C 898 and C 981. Highlights of text and figures are reprinted with permission from ASTM Committee C-24 of the American Society for Testing Materials.

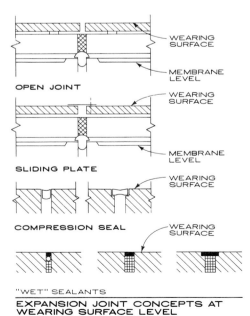

EXPANSION JOINT CONCEPTS AT MEMBRANE LEVEL

EXPANSION JOINT CONCEPTS AT WEARING SURFACE LEVEL

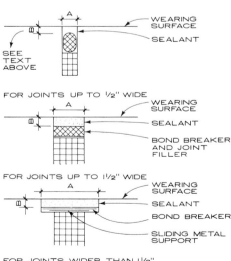

WET SEALANT DETAILS AT WEARING SURFACE

Charles J. Parise, FAIA, FASTM; Smith, Hinchman & Grylls Associates, Inc.; Detroit, Michigan

SUBSTRATE

The building deck or substrate referred to is reinforced cast-in-place structural concrete.

Polymeric, latex, or other organic chemical-based admixtures or modifiers can coat the concrete particles and reduce the ability of the membrane to bond to the substrate. Admixtures should not be used in the concrete unless determined that they are acceptable for use with the membrane.

The underside of the concrete deck should not have an impermeable barrier. A metal liner or coating that forms a vapor barrier on the underside traps moisture in the concrete and destroys or prevents the adhesive bond of the membrane to the upper surface of the concrete.

The surface should be of sufficiently rough texture to provide a mechanical bond for the membrane, but not so rough as to preclude achieving continuity of the membrane of the specified thickness across the surface.

The concrete should be cured a minimum of 7 days and aged a minimum of 28 days, including curing time, before application of the liquid-applied membrane. Curing is accomplished chemically with moisture and should not be construed as drying. Liquid or chemical curing compounds should not be used unless approved by the manufacturer of the liquid-applied membrane as the material may interfere with the bond of the membrane to the structural slab.

MEMBRANE

The membrane should be applied under dry, frost-free conditions on the surface as well as throughout the depth of the concrete slab. Use manufacturer's requirements for the particular membrane.

TERMINATION ON WALLS

A liquid-applied membrane, because of its inherent adhesive properties, may be terminated flush on the wall without the use of a reglet. However, the use of a reglet in a concrete wall has the advantage of providing greater depth protection at the terminal.

TERMINATION AT DRAINS

Drains should be designed with a wide flange or base as an integral part. The drain base should be set flush with the structural slab.

TREATMENT AT REINFORCED JOINTS

One recommended treatment of reinforced concrete joints in the structural slab is to apply a double layer of membrane over the crack. This type of detail is quite limited and implicitly relies on the membrane's crack-bridging ability. An alternative approach is to prevent the membrane from adhering to the substrate for a finite width centered on the joint or crack by means of a properly designed compatible bond-breaker tape.

TREATMENT AT NONREINFORCED JOINTS

Since the joints are not held together with reinforcing steel, some movement, however slight, should be anticipated and provided for, since the liquid-applied membrane has limited ability to take movement.

TREATMENT AT EXPANSION JOINTS

Gaskets and flexible preformed sheets lend themselves better to absorbing large amounts of movement. Since such materials, when used at an expansion joint, must be joined to the liquid-applied membrane, the watershed concept should be used.

PROTECTION BOARD

The liquid-applied membrane should be protected from damage prior to and during the remainder of deck construction. The proper timing of the application of the board is important and the manufacturer's printed instructions should be followed.

Reference: ASTM C 898. Highlights of text and figures are reprinted with permission from ASTM Committee C-24 of the American Society for Testing and Materials.

Charles J. Parise, FAIA, FASTM; Smith, Hinchman & Grylls Associates, Inc.; Detroit, Michigan

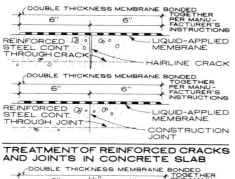

TREATMENT OF REINFORCED CRACKS AND JOINTS IN CONCRETE SLAB

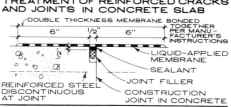

TREATMENT OF NONREINFORCED BUTTED JOINT IN CONCRETE SLAB

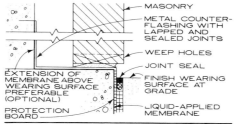

TERMINAL CONDITION WITH MASONRY ABOVE FINISH WEARING SURFACE AT GRADE

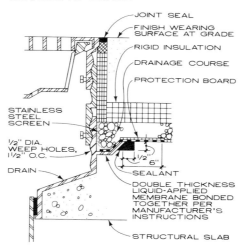

TERMINATION AT DRAIN

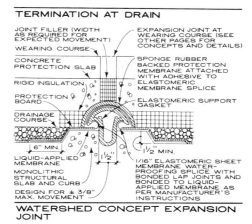

WATERSHED CONCEPT EXPANSION JOINT

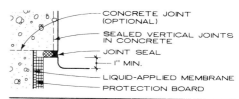

TERMINAL CONDITION ABOVE FINISH GRADE ON CONCRETE WALL

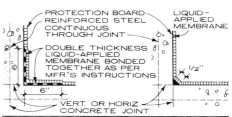

TURNUP DETAILS AT REINFORCED JOINT

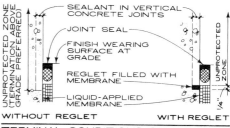

WITHOUT REGLET   WITH REGLET

TERMINAL CONDITIONS ON CONCRETE WALL BELOW FINISH WEARING SURFACE AT GRADE

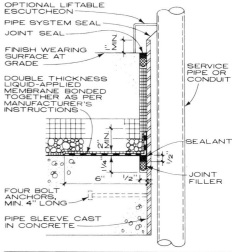

TERMINATION AT PIPE PENETRATIONS

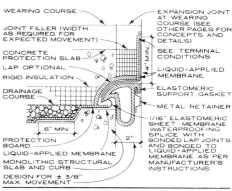

WATERSHED CONCEPT EXPANSION JOINT

SUBSTRATE

The building deck or substrate referred to is reinforced cast-in-place structural concrete.

The structural slab should have a finish of sufficiently rough texture to provide a mechanical bond for the membrane, but not so rough to preclude achieving continuity of the membrane across the surface.

The concrete should be cured a minimum of 7 days and aged a minimum of 28 days, including curing time, before application of the bituminous membrane. Curing is accomplished chemically with moisture and should not be construed as drying. Liquid or chemical curing compounds should not be used unless approved by the manufacturer of the built-up bituminous membrane as the material may interfere with the bond of the membrane to the structural slab.

MEMBRANE

A built-up bituminous waterproofing membrane consists of components joined together and bonded to its substrate at the site. The major membrane components include primers, bitumens, reinforcements, and flashing materials.

Surfaces to receive waterproofing must be clean, dry, reasonably smooth, and free of dust, dirt, voids, cracks, laitance, or sharp projections before application of materials.

Concrete surfaces should be uniformly primed to enhance the bond between the membrane and the substrate, so as to inhibit lateral movement of water.

The number of plies of membrane reinforcement required is dependent upon the head of water and strength required by the design function of the wearing surface. Plaza deck membranes should be composed of not less than three plies. The composition of the membrane is normally of a "shingle" or "ply-on-ply" (phased) construction.

For application temperatures, follow the recommendations of the manufacturers of the membrane materials.

Over reinforced structural slab joints, one ply of 6-in.-wide membrane reinforcement should be applied before application of the bituminous membrane.

Nonreinforced joints should receive a bead of compatible sealant in a recessed joint before application of the membrane.

At expansion joints, gaskets and flexible preformed sheets are required inasmuch as bituminous membranes have little or no movement capability. Since such materials must be joined to the bituminous membrane, the watershed concept should be used.

Reinforce all intersections with walls and corners with two layers of woven fabric embedded in hot bitumen.

Flashing membranes should extend above the wearing surface and the highest possible water level and not less than 150 mm (6 in.) onto the deck membrane.

The flashing should extend over the wall dampproofing or membrane waterproofing not less than 100 mm (4 in.).

Drains must be provided with a wide metal flange or base and set slightly below the drainage level. Metal flashing for the drain, if required, and the clamping ring should be set on the membrane in bituminous plastic cement. The metal flashing should be stripped in with a minimum of two plies of membrane reinforcement and three applications of bituminous plastic cement.

Penetrations through the membrane such as conduits and pipes should be avoided whenever possible. Penetrations must be flashed to a height above the anticipated water table that may extend above the wearing surface.

The built-up bituminous membrane should be protected from damage. Protection board should be placed on the waterproofing membrane when the final mopping is being placed. It will then be adhered to the membrane.

Reference: ASTM C 981. Highlights of text and figures are reprinted with permission from ASTM Committee C-24 of the American Society for Testing and Materials.

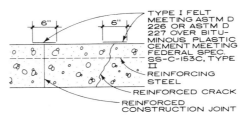

TREATMENT AT REINFORCED JOINTS

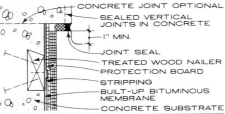

TERMINAL CONDITION ABOVE FINISH GRADE ON CONCRETE WALL

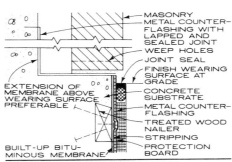

TERMINAL CONDITION WITH MASONRY ABOVE FINISH WEARING SURFACE AT GRADE

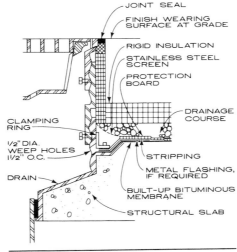

TERMINATION AT DRAIN

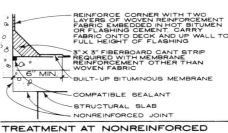

TREATMENT AT NONREINFORCED JOINTS

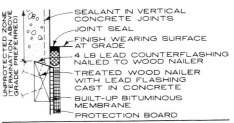

TERMINAL CONDITIONS ON CONCRETE WALL BELOW FINISH WEARING SURFACE AT GRADE

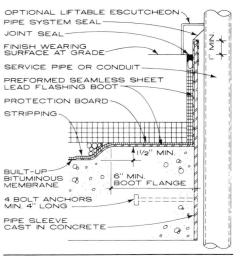

TERMINATION AT PIPE PENETRATIONS

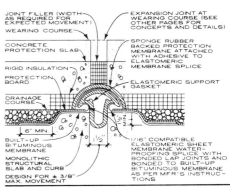

WATERSHED CONCEPT EXPANSION JOINT

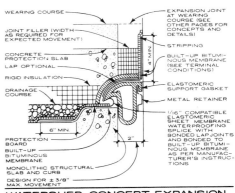

WATERSHED CONCEPT EXPANSION JOINT

Charles J. Parise, FAIA, FASTM; Smith, Hinchman & Grylls Associates, Inc.; Detroit, Michigan

WATERPROOFING

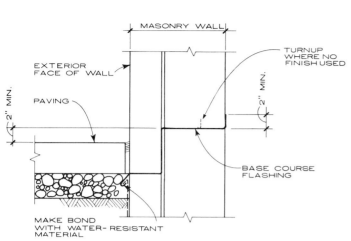

BASE COURSE AT PAVING AND WALL

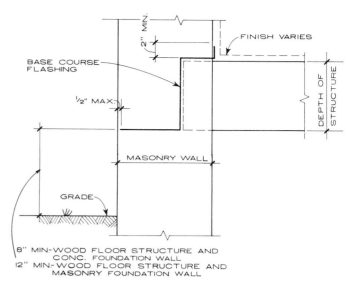

BASE COURSE AT FLOOR CONSTRUCTION

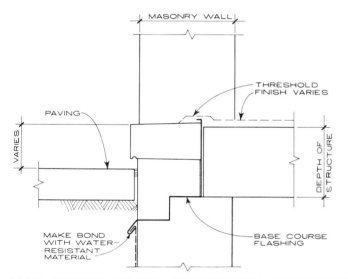

BASE COURSE AT SILL OF MASONRY CONSTRUCTION

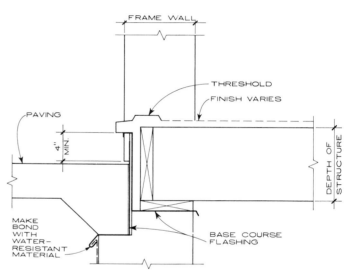

BASE COURSE AT SILL OF FRAME CONSTRUCTION

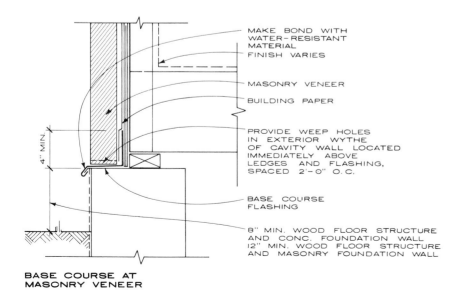

BASE COURSE AT MASONRY VENEER

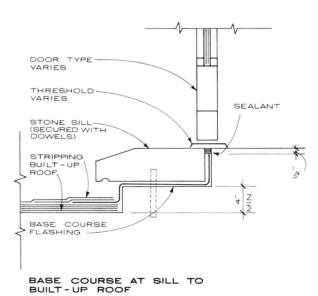

BASE COURSE AT SILL TO BUILT-UP ROOF

Michael Scott Rudden, The Stephens Associates P.C.—Architects; Albany, New York

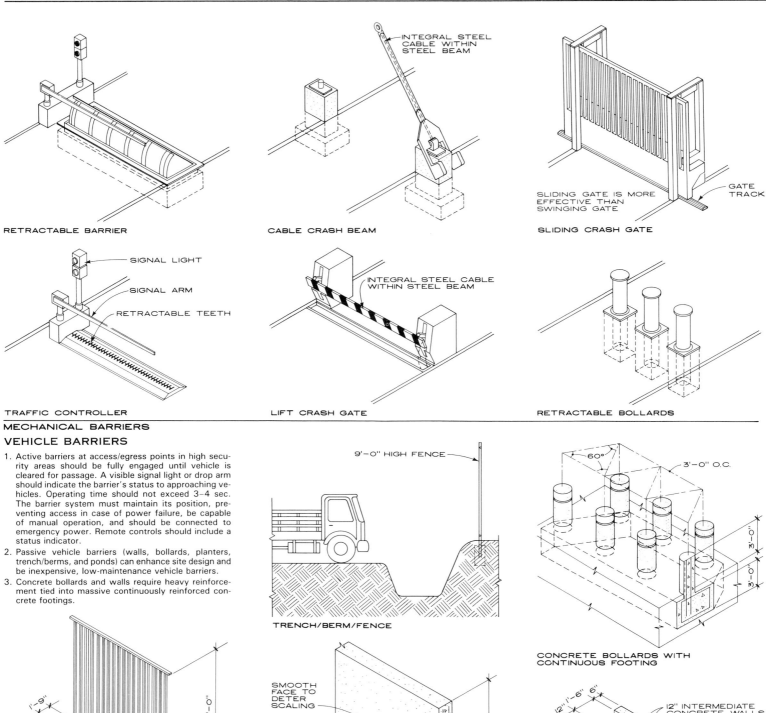

RETRACTABLE BARRIER

INTEGRAL STEEL CABLE WITHIN STEEL BEAM

CABLE CRASH BEAM

SLIDING GATE IS MORE EFFECTIVE THAN SWINGING GATE

GATE TRACK

SLIDING CRASH GATE

SIGNAL LIGHT

SIGNAL ARM

RETRACTABLE TEETH

TRAFFIC CONTROLLER

INTEGRAL STEEL CABLE WITHIN STEEL BEAM

LIFT CRASH GATE

RETRACTABLE BOLLARDS

MECHANICAL BARRIERS

VEHICLE BARRIERS

1. Active barriers at access/egress points in high security areas should be fully engaged until vehicle is cleared for passage. A visible signal light or drop arm should indicate the barrier's status to approaching vehicles. Operating time should not exceed 3–4 sec. The barrier system must maintain its position, preventing access in case of power failure, be capable of manual operation, and should be connected to emergency power. Remote controls should include a status indicator.
2. Passive vehicle barriers (walls, bollards, planters, trench/berms, and ponds) can enhance site design and be inexpensive, low-maintenance vehicle barriers.
3. Concrete bollards and walls require heavy reinforcement tied into massive continuously reinforced concrete footings.

9'-0" HIGH FENCE

TRENCH/BERM/FENCE

60°

3'-0" O.C.

3'-0"

3'-0"

CONCRETE BOLLARDS WITH CONTINUOUS FOOTING

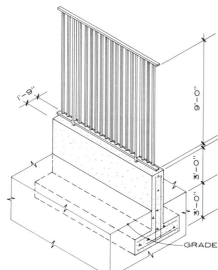

1'-9"

9'-0"

3'-0"

3'-0"

GRADE

FENCE ON BARRIER WALL

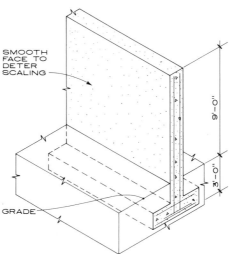

SMOOTH FACE TO DETER SCALING

9'-0"

3'-0"

GRADE

CONCRETE BARRIER WALL

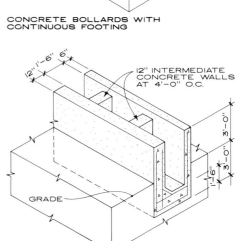

12" 1'-6" 6"

12" INTERMEDIATE CONCRETE WALLS AT 4'-0" O.C.

3'-0"

1'-6"

3'-0"

GRADE

CONCRETE PLANTER BARRIER

FIXED BARRIERS

Edwin Daly, AIA, and Ellen Delaney; Joseph Handwerger, Architects; Washington, D.C.
William G. Miner, AIA; Washington, D.C.

SPECIAL DOORS

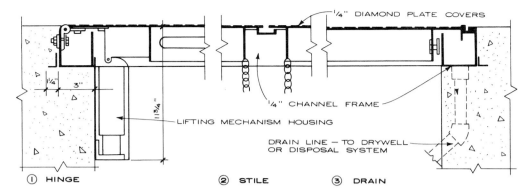

① HINGE   ② STILE   ③ DRAIN

DETAILS

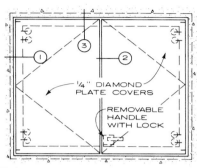

SECTION

PLAN

SIDEWALK DOOR

SIDEWALK DOORS are available in single and double leaf openings. Single leaf doors range in size from 2 ft to 3 ft 6 in. in 6 in. increments. Double leaf doors range in size from 4 to 6 ft in 1 ft increments. Special sizes are available.

Units are constructed in steel or aluminum. The door leafs are made of 1/4 in. diamond plate and are reinforced to withstand 300 psf of live load. Doors can be reinforced for greater loading conditions. The channel frames are made of 1/4 in. steel or aluminum with an anchor flange around the perimeter. Each door leaf is equipped with forged brass hinges, stainless steel pins, spring operators, and an automatic hold-open arm with release handle and is locked with a concealed snap lock. A drain coupling is provided to drain the internal gutter system. Safety chains are required to protect the opening.

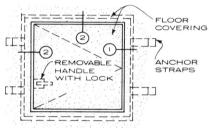

PLAN

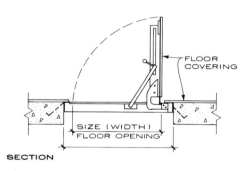

SECTION

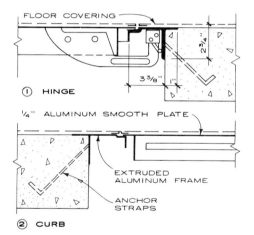

① HINGE   ② CURB

FLOOR DOOR

FLOOR DOORS are available in single and double leaf openings. Single leaf doors range in size from 2 ft to 3 ft 6 in. in 6 in. increments. Double leaf doors range in size from 4 to 6 ft in 1 ft increments. Special sizes are available. Units are constructed in aluminum.

The door leafs are made of 1/4 in. extruded aluminum. Doors are made to accept 1/8 or 3/16 in. flooring. Each leaf has cast steel hinges and torsion bars. Doors open by a removable handle and are locked with a concealed snap lock.

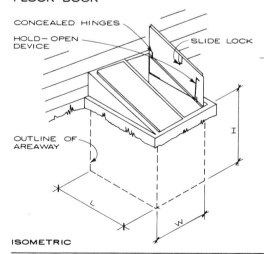

ISOMETRIC

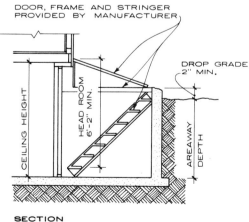

SECTION

CELLAR DOOR

CELLAR DOOR DIMENSIONS

TYPE	LENGTH	WIDTH	HEIGHT
S/L	3'-7 1/4''	4'-3''	4'-4''
O	4'-10''	3'-11''	2'-6''
B	5'-4''	4'-3''	1'-10''
C	6'-0''	4'-7''	1'-7 1/2''

AREAWAY DIMENSIONS (INSIDE)

TYPE	LENGTH	WIDTH	HEIGHT
S/L	3'-4''	3'-8''	3'-5 1/4''
O	4'-6''	3'-4''	4'-9 3/4''
B	5'-0''	3'-8''	5'-6''
C*	5'-8''	4'-0''	6'-2 1/4''

*Type C door can have a deeper areaway dimension with the use of stringer extensions.

Ronald C. Olech; SRGF, Inc., Architects; Champaign, Illinois

SPECIAL DOORS   5

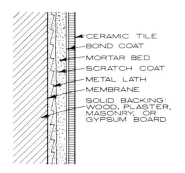

CEMENT MORTAR

Use over solid backing, over wood or metal studs. Preferred method for showers and tub enclosures. Ideal for remodeling.

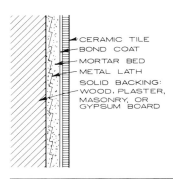

ONE COAT METHOD

Use for remodeling or on surfaces that present bonding problems. Preferred method of applying tile over gypsum plaster or gypsum board in showers and tub enclosures.

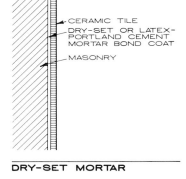

DRY-SET MORTAR

Use over gypsum board, plaster, exterior plywood, or other smooth, dimensionally stable surfaces. Use water-resistant gypsum board in wet areas.

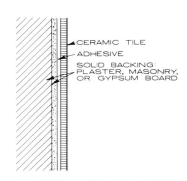

ORGANIC ADHESIVE

Use over gypsum board, plaster, exterior plywood, or other smooth, dimensionally stable surfaces. Use water-resistant gypsum board in wet areas.

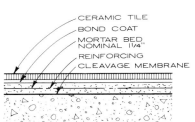

CEMENT MORTAR

Use over structural floors subject to bending and deflection. Reinforcing mesh mandatory; mortar bed nominal 1¼ in. thick and uniform.

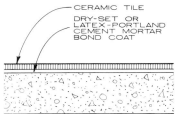

DRY-SET MORTAR

Use on level clean concrete where bending stresses do not exceed 1/360 of span and expansion joints are installed. Scarify existing concrete floors before installing tile.

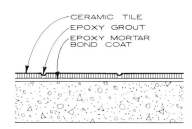

EPOXY MORTAR & GROUT

Use where moderate chemical exposure and severe cleaning methods are used, such as in commercial kitchens, dairies, breweries and food plants.

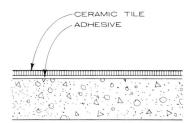

ORGANIC OR EPOXY ADHESIVE

Use over concrete floors in residential construction only. Will not withstand high impact or wheel loads. Not recommended in areas where temperatures exceed 140°F.

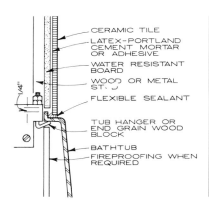

CERAMIC TILE TUB ENCLOSURE

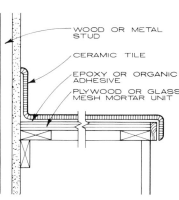

THIN-SET COUNTERTOP

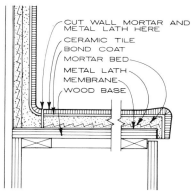

CEMENT MORTAR COUNTERTOP

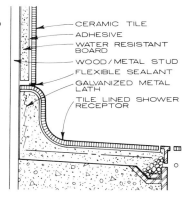

CERAMIC TILE SHOWER RECEPTOR AND WALL

TYPES OF MORTAR

PORTLAND CEMENT MORTAR

A mixture of portland cement and sand (for floor) or sand and lime (for walls) used for thick-bed installation.

DRY-SET MORTAR

A mixture of portland cement with sand and additives, imparting water retention that eliminates the need to soak tiles.

LATEX-PORTLAND CEMENT MORTAR

A mixture similar to dry-set but with latex (an emulsion of rubber or resin particles in water) added to replace all or part of the water in the mortar. It provides better adhesion, density and impact strength than dry-set mortar, and it is more flexible and resistant to frost damage.

MODIFIED EPOXY EMULSION MORTAR

As with epoxy mortars, this mixture contains a resin and hardener along with portland cement and sand. Although it is not as chemically resistant as epoxy mortar, it binds well. Compared with straight portland cement, it allows little or no shrinkage.

METHODS OF INSTALLATION

In a thick-bed process, tiles usually are applied over a portland cement mortar bed ¾ in. to 1¼ in. thick. The thickbed allows for accurate slopes or planes in the finished tile work and is not affected by prolonged contact with water. If the backing surface is damaged, cracked or unstable, a membrane should be used between the surface and the tile.

In a thin-set process, tiles are set or bonded to the surface with a thin coat of material varying from 1/32 in. to 1/8 in. thickness. Bonding materials used include dry-set mortar, latex-portland cement mortar, organic adhesive, and modified epoxy emulsion mortar. Thin-set application requires a continuous, stable and undamaged surface.

THIN-SET MORTAR WITHOUT PORTLAND CEMENT

EPOXY MORTAR

A two- or three-part mixture (resin and hardener with silica filler) used where chemical resistance is important. It has high bond strength and high resistance to impact. This mortar and furan mortar are the only two that can be recommended for use over steel plates.

EPOXY ADHESIVE

Mixture similar to epoxy mortar in bonding capability, but not as chemical or solvent resistant.

ORGANIC ADHESIVE

A one-part mastic mixture that requires no mixing. It remains somewhat flexible (as compared with portland cement mortar), and has good bond strength but should not be used for exterior or wet applications.

Tile Council of America, Inc.

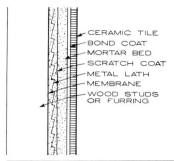

CEMENT MORTAR

Use over dry, well-braced wood studs or furring. Preferred method of installation in showers and tub or enclosures.

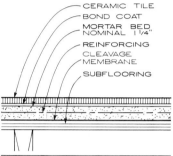

CEMENT MORTAR

Use over wood floors that are structurally sound and where deflection, including live and dead loads, does not exceed 1/360 of span.

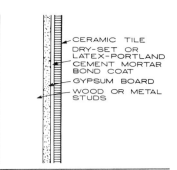

DRY-SET MORTAR

Use in dry interior areas in schools, institutions and commercial buildings. Do not use in areas where temperatures exceed 125° F.

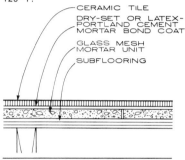

DRY-SET MORTAR

Use in light commercial and residential construction, deflection not to exceed 1/360, including live and dead loads. Waterproof membrane is required in wet areas.

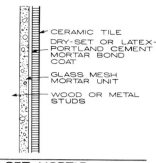

DRY-SET MORTAR WITH GLASS MESH MORTAR UNIT

Use in wet areas over well-braced wood or metal studs. Stud spacing should not exceed 16 in. o.c., and metal studs should be 20 ga. or heavier.

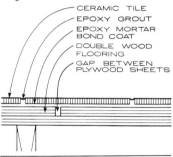

EPOXY MORTAR AND GROUT

Use in residential, normal commercial and light institutional construction. Recommended where resistance to water, chemicals or staining is needed.

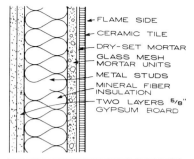

DRY-SET MORTAR (FIRE-RATED WALL)

Use where a fire resistance rating of 2 hours is required with tile face exposed to flame. Stud spacing not to exceed 16 in. o.c. and mortar bed min. thickness $^{3}/_{32}$ in.

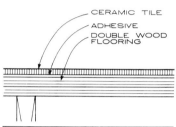

ORGANIC ADHESIVE

Use over wood or concrete floors in residential construction only. Not recommended in wet areas.

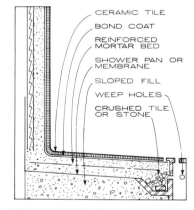

TILE SHOWER RECEPTOR

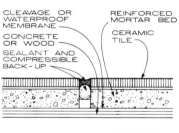
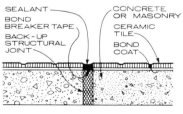
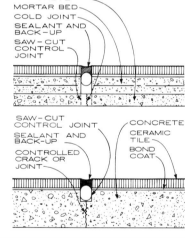

THRESHOLDS, SADDLES

VERTICAL AND HORIZONTAL EXPANSION JOINTS

FURAN MORTAR

A two-part mixture (furan resin and hardener) excellent for chemical resistant uses and its high temperatures (350°F.) tolerance.

GROUT

Grout is used to fill joints between tiles and is selected with a compatible mortar. Types include:

PORTLAND CEMENT BASED GROUTS

Include commercial portland cement grout, sand-portland cement grout, dry-set grout and latex-portland cement grout.

EPOXY GROUT

A two- or three-part mixture (epoxy resin hardener with silica sand filler) highly resistant to chemicals. It has great bond strength. This grout and furan grout are made for different chemical and solvent resistance.

FURAN RESIN GROUT

A two-part furan mixture (similar to furan mortar) that resists high temperatures and solvents.

MASTIC GROUT

A flexible one-part mixture.

SILICONE RUBBER GROUT

An elastomeric mixture based on silicone rubber. It has high bond strength, is resistant to water and staining, and remains flexible under freezing conditions.

Tile Council of America, Inc.

Terrazzo is a material composed of stone chips and cement matrix and is usually polished. There are four generally accepted types, classified by appearance:

1. STANDARD TERRAZZO: The most common type; relatively small chip sizes (#1 and #2 size chips).
2. VENETIAN TERRAZZO: Larger chips (size #3 through #8), with smaller chips filling the spaces between.
3. PALLADIANA: Random fractured slabs of marble up to approximately 15 in. greatest dimension, 3/8 to 1 in. thick, with smaller chips filling spaces between.
4. RUSTIC TERRAZZO: Uniformly textured terrazzo in which matrix is depressed to expose chips, not ground or only slightly ground.

MATRIX DATA

Two basic types exist: portland cement and chemical binders. Color pigments are added to create special effects. Limeproof mineral pigments or synthetic mineral pigments compatible with portland cement are required. Both white and grey portland cement is used depending on final color.

CHEMICAL BINDERS

All five types of chemical binders provide excellent chemical and abrasion resistance, except for latex, which is rated good.

1. EPOXY MATRIX: Two component resinous matrix.
2. POLYESTER MATRIX: Two component resinous matrix.
3. POLYACRYLATE MATRIX: Composite resinous matrix.
4. LATEX MATRIX: Synthetic latex matrix.
5. CONDUCTIVE MATRIX: Special formulated matrix to conduct electricity with regulated resistance, use in surgical areas and where explosive gases are a hazard.

PRECAST TERRAZZO

Several units are routinely available and almost any shape can be produced. Examples include: straight, coved, and splayed bases; window sills; stair treads and risers; shower receptors; floor tiles; and wall facings.

STONE CHIPS

Stone used in terrazzo includes all calcareous serpentine and other rocks capable of taking a good polish. Marble and onyx are the preferred materials. Quartz, granite, quartzite, and silica pebbles are used for rustic terrazzo and textured mosaics not requiring polishing.

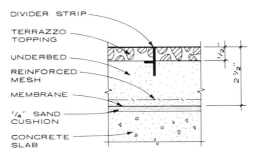

SAND CUSHION TERRAZZO

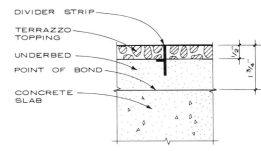

BONDED TERRAZZO

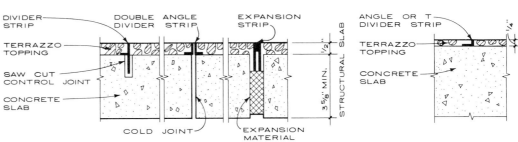

MONOLITHIC TERRAZZO

THIN-SET TERRAZZO

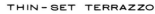

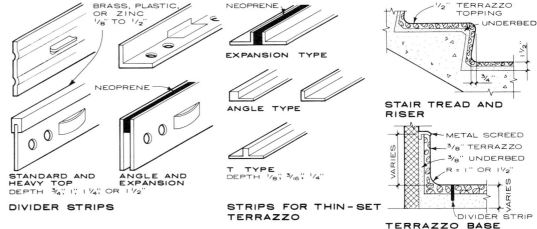

DIVIDER STRIPS

STRIPS FOR THIN-SET TERRAZZO

STAIR TREAD AND RISER

TERRAZZO BASE

TERRAZZO SYSTEMS

TERRAZZO SYSTEM	MINIMUM ALLOWANCE FOR FINISH	MINIMUM WEIGHT/ SQ FT	CONTROL JOINT STRIP LOCATION	SUGGESTED PANEL SIZE AND DIVIDER STRIP LOCATION	COMMENTS
Sand cushion terrazzo	2 1/2 ''	27 lb	At all control joints in structure	9 to 36 sq ft	Avoid narrow proportions (length no more than twice the width) and acute angles
Bonded underbed or strip terrazzo	1 3/4 ''	18 lb	At all control joints in structure	16 to 36 sq ft	Avoid narrow proportions as in sand cushion
Monolithic terrazzo	1/2 ''	7 lb	At all control joints in structure and at column centers or over grade beams where spans are great	At column centers in sawn or recessed slots maximum 24 x 24 ft	T or L strips usually provide decorative feature only
Thin-set terrazzo (chemical binders)	1/4 ''	3 lb	At all control joints	Only where structural crack can be anticipated	
Modified thin-set terrazzo	3/8 ''	4 1/2 lb	At all control joints	Only where structural crack can be anticipated	
Terrazzo over permanent metal forms	Varies, 3'' minimum	Varies	Directly over beam	Directly over joist centers and at 3 to 5 ft on center in the opposite direction	
Structural terrazzo	Varies, 4'' minimum	Varies	At all control joints at columns and at perimeter of floor	Deep strip (1 1/2 in. min.) at all column centers and over grade beams	Use divider strip at any location where structural crack can be anticipated

NOTES

1. Venetian and Palladiana require greater depth due to larger chip size; 2 3/4 in. minimum allowance for finish 28 lb/sq ft.
2. Divider and control joint strips are made of white alloy of zinc, brass, aluminum, or plastic. Aluminum is not satisfactory for portland cement matrix terrazzo; use brass and plastic in chemical binder matrix only with approval of binder manufacturer.
3. In exterior terrazzo, brass will tarnish and white alloy of zinc will deteriorate.

John C. Lunsford, AIA, Varney Sexton Sydnor Architects; Phoenix, Arizona

TERRAZZO

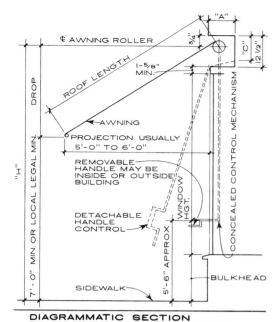

DIAGRAMMATIC SECTION RECESSED BOX INSTALLATION

AWNING MATERIALS:
1. Canvas
2. Interlocking metal slats
   a. aluminum
   b. bronze
   c. stainless steel
3. Fiberglass

AWNING OPERATORS:
1. Detachable handle control
2. Gear box & shaft (concealed or exposed) with removable handle inside or outside of building
3. Electric control

AWNING BOX CLEARANCES:

Recessed box sizes		"H"	"A"	"B"	"C"
A. lateral arm type	9'-6" to 11'-0"	10"	10 1/2"	10"
	9'-6" to 12'-0"	10 1/2"	12"	10"
	9'-6" to 14'-0"	11"	13 1/2"	10"
B. outrigger arm type	varies	6'-2"	6'-2"	6'-2"

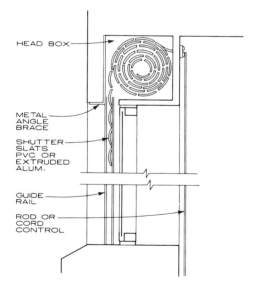

NOTE

Rolling shutters provide sun control not only by shading windows from direct sun rays but also by way of two dead airspaces—one between shutter and window, the other within the shutter extrusions to serve as insulation. The dead airspaces work as well in winter to prevent the escape of heat from the interior. In addition, shutters are useful as privacy and security measures. They can be installed in new or existing construction and are manufactured in standard window sizes.

ROLLING SHUTTERS

Graham Davidson, Architect; Washington, D.C.

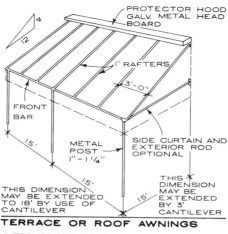

TERRACE OR ROOF AWNINGS

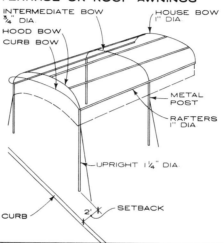

CANOPIES - LOW CURVED BOW SHOWN

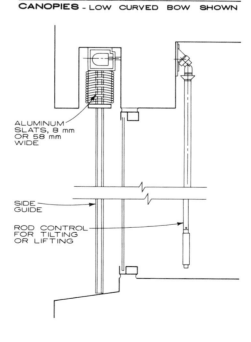

NOTE

External blinds protect the building interior from solar gain and glare, but can be raised partially or fully to the head when not needed. Manual or electric control is from inside the building.

EXTERNAL VENETIAN BLINDS

TERRACE OR ROOF AWNINGS

To provide complete sun protection and shade, the overall length of the awning bar should extend 3 in. past the glass line on both sides. For proper sunshade protection, awnings should project at least as far forward from the face of the window as the bottom of the window is below the front bar of the awning.

The wall measurement of an awning is the distance down the face of the building from the point where the awning attaches to the face of the building (or from the center of the roller in the case of the roller type awning).

The projection of an awning is the distance from the face of the building to the front bar of the awning in its correct projected position.

Right and left of an awning are your right and left as you are facing the awning looking into the building.

Framework consists of galvanized steel pipe, with non-rattling fittings. Awning is lace-on type canvas with rope reinforced eave. Protector hood is galvanized sheet metal or either bronze, copper, or aluminum.

Sizes of members should be checked by calculation for conditions not similar to those shown on this page.

Consult local building code for limitations on height and setback.

COVERED WALKWAYS

Covered walkways are available with aluminum fascia and soffit panels in a number of profiles. The fascia panels are supported with pipe columns and steel or aluminum structural members if necessary. Panels can cantilever up to 30% of span. Canopy designs can be supported from above.

Another method of providing covered exterior space is with stressed membrane structures. Using highly tensile synthetic fabric and cable in collaboration with compression members, usually metal, dynamic and versatile tentlike coverings can be created. Membrane structures are especially suited to temporary installations.

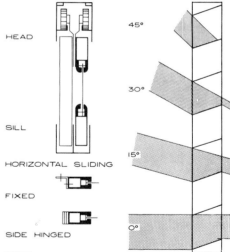

NOTE

These miniature external louvers shade windows from direct sunlight and glare while allowing a high degree of visibility, light, ventilation, insect protection, and daytime privacy. Much like a woven metal fabric, they are not strong architectural elements but present a uniform appearance in the areas covered. The solar screen is installed in aluminum frames and can be adapted to suit most applications.

SOLAR SCREEN SIZES

MATERIAL	LOUVERS	TILT	VERTICAL SPACING	SIZE (WIDTHS)
Aluminum	17"	17°	1" o.c.	18"-48"
Bronze	17", 23"	20°	1/2" o.c.	Up to 72 1/2"

Aluminum screens are available in black or light green. Bronze screens come in black only.

SOLAR SCREENS

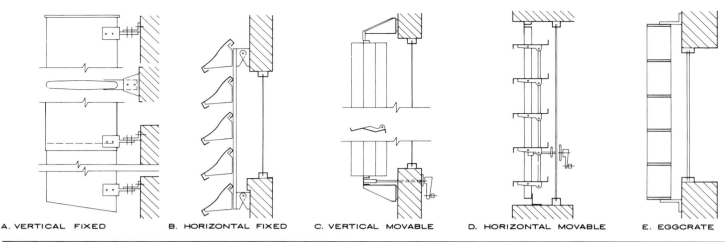

A. VERTICAL FIXED   B. HORIZONTAL FIXED   C. VERTICAL MOVABLE   D. HORIZONTAL MOVABLE   E. EGGCRATE

TYPICAL SUN SHADES AND CONTROLS

A. This device is effective on an east or west wall and can be attached at any degree of angle to facade. If slanted, it should incline to north. Fins are made in floor-to-floor lengths, capped at top and bottom, and telescoped top into bottom at intermediate levels.

B. This device is effective on any side of a building. Blades have a maximum length of 20 ft with supports of 6 ft on center.

C. Used on east or west side of building. This type may interfere with view. Many models are available up to 27 in. wide and 12 ft high.

D. Although this is effective on any side of a building, it is the least restrictive to view when used on the south side. It is usually hinged at the head for emergency exit and window washing. Blades are 9 in. deep; maximum width is 6 ft.

E. This type is very effective on southeast and southwest orientations. It is efficient in hot climates especially if bars can be tilted to more effective angles. All dimensions are variable according to desired function.

EXTERIOR SUN CONTROLS

The incidence of the sun's rays on a building transmits solar energy to the interior of the building. Since the heat gain through glass is particularly high, various forms of solar control for fenestration have been developed to reduce the use of mechanical equipment for cooling.

The most efficient of these is exterior shading, that is, avoiding the penetration of solar heat through the skin of the building. Exterior shading devices vary according to climate, orientation, and building function and are manufactured to suit specific conditions. They are strong design elements.

Sunshades (fixed horizontal or vertical fins, outriggers, and grills) shade glass completely or partially at critical times. Sun controls (movable horizontal or vertical fins) regulate the quantity of solar heat and light admitted through the glass, which is clear. Adjusting mechanisms can be manual or electric and can be automatically operated with time or photoelectric controls.

Aluminum, either sheet or extruded, is the standard material. Anodic and baked enamel coatings are available as finishes.

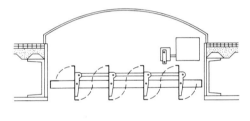

F. OUTRIGGER

F. Overhangs are most effectively used on the south side of a building. Wall brackets are made of cast aluminum. Projections greater than 6 ft require structural support or hangers.

G. SKYLIGHT SHUTTER

G. Perimeter framing should be designed to suit mounting conditions. Electrically operated shutters are available. Maximum width is 10 ft; length is unlimited.

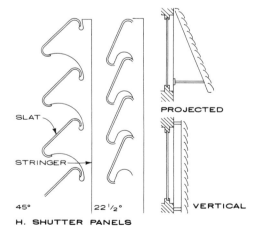

H. SHUTTER PANELS

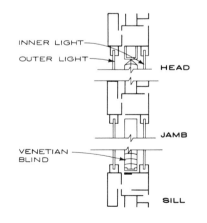

I. INTEGRAL VENETIAN BLINDS

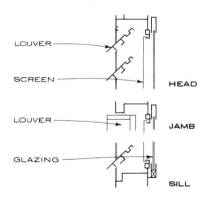

J. INTEGRAL HORIZONTAL SHADES

SPECIAL WINDOW TREATMENT

H. These panels are effective solar screens. The aluminum louvers are spaced to preserve the outside view and admit soft, diffused light while eliminating heat and glare. Horizontal slats snap onto stringer supports which can be easily attached to most structures.

I. This window type combines the thermal insulating values of dual glazing with the advantage of semi-external shading. An aluminum blind is provided between two pieces of glass, each in its own frame and each frame pivoted horizontally or vertically to make cleaning possible. The cavity between the two pieces of glass is ventilated to avoid condensation and to equalize air pressure.

The venetian blind can be tilted and, in some models, raised with controls on the interior window frame.

Window frames are constructed of aluminum, teak or pine.

J. A combination of exterior adjustable horizontal louvers and window frame, this window can be double hung, sliding, jalousie, or fixed. Louvers can be aluminum alloy extrusions, redwood, or glass.

Graham Davidson, Architect; Washington, D.C.

SUN CONTROL

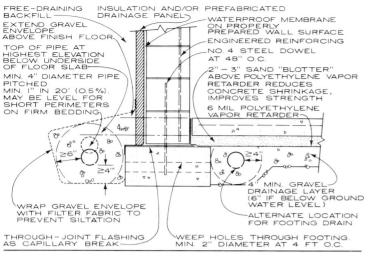

TYPICAL FOOTING CONDITION

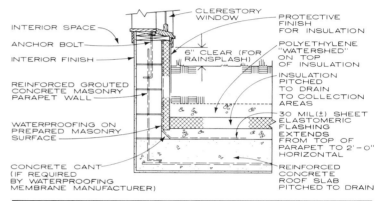

ROOF EDGE DETAIL

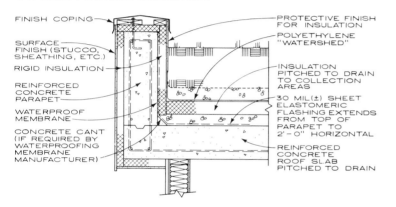

CONCRETE PERIMETER PARAPET

MASONRY INTERIOR PARAPET

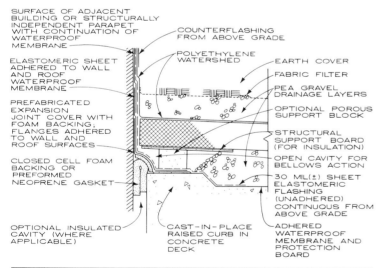

FLEXIBLE JOINT AT ROOF EDGE

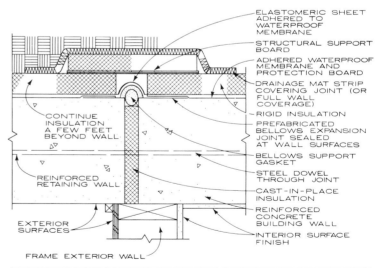

THERMAL BREAK AT RETAINING WING WALL (PLAN)

THERMAL CONSIDERATIONS

Exterior insulation keeps walls and roofs warm and at a stable temperature. This minimizes dimensional change and indoor surface condensation and keeps elastomeric waterproofing pliable. Exterior insulation consumes no indoor space, but it is sometimes attacked by rodents and insects. Extruded polystyrene is usually preferred for its resistance to water absorption. Roof insulation should be placed within the drainage layer so that it does not sit in water or impede drainage. Gravel is not always needed under the insulation, especially if the insulation is pitched to drain and is covered with polyethylene sheets. All seepage planes should be sloped a minimum of 1 in. in 4 ft.

Soil has little thermal resistance, so roof winter thermal performance depends largely on added insulation. Heat loss from earth-covered roofs is nearly constant at

$$Q = (T_1 - T_0)/R$$

where Q is heat loss in Btu/ft^2[hr]°F, T_1 and T_0 are indoor and outdoor air temperatures (°F) averaged over the preceding few days, and R is the thermal resistance of the overall roof assembly. Wet soil has an R value of slightly less than 1.0 per foot thickness.

Kenneth Labs; New Haven, Connecticut

STRUCTURAL CONSIDERATIONS

Earth sheltered structures are usually deeper and the loads greater than for basements. Hydrostatic and compaction loads add to the triangular soil loading on walls (Figure 1). Floors below water level are subjected to uplift of 62.4 psf per foot depth below water level and may require special design (Figure 2) to resist the load and to provide a uniform support plane for the waterproof membrane. Roof live loads in urban areas may include public assembly at 100 psf, in addition to soil, plants, and furnishings. Saturated soils and gravel are usually taken at 120 pcf. Tree loads are related to species and size. Tree weights can be estimated for preliminary design by the logarithmic relation

$$\log(\text{wt}) = x + 2.223 \log(\text{dia.}) + 0.339 \log(\text{ht})$$

where (wt) is in pounds, (dia.) is trunk diameter in inches at breast height, and (ht) is in feet. Forest trees range in x from 0.6 for fir to 0.8 for birch, with spruce and maple at about 0.7. The equation has not been tested for lawn trees, so it must be used with caution. Site investigation is important to determine soil bearing and drainage capacity, shearing strength, and water level. Hillside designs produce unbalanced lateral loads that may recommend interior wall buttressing.

LANDSCAPE CONSIDERATIONS

Rooftop plantings require adequate soil depth (Figure 3), underdrainage, and irrigation. Lightweight soil mixes reduce roof loads, but are not suitable under foot. Highly trafficked roofs may require special sandy soil mixes used for golf greens and athletic fields to resist compaction and root damage. Plant materials should be drought-resistant and hardier than normal, since roof soil may be colder than lawn soil.

DRAINAGE AND MOISTURE CONSIDERATIONS

Footing drains draw down the water table and prevent ponding in the backfill. Exterior location is more effective, but is subject to abuse during backfilling and to subsequent settlement. Underslab drains are easier to install correctly and are less likely to fail. Unless both are used, weep holes should be installed through the footing to connect underfloor and perimeter systems. A polyethylene sheet keeps water vapor from entering the slab, and through-joint flashing prevents capillary transfer of soil moisture through the footing to the wall. The waterproofing system must be suited to the structural system and the surface condition of the substrate. Plastic waterstops complicate joint forming and may conceal the source of leaks, disadvantages that usually outweigh whatever benefit they may provide. Chemical (e.g., bentonite base) waterstops do not have these disadvantages.

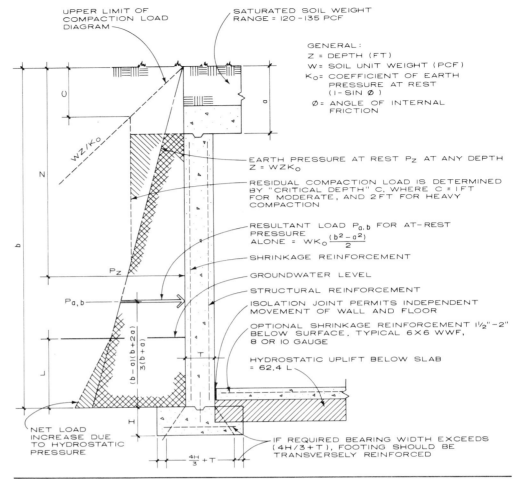

UPPER LIMIT OF COMPACTION LOAD DIAGRAM

SATURATED SOIL WEIGHT RANGE = 120 - 135 PCF

GENERAL:
Z = DEPTH (FT)
W = SOIL UNIT WEIGHT (PCF)
K_o = COEFFICIENT OF EARTH PRESSURE AT REST ($1 - \sin \emptyset$)
$\emptyset$ = ANGLE OF INTERNAL FRICTION

EARTH PRESSURE AT REST P_z AT ANY DEPTH Z = WZK_o

RESIDUAL COMPACTION LOAD IS DETERMINED BY "CRITICAL DEPTH" C, WHERE C = 1FT FOR MODERATE, AND 2FT FOR HEAVY COMPACTION

RESULTANT LOAD $P_{a,b}$ FOR AT-REST PRESSURE ALONE = $WK_o \frac{(b^2 - a^2)}{2}$

SHRINKAGE REINFORCEMENT

GROUNDWATER LEVEL

STRUCTURAL REINFORCEMENT

ISOLATION JOINT PERMITS INDEPENDENT MOVEMENT OF WALL AND FLOOR

OPTIONAL SHRINKAGE REINFORCEMENT 1½"–2" BELOW SURFACE, TYPICAL 6×6 WWF, 8 OR 10 GAUGE

HYDROSTATIC UPLIFT BELOW SLAB = 62.4 L

NET LOAD INCREASE DUE TO HYDROSTATIC PRESSURE

IF REQUIRED BEARING WIDTH EXCEEDS (4H/3+T), FOOTING SHOULD BE TRANSVERSELY REINFORCED

FIGURE 1 COMPOSITE LOAD DIAGRAM

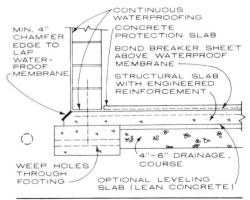

CONTINUOUS WATERPROOFING

CONCRETE PROTECTION SLAB

BOND BREAKER SHEET ABOVE WATERPROOF MEMBRANE

STRUCTURAL SLAB WITH ENGINEERED REINFORCEMENT

MIN. 4" CHAMFER EDGE TO LAP WATERPROOF MEMBRANE

4"–6" DRAINAGE COURSE

WEEP HOLES THROUGH FOOTING

OPTIONAL LEVELING SLAB (LEAN CONCRETE)

FIGURE 2 REINFORCED SLAB (GERMAN APPROACH)

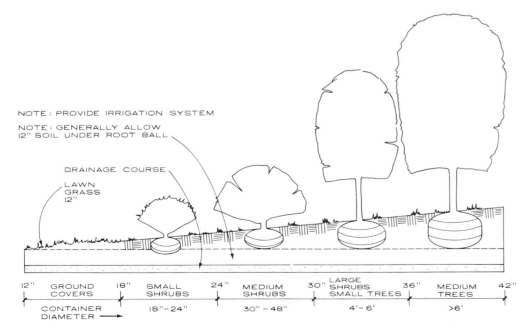

NOTE: PROVIDE IRRIGATION SYSTEM

NOTE: GENERALLY ALLOW 12" SOIL UNDER ROOT BALL

DRAINAGE COURSE

LAWN GRASS 12"

	GROUND COVERS		SMALL SHRUBS		MEDIUM SHRUBS		LARGE SHRUBS SMALL TREES		MEDIUM TREES	
12"		18"		24"		30"		36"		42"
CONTAINER DIAMETER →			18"–24"		30"–48"		4'–6'		>6'	

FIGURE 3 PLANT SOIL COVER REQUIREMENTS

Kenneth Labs; New Haven, Connecticut

RECOMMENDED REFERENCES

1. B. Anderson, "Waterproofing and the Design Professional," *The Construction Specifier*, March 1986, pp. 84–97.

2. J. Carmody and R. Sterling, *Earth Sheltered Housing Design*, 2nd Ed., Van Nostrand Reinhold, New York, 1985, 350 pp.

3. R. Sterling, W. Farnan, J. Carmody, *Earth Sheltered Residential Design Manual*, Van Nostrand Reinhold, New York, 1982, 252 pp.

4. U.S. Navy, *Earth Sheltered Buildings*, NAVFAC Design Manual 1.4, U.S. Government Printing Office, 1983.

5. Moreland Associates, *Earth Covered Buildings: An Exploratory Analysis for Hazard and Energy Performance*, Federal Emergency Management Agency, 1981.

5 EARTH SHELTERS

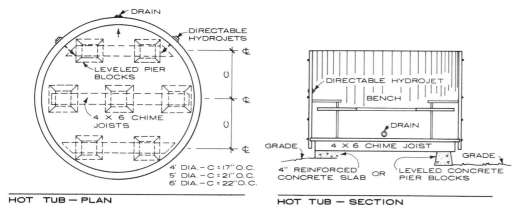

HOT TUB — PLAN

4' DIA. – C = 17" O.C.
5' DIA. – C = 21" O.C.
6' DIA. – C = 22" O.C.

DRAIN

DIRECTABLE HYDROJETS

LEVELED PIER BLOCKS

4 X 6 CHIME JOISTS

HOT TUB — SECTION

DIRECTABLE HYDROJET

BENCH

DRAIN

GRADE

4 X 6 CHIME JOIST

GRADE

4" REINFORCED CONCRETE SLAB or LEVELED CONCRETE PIER BLOCKS

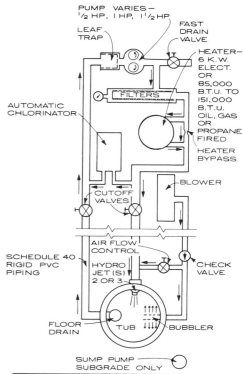

MECHANICAL SCHEMATIC

PUMP VARIES – ½ HP, 1 HP, 1½ HP

LEAF TRAP

FAST DRAIN VALVE

HEATER – 6 K.W. ELECT. OR 85,000 B.T.U. TO 151,000 B.T.U. OIL, GAS OR PROPANE FIRED

HEATER BYPASS

AUTOMATIC CHLORINATOR

FILTERS

BLOWER

CUTOFF VALVES

SCHEDULE 40 RIGID PVC PIPING

AIR FLOW CONTROL

HYDRO JET(S) 2 OR 3

CHECK VALVE

FLOOR DRAIN

TUB

BUBBLER

SUMP PUMP SUBGRADE ONLY

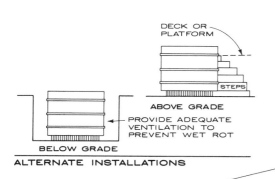

ALTERNATE INSTALLATIONS

DECK OR PLATFORM

STEPS

ABOVE GRADE

PROVIDE ADEQUATE VENTILATION TO PREVENT WET ROT

BELOW GRADE

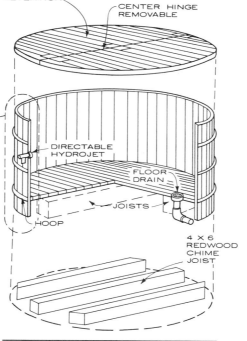

TUB COVER. TO MINIMIZE HEAT LOSS A COVER IS RECOMMENDED. A PRIMARY FOAM BLANKET LIES ON THE SURFACE OF THE WATER. THE SECONDARY 1 X 6 T & G REDWOOD COVER IS FOR SECURITY AND HEAT RETENTION

CENTER HINGE REMOVABLE

DIRECTABLE HYDROJET

FLOOR DRAIN

JOISTS

HOOP

4 X 6 REDWOOD CHIME JOIST

TYPICAL TUB

NOTES

Low profile tubs allow the bathers to sit directly on the floor with feet extended. Therapeutically, this style provides direct, close range hydromassage that comes from a floor bubbler. High profile tubs can accommodate more people per diameter foot and allows people to bath standing upright. Tub surfaces are normally left unsealed and will weather naturally to gray. Exterior can be stained or treated with silicone or oil resin to preserve the natural reddish finish. In high altitude, occasional repeated oil treatment is recommended. The size and sophistication of each tub is determined by capacity, budget, and preference for components. The most critical tub support components are the heater, filter system, chlorinator, and automatic cycling and temperature control system. Hydromassage jets are a significant part of every hot tub system. Many types of heaters are available: natural gas, electric, propane, and oil. Their sizes range from 50,000 to 175,000 Btu. All components should be approved and meet local codes and standards. Consult manufacturers for additional information. Tubs made of molded fiberglass with a smooth interior surface are generally referred to as SPAS. Their function and operation is similar to those of the hot tub.

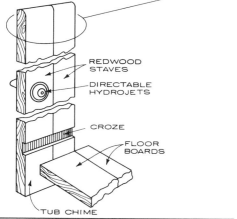

TYPICAL STAVE DETAIL

REDWOOD STAVES

DIRECTABLE HYDROJETS

CROZE

FLOOR BOARDS

TUB CHIME

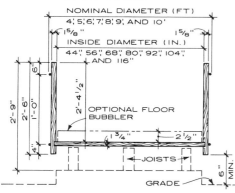

LOW PROFILE TUB

NOMINAL DIAMETER (FT)
4, 5, 6, 7, 8, 9, AND 10'

1⅝"   1⅝"

INSIDE DIAMETER (IN.)
44", 56", 68", 80", 92", 104", AND 116"

2'-9"   2'-6"   1'-0"   2'-4½"

OPTIONAL FLOOR BUBBLER

1¾"   2½"

4"

JOISTS

GRADE

6" MIN.

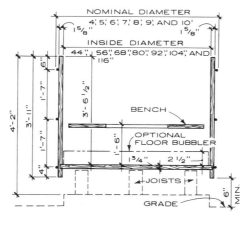

STANDARD TUB

NOMINAL DIAMETER
4, 5, 6, 7, 8, 9, AND 10'

1⅝"   1⅝"

INSIDE DIAMETER
44", 56", 68", 80", 92", 104", AND 116"

6"   1'-7"   3'-6½"   4'-2"   3'-11"   1'-7"   1'-6"

BENCH

OPTIONAL FLOOR BUBBLER

1¾"   2½"

4"

JOISTS

GRADE

6" MIN.

HOT TUB DIMENSIONS

	STANDARD TUB	LOW PROFILE TUB
NOM. DIA. (FT)	4 5 6 7 8 9 10	4 5 6 7 8 9 10
INSIDE DIA. (IN.)	44 56 68 80 92 104 116	44 56 68 80 92 104 116
NUMBER OF HOOPS	3 3 3 3 4 4	2 2 3 3 3 3
HOOP INTERVAL (IN.)	19 ± 1 IN.	12 ± 1 IN.
SEAT SECTIONS	2 3 4 5	SIT ON FLOOR

SEATING ARRANGEMENTS:

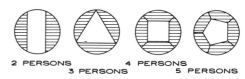

2 PERSONS

3 PERSONS

4 PERSONS

5 PERSONS

Jerry Graham; CTA Architects Engineers; Billings, Montana

SPECIAL CONSTRUCTION 5

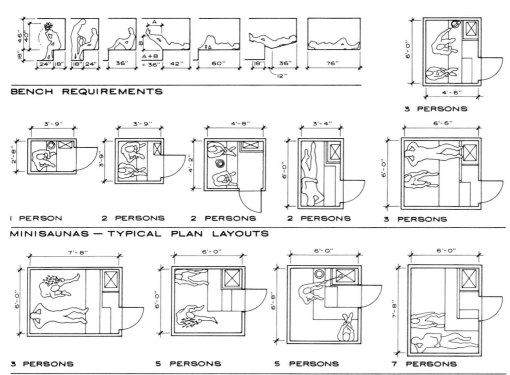

BENCH REQUIREMENTS

MINISAUNAS — TYPICAL PLAN LAYOUTS

1 PERSON   2 PERSONS   2 PERSONS   2 PERSONS   3 PERSONS   3 PERSONS

FAMILY SAUNAS — TYPICAL PLAN LAYOUTS

3 PERSONS   5 PERSONS   5 PERSONS   7 PERSONS

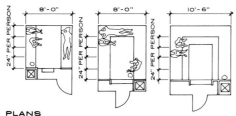

PLANS

PUBLIC SAUNAS

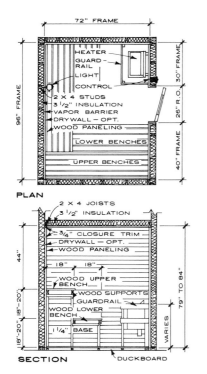

PLAN

SECTION

SAUNA ROOM CONSTRUCTION

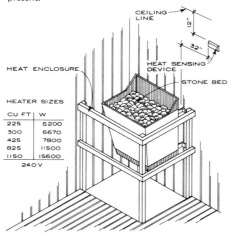

HEATER SIZES	
CU FT	W
225	5200
300	6670
425	7800
825	11500
1150	15600
240 V	

STOVE AND THERMOSTAT LOCATION

Jerry Graham; CTA Architects Engineers; Billings, Montana

DESIGN CONSIDERATIONS

The fundamental purpose of the sauna is to induce perspiration; the higher the temperature, the more quickly perspiration will begin.

The drier the air, the more heat one can stand. Temperatures on the platform can be as high as 212°F, 230°F, and 240°F. A little warm water thrown over the stove stones just before leaving the sauna produces a slightly humid wave of air that suddenly seems hotter and envelops the bather with an invisible glowing cloud, pleasantly stinging the skin. It is usually better to lie than to sit, for the temperature rises roughly 18°F for every 1 ft above the floor level; if one lies, heat is equally dispensed over the entire body. When lying down one may wish to raise one's feet against the wall or ceiling.

The expanded hot air in the sauna contains proportionately less oxygen than the denser atmosphere outside. Bathers sometimes experience faintness unless the air is changed regularly. An amount of fresh air enters each time the door is opened; this is insufficient, however. Normally two adjustable ventilators are built into the walls. One, the air inlet, is usually placed low near the stove. Fresh air should be drawn from outside and not from adjoining rooms where odors can be present.

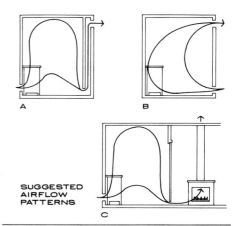

PANEL SAUNA VENTILATION

NATURAL VENTILATION

Air must flow freely into the room—inlet and outlet normally are on opposite walls and at approximately the same level. The inlet situated under the stove creates a strong updraft.

A. A flue or duct provides a chimney action that will pull air off the floor and out.

B. Inlet is low on the wall, with outlet high and directly above it. This ensures ventilation even if wind pressure exists on the wall containing the two ventilators because of the difference in air temperature at the two openings and the effect of normal convection.

C. Suggest fresh air from exterior with outlet through another room, fan, or fireplace.

HEATER: The heater depends on convection for air circulation. It is the preferred method, for the air in a sauna should be as static as possible to heat the sauna in 1 to 1½ hr.

INTERIOR PANELING: Tongue and grooved boards should be at least ⅝ in. thick, or thicker if possible because of the increased ability to absorb vapor and to retain the timber smell. Boards should not be wider than about six times their thickness. Blind nailing with galvanized or aluminum nails is common. Vapor barrier and insulation under the interior paneling must be completely vaporproof and heat resistant. Most conventional insulating materials are effective; mineral base is preferred; avoid using expanded polystyrene.

DOOR: The opening should be kept as small as possible to minimize loss of heat. Maximum height is 6 ft. Door must open outward as a safety measure. A close fitting rebate on all four sides is usually sufficient insurance against heat loss around the edges. The construction should approach the U value of the walls.

HARDWARE: Because of the weight of the door, a pair of 4 in. brass butt hinges with ball bearings are recommended. A heavy ball or roller catch keeps the door closed. Door handles are made of wood.

LIGHTING: The lighting must be indirect and the fitting unobtrusive. The best position for the light is above and slightly behind the bather's normal field of view. The switch is always outside the hot room.

TYPE OF WOOD: White or western red cedar and redwood are the materials suitable for sauna construction. They should be chosen based on their resistance to splitting and decay, color of the wood, and the thermal capacity of the wood. These woods stain badly by metal.

CEILING HEIGHT: The bigger the volume the more heat required; hence, keep the ceiling as low as possible within the limits imposed by the benches.

The main platform or bench will be about 39 in. above floor in a family sauna or at least 60 in. in a large public sauna. The ceiling is about 43 in. above the highest bench. Average family sauna ceiling height is 82 in., public 110 in.

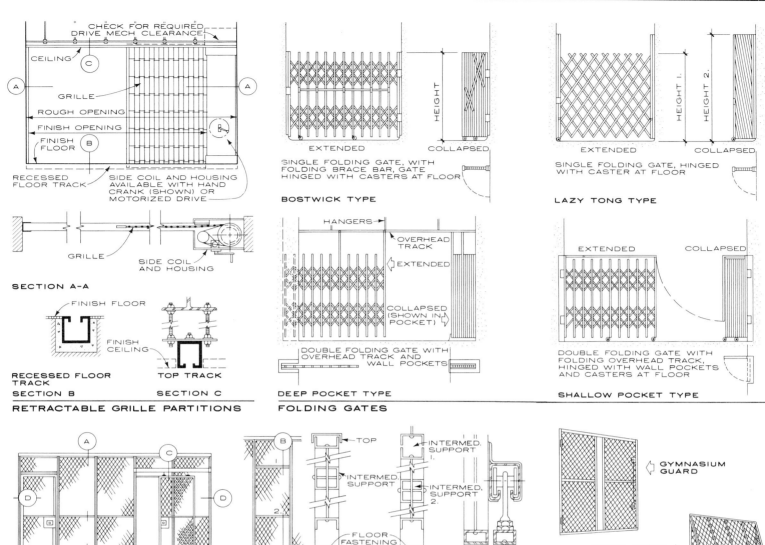

RETRACTABLE GRILLE PARTITIONS

SECTION A-A

RECESSED FLOOR TRACK SECTION B

TOP TRACK SECTION C

FOLDING GATES

SINGLE FOLDING GATE, WITH FOLDING BRACE BAR, GATE HINGED WITH CASTERS AT FLOOR

BOSTWICK TYPE

DOUBLE FOLDING GATE WITH OVERHEAD TRACK AND WALL POCKETS

DEEP POCKET TYPE

SINGLE FOLDING GATE, HINGED WITH CASTER AT FLOOR

LAZY TONG TYPE

DOUBLE FOLDING GATE WITH FOLDING OVERHEAD TRACK, HINGED WITH WALL POCKETS AND CASTERS AT FLOOR

SHALLOW POCKET TYPE

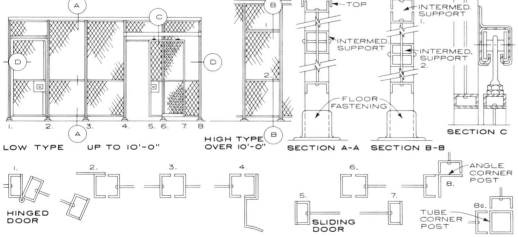

LOW TYPE   UP TO 10'-0"

HIGH TYPE OVER 10'-0"

SECTION A-A   SECTION B-B

SECTION C

HINGED DOOR

SLIDING DOOR

TUBE CORNER POST

SECTION D-D

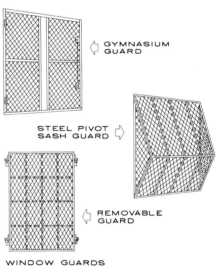

GYMNASIUM GUARD

STEEL PIVOT SASH GUARD

REMOVABLE GUARD

WINDOW GUARDS

RECOMMENDED USES FOR WIRE MESH PARTITIONS

MESH	PATTERN		WIRE SIZE	FRAMES	USES
1 1/4 "	◇	□	11	1" ⊏	Animal cages
1 1/2 "	◇		10	1" ⊏	Elevator shafts
1 3/4 "	◇		9	1 1/4 " ⊏	Fire escapes
2 "	◇		8	1 1/2 " ⊏	Cashier cages
2 "	◇		6	1 1/4 " "C"	Runways
				Channel 3/4 " ⊏	Stair enclosures Locker rooms Departmental divisions Stock rooms Tool rooms

OTHER USES FOR WOVEN WIRE MESH

MESH	PATTERN		WIRE SIZE	FRAMES	USES
3/4 "	◇	□	12	5/16 " ○ 3/4 " ⊏ 1" L	Air intake screens Bird screens
1 "	◇	□	12	3/8 " ○ 1" ⊏ 1" L	Basement window guards Shelves and trays Skylight guards
1 1/2 "	◇	□		3/8 " ○ 1" ⊏	Door and window guards
2 1/4 "	◇	□	7	7/16 " ○	Wire roof signs
2 1/2 "	◇		6	1 1/2 " ⊏	Fencing gratings

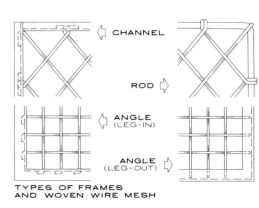

CHANNEL

ROD

ANGLE (LEG-IN)

ANGLE (LEG-OUT)

TYPES OF FRAMES AND WOVEN WIRE MESH

WIRE MESH PARTITIONS

Harnish, Morgan & Causey, Architects; Ontario, California

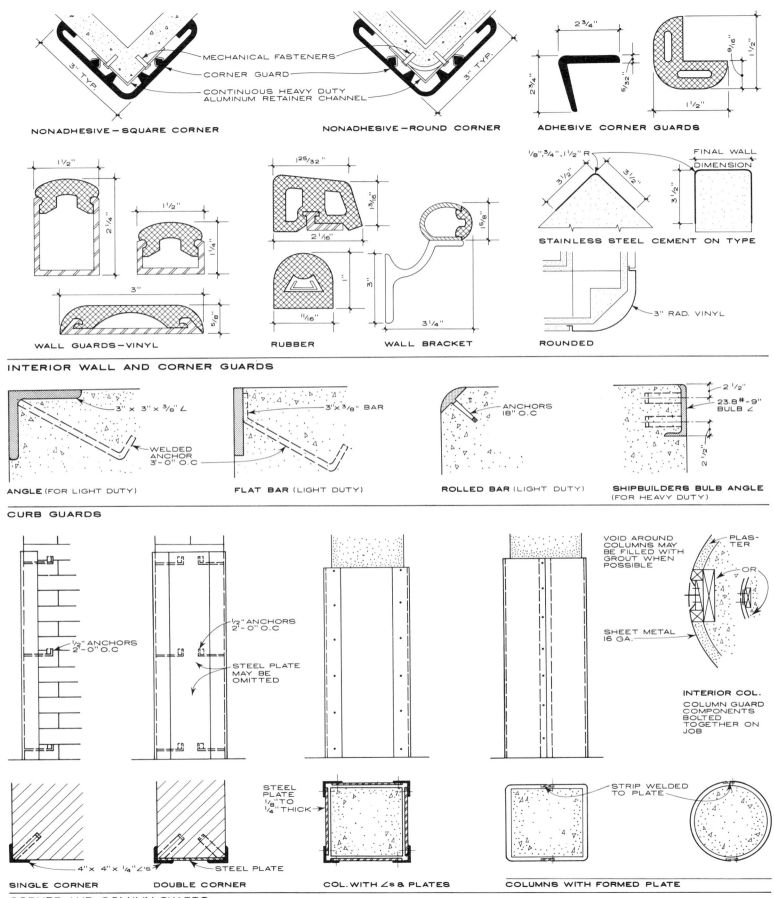

NONADHESIVE — SQUARE CORNER

MECHANICAL FASTENERS
CORNER GUARD
CONTINUOUS HEAVY DUTY ALUMINUM RETAINER CHANNEL

NONADHESIVE — ROUND CORNER

ADHESIVE CORNER GUARDS

WALL GUARDS — VINYL

RUBBER

WALL BRACKET

ROUNDED

STAINLESS STEEL CEMENT ON TYPE

FINAL WALL DIMENSION

3" RAD. VINYL

INTERIOR WALL AND CORNER GUARDS

ANGLE (FOR LIGHT DUTY)

3" x 3" x 3/8" ∠
WELDED ANCHOR 3'-0" O.C

FLAT BAR (LIGHT DUTY)

3" x 3/8" BAR

ROLLED BAR (LIGHT DUTY)

ANCHORS 18" O.C

SHIPBUILDERS BULB ANGLE
(FOR HEAVY DUTY)

2 1/2"
23.8 # -9" BULB ∠
2 1/2"

CURB GUARDS

1/2" ANCHORS 2'-0" O.C

1/2" ANCHORS 2'-0" O.C
STEEL PLATE MAY BE OMITTED

VOID AROUND COLUMNS MAY BE FILLED WITH GROUT WHEN POSSIBLE
PLASTER
OR
SHEET METAL 16 GA.

INTERIOR COL.
COLUMN GUARD COMPONENTS BOLTED TOGETHER ON JOB

SINGLE CORNER

4" x 4" x 1/4" ∠'s

DOUBLE CORNER

STEEL PLATE

COL. WITH ∠s & PLATES

STEEL PLATE 1/8" TO 1/4" THICK

COLUMNS WITH FORMED PLATE

STRIP WELDED TO PLATE

CORNER AND COLUMN GUARDS

John Sava; The Architects Collaborative, Inc.; Cambridge, Massachusetts
Vicente Cordero, AIA; Arlington, Virginia

5   **SPECIAL CONSTRUCTION**

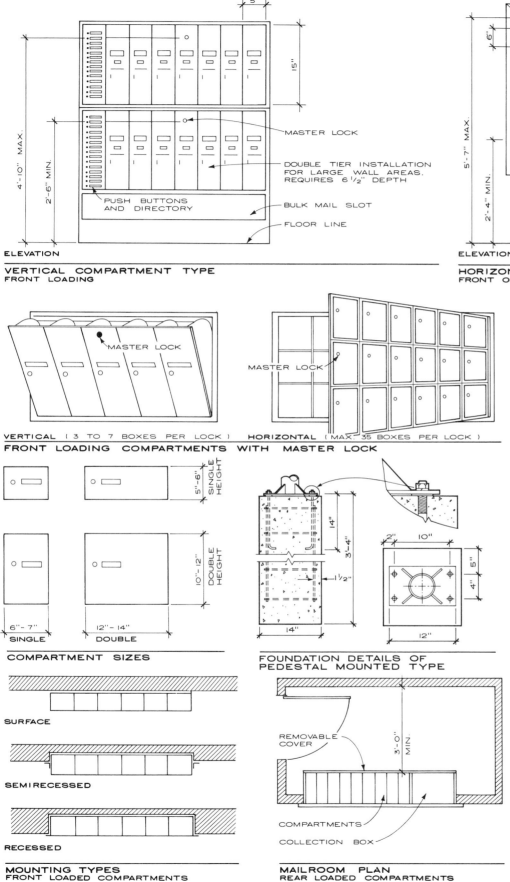

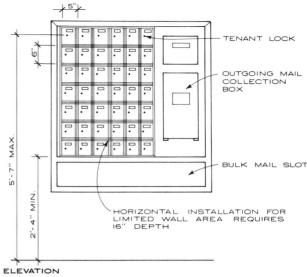

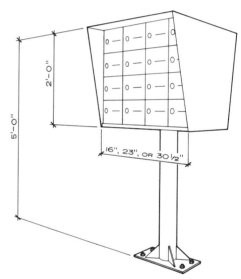

ELEVATION

VERTICAL COMPARTMENT TYPE
FRONT LOADING

MASTER LOCK

DOUBLE TIER INSTALLATION FOR LARGE WALL AREAS. REQUIRES 6½" DEPTH

PUSH BUTTONS AND DIRECTORY

BULK MAIL SLOT

FLOOR LINE

ELEVATION

HORIZONTAL COMPARTMENT TYPE
FRONT OR REAR LOADING

TENANT LOCK

OUTGOING MAIL COLLECTION BOX

BULK MAIL SLOT

HORIZONTAL INSTALLATION FOR LIMITED WALL AREA REQUIRES 16" DEPTH

MASTER LOCK

VERTICAL (3 TO 7 BOXES PER LOCK) **HORIZONTAL (MAX. 35 BOXES PER LOCK)**
FRONT LOADING COMPARTMENTS WITH MASTER LOCK

COMPARTMENT SIZES

SINGLE HEIGHT 5"-6"
DOUBLE HEIGHT 10"-12"
SINGLE 6"-7"
DOUBLE 12"-14"

FOUNDATION DETAILS OF PEDESTAL MOUNTED TYPE

PEDESTAL MOUNTED TYPE

MOUNTING TYPES
FRONT LOADED COMPARTMENTS

SURFACE
SEMIRECESSED
RECESSED

MAILROOM PLAN
REAR LOADED COMPARTMENTS

REMOVABLE COVER
COMPARTMENTS
COLLECTION BOX

GENERAL NOTES

1. Postal Service approved mail receptacles are required for apartment houses containing three or more apartments with a common building entrance and street number.
2. Individual compartments should be large enough to receive long letter mail 4½ in. wide and bulky magazines 14½ in. long and 3½ in. in diameter.
3. An outdoor installation should preferably be at least 15 ft from a street or public sidewalk, protected from driving rain, and visible from at least one apartment window.
4. All installations must be adequately lighted to afford better protection to the mail and enable carriers to read addresses on mail and names on boxes.
5. A directory, in alphabetical order, is required for installations with more than 15 compartments.
6. Each compartment group is supplied with mounting hardware for master lock.
7. Call buttons with telephone can be integrated into frame with mailboxes.
8. Depending on occupancy, a certain number of compartments shall be assigned to handicapped tenants. Key slots shall be no more than 48 in. from floor.
9. Use of collection boxes is subject to approval by local offices of the United States Postal Service.

Cohen, Karydas & Associates, Chartered; Washington, D.C.

SPECIAL CONSTRUCTION   5

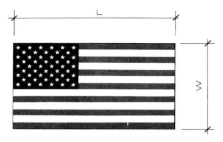

U.S. GOVERNMENT STANDARD L=1.9 W.

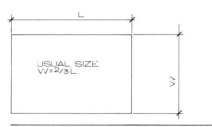

USUAL SIZE
W=2/3 L.

PROPORTIONS OF U.S. FLAG

U.S. FLAG SIZES AS MANUFACTURED AND USED

WIDTH	LENGTH	WIDTH	LENGTH
3'– 0''	5'– 0''	10'– 0''	18'– 0''
4'– 0''	6'– 0''	10'– 0''	19'– 0''
4'– 4''	5'– 6''	12'– 0''	20'– 0''
5'– 0''	8'– 0''	15'– 0''	25'– 0''
5'– 0''	9'– 6''	20'– 0''	30'– 0''
6'– 0''	10'– 0''	20'– 0''	38'– 0''
8'– 0''	12'– 0''	26'– 0''	45'– 0''
10'– 0''	15'– 0''		

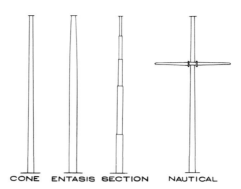

CONE   ENTASIS SECTION   NAUTICAL

Poles are manufactured in steel, aluminum, bronze, and fiberglass.

Flagpoles must be designed to withstand wind loads while the flag is flying. Design dimensions are dictated by the maximum wind load a pole is exposed to depending on geographical location, whether it is located in a city or open country, whether it is mounted at ground or on top of a building, and size of the flag to be flown. The combination wind load on pole and flag should always be considered. Refer to wind load tests conducted by the National Association of Architectural Metal Manufacturers. (NAAMM)

POLE STYLES

RELATION OF HEIGHT OF POLE TO HEIGHT OF BLDG.

HEIGHT OF POLE	HEIGHT OF BLDG.
20'– 0''	1 to 2 stories
25'– 0''	3 to 5 stories
33'– 0'' to 35'– 0''	6 to 10 stories
40'– 0'' to 50'– 0''	11 to 15 stories
60'– 0'' to 75'– 0''	over 15 stories

NOTE

This rule serves for preliminary assumptions.

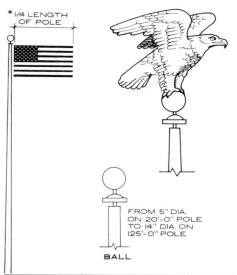

* 1/4 LENGTH OF POLE

FROM 5'' DIA. ON 20'-0'' POLE TO 14'' DIA. ON 125'-0'' POLE

BALL

POLE ON GROUND

SIZE OF FLAG IN RELATION TO POLE
RECOMMENDED FLAG SIZES

POLE	FLAG SIZE	POLE	FLAG SIZE
15'– 0''	3'– 0'' x 5'– 0''	50'– 0''	8'– 0'' x 12'– 0''
20'– 0''	4'– 0'' x 6'– 0''	60'– 0''	8'– 0'' x 12'– 0''
25'– 0''	4'– 0'' x 6'– 0''	65'– 0''	9'– 0'' x 15'– 0''
30'– 0''	5'– 0'' x 8'– 0''	70'– 0''	9'– 0'' x 15'– 0''
35'– 0''	5'– 0'' x 8'– 0''	80'– 0''	10'– 0'' x 15'– 0''
40'– 0''	6'– 0'' x 10'– 0''	90'– 0''	10'– 0'' x 15'– 0''
45'– 0''	6'– 0'' x 10'– 0''	100'– 0''	12'– 0'' x 18'– 0''

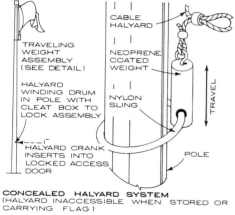

CABLE HALYARD

TRAVELING WEIGHT ASSEMBLY (SEE DETAIL)

NEOPRENE COATED WEIGHT

HALYARD WINDING DRUM IN POLE WITH CLEAT BOX TO LOCK ASSEMBLY

NYLON SLING

TRAVEL

HALYARD CRANK INSERTS INTO LOCKED ACCESS DOOR

POLE

CONCEALED HALYARD SYSTEM
(HALYARD INACCESSIBLE WHEN STORED OR CARRYING FLAG)

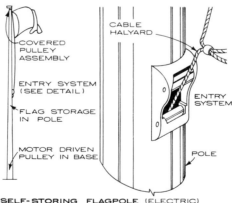

CABLE HALYARD

COVERED PULLEY ASSEMBLY

ENTRY SYSTEM (SEE DETAIL)

ENTRY SYSTEM

FLAG STORAGE IN POLE

MOTOR DRIVEN PULLEY IN BASE

POLE

SELF-STORING FLAGPOLE (ELECTRIC)
AUTOMATIC SOLAR CELL OR REMOTE SWITCH OPERATION

SPECIAL MECHANISMS FOR REMOTE OR VANDAL-PROOF OPERATION

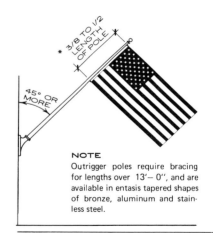

* 3/8 TO 1/2 LENGTH OF POLE

45° OR MORE

NOTE

Outrigger poles require bracing for lengths over 13'– 0'', and are available in entasis tapered shapes of bronze, aluminum and stainless steel.

OUTRIGGER POLES FOR FLAGS ON BUILDING FRONTS

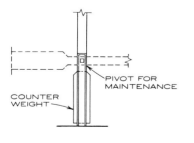

PIVOT FOR MAINTENANCE

COUNTER WEIGHT

TILTING POLE UNIT

METAL COLLAR

POLE

CAULKING

WEDGES

DRY SAND

CONCRETE

METAL TUBE

WEDGES

LIGHTNING PROTECTION

CONCRETE ANCHORS

10% OF POLE HGT.

3'-0'' MIN.

8''

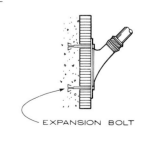

EXPANSION BOLT

FOUNDATION FOR GROUND SET POLES   **WALL MOUNTING FLAGPOLES**

FOUNDATION AND SURFACE MOUNTING DETAILS

5 **SPECIAL CONSTRUCTION**

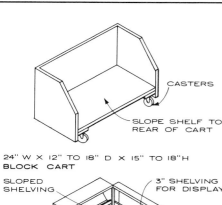

24" W × 12" TO 18" D × 15" TO 18"H
BLOCK CART

CASTERS

SLOPE SHELF TO REAR OF CART

SLOPED SHELVING

3" SHELVING FOR DISPLAY

10" SHELVING

36" W × 52"H
FOLDING BOOKCASE

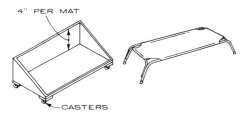

24" W × 3"D × 48"H SECTIONS
FOLDING BOOKSCREEN

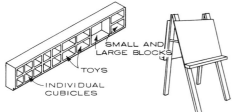

4" PER MAT

CASTERS

26"W × 14"D
REST MAT CART

22" TO 27"W × 54" TO 62"D × 12"H
STACKABLE REST COT

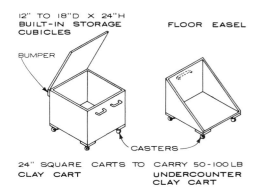

SMALL AND LARGE BLOCKS

TOYS

INDIVIDUAL CUBICLES

12" TO 18"D × 24"H
BUILT-IN STORAGE CUBICLES

FLOOR EASEL

BUMPER

CASTERS

24" SQUARE CARTS TO CARRY 50-100 LB
CLAY CART   **UNDERCOUNTER CLAY CART**

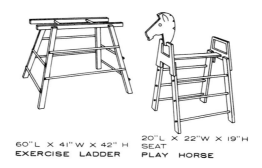

60"L × 41"W × 42" H
EXERCISE LADDER

20"L × 22"W × 19"H SEAT
PLAY HORSE

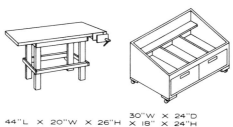

44"L × 20"W × 26"H
WORKBENCH

30"W × 24"D × 18" × 24"H
CARPENTRY TOOL CART

LARGE INSTRUMENT STORAGE

RECORD STORAGE

CASSETTE AND CASSETTE PLAYER STORAGE

RUBBER TIRES

SMALL INSTRUMENT STORAGE

54"W × 18"D × 28"H
MUSIC CART

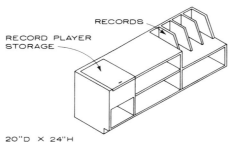

RECORDS

RECORD PLAYER STORAGE

20"D × 24"H
RECORD PLAYER AND STORAGE UNIT

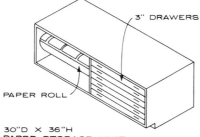

3" DRAWERS

PAPER ROLL

30"D × 36"H
PAPER STORAGE UNIT

HATS

COATS

BENCH

SHOES

12" MODULAR WIDTH × 14"D × 52" H

12"

LOCKER UNIT

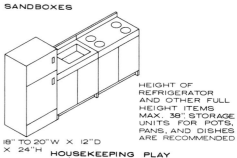

MOLDED PLASTIC LINER

TOY STORAGE UNDER HINGED 10" SEATS

24"W × 48"L × 24" H 6"-8" DEEP BOX FOR SAND OR WATER

96"SQ. × 18"H
96" × 72" × 18"H

SANDBOXES

HEIGHT OF REFRIGERATOR AND OTHER FULL HEIGHT ITEMS MAX. 38". STORAGE UNITS FOR POTS, PANS, AND DISHES ARE RECOMMENDED

18" TO 20"W × 12"D × 24"H
HOUSEKEEPING PLAY

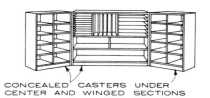

62"L × 24"W × 36"H
INDOOR SLIDE

SHELVES MOVABLE IN 2" INTERVALS

CONCEALED CASTERS UNDER CENTER AND WINGED SECTIONS

46"W (CLOSED) × 14"D × 34"H
FOLDING STORAGE UNIT

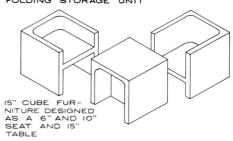

15" CUBE FURNITURE DESIGNED AS A 6" AND 10" SEAT AND 15" TABLE

PRESCHOOL AND KINDERGARTEN SEATING

GENERAL CHAIR AND TABLE REQUIREMENTS

AGE OF CHILD	CHAIR SEAT HEIGHT				TABLE HEIGHT
	8"	10"	12"	14"	
2 years	80%	20%			—
3 years	40%	50%	10%		18"
4 years		25%	75%		20"
5 years			75%	25%	22"

Kent Wong; Hewlett, Jamison, Atkinson & Luey; Portland, Oregon

GENERAL INFORMATION

Most air structures are primarily designed to resist wind loads. Mechanical blowers must maintain 3 to 5 psf pressure inside the structure at all times. Architectural elements of the building must be detailed to avoid loss of air pressure. Normal entering and exiting should be through revolving doors, while emergency exiting is provided through pressure balanced doors, and vehicles pass through air locks. Avoid using interior furnishings that could possibly puncture the structural membrane. Automatic auxiliary fans should be activated in the event of a pressure drop due to primary power failure.

The structural membrane is usually a nylon, fiberglass, or polyester fabric coated with polyvinyl chloride. Such skins have a life span from 7 to 10 years, and provide fire retardation that passes NFPA 701. A urethane topcoat will reduce dirt adhesion and improve service life. New Teflon coated fiberglass membranes have a life expectancy of more than 25 years. This material is incombustible, passing NFPA 70, with flame spread rating = 10, smoke developed = 50, and fuel contributed = 10. An acoustical liner (NCR = 0.65) is also available.

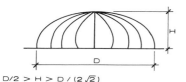

$$D/2 > H > D/(2\sqrt{2})$$

SPAN LIMITATIONS	VAULT	DOME
Without cables	D = 120' - 0''	D = 150' - 0''
With cables	D = 400' - 0''	D = 600' - 0''

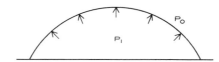

SINGLE MEMBRANE $P_I > P_O$

This is the most common type of air structure. The internal pressure (P_1) is kept approximately 0.03 psi above the external atmospheric pressure (P_0). It is this pressure difference that keeps the dome inflated.

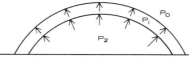

DOUBLE MEMBRANE $P_2 > P_I > P_O$

The airspace between the two membranes is used for insulation and security. If the outer skin is punctured the inner skin will remain standing. Both single and double membrane air structures require the constant use of blowers to keep them inflated.

AIR SUPPORTED

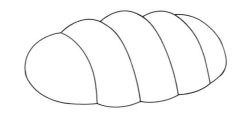

VAULT

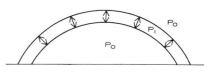

DUAL MEMBRANE $P_I > P_O$

Here the internal and external pressures are the same. Only the area between the skins is pressurized. The inflated area of a dual membrane structure can be sealed, thus eliminating the need for constant use of blowers.

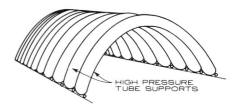

HIGH PRESSURE TUBE SUPPORTS

AIR INFLATED

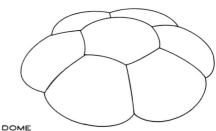

DOME

BASIC CONFIGURATIONS

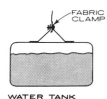

WATER TANK

FABRIC CLAMP

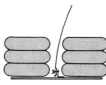

SAND BAGS

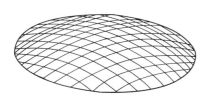

SCREW PLUG

SOCKET SET IN CONCRETE SLAB

EYE HOOK

EARTH ANCHOR

SCREW BLADE

C-PROFILE   MEMBRANE

STRADDLING DOWEL

CABLE

GRADE BEAM

ROD SET IN CONCRETE PIER

ANGLE CLAMP

ANCHORAGE DETAILS

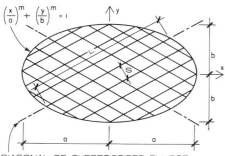

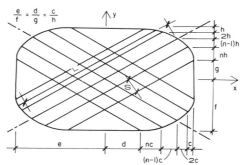

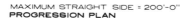

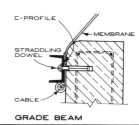

FABRIC CLAMP
COMPRESSION RING
CABLE SOCKET

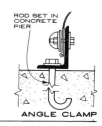

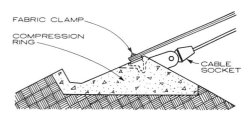

$$\left(\frac{x}{a}\right)^m + \left(\frac{y}{b}\right)^m = 1$$

DIAGONAL OF SUPERSCRIBED ELLIPSE
MAXIMUM CABLE SPACING = 50'-0''

SUPERELLIPSE PLAN

KEY TO NOTATIONS
a/b—One half of major/minor axes of superellipse.
s—Cable spacing.
L—Length of cable along diagonal of superscribed rectangle of proportions 2a and 2b.
e/f—One half of major/minor axes of superscribed

$$\frac{e}{f} = \frac{d}{g} = \frac{c}{h}$$

h
2h
(n-1)h
nh
g
f

e   d   nc   c
(n-1)c   2c

MAXIMUM STRAIGHT SIDE = 200'-0''
PROGRESSION PLAN

rectangle of plan progression.
d/g—One half of straight sides of and parallel to the major/minor axes of the plan progression.
c, 2c, (n-1)c, nc/h, 2h, (n-1)h, nh—The sequences of curve coordinates parallel to the major/minor axes of the plan progression.

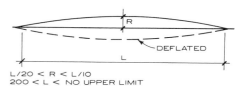

R
DEFLATED
L

$$L/20 < R < L/10$$
$$200 < L < \text{NO UPPER LIMIT}$$

STRUCTURAL CONSIDERATIONS

Membrane strengths up to 1000 lb/in. are available; a safety factor of 4 for short term loading and 8 for long term loading is required. The membrane must be patterned to carry loads without wrinkling. Structural behavior is nonlinear with large displacements. The roof shape shall be established such that the horizontal components of the cable forces result in minimum bending moment in the compression ring under maximum loads. The skewed symmetry indicated permits this condition to be realized. Consult specialist in air structures to integrate structural and architectural requirements.

LONG SPAN STRUCTURES

Geiger-Berger Associates, P.C.; New York, New York

SPECIAL CONSTRUCTION

REFERENCES

GENERAL REFERENCES

Time-Saver Standards for Site Planning, 1984, Joseph DeChiara and Lee E. Koppleman, McGraw-Hill

Time-Saver Standards for Landscape Architecture, 1988, Charles W. Harris and Nicholas T. Dines, McGraw-Hill

Graphic Standards for Landscape Architecture, 1986, Richard L. Austin, Thomas R. Dunbar, J. Kip Hulvershorn, and Kim W. Todd, Van Nostrand Reinhold

Site Details, 1989, Geogory W. Jameson and Michael A. Versen, Van Nostrand Reinhold

Site Design and Construction Detailing, 2nd ed., 1986, Theodore D. Walker, PDA Publishers

Building Construction: Site and Below-Grade Systems, 1990, James Ambrose, Van Nostrand Reinhold

Earth Sheltered Homes: Plans and Designs, 1981, Donna Aherns, Tom Ellison, and Ray Sterling, Underground Space Center, University of Minnesota, Van Nostrand Reinhold

Architect's Detail Library, 1990, Fred A. Stitt, Van Nostrand Reinhold

Simplified Design of Building Foundations, 2nd ed., 1988, James Ambrose, Wiley

Standard Handbook for Civil Engineers, 1983, 3rd ed., Frederick S. Merritt, McGraw-Hill

Structural Details for Concrete Construction, 1988, Morton Newman, McGraw-Hill

Structural Details for Masonry Construction, 1988, Morton Newman, McGraw-Hill

DATA SOURCES: ORGANIZATIONS

American National Standards Institute (ANSI), 135

American Society for Testing and Materials (ASTM), 117, 130, 137

American Wood Preservers Institute (AWP), 116

American–German Industries, 163

Architectural Press Limited, 116

Bilco Company, 159

Birdair Structures, 174

Blumcraft of Pittsburgh, 145

Bommer Associates, 171

Brick Institute of America (BIA), 136, 137, 138

Brown Manufacturing Company, 164

Building Stone Institute (BSI), 139

California Hot Tub Company, 167

California Redwood Association (CRA), 132

Clearview Corporation, 164

Columbia Cascade Timber Company, 122

Community Playthings, 173

Compackager, Inc., 173

CONTECH-Construction Techniques, Inc., 118

Creative Playthings, 173

Disco Aluminum Products Company, 164

Environmental Protection Agency (EPA), 116

Gametime, Inc., 123

Grass Pavers Limited, 118

Iron Mountain Forge, 122

Julius Blum and Company, Inc., 145

Koolshade Corporation, 163

Landscape Structures, Inc., 122, 123

Learning World, Inc., 173

Manhattan American Terrazzo Strip Company, 162

National Cement Products, 118

National Concrete Masonry Association (NCMA), 130

National Fire Protection Association (NFPA), 174

National Terrazzo and Mosaic Association, Inc. (NTMA), 162

Occupational Safety and Health Administration (OSHA), 119

Outdoor Advertising Association of America, Inc. (OAAA), 125

Pawling Rubber Company, 170

Playworld Systems, 122, 123

Portland Cement Association (PCA), 116, 133

Simpson Company, 146, 147

Tile Council of America, Inc. (TCA), 160

Underpinning and Foundation Construction, Inc., 117

U.S. Postal Service (USPS), 171

Willard Shutter Corporation, 164

DATA SOURCES: PUBLICATIONS

Architectural Sheet Metal Manual, Sheet Metal and Air Conditioning Contractors National Association, Inc. (SMACNA), 157

BOCA Basic Building Code, Building Officials and Code Administrators International (BOCA), 135

CRSI Handbook, 1984 ed., Concrete Reinforcing Steel Institute, 127

Construction Measurements, B. Austin Barry, Wiley, 143

Fountains and Pools, C. Douglas Aurand, PDA Publishers, 126

Handbook of Landscape Architectural Construction, E. Byron McCulley and Jot D. Carpenter, Landscape Architecture Foundation, Inc., 126

Masonry Design and Detailing, Christine Beall, McGraw-Hill, 126, 136, 137

Pile Foundations, Robert D. Chelus, Wiley, 117

Underground Waterproofing, Brent Anderson, WEBCO Publishing, 153

Various Foundation Waterproofing Methods and Conditions, Bob Bates Associates, 153

CHAPTER 6

SITE UTILITIES AND SERVICES

SITE IMPROVEMENTS   178

SEWERAGE AND DRAINAGE   180

WATER DISTRIBUTION   188

ELECTRIC RESISTANCE HEATING   189

HIGH VOLTAGE DISTRIBUTION   190

LIGHTNING PROTECTION   191

CONSIDERATIONS

The following factors must be considered when installing or renovating outdoor lighting systems:

1. In general, overhead lighting is more efficient and economical than low level lighting.
2. Fixtures should provide an overlapping pattern of light at a height of about 7 ft.
3. Lighting levels should respond to site hazards such as steps, ramps, and steep embankments.
4. Posts and standards should be placed so that they do not create hazards for pedestrians or vehicles.

NOTES

1. Because of their effect on light distribution, trees and shrubs at present height and growth potential should be considered in a lighting layout.
2. It is recommended to use manufacturer-provided lighting templates sized for fixture type, wattage, pole height, and layout scale.
3. Color rendition should be considered when selecting light source. When possible, colors should be selected under proposed light source.
4. Light pollution to areas other than those to be illuminated should be avoided.

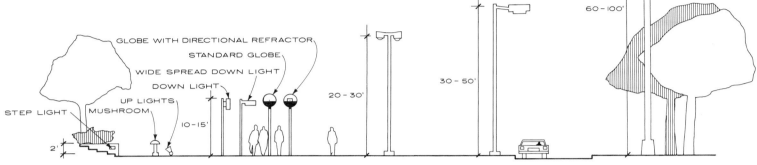

LOW LEVEL LIGHTING

1. Heights below eye level.
2. Very finite patterns with low wattage capabilities.
3. Incandescent, fluorescent, and high-pressure sodium, 5 to 150 watt lamps.
4. Lowest maintenance requirements, but highly susceptible to vandals.

MALL AND WALKWAY LIGHTING

1. 10 ft. to 15 ft. heights average for multiuse areas. Wide variety of fixtures and light patterns.
2. Mercury, metal halide, or high-pressure sodium, 70 to 250 watt lamps.
3. Susceptible to vandals.

SPECIAL PURPOSE LIGHTING

1. 20 ft. to 30 ft. heights average.
2. Recreational, commercial, residential, industrial.
3. Mercury, metal halide, or high-pressure sodium, 200 to 400 watt lamps.
4. Fixtures maintained by gantry.

PARKING AND ROADWAY LIGHTING

1. 30 ft. to 50 ft. heights average.
2. Large recreational, commercial, industrial areas, highways.
3. Mercury, metal halide, or high-pressure sodium, 400 to 1000 watt lamps.
4. Fixtures maintained by gantry.

HIGH MASTLIGHTING

1. 60 ft. to 100 ft. heights average.
2. Large areas—parking, recreational, highway interchanges.
3. Metal halide or high-pressure sodium, 1000 watt lamps.
4. Fixtures must lower for maintenance.

DEFINITIONS

A lumen is a unit used for measuring the amount of light energy given off by a light source. A footcandle is a unit used for measuring the amount of illumination on a surface. The amount of usable light from any given source is partially determined by the source's angle of incidence and the distance to the illuminated surface. See Chapter 1 on illumination.

NOTE

All exterior installations must be provided with ground fault interruption circuit.

RECOMMENDED LIGHTING LEVELS IN FOOTCANDLES

	COMMERCIAL	INTERMEDIATE	RESIDENTIAL
PEDESTRIAN AREAS			
Sidewalks	0.9	0.6	0.2
Pedestrian ways	2.0	1.0	0.5
VEHICULAR ROADS			
Freeway*	0.6	0.6	0.6
Major road and expressway*	2.0	1.4	1.0
Collector road	1.2	0.9	0.6
Local road	0.9	0.6	0.4
Alleys	0.6	0.4	0.2
PARKING AREAS			
Self-parking	1.0	—	—
Attendant parking	2.0	—	—
Security problem area	—	—	5.0
Minimum for television viewing of important interdiction areas	10.0	10.0	10.0
BUILDING AREAS			
Entrances	5.0	—	—
General grounds	1.0	—	—

*Both mainline and ramps.

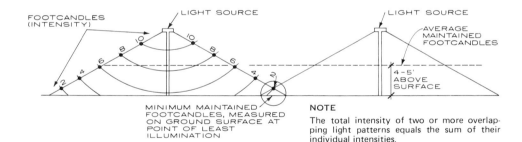

MEASURING LIGHT INTENSITY IN FOOTCANDLES

NOTE

The total intensity of two or more overlapping light patterns equals the sum of their individual intensities.

1. CUTOFF means that maximum of 10 percent of light source lumens fall outside of TRL area.
2. SEMICUTOFF means that maximum of 30 percent of light source lumens fall outside of the TRL area.
3. NONCUTOFF means that no control limitations exist.

CUTOFF TERMINOLOGY
(NOTE: "CUTOFF" IS MEASURED ALONG TRL.)

NOTE

Degree of cutoff is determined by one of the following:

(a) design of fixture housing
(b) incorporation of prismatic lens over light source
(c) addition of shield to fixture on "house side"

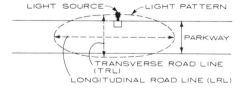

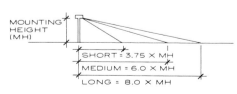

TYPES OF DISTRIBUTION
(NOTE: DISTRIBUTION IS MEASURED ALONG LRL)

Johnson, Johnson & Roy, Inc.; Ann Arbor, Michigan
Dewey Hou; Tomblinson Harburn Associates; Flint, Michigan

SITE IMPROVEMENTS

SPRINKLER SYSTEMS

Spray: For residential or commercial planting beds, shrub areas, ground covers, and trees. Available in various arc and strip patterns. 2 in. to 12 in. pop-up shrub heads common. Recommended operating pressure: 20-50 psi.

Stream rotor: For residential or commercial small to large turf areas, slopes, ground covers, and planting beds. Available in various arc patterns. 3 in. to 12 in. pop-up shrub heads common. Recommended operating pressure: 35-60 psi.

Rotary (gear driven): For residential or commercial large turf areas, sports fields, parks, and cemeteries. Available in various arc patterns. 2 in. to 4 in. pop-up and shrub heads common. Recommended operating pressure: 25-90 psi.

Agricultural: For dust control, ground cover, nurseries, and frost protection. Available in different trajectory angles and nozzle volumes. Recommended operating pressure: 20-100 psi.

Drip: For special residential, commercial, and agricultural problems such as hillsides or individual plantings, or where excessive runoff, overspray, and wasted water are problems. Recommended operating pressure: 10-40 psi.

DESIGN FACTORS

Supply line size, meter, available water pressure, code restrictions, type and scale of growing material, and soil conditions govern the type of system, spray heads, and pipe size used.

TYPES OF CONTROL SYSTEMS

Quick coupler: This system normally is under pressure. A key is inserted into a spray head where water is needed.

Manual: This system is turned on with a valve, all heads in place.

Automatic: The two basic types are hydraulic, in which the signal between the controller and the valves is transmitted through fluid pressure in control tubing, and electric, in which the signal is transmitted to the valves directly through buried wire. Electric is the more common system. It is operated from a central control unit.

PIPE

Polyvinyl chloride or polyethylene piping, easily cut and connected, commonly is used. Steel and copper pipe also are used. Pipe sleeves should be preset under walks and through walls for ease of installation and future extension of the system.

PRECIPITATION RATES

The amount of water applied to turf areas must be adjusted according to the species of grass, the traffic it receives, subsoil conditions, and surface gradient.

BACKFLOW PREVENTERS

A cross-connection device protects the potable water supply from contaminants caused by backsiphonage or backpressure. Many state and local plumbing codes require the use of such a device on an irrigation system. Types of cross-connections include atmospheric vacuum breakers, pressure vacuum breakers, double check valves, and reduced pressure valves.

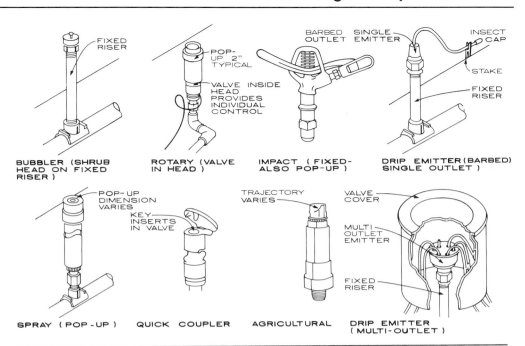

SPRAY HEADS

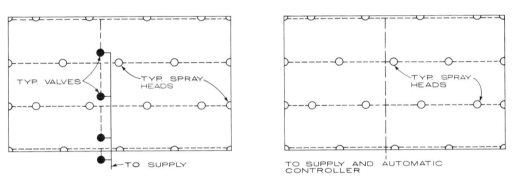

TYPICAL LAYOUTS

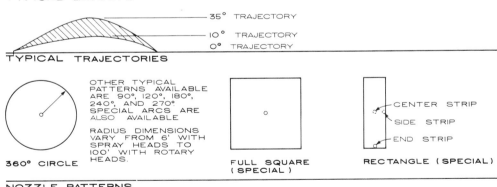

NOZZLE PATTERNS

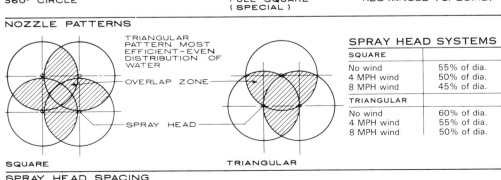

SPRAY HEAD SPACING

SPRAY HEAD SYSTEMS	
SQUARE	
No wind	55% of dia.
4 MPH wind	50% of dia.
8 MPH wind	45% of dia.
TRIANGULAR	
No wind	60% of dia.
4 MPH wind	55% of dia.
8 MPH wind	50% of dia.

Robert K. Sherrill; Wilkes, Faulkner, Jenkins & Bass; Washington, D.C.

SITE IMPROVEMENTS

GENERAL NOTES

Seepage and runoff each require special engineering designs to protect against potential water damage. Drainage systems intercept and dispose of the water flow to prevent inordinate damage to an area or facility from seepage and direct runoff.

Subsurface drainage systems are designed to lower the natural water table, to intercept underground flow, and to dispose of infiltration percolating down through soils from surface sources. These systems typically are used under floors, around foundations, in planters, and under athletic fields and courts. Each system must be provided with a positive outfall either by pumped discharge or gravity drain above expected high water levels.

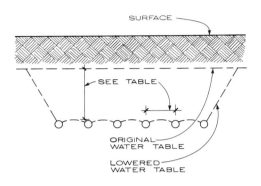

SECTION

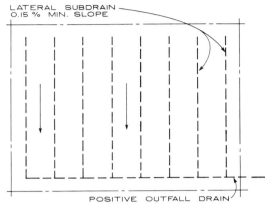

PLAN

Drain layout varies to meet need. May be grid, parallel, herringbone, or random pattern to fit topography.

Depths indicated in table below are minimum range. Greater depths may be required to prevent frost heave in colder climates or where soils have a high capillarity.

FOOTING DRAIN

TYPICAL SECTION

If perforated drain is used, it should be installed with the holes facing down.

When used to intercept sidehill seepage, the bottom of the trench should be cut into underlying impervious material a minimum of 6 in.

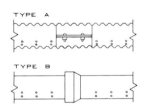
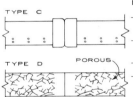

SUBSURFACE DRAIN PIPES IN GENERAL USE

DRAIN PIPES

DRAIN TYPE	MATERIAL	JOINT
A	Corrugated metal Flexible plastic	Collars
B	Concrete Clay tile	Bell and spigot
C	Rigid plastic	Sleeve socket
D	Porous concrete	Tongue and groove

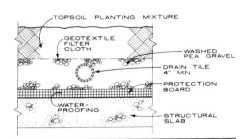

PLANTER DRAIN

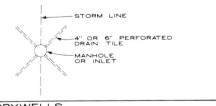

DRYWELLS

Drywells provide an underground disposal system for surface runoff. Their effectiveness is in direct proportion to the porosity of surrounding soils, and they are efficient only for draining small areas. High rainfall runoff rates cannot be absorbed at the considerably lower percolation rates of most soils; the difference is stored temporarily in the drywell. Efficiency is reduced during extended periods of wet weather when receiving soils are saturated and the well is refilled prior to draining completely.

DEPTH AND SPACING OF SUBDRAINS RECOMMENDED FOR VARIOUS SOIL CLASSES

SOIL CLASSES	PERCENTAGE OF SOIL SEPARATES			DEPTH OF BOTTOM OF DRAIN (FT.)	DISTANCE BETWEEN SUBDRAINS (FT.)
	SAND	SILT	CLAY		
Sand	80–100	0–20	0–20	3–4 / 2–3	150–300 / 100–150
Sandy loam	50–80	0–50	0–20	3–4 / 2–3	100–150 / 85–100
Loam	30–50	30–50	0–20	3–4 / 2–3	85–100 / 75–85
Silt loam	0–50	50–100	0–20	3–4 / 2–3	75–85 / 65–75
Sandy clay loam	50–80	0–30	20–30	3–4 / 2–3	65–75 / 55–65
Clay loam	20–50	20–50	20–30	3–4 / 2–3	55–65 / 45–55
Silty clay loam	0–30	50–80	20–30	3–4 / 2–3	45–55 / 40–45
Sandy clay	50–70	0–20	30–50	3–4 / 2–3	40–45 / 35–40
Silty clay	0–20	50–70	30–50	3–4 / 2–3	35–40 / 30–35
Clay	0–50	0–50	30–100	3–4 / 2–3	30–35 / 25–30

Harold C. Munger, FAIA; Munger Munger + Associates Architects, Inc.; Toledo, Ohio
Kurt N. Pronske, P.E.; Reston, Virginia

SEWERAGE AND DRAINAGE

SURFACE DRAINAGE SYSTEMS: Designed to collect and dispose of rainfall runoff. There are two basic types. One, a ditch/swale and culvert, or open system, is generally used in less densely populated and more open areas where natural surfaces predominate. In urbanized areas where much of the land is overbuilt, the second type is used—the pipe, inlet/catchbasin and manhole, or closed system. Combinations of the two are quite common where terrain and density dictate.

GENERAL NOTES

1. Lay out grades to allow safe flow away from building if drains becomes blocked.
2. It is generally more economical to keep water on surface as long as possible.
3. Consider the possibility of ice forming on surface when determining slopes for vehicles and pedestrians.
4. Determine which design criteria are set by code or governmental agency, such as intensity and duration of rain storm and allowable runoff.
5. Formulas given are for approx. only. A qualified engineer should be consulted to design the system.

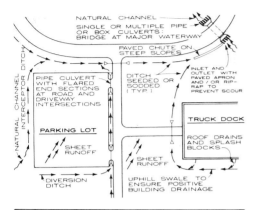

OPEN SYSTEM

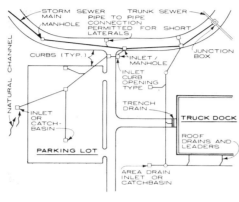

CLOSED SYSTEM

SITE PLAN—EXAMPLE

$$\frac{\text{AREA} = 10,000 \text{ SQ FT}}{43,560 \text{ SQ FT/ACRE}} = 0.23 \text{ ACRES}$$

ASPHALT SURFACE C=0.9

RATIONAL FORMULA

Q = CIA

Q = Flow (cu ft/sec)
C = From table (Approximate Values for C)
I = Intensity (in./hr)
Obtain from local code requirements
A = Area of site (acres)

EXAMPLE: Assume local code requires I = 5 in./hr

Q = CIA
Q = 0.9(5)0.23
 = 1.04 cu ft/sec
 = Approximate volume of water entering the V-channel per second from the parking lot

Note: Simplified method of calculation for areas of less than 100 acres.

APPROXIMATE METHOD FOR CALCULATING RUNOFF

APPROXIMATE VALUES FOR C

Roofs	0.95–1.00
Pavement	0.90–1.00
Roads	0.30–0.90
Bare soil	
Sand	0.20–0.40
Clay	0.30–0.75
Grass	0.15–0.60
Developed land	
Commercial	0.60–0.75
High-density residential	0.50–0.65
Low-density residential	0.30–0.55

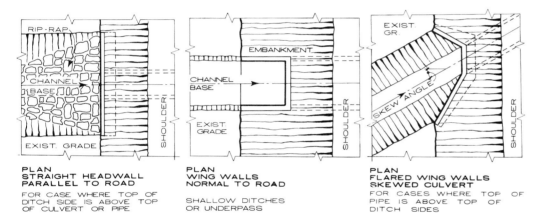

PLAN STRAIGHT HEADWALL PARALLEL TO ROAD

FOR CASE WHERE TOP OF DITCH SIDE IS ABOVE TOP OF CULVERT OR PIPE

PLAN WING WALLS NORMAL TO ROAD

SHALLOW DITCHES OR UNDERPASS

PLAN FLARED WING WALLS SKEWED CULVERT

FOR CASES WHERE TOP OF PIPE IS ABOVE TOP OF DITCH SIDES

HEADWALL DESIGN AS CONTROLLED BY TOPOGRAPHY

n VALUES FOR MANNING FORMULA

CHANNEL SURFACE	n
Cast iron	0.012
Corrugated steel	0.032
Clay tile	0.014
Cement grout	0.013
Concrete	0.015
Earth ditch	0.023
Cut rock channel	0.033
Winding channel	0.025

NOTES

1. Determine velocity with Manning formula.
2. Check flow with formula Q = Va
 a = Cross-sectional area of water in sq ft.
3. For a given Q, adjust channel shape, size, and/or slope to obtain desired velocity (noneroding for earth and grass ditches, etc.)

APPROXIMATE METHOD FOR SIZING CHANNELS

Fred W. Hegel, AIA; Denver, Colorado
Seelye, see data sources

MANNING FORMULA

$$V = \left(\frac{1.486}{n}\right) r^{0.67} S^{0.5}$$

 = Velocity (ft/sec)
n = From table (n Values for Manning Formula)
r = Hydraulic radius
See Channel Properties for derivation of r

$$S = \text{Slope} \left(\frac{\text{drop in ft}}{\text{length in ft}}\right)$$

EXAMPLE: Assume concrete V-channel

W = 2 ft
h = 0.5 ft
S = 0.005   (see site plan—example)
r = 0.37 (calculated using V-channel properties)

$$V = \left(\frac{1.486}{0.015}\right)(0.37)^{0.67}(0.005)^{0.5}$$

 = 2.6 ft/sec (see runoff velocity table)

CHECK FLOW

Q = Va (a from Channel Properties)
 = 2.6 (0.5) = 1.3 cu ft/sec
1.04 cu ft/sec required from example above using the Rational Formula; therefore, flow is OK.

$$a = Wh$$
$$p = 2h + W$$
$$r = \frac{Wh}{2h + W}$$

$$a = eh$$
$$p = 2(e^2 + h^2)^{1/2}$$
$$r = \frac{eh}{2(e^2 + h^2)^{1/2}}$$

$$a = h(W_2 + e)$$
$$p = W_2 + 2(e^2 + h^2)^{1/2}$$
$$r = \frac{h(W_2 + e)}{W_2 + 2(e^2 + h^2)^{1/2}}$$

$$a = \pi h^2/2$$
$$p = \pi h$$
$$r = \frac{2}{h}$$

a = AREA OF WATER SECTION
p = WETTED PERIMETER
r = a/p = HYDRAULIC RADIUS

CHANNEL PROPERTIES

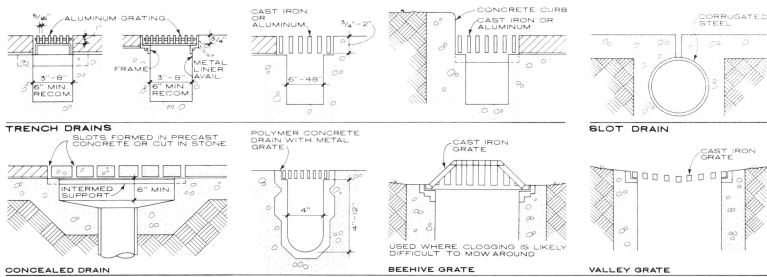

TRENCH DRAINS

SLOT DRAIN

DRAIN INLETS TO UNDERGROUND SYSTEM

CONCEALED DRAIN

USED WHERE CLOGGING IS LIKELY DIFFICULT TO MOW AROUND

BEEHIVE GRATE

VALLEY GRATE

USE GRATING DESIGNED FOR EXTERIOR USE AND CORRECT WHEEL LOAD

GRATING DESIGNS—STANDARD

GRATE SIZING

Most gratings are oversized to prevent a buildup of water. See manufacturers' catalogs for free area.

Formula shown for sizing gratings is based on a given allowable depth of water (d) over the grating.

$$Q = .66 \, CA \, (64.4 \, d)^{.5}$$

A = Free area (square feet)
d = Allowable depth of water above grate (feet)
C = Orifice coefficient
   .6 for square edges
   .8 for round edges
.66 = Clogging factor

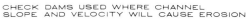

CHECK DAMS USED WHERE CHANNEL SLOPE AND VELOCITY WILL CAUSE EROSION

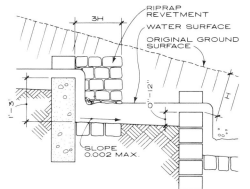

RIPRAP REVETMENT
WATER SURFACE
ORIGINAL GROUND SURFACE

SLOPE 0.002 MAX.

CHECK DAMS

DETENTION

Check with local code requirements for control of storm water. Many require runoff to be maintained at predevelopment rates. This is accomplished with a detention facility upstream of a controlled outlet structure. The detention basin may be a structure or a paved or grass basin. If soil types permit, seepage may be used to dispose of runoff accumulated in a grass basin. The volume of detention required can be approximated by the following formula:

AMOUNT OF DETENTION:

$$Vol. = (C_{dev.} - C_{hist.})AD$$

D = Design storm depth (inches)
A = Area site (acres)
$C_{dev.}$ = C from table for developed land
$C_{hist.}$ = C from table for land prior to development

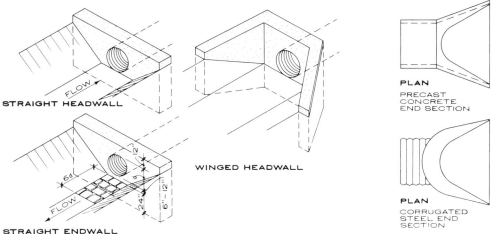
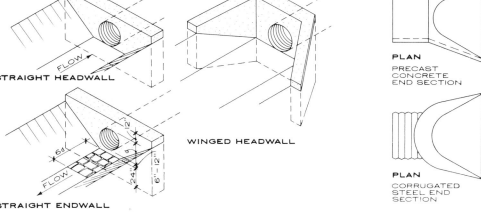

STRAIGHT HEADWALL

WINGED HEADWALL

STRAIGHT ENDWALL

PLAN
PRECAST CONCRETE END SECTION

PLAN
CORRUGATED STEEL END SECTION

HEADWALLS AND ENDWALLS

SLOPES

DESCRIPTION	MIN. %	MAX. %	REC. %
Grass (mowed)	1	25	1.5–10
(athletic field)	.5	2	1
Walks (Long.)	.5	12*	1.5
(Transv.)	1	4	1–2
Streets (Long.)	.5	20	1–10
Parking	1	5	2–3
Channels			
Grass swale	1	8	1.5–2
Paved swale	.5	12	4–6

*8.3% max. for handicapped

RUN-OFF VELOCITY

VELOCITIES CHANNEL	MIN. FT/SEC	MAX. FT/SEC
Grass	2	4
Concrete	2	10
Gravel	2	3
Asphalt	2	7.5
Sand	5	1.5

Fred W. Hegel, AIA; Denver, Colorado
Seelye; Landphair and Klatt; see data sources

SEWERAGE AND DRAINAGE

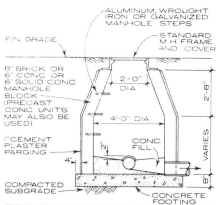

COMBINED OR SANITARY SEWER MANHOLE

NOTES

1. Parging may be omitted in construction of storm sewer manholes.
2. Brick and block walls to be as shown for manholes up to 12 ft deep. For that part of manhole deeper than 12 ft, brick and block walls shall be 12 in. thick. Manholes over 12 ft deep shall have a 12 in. thick base.

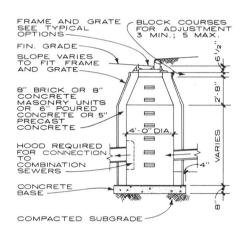

CATCH BASIN

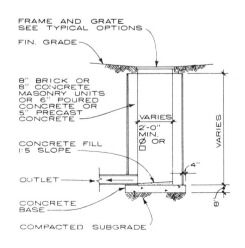

INLET

Kurt N. Pronske, P.E.; Reston, Virginia

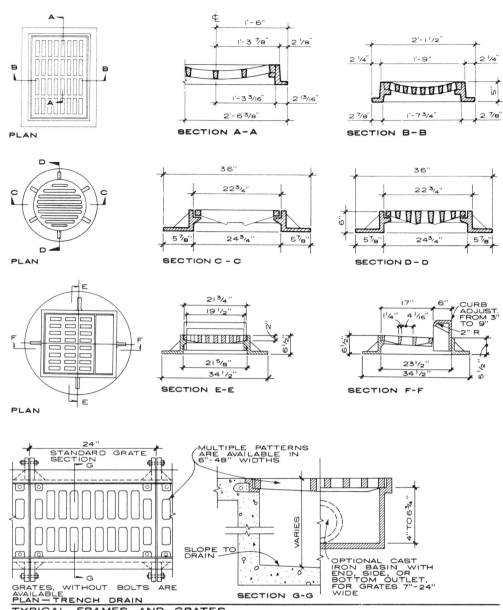

PLAN—TRENCH DRAIN

TYPICAL FRAMES AND GRATES

NOTES

1. A great number of standard shapes and sizes of frames and grates are available. They are constructed of cast or ductile iron for light or heavy duty loading conditions. The available shapes are shown above: round, rectangular or square, and linear. In addition, grates may be flat, concave, or convex. Manufacturers' catalogs and local foundries should be consulted for the full range of castings.

2. Drainage structures with grated openings should be located on the periphery of traveled ways or beyond to minimize their contact with pedestrian or vehicular traffic. Grates that will be susceptible to foot or narrow wheel contact must be so constructed as to prevent penetration by heels, crutch and cane tips, and slim tires, but still serve to provide sufficient drainage. This can be done by reducing the size of each unit opening and increasing the overall size or number of grates. Where only narrow wheel use is expected, slotted gratings can be used if the slots are oriented transversely to the direction of traffic.

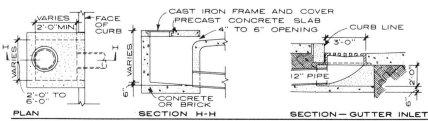

CURB INLET

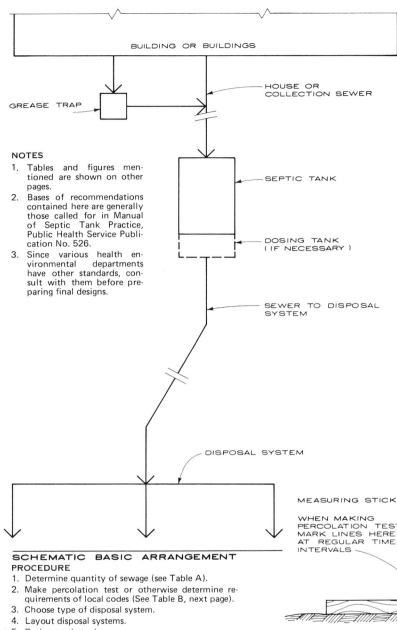

SCHEMATIC BASIC ARRANGEMENT

TABLE A QUANTITIES OF SEWAGE FLOWS

TYPE OF ESTABLISHMENT	GALLONS PER PERSON PER DAY
Airports (per passenger)	5
Bathhouses and swimming pools	10
Camps	
Campground with central comfort stations	35
Day camps (no meals served)	15
Resort camp (night and day) with limited plumbing	50
Cottages and small dwelling with seasonal occupancy[1]	50
Country clubs (per resident member)	100
Country clubs (per nonresident member present)	25
Dwellings	
Boarding houses[1]	50
Multiple family dwellings (apartments)	60
Single family dwellings[1]	75
Factories (gallons per person, per shift, exclusive of industry wastes)	35
Hospitals (per bed space)	250+
Hotels with private baths (2 persons per room)[2]	60
Institutions other than hospitals (per bed space)	125
Laundries, self-service (gallons per wash, i.e., per customer)	50
Mobile home parks (per space)	250
Picnic parks (toilet wastes only, per picnicker)	5
Picnic parks with bathhouses, showers, and flush toilets	10
Restaurants (toilets and kitchen wastes per patron)	10
Restaurants (kitchen wastes per meal served)	3
Restaurants (additional for bars and cocktail lounges)	2
Schools	
Boarding	100
Day, with gyms, cafeteria, and showers	25
Service stations (per vehicle served)	10
Theaters	
Movie (per auditorium seat)	5
Drive-in (per car space)	5
Travel trailer parks with individual water and sewer hookups	100
Workers	
Day, at schools and offices (per shift)	15

NOTES
1. Two people per bedroom.
2. Use also for motels.

NOTES

1. Tables and figures mentioned are shown on other pages.
2. Bases of recommendations contained here are generally those called for in Manual of Septic Tank Practice, Public Health Service Publication No. 526.
3. Since various health environmental departments have other standards, consult with them before preparing final designs.

PROCEDURE

1. Determine quantity of sewage (see Table A).
2. Make percolation test or otherwise determine requirements of local codes (See Table B, next page).
3. Choose type of disposal system.
4. Layout disposal systems.
5. Design septic tank.
6. Use dosing tank, diversion box and/or trap where necessary.

MATERIALS

Piping may be salt glazed clay bell and spigot, tile pipe, asbestos cement or concrete bell and spigot. If near well or any other water supply, use cast iron.

Where trees or shrubs may cause root stoppage in clay pipe, use cast iron.

Use bituminous joints or rubber ring type joints for clay, concrete, or asbestos cement pipe; use lead for cast iron pipe.

SIZE

4 in. diameter for small installations; 6 in. is better in all cases.

GRADE

In northern latitudes, start sewer approximately 3 ft below grade. In southern latitudes, sewer may start just below grade.

PITCH

Pitch 4 in. sewer $\frac{1}{4}$ in./ft minimum. Pitch 6 in. sewer $\frac{1}{8}$ in./ft minimum.

PROCEDURE

First soak hole by filling at least 12 in. over gravel with water and continue to refill with water so that hole is soaked for 24 hr. After 24 hr adjust the depth of water over the gravel to approximately 6 in. Now measure the drop in water level over a 30 min period.

NOTE: THIS TEST IS RECOMMENDED BY THE ENVIRONMENTAL PROTECTION AGENCY. CHECK LOCAL REQUIREMENTS FOR OTHER TEST CONDITIONS

METHOD OF MAKING PERCOLATION TEST

Jack L. Staunton, P.E.; Staunton and Freeman, Consulting Engineers; New York, New York

SEWERAGE AND DRAINAGE

TABLE B. ALLOWABLE RATE OF SEWAGE APPLICATION TO A SOIL ABSORPTION SYSTEM

PERCOLATION RATE [TIME (MIN) FOR WATER TO FALL 1 IN.]	MAXIMUM RATE OF SEWAGE APPLICATION (GAL/SQ FT/DAY)[1] FOR ABSORPTION TRENCHES,[2] SEEPAGE BEDS, AND SEEPAGE PITS[3]	PERCOLATION RATE [TIME (MIN) FOR WATER TO FALL 1 IN.]	MAXIMUM RATE OF SEWAGE APPLICATION (GAL/SQ FT/DAY)[1] FOR ABSORPTION TRENCHES,[2] SEEPAGE BEDS, AND SEEPAGE PITS[3]
1 or less	5.0	10	1.6
2	3.5	15	1.3
3	2.9	30[4]	0.9
4	2.5	45[4]	0.8
5	2.2	60[4, 5]	0.6

NOTES

1. Not including effluents from septic tanks that receive wastes from garbage grinders and automatic washing machines.
2. Absorption area is figured as trench bottom area and includes a statistical allowance for vertical sidewall area.
3. Absorption area for seepage pits is effective sidewall area.
4. Over 30 is unsuitable for seepage pits.
5. Over 60 is unsuitable for absorption systems.

If permissible, use sand filtration system. For subsurface sand filters use 1.15 gal/sq ft/day.

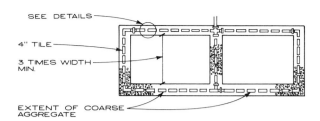

ABSORPTION TRENCH ARRANGEMENT FOR LEVEL GROUND FOR HOUSEHOLD DISPOSAL

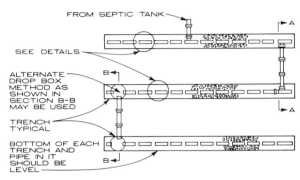

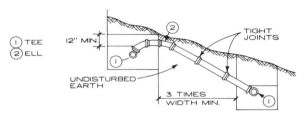

SECTION A-A

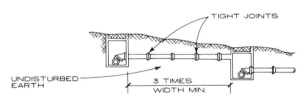

SECTION B-B

ABSORPTION TRENCH ARRANGEMENT FOR HILLY SITE FOR HOUSEHOLD DISPOSAL

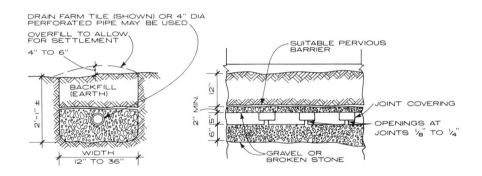

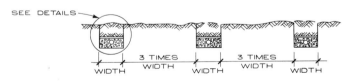

ABSORPTION TRENCH SYSTEM DETAILS

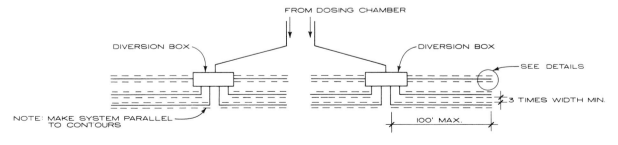

ABSORPTION TRENCH ARRANGEMENT FOR INSTITUTIONAL AND LIGHT COMMERCIAL DISPOSAL

Jack L. Staunton, P.E.; Staunton and Freeman, Consulting Engineers; New York, New York

SEWERAGE AND DRAINAGE

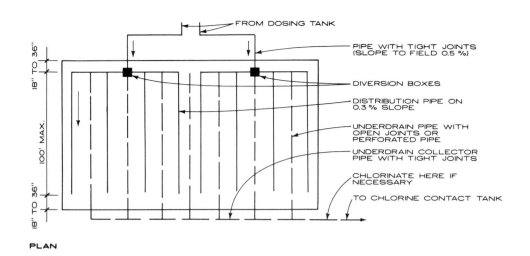

FROM DOSING TANK

PIPE WITH TIGHT JOINTS (SLOPE TO FIELD 0.5 %)

DIVERSION BOXES

DISTRIBUTION PIPE ON 0.3 % SLOPE

UNDERDRAIN PIPE WITH OPEN JOINTS OR PERFORATED PIPE

UNDERDRAIN COLLECTOR PIPE WITH TIGHT JOINTS

CHLORINATE HERE IF NECESSARY

TO CHLORINE CONTACT TANK

18" TO 36"

100' MAX.

18" TO 36"

PLAN

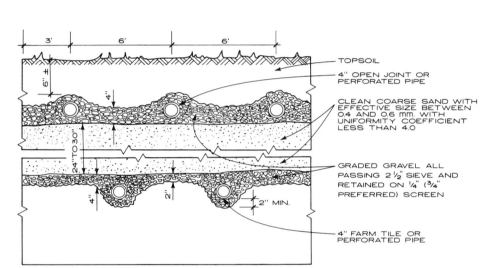

TOPSOIL

4" OPEN JOINT OR PERFORATED PIPE

CLEAN COARSE SAND WITH EFFECTIVE SIZE BETWEEN 0.4 AND 0.6 mm. WITH UNIFORMITY COEFFICIENT LESS THAN 4.0

GRADED GRAVEL ALL PASSING 2 1/2" SIEVE AND RETAINED ON 1/4" (3/4" PREFERRED) SCREEN

4" FARM TILE OR PERFORATED PIPE

2" MIN.

24" TO 30"

SECTIONAL ELEVATION

SUBSURFACE SAND FILTER

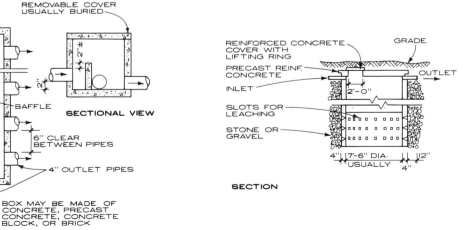

REMOVABLE COVER USUALLY BURIED

6" MIN.

6" MIN.

INLET

BAFFLE

6" CLEAR BETWEEN PIPES

4" OUTLET PIPES

SECTIONAL VIEW

BOX MAY BE MADE OF CONCRETE, PRECAST CONCRETE, CONCRETE BLOCK, OR BRICK

PLAN

DIVERSION BOX

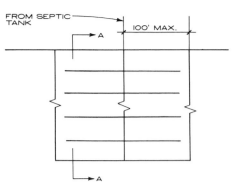

FROM SEPTIC TANK

100' MAX.

A

A

PLAN

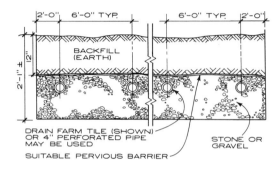

2'-0"   6'-0" TYP.   6'-0" TYP.   2'-0"

BACKFILL (EARTH)

±2'

2'-1"±

DRAIN FARM TILE (SHOWN) OR 4" PERFORATED PIPE MAY BE USED

SUITABLE PERVIOUS BARRIER

STONE OR GRAVEL

SECTION A-A

SEEPAGE BED

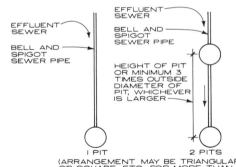

EFFLUENT SEWER

EFFLUENT SEWER

BELL AND SPIGOT SEWER PIPE

BELL AND SPIGOT SEWER PIPE

HEIGHT OF PIT OR MINIMUM 3 TIMES OUTSIDE DIAMETER OF PIT, WHICHEVER IS LARGER

1 PIT

2 PITS

(ARRANGEMENT MAY BE TRIANGULAR OR SQUARE, ETC., FOR MORE THAN 2 PITS)

ARRANGEMENT

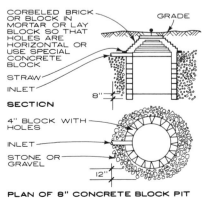

REINFORCED CONCRETE COVER WITH LIFTING RING

GRADE

PRECAST REINF. CONCRETE

INLET

OUTLET

2'-0"

SLOTS FOR LEACHING

STONE OR GRAVEL

4"   7'-6" DIA. USUALLY   12"
4"

SECTION

CORBELED BRICK OR BLOCK IN MORTAR OR LAY BLOCK SO THAT HOLES ARE HORIZONTAL OR USE SPECIAL CONCRETE BLOCK

GRADE

STRAW

INLET

8"

SECTION

4" BLOCK WITH HOLES

INLET

STONE OR GRAVEL

12"

PLAN OF 8" CONCRETE BLOCK PIT

SEEPAGE PITS

Jack L. Staunton, P.E.; Staunton and Freeman, Consulting Engineers; New York, New York

SEWERAGE AND DRAINAGE

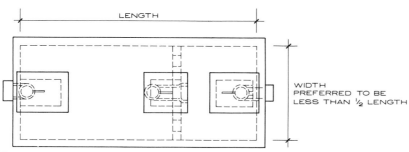

LENGTH

WIDTH PREFERRED TO BE LESS THAN ½ LENGTH

PLAN

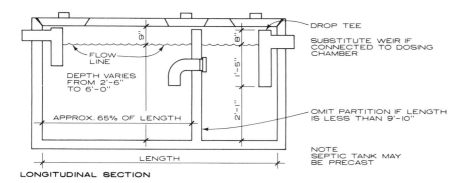

DROP TEE

SUBSTITUTE WEIR IF CONNECTED TO DOSING CHAMBER

FLOW LINE

DEPTH VARIES FROM 2'-6" TO 6'-0"

APPROX. 65% OF LENGTH

OMIT PARTITION IF LENGTH IS LESS THAN 9'-10"

NOTE SEPTIC TANK MAY BE PRECAST

LENGTH

LONGITUDINAL SECTION

SEPTIC TANK

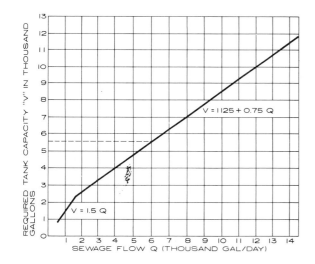

$$V = 1125 + 0.75 Q$$

$$V = 1.5 Q$$

REQUIRED TANK CAPACITY "V" IN THOUSAND GALLONS

SEWAGE FLOW Q (THOUSAND GAL/DAY)

DETERMINATION OF SEPTIC TANK VOLUME

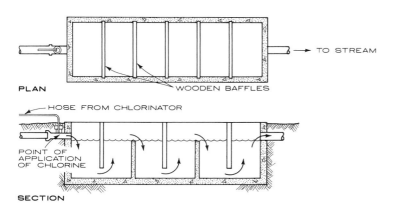

TO STREAM

PLAN

WOODEN BAFFLES

HOSE FROM CHLORINATOR

POINT OF APPLICATION OF CHLORINE

SECTION

CHLORINE CONTACT CHAMBER

Jack L. Staunton, P.E.; Staunton and Freeman, Consulting Engineers; New York, New York

NOTES
• DOSE FROM CHAMBER TO EQUAL ¾ OF FARM TILE OR PERFORATED PIPE IN ONE FIELD
• PIPES MAY BE SUBSTITUTED FOR SIPHONS IF CONDITION DICTATES

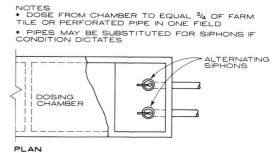

ALTERNATING SIPHONS

DOSING CHAMBER

PLAN

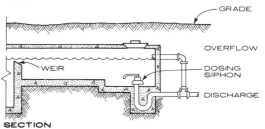

GRADE

OVERFLOW

WEIR

DOSING SIPHON

DISCHARGE

SECTION

DOSING CHAMBER WITH ALTERNATING SIPHONS

NOTE GREASE TRAPS TO BE USED ONLY IF THEY ARE CLEANED DAILY

PLAN (TOP REMOVED)

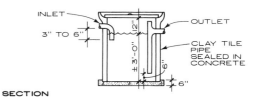

INLET

3" TO 6"

OUTLET

CLAY TILE PIPE SEALED IN CONCRETE

SECTION

PLAN (TOP REMOVED)

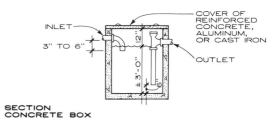

COVER OF REINFORCED CONCRETE, ALUMINUM, OR CAST IRON

INLET

3" TO 6"

OUTLET

SECTION CONCRETE BOX

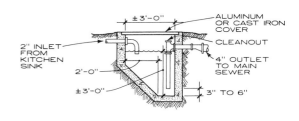

ALUMINUM OR CAST IRON COVER

CLEANOUT

2" INLET FROM KITCHEN SINK

4" OUTLET TO MAIN SEWER

2'-0"

±3'-0"

±3'-0"

3" TO 6"

TYPICAL GREASE TRAPS

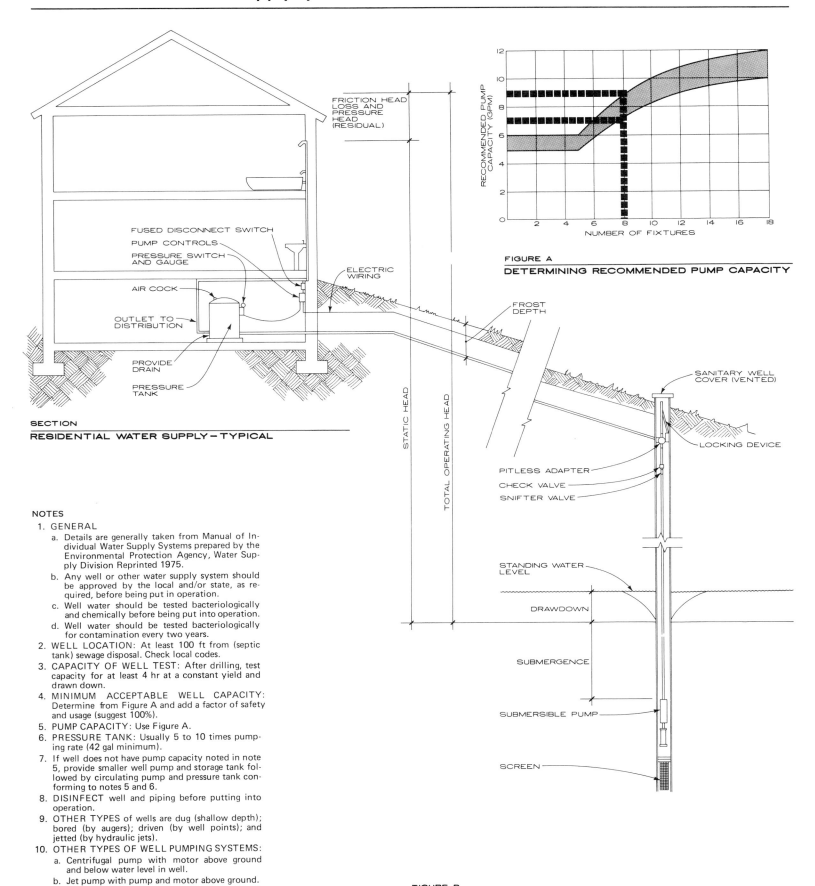

FIGURE A

DETERMINING RECOMMENDED PUMP CAPACITY

SECTION

RESIDENTIAL WATER SUPPLY—TYPICAL

NOTES

1. GENERAL
   a. Details are generally taken from Manual of In-
      dividual Water Supply Systems prepared by the
      Environmental Protection Agency, Water Sup-
      ply Division Reprinted 1975.
   b. Any well or other water supply system should
      be approved by the local and/or state, as re-
      quired, before being put in operation.
   c. Well water should be tested bacteriologically
      and chemically before being put into operation.
   d. Well water should be tested bacteriologically
      for contamination every two years.
2. WELL LOCATION: At least 100 ft from (septic
   tank) sewage disposal. Check local codes.
3. CAPACITY OF WELL TEST: After drilling, test
   capacity for at least 4 hr at a constant yield and
   drawn down.
4. MINIMUM ACCEPTABLE WELL CAPACITY:
   Determine from Figure A and add a factor of safety
   and usage (suggest 100%).
5. PUMP CAPACITY: Use Figure A.
6. PRESSURE TANK: Usually 5 to 10 times pumping rate (42 gal minimum).
7. If well does not have pump capacity noted in note
   5, provide smaller well pump and storage tank followed by circulating pump and pressure tank con-
   forming to notes 5 and 6.
8. DISINFECT well and piping before putting into
   operation.
9. OTHER TYPES of wells are dug (shallow depth);
   bored (by augers); driven (by well points); and
   jetted (by hydraulic jets).
10. OTHER TYPES OF WELL PUMPING SYSTEMS:
    a. Centrifugal pump with motor above ground
       and below water level in well.
    b. Jet pump with pump and motor above ground.
    c. Direct or reciprocating pumps in the well with
       motor above ground.

FIGURE B

DRILLED WELL—SECTION

Jack L. Staunton, P.E.; Staunton and Freeman, Consulting Engineers; New York, New York

WATER DISTRIBUTION

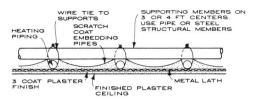

PIPES IN SUSPENDED PLASTER CEILING

In a suspended plaster ceiling both the lath and the heating coils are securely wired to the support members so that the lath is below but in good contact with the coils. Plaster is then applied to the lath to embed the tubes. Some local codes may prohibit this assembly.

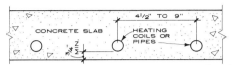

COILS IN STRUCTURAL CONCRETE SLAB

Heating pipes can be embedded in the lower portion of a concrete slab. If plaster is to be applied to the concrete, the piping may be placed directly on the wood forms. The minimum coverage for an exposed concrete slab is generally $3/4$ in. but may vary with local codes.

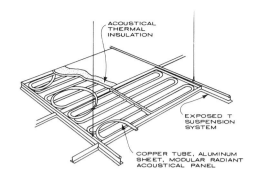

METAL CEILING PANELS

Metal panel ceiling systems use copper tubing bonded to an aluminum panel which can be mounted into a standard suspended ceiling grid. An insulating blanket is required to reduce the upward flow of heat from the metal panel. The heating pipes can be connected in either a sinuous or parallel flow welded system. A ceiling panel system can also be used for cooling purposes if chilled water is supplied through the tubes.

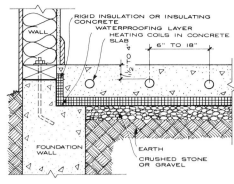

COILS IN FLOOR SLAB ON GRADE

Plastic, ferrous, or nonferrous heating pipes are used in floor slabs that rest on grade. It is recommended that perimeter insulation be used to reduce thermal losses at the edges. Coils should be embedded completely in the concrete slab and should not rest on an interface. Supports used to position the coils while pouring the slab should be nonabsorbent and inorganic. A layer of waterproofing should be placed above grade to protect insulation and piping.

LIQUID RADIANT HEATING SYSTEMS

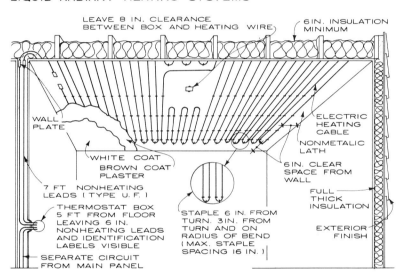

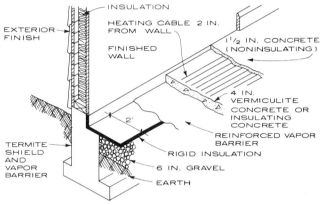

ELECTRIC HEATING CABLE IN CONCRETE SLAB

Electric heating cables embedded in plaster ceilings or concrete floors or laminated in gypsum board construction are factory-assembled units furnished in standard lengths from 75 to 1800 ft. Standard cable assemblies are normally rated at 2.75 W/linear ft and are available for 120, 208 and 240 V.

ELECTRIC RADIANT HEATING SYSTEMS

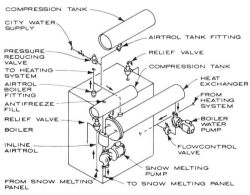

BOILER AND HEAT EXCHANGER

DRIVEWAY PIPING PLAN

EXPANSION JOINT IN CONCRETE WALK OR DRIVEWAY

HEATING CABLE IN ASPHALT

SNOW MELTING SYSTEMS

Snow melting systems for driveways and sidewalks can be of the ethylene-glycol type, hot oil or electric cables. The hot liquid types use a central hot water boiler with a heat exchanger that pumps the fluid through tubes embedded in the asphalt pavement.

W. S. Fleming and Associates, Inc.; Fayetteville, New York

Vents, drains, slab pitch, and expansion joints must be provided for in the initial design. A $3/4$ in. pipe or tube on 12 in. centers is used as a standard coil. Header pipes are normally $1 1/2$ in. in diameter. Piping should be supported with a minimum of 2 in. of concrete above and below the pipe.

If piping must pass through a concrete expansion joint, provision should be made to avoid any stresses on the tubing. By dipping the tube below the expansion joint any movement or heaving in the slab can be accommodated. All piping below the level of the concrete slab must be waterproofed and covered with insulation.

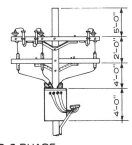

SINGLE OR 3 PHASE

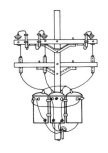

3 PHASE

OVERHEAD TRANSFORMER

OVERHEAD TRANSFORMER: Three-phase transformers are available up to 500 kVA in a single unit. Three single-phase units can total to 1500 kVA with adequate platform support. Service lateral to building can be either overhead or underground.

Typical dimensions for 13 and 23 kV. See the National Electrical Safety Code (ANSI C2) for required clearances; 6 in. if overhead ground wire is not provided.

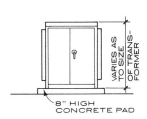

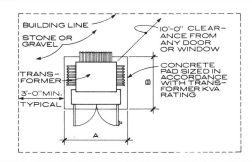

PAD MOUNTED TRANSFORMER

High voltage compartment requires 10 ft clearance for on-off operation of the insulated stick located on the transformer (known as "hot stick" operation).

		A	B
Typical pad sizes:	75– 500 KVA	70 in.	58 in.
	750–2500 KVA	87 in.	70 in.

PAD MOUNTED TRANSFORMER: Pad mounted transformers with weatherproof tamperproof enclosure permit installation at ground level without danger from exposed live parts. Three phase units up to 2500 kVA are available and are normally used with underground primary and secondary feeders.

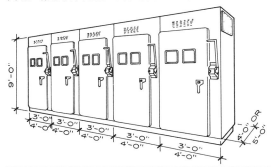

PRIMARY SWITCHGEAR

PRIMARY SWITCHGEAR: Where the owner's buildings cover a large area such as a college campus or medical center, the application usually requires the use of medium voltages of 5 kV to 34 kV for distribution feeders. Therefore, the utility company will terminate their primary feeders on the owner's metal clad or metal enclosed switchgear. This switchgear may be interior or exterior weatherproof construction. Code clearance in front and back of board must be provided in accordance with the National Electric Code.

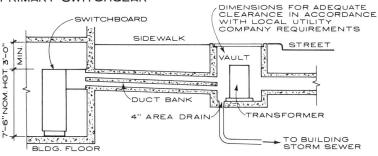

UNDERGROUND VAULT

UNDERGROUND VAULT. Underground vaults are generally used for utility company transformers where all distribution feeders are underground. These systems usually constitute a network or spot network. Vaults often are located below the sidewalks and have grating tops.

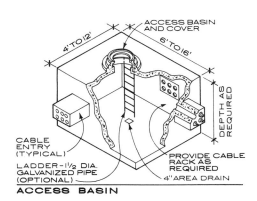

ACCESS BASIN

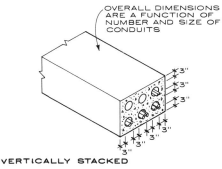

VERTICALLY STACKED

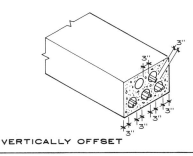

VERTICALLY OFFSET

UNDERGROUND DUCT BANK

William Tao & Associates, Inc., Consulting Engineers; St. Louis, Missouri
Dennis W. Wolbert; Everett I. Brown Company; Indianapolis, Indiana

HIGH VOLTAGE DISTRIBUTION

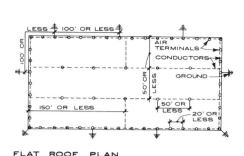

FLAT ROOF PLAN

ROOF LAYOUT PLANS

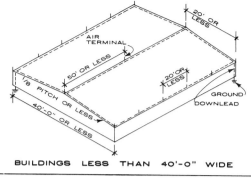

BUILDINGS LESS THAN 40'-0" WIDE   BUILDINGS GREATER THAN 40'-0" WIDE

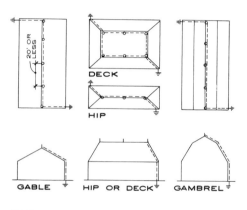

DECK

HIP

GABLE   HIP OR DECK   GAMBREL

PITCH ROOF TYPES

OVERALL SYSTEMS DESIGN

1. Air terminals shall be located around the perimeter of flat roof buildings and along the ridge of pitched roof buildings spaced at 20 ft on center maximum and located not more than 2 ft from ridge ends, outside corners, and edges of building walls.
2. Full size main conductors shall interconnect all air terminals.
3. Additional air terminals shall be located in the center of large open flat roofs at spacings not to exceed 50 ft maximum.
4. Cable runs connecting these center roof air terminals shall not exceed 150 ft in length without a lead back to the perimeter cable.
5. Gently sloping roofs are classed as flat under the rules shown above and are protected in the same fashion as flat roof.
6. Download cables to ground shall be connected to the roof perimeter cable at a maximum spacing of 100 ft on center. Buildings having a perimeter of 250 to 300 ft shall have three downloads. For each additional 100 ft or fraction thereof add one download.
7. No building or structure shall have less than two downloads.

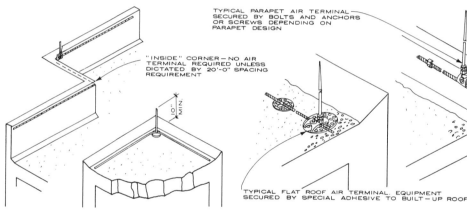

AIR TERMINALS

GENERAL NOTES

A lightning protection system is an integrated arrangement of air terminals, bonding connections, arrestors, splicers, and other fittings installed on a structure in order to safely conduct to ground any lightning discharge to the structure.

Lightning protection systems and components are grouped into three categories (U.L. classes) based on building height and intended applications. Class I equipment and systems are for ordinary buildings under 75 ft in height, Class II is for those over 75 ft in height, and Class II Modified is a specialty area covering only large, heavy duty stacks and chimneys similar to those used at power plants, for example. Each of these types of systems consists of five or six major groups of components:

1. Air terminals (lightning rods) located on the roof and building projections.
2. Main conductors that tie the air terminals together and interconnect with the grounding system.
3. Bonds to metal roof structures and equipment.
4. Arrestors to prevent powerline surge damage.
5. Ground terminals, typically rods or plates driven or buried in the earth.
6. Tree protection (usually applicable only to residential work).

Each of these types of equipment and the methods for their installation are covered in the following drawings.

Beyond these material requirements, other factors to be considered relative to lightning protection systems include (a) selection of codes for compliance, (b) inspection criteria (again based on code), (c) criteria to evaluate competency of installing personnel, and (d) requirement for annual inspection and maintenance.

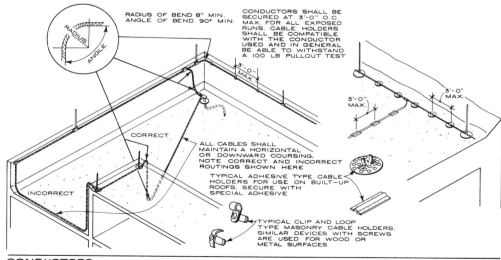

CONDUCTORS

Douglas J. Franklin; Thompson Lightning Protection, Inc.; St. Paul, Minnesota

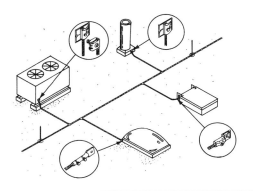
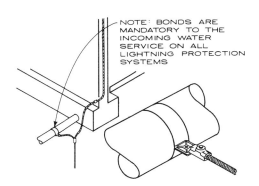

NOTE: BONDS ARE MANDATORY TO THE INCOMING WATER SERVICE ON ALL LIGHTNING PROTECTION SYSTEMS

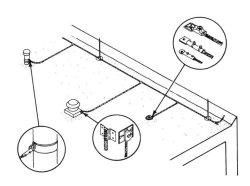

BONDING

NOTES

There are two classes of equipment that require bonding to the lightning protection systems.

1. METAL BODIES OF CONDUCTANCE: Larger metal objects located on the roof and subject to direct lightning strike. These objects must be bonded using full size conductor and fittings regardless of their location on the roof. Typical examples as shown include plumbing vents, exhaust fans, air-conditioning units, metal stacks, skylite frames, and roof hatches. Television and radio antennas must also be bonded.

2. METAL BODIES OF INDUCTANCE: Smaller objects such as roof drains, gutters, downspouts, flashings, coping, and expansion joint caps. These require bonding only if within 6 ft of the system.

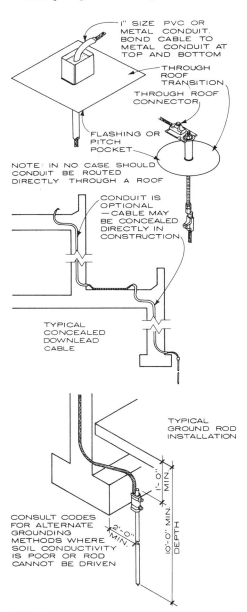

I" SIZE PVC OR METAL CONDUIT. BOND CABLE TO METAL CONDUIT AT TOP AND BOTTOM

THROUGH ROOF TRANSITION

THROUGH ROOF CONNECTOR

FLASHING OR PITCH POCKET

NOTE: IN NO CASE SHOULD CONDUIT BE ROUTED DIRECTLY THROUGH A ROOF

CONDUIT IS OPTIONAL — CABLE MAY BE CONCEALED DIRECTLY IN CONSTRUCTION

TYPICAL CONCEALED DOWNLEAD CABLE

TYPICAL GROUND ROD INSTALLATION

CONSULT CODES FOR ALTERNATE GROUNDING METHODS WHERE SOIL CONDUCTIVITY IS POOR OR ROD CANNOT BE DRIVEN

1'-0" MIN.
2'-0" MIN.
10'-0" MIN. DEPTH

DOWNLEADS AND GROUNDS

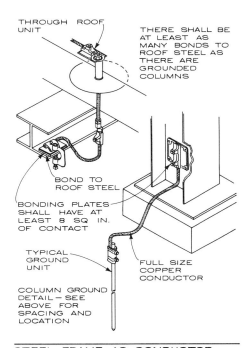

THROUGH ROOF UNIT

THERE SHALL BE AT LEAST AS MANY BONDS TO ROOF STEEL AS THERE ARE GROUNDED COLUMNS

BOND TO ROOF STEEL

BONDING PLATES SHALL HAVE AT LEAST 8 SQ IN. OF CONTACT

TYPICAL GROUND UNIT

FULL SIZE COPPER CONDUCTOR

COLUMN GROUND DETAIL — SEE ABOVE FOR SPACING AND LOCATION

STEEL FRAME AS CONDUCTOR

NOTE

In some cases, especially on tall structures, it may be advantageous to substitute the steel frame of a structure for portions of the usual conductor system, normally the downleads. Connections are made to cleaned areas of the building steel, at grade and roof level, and the columns serve to connect the roof and ground systems.

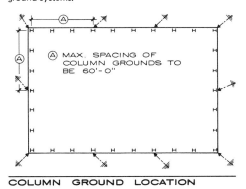

(A) MAX. SPACING OF COLUMN GROUNDS TO BE 60'-0"

COLUMN GROUND LOCATION

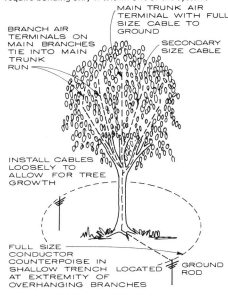

MAIN TRUNK AIR TERMINAL WITH FULL SIZE CABLE TO GROUND

BRANCH AIR TERMINALS ON MAIN BRANCHES TIE INTO MAIN TRUNK RUN

SECONDARY SIZE CABLE

INSTALL CABLES LOOSELY TO ALLOW FOR TREE GROWTH

FULL SIZE CONDUCTOR COUNTERPOISE IN SHALLOW TRENCH LOCATED AT EXTREMITY OF OVERHANGING BRANCHES

GROUND ROD

TREE INSTALLATION
OTHER CONSIDERATIONS

1. Arresters should be installed on the electric and telephone services and on all radio and television lead-ins to a structure. Responsibility and jurisdiction for the installation of these devices can vary with locality so that special consideration may have to be given to these items.

2. Trees adjacent to residences pose another special hazard. It is recommended that all trees taller than an adjacent structure that are within 10 ft be fully protected. Consult codes or manufacturer for recommendations on materials and installation requirements.

3. On-site inspections and certification of completed systems, installer competency certification, and guaranteed inspection/maintenance options are all available under existing standards. Consult codes and standards for specifics.

REFERENCES

The following codes, technical sources, and quality control procedures are standards for lightning protection systems.

1. LIGHTNING PROTECTION INSTITUTE: "Installation Code L.P.I.—175."

2. UNDERWRITERS LABORATORIES: Master Labeled program under "U.L. Installation Requirements 96A."

3. NATIONAL FIRE PROTECTION ASSOCIATION: "Lightning Protection Code N.F.P.A. 78."

Douglas J. Franklin; Thompson Lightning Protection, Inc.; St. Paul, Minnesota

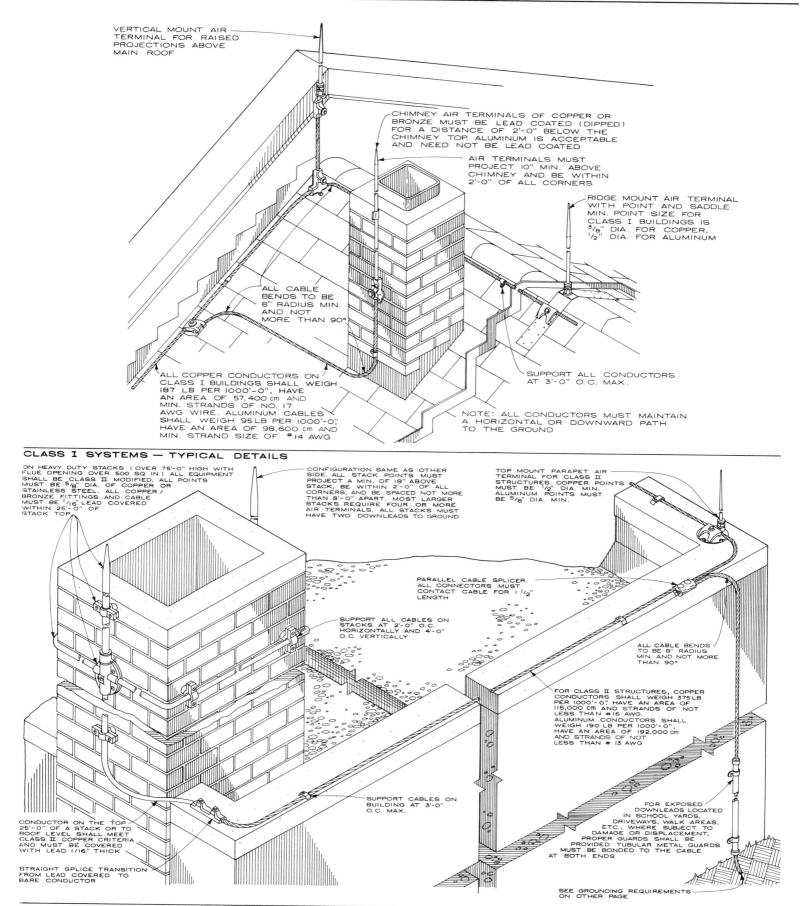

VERTICAL MOUNT AIR TERMINAL FOR RAISED PROJECTIONS ABOVE MAIN ROOF

CHIMNEY AIR TERMINALS OF COPPER OR BRONZE MUST BE LEAD COATED (DIPPED) FOR A DISTANCE OF 2'-0" BELOW THE CHIMNEY TOP. ALUMINUM IS ACCEPTABLE AND NEED NOT BE LEAD COATED

AIR TERMINALS MUST PROJECT 10" MIN. ABOVE CHIMNEY AND BE WITHIN 2'-0" OF ALL CORNERS

RIDGE MOUNT AIR TERMINAL WITH POINT AND SADDLE. MIN. POINT SIZE FOR CLASS I BUILDINGS IS 3/8" DIA. FOR COPPER, 1/2" DIA. FOR ALUMINUM

ALL CABLE BENDS TO BE 8" RADIUS MIN. AND NOT MORE THAN 90°

SUPPORT ALL CONDUCTORS AT 3'-0" O.C. MAX.

ALL COPPER CONDUCTORS ON CLASS I BUILDINGS SHALL WEIGH 187 LB PER 1000'-0", HAVE AN AREA OF 57,400 cm AND MIN. STRANDS OF NO. 17 AWG WIRE. ALUMINUM CABLES SHALL WEIGH 95 LB PER 1000'-0", HAVE AN AREA OF 98,600 cm AND MIN. STRAND SIZE OF #14 AWG

NOTE: ALL CONDUCTORS MUST MAINTAIN A HORIZONTAL OR DOWNWARD PATH TO THE GROUND

CLASS I SYSTEMS — TYPICAL DETAILS

ON HEAVY DUTY STACKS (OVER 75'-0" HIGH WITH FLUE OPENING OVER 500 SQ IN) ALL EQUIPMENT SHALL BE CLASS II MODIFIED. ALL POINTS MUST BE 5/8" DIA. OF COPPER OR STAINLESS STEEL. ALL COPPER/BRONZE FITTINGS AND CABLE MUST BE 1/16" LEAD COVERED WITHIN 25'-0" OF STACK TOP

CONFIGURATION SAME AS OTHER SIDE. ALL STACK POINTS MUST PROJECT A MIN. OF 18" ABOVE STACK, BE WITHIN 2'-0" OF ALL CORNERS, AND BE SPACED NOT MORE THAN 8'-0" APART. MOST LARGER STACKS REQUIRE FOUR OR MORE AIR TERMINALS. ALL STACKS MUST HAVE TWO DOWNLEADS TO GROUND

TOP MOUNT PARAPET AIR TERMINAL FOR CLASS II STRUCTURES. COPPER POINTS MUST BE 1/2" DIA. MIN. ALUMINUM POINTS MUST BE 5/8" DIA. MIN.

PARALLEL CABLE SPLICER. ALL CONNECTORS MUST CONTACT CABLE FOR 1 1/2" LENGTH

SUPPORT ALL CABLES ON STACKS AT 2'-0" O.C. HORIZONTALLY AND 4'-0" O.C. VERTICALLY

ALL CABLE BENDS TO BE 8" RADIUS MIN. AND NOT MORE THAN 90°

FOR CLASS II STRUCTURES, COPPER CONDUCTORS SHALL WEIGH 375 LB PER 1000'-0", HAVE AN AREA OF 115,000 cm AND STRANDS OF NOT LESS THAN #16 AWG. ALUMINUM CONDUCTORS SHALL WEIGH 190 LB PER 1000'-0", HAVE AN AREA OF 192,000 cm AND STRANDS OF NOT LESS THAN #13 AWG

CONDUCTOR ON THE TOP 25'-0" OF A STACK OR TO ROOF LEVEL SHALL MEET CLASS II COPPER CRITERIA AND MUST BE COVERED WITH LEAD 1/16" THICK

STRAIGHT SPLICE TRANSITION FROM LEAD COVERED TO BARE CONDUCTOR

SUPPORT CABLES ON BUILDING AT 3'-0" O.C. MAX.

FOR EXPOSED DOWNLEADS LOCATED IN SCHOOL YARDS, DRIVEWAYS, WALK AREAS, ETC., WHERE SUBJECT TO DAMAGE OR DISPLACEMENT, PROPER GUARDS SHALL BE PROVIDED. TUBULAR METAL GUARDS MUST BE BONDED TO THE CABLE AT BOTH ENDS

SEE GROUNDING REQUIREMENTS ON OTHER PAGE

CLASS II SYSTEMS — TYPICAL DETAILS

Douglas J. Franklin; Thompson Lightning Protection, Inc.; St. Paul, Minnesota

REFERENCES

GENERAL REFERENCES

Mechanical and Electrical Equipment of Buildings, 7th ed., 1986, Benjamin Stein, John S. Reynolds, and William J. McGuinness, Wiley

Handbook of Utilities and Services for Buildings, 1990, Cyril M. Harris, McGraw-Hill

Standard Handbook for Civil Engineers, 3rd ed., 1983, Frederick S. Merritt, McGraw-Hill

DATA SOURCES: ORGANIZATIONS

American Society of Heating, Refrigerating, and Air Conditioning Engineers (ASHRAE), 189

Barry Pattern and Foundry Company, Inc., 182

Bell and Gossett (ITT), 189

Contech Construction Products Inc., 182

Environmental Protection Agency (EPA), 184, 185, 186, 187

Lightning Protection Institute (LPI), 191, 192, 193

Metalines, Inc., 182

National Electric Code (NEC), 190

National Fire Protection Association (NFPA), 191, 192, 193

Neenah Foundry Company, 182

Polydrain, 182

Toro Company, 179

Underwriters Laboratories, Inc. (UL), 191, 192, 193

Walker Porsowall Pipe Company, 180

DATA SOURCES: PUBLICATIONS

Data Book for Civil Engineers, Vol. 1: Design, 1945, Elwyn E. Seelye, Wiley, reprinted with permission, 181, 182

Landscape Architecture Construction, 1979, Harlow C. Landphair and Fred Klatt, Jr., Elsevier, 181, 182

Manual of Individual Water Supply Systems, Environmental Protection Agency (EPA), 188

Site Design and Construction Detailing, 1978, Theodore Walker, PDA Publishers, 182

Turf Irrigation Manual, James A. Watkins, Telsco Industries, 179

CHAPTER **7**

SPORTS

INDOOR SPORTS	196
OUTDOOR SPORTS	201
AQUATICS	215
WINTER SPORTS	226
BOATING	228
AIR SPORTS	230
TRAINING ROOMS	231
EQUESTRIAN	232

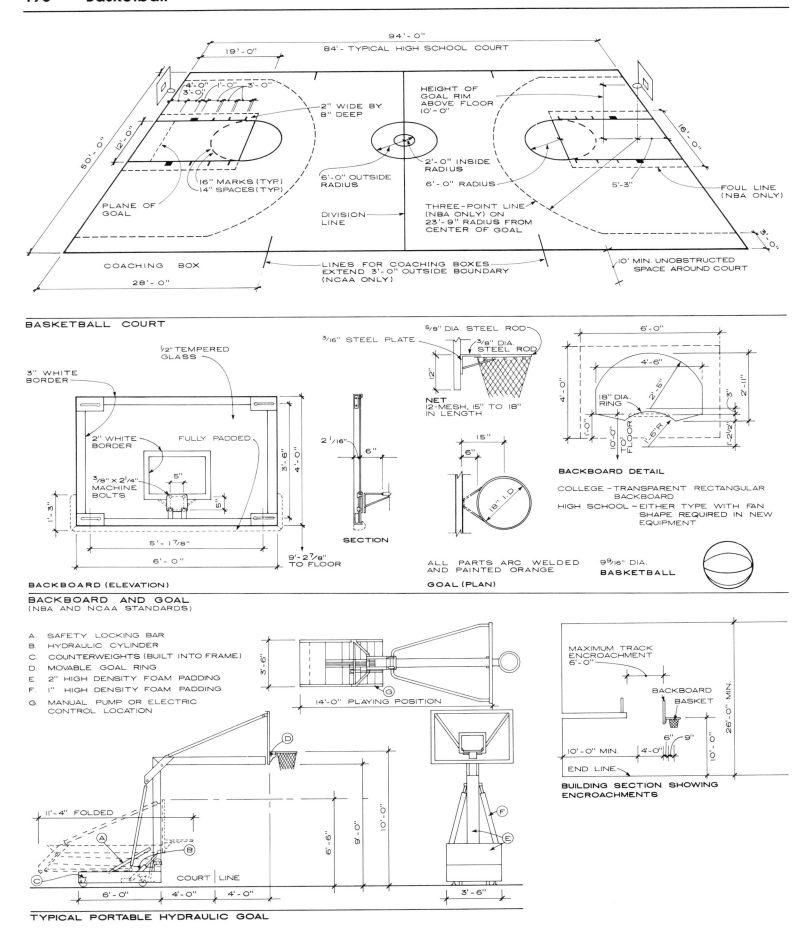

94'-0"
84'- TYPICAL HIGH SCHOOL COURT
19'-0"
4'-0" 1'-0" 3'-0"
3'-0"
50'-0"
12'-0"
2" WIDE BY 8" DEEP
HEIGHT OF GOAL RIM ABOVE FLOOR 10'-0"
16'-0"
16" MARKS (TYP.)
14" SPACES (TYP.)
2'-0" INSIDE RADIUS
6'-0" OUTSIDE RADIUS
6'-0" RADIUS
5'-3"
FOUL LINE (NBA ONLY)
PLANE OF GOAL
DIVISION LINE
THREE-POINT LINE (NBA ONLY) ON 23'-9" RADIUS FROM CENTER OF GOAL
COACHING BOX
LINES FOR COACHING BOXES EXTEND 3'-0" OUTSIDE BOUNDARY (NCAA ONLY)
3'-0"
10' MIN. UNOBSTRUCTED SPACE AROUND COURT
28'-0"

BASKETBALL COURT

1/2" TEMPERED GLASS
3" WHITE BORDER
2" WHITE BORDER
FULLY PADDED
3/8" x 2 1/4" MACHINE BOLTS
5"
5"
1'-3"
3'-6"
4'-0"
5'-1 7/8"
6'-0"
9'-2 7/8" TO FLOOR

BACKBOARD (ELEVATION)

BACKBOARD AND GOAL
(NBA AND NCAA STANDARDS)

A. SAFETY LOCKING BAR
B. HYDRAULIC CYLINDER
C. COUNTERWEIGHTS (BUILT INTO FRAME)
D. MOVABLE GOAL RING
E. 2" HIGH DENSITY FOAM PADDING
F. 1" HIGH DENSITY FOAM PADDING
G. MANUAL PUMP OR ELECTRIC CONTROL LOCATION

5/8" DIA. STEEL ROD
3/16" STEEL PLATE
3/8" DIA. STEEL ROD
12"
NET
12-MESH, 15" TO 18" IN LENGTH
2 1/16"
6"
SECTION

15"
6"
18" I.D.
ALL PARTS ARC WELDED AND PAINTED ORANGE
GOAL (PLAN)

6'-0"
4'-6"
2'-5"
18" DIA. RING
4'-0"
1'-0"
10'-0" TO FLOOR
1'-6"R
3"
2'-11"
1'-2 1/2"
BACKBOARD DETAIL

COLLEGE - TRANSPARENT RECTANGULAR BACKBOARD
HIGH SCHOOL - EITHER TYPE WITH FAN SHAPE REQUIRED IN NEW EQUIPMENT

9 9/16" DIA.
BASKETBALL

3'-6"
14'-0" PLAYING POSITION
D
11'-4" FOLDED
A
B
C
COURT LINE
6'-0" 4'-0" 4'-0"
6'-6"
9'-0"
10'-0"
F
E
3'-6"

TYPICAL PORTABLE HYDRAULIC GOAL

MAXIMUM TRACK ENCROACHMENT 6'-0"
BACKBOARD
BASKET
26'-0" MIN.
10'-0" MIN.
4'-0"
6" 9"
10'-0"
END LINE

BUILDING SECTION SHOWING ENCROACHMENTS

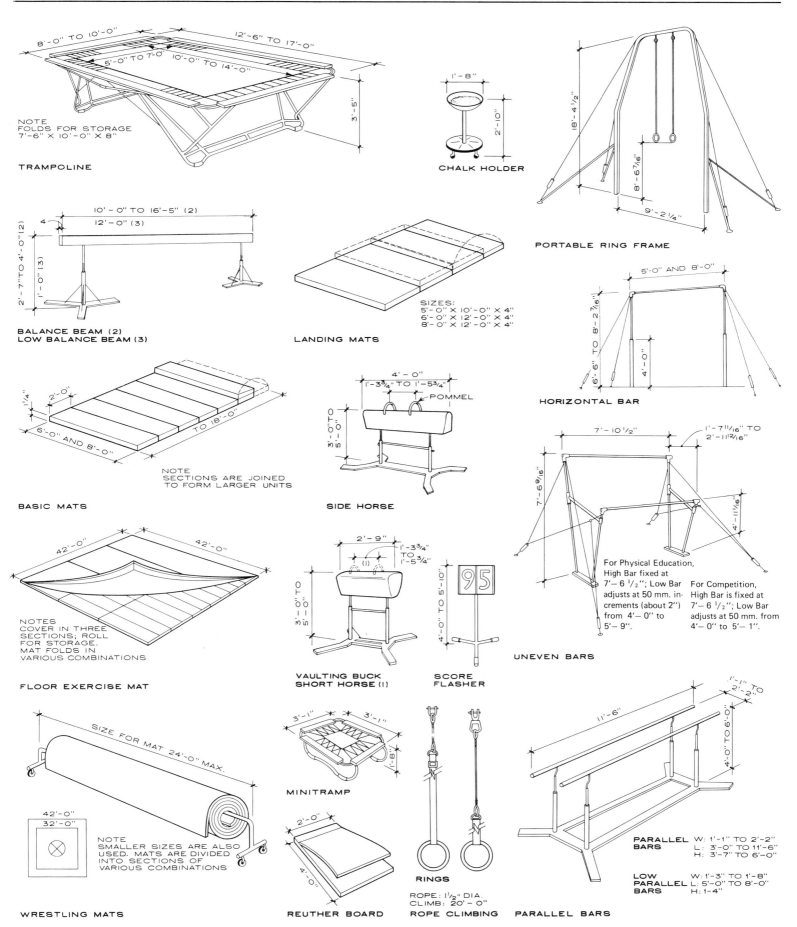

TRAMPOLINE

NOTE
FOLDS FOR STORAGE
7'-6" X 10'-0" X 8"

8'-0" TO 10'-0"
12'-6" TO 17'-0"
5'-0" TO 7'-0"
10'-0" TO 14'-0"
3'-5"

CHALK HOLDER

1'-8"
2'-0"

PORTABLE RING FRAME

18'-4 1/2"
8'-6 7/16"
9'-2 1/4"

BALANCE BEAM (2)
LOW BALANCE BEAM (3)

10'-0" TO 16'-5" (2)
12'-0" (3)
4
2'-7" TO 4'-0" (2)
1'-0" (3)

LANDING MATS

SIZES:
5'-0" X 10'-0" X 4"
6'-0" X 12'-0" X 4"
8'-0" X 12'-0" X 4"

HORIZONTAL BAR

5'-0" AND 8'-0"
6'-6" TO 8'-2 7/16"
4'-0"

BASIC MATS

1 1/4"
2'-0"
6'-0" AND 8'-0"
TO 18'-0"

NOTE
SECTIONS ARE JOINED
TO FORM LARGER UNITS

SIDE HORSE

4'-0"
1'-3 3/4" TO 1'-5 3/4"
POMMEL
3'-0" TO 5'-0"

UNEVEN BARS

7'-10 1/2"
1'-7 11/16" TO 2'-11 12/16"
7'-6 9/16"
4'-11 1/16"

For Physical Education,
High Bar fixed at
7'-6 1/2"; Low Bar
adjusts at 50 mm. in-
crements (about 2")
from 4'-0" to
5'-9".

For Competition,
High Bar is fixed at
7'-6 1/2"; Low Bar
adjusts at 50 mm. from
4'-0" to 5'-1".

FLOOR EXERCISE MAT

42'-0"
42'-0"

NOTES
COVER IN THREE
SECTIONS; ROLL
FOR STORAGE.
MAT FOLDS IN
VARIOUS COMBINATIONS

VAULTING BUCK
SHORT HORSE (1)

2'-9"
1'-3 3/4"
TO
1'-5 3/4"
(1)
3'-0" TO 5'-0"

SCORE
FLASHER

95
4'-0" TO 5'-10"

WRESTLING MATS

SIZE FOR MAT 24'-0" MAX.

42'-0"
32'-0"
⊗

NOTE
SMALLER SIZES ARE ALSO
USED. MATS ARE DIVIDED
INTO SECTIONS OF
VARIOUS COMBINATIONS

MINITRAMP

3'-1"
3'-1"
1'-8"

REUTHER BOARD

2'-0"
4'-0"

RINGS

RINGS

ROPE: 1 1/2" DIA.
CLIMB: 20'-0"

ROPE CLIMBING

PARALLEL BARS

11'-6"
1'-1" TO 2'-2"
4'-0" TO 6'-0"

PARALLEL   W: 1'-1" TO 2'-2"
BARS   L: 3'-0" TO 11'-6"
           H: 3'-7" TO 6'-0"

LOW   W: 1'-3" TO 1'-8"
PARALLEL   L: 5'-0" TO 8'-0"
BARS   H: 1-4"

John C. Lunsford, AIA, Varney Sexton Sydnor Associates; Phoenix, Arizona

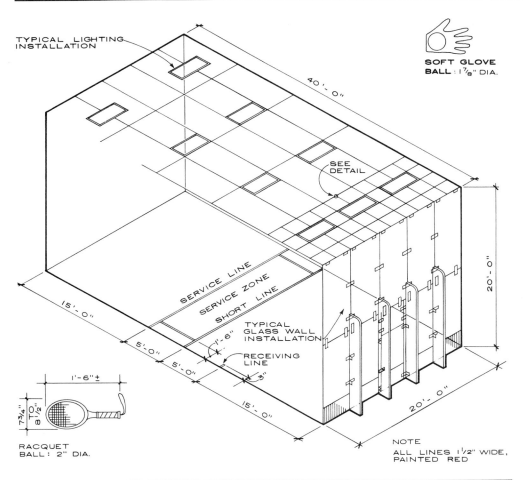

TYPICAL LIGHTING INSTALLATION

SOFT GLOVE BALL : 1 7/8" DIA.

40'-0"

20'-0"

15'-0"

SERVICE LINE

SERVICE ZONE

SHORT LINE

SEE DETAIL

TYPICAL GLASS WALL INSTALLATION

RECEIVING LINE

5'-0"

5'-0"

1'-6"

3"

15'-0"

20'-0"

1'-6"±

7 3/4" TO 8 1/2"

RACQUET BALL : 2" DIA.

NOTE
ALL LINES 1 1/2" WIDE, PAINTED RED

HANDBALL / RACQUETBALL / PADDLEBALL COURT

TYPICAL WALL PANELS 4'-0" x 8'-0" TONGUE AND GROOVE PARTICLE BOARD

SERVICE LINE 6'-6" A.F.F. (S) 8'-2" A.F.F. (D)

22'-0" (S)
31'-0" (D)

9"

8 1/4"

1/2"

2'-3"

RACQUET BALL : 1 3/4" DIA.

16'-0" (S)
20'-0" (D)

10'-0" (S)
14'-0" (D)

12'-0" (S)
15'-0" (D)

6'-6" (S)
7'-0" (D)

TELLTALE 18 GAUGE SHEET METAL WITH 2" BEVEL AT 45° SLOPE; TOP EDGE 1'-5" ABOVE FLOOR FINISH

4'-6" RADIUS

SERVICE COURT

FLUSH MOUNTED DOOR

32'-0" (S)
45'-0" (D)

10'-0" (S)
15'-0" (D)

9'-3" (S)
12'-6" (D)

18'-6" (S)
25'-0" (D)

NOTE
ALL LINES 1" WIDE, PAINTED RED

SQUASH COURT

Timothy B. McDonald; Washington, D.C.

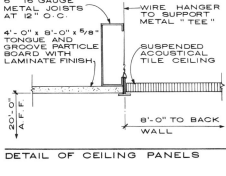

6" 16 GAUGE METAL JOISTS AT 12" O.C.

WIRE HANGER TO SUPPORT METAL "TEE"

4'-0" x 8'-0" x 5/8" TONGUE AND GROOVE PARTICLE BOARD WITH LAMINATE FINISH

SUSPENDED ACOUSTICAL TILE CEILING

20'-0" A.F.F.

8'-0" TO BACK WALL

DETAIL OF CEILING PANELS

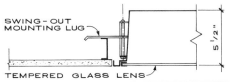

SWING-OUT MOUNTING LUG

5 1/2"

TEMPERED GLASS LENS

DETAIL OF LIGHT FIXTURE

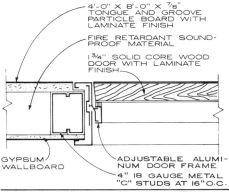

4'-0" X 8'-0" X 7/8" TONGUE AND GROOVE PARTICLE BOARD WITH LAMINATE FINISH

FIRE RETARDANT SOUND-PROOF MATERIAL

1 3/4" SOLID CORE WOOD DOOR WITH LAMINATE FINISH

GYPSUM WALLBOARD

ADJUSTABLE ALUMINUM DOOR FRAME

4" 18 GAUGE METAL "C" STUDS AT 16" O.C.

DETAIL OF FLUSH MOUNTED DOOR AT JAMB

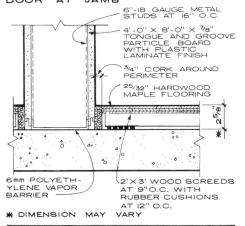

6"-18 GAUGE METAL STUDS AT 16" O.C.

4'-0" X 8'-0" X 7/8" TONGUE AND GROOVE PARTICLE BOARD WITH PLASTIC LAMINATE FINISH

3/4" CORK AROUND PERIMETER

25/32" HARDWOOD MAPLE FLOORING

2 5/8"

6mm POLYETHYLENE VAPOR BARRIER

2' X 3' WOOD SCREEDS AT 9" O.C. WITH RUBBER CUSHIONS AT 12" O.C.

＊ DIMENSION MAY VARY

SECTION AT COMMON SIDE WALL THROUGH FLOOR

NOTES

1. Materials and installation of glass wall system shall comply with safety and performance criteria for walls established by the standards of the International Squash Racquets Federation, the American Association of Racquetsports Manufacturers and Suppliers, and B.O.C.A.

2. For racquetball courts, temperature and humidity shall be maintained during storage, installation and thereafter as follows: temperature range is 65°-78°F. and humidity to be controlled between 40% and 60% at all times.

3. All dimensions shown are finished court dimensions. D - doubles; S - singles

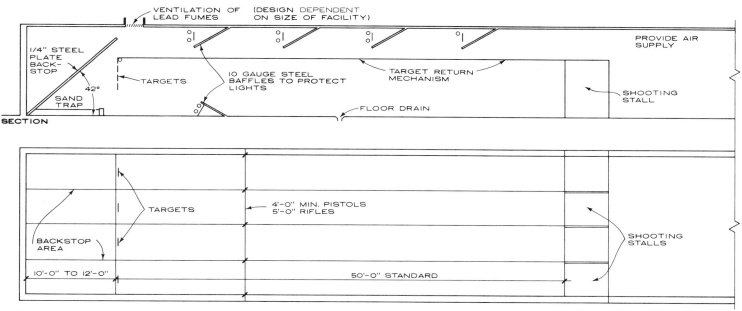

VENTILATION OF LEAD FUMES (DESIGN DEPENDENT ON SIZE OF FACILITY)

PROVIDE AIR SUPPLY

1/4" STEEL PLATE BACK-STOP

42°

SAND TRAP

TARGETS

10 GAUGE STEEL BAFFLES TO PROTECT LIGHTS

TARGET RETURN MECHANISM

SHOOTING STALL

FLOOR DRAIN

SECTION

BACKSTOP AREA

TARGETS

4'-0" MIN. PISTOLS 5'-0" RIFLES

SHOOTING STALLS

10'-0" TO 12'-0"

50'-0" STANDARD

PLAN

DESIGN PROBLEMS

When planning a firearms range, the following safety considerations must be made:

1. Placement of traps; use of stalls and placement of firing line; provision for space for spectators; protection from ricochet; prevention of spilled powder explosions.
2. Ventilation adequate to dissipate lead fumes.
3. Noise abatement.
4. Lighting.

The use of range design consultants is advisable. Contact the National Rifle Association for information.

TARGET SHOOTING

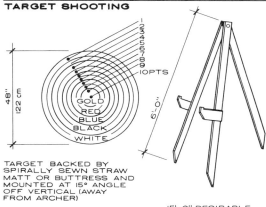

1 2 3 4 5 6 7 8 9 10PTS

GOLD
RED
BLUE
BLACK
WHITE

48" 122 cm

6'-0"

TARGET BACKED BY SPIRALLY SEWN STRAW MATT OR BUTTRESS AND MOUNTED AT 15° ANGLE OFF VERTICAL (AWAY FROM ARCHER)

Archery ranges should be orientated, in the northern hemisphere, so the archer is facing north ±45°. The range surface is to be turf, and free from obstructions or hard objects; likewise, spaces behind and to either side should be clear.

Target backings are made of stitched compressed straw rope called mat or buttress. Targets are made of thick paper with five concentric color zones. Both the mat and target are slanted at a 15° angle off vertical away from the archer.

Modern bows often are wood composites, fiberglass, and graphite. Lengths vary from 72 in. (1.82 M) to 62 in. (1.57 M). Bows are categorized by their draw weight, the amount of energy needed to pull a 28 in. (71 cm) arrow to full draw. Male archers usually use a 50 lb. to 55 lb. bow; female archers usually use 35 lb. to 40 lb. bow.

Arrow shafts are made of wood, graphite, or aluminum tubing. The flecking is made of plastic or feathers.

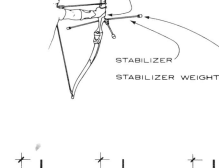

LIMBS

SIGHT APPARATUS

HAND GRIP

STABILIZER

STABILIZER WEIGHT

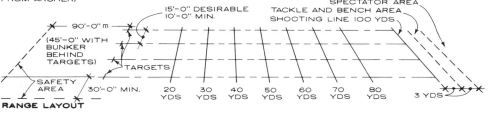

15'-0" DESIRABLE 10'-0" MIN.

SPECTATOR AREA
TACKLE AND BENCH AREA
SHOOTING LINE 100 YDS

90'-0" m

(45'-0" WITH BUNKER BEHIND TARGETS)

TARGETS

SAFETY AREA

30'-0" MIN.

20 YDS 30 YDS 40 YDS 50 YDS 60 YDS 70 YDS 80 YDS 3 YDS

RANGE LAYOUT

ARCHERY

Wooden nonskid flooring is ideal. A rubber piste is used on slippery floors. When a special metallic piste is used, a rubber mat must be placed beneath it to prevent hits on the floor being registered by the electronic scoring device. In competitive fencing, the score is kept by an electronic apparatus, which records each hit, and is linked to the fencers by wires. The wires are kept from trailing the ground by a spring-loaded spool. These spools often are recessed in a pit at each end of the piste.

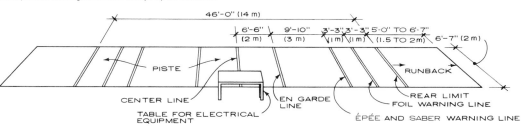

46'-0" (14 m)

6'-6" (2 m) 9'-10" (3 m) 3'-3" (1 m) 3'-3" (1 m) 5'-0" TO 6'-7" (1.5 TO 2m) 6'-7" (2 m)

PISTE

CENTER LINE

TABLE FOR ELECTRICAL EQUIPMENT

EN GARDE LINE

RUNBACK

REAR LIMIT
FOIL WARNING LINE

ÉPÉE AND SABER WARNING LINE

FENCING

3'-0" (90 cm)   17⁵/₈ OZ (500 G)

3'-0" (90 cm)   27¹/₈ OZ (770 G)

2'-11¹/₈" (88 cm)   17⁵/₈ OZ (500 G)

FOIL FRENCH HANDLE

ÉPÉE AMERICAN HANDLE

SABER

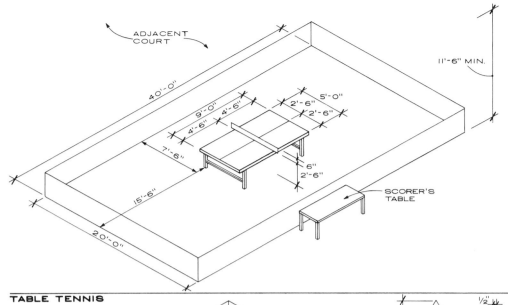

TABLE TENNIS

NOTES

Flooring should be level, slightly resilient, and not of non-skid material. Walls should be uniformly dark nongloss background to provide enough contrast to help players follow the ball. Lighting often varies for different standards of play, but 150-500 lumens at table height is the acceptable range. This should not be fluorescent or natural lighting, but preferably tungsten halogen. Sectional tables are stored upright when not in use.

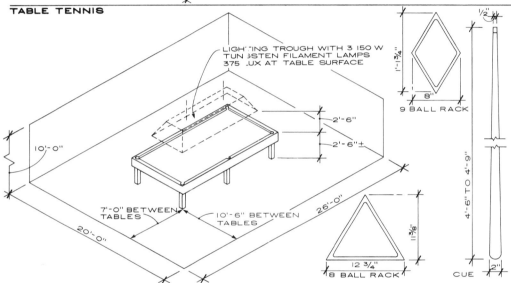

BILLIARDS / POCKET BILLIARDS / SNOOKER

The flooring must be level permanently and be able to withstand point loads. Traditionally designed billiard tables weigh about 1.5 tons spread over eight legs. Lighting must not produce harsh shadows, but some modeling of the balls is desirable. Direct or reflected glare should be avoided, and true color rendering is important in snooker. An overall bright light is needed for each table; natural lighting is not essential. Lighting at the table surface should be approximately 375 lumens, which can be achieved by three 150-watt tungsten filament lamps suspended in a lighting trough. Fluorescent lamps are unacceptable. Some sound insulation is required to prevent distractions from noise outside the playing area.

TYPE OF TABLE	PLAYING SURFACE W.	L.	TABLE SIZE W.	L.
ENGLISH (SNOOKER)	5'-9''	11'-6''	5'-9''	12'-9''
STANDARD POOL OR BILL.	5'-0''	10'-0''	5'-9''	10'-9''
STANDARD POOL OR BILL.	4'-6''	9'-0''	5'-3''	9'-9''
STANDARD POOL OR BILL.	4'-0''	8'-0''	4'-9''	8'-9''
JUNIOR POOL	3'-6''	7'-0''	4'-3''	7'-9''
JUNIOR POOL	3'-0''	6'-0''	3'-9''	6'-9''

TABLE HEIGHT 2'-6" ±

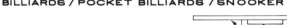

A dart board in a hanging box needs no additional storage. Lighting can be artificial, natural, or both. An adjustable spotlight is advisable. For safety reasons, the playing area should be placed away from doorways and traffic ways. Walls around the board should be surfaced with a material that will not be defaced by the darts.

DARTS

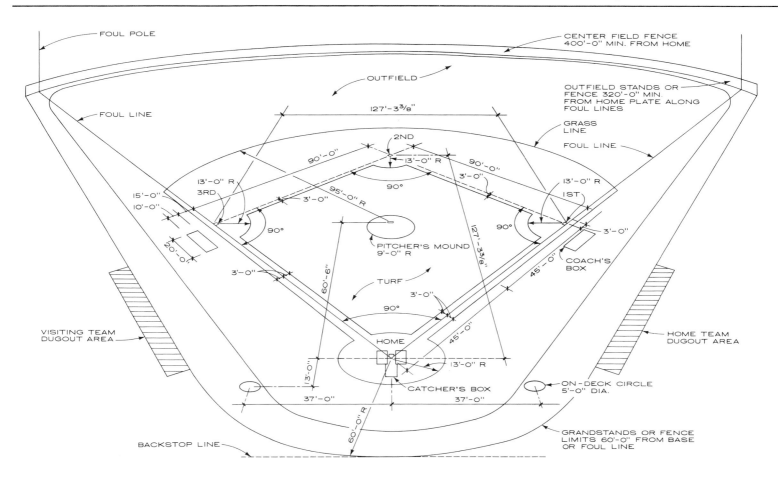

FOUL POLE

CENTER FIELD FENCE 400'-0" MIN. FROM HOME

OUTFIELD

FOUL LINE

OUTFIELD STANDS OR FENCE 320'-0" MIN. FROM HOME PLATE ALONG FOUL LINES

127'-3 3/8"

GRASS LINE

2ND

FOUL LINE

90'-0"

13'-0" R

90'-0"

3'-0"

13'-0" R
3RD

13'-0" R
3'-0"

90°

13'-0" R
1ST

15'-0"

95'-0" R

10'-0"

3'-0"

90°

90°

3'-0"
COACH'S BOX

20'-0"

PITCHER'S MOUND 9'-0" R

60'-6"

127'-3 3/8"

VISITING TEAM DUGOUT AREA

3'-0"

TURF

45'-0"

HOME TEAM DUGOUT AREA

3'-0"

90°

HOME

45'-0"

3'-0"

13'-0" R

ON-DECK CIRCLE 5'-0" DIA.

CATCHER'S BOX

37'-0"

37'-0"

GRANDSTANDS OR FENCE LIMITS 60'-0" FROM BASE OR FOUL LINE

60'-0" R

BACKSTOP LINE

NOTE

This information is for preliminary planning and design only. For final layouts and design, investigate current rules and regulations of the athletic organization or other authority whose standards will govern.

ORIENTATION

No standard—consider time of day for games; months when played; location of field, surrounding buildings and stands. East-northeast recommended by NCAA (home plate to center field).

BASEBALL FIELD

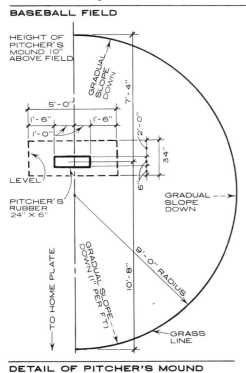

HEIGHT OF PITCHER'S MOUND 10" ABOVE FIELD

GRADUAL SLOPE DOWN

7'-4"

5'-0"

1'-6"

1'-6"

2'-0"

1'-0"

34"

LEVEL

6"

PITCHER'S RUBBER 24" × 6"

GRADUAL SLOPE DOWN

GRADUAL SLOPE DOWN (1" PER FT)

9'-0" RADIUS

TO HOME PLATE

10'-8"

GRASS LINE

DETAIL OF PITCHER'S MOUND

5 3/32" DIAMETER

3 13/16" DIAMETER

3 1/2" DIAMETER

SOFTBALL

2 13/16" TO 2 29/32" DIAMETER

BASEBALL

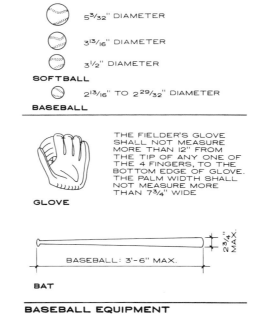

THE FIELDER'S GLOVE SHALL NOT MEASURE MORE THAN 12" FROM THE TIP OF ANY ONE OF THE 4 FINGERS, TO THE BOTTOM EDGE OF GLOVE. THE PALM WIDTH SHALL NOT MEASURE MORE THAN 7 3/4" WIDE

GLOVE

2 3/4" MAX.

BASEBALL: 3'-6" MAX.

BAT

BASEBALL EQUIPMENT

1'-3"

1'-3"

1ST AND 3RD

1'-3"

BASE LINES

7 1/2"

2ND

BASES

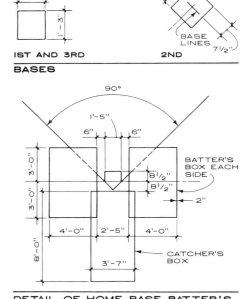

90°

1'-5"

6"

6"

3'-0"

8 1/2"

3'-0"

8 1/2"

2"

4'-0"

2'-5"

4'-0"

8'-0"

3'-7"

BATTER'S BOX EACH SIDE

CATCHER'S BOX

DETAIL OF HOME BASE BATTER'S AND CATCHER'S BOX

Richard J. Vitullo; Washington Grove, Maryland

NOTES

Base lines should be level; if the diamond must pitch, the slope should not be more than 2 percent from third to first base, or vice versa. The minimum slope on turf areas outside the skinned area is 1 percent when there is good subsoil drainage, 2.5 percent when drainage is poor.

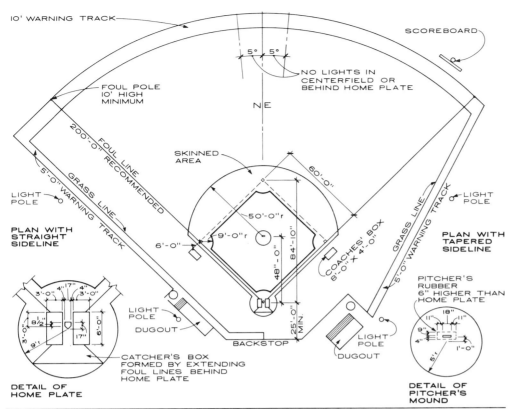

PLAN OF LITTLE LEAGUE BASEBALL FIELD

- 10' WARNING TRACK
- SCOREBOARD
- 5° 5°
- NO LIGHTS IN CENTERFIELD OR BEHIND HOME PLATE
- NE
- FOUL POLE 10' HIGH MINIMUM
- SKINNED AREA
- 200'-0" RECOMMENDED
- FOUL LINE
- 5'-0" WARNING TRACK
- GRASS LINE
- LIGHT POLE
- 60'-0"
- 50'-0" r
- 9'-0" r
- 6'-0"
- 48'-0"
- 84'-0"
- COACHES' BOX 8'-0" X 4'-0"
- 25'-0" MIN.
- BACKSTOP
- GRASS LINE
- 5'-0" WARNING TRACK
- LIGHT POLE
- PLAN WITH TAPERED SIDELINE
- PITCHER'S RUBBER 6" HIGHER THAN HOME PLATE
- LIGHT POLE
- DUGOUT
- LIGHT POLE
- DUGOUT
- PLAN WITH STRAIGHT SIDELINE
- 3'-0" 4" 17" 4" 3'-0"
- 8½"
- 3'-0"
- 9'r
- 17"
- 6'-0"
- LIGHT POLE
- DUGOUT
- CATCHER'S BOX FORMED BY EXTENDING FOUL LINES BEHIND HOME PLATE
- DETAIL OF HOME PLATE
- 11" 18" 11"
- 9"
- 4"
- 1'-0"
- 5'
- DETAIL OF PITCHER'S MOUND

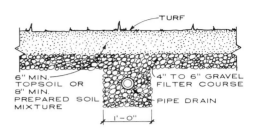

SECTION OF TURF AND SUBSOIL DRAIN

- TURF
- 6" MIN. TOPSOIL OR 8" MIN. PREPARED SOIL MIXTURE
- 4" TO 6" GRAVEL FILTER COURSE
- PIPE DRAIN
- 1'-0"

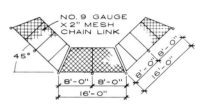

PLAN

- NO. 9 GAUGE X 2" MESH CHAIN LINK
- 45°
- 8'-0" 8'-0" 8'-0" 8'-0"
- 16'-0" 16'-0"

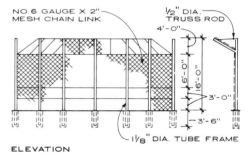

ELEVATION

SOFTBALL BACKSTOP

- NO. 6 GAUGE X 2" MESH CHAIN LINK
- ½" DIA. TRUSS ROD
- 4'-0"
- 6'-0" 16'-0"
- 3'-0"
- 3'-6"
- 1⅛" DIA. TUBE FRAME

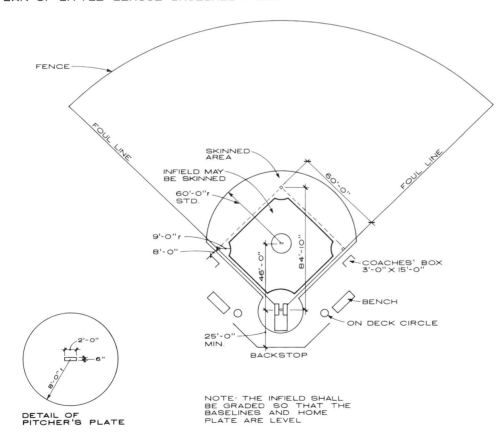

PLAN OF SOFTBALL FIELD

- FENCE
- FOUL LINE
- SKINNED AREA
- INFIELD MAY BE SKINNED
- 60'-0" r STD.
- 9'-0" r
- 8'-0"
- 60'-0"
- 46'-0"
- 84'-0"
- FOUL LINE
- COACHES' BOX 3'-0" X 15'-0"
- BENCH
- ON DECK CIRCLE
- 25'-0" MIN.
- BACKSTOP
- 2'-0"
- 6"
- 8'-0"
- DETAIL OF PITCHER'S PLATE
- NOTE: THE INFIELD SHALL BE GRADED SO THAT THE BASELINES AND HOME PLATE ARE LEVEL

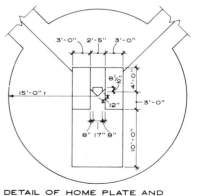

DETAIL OF HOME PLATE AND CATCHER'S BOX

- 3'-0" 2'-5" 3'-0"
- 8½"
- 4'-0"
- 15'-0" r
- 12"
- 3'-0"
- 8" 17" 8"
- 10'-0"

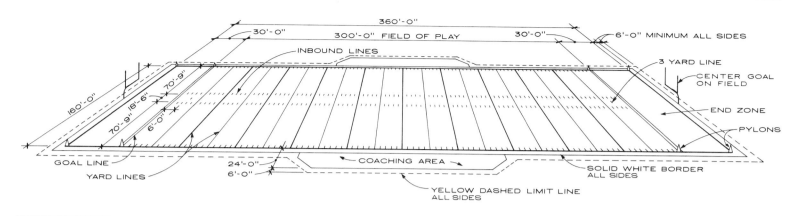

FOOTBALL - NATIONAL FOOTBALL LEAGUE (NFL)

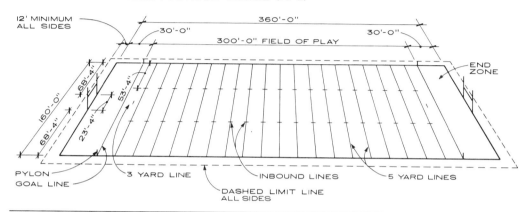

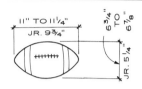

FOOTBALL

FOOTBALL - NATIONAL COLLEGIATE ATHLETIC ASSOCIATION (NCAA)

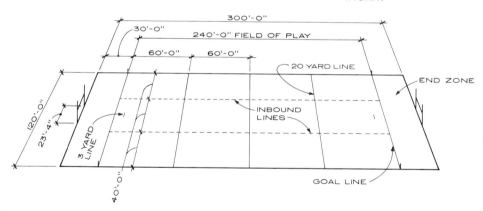

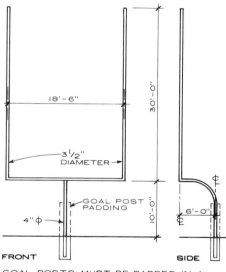

GOAL POSTS MUST BE PADDED IN A MANNER PRESCRIBED BY THE LEAGUE
GOAL POSTS (NFL)

TOUCH AND FLAG FOOTBALL

PROFESSIONAL FOOTBALL (NFL)

The playing field is 360 ft. long by 160 ft. wide. Preferred orientation is with long axis northwest-southeast with no recommended slope. (For further information, contact the NFL.) All lines are 4 in. wide except the goal lines and yellow lines, which are 8 in. wide. All lines are marked with a nontoxic material.

The football, a prolate spheroid with a long axis of 11 in. to 11¼ in., weighs from 14 oz. to 15 oz.

NCAA FOOTBALL

The playing field is 300 ft. long by 160 ft. wide with an additional 12 ft. allowed for on all sides. Preferred orientation is with the long axis northwest-southeast. Grading of the field should be from the centerline. Subsoil drainage may be necessary. All field dimension lines are 4 in. wide,

and are marked with a white, nontoxic material. All measurements are from the wide edge of lines marking boundaries. End zone marking should not overlap goal lines, side lines, and end lines. Location of inbound lines is 53 ft. 4 in. for college football. Marks should be 4 in. wide by 2 ft. long.

TOUCH AND FLAG FOOTBALL

The playing field is 300 ft. long by 120 ft. wide with an additional 6 ft. allowed for on all sides. Preferred orientation is for the long axis to run northwest-southeast. The recommended slope of 1 percent for proper drainage should run away from each side of the center long axis. All measurements are from the inside edge of the lines, which are 4 in. wide and are marked with a white, nontoxic material.

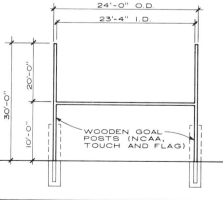

GOAL POSTS

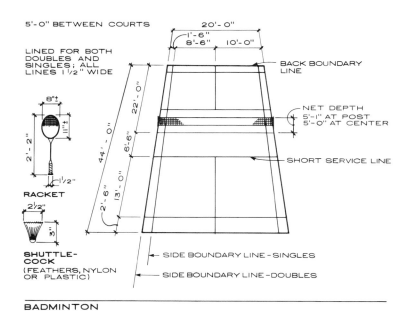

5'-0" BETWEEN COURTS

LINED FOR BOTH
DOUBLES AND
SINGLES; ALL
LINES 1½" WIDE

20'-0"

1'-6"
8'-6"   10'-0"

BACK BOUNDARY
LINE

NET DEPTH
5'-1" AT POST
5'-0" AT CENTER

SHORT SERVICE LINE

8"±
11"±
2'-2"
1½"

RACKET

2½"
3"

**SHUTTLE-
COCK**
(FEATHERS, NYLON
OR PLASTIC)

44'-0"   22'-0"   6'-6"   13'-0"   2'-6"

SIDE BOUNDARY LINE—SINGLES

SIDE BOUNDARY LINE—DOUBLES

BADMINTON

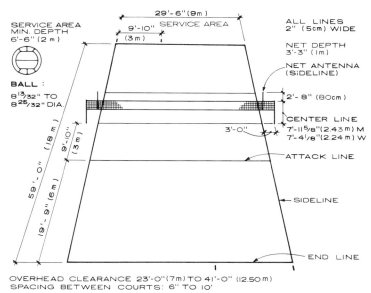

SERVICE AREA
MIN. DEPTH
6'-6" (2 m)

29'-6" (9m)
9'-10"   SERVICE AREA
(3 m)

ALL LINES
2" (5cm) WIDE

NET DEPTH
3'-3" (1m)

NET ANTENNA
(SIDELINE)

2'-8" (80cm)

CENTER LINE

3'-0"   7'-11⅝"(2.43m) M
7'-4⅛"(2.24m) W

ATTACK LINE

SIDELINE

END LINE

BALL :
8¹³⁄₃₂" TO
8²⁵⁄₃₂" DIA.

59'-0" (18m)   9'-10" (3m)   19'-9" (6m)

OVERHEAD CLEARANCE 23'-0"(7m) TO 41'-0" (12.50m)
SPACING BETWEEN COURTS: 6" TO 10'

VOLLEYBALL

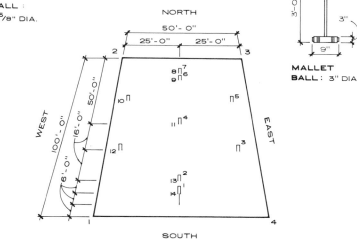

1'-5½"
8½"
9"

RACKET
BALL : PUNCTURED
TENNIS
BALL

20'-0"
10'-0"

ALL LINES
2" WIDE

NET HEIGHT
2'-7" AT POST
2'-6" AT CENTER

POST 1'-6" AWAY
FROM SIDELINE

SIDELINE

SERVICE LINE

BASELINE

50'-0"   25'-0"   22'-0"   3'-0"

SPACE BEHIND EACH BASELINE TO BACK FENCE : 15'-0" MIN.
SPACE FROM EACH SIDELINE TO SIDE FENCE : 10'-0" MIN.
FENCE SHALL BE 8'-0" HIGH UNLESS OTHERWISE NOTED

PADDLE   TENNIS

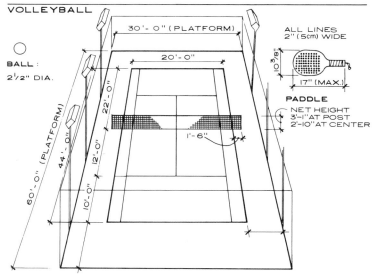

30'-0" (PLATFORM)
20'-0" (PLATFORM)

ALL LINES
2" (5cm) WIDE

10⅜"
17" (MAX.)

PADDLE

NET HEIGHT
3'-1" AT POST
2'-10" AT CENTER

BALL :
2½" DIA.

60'-0" (PLATFORM)   44'-0"   22'-0"   12'-0"   10'-0"   1'-6"

PLATFORM   TENNIS

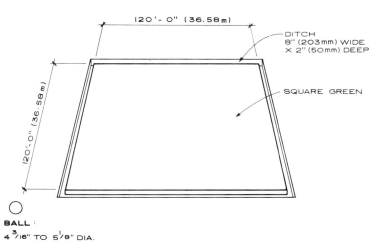

BALL :
3⅝" DIA.

NORTH

50'-0"
25'-0"   25'-0"

2   3

8⌐7
9⌐6

10⌐   ⌐5

11⌐4

12⌐   ⌐3

13⌐2
14⌐1

WEST   EAST

100'-0"   50'-0"   6'-0"   6'-0"

1   4

SOUTH

3'-0"
3"
9"

MALLET
BALL : 3" DIA.

CROQUET

120'-0" (36.58m)

DITCH
8" (203mm) WIDE
X 2" (50mm) DEEP

SQUARE GREEN

120'-0" (36.58m)

BALL :
4³⁄₁₆" TO 5⅛" DIA.

LAWN   BOWLING

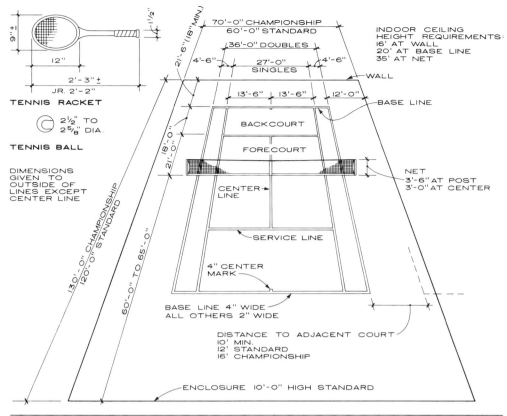

TENNIS RACKET

TENNIS BALL

2½" TO
2⅝" DIA.

DIMENSIONS
GIVEN TO
OUTSIDE OF
LINES EXCEPT
CENTER LINE

70'-0" CHAMPIONSHIP
60'-0" STANDARD
36'-0" DOUBLES
27'-0" SINGLES
4'-6"   4'-6"

INDOOR CEILING
HEIGHT REQUIREMENTS:
16' AT WALL
20' AT BASE LINE
35' AT NET

WALL

BASE LINE

13'-6"   13'-6"   12'-0"

BACKCOURT

FORECOURT

CENTER
LINE

NET
3'-6" AT POST
3'-0" AT CENTER

SERVICE LINE

4" CENTER
MARK

BASE LINE 4" WIDE
ALL OTHERS 2" WIDE

DISTANCE TO ADJACENT COURT
10' MIN.
12' STANDARD
16' CHAMPIONSHIP

130'-0" CHAMPIONSHIP
120'-0" STANDARD

60'-0" TO 65'-0"

ENCLOSURE 10'-0" HIGH STANDARD

TENNIS COURT

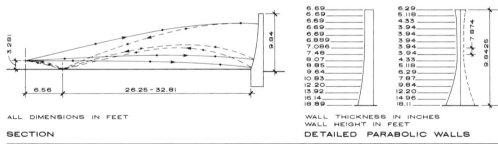

ALL DIMENSIONS IN FEET

3.281   9.84

6.56   26.25 - 32.81

SECTION

PRACTICE COURT

6.69	6.29
6.69	5.118
6.69	4.33
6.69	3.94
6.69	3.94
6.889	3.94
7.086	3.94
7.48	3.94
8.07	4.33
8.85	5.118
9.64	6.29
10.83	7.87
12.20	9.84
13.92	12.20
16.14	14.96
18.89	18.11

7.874   9.8425

WALL THICKNESS IN INCHES
WALL HEIGHT IN FEET

DETAILED PARABOLIC WALLS

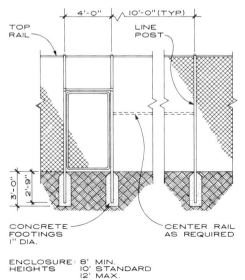

TOP
RAIL

LINE
POST

4'-0"   10'-0" (TYP.)

CONCRETE
FOOTINGS
1" DIA.

CENTER RAIL
AS REQUIRED

ENCLOSURE: 8' MIN.
HEIGHTS   10' STANDARD
            12' MAX.

ELEVATION OF ENCLOSURE

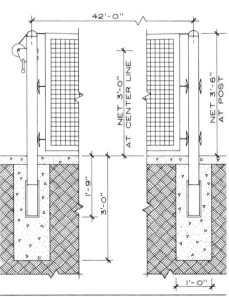

42'-0"

NET 3'-0"
AT CENTER LINE

NET 3'-6"
AT POST

1'-9"

3'-0"

1'-0"

TENNIS POSTS

ORIENTATION

For the northern states the north-south orientation is recommended. North-northwest by south-southeast at approximately 22° (true north) is recommended for outdoor courts south of the 41st parallel. Particular site characteristics, length of tennis season, and latitude should be taken into consideration when deciding on the most desirable court orientation angle.

NOTES

1. SURFACE DRAINAGE: Pitch 1 in. per 10 ft for porous and nonporous courts. Each court should be in one plane and pitch side to side; never up or down to middle court.
2. SUBSOIL DRAINAGE: Need for drainage systems depends on soil conditions.

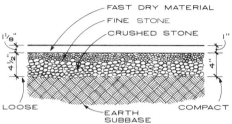

FAST DRY MATERIAL
FINE STONE
CRUSHED STONE

1⅛"   1"
4½"   4"

LOOSE   EARTH   COMPACT
         SUBBASE

FAST-DRYING SURFACE

Fast-drying courts are successive layers of crushed green stone or burnt brick and finely ground rock particles mixed with a chemical binder. This surface provides a uniform bounce and allows sliding. A sprinkler system, frequent maintenance, and annual resurfacing are recommended.

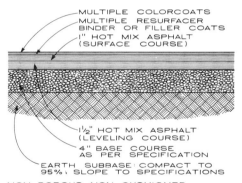

MULTIPLE COLORCOATS
MULTIPLE RESURFACER
BINDER OR FILLER COATS
1" HOT MIX ASPHALT
(SURFACE COURSE)

1½" HOT MIX ASPHALT
(LEVELING COURSE)
4" BASE COURSE
AS PER SPECIFICATION
EARTH SUBBASE: COMPACT TO
95%; SLOPE TO SPECIFICATIONS

NON-POROUS NON-CUSHIONED SURFACE

Hot mix asphalt is a mixture of asphalt and aggregate laid in place and compacted before cooling. This surface is laid on a 4 in. base of stone, gravel or perforated macadam, depending on soil conditions.

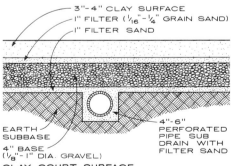

3"-4" CLAY SURFACE
1" FILTER (1/16"-1/4" GRAIN SAND)
1" FILTER SAND

EARTH
SUBBASE
4" BASE
(1/8"-1" DIA. GRAVEL)

4"-6"
PERFORATED
PIPE SUB
DRAIN WITH
FILTER SAND

CLAY COURT SURFACE

Clay courts are constructed on a system of open drain tiles overlaid by a bed of gravel sandwiched between two filter layers of sand or fine gravel, and topped by a thick (3 in.-4 in.) layer of clay. A clay surface also allows sliding and a uniform bounce.

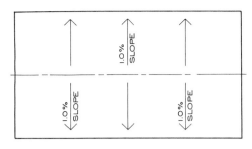

PREFERRED GRADING

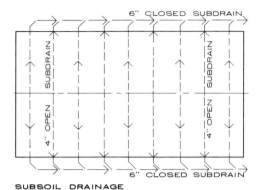

SUBSOIL DRAINAGE

RECTANGULAR SPORTS FIELDS

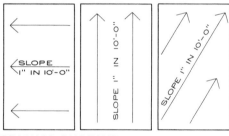

DRAINAGE DIAGRAMS

SPORTS COURTS

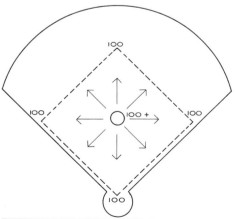

BASEBALL, SOFTBALL DIAMONDS

NOTE

It is preferable that the base lines be level. If the diamond must pitch, the average slope shall be 2.0% from first base to third base or vice versa.

The minimum slope for drainage on turf areas outside the skinned area is 1.0% when adequate subsoil drainage is provided. The maximum is 2.5%.

Sheryl Maletic; Tomblinson Harburn Associates; Flint, Michigan
J. Paul Raeder; Beckett Raeder Rankin, Inc.; Ann Arbor, Michigan
Lawrence Cook & Associates; Falls Church, Virginia

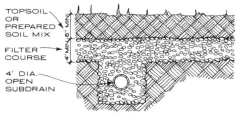

NATURAL TURF

SAND CLAY

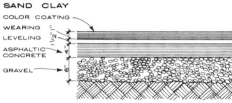

BITUMINOUS CONCRETE

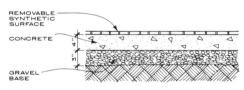

SYNTHETIC SURFACE

PLAYING SURFACES

TYPICAL GRADING AND DRAINAGE DETAILS

COURT SURFACES

Paved playing surfaces should be in one plane and pitched from side to side, end to end, or corner to corner diagonally, instead of in two planes pitched to or from the net. Minimum slope should be 1 in. in 10 ft. Subgrade should slope in the same direction as the surface. Perimeter drains may be provided for paved areas. Underdrains are not recommended beneath paved areas.

PLAYING FIELDS

Preferred grading for rectangular field is a longitudinal crown with 1% slope from center to each side.

Grading may be from side to side or corner to corner diagonally if conditions do not permit the preferred grading.

Subsoil drainage is to slope in the same direction as the surface. Subdrains and filter course are to be used only when subsoil conditions require. Where subsoil drainage is necessary, the spacing of subdrains is dependent on local soil conditions and rainfall.

Subdrains are to have a minimum gradient of 0.15%.

Baseball and softball fields should be graded so that the bases are level.

LINE PAINTING

All line markings should be acrylic water base paint only. Oil base or traffic paints crack, craze, or peel. Spray painting usually is used. High quality courts should be hand painted. Accuracy of track layouts should be verified by registered land surveyor.

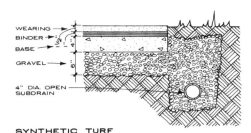

SYNTHETIC TURF

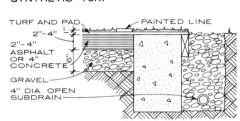

FABRIC TYPE ARTIFICIAL TURF WITH ASPHALT OR CONCRETE BASE

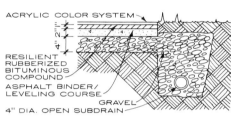

RUBBERIZED ASPHALT SURFACE

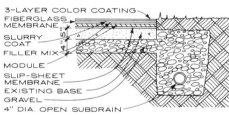

RESURFACING ASPHALT COLOR SYSTEM

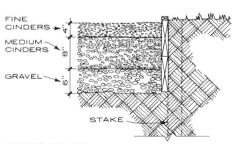

CINDER TRACK

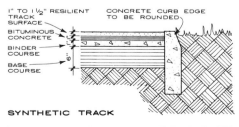

SYNTHETIC TRACK

EDGE CONDITIONS

OUTDOOR SPORTS

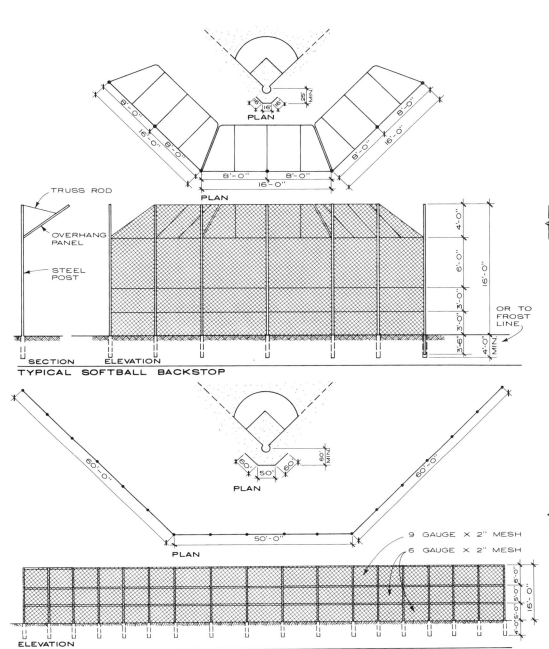

PLAN

PLAN

TRUSS ROD

OVERHANG PANEL

STEEL POST

SECTION   ELEVATION

TYPICAL SOFTBALL BACKSTOP

9 GAUGE × 2" MESH

6 GAUGE × 2" MESH

PLAN

ELEVATION

REGULATION BASEBALL BACKSTOP

BASKETBALL STANDARDS

Backboard support shall have minimum overhang of 4 ft for NCAA with a minimum post diameter of 3½ in. O.D.

Regulation AAU, 5 ft 5 in. overhang, and optional NCAA 4 ft to 6 ft overhang also require a minimum post diameter of 4½ in. O.D.

Footing is to be concrete with a minimum 2 ft diameter and 4 ft depth.

Method of bracing and backboard support varies with manufacturer.

BACKSTOP SIZE AND DIMENSION

Height and width of baseball backstops are to be determined by sports authorities and local requirements.

PIPE SIZES

Posts for backstop heights up to 16 ft: use 3 in. O.D.

Posts for backstop heights 18 ft to 24 ft: use 4 in. O.D.

Top, intermediate, and bottom rails: 1⅝ in. O.D.

WIRE MESH FABRIC

Fabric shall be chain link with galvanized coating or aluminized. (Optional polyvinyl chloride coated steel.)

J. Paul Raeder; Beckett Raeder Rankin, Inc.; Ann Arbor, Michigan
Lawrence Cook & Associates; Falls Church, Virginia

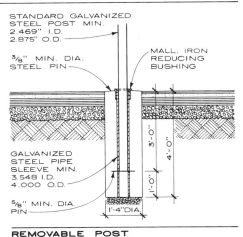

STANDARD GALVANIZED STEEL POST MIN. 2.469" I.D. 2.875" O.D.

MALL. IRON REDUCING BUSHING

⅜" MIN. DIA. STEEL PIN

GALVANIZED STEEL PIPE SLEEVE MIN. 3.548 I.D. 4.000 O.D.

⅝" MIN. DIA. PIN

1'-4" DIA.

REMOVABLE POST

All ferrous metal parts are to be hot dip galvanized after fabrication.

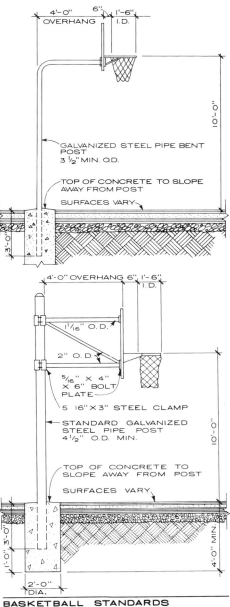

4'-0" OVERHANG   6"   1'-6" I.D.

GALVANIZED STEEL PIPE BENT POST 3½" MIN. O.D.

TOP OF CONCRETE TO SLOPE AWAY FROM POST

SURFACES VARY

4'-0" OVERHANG 6" 1'-6" I.D.

1 1/16" O.D.

2" O.D.

5/16" × 4" × 6" BOLT PLATE

5 16"×3" STEEL CLAMP

STANDARD GALVANIZED STEEL PIPE POST 4½" O.D. MIN.

TOP OF CONCRETE TO SLOPE AWAY FROM POST

SURFACES VARY

2'-0" DIA.

BASKETBALL STANDARDS

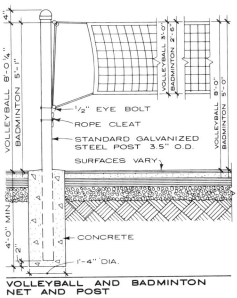

VOLLEYBALL 8'-0¼"
BADMINTON 5'-1"

VOLLEYBALL 3'-0"
BADMINTON 2'-6"

VOLLEYBALL 8'-0"
BADMINTON 5'-0"

½" EYE BOLT

ROPE CLEAT

STANDARD GALVANIZED STEEL POST 3.5" O.D.

SURFACES VARY

CONCRETE

1'-4" DIA.

VOLLEYBALL AND BADMINTON NET AND POST

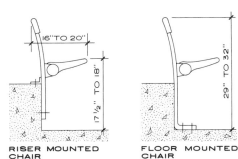
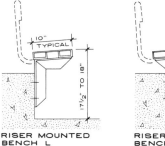
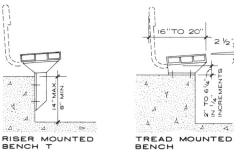
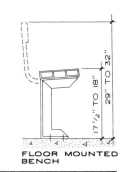

RISER MOUNTED CHAIR   FLOOR MOUNTED CHAIR   RISER MOUNTED BENCH L   RISER MOUNTED BENCH T   TREAD MOUNTED BENCH   FLOOR MOUNTED BENCH

STANDARD SEATS AND SEAT SUPPORTS

SEATING CAPACITY

Allow 18 in. of bleacher length per person per row. Normal aisle width of 36 in. reduces seating capacity by two seats per row x number of rows x number of aisles. See table below.

SAFETY AREAS

1. BASEBALL FIELDS: Minimum 60 ft from seating to foul line or baseline at each side of home plate.
2. SOFTBALL FIELDS: Minimum 25 ft from seating to foul line or baseline at each side of home plate.
3. BASKETBALL COURTS: Minimum 6 ft from seating to court sides, 8 in. minimum to court ends.
4. SWIMMING POOLS: Minimum 5 ft from seating to pool decks. Spectator area must be separate from pool area to avoid mixing dry and wet traffic.

STADIUM SEATING

Concrete risers and treads with seating attached. See typical seats and seat supports above.

FIXED GRANDSTAND

8 in. rise with 24 in. row spacing typical. Available options include front, end, and back rails, crosswalks, ramps, stairs, aisles, vomitories, closed risers, double foot plates, folding seat backs, and waterproof covers of metal or fiberglass for resurfacing existing wooden bleachers.

PORTABLE BLEACHERS

3, 4, or 5 row sections typical. Transportable options include wheels and trailer attachments. Bleachers of up to 25 rows may be assembled of portable sections.

TELESCOPIC BLEACHERS

1. LOWRISE: 9⅝ in. normal rise for most uses. 22 in. minimum row spacing gives maximum seating capacity. 24 in. spacing gives greater leg room. 30 or 32 in. spacing provides extra passage and leg room space and space for optional folding back rests.
2. HIGHRISE: Models with 11⅝ or 16 in. risers are suggested for pools, balconies, hockey rinks, or similarly difficult viewing situations where seating must be banked more steeply than is normal.

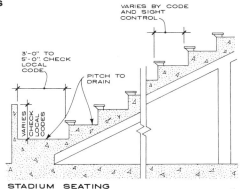

STADIUM SEATING

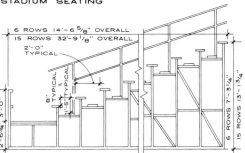

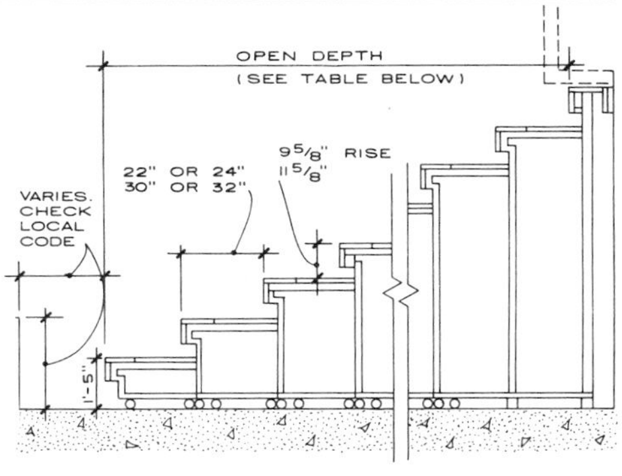

FIXED GRANDSTAND (ELEVATED)

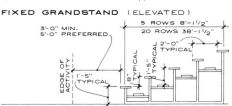

PORTABLE BLEACHERS

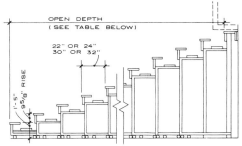

TELESCOPIC BLEACHERS (HIGHRISE)

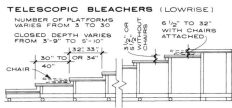

TELESCOPIC BLEACHERS (LOWRISE)

TELESCOPIC PLATFORM

SEATING CAPACITY

LENGTH (FT)

ROW	8	12	16	20	24	28	32	36	40
3	16	24	32	40	48	56	64	72	80
4	21	32	42	53	64	74	85	96	106
5	26	40	53	66	80	93	106	120	133
6	32	48	64	80	96	112	128	144	160
7	37	56	74	93	112	130	149	168	186
8	42	64	85	106	128	149	170	192	213
9	48	72	96	120	144	168	192	216	240
10	53	80	106	133	160	186	213	240	266
12	64	96	128	160	192	224	256	288	320
14	74	112	149	186	224	261	298	336	373
16	85	128	170	213	256	298	341	384	426
18	96	144	192	240	288	336	384	432	480
20	106	160	213	266	320	373	426	480	533

NOTE: Consult manufacturers for additional information.

GRANDSTANDS AND BLEACHERS DIMENSIONS

ROW	OPEN DEPTH				9⅝" RISE CLOSED DEPTH		11⅝" AND 16" RISE CLOSED DEPTH	
	22"	24"	30"	32"	22" OR 24"	30" OR 32"	22" OR 24"	30" OR 32"
3	4'-11½"	5'-1½"	6'-3½"	6'-5½"	3'-1 13/16"	3'-9 13/16"	3'-1 13/16"	3'-9 13/16"
4	6'-9½"	7'-1½"	8'-9½"	9'-1½"	3'-2 1/8"	3'-10 1/8"	3'-2 1/8"	3'-10 1/8"
5	8'-7½"	9'-1½"	11'-3½"	11'-9½"	3'-2 7/16"	3'-10 7/16"	3'-2 7/16"	3'-10 7/16"
6	10'-5½"	11'-1½"	13'-9½"	14'-5½"	3'-2¾"	3'-10¾"	3'-2¾"	3'-10¾"
7	12'-3½"	13'-1½"	16'-3½"	17'-1½"	3'-3 1/16"	3'-11 1/16"	3'-3 1/16"	3'-11 1/16"
8	14'-1½"	15'-1½"	18'-9½"	19'-9½"	3'-3 3/8"	3'-11 3/8"	3'-3 3/8"	3'-11 3/8"
9	15'-11½"	17'-1½"	21'-3½"	22'-5½"	3'-3 11/16"	3'-11 11/16"	3'-3 11/16"	3'-11 11/16"
10	17'-9½"	19'-1½"	23'-9½"	25'-1½"	3'-4"	4'-0"	3'-4"	4'-0"
12	21'-5½"	23'-1½"	28'-9½"	30'-5½"	3'-4 5/8"	4'-0 5/8"	3'-4 5/8"	4'-0 5/8"
14	25'-1½"	27'-1½"	33'-9½"	35'-9½"	3'-5¼"	4'-1¼"	NOTE: For 11⅝" rise of 18 or more rows and 16" rise of 13 or more rows check with manufacturer for modified closed depth dimensions.	
16	28'-9½"	31'-1½"	38'-9½"	41'-1½"	3'-5 7/8"	4'-1 7/8"		
18	32'-5½"	35'-1½"	43'-9½"	46'-5½"	3'-6½"	4'-2½"		
20	36'-1½"	39'-1½"	48'-9½"	51'-9½"	3'-7 1/8"	4'-3 1/8"		

Erik Johnson; Lawrence Cook & Associates; Falls Church, Virginia
David W. Johnson; Washington, D.C.

FACTORS INFLUENCING DESIGN

The layout of circulation routes for spectators is affected by the means of egress requirements in leading standards and model building codes. Changes to these standards and codes were based on recommendations developed in 1985 by the Board for Coordination of Model Codes (BCMC) and by committees responsible for National Fire Protection Association (NFPA) standards (particularly NFPA 101-1988 and NFPA 102-1986).

These changes, whether or not reflected in the legal requirements establishing the standards or codes in a particular area, provide a good technical base for using alternative methods of circulation route planning. Incorporating these changes in the planning process requires a firm grasp of underlying principles and would benefit from assistance from a consultant.

Improved design standards for spectator circulation are a result of growing sensitivity to environmental quality and accidents which are sometimes followed by litigation.

MORE FLEXIBLE EGRESS RULES FOR LARGE BUILDINGS

Changes introduced in NFPA 102-1986 provide flexible egress requirements for open-air or enclosed spectator facilities in larger buildings that qualify as ''smoke-protected assembly seating.'' They address the longer egress time that may be acceptable because of greater control of fire hazards, higher ceilings that keep smoke from blocking egress routes, and similar more flexible rules.

Flexibility in egress requirements also may be applicable in intermediate-sized facilities other than large stadia and arenas. Egress requirements may differ by a factor of five, depending on facility size. Generally, to be treated as smoke-protected assembly seating, all hazards—not only fire—must be addressed. Also, a ''life safety evaluation'' must be conducted which is acceptable to the authority having jurisdiction. Expert advice on life and fire safety engineering should be retained for a life safety evaluation.

AISLES

Requirements governing provision of aisles in bleacher seating have, in many cases, been made more stringent. For example, NFPA 102-1986 extended aisle requirements. Some bleacher seating formerly permitted to be without aisles must now be provided with aisles. Missteps and falls, plus normal inconvenience to patrons, are more likely to occur on surfaces serving as seating rather than on designated aisles.

LOCATION OF AISLES

Liberalized requirements for locating aisles reinterpret such traditional principles as the following.

Path redundancy: Except for travel over short distances, as in a short row of seats served by only one aisle, all spectators must have a choice of at least two egress routes from their seat.

Common path of travel along a row of seats served by a single aisle usually should not exceed 30 ft (9 m) to the point where there are two paths of egress.

Common path of travel or dead end in an aisle often will be compensated for by the path redundancy of the rows of seats served by such aisles at each end of the rows. Blockage of one aisle simply means that spectator movement occurs along rows to the next aisle (and on to the next if necessary). Beyond general limits, noted below, the length and spacing of rows providing such alternative routes may be regulated as follows.

For facilities not providing smoke-protected assembly seating, requirements may call for:

1. Rows to be no longer than 25 seats
2. 12 in. (305 mm) clear width between rows plus 0.6 in. (15 mm) for each additional seat beyond 7 in the row.

For facilities providing smoke-protected assembly seating, requirements may be relaxed to permit:

1. Rows to be no longer than 40 seats
2. 12 in. (305 mm) clear width between rows plus 0.3 in. (8 mm) for each additional seat beyond 14 in the row.

Minimum clear widths: Building upon a principle established with the rules for continental seating, changes in rules for minimum clearances between seat rows and maximum number of seats per row may allow rows to contain up to 100 seats if served by aisles at both ends. Rules on common path of travel (dead ends) limit other aisles to 30–50 ft (9–15 m) lengths. Row length and spacing are interrelated; longer rows require greater clearance between rows:

1. 12 in. (303 mm) plus 0.3 in. (8 mm) for each seat beyond 14 in a row served by two aisles
2. 12 in. (305 mm) plus 0.6 in. (15 mm) for each seat beyond 7 in a row served by only one aisle.

Seat row length limits, beyond which increased spacing is required, may be increased by as much as 50% for larger facilities providing smoke-protected assembly seating.

AISLE WIDTH

Aisle width also may be subject to newer minimums that take greater account of whether steps are used. Aisle stairs should be:

1. 48 in. (1220 mm) wide at treads and between seats to either side
2. 36 in. (910 mm) wide at treads and clear with seats to one side only
3. If serving five or fewer rows on one side of a handrail, the clear width only is required to be 23 in. (584 mm).

Width for capacity: Changes in the way egress capacity is credited allow more flexibility in aisle width calculation, with small increments in width adding to egress capacity.

1. Level or ramped routes should provide at least 0.2 in. (5 mm) of clear width per person
2. Aisle stairs should provide at least 0.3 in. (8 mm) of clear width per person. Handrails can be within this clear width and should be provided in this case
3. Aisle stairs with risers higher than 7 in. (178 mm) decrease efficiency and safety, requiring the width per person to be increased by 2% for each extra 0.1 in. (3 mm) of height. The maximum height of 9 in. (229 mm), however, is permitted only if sightlines dictate steep seating decks and aisles.

Smoke-protected assembly seating in intermediate-sized and larger buildings may have reduced width requirements for capacity. Depending on the code in use, the incremental widths noted above may be reduced by a factor of five for the largest facilities with intermediate width increments applying, on a sliding scale, to intermediate-sized ones.

AISLE DETAILS

Handrails are increasingly required on all aisle stairs. Such aisles are subject to all the hazards of stairs in addition to flight lengths, step geometry, use conditions, and profusion of visual distraction. Prudent design calls for functional handrails on all stairs, including aisle stairs and moderately sloped stairs in lower-level seating areas. Ramped aisles also can benefit from handrails and may be a code requirement.

Handrails in the middle of aisles should have gaps every 3 to 5 rows, allowing people to move to the other side of the aisle. Height should be as high as sightlines permit. An intermediate height handrail should be provided for children and to deter people from ducking under the rail. Handrails should be finished with a light or reflective color to reduce heating in full sun.

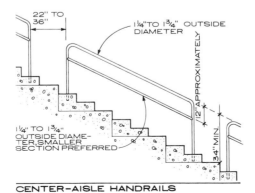

CENTER-AISLE HANDRAILS

STEP DETAILS

Contrary to much traditional practice, all treads within an aisle stair must be uniform in size. Single or double intermediate steps between seating platforms must not be made smaller so that a larger area is available at the seating platform for entry to and egress from rows. Entry and egress is not compromised by making all steps similar. Safety, as well as comfortable movement along the aisle, is seriously reduced by varying tread size.

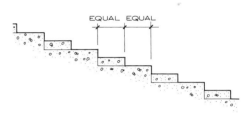

AISLE STAIR TREAD UNIFORMITY

Often overlooked during the planning of spectator facilities is the proper design and placement of seating platforms and infill steps forming the aisles. Dimensional nonuniformities between steps should be kept under 3/16 in. (5 mm) between steps. Faulty workmanship and inspection may result in a spectator's fall and subsequent litigation. Step dimensions and all other aspects of aisle design should adhere to general principles of stair safety: a tread (run) of at least 11 in. (279 mm) and riser heights of over 4 in. (100 mm), but not more than 7 in. (178 mm). Tread depth is the most important dimension. Compromises forced by sightlines and resulting steep seating decks are more acceptable in the height of risers. Codes may permit aisle stair risers to be up to 9 in. (229 mm) high.

Tread nosing marking: Stair visibility, particularly for descent, is especially critical in the complex visual settings found in spectator seating facilities. All treads should be marked with a contrasting marking stripe, 1–2 in. (25–51 mm) wide at the nosing. For concrete treads, special durable coatings such as epoxy are available that have a slip-resistant surface. These coatings, similar to concrete, have a good surface for slip resistance when not too highly finished. Chemically treating carpet produces a durable marking stripe. Nosing caps and tapes can be tripping hazards, may work loose, and are not recommended.

Where adjacent riser heights differ by more than 3/16 in. (5 mm) due to changes in seat deck slope, for improving sightlines, distinctive tread nosing marking should be provided to indicate unavoidable differences in step dimensions. Hazard yellow may be the most appropriate color to use where missteps and falls are likely. Spectators have a right to be warned of dangers.

VOMITORIES VERSUS CROSS AISLES

Cross aisles, unless located with no seating behind them, will invariably cause difficulties with sightlines, spectator circulation, or both. A vomitory, an opening piercing a bank of seats, is a better way of providing access to and egress from an aisle serving seating rows. The key is designing for the minimum number and variety of steps to be negotiated in moving from a seat to a concourse.

Vomitory–aisle configurations are of two common types—symmetrical and nonsymmetrical. The nonsymmetrical type is preferred for minimizing sightline interference for seats located above the vomitory. To optimize spectator flow into the vomitory, the aisle feeding into the vomitory from below should be offset from aisles feeding in from above.

CONSULTANTS

Expert safety guidance should be sought for the following situations:

1. Smoke protected assembly seating
2. Requirement for a life safety evaluation
3. Local codes not based on a current model code
4. Retrofit of existing spectator facilities
5. Seating decks steeper than 33°
6. Serious unavoidable nonuniformities in stairs.

Jake Pauls, Life Safety Specialist; Hughes Associates, Inc.; Wheaton, Maryland

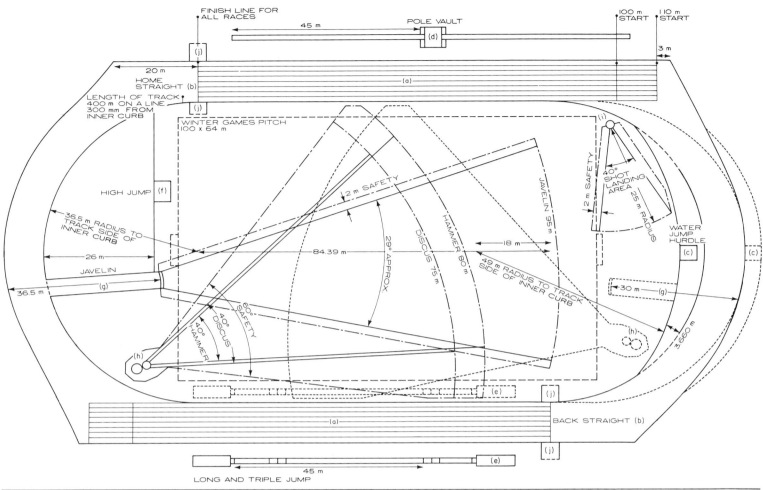

LAYOUT GUIDE FOR 400 m RUNNING TRACK AND FIELD EVENT LOCATIONS

(a) Number of lanes
(b) Straights
(c) Steeplechase and water jump
(d) Pole vault
(e) Long and triple jumps
(f) High jump
(g) Javelin
(h) Hammer and discus in cage
(i) Putting and shot
(j) Paved areas

NATIONAL AND INTERNATIONAL COMPETITION

The diagram indicates how a 400 m track with a synthetic surface might be laid out for national and international competition. Different arrangements are possible to suit particular circumstances. For high level competition, however, alternatives for the siting of the throwing circles are of necessity limited if maximum distances are to be safely thrown. For Rules of Competition reference should be made to the Handbook of the International Amateur Athletic Federation.

TRACK AND LANES

The length of the running track should be not less than 400 m. The track should be not less than 7.32 m in width and should, if possible, be bordered on the inside with concrete or other suitable material, approximately 50 mm high, minimum 50 mm wide. The curb may be raised to permit surface water to drain away, in which case a maximum height of 65 mm must not be exceeded.

Where it is not possible for the inner edge of the running track to have a raised border, the inner edge shall be marked with lines 50 mm wide.

The measurement shall be taken 0.30 m outward from the inner border of the track or, where no border exists, 0.20 m from the line marking the inside of the track.

In all races up to and including 400 m, each competitor shall have a separate lane, with a minimum width

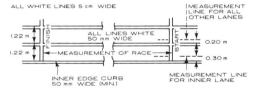

METHOD OF MARKING LANES

of 1.22 m and a maximum width of 1.25 m to be marked by lines 50 mm in width. The inner lane shall be measured as stated in the preceding text, but the remaining lanes shall be measured 0.20 m from the outer edges of the lines.

In international meetings the track should allow for at least six lanes and, where possible, for eight lanes, particularly for major international events.

The maximum allowance for lateral inclination of tracks shall not exceed 1 : 100, and the inclination in the running direction shall not exceed 1 : 1000.

The lateral inclination of the track should wherever possible be toward the inside lane.

SURFACE

Synthetic materials provide a consistently good surface capable of continuous and unlimited use in most weather conditions. Maintenance is minimal, consisting of periodic cleaning by hosing down or brushing, the repainting when necessary of the line markings, and an occasional repair.

Cinder surfaces require considerable maintenance by a skilled groundsman every time a track is used. They are not all-weather and seldom provide a consistently good running surface. They are, however, much cheaper to construct and are suitable for club use and training.

On cinder tracks an extra lane is necessary so that

sprint and hurdle events can be run on the six outer lanes to avoid the inner lane, which is subject to heavy use during long distance events.

ORIENTATION

It is often difficult to reconcile the requirements of wind directions and the need to avoid an approach into the setting sun. For these reasons it is now becoming common practice to provide, where possible, alternative directions for running, jumping, and throwing.

NUMBER OF LANES

Synthetic all-weather:

International competition:	8 lanes (9.76 m)
Area or regional competition:	6 lanes (7.32 m)

Cinder:

International competition:	8 lanes (9.76 m)
	9 lanes (straights)
Area or regional competition:	7 lanes (8.54 m)

THE FINISH

Two white posts shall denote the extremities of the finish line, and shall be placed at least 30 cm from the edge of the track.

The finish posts shall be of rigid construction about 1.4 m high, 80 mm wide, and 20 mm thick.

FORMULA FOR OTHER TRACK PROPORTIONS

Where a track of wider or narrower proportions or of different length is required, the appropriate dimensions can be calculated from the following formula:

$$L = 2P + 2\ (R + 300\ mm)$$

where L = length of track (m)
    P = length of parallels or distance apart of centers of curves (m)
    R = radius to track side of inner curb (m)
    π = 3.1416 (not 22/7)

It is recommended that the radius of the semicircles should not normally be less than 32 m or more than 42 m for a 400 m circuit.

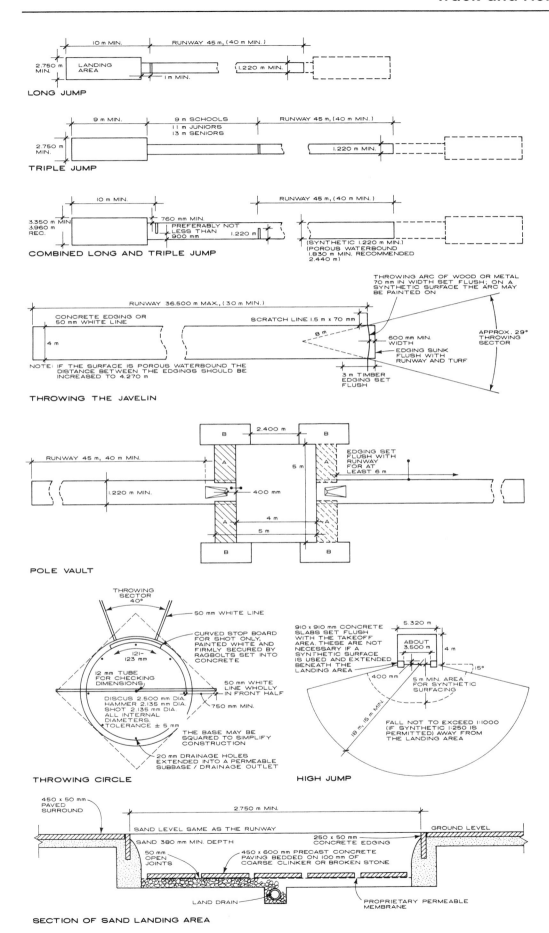

LONG JUMP

TRIPLE JUMP

COMBINED LONG AND TRIPLE JUMP

THROWING THE JAVELIN

NOTE: IF THE SURFACE IS POROUS WATERBOUND THE DISTANCE BETWEEN THE EDGINGS SHOULD BE INCREASED TO 4.270 m.

POLE VAULT

THROWING CIRCLE

HIGH JUMP

SECTION OF SAND LANDING AREA

400 m TRACK AND FIELD EVENTS— CONSTRUCTION DETAILS

These details are based on international standards. For additional information consult the IAAF, which is the International Amateur Athletic Federation. These details were provided by the National Playing Fields Association, London, England.

NOTE

To avoid adverse wind conditions during competition, landing areas for the long and triple jumps are desirable at both ends of the runway. A surround of paving slabs (450 x 600 mm) is an advantage. Takeoff board to be of wood or other suitable rigid material, set level with surface and painted white. See detail.

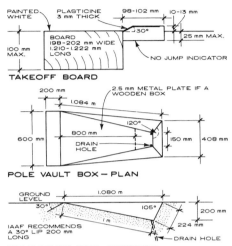

TAKEOFF BOARD

POLE VAULT BOX – PLAN

POLE VAULT BOX – SECTION

POLE VAULT

A = Detachable soft landing units each 1 x 2 m.
B = Concrete platforms each 1 x 2.450 m x 75 mm thick minimum and set level with runway surface.

The soft landing area to be 5 x 5 m minimum. The distance between uprights or extension arms to be 3.660 m minimum/4.370 m maximum. A larger soft landing unit with a 1.300 m extension for the pole vault box cutout giving a total size of 5 x 6.300 m may be provided. The diagram shows a double runway with detachable A units and thus gives a choice of runways according to the wind direction.

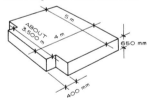

HIGH JUMP SOFT LANDING AREA

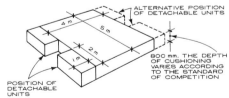

POLE VAULT SOFT LANDING AREA

For outdoor use soft landing units should be laid on duckboards on an ash base or other suitable materials (e.g., precast concrete paving on a porous base with 50 mm open joints).

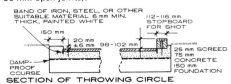

SECTION OF THROWING CIRCLE

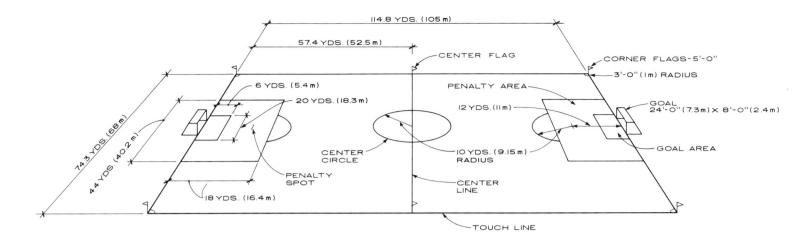

SOCCER - NORTH AMERICAN SOCCER LEAGUE
U.S. SOCCER FEDERATION

SOCCER - NORTH AMERICAN SOCCER LEAGUE
U.S. SOCCER FEDERATION

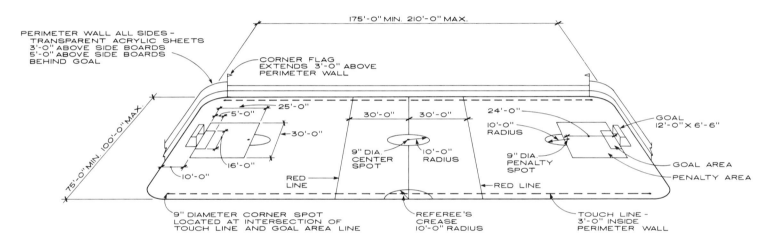

NOTE: OVERALL FIELD DIMENSIONS DEPEND ON AVAILABLE PLAYING SURFACE.

INDOOR SOCCER - MAJOR INDOOR SOCCER LEAGUE

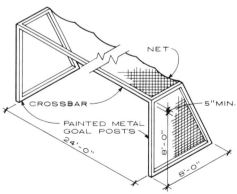

GOAL

The goal posts and crossbar shall not exceed 5 in. nor be less than 4 in. wide and shall present a flat surface to the playing field. The net must be attached to the ground, goal posts, and crossbar. It must extend back and level with the crossbar for 2 ft. 0 in. (.61 M).

SOCCER GOAL

27" (68.58CM) IN CIRCUMFERENCE 14 TO 16 OZ. (453-897 GRAMS)

BALL

The ball's surface has thirty-odd black and white panels that enable the players to estimate its direction and speed of spin.

NOTES AND DEFINITIONS

All dimensions shown are to the inside edge of lines. All lines are to be white and 2 in. wide, except the centerline, which is 5 in. wide.

The long-field orientations in the northern hemisphere should be northwest-southeast for best sun angle during the fall playing season. The preferred drainage is a longitudinal crown with a 1 percent slope from center to each side.

Touchlines are the side boundaries, which are 114 yards (105 M) long.

The centerline is 5 in. (12.7 cm) wide and divides the playing field in half.

The center circle is a 10 yard (9 M) radius from the center of the centerline. At the beginning of each half the ball is kicked off from this circle by one team or the other.

The goal area is the smaller of the two rectangular zones: 20 yards (18.3 M) wide, 6 yards (5.4 M) in front of each goal. Other players can enter the goal area but cannot charge the goalie when he does not have the ball.

The penalty area is the larger of the two rectangular zones: 44 yards (40 M) wide, 18 yards (16.4 M) deep. A major rule infraction in this area allows the other team a penalty kick from the penalty spot.

Refer to rule setting body involved for actual dimensions required. Information shown here is for initial planning only.

Besides all the architectural differences between indoor and outdoor soccer, the natures of the games are deeply contrasted. Refer to the governing bodies, the Major Indoor Soccer League, the U.S. Soccer Federation, the North American Soccer League.

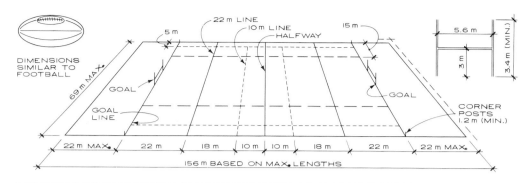

RUGBY

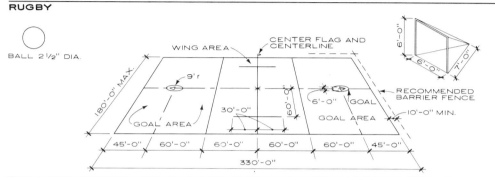

RUGBY

BALL 2½" DIA.

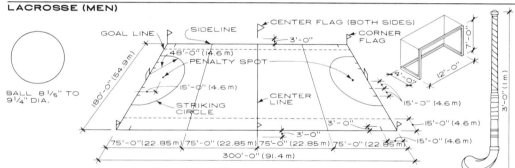

LACROSSE (MEN)

BALL 8⅛" TO 9¼" DIA.

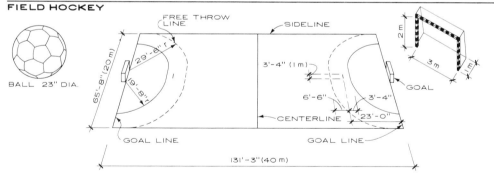

FIELD HOCKEY

BALL 23" DIA.

TEAM HANDBALL

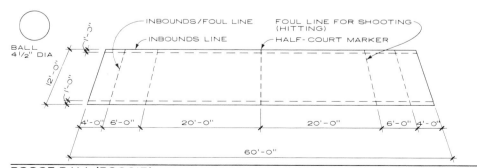

BALL 4½" DIA.

BOCCE BALL (BOCCIE)

RUGBY

The playing field is 156 m x 69 m with an additional 3 m safety zone recommended on all sides. The preferred long axis orientation is northwest–southeast; recommended grading is a 1% slope from each side of the axis. All measurements are from the inside line edges, which are marked with a white, nontoxic material.

MEN'S LACROSSE

The playing field is 330 ft (100.58 m) long and from 160 to 180 ft (48–55m) wide, with an additional 20 ft (60.10 m) recommended on all sides. The preferred long axis orientation is northwest–southeast and preferred drainage is a 1% slope away from each side of the longitudinal axis. All dimensions shown are to the inside of the lines except for the centerline. Lines are 2 in. wide and marked with a white, nontoxic material. Flexible flag markers are placed at each corner and on field sidelines at the centerline.

Diameter of the lacrosse ball is 2½ in.; the stick is 3 ft to 6 ft in length.

Further information is available from the National Collegiate Athletic Association.

FIELD HOCKEY

The playing field is 300 ft (91.4 m) x 180 ft (54.9 m) with an additional 10 ft (3.05 m) safety zone recommended on all sides. The preferred long axis orientation is northwest–southeast. Recommended grading is a 1% slope on each side of the longitudinal axis. All measurements shown are from the inside line edges. Lines are 3 in. wide, and marked with a white, nontoxic material.

The field hockey ball is 8⅛ in. to 9¼ in. (20.8–23.5 cm) in circumference and weighs 5½ oz. (156 g). The stick is 3 ft (1 m) long with a wooden head and cane handle with a cork or rubber insert.

Further information is available from the United States Field Hockey Association.

INDOOR TEAM HANDBALL

The playing field is 131 ft 4 in. (40 m) x 65 ft 8 in. (20 m) with an additional 6 ft (2 m) unobstructed space on all sides. Preferred orientation is northwest–southeast along the longitudinal axis with a 1% slope away from each side of that axis. All dimensions shown are from the inside line edges except the centerline. All lines are 2 in. wide and marked with a white, nontoxic material.

The men's handball is 23 in. (58.4 cm) in circumference and weighs 16 oz. (453.6 g).

BOCCE

The court is 60 ft (18.28 m) x 12 ft (3.65 m). Although orientation is of minor importance, it is preferred that the long axis run north–south. The surface should be flat without slope when it is stone, dust, or clay with adequate underdrainage and 1 percent slope in any direction when turf.

The ball is 4½ in. in diameter and weighs 32 oz.

Further information is available from the International Bocce Association, Inc.

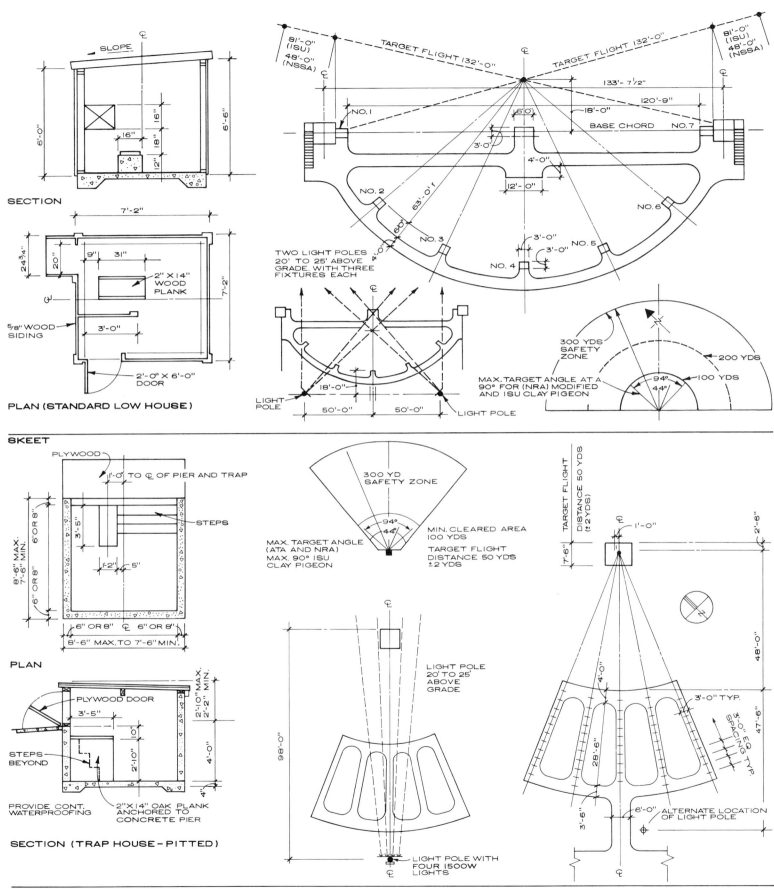

SECTION

PLAN (STANDARD LOW HOUSE)

SKEET

PLAN

SECTION (TRAP HOUSE – PITTED)

TRAP

NOTES

1. The drawings below illustrate the use of a 7-point dimension grid that expresses the minimum desirable dimensions to be used when either specifying or designing a rectangular shaped pool for residential use.
2. Width, length, and depth dimensions may apply to residential pools of any shape.
3. The minimum length with diving board and wading area is 28 ft. The average length of a residential pool is 28 to 40 ft.
4. Standards for residential swimming pools have been published by the National Spa and Pool Institute (1974).

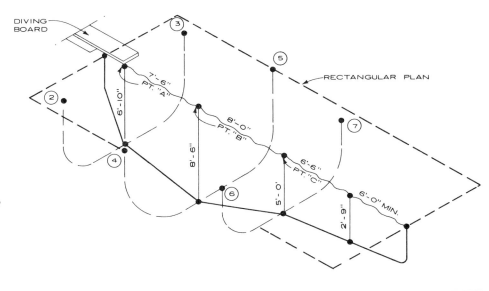

ISOMETRIC OVERLAY VIEW

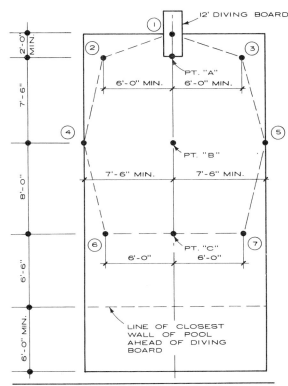

7-POINT GRID DIMENSION PLAN

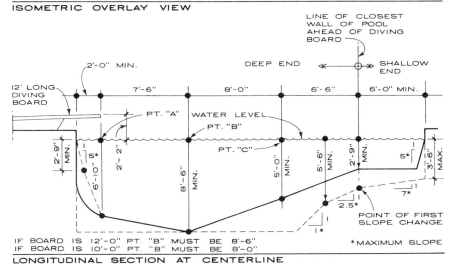

IF BOARD IS 12'-0" PT. "B" MUST BE 8'-6"
IF BOARD IS 10'-0" PT. "B" MUST BE 8'-0"

LONGITUDINAL SECTION AT CENTERLINE

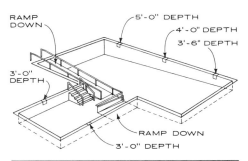

HANDICAPPED POOL ACCESS

Haver, Nunn and Collamer; Phoenix, Arizona

PERMITS AND RESTRICTIONS

Required in most areas from building, health, plumbing, and electrical departments and zoning boards. Check for setback restrictions and easements covering power and telephone lines, sewers, and storm drains.

SITE CONSIDERATIONS

Check the site for the following conditions, each of which will considerably increase the cost.

1. Fill that is more than 3 ft below pool deck.
2. Hard rock that requires drilling and blasting.
3. Underground water or springs that necessitate pumping or drains.
4. Accessibility of the site for mechanical equipment, minimum entry 8 ft wide by 7 ft 8 in. high, with a grade easy enough for a truck to reach the site.
5. Place the pool where it will get the most sun during swimming season. If possible, place deep end so a diver dives away from, not into, the afternoon sun. Avoid overhanging tree branches near the pool.
6. The slope of the site should be as level as possible; a steep slope requires retaining walls for the pool.
7. The surface deck around the pool should be of a slip-resistant surface.
8. A surrounding fence is recommended to protect pool area from unwanted visitors and to prevent accidents.

CONSTRUCTION AND SHAPES

Pools may be made of reinforced concrete (poured on the job, precast, or gunite sprayed), concrete block, steel, aluminum, or plastic with or without block backup. Concrete, aluminum, fiberglass, and steel pools are available in any shape—rectangular, square, kidney, oval or free form. Complete plastic installations and plastic pool liners with various backups are available only in manufacturers' standard shapes and sizes.

A rectangular pool is the most practical if site permits, since it gives the longest swimming distance.

POOL CAPACITY

Rule of thumb: 36 sq ft for each swimmer, 100 sq ft for each diver. A pool of 20 x 40 ft accommodates 14 persons at a time, but since not everyone is in the pool at once, pool and surroundings are adequate for 30 to 40 people.

FILTER REQUIREMENTS

Filter, motor, and electrical equipment shall be sheltered and waterproofed.

GENERAL

Public pools are generally considered to be those that belong to municipalities, schools, country clubs, hotels, motels, apartments, and resorts. Permits for their construction are required in most areas from local and state boards of health as well as the departments of building, plumbing, and electricity.

Community pools should be integrated with existing and projected recreational facilities, such as picnic areas and parks, for maximum usage. Transportation access should be good, and there should be ample parking space. In a hot climate, enough shade should be provided, particularly in the lounging areas, and so located that it can be easily converted to spectator space by erecting bleachers.

POOL DESIGN

Formerly most public pools were designed to meet competitive swimming requirements. The trend today is to provide for all-around use. The following should be considered:

1. Ratio of shallow water to deep water. Formerly 60% of pool area 5 ft deep and less was considered to be adequate. Now 80% is considered more realistic.
2. Ratio of loungers to bathers. Generally, no more than one-third of people attending a public pool are in the water at one time. Consequently the 6 to 8 ft walks formerly surrounding pools and used for lounging have been enlarged so that lounging area now approximates pool size.
3. For capacity formula see "Public Swimming Pool Capacity" diagram on another page.

RECOMMENDED DIMENSIONS

RELATED DIVING EQUIPMENT		MINIMUM DIMENSIONS								MINIMUM WIDTH OF POOL AT:		
MAX. BOARD LENGTH	MAX. HEIGHT OVER WATER	D_1	D_2	R	L_1	L_2	L_3	L_4	L_5	PT. A	PT. B	PT. C
10'	$2/3$ m 26''	2.13 m 7'-0''	2.59 m 8'-6''	1.68 m 5'-6''	0.76 m 2'-6''	2.44 m 8'-0''	3.20 m 10'-6''	2.13 m 7'-0''	8.53 m 28'-0''	4.88 m 16'-0''	5.49 m 18'-0''	5.49 m 18'-0''
12'	$3/4$ m 30''	2.29 m 7'-6''	2.74 m 9'-0''	1.83 m 6'-0''	0.91 m 3'-0''	2.74 m 9'-0''	3.66 m 12'-0''	1.22 m 4'-0''	8.53 m 28'-0''	5.49 m 18'-0''	6.10 m 20'-0''	6.10 m 20'-0''
16'	1 m	2.59 m 8'-6''	3.05 m 10'-0''	2.13 m 7'-0''	1.22 m 4'-0''	3.05 m 10'-0''	4.57 m 15'-0''	0.61 m 2'-0''	9.45 m 31'-0''	6.10 m 20'-0''	6.71 m 22'-0''	6.71 m 22'-0''
16'	3 m	3.35 m 11'-0''	3.66 m 12'-0''	2.59 m 8'-6''	1.83 m 6'-0''	3.20 m 10'-6''	6.40 m 21'-0''	0	11.43 m 37'-6''	6.70 m 22'-0''	7.32 m 24'-0''	7.32 m 24'-0''

Data source: National SPA and Swimming Pool Institute.

L_2, L_3, and L_4 combined represent the minimum distance from the tip of board to pool wall opposite diving equipment.

For board heights exceeding 3 m or for platform diving facilities; comply with dimensional requirements of FINA, USS, NCAA, N.F., etc.

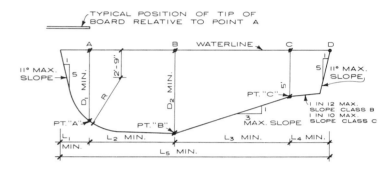

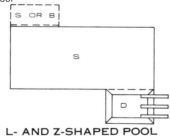

T-SHAPED POOL

Provides large shallow area(s). Diving area off to one side. Water in large part of pool from 3 ft 6 in. to 5 ft deep, adequate for regular competitive events.

L- AND Z-SHAPED POOL

These two shapes generally desired for large 50 m pools.

NOTE: Placement of boards shall observe the following minimum dimensions. With multiple board installations minimum pool widths must be increased accordingly.

1 m or deck level board to pool side	9' (2.74 m)
3 m board to pool side	11' (3.35 m)
1 m or deck level board to 3 m board	10' (3.05 m)
1 m or deck level to another 1 m or deck level board	8' (2.44 m)
3 m to another 3 m board	10' (3.05 m)

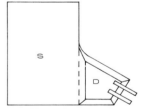

RECTANGULAR POOL

Standard design. Good for competitive swimming and indoor pool design. Shallow area often inadequate.

FAN SHAPED POOL

Successful where there is a high percentage of children. Largest area for shallow depth. Deep area can be roped off or separated by bulkhead.

FREE FORM POOL

Kidney and oval shapes are the most common free forms. Use only where competitive meets are not a consideration.

MODIFIED L POOL

Provides for separate diving area. Shallow area with 4 ft min. depth may be roped off for competitive meets.

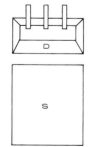

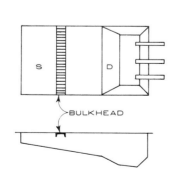

MULTIPLE POOLS

Separate pools for beginners, divers, and swimmers. Ultimate in desirability especially if pool is intended for large numbers of people. Variation at left shows single pool and bulkhead over it with advantage that swimmers are kept out of area reserved for beginners. Both designs may use common filtration system.

WADING POOLS

Generally provided in connection with community and family club pools. Placed away from swimming area to avoid congestion. If near swimming pool, wading area should be fenced off for children's protection. To add play appeal provide spray fittings and small fountains in pool. Also provide seats and benches for adults who accompany children to pool.

PUBLIC POOL SHAPES

NOTE: S = swimming pool, D = diving pool, B = beginners' pool.

R. Jackson Smith, AIA; Designed Environments, Inc.; Stamford, Connecticut
National Swimming Pool Institute; Washington, D.C.

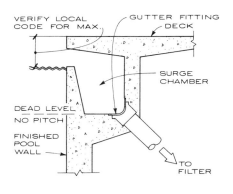

FULLY RECESSED OVERFLOW GUTTER

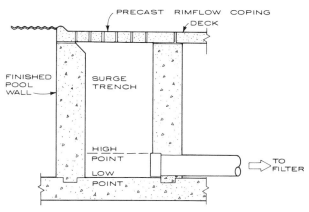

RIMFLOW SYSTEM

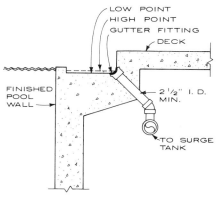

ROLL-OUT OVERFLOW GUTTER

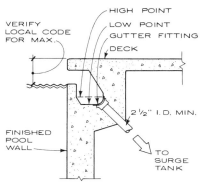

FULLY RECESSED GUTTER

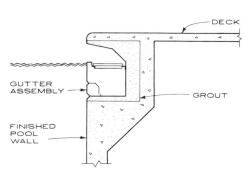

STAINLESS STEEL RECESSED SKIMMER

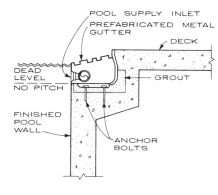

PREFABRICATED OVERFLOW GUTTER

PERIMETER OVERFLOW SYSTEMS

NOTES

1. A perimeter overflow system must be provided on all public swimming pools. It must be designed and constructed so that the water level of the pool is maintained at the operating level of the overflow rim or weir device. Dimension from the deck to the water level is determined by applicable codes.

2. Perimeter type overflow systems, when used as the only overflow system on the pool, must extend around a minimum 50% of the swimming pool perimeter. Perimeter overflow systems must be connected to the circulation system with a system surge capacity of not less than 1 gal/sq ft of pool surface.

3. The perimeter overflow system in combination with the upper rim of the pool must constitute a handhold. It must be designed to prevent the entrapment of swimmer's arms, legs, or feet and to permit inspection and cleaning.

4. The hydraulic capacity of the overflow system must be sufficient to handle 100% of the circulation flow.

5. When roll-out or flush deck type of perimeter overflows are used on competitive pools, the ends of the pool must be provided with a visual barrier that can be seen by swimmers.

6. Perimeter overflows are commonly used on public swimming pools. Some state health departments do not approve skimmers on public swimming pools that exceed a certain surface area. Current state codes or swimming pool regulations must be checked to determine limits of use, minimum dimensions, and other factors dealing with overflow design.

7. Metal swimming pool systems are available that have a built-in perimeter overflow. In addition to the overflow channel, the metal liner may also contain the return waterline from the filtration system. A metal liner that incorporates a cove between wall and floor is desirable to facilitate cleaning.

8. Deck areas adjoining the overflow system are generally required to slope away from it to separate drains. When deck is sloped to pool overflow, provide for diverting pool overflow to waste during deck cleaning.

National Swimming Pool Institute; Washington, D.C.

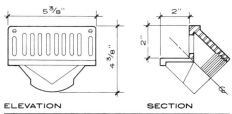

FLAT TYPE GUTTER FITTINGS

PLAN   SECTION

ANGLE TYPE GUTTER FITTINGS

ELEVATION   SECTION

9. Perimeter type overflows may be custom built to conform to the design selected. Ceramic tile is the preferred material for the top 6 in. of the pool wall, the pool rim, the gutter, and the deck for indoor swimming pools. Gratings for deep overflow gutters may be of precast concrete, plastic, or metal.

10. Proprietary overflow systems are available that have the characteristics of many of the perimeter overflow types shown. Stainless steel is commonly used because of its corrosion resistance. Aluminum overflow systems have a coating or enamel finish. Slotted precast concrete units are also available.

11. Surfaces subject to traffic must be nonslip.

SURFACE SKIMMERS

When surface skimmers are used, one must be provided for each 500 sq ft, or fraction thereof, of the pool surface. When two or more skimmers are used, they must be located so as to maintain effective skimming action over the entire surface of the swimming pool. Skimmers may not be permitted on larger pools. See local health department codes for limitation on public pools. Skimmers are not recommended for competitive pools.

Surface skimmers are available from many swimming pool suppliers. Metal or plastic units are available in various capacities. An access cover in the deck permits removal and cleaning of the strainer. Surface skimmers should comply with the joint National Swimming Pool Institute—National Sanitation Foundation performance standards.

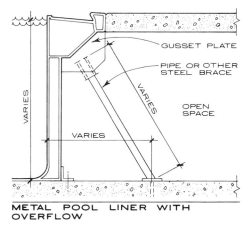

METAL POOL LINER WITH OVERFLOW

Often used in rooftop or other above grade installations where weight is a primary factor in design.

LENGTH OF POOLS

25 yards is the minimum length for American records, and meets interscholastic and intercollegiate requirements. (Pool should be 75 ft-1½ in. long to allow for electronic timing panels at one end.)

Standards for international competition are shown on 50 meter pool page.

WIDTH OF POOLS

Drawing below shows 7 ft lanes with pool width of 45 ft (6 lanes). Strictly competitive pools should have 8 ft lanes, with pool width of 83 ft (10 lanes). Minimum widths include additional 18 in. width outside lanes on both sides of pool.

NOTES

Gutters at sides of pool are desirable to reduce wave action in swimming meets or water polo. See lighting standards and diving board standards on other pages of this series for additional requirements for competitive pools.

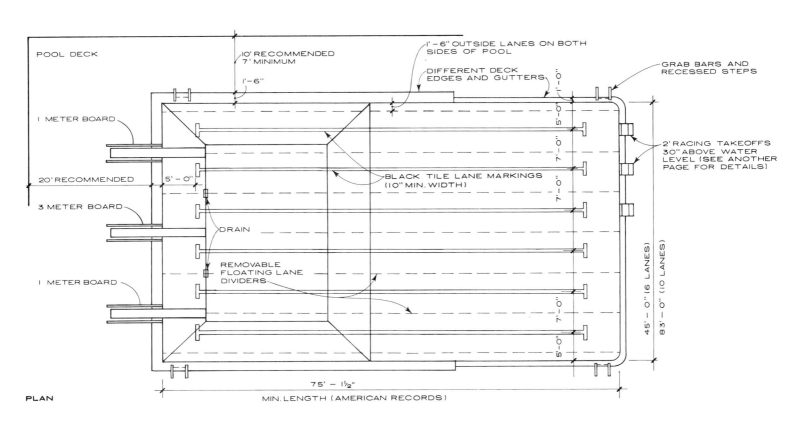

PLAN

25 YARD POOL

LONGITUDINAL SECTION

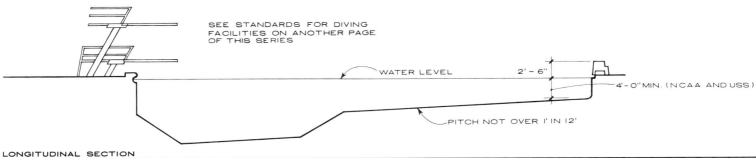

Swimming pool capacity requirements vary from one locality to another: check local regulations. The following is suggested by the American Public Health Association.

FORMULA DERIVATION:

ZONE A Diving area defined by 10 ft radius from diving board or platform. 12 divers per board; 2–3 in water, the rest on shore. Or allow 300 sq ft of pool water surface per board.

ZONE B Swimming area; 24 sq ft per swimmer. Based on volume displaced by each swimmer (⅘ square of average ht) and adjusted by the number of swimmers using pool at one time (⅔ total swimmers).

ZONE C Nonswimmer area. 10 sq ft per person. Based on volume displaced by person (½ area allowed per swimmer) and adjusted by number not using water—50% (in some pools with large number of nonswimmers, figure may be as high as 75%).

FORMULA:

$$\text{Max. pool capacity} = 12 \times \text{No. diving boards or platforms} + \frac{\text{Area Zone B}}{24} + \frac{\text{Area Zone C}}{10}$$

PUBLIC SWIMMING POOL CAPACITY

R. Jackson Smith, AIA; Designed Environments, Inc.; Stamford, Connecticut

AQUATICS

GENERAL NOTES

For judging competitive meets, FINA officials recommend the springboard and diving platform arrangement indicated below in plan. Diving dimensions meet minimum FINA standards. Fifty meters is minimum length for world records.

NOTE

*Length should be 50.03 m allowing an extra .03 m to compensate for possible future tile facing, structural defects and electrical timing panels.

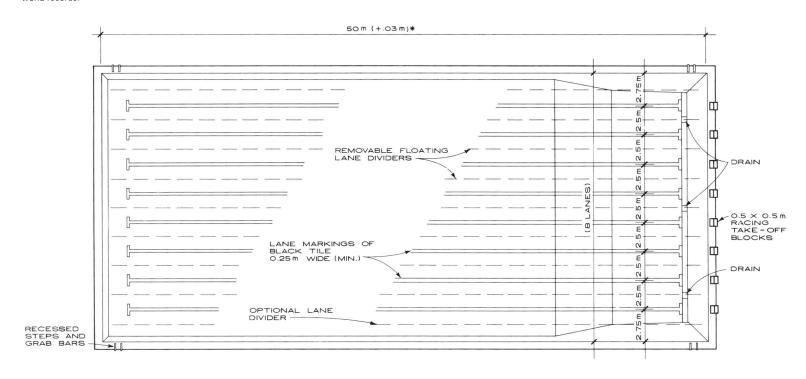

50 m (+.03 m)*

(8 LANES)

2.75 m
2.5 m
2.5 m
2.5 m
2.5 m
2.5 m
2.5 m
2.5 m
2.75 m

REMOVABLE FLOATING LANE DIVIDERS

LANE MARKINGS OF BLACK TILE 0.25 m WIDE (MIN.)

OPTIONAL LANE DIVIDER

DRAIN

0.5 X 0.5 m RACING TAKE-OFF BLOCKS

DRAIN

RECESSED STEPS AND GRAB BARS

PLAN

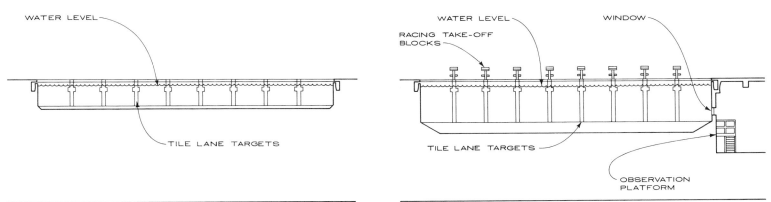

WATER LEVEL

TILE LANE TARGETS

CROSS SECTION

WATER LEVEL

RACING TAKE-OFF BLOCKS

WINDOW

TILE LANE TARGETS

OBSERVATION PLATFORM

CROSS SECTION

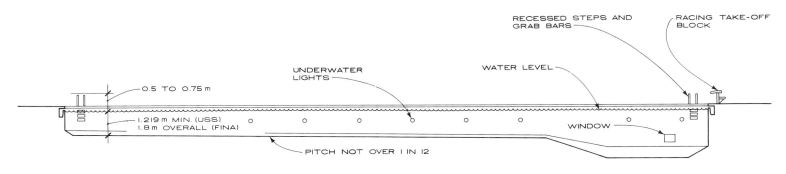

RECESSED STEPS AND GRAB BARS

RACING TAKE-OFF BLOCK

UNDERWATER LIGHTS

WATER LEVEL

0.5 TO 0.75 m

1.219 m MIN. (USS)
1.8 m OVERALL (FINA)

PITCH NOT OVER 1 IN 12

WINDOW

LONGITUDINAL SECTION

Flewelling & Moody; Los Angeles, California
Richard J. Vitullo; Washington Grove, Maryland

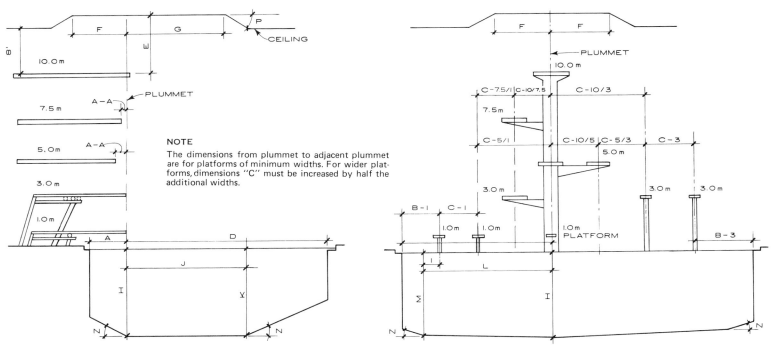

DIAGRAMMATIC LONGITUDINAL SECTION   DIAGRAMMATIC CROSS SECTION

NOTE

The dimensions from plummet to adjacent plummet are for platforms of minimum widths. For wider platforms, dimensions "C" must be increased by half the additional widths.

FINA INTERNATIONAL AMATEUR SWIMMING AND DIVING FEDERATION STANDARDS

			SPRINGBOARDS			PLATFORMS							
			1 METER	3 METER	1 METER	3 METER	5 METER		7.5 METER		10 METER		
DIMENSIONS FOR DIVING FACILITIES		LENGTH	5.0	5.0	4.5	5.0	6.0		6.0		6.0		
		WIDTH	0.5	0.5	0.6	0.8	1.5		1.5		2.0		
		HEIGHT	1.0	3.0	1.0	0.8	5.0		7.5		10.0		
A	FROM PLUMMET: BACK TO POOL WALL	DESIG.	A-1	A-3	A-1 (PL)	A-3 (PL)	A-5		A-7.5		A-10		
		MIN.	1.50	1.50	0.75	1.25	1.25		1.50		1.50		
		PREF.	1.80	1.80			1.50						
A-A	FROM PLUMMET: BACK TO PLATFORM DIRECTLY BELOW	DESIG.					AA-5/1		A-7.5/3		AA-10/5		
		MIN.					0.75		0.75		0.75		
		PREF.							1.50		1.50		
B	FROM PLUMMET: TO POOL WALL AT SIDE	DESIG.	B-1	B-3	B-1 (PL)	B-3 (PL)	B-5		B-7.5		B-10		
		MIN.	2.50	3.50	2.30	2.90	4.25		4.50		5.25		
		PREF.	3.00										
C	FROM PLUMMET TO ADJACENT PLUMMET	DESIG.	C-1	C-3	C-3/1	C-1/1 (PL)	C-3/1 (PL)	C-5/3 (PL)	C-5/1	C-7.5/3/1	C-10/7.5	C-10/7.5/3	C-10/3/1
		MIN.	2.40	2.60	2.60	1.65	2.10	2.10	2.10	2.10	2.50	2.75	2.75
		PREF.	2.40	2.40	1.4/3.0								
D	FROM PLUMMET TO POOL WALL AHEAD	DESIG.	D-1	D-3	D-1 (PL)	D-3 (PL)	D-5		D-7.5		D-10		
		MIN.	9.00	10.25	8.00	9.50	10.25		11.00		13.50		
		PREF.											
E	PLUMMET, FROM BOARD TO CEILING OVERHEAD	DESIG.	E-1	E-3	E-1 (PL)	E-3 (PL)	E-5		E-7.5		E-10		
		MIN.	5.00	5.00	3.00	3.00	3.00		3.20		3.40		
		PREF.					3.40		3.40		5 00		
F	CLEAR OVERHEAD, BEHIND AND EACH SIDE OF PLUMMET	DESIG.	F-1 E-1	F-3 E-3	F-1 (PL)	F-3 (PL)	F-5 E-5	F-7.5 E-7.5		F-10 E-10			
		MIN.	2.50 5.00	2.50 5.00	2.75	2.75	2.75 3.00	2.75 3.20		2.75 3.40			
		PREF.					3.40	3.40		5.00			
G	CLEAR OVERHEAD, AHEAD OF PLUMMET	DESIG.	G-1 E-1	G-3 E-3	G-1 (PL)	G-3 (PL)	G-5 E-5	G-7.5 E-7.5		G-10 E-10			
		MIN.	5.00 5.00	5.00 5.00	5.00	5.00	5.00 3.00	5.00 3.20		6.00 3.40			
		PREF.					3.40	3.40		5.00			
H	DEPTH OF WATER AT PLUMMET	DESIG.	H-1	H-3	H-1 (PL)	H-3 (PL)	H-5		H-7.5		H-10		
		MIN.	3.40	3.80	3.40	3.60	3.40		4.10		4.50		
		PREF.	3.80	4.00		3.80	4.00		4.50		5.00		
J-K	DISTANCE, DEPTH OF WATER, AHEAD OF PLUMMET	DESIG.	J-1 K-1	J-3 K-3	J/K-1 (PL)	J/K-3 (PL)	J-5 K-5	J-7.5 K-7.5		J-10 K-10			
		MIN.	5.00 3.30	6.00 3.70	5.0/3.3	6.0/3.3	6.00 3.70	8.00 4.00		11.00 4.25			
		PREF.	3.70	3.90		3.70	3.90	4.40		4.75			
L-M	DISTANCE, DEPTH OF WATER, EACH SIDE OF PLUMMET	DESIG.	L-1 M-1	L-3 M-3	L/M-1 (PL)	L/M-3 (PL)	L-5 M-5	L-7.5 M-7.5		L-10 M-10			
		MIN.	2.50 3.30	3.25 3.70	2.05/3.3	2.65/3.5	4.25 3.70	4.50 4.00		5.25 4.25			
		PREF.	3.70	3.90		3.70	3.90	4.40		4.75			
N P	MAXIMUM ANGLE OF SLOPE TO REDUCE DIMENSIONS BEYOND FULL REQUIREMENTS	POOL BOTTOM	= 30 Degrees (Approximately 1 ft vertical to 2 ft horizontal)										
		CEILING HEIGHT	= 30 Degrees										

R. Jackson Smith, AIA; Designed Environments, Inc.; Stamford, Connecticut

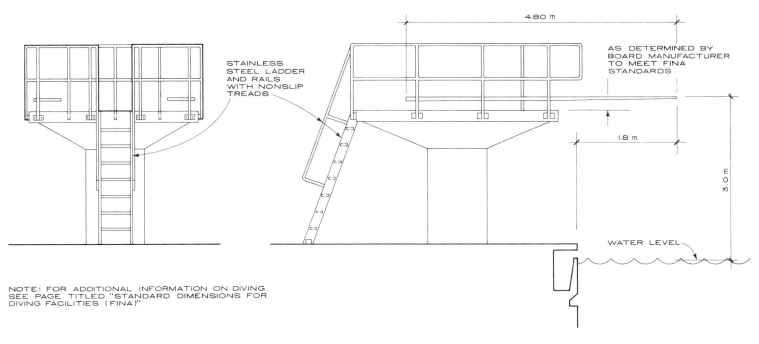

STAINLESS STEEL LADDER AND RAILS WITH NONSLIP TREADS

4.80 m

AS DETERMINED BY BOARD MANUFACTURER TO MEET FINA STANDARDS

1.8 m

3.0 m

WATER LEVEL

NOTE: FOR ADDITIONAL INFORMATION ON DIVING SEE PAGE TITLED "STANDARD DIMENSIONS FOR DIVING FACILITIES (FINA)"

REAR ELEVATION   SIDE ELEVATION

3 METER DIVING BOARD

GENERAL NOTES

Both 1 m and 3 m boards are required for amateur, collegiate, and international meets. All boards shall have a nonslip surface. Consult FINA Handbook. FINA is the Fédération Internationale de Natation Amateur.

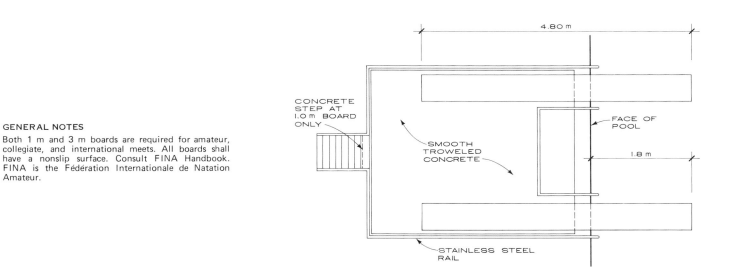

4.80 m

CONCRETE STEP AT 1.0 m BOARD ONLY

SMOOTH TROWELED CONCRETE

FACE OF POOL

1.8 m

STAINLESS STEEL RAIL

PLAN

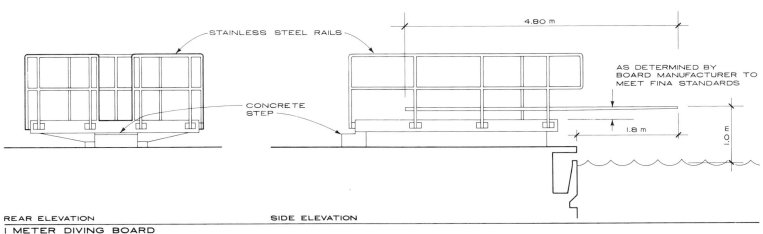

STAINLESS STEEL RAILS

CONCRETE STEP

4.80 m

AS DETERMINED BY BOARD MANUFACTURER TO MEET FINA STANDARDS

1.8 m

1.0 m

REAR ELEVATION   SIDE ELEVATION

I METER DIVING BOARD

Flewelling & Moody; Los Angeles, California
Richard J. Vitullo; Washington Grove, Maryland

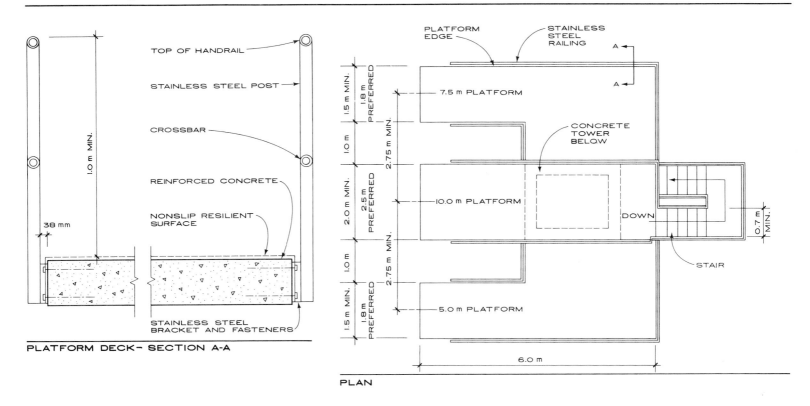

TOP OF HANDRAIL

STAINLESS STEEL POST

CROSSBAR

REINFORCED CONCRETE

NONSLIP RESILIENT SURFACE

STAINLESS STEEL BRACKET AND FASTENERS

1.0 m MIN.

38 mm

PLATFORM DECK- SECTION A-A

PLATFORM EDGE

STAINLESS STEEL RAILING

7.5 m PLATFORM

10.0 m PLATFORM

5.0 m PLATFORM

CONCRETE TOWER BELOW

DOWN

STAIR

1.5 m MIN. / 1.8 m PREFERRED

1.0 m / 2.75 m MIN.

2.0 m MIN. / 2.5 m PREFERRED

1.0 m / 2.75 m MIN.

1.5 m MIN. / 1.8 m PREFERRED

0.7 m MIN.

6.0 m

PLAN

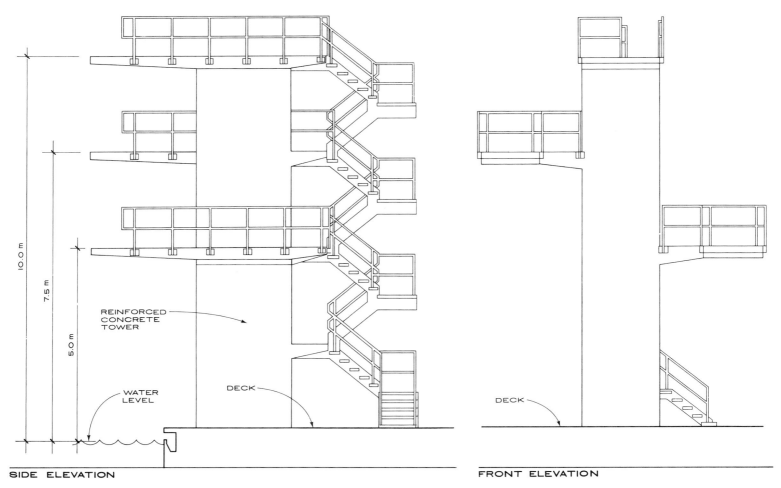

10.0 m

7.5 m

5.0 m

REINFORCED CONCRETE TOWER

WATER LEVEL

DECK

SIDE ELEVATION

DECK

FRONT ELEVATION

Flewelling & Moody; Los Angeles, California
Richard J. Vitullo; Washington Grove, Maryland

7   **AQUATICS**

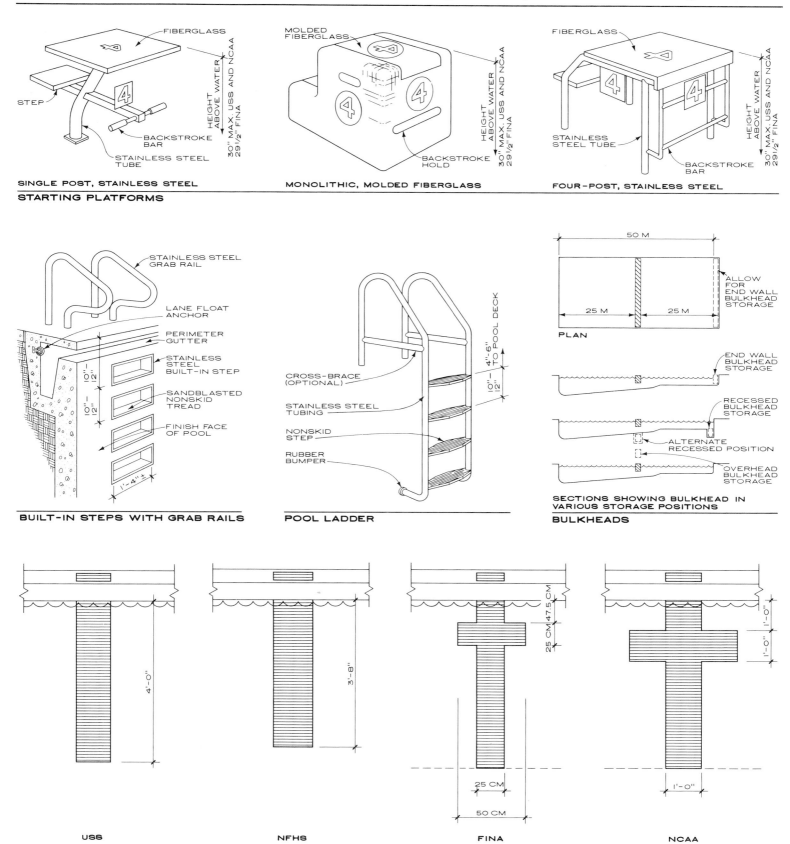

STARTING PLATFORMS

- SINGLE POST, STAINLESS STEEL
- MONOLITHIC, MOLDED FIBERGLASS
- FOUR-POST, STAINLESS STEEL

BUILT-IN STEPS WITH GRAB RAILS

POOL LADDER

BULKHEADS

USS   NFHS   FINA   NCAA

NOTE: COLOR OF END WALL TARGETS SHOULD BE DARK AND CONTRASTING TO THE GENERAL COLOR OF THE POOL (BLACK PREFERABLE)

END WALL TARGETS

Richard J. Vitullo; Washington Grove, Maryland

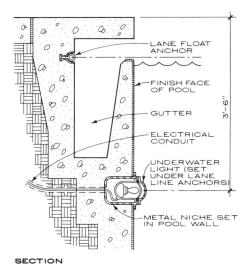

SECTION
GUTTER DETAIL SHOWING UNDERWATER LIGHTING

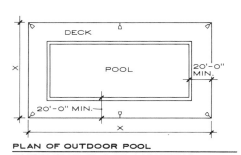

PLAN OF OUTDOOR POOL
OVERHEAD FLOOD LIGHTING

NOTE

Distance ''x'' for spacing of lights not to exceed four times the actual mounting height of lamp in light fixture. For outdoor above-water lighting, flood lights should be mounted at least 20 ft above the water. Select lamps to allow 1.0 W/sq ft minimum for flood lights. Consult USS or NCAA for specific requirements for championship meets. USS rules for championship meets require a minimum of 40 fc 3 ft above the water surface. For interior above-water lighting, concentration of 100 fc is recommended and should be directly over turning end and finish line. (This is a specific requirement for national championship meets.) A power source for additional lighting should be available for use with television, movies, and special events. Buildings housing indoor pools should not have deck-level windows in walls facing pool ends to prevent glare. Deck-level windows at side should be tinted.

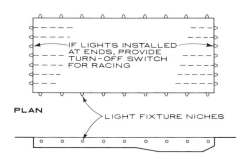

PLAN

SECTION
UNDERWATER POOL LIGHTING

NOTES FOR WET AND DRY NICHE UNDERWATER LIGHTS

Underwater lighting type and dimensions should be in accordance with NEC (article 680) regulations.

Underwater lights will require 0.5 to 2.0 W/sq ft of water area and should be sized accordingly.

Box connections for dry or wet niches should be a minimum of 4 ft 0 in. away from the side wall of the pool and 8 in. above the deck. Low voltage wiring should be used for all dry or wet niche lighting fixtures. This requires a transformer located, by code, a specific distance away from pool wall and above deck.

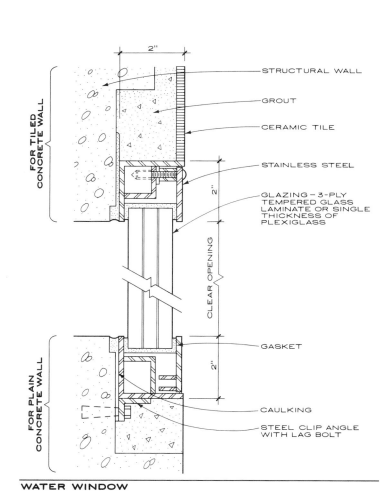

WATER WINDOW

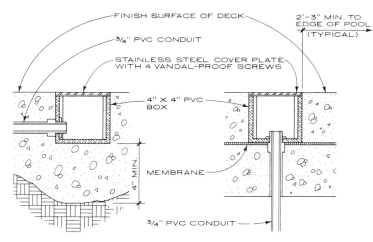

SLAB ON GRADE   **SUSPENDED SLAB**
ELECTRONIC TIMING DECK BOXES

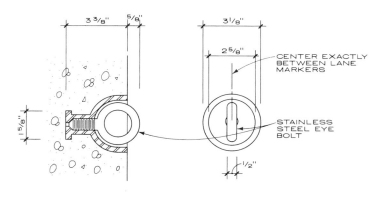

SECTION   **ELEVATION**
LANE FLOAT ANCHOR

Flewelling & Moody; Los Angeles, California
Richard J. Vitullo; Washington Grove, Maryland

7 AQUATICS

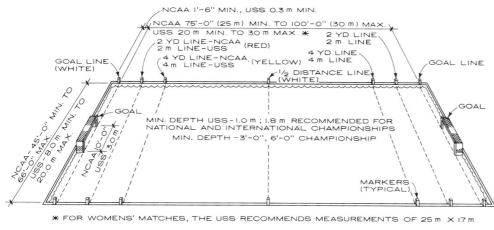

NCAA 1'-6" MIN., USS 0.3 m MIN.

NCAA 75'-0" (25 m) MIN. TO 100'-0" (30 m) MAX.
USS 20 m MIN. TO 30 m MAX. ✳

2 YD LINE-NCAA   2 YD LINE
2 m LINE-USS (RED)   2 m LINE

GOAL LINE   4 YD LINE-NCAA (YELLOW)   4 YD LINE
(WHITE)   4 m LINE-USS   4 m LINE   GOAL LINE

GOAL   GOAL

½ DISTANCE LINE
(WHITE)

MIN. DEPTH USS - 1.0 m ; 1.8 m RECOMMENDED FOR
NATIONAL AND INTERNATIONAL CHAMPIONSHIPS
MIN. DEPTH - 3'-0", 6'-0" CHAMPIONSHIP

MARKERS
(TYPICAL)

NCAA - 45'-0" MIN. TO
66'-0" MAX.
USS - 8.0 m MIN. TO
20.0 m MAX.

✳ FOR WOMENS' MATCHES, THE USS RECOMMENDS MEASUREMENTS OF 25 m × 17 m

NOTES

Distinctive marks must be provided on both sides of field of play indicating goal lines, 2 and 4 yd (or meter) lines, and ½ distance between goal lines. These must be clearly visible from any position within the field of play. Allow sufficient space on walkways so referees may move freely from end to end of field of play. Provide space at goal lines for goal judges.

GOAL REQUIREMENTS

Posts and crossbar, rigid and perpendicular. USS, wood or metal, 3 in. sq, painted white; NCAA, metal 1½ in. diameter, painted yellow or orange. Nets to hang loosely on frame. For USS, the underside of the crossbar must be 0.90 m above water surface when water is 1.50 m or more in depth, and 2.40 m from the bottom of the bath when the depth of the water is less than 1.50 m.

Frames are custom made, with bracing placed where necessary. It is recommended that they be collapsible for easy storage. Anchorage methods depend on pool design, with those above commonly used, or brass couplings may be placed in pool walls to which frame is attached. If pool is longer than required length, one of the goals may be floated and anchored with guy wires.

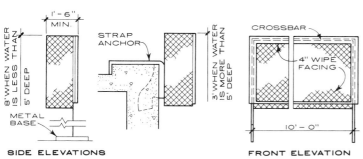

1'-6"
MIN.

8' WHEN WATER
IS LESS THAN
5' DEEP

3' WHEN WATER
IS MORE THAN
5' DEEP

STRAP
ANCHOR

METAL
BASE

SIDE ELEVATIONS
NCAA GOALS

CROSSBAR

4" WIPE
FACING

FRONT ELEVATION

10' - 0"

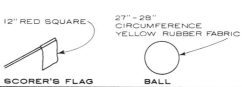

12" RED SQUARE

SCORER'S FLAG

27" - 28"
CIRCUMFERENCE
YELLOW RUBBER FABRIC

BALL

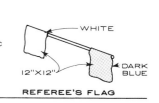

WHITE

12"×12"

DARK
BLUE

REFEREE'S FLAG

WATER POLO

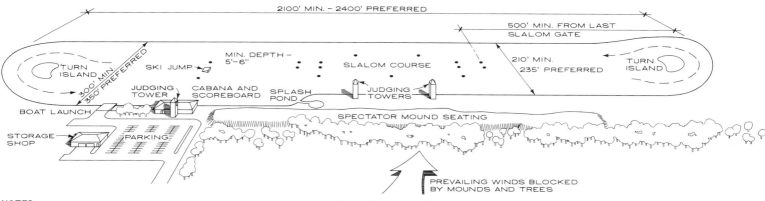

2100' MIN. - 2400' PREFERRED

500' MIN. FROM LAST
SLALOM GATE

TURN
ISLAND

SKI JUMP

MIN. DEPTH -
5'-6"

SLALOM COURSE

210' MIN.
235' PREFERRED

TURN
ISLAND

300' MIN.
350' PREFERRED

JUDGING
TOWER

CABANA AND
SCOREBOARD

SPLASH
POND

JUDGING
TOWERS

BOAT LAUNCH

SPECTATOR MOUND SEATING

STORAGE
SHOP

PARKING

PREVAILING WINDS BLOCKED
BY MOUNDS AND TREES

NOTES

1. To decrease turbidity caused by boat wake, an island running down the center of the lake may be built in addition to turn islands. Floating breakwaters may also

be used; islands should be riprapped to prevent soil erosion.

2. A gradual (ratio 6 : 1) sandy slope along shorelines lets wave action die without rolling back.

WATER SKI LAKE

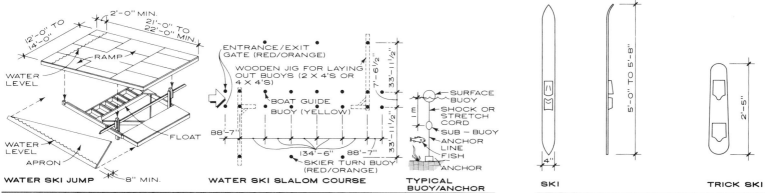

2'-0" MIN.

21'-0" TO
22'-0" MIN.

12'-0" TO
14'-0"

RAMP

WATER
LEVEL

WATER
LEVEL

APRON

FLOAT

WATER SKI JUMP

8" MIN.

ENTRANCE/EXIT
GATE (RED/ORANGE)

WOODEN JIG FOR LAYING
OUT BUOYS (2 × 4'S OR
4 × 4'S)

BOAT GUIDE
BUOY (YELLOW)

7' - 6½"

33'-11½"

33'-11½"

88'-7"

134'-6"

88'-7"

SKIER TURN BUOY
(RED/ORANGE)

SURFACE
BUOY

SHOCK OR
STRETCH
CORD

SUB - BUOY

ANCHOR
LINE
FISH

ANCHOR

WATER SKI SLALOM COURSE

TYPICAL
BUOY/ANCHOR

SKI

5'-0" TO 5'-8"

4"

TRICK SKI

2'-5"

WATER SKIING AND JUMPING

Richard J. Vitullo; Washington Grove, Maryland

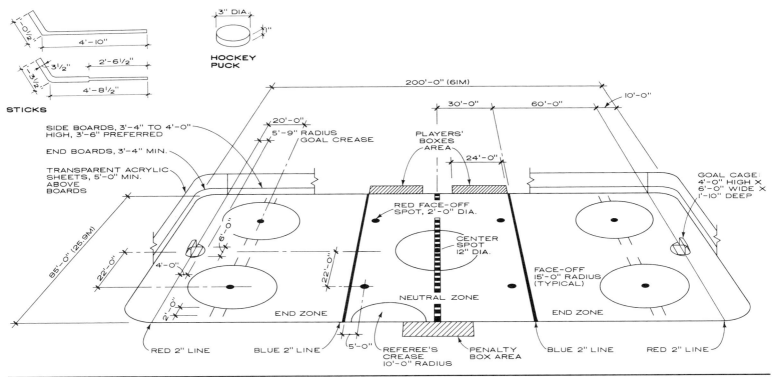

STICKS

HOCKEY PUCK

ICE HOCKEY

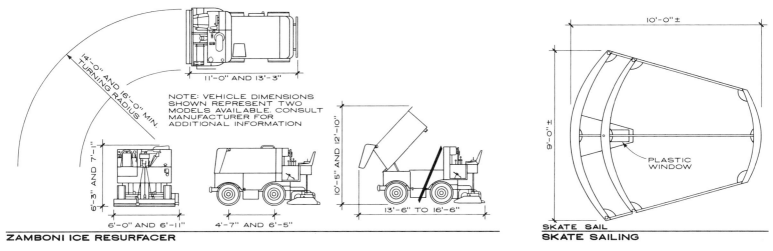

ZAMBONI ICE RESURFACER

NOTE: VEHICLE DIMENSIONS SHOWN REPRESENT TWO MODELS AVAILABLE. CONSULT MANUFACTURER FOR ADDITIONAL INFORMATION

SKATE SAIL

PLASTIC WINDOW

SKATE SAILING

CURLING EQUIPMENT

HANDLE

STONE

CURLING

Richard J. Vitullo; Washington Grove, Maryland

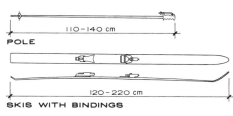

POLE

SKIS WITH BINDINGS

BOOT

BASIC EQUIPMENT

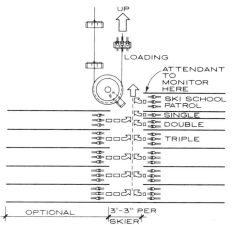

LIFT MAZE

LIFT MAZE AREA REQUIRED FOR 10-MINUTE LIFT LINE

LIFT TYPE	WIDTH (EACH ROW)	AREA (SQ FT)
Double	5 ft 0 in.	2500
Triple	7 ft 6 in.	3750
Quad	10 ft 0 in.	5000

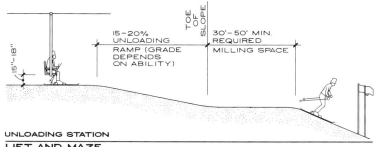

UNLOADING STATION

LIFT AND MAZE

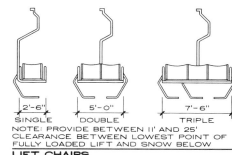

LIFT CHAIRS

NOTE: PROVIDE BETWEEN 11' AND 25' CLEARANCE BETWEEN LOWEST POINT OF FULLY LOADED LIFT AND SNOW BELOW

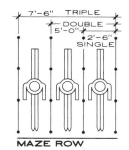

MAZE ROW

NOTE

Lift mazes to be located downhill of or to the side of loading point.

Mazes to be graded as flat as possible.

Approach to loading point to be graded at 3% downhill for distance of 50 ft minimum.

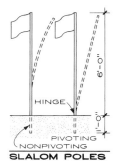

SLALOM POLES

VERTICAL DROP AND GATE SPECIFICATIONS FOR FIS AND USSA COURSES

EVENT	FIS DROP (M) MIN.	FIS DROP (M) MAX.	NO. OF GATES MIN.	NO. OF GATES MAX.	USSA DROP (M) MIN.	NO. OF GATES MIN.
DOWNHILL						
One-run:						
men	500	1000			400	
women	500	700			400	
Two-run						
(each)	450					
SLALOM						
Men	140	220	52	78	120	42
Women	120	180	42	63	120	42
GIANT SLALOM						
Men	250	400	30	60	250	33
Women	250	350	30	53	250	33
SUPER GIANT SLALOM						
Men	500	650	35	65	350	30
Women	350	500	30	50	350	30

FIS = Federation Internationale de Ski

USSA = United States Ski Association

ACCEPTABLE TERRAIN GRADIENTS FOR SLOPES AND TRAILS

SKILL LEVEL	TERRAIN GRADIENTS LOW	HIGH
Beginner/novice	8%	25%
Intermediate	15%	40%
Advanced intermediate/expert	25%	70%
Average Olympic downhill	23%	30%

BASE LODGE

Base lodge size in sq ft = (mountain capacity/seat turn-over rate x sq ft/person.

Seat turnover rate—number of persons served per seat per day depends upon weather and temperature.

Typically: 3 (cold/overcast)
5 (warm/clear)

Typical sq ft/person at ski lodge:
30 (local ski area)
35 (destination ski area)

Edge of lodge to be: minimum 100 ft
optimal 150 ft
suitable 100–300 ft
from lift terminals.

Stairs with long treads (14–16 in.) and low risers (6 in.) to accommodate ski boots.

Protect entry/doorways from snowfall/dripping.

Locate windows above snow level.

Ski rental space = 3 sq ft per rental setup (skis, boots, poles).

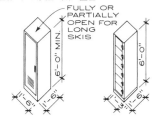

SEASON LOCKER   **COIN-OPERATED LOCKER**

LOCKERS

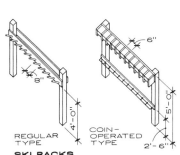

REGULAR TYPE   **COIN-OPERATED TYPE**

SKI RACKS

LOCKERS AND SKI RACKS

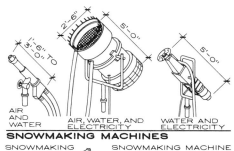

AIR AND WATER   **AIR, WATER, AND ELECTRICITY**   **WATER AND ELECTRICITY**

SNOWMAKING MACHINES

SNOWMAKING MACHINE MOUNT   **SNOWMAKING MACHINE MOUNT**

SNOWMAKING MACHINE CARRIAGE   **SNOWMAKING MACHINE SLED**

MAINTENANCE AND SNOWMAKING EQUIPMENT

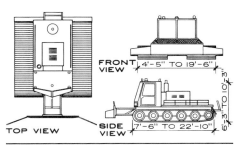

FRONT VIEW   **TOP VIEW**   **SIDE VIEW**

OVERSNOW VEHICLES

MAINTENANCE BUILDING

Area required: 100 sq ft per oversnow vehicle includes vehicle storage, parts and general storage, office, toilets. Does not include snowmaking system.

Doors: 16–20 ft wide, 14–16 ft high for main vehicle entry doors.

Eliot W. Goldstein, AIA, and Chan Li Lin; James Goldstein & Partners; Millburn, New Jersey

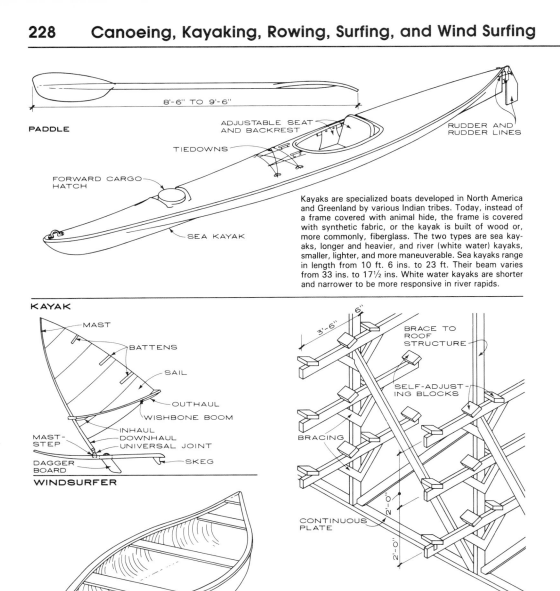

PADDLE

8'-6" TO 9'-6"

ADJUSTABLE SEAT
AND BACKREST

RUDDER AND
RUDDER LINES

TIEDOWNS

FORWARD CARGO
HATCH

SEA KAYAK

Kayaks are specialized boats developed in North America and Greenland by various Indian tribes. Today, instead of a frame covered with animal hide, the frame is covered with synthetic fabric, or the kayak is built of wood or, more commonly, fiberglass. The two types are sea kayaks, longer and heavier, and river (white water) kayaks, smaller, lighter, and more maneuverable. Sea kayaks range in length from 10 ft. 6 ins. to 23 ft. Their beam varies from 33 ins. to 17½ ins. White water kayaks are shorter and narrower to be more responsive in river rapids.

KAYAK

MAST

BATTENS

SAIL

OUTHAUL

WISHBONE BOOM

INHAUL

MAST-STEP

DOWNHAUL

UNIVERSAL JOINT

DAGGER BOARD

SKEG

WINDSURFER

BRACE TO ROOF STRUCTURE

3'-6"   6"

SELF-ADJUSTING BLOCKS

BRACING

2'-0"

CONTINUOUS PLATE

2'-0"

ROWING SHELL STORAGE RACK

Storage for rowing shells requires: two racks 8 feet apart for single and double; three racks 8 feet apart for eight-oared. Shells used daily should not be stored higher than 6 ft. Storage racks can be adapted easily to hold kayaks or canoes by adjusting the spacing between racks and the height between horizontal members.

Racing shells, built primarily of carbon fiber or plastic, are narrow and unstable in the water. There are two rowing styles: sweep rowing, where oarsmen work one oar with both hands; and sculling, where each oarsman works two oars, one in each hand. Sweeps are 12 ft. to 13 ft. long; sculling oars are 9 ft. 6 ins. to 10 ft. long.

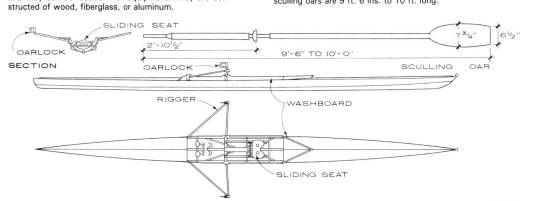

4'-0" TO 6'-0" IN 3" INCR.

PADDLE

CANOE

Canoes have shallow draft, and they range in length from 12 ft. to 35 ft. They can be paddled, sailed, or motored, and they can be loaded with equipment. They are constructed of wood, fiberglass, or aluminum.

SLIDING SEAT

OARLOCK

SECTION

2'-10½"

OARLOCK

9'-6" TO 10'-0"

7¾"   6½"

SCULLING   OAR

RIGGER

WASHBOARD

SLIDING SEAT

ROWING SHELL

Timothy B. McDonald; Washington, D.C.

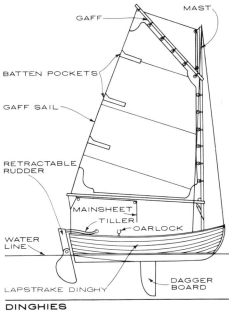

GAFF

MAST

BATTEN POCKETS

GAFF SAIL

RETRACTABLE RUDDER

MAINSHEET

TILLER

OARLOCK

WATER LINE

LAPSTRAKE DINGHY

DAGGER BOARD

DINGHIES

Dinghies are small boats used as auxiliaries to larger craft. They also can be sailed and raced on their own. They vary in length from 6 ft. to 16 ft., and they are 2 ft. 10 ins. to 5 ft. 6 ins. in beam. They are constructed of wood or fiberglass, and they can be rigged for sail, rowing, or motoring.

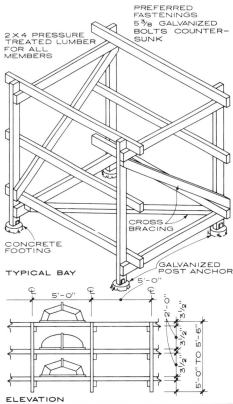

PREFERRED FASTENINGS
5⅜ GALVANIZED BOLTS COUNTERSUNK

2 X 4 PRESSURE TREATED LUMBER FOR ALL MEMBERS

CROSS BRACING

CONCRETE FOOTING

GALVANIZED POST ANCHOR

TYPICAL BAY

5'-0"

5'-0"

2'-0"

3½"   3½"   3½"

5'-0" TO 5'-6"

ELEVATION

DINGHY STORAGE RACK

Dinghy racks store the small boats year round, and should be weather-treated. The rack members are fastened with countersunk bolts to avoid damaging dinghies. Racks must be able to support the weight of the boats and anyone climbing on the racks.

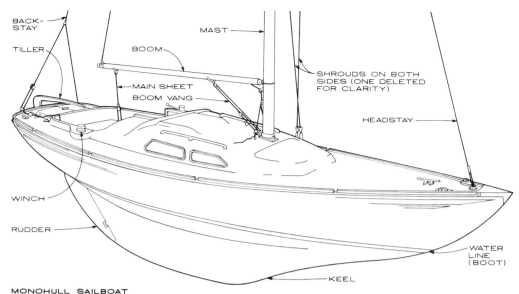

MONOHULL SAILBOAT

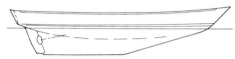

FULL KEEL

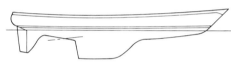

FIN KEEL

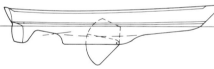

FIN KEEL / CENTER BOARD

CENTER BOARD

MONOHULL - BASIC UNDERWATER HULL SHAPES

MULTIHULL

DEFINITIONS

1. Length overall—LOA—boat's greatest length excluding bowsprits rudder or other extensions.
2. Length of water line—LWL—boat's greatest length at the water level excluding extensions such as rudders.
3. Beam—boat's maximum breadth.
4. Draft—distance from the waterline to the bottom of the boat's keel determining the least depth of water the boat can operate in: i.e., the amount it draws.
5. Displacement—weight of the water that the boat displaces.

NOTES FOR BASIC RIGS

LATEEN

Ancestor of the fore and aft rigs shown here. It dates back thousands of years and is still used in many parts of the world.

CATBOAT RIG

Traditionally puts a lot of sail area on one short mast, as shown here, which is stepped far forward in the boat.

SLOOP

Design with two basic sails, mainsail and headsail; the latter, called a "fractional rig," is set either to the masthead or some distance below the masthead.

CUTTER

Like the sloop, a cutter rig has one mast carrying two headsails instead of one. The inner sail is the forestay sail and the outer sail is the jib.

YAWL

Unlike the sloop or cutter, the yawl is a two masted rig consisting of a mainmast and a mizzen mast that is stepped abaft (behind) the rudder post. The mizzen sail is much smaller than the main sail.

KETCH

Like the yawl, the ketch is also a two-masted rig; however, the mizzen mast is stepped forward of the rudder post and is larger than the yawl's mizzen. This placement dictates a smaller mainsail.

SCHOONER

Usually two-masted but can be three-masted. Commonly the foremast is the shorter of the two, and may be gaff or marconi rigged or at times a combination of both.

A combination of mast and rigging placement (where the mast is stepped), along with size, type and number of sails, make up the main differences in sailboat rigs. Today the most common is the marconi rig distinguished by a triangular mainsail, but it is not unusual for boats to be rigged with a traditional gaff, which is a four-sided sail that hangs from a spar called a gaff. In some instances marconi and gaff rigs are used together as shown on the schooner below.

Headsails are triangular sails set ahead of the mast. Basic headsails are the jib, working jib, staysail, and genoa. The working jib, unlike other jibs, does not overlap the mast and is often attached to a boom for easier control. Jibs and genoas do overlap the mast and mainsail. The forestaysail is combined with the jib to create a double-headsail and is used primarily on cutters and schooners.

Spinnakers, usually the largest sail set before the mast, come in several different shapes and sizes according to use.

EXAMPLES

	LOA	LWL	BEAM	DRAFT	
FULL KEEL BOATS					
Folkboat	25'-10"	19'-10"	7'-4"	3'-11"	
Cape Dory 45	45'-3"	33'-6"	13'-0"	6'-3"	
FIN KEEL BOATS					
Tartan 28	28'-3"	23'-3"	9'-10"	4'-11"	
O'Day 35	35'-0"	28'-9"	11'-3"	5'-7"	
FIN/CENTERBOARD				UP	DOWN
Cape Dory (270)	27'-3"	20'-9"	9'-5"	3'-0"	7'-0"
Tartan 37	37'-3"	28'-6"	11'-9"	4'-2"	7'-9"
CENTERBOARD				UP	DOWN
Sunfish	13'-10"	13'-10"	4'-1/2"	3"	2'-8"
Laser	13'-10"	12'-6"	4'-6"	6"	2'-8"
El Toro	8'-0"	7'-0"	3'-10"	3"	1'-10"
MULTIHULLS					
Hobie 16	16'-7"	15'-9"	7'-11"	10"	

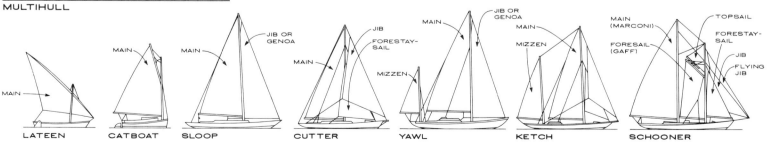

BASIC BOAT RIGS

Timothy B. McDonald; Washington, D.C.

HOT-AIR AND GAS BALLOONS

CLASS	VOLUME CFx1000	DIAMETER (FT)	HEIGHT (FT)	CREW
AX–1	8.5	25	28	1
AX–2	12.2–14	28–32	28–37	1
AA/AX–3	17–22	30–34	30–45	1–3
AA/AX–4	27.5–33.4	34–41	34–67	1–6
AA/AX–5	37.1–45	39–46	46–73	1–6
AA/AX–6	55–59.3	47–50	51–80	1–6
AX–7	60–77.7	50–56	53–64	1–4
AX–8	80–106	54–62	57–72	3–6
AX–9	139–160	N/A	N/A	4–12

NOTE: Deflated balloon including burner can be stored in the crew basket for transporting in a small pickup truck.

BALLOONS

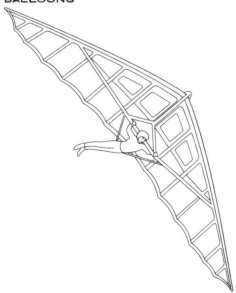

FLEXIBLE WING HANG GLIDER

SPAN	LEADING EDGE	KEEL	WEIGHT (LB)
24 ft 9 in. to 38 ft 2 in.	16 ft 0 in. to 21 ft 0 in.	7 ft 2 in. to 13 ft 5 in.	41 to 78

HANG GLIDERS

Marr Knapp Crawfis Associates, Inc.; Mansfield, Ohio
Jane's All the World's Aircraft, 82–83

LIGHT PLANES (MICROLIGHTS) USUALLY DRIVEN BY LIGHT, LOW-POWERED ENGINES

WING SPAN	LENGTH	HEIGHT	PROPELLER	WEIGHT EMPTY (LB)
30 ft to 37 ft	10 ft 6 in. to 19 ft 6 in.	5 ft 6 in. to 10 ft 0 in.	3 ft 6 in. to 4 ft 6 in.	120 to 245

NOTE: Physical sizes for models with solar-powered electrical motors exceed the data given above.

LIGHT/MICRO PLANES

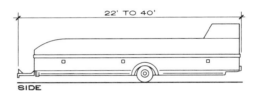

SIDE

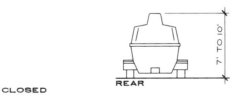

CLOSED

REAR

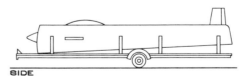

SIDE

OPEN
SAILPLANE TRAILERS

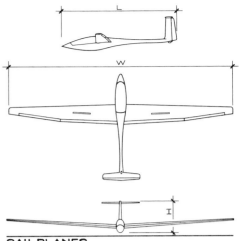

SAILPLANES

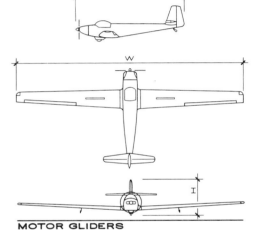

MOTOR GLIDERS

SOARING

1. Sailplanes with winch or auto-tow launch: constructed of aluminum, fiberglass, carbon composites, wood, specially treated fabric stretched over metal tubing, or any combination of these materials.

Size ranges:
Wingspan (W) from under 40 to over 72 ft.
Fuselage (L) from 20 to 30 ft.
Height (H) from 3 to 9.3 ft.
Empty weight from 250 (one seat) to 1,000 lb (three-seat models).

Major design classes for national competitions:
Open class: Wingspan over 72 ft (22 m).
15-m class: Wingspan up to 49.2 ft (15 m) with modifications to increase performance.
Standard class: Similar to 15-m class, no flaps.
Sports class: For older, lower performance models, including home-builts and sailplanes not qualifying for other classes.

2. Motor gliders, self-launching or with auxiliary power engines for use after auto-tow launch: various designs available fully manufacturer assembled or in kit.

Manufacturer-assembled motor gliders are similar in size to sailplanes. Wingspans range from 40 to 68 ft. Landing runs range from 300 to under 1,000 ft.

Kit-built motor gliders offer wingspans from as little as 15 ft 8 in. to approximately 42 ft, with a wide range of specifications.

Source: Soaring Society of America, P.O. Box 66071, Los Angeles, CA 90066.

SOARING

RECOMMENDED READING

Jane's All the World's Aircraft, Jane's Publishing Company Limited, 238 City Road, London EC1V 2PU, England.

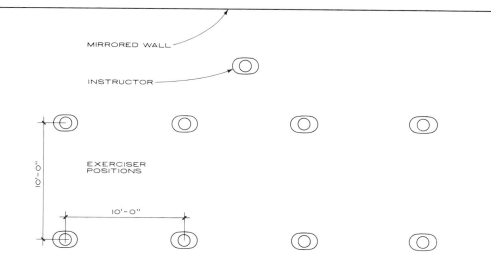

MIRRORED WALL

INSTRUCTOR

EXERCISER POSITIONS

10'-0"

10'-0"

AEROBICS TRAINING AREA

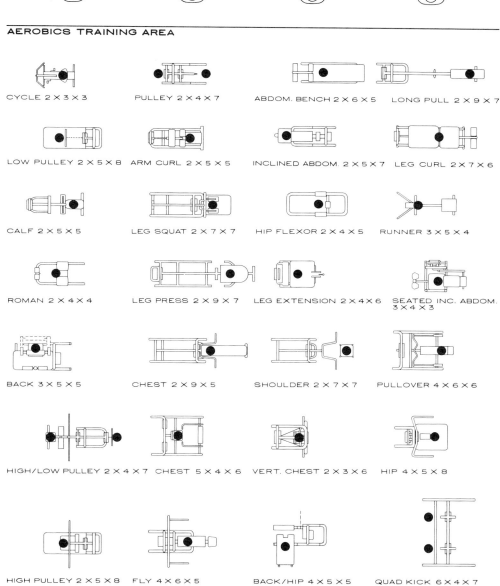

CYCLE 2 X 3 X 3

PULLEY 2 X 4 X 7

ABDOM. BENCH 2 X 6 X 5

LONG PULL 2 X 9 X 7

LOW PULLEY 2 X 5 X 8

ARM CURL 2 X 5 X 5

INCLINED ABDOM. 2 X 5 X 7

LEG CURL 2 X 7 X 6

CALF 2 X 5 X 5

LEG SQUAT 2 X 7 X 7

HIP FLEXOR 2 X 4 X 5

RUNNER 3 X 5 X 4

ROMAN 2 X 4 X 4

LEG PRESS 2 X 9 X 7

LEG EXTENSION 2 X 4 X 6

SEATED INC. ABDOM. 3 X 4 X 3

BACK 3 X 5 X 5

CHEST 2 X 9 X 5

SHOULDER 2 X 7 X 7

PULLOVER 4 X 6 X 6

HIGH/LOW PULLEY 2 X 4 X 7

CHEST 5 X 4 X 6

VERT. CHEST 2 X 3 X 6

HIP 4 X 5 X 8

HIGH PULLEY 2 X 5 X 8

FLY 4 X 6 X 5

BACK/HIP 4 X 5 X 5

QUAD KICK 6 X 4 X 7

● INDICATES APPROXIMATE USER POSITION. PROXIMITY TO WALL AND OTHER MACHINES VARIES. DIMENSIONS TO NEAREST FOOT W X D X H

WEIGHT TRAINING MACHINES

Frederick C. Krenson, AIA; Rosser Fabrap International; Atlanta, Georgia

AEROBICS

Aerobics is taught in a classroom setting. Space requirements are 100 sq ft per person plus an instructor. Flooring should be firm but resilient, such as a court floor. Ceilings should be acoustically absorptive. One or two walls should be mirrored, and stretching bars should be provided. The instructor's area at the front of the room may include voice amplification and a control or sound system. Use of videotape for teaching purposes should be considered.

TRAINING EQUIPMENT

Exercise and weight training equipment is available from a variety of manufacturers. Combinations of equipment, or circuits, can be arranged to develop particular muscle groups or endurance. Equipment manufacturers can assist with proper spacing and clearances. Overall supervision of training areas is recommended, both for equipment safety and proper conditioning use. Ceiling height should be as required by equipment, but should not be less than 10 ft high. Training room arrangement may include mirrors on one or two walls, computerization of certain pieces of equipment, a record-keeping area for users, soft flooring to reduce impact noise, as well as other acoustical treatment. The weight of the machinery and proper ventilation should be considered. Other pieces of equipment such as treadmills and exercycles may be research related and require ancillary monitoring and data-keeping equipment. Loose equipment, such as dumbbells and barbells, complements power racks and may be preferred by some users or programs. Olympic weights and an Olympic lifting platform may be coordinated with a videotaping system.

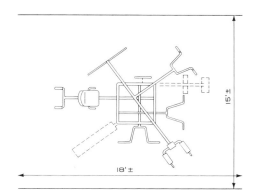

15' ±

18' ±

NOTE

The multiple station machine combines the functions of a variety of individual training devices into one machine. It is less costly than multiple machines and requires less space.

MULTIPLE STATION

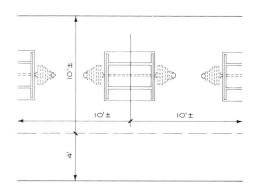

10' ±

10' ±

10' ±

4'

NOTE

The power rack is designed for confined free weights. It often involves a user, spotters, coaches, and observers and may be placed in front of mirrors. This machine should be on soft flooring such as rubber. Benches and other accessories may be used with the power rack.

POWER RACK

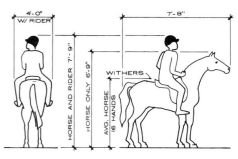

ONE HAND EQUALS 4"

CLEARANCES FOR HORSE AND RIDER

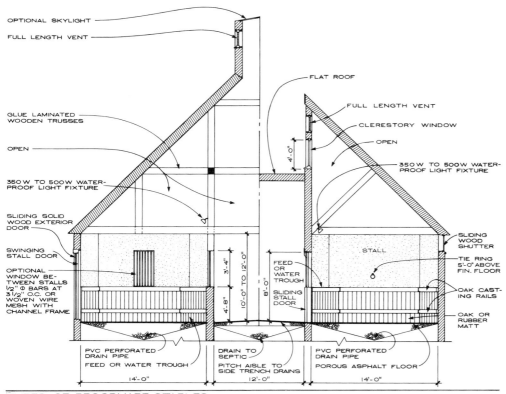

TYPES OF BROODMARE STABLES

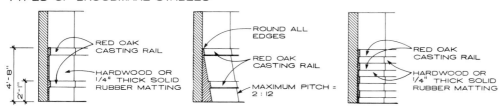

TYPICAL STALL TREATMENT FOR CASTING PREVENTION

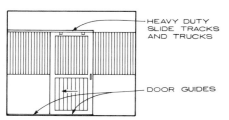

TYPICAL SLIDING AISLE DOOR

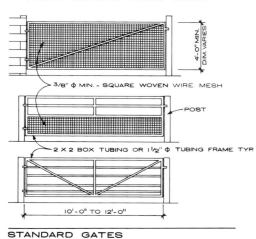

STANDARD GATES

Theodore M. Ceraldi & Associates, Architects; Nyack, New York

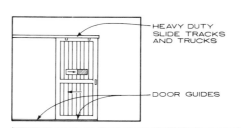

SOLID WOOD FOALING STALL WITH VIEW THROUGH

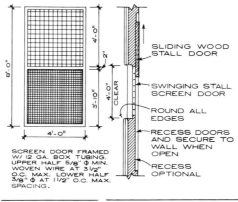

BROODMARE STALL SCREEN   **BROODMARE EXTERIOR STALL DOOR PLAN**

NOTES

Barns: masonry and glue-laminated construction for fire-resistance. Stalls: furred out, finished with red oak, hardwood, or ¼ in. rubber matting. Casting rails: 2 in. x 6 in. red oak, edges rounded, sealed with boiled linseed oil. Countersink fastener heads, plug. Stall corners: rounded or 45° walls to casting rail. Ventilation: high open slots with optional sliding wood shutter. Windows: safety glass only, minimum of 8 ft. above floor. Floor: 3 in. porous asphalt (percolation of one gallon in ten seconds) over 18 in. crushed stone with a porous drain pipe pitched to take effluent away from barn areas. Check local codes on septic requirements. Floors: rough concrete or skid-resistant brick pavers with a central floor drain to catch basin. Grates: cast iron or pre-cast concrete centered in stall with perforations no larger than 1 in. diameter or 1 in. sq. Floor: sloped to center drain. Provide optional infrared heaters in all horse wash areas at maximum 10 ft. above floor. Aisle floors: porous asphalt, paving bricks set in 2 in. sand, or diamond scored concrete with trench drains to each side.

Tack room area varies with the type of stable. Riding stables have at least one bridle and saddle per horse or pony. Saddle and bridle racks can be fastened in rows, one over another. Additional space is needed for groom equipment, sometimes stored in tack trunks. In broodmare stables, tack is mainly halters and grooming supplies. Tack room and foaling stall must be heated. Foaling stall heat: controllable to raise it as quickly as possible to 75° minimum and to maintain it. Foaling stall floor: seamless, rubberized material, minimum 1 in. thick, texturized, and pitched to a separate drain and catch basin (not connected to main barn drainage). Rubberized flooring turned up the walls, minimum of 24 in. Foaling stall adjoined by the situp room (also heated) with a one-way unbreakable glass panel and/or slide shutter for the groom to observe.

All feed and grain storage bins are lined with galvanized steel for vermin control. Feed amounts vary widely. As a guideline, a horse under medium to heavy workload is fed 15 lbs. of grain plus hay per day. All hay and bedding must be stored in a separate dry barn due to fire risk. As horses are grazing animals, hay mangers are not recommended; place hay in a corner on the stall floor. All roofs should have a minimum 7/12 pitch and continuous full length vents under the eaves and at ridges. Sliding doors are preferable. All swinging dutch doors or full doors should have a 180° swing to wall and fasten. Stalls should have heavy duty slide bolts, kick over bolts, and/or locking pins. All hardware should be smooth with no sharp protrusions and inaccessible to horses at the stalls. All light fixtures should be guarded and/or waterproofed. Light switches: located in a central panel away from wet areas. Lighting levels vary. Depending on the program, stalls are lighted with a single floodlight over the inside stall door at the ceiling or 10 ft. to 12 ft. above finished floor. Aisles can be lighted by incandescent or fluorescent lamps. Broodmares and stallions require brighter light and lighting programs to keep fertility levels maximized (approximately 100 foot candles should be achieved at 5 ft. 0 in. above finished floor per stall). Aisles may have lower light levels of 40 foot candles, except examination or display areas, which must have additional light available on demand.

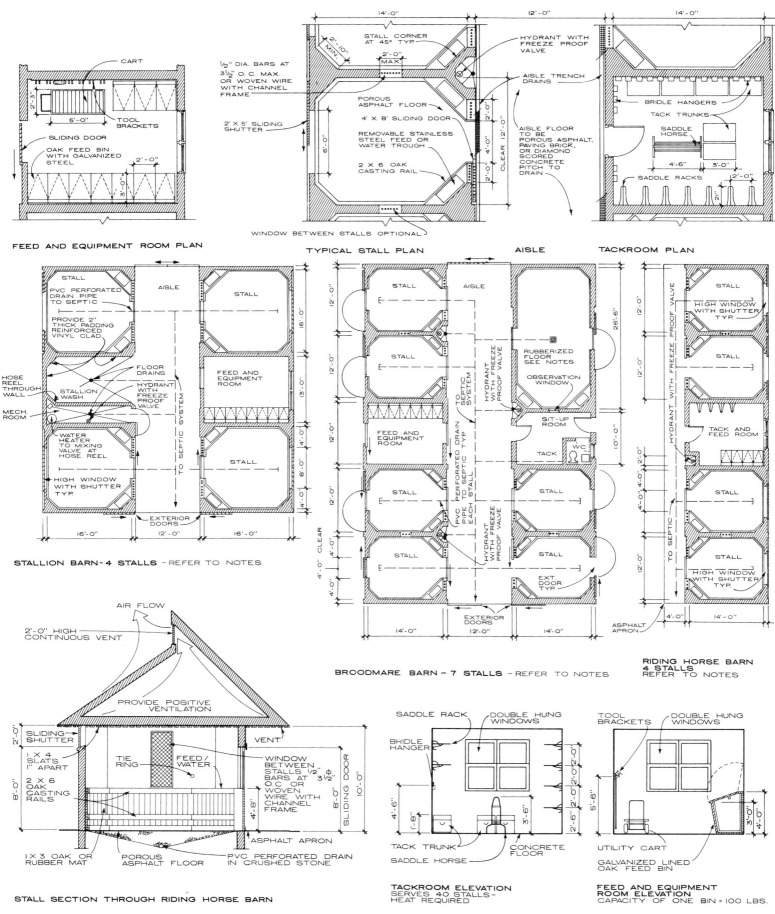

FEED AND EQUIPMENT ROOM PLAN

TYPICAL STALL PLAN

AISLE

TACKROOM PLAN

STALLION BARN-4 STALLS - REFER TO NOTES

BROODMARE BARN - 7 STALLS - REFER TO NOTES

RIDING HORSE BARN 4 STALLS REFER TO NOTES

STALL SECTION THROUGH RIDING HORSE BARN

TACKROOM ELEVATION
SERVES 40 STALLS - HEAT REQUIRED

FEED AND EQUIPMENT ROOM ELEVATION
CAPACITY OF ONE BIN = 100 LBS.

Theodore M. Ceraldi & Associates, Architects; Nyack, New York

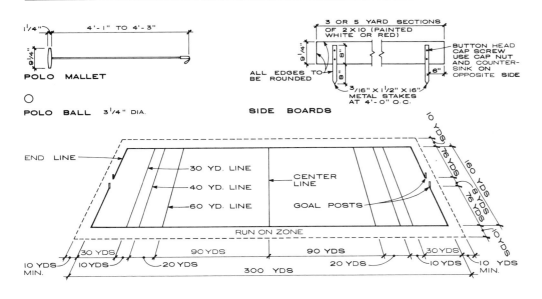

POLO MALLET

POLO BALL 3¼" DIA.

SIDE BOARDS

OUTDOOR POLO FIELD

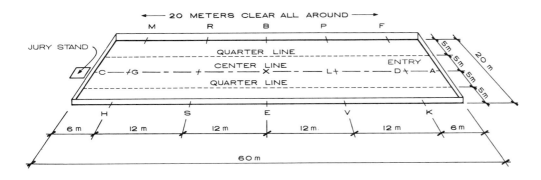

STANDARD DRESSAGE ARENA

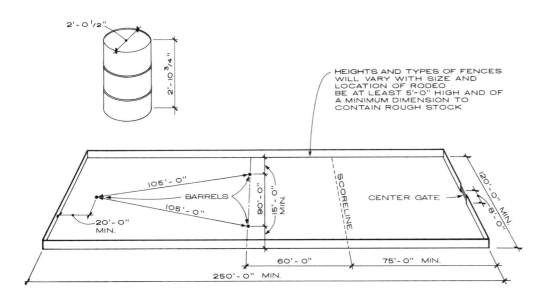

STANDARD BARREL COURSE

Theodore M. Ceraldi & Associates, Architects; Nyack, New York

POLO

Outdoor or high goal polo is played with two teams of four players each. There can be as many as forty horses per team, and stabling and picket areas are needed for the horses. Spectator stands to accommodate three to six thousand people are needed, depending on the level of play.

The field surface should be grass cut smooth and short enough for the ball to roll straight and easily. The field side boundaries are 10 in. high side boards with a minimum of 10 yards run on, known as the safety zone, beyond. Goal posts must be vertical and light enough to break upon collision. Goal posts are 10 ft. high, and 8 yds. apart. About twenty balls are used in a game.

Arena polo is played at smaller clubs or indoors where less space is available. A playing area of 300 ft. by 150 ft. is considered ideal. Goals, at opposite ends of the field, are 10 ft. in width by 12 ft. in height, inside measurement. In smaller arenas the goal size may be reduced, but to not less than 8 ft. in width by 10 ft.in height. The arena shall be clearly marked at the center and at points 15 yds. and 25 yds. perpendicular to each goal. The inflated arena polo ball shall be not less than 4¼ in. nor more than 4½ in. in diameter.

Further information: United States Polo Association, Oak Brook, Ill.

DRESSAGE

The arena should be on as level ground as possible. The standard arena is 60 meters x 20 meters. The small arena is 40 meters x 20 meters. The enclosure itself should consist of a low fence about 0.30 meters high. The part of the fence at letter A should be easily removable to let competitors in and out of the arena. Arenas must be separated from the public by a distance of not less than 20 meters.

The letters, clearly marked, should be placed outside the enclosure about 0.50 meters from the fence. A red line painted on the fence 20 cm. high locates the exact point of the letters on the track. The center line, throughout its length, and the three points D, X, and G should be as clearly marked as possible, without frightening the horses. It is recommended, on grass arenas, to mow the grass on the center line shorter than other parts of the arena, and on a sand arena, to roll or rake the center line.

An exercise area must be provided far enough away from the arena so as not to disturb the competitors.

SHOW

Horse show rings vary in size according to type of activity performed. A basic outdoor ring size for hunters and jumpers is 150 ft.x 300 ft. Combined training requires a stadium show ring of 80 meters x 80 meters, as well as a dressage ring. The appropriate breed or show association should be contacted for current and specific regulations.

Flat classes need a level arena with solid footing. There should be one definite opening for an 'in' gate; preferable are separate openings for in and out gates. Rings for flat classes should be large enough to accommodate comfortably the number of horses.

Show management must provide sufficient area for schooling horses. It is recommended that separate schooling areas be provided for hunters and jumpers since different types of jumps are used for each. Jumps may vary from a single jump consisting of a single bar 4 in. in diameter and 6 ft. long, hung in cups from two uprights, to various combinations of two and three fences, water jumps, banks, and ditches—depending on the skill level of the class.

Further information: American Horse Show Association, New York, N.Y.

RODEO

Rodeo consists of several events involving timed contests such as calf roping and barrel riding, and rough stock events such as steer wrestling and bull riding. Arenas may vary in size but must be enclosed with fencing to control the various livestock. Barriers and chutes for timed events should be at the opposite end of arena from chutes for rough stock events. Stables, pens, and corrals for holding stock must be provided, as well as area for contestants to exercise their animals. Grandstand seating is standard; the number of spectators varies with the number and competition level of rodeo participants.

Barrels must be regulation 55 gal. size metal or rubber and enclosed on both ends.

Further information: International Professional Rodeo Association, Pauls Valley, Okla.

REFERENCES

DATA SOURCES; ORGANIZATIONS

Amateur Athletic Union (AAU), 207

American Locker Security Systems, Inc., 227

American Public Health Association (APHA), 218

American Water Ski Association, 225

Federation Internationale de Natation Amateur (FINA), 215, 218, 220

Hussey Manufacturing Company, Inc., 208

International Amateur Athletic Federation (IAAF), 210, 211

International Professional Rodeo Association (IPRA), 234

KDI Paragon, Inc., 223, 224

Larchmont Engineering, Inc., 227

National Collegiate Athletic Association (NCAA), 207

National Hockey League, 226

National Playing Fields Association (NPFA), 210, 211

National Swimming Pool Institute (NSPI), 215, 217

Skate Sailing Association of America, 226

Snow Machines, Inc., 227

Sno-Engineering, Inc., 227

Southwood Corporation, 231

Universal Gym Equipment, 231

U.S. Water Polo, Inc., 225

Young Men's Christian Association (YMCA), 217

DATA SOURCES: PUBLICATIONS

1985 Roundup of Over-Snow Vehicles, Nils Ericksen, Ski Area Management Magazine, 227

1986 Alpine Skiing Competition Guide, USSA, 227

American Horse Show Association Rule Book, 1984–85 ed., American Horse Show Association (AHSA), 234

Developing an Urban Ski Facility, James Branch, Ski Area Management Magazine, 227

Jane's All the World's Aircraft, 1979–80 ed. and 1982–83 ed., John W. Taylor, Jane's USA, a Division of Franklin Watts, 230

Soaring in America, 1983, Soaring Society of America, 230

United States Polo Association Rule Book, United States Polo Association (USPA), 234

CHAPTER **8**

MISCELLANEOUS DATA

GRAPHIC STANDARDS	238
GRAPHIC METHODS	240
MATHEMATICAL DATA	245
WEIGHTS OF MATERIALS	246
METRIC CONVERSION	247

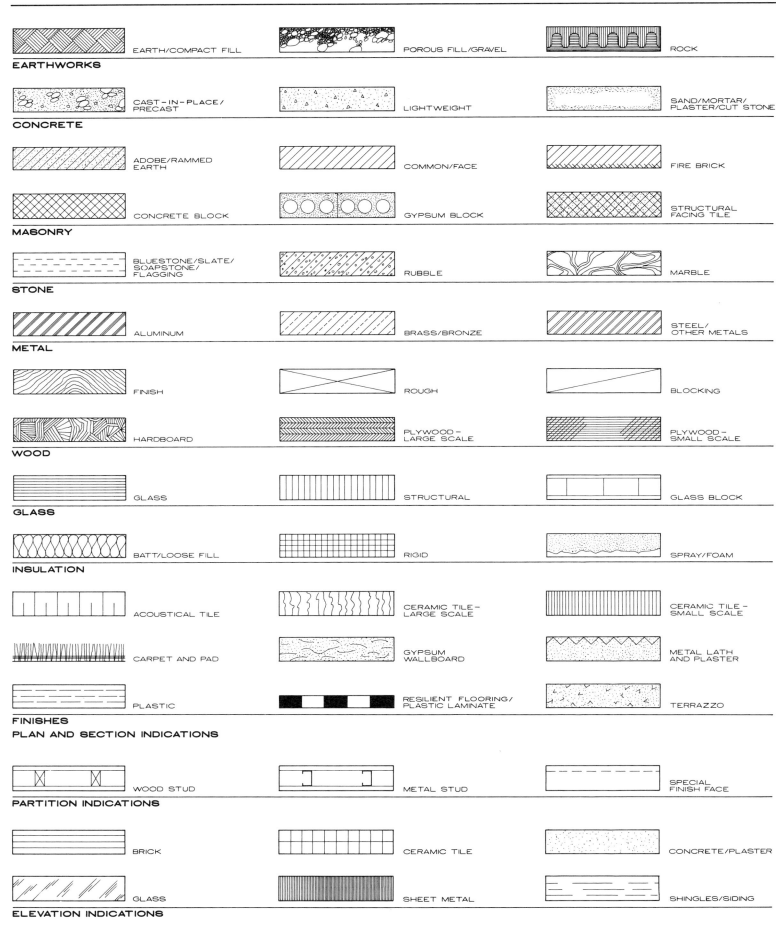

EARTH/COMPACT FILL

POROUS FILL/GRAVEL

ROCK

EARTHWORKS

CAST-IN-PLACE/PRECAST

LIGHTWEIGHT

SAND/MORTAR/PLASTER/CUT STONE

CONCRETE

ADOBE/RAMMED EARTH

COMMON/FACE

FIRE BRICK

CONCRETE BLOCK

GYPSUM BLOCK

STRUCTURAL FACING TILE

MASONRY

BLUESTONE/SLATE/SOAPSTONE/FLAGGING

RUBBLE

MARBLE

STONE

ALUMINUM

BRASS/BRONZE

STEEL/OTHER METALS

METAL

FINISH

ROUGH

BLOCKING

HARDBOARD

PLYWOOD-LARGE SCALE

PLYWOOD-SMALL SCALE

WOOD

GLASS

STRUCTURAL

GLASS BLOCK

GLASS

BATT/LOOSE FILL

RIGID

SPRAY/FOAM

INSULATION

ACOUSTICAL TILE

CERAMIC TILE-LARGE SCALE

CERAMIC TILE-SMALL SCALE

CARPET AND PAD

GYPSUM WALLBOARD

METAL LATH AND PLASTER

PLASTIC

RESILIENT FLOORING/PLASTIC LAMINATE

TERRAZZO

FINISHES

PLAN AND SECTION INDICATIONS

WOOD STUD

METAL STUD

SPECIAL FINISH FACE

PARTITION INDICATIONS

BRICK

CERAMIC TILE

CONCRETE/PLASTER

GLASS

SHEET METAL

SHINGLES/SIDING

ELEVATION INDICATIONS

John Ray Hoke, Jr., AIA; Washington, D.C.

GRAPHIC STANDARDS

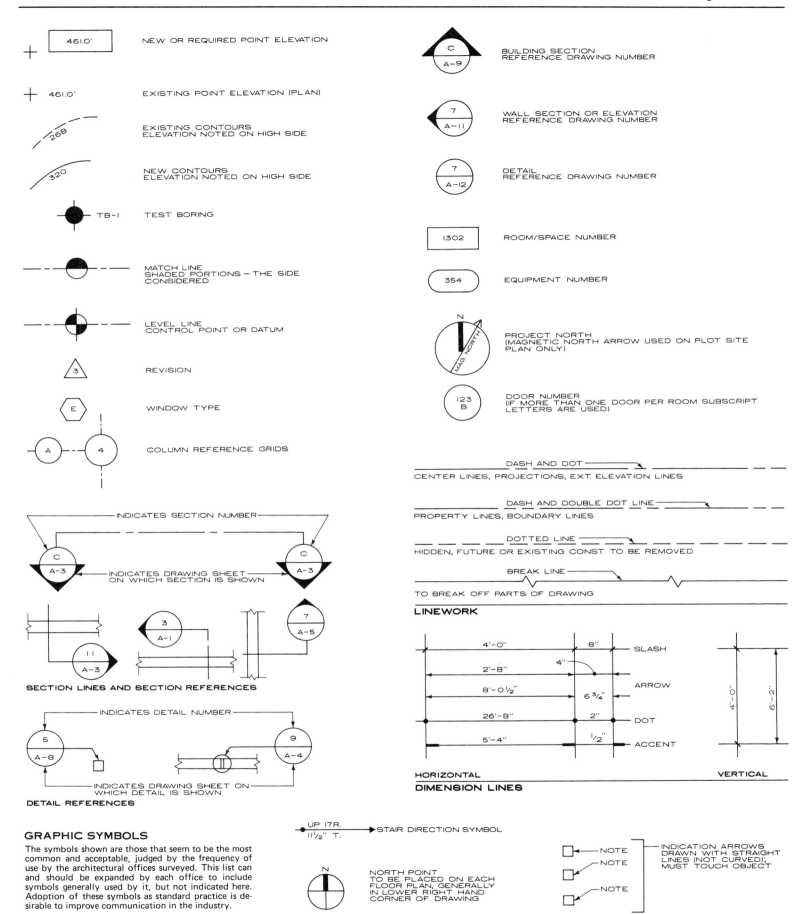

GRAPHIC SYMBOLS

The symbols shown are those that seem to be the most common and acceptable, judged by the frequency of use by the architectural offices surveyed. This list can and should be expanded by each office to include symbols generally used by it, but not indicated here. Adoption of these symbols as standard practice is desirable to improve communication in the industry.

John Ray Hoke, Jr., AIA; Washington, D.C.

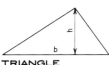

TRIANGLE
AREA = ½ ANY ALTITUDE X ITS BASE (ALTITUDE IS PERPENDICULAR DISTANCE TO OPPOSITE VERTEX OR CORNER.)
$A = \frac{1}{2} b \times h$

TRAPEZUM (IRREGULAR QUADRILATERAL)
AREA = DIVIDE FIGURE INTO TWO TRIANGLES AND FIND AREAS AS ABOVE

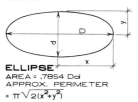

ELLIPSE
AREA = .7854 Dd
APPROX. PERIMETER
$= \pi \sqrt{2(x^2 + y^2)}$

TRAPEZOID
AREA = ½ SUM OF PARALLEL SIDES X ALTITUDE
$A = h\frac{(a+b)}{2}$

PARALLELOGRAM
AREA = EITHER SIDE X ALTITUDE

PARABOLA
AREA $= \frac{4 hb}{3}$

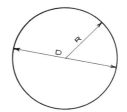

CIRCLE
AREA $= \frac{\pi D^2}{4} = \pi R^2$
CIRCUMFERENCE $= 2\pi R = \pi D$
($\pi = 3.14159265359$)

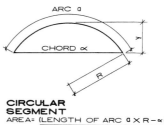

CIRCULAR SEGMENT
AREA = (LENGTH OF ARC $a \times R - a(R-y)$) /2
CHORD $a = 2\sqrt{2yR - y^2}$
$= 2R \sin \frac{A°}{2}$

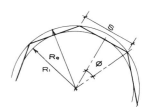

REGULAR POLYGON
AREA $= \frac{nSR_i}{2}$
(n = NUMBER OF SIDES)
ANY SIDE $S = 2\sqrt{R_o^2 - R_i^2}$
$R_i = \frac{S}{2 \tan \phi}$ $R_o = \frac{S}{2 \sin \phi}$

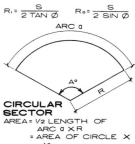

CIRCULAR SECTOR
AREA = ½ LENGTH OF ARC $a \times R$
= AREA OF CIRCLE X $\frac{A°}{360}$
$= 0.0087 R^2 A°$
ARC $a = \frac{\pi R A°}{180°} = 0.0175 R A°$

GEOMETRIC PROPERTIES OF PLANE FIGURES

SPHERE
VOLUME $= \frac{4\pi R^3}{3} = 0.5236 D^3$
SURFACE $= 4\pi R^2 = \pi D^2$

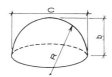

SEGMENT OF SPHERE
VOLUME $= \frac{\pi b^2 (3R - b)}{3}$ (OR SECTOR − CONE)
SURFACE $= 2\pi Rb$ (NOT INCLUDING SURFACE OF CIRCULAR BASE)

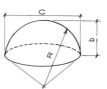

SECTOR OF SPHERE
VOLUME $= \frac{2\pi R^2 b}{3}$
SURFACE $= \frac{\pi R (4b + c)}{2}$ (OR: SEGMENT + CONE)

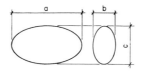

ELLIPSOID
VOLUME $= \frac{\pi abc}{6}$
SURFACE: NO SIMPLE RULE

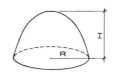

PARABOLOID OF REVOLUTION
VOLUME = AREA OF CIRCULAR BASE X ½ ALTITUDE.
SURFACE: NO SIMPLE RULE

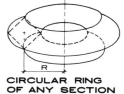

CIRCULAR RING OF ANY SECTION
R = DISTANCE FROM AXIS OF RING TO TRUE CENTER OF SECTION
VOLUME = AREA OF SECTION X $2\pi R$
SURFACE = PERIMETER OF SECTION X $2\pi R$ (CONSIDER THE SECTION ON ONE SIDE OF AXIS ONLY)

VOLUMES AND SURFACES OF DOUBLE - CURVED SOLIDS

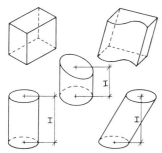

ANY PRISM OR CYLINDER, RIGHT OR OBLIQUE, REGULAR OR IRREGULAR.
Volume = area of base x altitude
Altitude = distance between parallel bases, measured perpendicular to the bases. When bases are not parallel, then Altitude = perpendicular distance from one base to the center of the other.

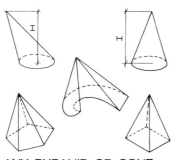

ANY PYRAMID OR CONE, RIGHT OR OBLIQUE, REGULAR OR IRREGULAR.
Volume = area of base x 1/3 altitude
Altitude = distance from base to apex, measured perpendicular to base.

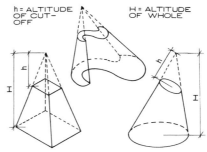

ANY FRUSTUM OR TRUNCATED PORTION OF THE SOLIDS SHOWN
Volume: From the volume of the whole solid, if complete, subtract the volume of the portion cut off.
The altitude of the cut-off part must be measured perpendicular to its own base.

SURFACES OF SOLIDS
The area of the surface is best found by adding together the areas of all the faces.

The area of a right cylindrical surface = perimeter of base x length of elements (average length if other base is oblique).

The area of a right conical surface = perimeter of base x 1/2 length of elements.

There is no simple rule for the area of an oblique conical surface, or for a cylindrical one where neither base is perpendicular to the elments. The best method is to construct a development, as if making a paper model, and measure its area by one of the methods given on the next page.

VOLUMES AND SURFACES OF TYPICAL SOLIDS

GRAPHIC METHODS

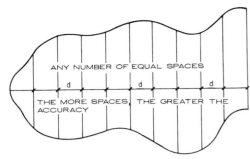

TO FIND THE AREA OF AN IRREGULAR PLANE FIGURE

1. Divide the figure into parallel strips by equally spaced parallel lines.

2. Measure the length of each of the parallel lines.

3. Obtain a summation of the unit areas by one of these 3 "rules".

TRAPEZOID RULE

Add together the length of the parallels, taking the first and last at $1/2$ value, and multiply by the width of the internal "d". This rule is sufficiently accurate for estimating and other ordinary purposes.

SIMPSON'S RULE

Add the parallels, taking the first and last at full value, second, the fourth, sixth, etc. from each end at 4 times full value, and the third, fifth, seventh, etc. from each end at 2 times the value, then multiply by $1/3$ d. This rule works only for an even number of spaces and is accurate for areas bounded by smooth curves.

DURAND'S RULE

Add the parallels taking the first and last at $5/12$ value, the second from each end at $13/12$ value, and all others at full value, then multiply by d. This rule is the most accurate for very irregular shapes.

NOTE

Irregular areas may be directly read off by means of a simple instrument called a Planimeter.

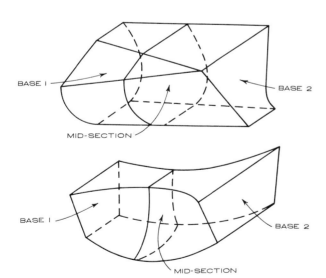

TO FIND THE VOLUME OF AN IRREGULAR FIGURE BY THE PRISMATOID FORMULA

Construct a section midway between the bases. Add 4 to the sum of the areas of the 2 bases and multiply the quantity by the area of the mid-section. Then multiply the total by $1/6$ the perpendicular distance between the bases.

V = [(area of base$_1$ + area of base$_2$ + 4) (area of midsection) x $1/6$ perpendicular distance between bases.

This formula is quite accurate for any solid with two parallel bases connected by a surface of straight line elements (upper figure), or smooth simple curves (lower figure).

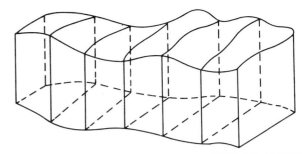

TO FIND THE VOLUME OF A VERY IRREGULAR FIGURE BY THE SECTIONING METHOD

1. Construct a series of equally spaced sections or profiles.

2. Determine the area of each section by any of the methods shown at left (preferably with a Planimeter).

3. Apply any one of the 3 summation "rules" given at left, to determine the total volume.

This method is in general use for estimating quantities of earthwork, etc.

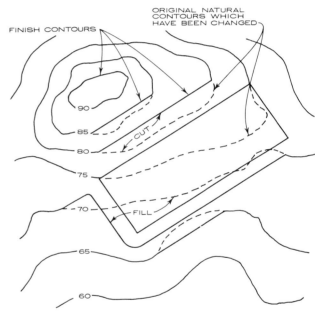

TO FIND THE VOLUME OF CUT AND FILL DIRECTLY FROM THE CONTOUR PLAN

1. Draw "finish" and "original" contours on same contour map.

2. Measure the differential areas between new and old contours of each contour and enter in columns according to whether cut or fill.

3. Add up each column and multiply by the contour interval to determine the volume in cubic feet.

EXAMPLE

CONTOUR	CUT		FILL	
85		300		
80		960		
75	2,460 − 2 =	1,230	3,800 − 2 =	1,900
70		20		2,200
		9,200		6,800
		x5		x5
TOTALS		46,000 cu. ft.		34,000 cu. ft.

NOTE

1. Where a cut or fill ends directly on a contour level use $1/2$ value.

2. The closer the contour interval, the greater the accuracy.

This method is more rapid than the sectioning method, and is sufficiently accurate for simple estimating purposes and for balancing of cut and fill.

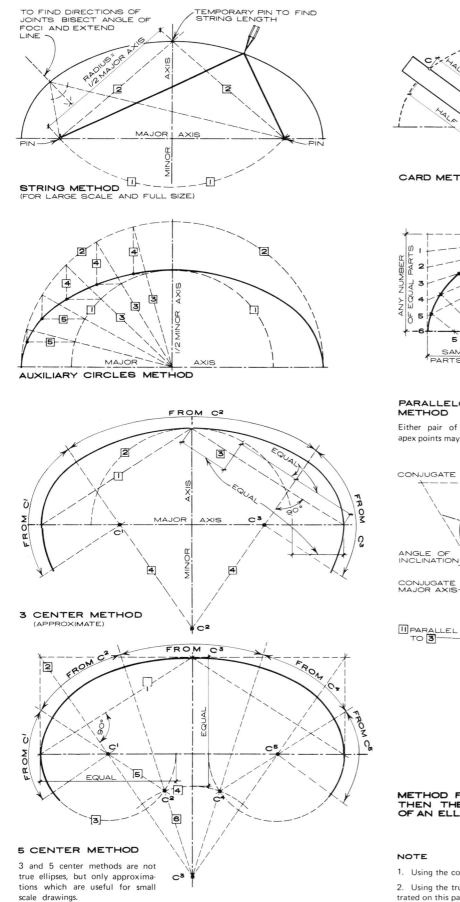

TO FIND DIRECTIONS OF JOINTS BISECT ANGLE OF FOCI AND EXTEND LINE

TEMPORARY PIN TO FIND STRING LENGTH

RADIUS = 1/2 MAJOR AXIS

AXIS

MAJOR AXIS

MINOR

PIN

PIN

STRING METHOD
(FOR LARGE SCALE AND FULL SIZE.)

1/2 MINOR AXIS

MAJOR   AXIS

AUXILIARY CIRCLES METHOD

FROM C²

FROM C¹

FROM C³

EQUAL

EQUAL

90°

AXIS

MAJOR   AXIS

C¹

C³

MINOR

3 CENTER METHOD
(APPROXIMATE)

FROM C²

FROM C³

FROM C⁴

FROM C¹

FROM C⁵

90°

C¹

C⁵

EQUAL

EQUAL

C²

C⁴

C³

5 CENTER METHOD

3 and 5 center methods are not true ellipses, but only approximations which are useful for small scale drawings.

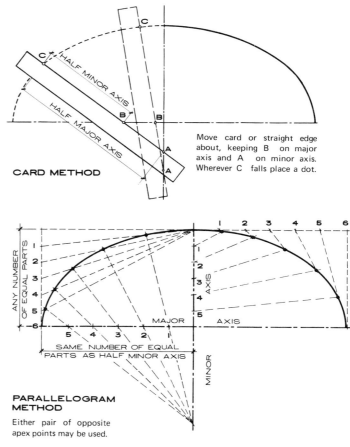

C

HALF MINOR AXIS

B

B

HALF MAJOR AXIS

A

A

CARD METHOD

Move card or straight edge about, keeping B on major axis and A on minor axis. Wherever C falls place a dot.

ANY NUMBER OF EQUAL PARTS

1 2 3 4 5 6

MAJOR   AXIS

SAME NUMBER OF EQUAL PARTS AS HALF MINOR AXIS

MINOR

PARALLELOGRAM METHOD

Either pair of opposite apex points may be used.

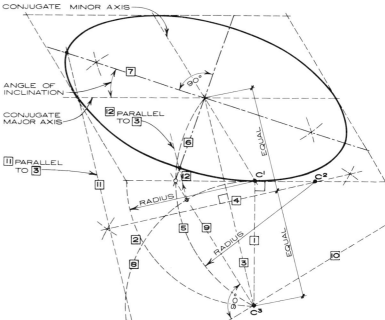

CONJUGATE MINOR AXIS

90°

ANGLE OF INCLINATION

7

CONJUGATE MAJOR AXIS

12 PARALLEL TO 3

6

11 PARALLEL TO 3

12

C¹

C²

RADIUS

11

4

EQUAL

5 9

2

RADIUS

1

8

3

90°

10

C³

METHOD FOR FINDING THE ANGLE OF INCLINATION AND THEN THE TRUE LENGTHS OF THE MAJOR & MINOR AXES OF AN ELLIPSE TO BE INSCRIBED WITHIN A PARALLELOGRAM

NOTE

1. Using the conjugate axes, the ellipse can be drawn directly by using the parallelogram method.

2. Using the true lengths of the axes, the ellipse may be drawn with any one of the methods illustrated on this page.

8

GRAPHIC METHODS

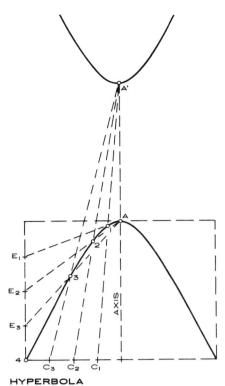

HYPERBOLA
PARALLELOGRAM METHOD
GIVEN:

Axis, two apexes (A and A') and a chord.

1. Draw surrounding parallelogram.
2. Divide chord in whole number of equal spaces (C_1, C_2, C_3, etc.).
3. Divide edge of parallelogram into same integral number of equal spaces (E_1, E_2, E_3, etc.).
4. Join A to points E on edge; join A' to points C on chord. Intersection of these rays are points on curve.

This method can be used equally well for any type of orthogonal or perspective projection, as shown by example of ellipse.

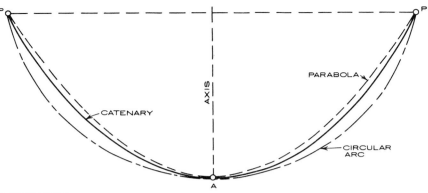

CATENARY

A catenary curve lies between a parabola and a circular arc drawn through the same three points, but is closer to the parabola. The catenary is not a conic section. The easiest method of drawing it is to tilt the drafting board and hang a very fine chain on it, and then prick guide points through the links of the chain.

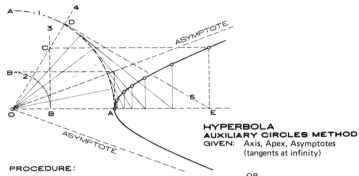

HYPERBOLA
AUXILIARY CIRCLES METHOD
GIVEN: Axis, Apex, Asymptotes (tangents at infinity)

PROCEDURE:

1. Draw auxiliary circles with OB and OA as radii: note $\frac{OB}{OA}$ = slope of asymptote.
2. Erect perpendicular 3 where circle 2 intersects axis.
3. Draw any line 4 through 0, intersecting circle 1 at B and line 3 at C.
4. Draw line 5 through C parallel to axis.
5. Draw tangent 6 at D, intersecting axis at E.
6. Erect perpendicular 7 at E, intersecting 5 at P, a point on hyperbola.

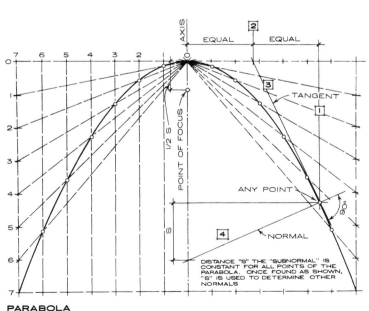

PARABOLA
PARALLELOGRAM METHOD

This method is comparable to the "Parallelogram Method" shown for the hyperbola above and the ellipse on previous page. The other apex 'A' is at infinity.

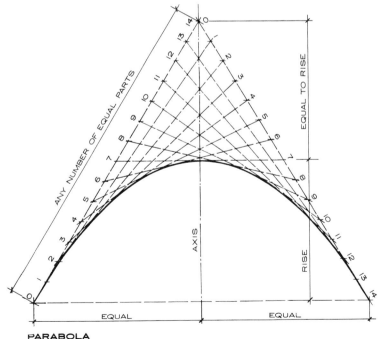

PARABOLA
ENVELOPE OF TANGENTS

This method does not give points on the curve, but a series of tangents within which the parabola can be drawn.

H. Seymour Howard, Jr.; Oyster Bay, New York

GRAPHIC METHODS

8

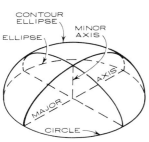

OBLATE SPHEROID

An ellipse rotated about its minor axis.

NOTES

1. The dome shapes shown above are SURFACES OF POSITIVE CUR-VATURE, that is, the centers of both principal radii of curvature are on the same side of the surface.

2. SURFACES OF NEGATIVE CURVATURE (saddle shapes) such as those shown below, are surfaces in which the centers of the two principal radii of curvature are on opposite sides of the surface.

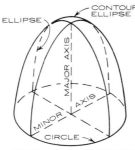

PROLATE SPHEROID

An ellipse rotated about its major axis.

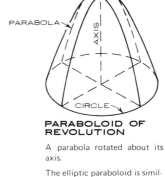

PARABOLOID OF REVOLUTION

A parabola rotated about its axis.

The elliptic paraboloid is similar, but its plan is an ellipse instead of circle, and vertical sections are varying parabolas.

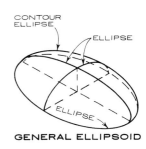

GENERAL ELLIPSOID

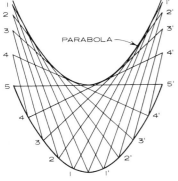

HYPERBOLIC PARABOLOID

(STRAIGHT LINE BOUNDARIES)
This shape and the hyperboloid of one sheet are the only two doubly ruled curved surfaces.

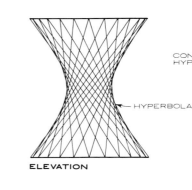

ELEVATION   **PROJECTION**

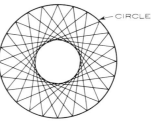

PLAN
HYPERBOLOID OF REVOLUTION
(OR HYPERBOLOID OF ONE SHEET)

NOTE

This shape is a doubly ruled surface, which can also be drawn with ellipses as plan sections instead of the circles shown.

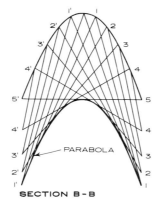

SECTION A-A   **SECTION B-B**

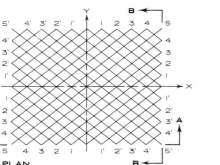

PLAN
HYPERBOLIC PARABOLOID
(PARABOLA BOUNDARIES)

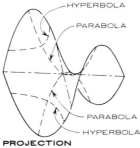

PROJECTION

SECTION

RULINGS IN PARALLEL PLANES

PLAN
CONOID
(SINGLY RULED SURFACE)

ELEVATION

ANY CURVE

PROJECTION

DECIMALS OF A FOOT

FRACTION	DECIMAL	FRACTION	DECIMAL	FRACTION	DECIMAL
1/16	0.0052	4-1/16	0.3385	8-1/16	0.6719
1/8	0.0104	4-1/8	0.3438	8-1/8	0.6771
3/16	0.0156	4-3/16	0.3490	8-3/16	0.6823
1/4	0.0208	4-1/4	0.3542	8-1/4	0.6875
5/16	0.0260	4-5/16	0.3594	8-5/16	0.6927
3/8	0.0313	4-3/8	0.3646	8-3/8	0.6979
7/16	0.0365	4-7/16	0.3698	8-7/16	0.7031
1/2	0.0417	4-1/2	0.3750	8-1/2	0.7083
9/16	0.0469	4-9/16	0.3802	8-9/16	0.7135
5/8	0.0521	4-5/8	0.3854	8-5/8	0.7188
11/16	0.0573	4-11/16	0.3906	8-11/16	0.7240
3/4	0.0625	4-3/4	0.3958	8-3/4	0.7292
13/16	0.0677	4-13/16	0.4010	8-13/16	0.7344
7/8	0.0729	4-7/8	0.4063	8-7/8	0.7396
15/16	0.0781	4-15/16	0.4115	8-15/16	0.7448
1-	0.0833	5-	0.4167	9-	0.7500
1-1/16	0.0885	5-1/16	0.4219	9-1/16	0.7552
1-1/8	0.0938	5-1/8	0.4271	9-1/8	0.7604
1-3/16	0.0990	5-3/16	0.4323	9-3/16	0.7656
1-1/4	0.1042	5-1/4	0.4375	9-1/4	0.7708
1-5/16	0.1094	5-5/16	0.4427	9-5/16	0.7760
1-3/8	0.1146	5-3/8	0.4479	9-3/8	0.7813
1-7/16	0.1198	5-7/16	0.4531	9-7/16	0.7865
1-1/2	0.1250	5-1/2	0.4583	9-1/2	0.7917
1-9/16	0.1302	5-9/16	0.4635	9-9/16	0.7969
1-5/8	0.1354	5-5/8	0.4688	9-5/8	0.8021
1-11/16	0.1406	5-11/16	0.4740	9-11/16	0.8073
1-3/4	0.1458	5-3/4	0.4792	9-3/4	0.8125
1-13/16	0.1510	5-13/16	0.4844	9-13/16	0.8177
1-7/8	0.1563	5-7/8	0.4896	9-7/8	0.8229
1-15/16	0.1615	5-15/16	0.4948	9-15/16	0.8281
2-	0.1667	6-	0.5000	10-	0.8333
2-1/16	0.1719	6-1/16	0.5052	10-1/16	0.8385
2-1/8	0.1771	6-1/8	0.5104	10-1/8	0.8438
2-3/16	0.1823	6-3/16	0.5156	10-3/16	0.8490
2-1/4	0.1875	6-1/4	0.5208	10-1/4	0.8542
2-5/16	0.1927	6-5/16	0.5260	10-5/16	0.8594
2-3/8	0.1979	6-3/8	0.5313	10-3/8	0.8646
2-7/16	0.2031	6-7/16	0.5365	10-7/16	0.8698
2-1/2	0.2083	6-1/2	0.5417	10-1/2	0.8750
2-9/16	0.2135	6-9/16	0.5469	10-9/16	0.8802
2-5/8	0.2188	6-5/8	0.5521	10-5/8	0.8854
2-11/16	0.2240	6-11/16	0.5573	10-11/16	0.8906
2-3/4	0.2292	6-3/4	0.5625	10-3/4	0.8958
2-13/16	0.2344	6-13/16	0.5677	10-13/16	0.9010
2-7/8	0.2396	6-7/8	0.5729	10-7/8	0.9063
2-15/16	0.2448	6-15/16	0.5781	10-15/16	0.9115
3-	0.2500	7-	0.5833	11-	0.9167
3-1/16	0.2552	7-1/16	0.5885	11-1/16	0.9219
3-1/8	0.2604	7-1/8	0.5938	11-1/8	0.9271
3-3/16	0.2656	7-3/16	0.5990	11-3/16	0.9323
3-1/4	0.2708	7-1/4	0.6042	11-1/4	0.9375
3-5/16	0.2760	7-5/16	0.6094	11-5/16	0.9427
3-3/8	0.2813	7-3/8	0.6146	11-3/8	0.9479
3-7/16	0.2865	7-7/16	0.6198	11-7/16	0.9531
3-1/2	0.2917	7-1/2	0.6250	11-1/2	0.9583
3-9/16	0.2969	7-9/16	0.6302	11-9/16	0.9635
3-5/8	0.3021	7-5/8	0.6354	11-5/8	0.9688
3-11/16	0.3073	7-11/16	0.6406	11-11/16	0.9740
3-3/4	0.3125	7-3/4	0.6458	11-3/4	0.9792
3-13/16	0.3177	7-13/16	0.6510	11-13/16	0.9844
3-7/8	0.3229	7-7/8	0.6563	11-7/8	0.9896
3-15/16	0.3281	7-15/16	0.6615	11-15/16	0.9948
4-	0.3333	8-	0.6667	12-	1.0000

DECIMALS OF AN INCH

FRACTION	DECIMAL
1/64	0.015625
1/32	0.03125
3/64	0.046875
1/16	0.0625
5/64	0.078125
3/32	0.09375
7/64	0.109375
1/8	0.125
9/64	0.140625
5/32	0.15625
11/64	0.171875
3/16	0.1875
13/64	0.203125
7/32	0.21875
15/64	0.234375
1/4	0.250
17/64	0.265625
9/32	0.28125
19/64	0.296875
5/16	0.3125
21/64	0.328125
11/32	0.34375
23/64	0.359375
3/8	0.375
25/64	0.390625
13/32	0.40625
27/64	0.421875
7/16	0.4375
29/64	0.453125
15/32	0.46875
31/64	0.484375
1/2	0.500
33/64	0.515625
17/32	0.53125
35/64	0.546875
9/16	0.5625
37/64	0.578125
19/32	0.59375
39/64	0.609375
5/8	0.625
41/64	0.640625
21/32	0.65625
43/64	0.671875
11/16	0.6875
45/64	0.703125
23/32	0.71875
47/64	0.734375
3/4	0.750
49/64	0.765625
25/32	0.78125
51/64	0.796875
13/16	0.8125
53/64	0.828125
27/32	0.84375
55/64	0.859375
7/8	0.875
57/64	0.890625
29/32	0.90625
59/64	0.921875
15/16	0.9375
61/64	0.953125
31/32	0.96875
63/64	0.984375
1"	1.000

BRICK AND BLOCK MASONRY	PSF
4" brickwork	40
4" concrete block, stone or gravel	34
4" concrete block, lightweight	22
4" concrete brick, stone or gravel	46
4" concrete brick, lightweight	33
6" concrete block, stone or gravel	50
6" concrete block, lightweight	31
8" concrete block, stone or gravel	55
8" concrete block, lightweight	35
12" concrete block, stone or gravel	85
12" concrete block, lightweight	55

CONCRETE		PCF
Plain	Cinder	108
	Expanded slag aggregate	100
	Expanded clay	90
	Slag	132
	Stone and cast stone	144
Reinforced	Cinder	111
	Slag	138
	Stone	150

FINISH MATERIALS	PSF
Acoustical tile unsupported per 1/2"	0.8
Building board, 1/2"	0.8
Cement finish, 1"	12
Fiberboard, 1/2"	0.75
Gypsum wallboard, 1/2"	2
Marble and setting bed	25-30
Plaster, 1/2"	4.5
Plaster on wood lath	8
Plaster suspended with lath	10
Plywood, 1/2"	1.5
Tile, glazed wall 3/8"	3
Tile, ceramic mosaic, 1/4"	2.5
Quarry tile, 1/2"	5.8
Quarry tile, 3/4"	8.6
Terrazzo 1", 2" in stone concrete	25
Vinyl tile, 1/8"	1.33
Hardwood flooring, 25/32"	4
Wood block flooring, 3" on mastic	15

FLOOR AND ROOF (CONCRETE)		PSF
Flexicore, 6" precast lightweight concrete		30
Flexicore, 6" precast stone concrete		40
Plank, cinder concrete, 2"		15
Plank, gypsum, 2"		12
Concrete, reinforced, 1"	Stone	12.5
	Slag	11.5
	Lightweight	6-10
Concrete, plain, 1"	Stone	12
	Slag	11
	Lightweight	3-9

FUELS AND LIQUIDS	PCF
Coal, piled anthracite	47-58
Coal, piled bituminous	40-54
Ice	57.2
Gasoline	75
Snow	8
Water, fresh	62.4
Water, sea	64

GLASS	PSF
Polished plate, 1/4"	3.28
Polished plate, 1/2"	6.56
Double strength, 1/8"	26 oz
Sheet A, B, 1/32"	45 oz
Sheet A, B, 1/4"	52 oz

Insulating glass 5/8" plate with airspace	3.25
1/4" wire glass	3.5
Glass block	18

INSULATION AND WATERPROOFING	PSF
Batt, blankets per 1" thickness	0.1-0.4
Corkboard per 1" thickness	0.58
Foamed board insulation per 1" thickness	2.6 oz
Five-ply membrane	5
Rigid insulation	0.75

LIGHTWEIGHT CONCRETE	PSF
Concrete, aerocrete	50-80
Concrete, cinder fill	60
Concrete, expanded clay	85-100
Concrete, expanded shale-sand	105-120
Concrete, perlite	35-50
Concrete, pumice	60-90

METALS	PCF
Aluminum, cast	165
Brass, cast, rolled	534
Bronze, commercial	552
Bronze, statuary	509
Copper, cast or rolled	556
Gold, cast, solid	1205
Gold coin in bags	509
Iron, cast gray, pig	450
Iron, wrought	480
Lead	710
Nickel	565
Silver, cast, solid	656
Silver coin in bags	590
Tin	459
Stainless steel, rolled	492-510
Steel, rolled, cold drawn	490
Zinc, rolled, cast or sheet	449

MORTAR AND PLASTER	PCF
Mortar, masonry	116
Plaster, gypsum, sand	104-120

PARTITIONS	PSF
2 x 4 wood stud, GWB, two sides	8
4" metal stud, GWB, two sides	6
4" concrete block, lightweight, GWB	26
6" concrete block, lightweight, GWB	35
2" solid plaster	20
4" solid plaster	32

ROOFING MATERIALS	PSF
Built up	6.5
Concrete roof tile	9.5
Copper	1.5-2.5
Corrugated iron	2
Deck, steel without roofing or insulation	2.2-3.6
Fiberglass panels (2 1/2" corrugated)	5-8 oz
Galvanized iron	1.2-1.7
Lead, 1/8"	6-8
Plastic sandwich panel, 2 1/2" thick	2.6
Shingles, asphalt	1.7-2.8
Shingles, wood	2-3
Slate, 3/16" to 1/4"	7-9.5
Slate, 3/8" to 1/2"	14-18
Stainless steel	2.5
Tile, cement flat	13
Tile, cement ribbed	16
Tile, clay shingle type	8-16
Tile, clay flat with setting bed	15-20

Wood sheathing per inch	3

SOIL, SAND, AND GRAVEL	PCF
Ashes or cinder	40-50
Clay, damp and plastic	110
Clay, dry	63
Clay and gravel, dry	100
Earth, dry and loose	76
Earth, dry and packed	95
Earth, moist and loose	78
Earth, moist and packed	96
Earth, mud, packed	115
Sand or gravel, dry and loose	90-105
Sand or gravel, dry and packed	100-120
Sand or gravel, dry and wet	118-120
Silt, moist, loose	78
Silt, moist, packed	96

STONE (ASHLAR)	PCF
Granite, limestone, crystalline	165
Limestone, oolitic	135
Marble	173
Sandstone, bluestone	144
Slate	172

STONE VENEER	PSF
2" granite, 1/2" parging	30
4" granite, 1/2" parging	59
6" limestone facing, 1/2" parging	55
4" sandstone or bluestone, 1/2" parging	49
1" marble	13
1" slate	14

STRUCTURAL CLAY TILE	PSF
4" hollow	23
6" hollow	38
8" hollow	45

STRUCTURAL FACING TILE	PSF
2" facing tile	14
4" facing tile	24
6" facing tile	34
8" facing tile	44

SUSPENDED CEILINGS	PSF
Mineral fiber tile 3/4", 12" x 12"	1.2-1.57
Mineral fiberboard 5/8", 24" x 24"	1.4
Acoustic plaster on gypsum lath base	10-11

WOOD	PCF
Ash, commercial white	40.5
Birch, red oak, sweet and yellow	44
Cedar, northern white	22.2
Cedar, western red	24.2
Cypress, southern	33.5
Douglas fir (coast region)	32.7
Fir, commercial white; Idaho white pine	27
Hemlock	28-29
Maple, hard (black and sugar)	44.5
Oak, white and red	47.3
Pine, northern white sugar	25
Pine, southern yellow	37.3
Pine, ponderosa, spruce: eastern and sitka	28.6
Poplar, yellow	29.4
Redwood	26
Walnut, black	38

NOTE

To establish uniform practice among designers, it is desirable to present a list of materials generally used in building construction, together with their proper weights. Many building codes prescribe the minimum weights of only a few building materials. It should be noted that there is a difference of more than 25% in some cases.

MEASUREMENT OF LENGTH

The basic SI unit of length is the meter. Fractions or multiples of the base unit are expressed with prefixes, only some of which are recommended for construction. In order to be clear, avoid those prefixes that are not specifically recommended for construction.

Common SI units for length as used in construction are:

UNIT NAME	SYMBOL	COMMENT	COMPUTER SYMBOL
Meter	m	Also spelled metre	M
Millimeter	mm	0.001 meter	MM
Kilometer	km	1000 meters	KM
Micrometer	um	0.000 001 meter	UM

Note: Centimeter is not recommended for construction.

The recommended unit for dimensioning buildings is the millimeter. The use of the meter would be limited to large dimensions, such as levels, overall dimensions, and engineering computations. Meters are also used for estimating and land surveying. On architectural drawings, dimensions require no symbol if millimeters are consistently used.

Kilometers are used for transportation and surveying. Micrometers would be used for thicknesses of materials, such as coatings.

Conversion factors for length are shown below:

METRIC	CUSTOMARY
1 meter	3.280 84 feet or 1.093 61 yards
1 millimeter	0.039 370 1 inch
1 kilometer	0.621 371 mile or 49.709 6 chains
1 micrometer	0.000 393 7 inch or 0.3937 mils

CUSTOMARY	METRIC
1 mile	1.609 344 km
1 chain	20.1168 m
1 yard	0.9144 m
1 foot	0.3048 m 304.8 mm
1 inch	25.4 mm

(1 U.S. survey foot = 0.304 800 6 m.)

The recommended linear basic module for construction is 100 mm in the United States. See page on dimensional coordination for application of this basic module. This is very close to the 4 in. module in general use for light construction. Scales of drawing relate to units of length. Use meters on all drawings with scale ratios between 1:200 and 1:2000. Use millimeters on drawings with scale ratios between 1:1 and 1:200.

MEASUREMENT OF AREA

There are no basic SI metric units for area. Rather, area units are derived from units for length, as follows:

UNIT NAME	SYMBOL	COMMENT
Square meter	m²	1 m² = 10⁶ mm²
Square millimeter	mm²	
Square kilometer	km²	Land area
Hectare	ha	1 ha = 10 000 m²

Note that the hectare, although not an SI unit, is acceptable as a supplemental unit. It is used for surface measurement of land and water only.

At times, area is expressed by linear dimensions such as 40 mm x 90 mm; 300 x 600. Normally the width is written first and depth or height second.

The square centimeter is not recommended for construction. Such measurements may be converted to millimeters (1 cm² = 100 mm²) or to meters (1 cm² = 10⁻⁴ m² = 0.0001 m²).

Conversion factors for area are shown below.

METRIC	CUSTOMARY
1 km²	0.386 101 mile² (U.S. Survey)
1 ha	2.471 04 acre (U.S. Survey)
1 m²	10.7639 ft² 1.195 99 yd²
1 mm²	0.001 550 in.²

CUSTOMARY	METRIC
1 mile² (U.S. Survey)	2.590 00 km²
1 acre (U.S. Survey)	0.404 687 ha 4046.87 m²
1 yd²	0.836 127 m²
1 ft²	0.092 903 m²
1 in.²	645.16 mm²

MEASUREMENT OF VOLUME AND SECTION MODULUS

There are no basic SI metric units for volume, but these are derived from units for length as well as non-SI units that are acceptable for use.

UNIT NAME	SYMBOL	COMMENT
Cubic meter	m³	1 m³ = 1000 L
Cubic millimeter	mm³	
Liter	L	Volume of fluids
Milliliter	mL	1 mL = 1 cm³
Cubic centimeter	cm³	1 cm³ = 1000 mm³

In construction, the cubic meter is used for volume and capacity of large quantities of earth, concrete, sand, and so on. It is preferred for all engineering purposes.

The section modulus is also expressed as unit of length to the third power (m³ and mm³).

Conversion factors are listed below.

VOLUME, MODULUS OF SECTION

METRIC	CUSTOMARY
1 m³	0.810 709 x 10³ acre ft 1.307 95 yd³ 35.3147 ft³ 423.776 board ft
1 mm³	61.0237 x 10⁻⁶ in.³

CUSTOMARY	METRIC
1 acre ft	1233.49 m³
1 yd³	0.764 555 m³
100 board ft	0.028 316 8 m³
1 ft³	16.387 1 mm³ 28 3168 1 (cm³)
1 in.³	16.3871 mL(cm³)

LIQUID, CAPACITY

METRIC	CUSTOMARY
1 L	0.035 3147 ft³ 0.264 172 gal (U.S.) 1.056 69 qt (U.S.)
1 mL	0.061 023 7 in.³

CUSTOMARY	METRIC
1 gal (U.S. liquid)	3.785 41 L
1 qt (U.S. liquid)	946.353 mL
1 pt (U.S. liquid)	473.177 mL
1 fl oz (U.S.)	29.5735 mL

NOTE: 1 gal (U.K.) = approximately 1.2 gal (U.S.).

MEASUREMENT OF MASS

The SI metric system recommends the use of the word mass in place of the more common word weight, because weight refers specifically to the pull of gravity, which can vary in different locations. The SI system also separates the concept of mass from that of force.

SI metric units and other acceptable units for mass are:

UNIT NAME	SYMBOL	COMMENT
Kilogram	kg	Most used
Gram	g	
Metric ton	t	1 t = 1000 kg

The kilogram is based on a prototype, and unlike other SI units cannot be derived without reference to the international prototype kilogram maintained under specified conditions at the International Bureau of Weights and Measures (BIPM) near Paris, France.

Conversion factors are listed below.

METRIC	CUSTOMARY
1 kg	2.204 62 lb (avoirdupois) 35.2740 02 oz (avoirdupois)
1 metric ton	1.102 31 ton (short, 2000 lb) 2204.62 lb
1 g	0.035 274 oz 0.643 015 pennyweight

CUSTOMARY	METRIC
1 ton (short)	0.907 185 metric ton (megagram) 907.185 kg
1 lb	0.453 592 kg
1 oz	28.3495 9 g
1 pennyweight	1.555 17 g

NOTE: A long ton (2240 lb) = 1016.05 kg or 1.016 05 metric ton.

TIME

The SI unit for time is the second, from which other units of time are derived. In construction measurements, such as flow rates, the use of minutes is not recommended, so that cubic meters per second, liters per second, or cubic meters per hour would be normally used. Time symbols are as follows:

Second	s
Minute	min
Hour	h
Day	d
Month	—
Year	a (365 days or 31 536 000 seconds)

For clarity, international recommendations for writing time and dates are as follows:

Time   Express by hour/minute/second on a 24 hour day:

03:20:30
16:45

Dates   Express by year/month/day:

1978-06-30
1978 06 30 (second preference)
19780630 (computer entry)

MEASUREMENT OF TEMPERATURE

The SI base unit of temperature is the Kelvin, which is a scale based on absolute zero. The allowable unit Celsius is equal to the Kelvin unit except that 0° Celsius is the freezing point of water. Thus a temperature listed in degrees Celsius plus 275.15 degrees is the temperature in degrees Kelvin. Celsius is in common use for construction, not Kelvin.

CUSTOMARY	METRIC
1°F	0.555 556°C 5/9° C or 5/9 K

METRIC	CUSTOMARY
1°C	1 K 1.8°F

NOTE: Centigrade is not recognized as part of the SI system.

PLANE ANGLE

While the SI unit for plane angle is the radian, the customary units degree (°), minute ('), and second ('') of arc will be retained in most applications in construction, engineering, and land surveying.

CUSTOMARY	METRIC
1°	(π/180) rad

REFERENCES

DATA SOURCES; ORGANIZATIONS

American Society for Testing and Materials (ASTM), 247

National Solid Wastes Management Association, 246

CHAPTER 9

HISTORIC CONSTRUCTION

The following materials are reproduced from two books—one that was published just before and the other just after the United States involvement in World War II. They present details and data for forms of construction that were widely used in the period of the early- to mid-twentieth century.

From:
Architectural Graphic Standards, Third Edition, Ramsey and Sleeper, Wiley, 1941.

RETAINING WALLS 250

FOOTINGS & FOUNDATIONS 251

EXTERIOR STEPS 252

MASONRY WALL THICKNESS 253

REINFORCING 254

BRICK WALLS 255

ADOBE 256

STONEWORK 257

TERRA COTTA 262

WATERPROOFING 264

WIRE FENCES 268

MARBLE WORK 269

SEWERAGE AND DRAINAGE 270

PAVING 276

GARAGES AND PARKING 280

WOOD FENCES 281

PARK EQUIPMENT 282

SWIMMING POOLS 283

From:
Data Book for Civil Engineers: Design, Elwyn E. Seelye, Wiley, 1945.

ROADS 287

DOCKS AND PIERS 297

DRAINAGE CONTROL 299

SEWAGE TREATMENT 306

WATER SUPPLY 309

RETAINING WALLS

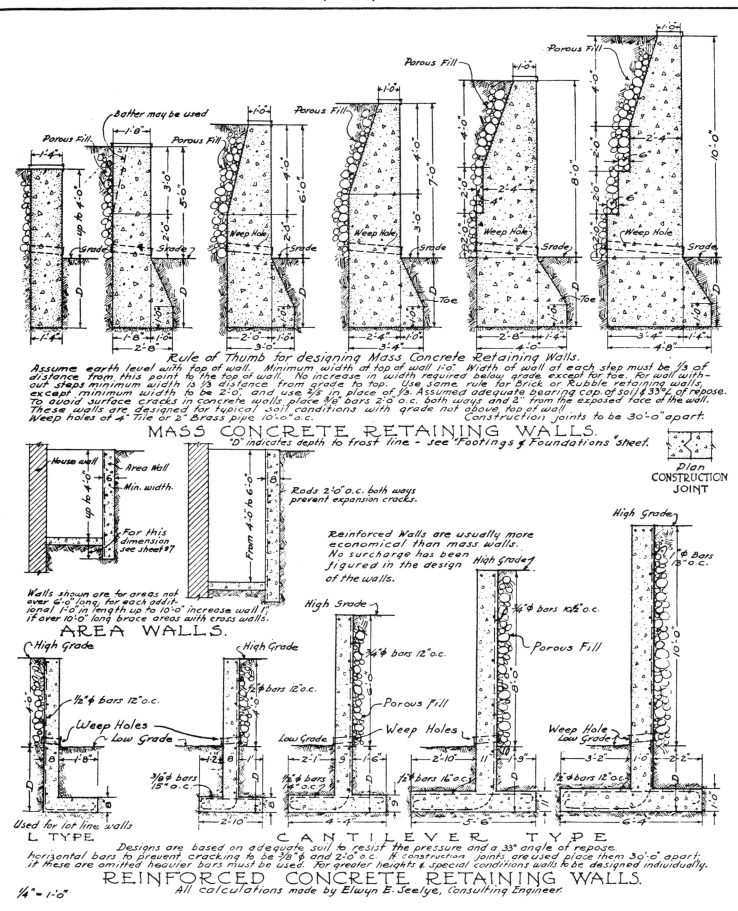

Rule of Thumb for designing Mass Concrete Retaining Walls.

Assume earth level with top of wall. Minimum width at top of wall 1'-0". Width of wall at each step must be ⅓ of distance from this point to the top of wall. No increase in width required below grade except for toe. For wall without steps minimum width is ⅓ distance from grade to top. Use same rule for Brick or Rubble retaining walls, except minimum width to be 2'-0", and use ⅖ in place of ⅓. Assumed adequate bearing cap. of soil & 33° ∠ of repose. To avoid surface cracks in concrete walls place ⅜" bars 2'-0" o.c. both ways and 2" from the exposed face of the wall. These walls are designed for typical soil conditions with grade not above top of wall. Weep holes of 4" Tile or 2" Brass pipe 10'-0" o.c.   Construction joints to be 30'-0" apart.

MASS CONCRETE RETAINING WALLS.
"D" indicates depth to frost line - see "Footings & Foundations" sheet.

Plan
CONSTRUCTION
JOINT

Rods 2'-0" o.c. both ways prevent expansion cracks.

Reinforced Walls are usually more economical than mass walls. No surcharge has been figured in the design of the walls.

Walls shown are for areas not over 6'-0" long; for each additional 1'-0" in length up to 10'-0" increase wall 1"; if over 10'-0" long brace areas with cross walls.

AREA WALLS.

Used for lot line walls
L TYPE   CANTILEVER   TYPE

Designs are based on adequate soil to resist the pressure and a 33° angle of repose. Horizontal bars to prevent cracking to be ⅜"ø and 2'-0" o.c. If construction joints are used place them 30'-0" apart. If these are omitted heavier bars must be used. For greater heights & special conditions walls to be designed individually.

REINFORCED CONCRETE RETAINING WALLS.
All calculations made by Elwyn E. Seelye, Consulting Engineer.

¼" = 1'-0"

FOOTINGS & FOUNDATIONS

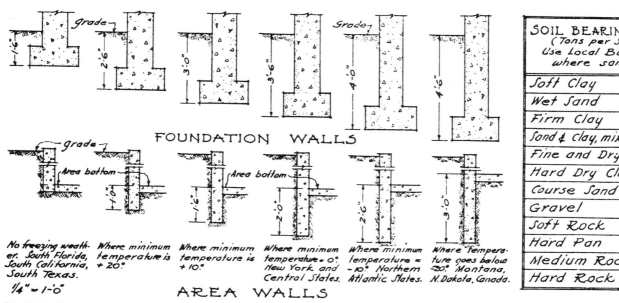

FOUNDATION WALLS

SOIL BEARING CAPACITIES (Tons per Square Foot) Use Local Building Code where same exists.	
Soft Clay	1
Wet Sand	2
Firm Clay	2
Sand & Clay, mixed or in layers	2
Fine and Dry Sand	3
Hard Dry Clay	4
Course Sand	4
Gravel	6
Soft Rock	8
Hard Pan	10
Medium Rock	15
Hard Rock	40

No freezing weather. South Florida, South California, South Texas.

Where minimum temperature is +20°.

Where minimum temperature is +10°.

Where minimum temperature = 0° New York and Central States.

Where minimum temperature = -10° Northern Atlantic States.

Where temperature goes below -20° Montana, N.Dakota, Canada.

¼" = 1'-0"

AREA WALLS

DEPTH OF FOUNDATION WALLS

Same Dimensions apply with Brick or Stone Walls.

Minimum temperature (Fahrenheit) means that these temperatures are reached for periods of days and not just for a few hours. These minimum temperatures are 10° to 15° above lowest recorded and are the same as used for calculating heating requirements. Consult Building Code for depth requirements where same exists

DEPTHS REQUIRED BY BUILDING CODES

	Below grade.				
Atlanta, Ga.		Halifax, Canada.	4'-0"	Omaha, Neb	3'-0"
Baltimore, Md.	3'-0"	Jacksonville, Florida	1'-0"	Portland, Ore.	No mention.
Boston, Mass.	4'-0"	Kansas City, Mo.	3'-0"	Philadelphia, Pa.	3'-0"
Butte, Mont.	3'-0"	Louisville, Kentucky	2'-6"	St. Paul, Minn.	4'-0"
Chicago, Ill.	4'-0"	Milwaukee, Wis.	5'-0"	St. Louis, Mo.	2'-6"
Denver, Col.	1'-6"	Minneapolis, Minn.	No mention.	Salt Lake City.	No mention.
Detroit, Mich.	3'-6"	New Orleans, La	No mention.	Seattle, Wash.	1'-6"
El Paso, Texas.	No mention.	New York, N.Y.	4'-0"	Washington, D.C.	No mention.
		Winnipeg, Canada.	No mention.		

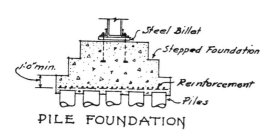

PILE FOUNDATION

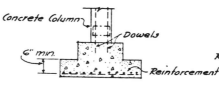

REINFORCED CONCRETE ON SPREAD FOOTING

FOOTING FOR LIGHT WALL

Such as for House, School etc. Check load per square foot with soil bearing capacity.

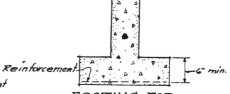

FOOTING FOR HEAVY WALL

Cantilever Span type to be designed for individual cases.

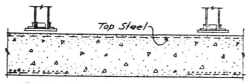

COMBINED FOUNDATION.

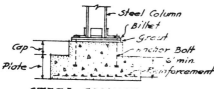

STEEL COLUMN ON SPREAD FOOTING

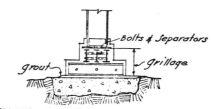

STEEL GRILLAGE FOUNDATION

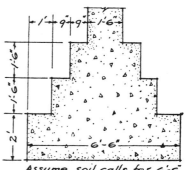

Assume soil calls for 6'-6" wide footing, depth of steps to be twice their projection

MASS CONCRETE FOOTING HEAVY WALL or CHIMNEY.

TYPICAL FOOTINGS

¼" = 1'-0"   Data approved by Elwyn E. Seelye Consulting Engineer.

EXTERIOR STEPS

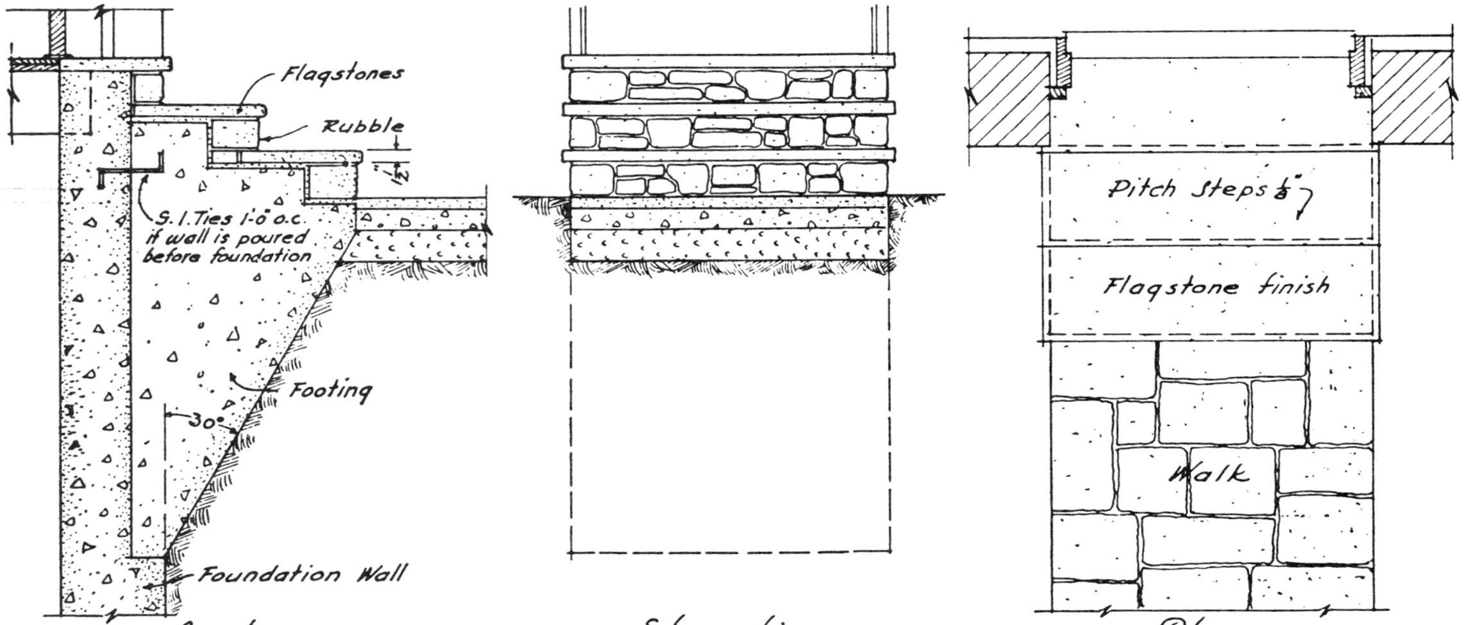

Flagstones
Rubble
1/2
S. I. Ties 1'-0" o.c. if wall is poured before foundation
Footing
30°
Foundation Wall
Pitch Steps 1/8"
Flagstone finish
Walk

Section Elevation Plan

SLOPE-BACK FOUNDATION for ENTRANCE STEPS

This type of footing will stay in place, but becomes uneconomical when there are more than three or four steps.
1/2"=1'-0"

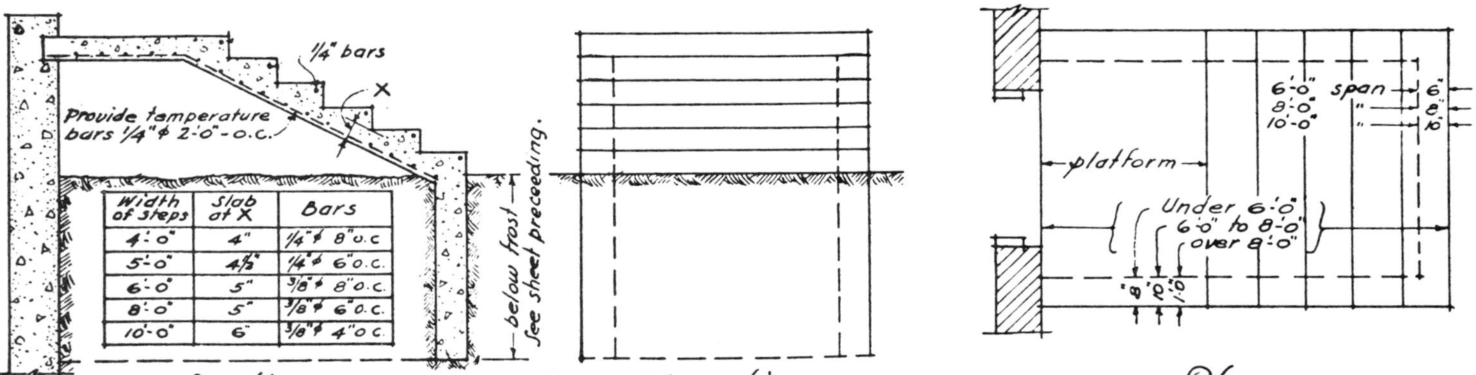

1/4" bars
X
Provide temperature bars 1/4"φ 2'-0" o.c.
below frost
See sheet preceeding.
6'-0" span
8'-0"
10'-0"
6"
8"
10"
platform
Under 6'-0"
6'-0" to 8'-0"
over 8'-0"
8"
10"
1'-0"

Width of steps	Slab at X	Bars
4'-0"	4"	1/4"φ 8" o.c.
5'-0"	4½"	1/4"φ 6" o.c.
6'-0"	5"	3/8"φ 8" o.c.
8'-0"	5"	3/8"φ 6" o.c.
10'-0"	6"	3/8"φ 4" o.c.

Section Elevation Plan

SELF SUPPORTING SLAB FOR STEPS AND PLATFORM

DIAGRAMS of CONCRETE STEPS for RESIDENTIAL WORK

Finish is not indicated but slabs will take slate, flag or other finish.
1/4"=1'-0"

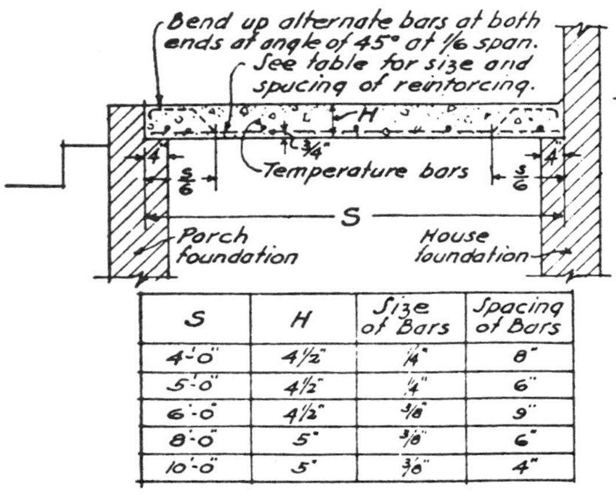

Bend up alternate bars at both ends at angle of 45° at 1/6 span. See table for size and spacing of reinforcing.
H
3/4
4
S/6
Temperature bars
S
Porch foundation
House foundation

S	H	Size of Bars	Spacing of Bars
4'-0"	4½"	¼"	8"
5'-0"	4½"	¼"	6"
6'-0"	4½"	3/8"	9"
8'-0"	5"	3/8"	6"
10'-0"	5"	3/8"	4"

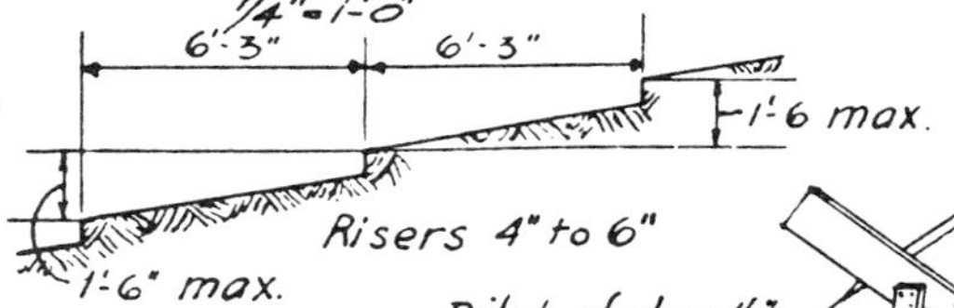

6'-3"
6'-3"
1'-6 max.
Risers 4" to 6"
1'-6" max.

RAMP & STEP

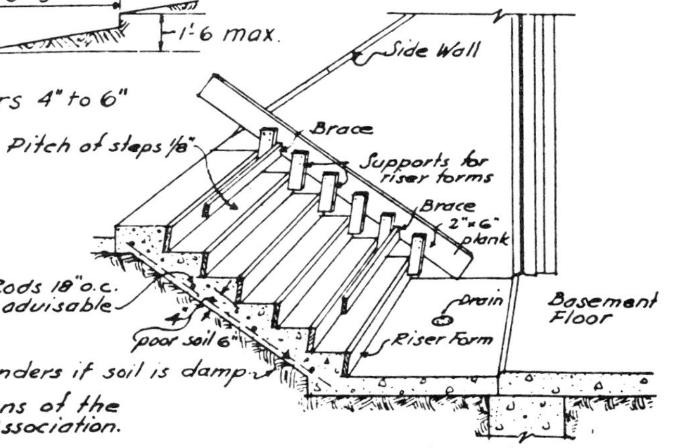

Side Wall
Brace
Pitch of steps 1/8"
Supports for riser forms
Brace 2"×6" plank
3/8" Rods 18" o.c. are advisable
4" poor soil 6"
Drain
Basement Floor
Riser Form
Cinders if soil is damp

Recommendations of the Portland Cement Association.

REINFORCED CONCRETE PORCH FLOOR CONCRETE BASEMENT STEPS

STEPS ETC; CONCRETE, FLAGSTONE and BLUESTONE

Calculations checked by Elwyn E. Seelye, Structural Engineer.

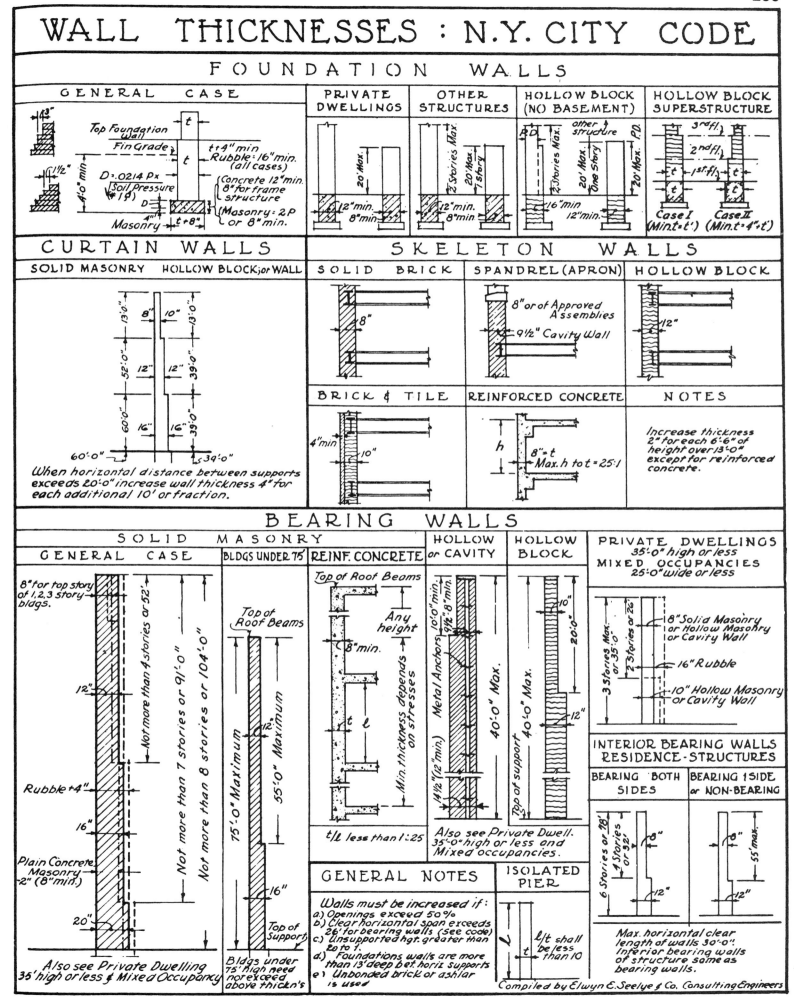

WALL THICKNESSES : N.Y. CITY CODE

REINFORCING BARS

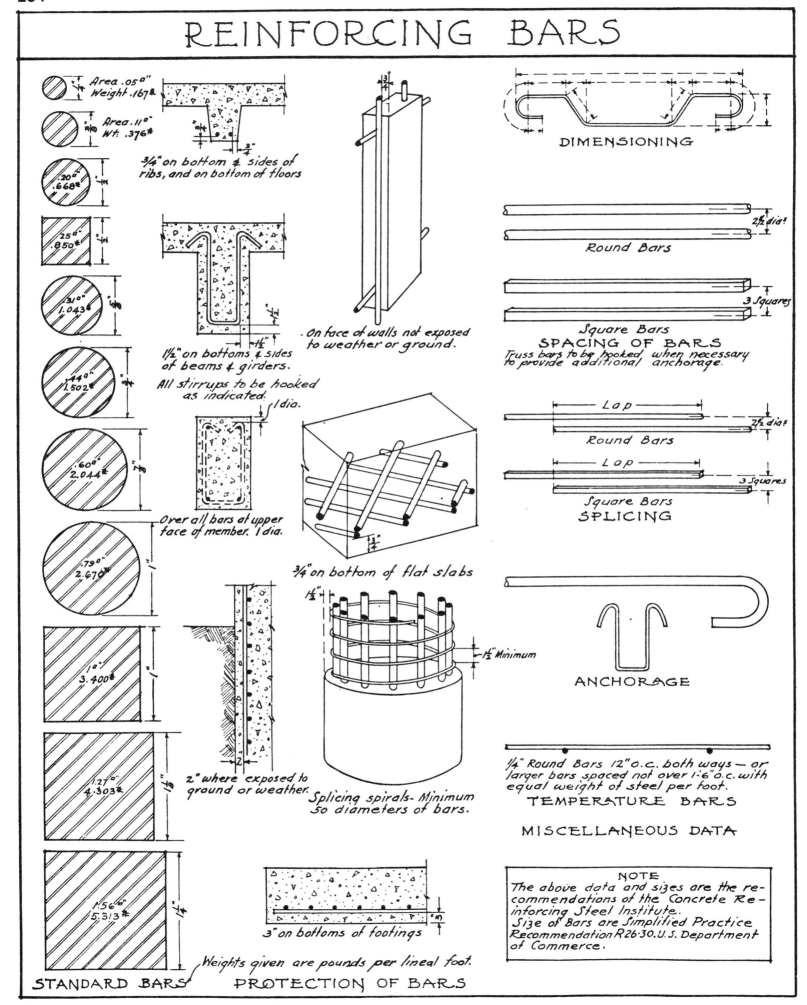

STANDARD BARS

- Area .05☐" Weight .167#
- Area .11☐" Wt .376#
- .20☐" .668#
- .25☐" .850#
- .31☐" 1.043#
- .44☐" 1.502#
- .60☐" 2.044#
- .79☐" 2.670#
- 3.400#
- 1.27☐" 4.303#
- 1.56☐" 5.313#

PROTECTION OF BARS

3/4" on bottom & sides of ribs, and on bottom of floors

1½" on bottoms & sides of beams & girders. All stirrups to be hooked as indicated.

Over all bars at upper face of member. 1 dia.

On face of walls not exposed to weather or ground.

3/4" on bottom of flat slabs

2" where exposed to ground or weather.

Splicing spirals- Minimum 50 diameters of bars.

3" on bottoms of footings

Weights given are pounds per lineal foot.

DIMENSIONING

2½ dia. Round Bars

3 Squares Square Bars

SPACING OF BARS

Truss bars to be hooked when necessary to provide additional anchorage.

Lap — Round Bars — 2½ dia.

Lap — Square Bars — 3 Squares

SPLICING

ANCHORAGE

¼" Round Bars 12" o.c. both ways — or larger bars spaced not over 1'-6" o.c. with equal weight of steel per foot.

TEMPERATURE BARS

MISCELLANEOUS DATA

NOTE
The above data and sizes are the recommendations of the Concrete Reinforcing Steel Institute. Size of Bars are Simplified Practice Recommendation R26-30. U.S. Department of Commerce.

BRICK—CAVITY & SERPENTINE WALLS

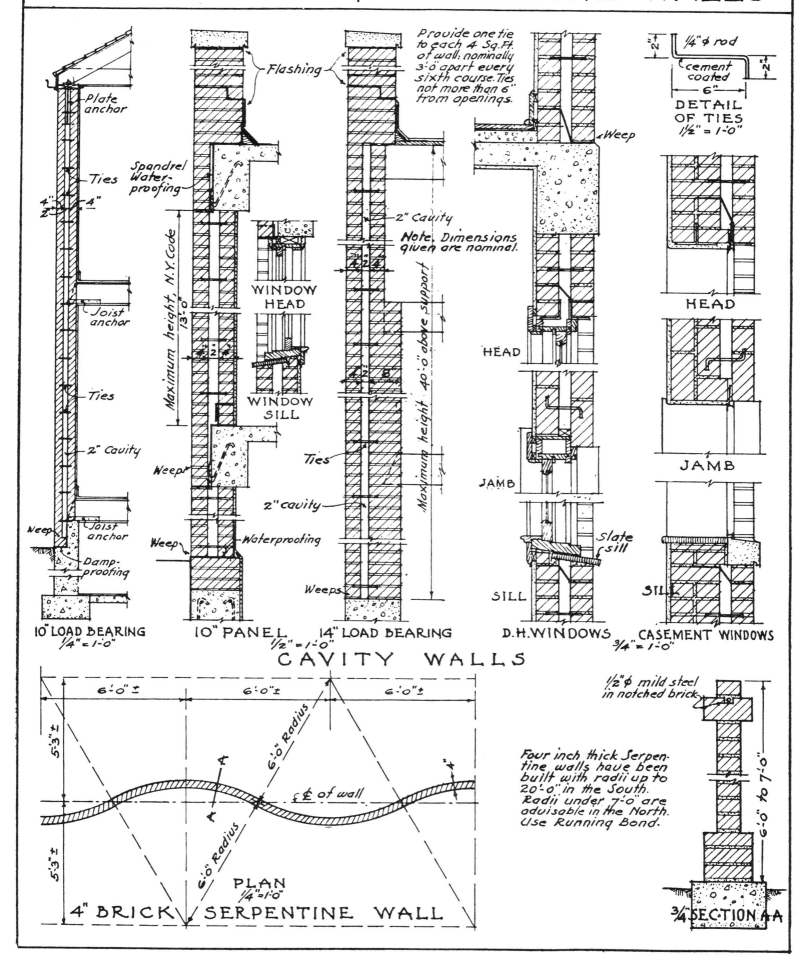

Provide one tie to each 4 Sq.Ft. of wall: nominally 3'-0" apart every sixth course. Ties not more than 6" from openings.

Flashing

Plate anchor

Ties

4" 4"
2"

Spandrel Water-proofing

Joist anchor

WINDOW HEAD

Note. Dimensions given are nominal.

2" cavity

Maximum height, N.Y.Code 13'-0"

Ties

2" Cavity

WINDOW SILL

Weep

Weeps

Weep

Weep

Maximum height 40'-0" above support

Ties

2" cavity

Waterproofing

Joist anchor

Damp-proofing

10" LOAD BEARING
1/4" = 1'-0"

10" PANEL
1/2" = 1'-0"

14" LOAD BEARING

Weeps

Weep

DETAIL OF TIES
1 1/2" = 1'-0"
1/4" ⌀ rod
cement coated
2" 2"
6"

HEAD

Weep

JAMB

Slate sill

SILL

D.H. WINDOWS
3/4" = 1'-0"

HEAD

JAMB

SILL

CASEMENT WINDOWS

CAVITY WALLS

6'-0"±   6'-0"±   6'-0"±

5'-3"±

6'-0" Radius

A

℄ of wall

A

6'-0" Radius

5'-3"±

PLAN
1/4" = 1'-0"

4" BRICK SERPENTINE WALL

1/2" ⌀ mild steel in notched brick

Four inch thick Serpentine walls have been built with radii up to 20'-0" in the South. Radii under 7'-0" are advisable in the North. Use Running Bond.

6'-0" to 7'-0"

3/4" SECTION AA

ADOBE DETAILS

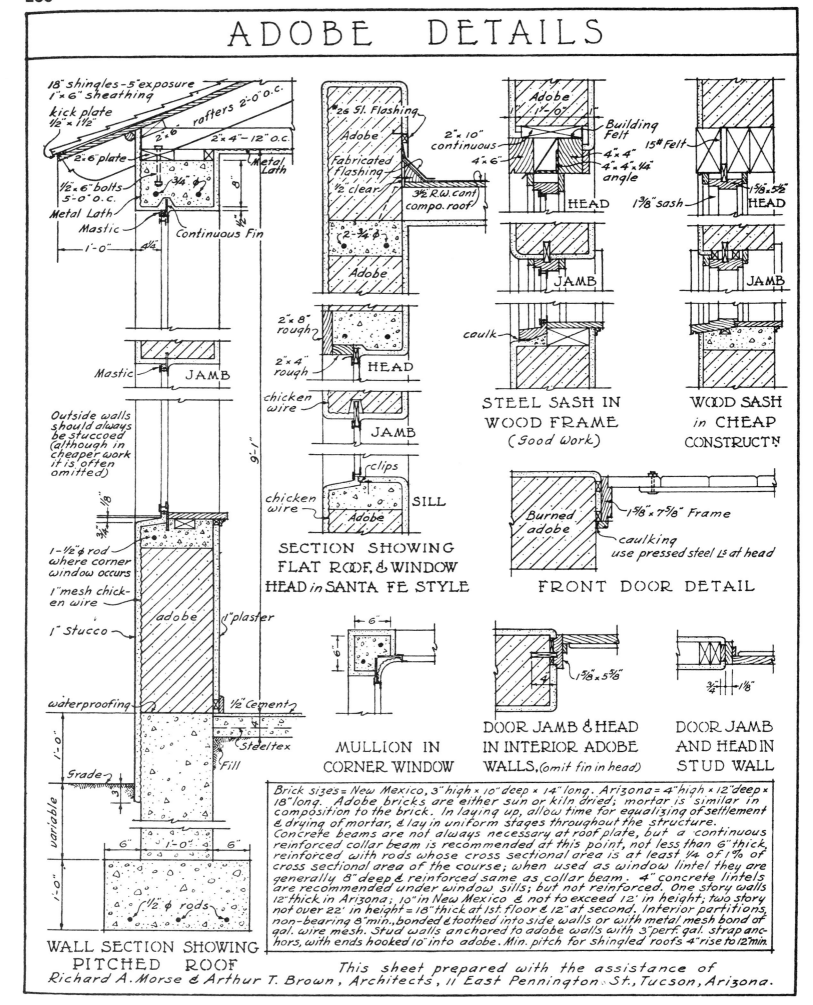

18" shingles – 5" exposure
1" × 6" sheathing
kick plate
1/2" × 1 1/2"
rafters 2'-0" o.c.
2" × 6"
2" × 4" – 12" o.c.
Metal Lath
2" × 6" plate
1/2" × 6" bolts
5'-0" o.c.
3/4" ⌀
Metal Lath
Mastic
Continuous Fin
1'-0"
4 1/4"
JAMB
Mastic

Outside walls should always be stuccoed (although in cheaper work it is often omitted)

3/4" 1/8"
1-1/2" ⌀ rod where corner window occurs
1" mesh chicken wire
1" Stucco
adobe
1" plaster
9'-1"
waterproofing
1/2" Cement
Steeltex
Fill
Grade
3"
variable
1'-0"
6" 1'-0" 6"
1'-0"
1/2" ⌀ rods

WALL SECTION SHOWING PITCHED ROOF

#26 Sl. Flashing
Adobe
Fabricated Flashing
1/2" clear
2" × 10" continuous
4" × 6"
3 1/2" R.W. cant compo. roof
Adobe
2-3/4" ⌀
Adobe
2" × 8" rough
2" × 4" rough
HEAD
chicken wire
JAMB
clips
chicken wire
SILL
Adobe

SECTION SHOWING FLAT ROOF & WINDOW HEAD in SANTA FE STYLE

Adobe 1'-0"
Building Felt
2" × 10" continuous
4" × 6"
4" × 4"
4" × 4" × 1/4" angle
HEAD
JAMB
caulk

STEEL SASH IN WOOD FRAME (Good Work)

15# Felt
1 5/8" × 5 1/2"
1 3/8" sash
HEAD
JAMB

WOOD SASH in CHEAP CONSTRUCT'N

Burned adobe
1 5/8" × 7 5/8" Frame
caulking use pressed steel Ls at head

FRONT DOOR DETAIL

6"
6"

MULLION IN CORNER WINDOW

4"
1 5/8" × 5 5/8"

DOOR JAMB & HEAD IN INTERIOR ADOBE WALLS, (omit fin in head)

3/4" 1/8"

DOOR JAMB AND HEAD IN STUD WALL

Brick sizes = New Mexico, 3" high × 10" deep × 14" long. Arizona = 4" high × 12" deep × 18" long. Adobe bricks are either sun or kiln dried; mortar is similar in composition to the brick. In laying up, allow time for equalizing of settlement & drying of mortar, & lay in uniform stages throughout the structure.
Concrete beams are not always necessary at roof plate, but a continuous reinforced collar beam is recommended at this point, not less than 6" thick, reinforced with rods whose cross sectional area is at least 1/4 of 1% of cross sectional area of the course; when used as window lintel they are generally 8" deep & reinforced same as collar beam. 4" concrete lintels are recommended under window sills; but not reinforced. One story walls 12" thick in Arizona; 10" in New Mexico & not to exceed 12' in height; two story not over 22' in height = 18" thick at 1st. floor & 12" at second. Interior partitions, non-bearing 8" min., bonded & toothed into side walls or with metal mesh bond of gal. wire mesh. Stud walls anchored to adobe walls with 3" perf. gal. strap anchors, with ends hooked 10" into adobe. Min. pitch for shingled roofs 4" rise to 12" min.

This sheet prepared with the assistance of
Richard A. Morse & Arthur T. Brown, Architects, 11 East Pennington St., Tucson, Arizona.

CUT STONE

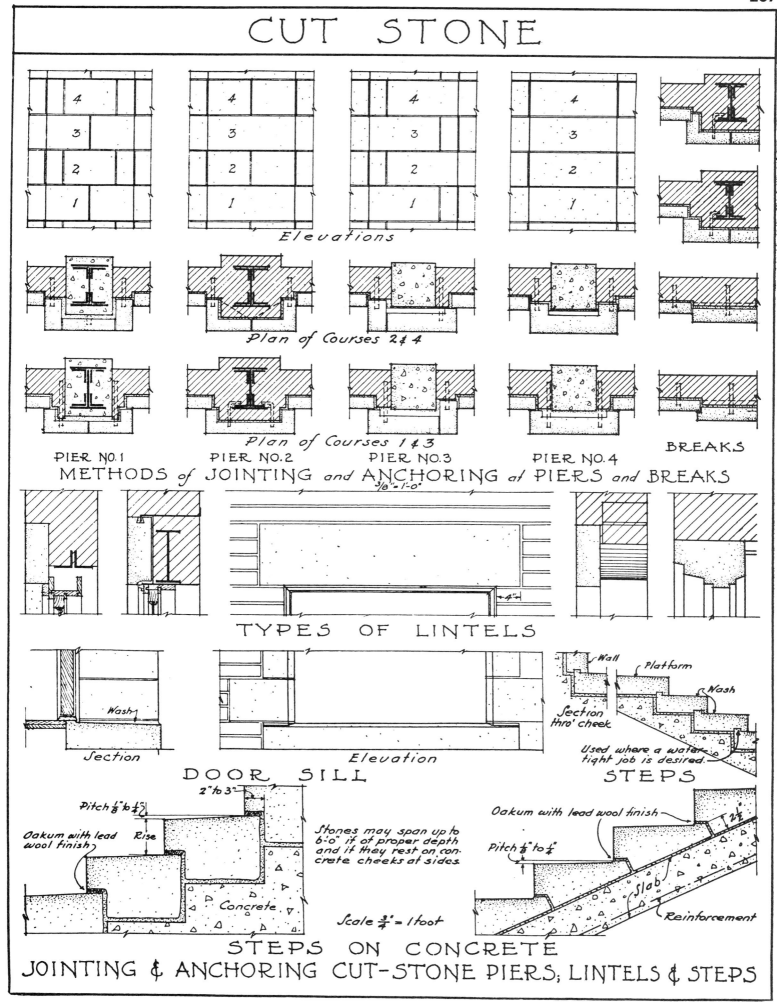

Elevations

Plan of Courses 2 & 4

Plan of Courses 1 & 3

PIER NO.1   PIER NO.2   PIER NO.3   PIER NO.4   BREAKS

METHODS of JOINTING and ANCHORING at PIERS and BREAKS

3/8" = 1'-0"

4"

TYPES OF LINTELS

Wash

Section   *Elevation*

DOOR SILL

Wall   *Platform*   *Nash*

Section thro' cheek

Used where a water-tight job is desired.

STEPS

Pitch ⅛" to ¼"   2" to 3"   *Rise*

Oakum with lead wool finish

Stones may span up to 6'-0" if of proper depth and if they rest on concrete cheeks at sides.

Concrete

Scale ¾" = 1 foot

Oakum with lead wool finish

Pitch ⅛" to ¼"   2½"

Slab

Reinforcement

STEPS ON CONCRETE

JOINTING & ANCHORING CUT-STONE PIERS, LINTELS & STEPS

CUT STONE

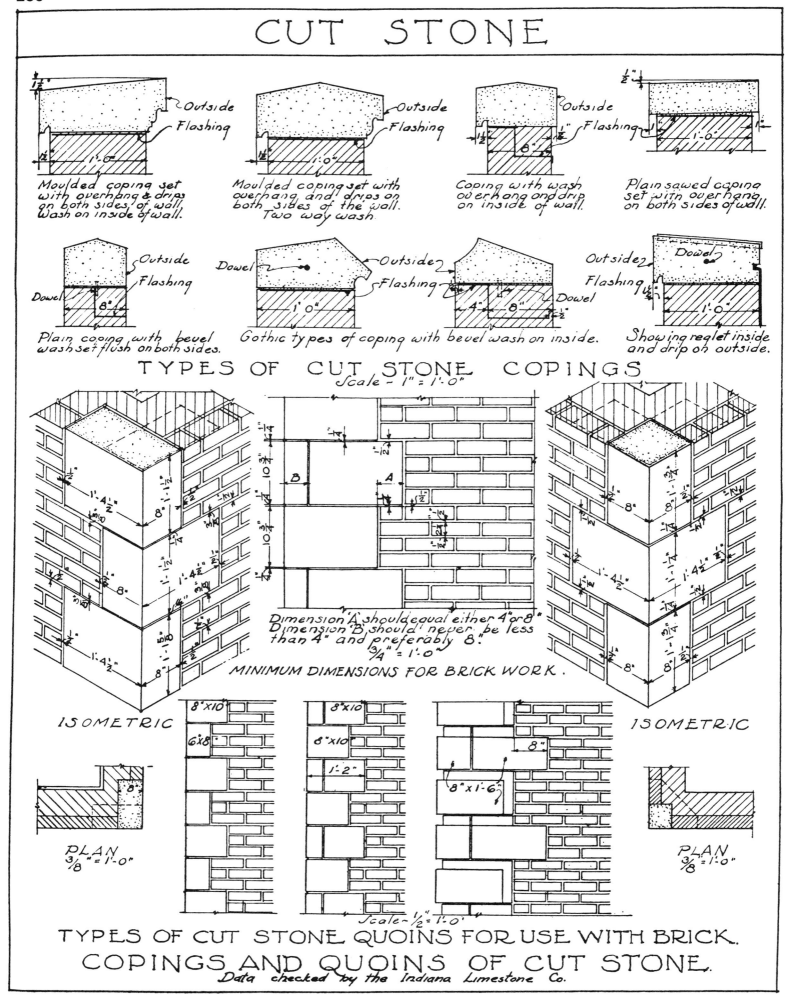

Moulded coping set with overhang & drips on both sides of wall. Wash on inside of wall.

Moulded coping set with overhang and drips on both sides of the wall. Two way wash.

Coping with wash overhang and drip on inside of wall.

Plain sawed coping set with overhang on both sides of wall.

Plain coping with bevel wash set flush on both sides.

Gothic types of coping with bevel wash on inside.

Showing reglet inside and drip on outside.

TYPES OF CUT STONE COPINGS

Scale - 1" = 1'-0"

Dimension "A" should equal either 4" or 8". Dimension "B" should never be less than 4" and preferably 8".

3/4" = 1'-0"

MINIMUM DIMENSIONS FOR BRICK WORK.

ISOMETRIC

ISOMETRIC

PLAN
3/8" = 1'-0"

PLAN
3/8" = 1'-0"

Scale - 1/2" = 1'-0"

TYPES OF CUT STONE QUOINS FOR USE WITH BRICK.

COPINGS AND QUOINS OF CUT STONE.

Data checked by the Indiana Limestone Co.

STONE WORK

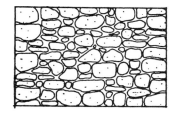
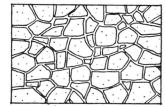

UNCOURSED FIELDSTONE ROUGH OR ORDINARY.

POLYGONAL, MOSAIC OR RANDOM.

COURSED

Laid of stratified stone fitted on job. It is between rubble & ashlar. Finish is quarry face, seam face or split. Called rubble ashlar in granite.

TYPES OF RUBBLE MASONRY

SQUARED-STONE MASONRY.

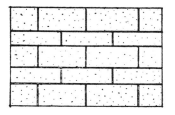
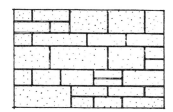
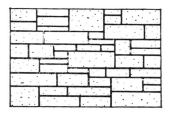
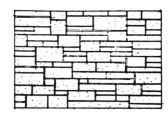

RANGE. Coursed

BROKEN RANGE.

RANDOM Interrupted coursed

RANGE. Coursed (Long stones)

TYPES OF ASHLAR MASONRY
This is stone that is sawed, dressed, squared or Quarry faced.

ELEVATIONS SHOWING FACE JOINTING FOR STONE.

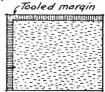

For both hard and soft stones. Rock or Pitch Face.

Smooth, but saw mark visible. All stones. Sawed Finish (Gang).

More marked than sawed. Soft stones. Shot Sawed (Rough).

Smooth finish with some texture. Soft stones. Machine Finish (Planer).

May be coarse, medium or fine. Usually on hard stones. Pointed Finish.

After pointing on hard stones. Pean Hammered.

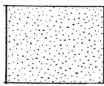

For soft stones. Bush-hammered.

All stones. Used much on granite. 4 to 8 cut in 1/8". Patent Bush-hammer.

For soft stones. Drove or Boasted.

Random For soft stones. Hand Tooled.

Tool marks may be 2 to 10 per inch. Machine Tooled.

For soft stones. Tooth-chisel.

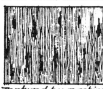

Random For soft stones. Crandalled.

Textured by machine For Limestone. Plucker Finish.

Very smooth. For Limestone. Done by machine. Carborundum Finish.

Smooth All stones. May use sand or carborundum. Rubbed (Wet).

Very Smooth Marble, granite. For interior work. Soft stones. Honed (rubbed first).

Very smooth Has high gloss. Marble and Granite. Polished (honed first).

STONE FINISHES.
Seam face and split face (or quarry face) not shown as they are not worked finishes.

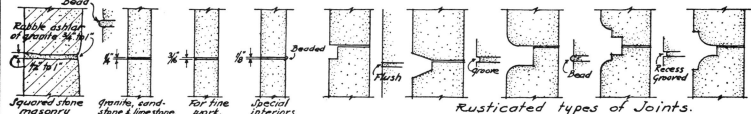

Rusticated types of Joints.

STONE JOINTS
TYPES, FINISH AND JOINTING OF STONE MASONRY.
A perch is nominally 16'-6" long, 1'-0" high & 1'-6" thick = 24¾ cu.ft. In some localities 16'2 & 22 cu.ft. are used.

STONE WORK

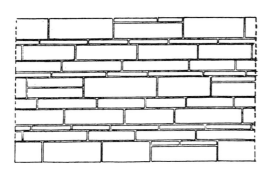

· FOUR · UNIT, LONG TYPE · RANGE · WORK ·
Average length of Stones four times height
· BROKEN RANGE ·

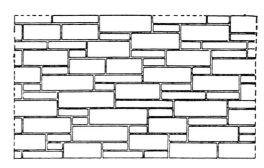

· TWO · UNIT, MEDIUM · TYPE · RANDOM · ASHLAR ·
Average length of larger Stones is three times height.

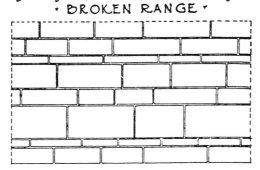

· FOUR · UNIT, MEDIUM · TYPE · RANGE · WORK ·
Average length of Stones about 2½ times their height.
· RANGE ·

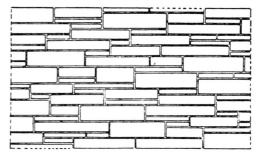

THREE · UNIT, LONG TYPE · RANDOM · ASHLAR ·
Average length of Stones 4 times height or more .

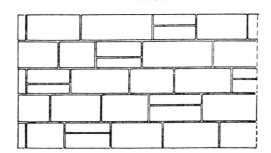

· EQUAL · COURSE · HEIGHTS ·
With occasional units divided by horizontal joints.
· BROKEN RANGE ·

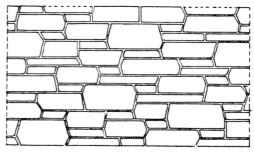

· THREE · UNIT · RANDOM · ASHLAR ; ANGULAR · BROKEN · END ·
Average length of larger Stones 2 times their height.
Joints ¾" thick.

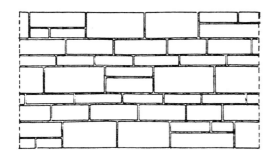

· · THREE · UNIT · RANGE · WORK ·
With occasional Horizontal joints in the higher Courses.
· BROKEN · RANGE ·

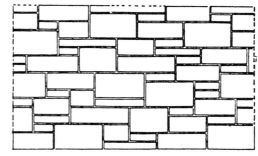

· THREE · UNIT · MEDIUM · TYPE · RANDOM · ASHLAR ·
· Average length of larger Stones about twice the height.

This type of Stone is delivered in strips & jointed to length at the job. Joints all ½" except where noted ¾" · ~ .

· RANGE & BROKEN RANGE ·   **· RANDOM · RANGE ·**

· Scale :~ ¼" = 1'·0" ·

· JOINTING · OF · STRIP · LIMESTONE · ASHLAR ·

~ ~ Recommendations of the "INDIANA LIMESTONE Co." ~

STONE WALLS

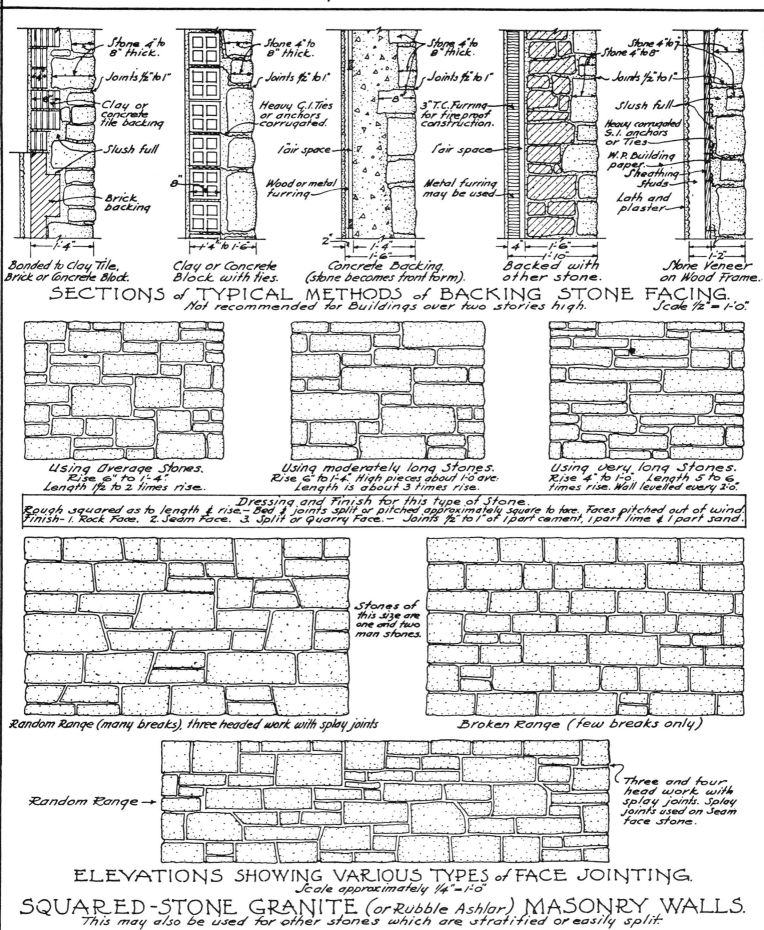

Bonded to Clay Tile, Brick or Concrete Block. — Stone 4" to 8" thick. Joints ½" to 1". Clay or concrete tile backing. Slush full. Brick backing. 1'-4"

Clay or Concrete Block with ties. — Stone 4" to 8" thick. Joints ½" to 1". Heavy G.I. Ties or anchors corrugated. 1" air space. Wood or metal furring. 8". 1'-4" to 1'-6".

Concrete Backing. (stone becomes front form). — Stone 4" to 8" thick. Joints ½" to 1". 8". 1" air space. Metal furring may be used. 2". 1'-4". 1'-6".

Backed with other stone. — 3" T.C. Furring for fireproof construction. 4". 1'-6". 1'-10".

Stone Veneer on Wood Frame. — Stone 4" to 7". Stone 4" to 8". Joints ½" to 1". Slush full. Heavy corrugated S.I. anchors or Ties. W.P. Building paper. Sheathing. Studs. Lath and plaster. 1'-2".

SECTIONS of TYPICAL METHODS of BACKING STONE FACING.
Not recommended for Buildings over two stories high.   Scale ½" = 1'-0"

Using average Stones. Rise 6" to 1'-4". Length 1½ to 2 times rise.

Using moderately long Stones. Rise 6" to 1'-4". High pieces about 1'-0" ave. Length is about 3 times rise.

Using very long Stones. Rise 4" to 1'-0". Length 5 to 6 times rise. Wall levelled every 2'-0".

Dressing and Finish for this type of Stone.
Rough squared as to length & rise.— Bed & joints split or pitched approximately square to face. Faces pitched out of wind. Finish— 1. Rock Face. 2. Seam Face. 3. Split or Quarry Face. — Joints ½" to 1" of 1 part cement, 1 part lime & 1 part sand.

Random Range (many breaks), three headed work with splay joints

Stones of this size are one and two man stones.

Broken Range (few breaks only)

Random Range →

Three and four head work with splay joints. Splay joints used on Seam face stone.

ELEVATIONS SHOWING VARIOUS TYPES of FACE JOINTING.
Scale approximately ¼" = 1'-0"

SQUARED-STONE GRANITE (or Rubble Ashlar) MASONRY WALLS.
This may also be used for other stones which are stratified or easily split.

ARCHITECTURAL TERRA COTTA

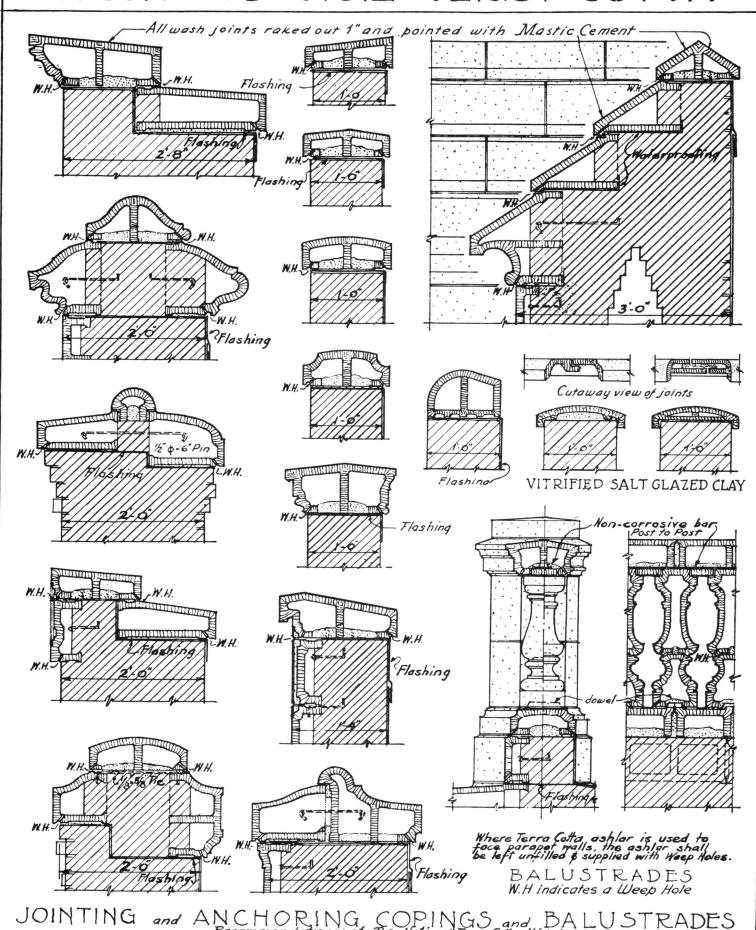

All wash joints raked out 1" and pointed with Mastic Cement

Flashing

W.H.
W.H.
W.H.
2'-8"
Flashing
W.H.

1'-0"
Flashing

W.H.
W.H.
2'-0"
Flashing

W.H.

Waterproofing

W.H.

3'-0"

W.H.
W.H.
1/2" φ×6" Pin
Flashing
W.H.

1'-0"

Flashing

2'-0"

1'-0"

Cutaway view of joints

1'-0"
1'-0"

VITRIFIED SALT GLAZED CLAY

W.H.
W.H.
2'-0"
Flashing
W.H.

W.H.
W.H.
Flashing

Flashing

Non-corrosive bar
Post to Post

W.H.

dowel

W.H.
W.H.
2'-0"
Flashing

W.H.
2'-0"
Flashing

Flashing

Where Terra Cotta ashlar is used to
face parapet walls, the ashlar shall
be left unfilled & supplied with Weep Holes.

BALUSTRADES
W.H indicates a Weep Hole

JOINTING and ANCHORING COPINGS and BALUSTRADES

Recommendations of The National Terra Cotta Mfrs. Association.
3/4" = 1'-0"

ARCHITECTURAL TERRA COTTA

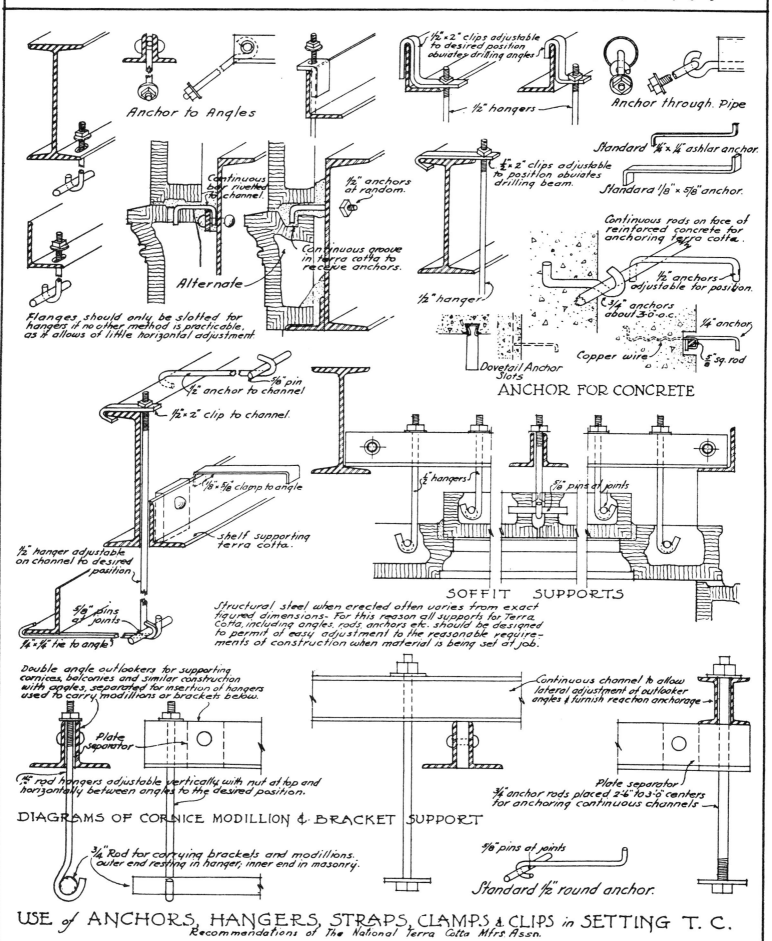

Anchor to Angles

½"x 2" clips adjustable to desired position obviates drilling angles

½" hangers

Anchor through Pipe

Continuous bar rivetted to channel.

½" anchors at random.

¼"x 2" clips adjustable to position obviates drilling beam.

Standard ¾" x ¼" ashlar anchor.

Standard ⅛" x ⅝" anchor.

Continuous groove in terra cotta to receive anchors.

Alternate

½" hanger

Continuous rods on face of reinforced concrete for anchoring terra cotta.

½" anchors adjustable for position.

¾" anchors about 3'-0" o.c.

¼" anchor

Copper wire

⅜" sq. rod

Flanges should only be slotted for hangers if no other method is practicable, as it allows of little horizontal adjustment.

Dovetail Anchor Slots

ANCHOR FOR CONCRETE

½" anchor to channel

⅝" pin

½" x 2" clip to channel.

⅛" x ⅝" clamp to angle

shelf supporting terra cotta.

½" hanger adjustable on channel to desired position

½" hangers

⅝" pins at joints

⅝" pins at joints

¼" x ¼" tie to angle.

SOFFIT SUPPORTS

Structural steel when erected often varies from exact figured dimensions. For this reason all supports for Terra Cotta, including angles, rods, anchors etc. should be designed to permit of easy adjustment to the reasonable requirements of construction when material is being set at job.

Double angle outlookers for supporting cornices, balconies and similar construction with angles, separated for insertion of hangers used to carry modillions or brackets below.

Plate separator

Continuous channel to allow lateral adjustment of outlooker angles & furnish reaction anchorage.

½" rod hangers adjustable vertically with nut at top and horizontally between angles to the desired position.

Plate separator

¾" anchor rods placed 2'-6" to 3'-0" centers for anchoring continuous channels.

DIAGRAMS OF CORNICE MODILLION & BRACKET SUPPORT

¾" Rod for carrying brackets and modillions. outer end resting in hanger; inner end in masonry.

⅝" pins at joints

Standard ½" round anchor.

USE of ANCHORS, HANGERS, STRAPS, CLAMPS & CLIPS in SETTING T. C.

Recommendations of The National Terra Cotta Mfrs. Assn.

WATERPROOFING

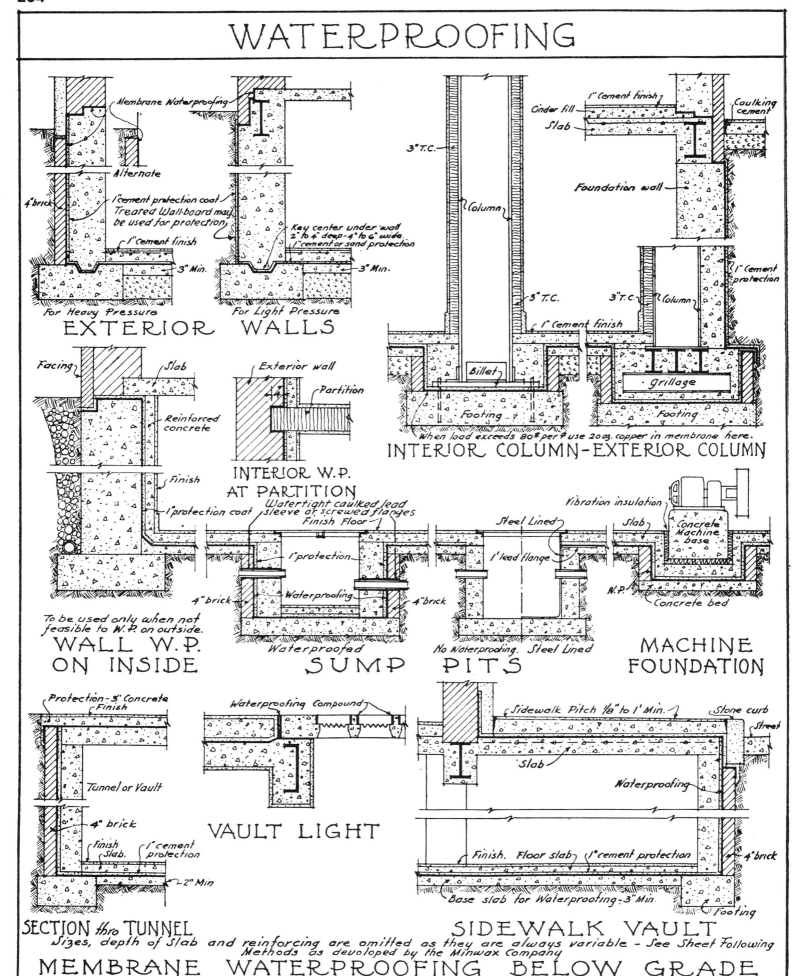

EXTERIOR WALLS

Membrane Waterproofing

Alternate

1" cement protection coat
Treated Wall-board may be used for protection

1" cement finish

4" brick

3" Min.

For Heavy Pressure

Key center under wall 2" to 4" deep-4" to 6" wide
1" cement or sand protection

3" Min.

For Light Pressure

INTERIOR COLUMN-EXTERIOR COLUMN

1" cement finish

Cinder fill

Slab

3" T.C.

Column

Foundation wall

Caulking cement

1" cement protection

3" T.C.

Column

Billet

1" cement finish

Footing

Grillage

Footing

When load exceeds 80# per # use 20 oz. copper in membrane here.

WALL W.P. ON INSIDE

Facing

Reinforced concrete

Finish

1" protection coat

To be used only when not feasible to W.P. on outside.

INTERIOR W.P. AT PARTITION

Slab

Exterior wall

Partition

SUMP PITS

Watertight caulked lead sleeve or screwed flanges
Finish Floor

1" protection

Waterproofing

4" brick

4" brick

Waterproofed

Steel Lined

1' lead flange

No Waterproofing. Steel Lined

MACHINE FOUNDATION

Vibration insulation

Slab

Concrete Machine base

W.P.

Concrete bed

SECTION thro TUNNEL

Protection-3" Concrete Finish

Tunnel or Vault

4" brick

Finish Slab.

1" cement protection

2" Min

VAULT LIGHT

Waterproofing Compound

SIDEWALK VAULT

Sidewalk Pitch 1/8" to 1' Min.

Stone curb

Street

Slab

Waterproofing

Finish. Floor slab

1" cement protection

4" brick

Base slab for Waterproofing-3" Min.

Footing

Sizes, depth of slab and reinforcing are omitted as they are always variable - See Sheet Following
Methods as developed by the Minwax Company

MEMBRANE WATERPROOFING BELOW GRADE

3/8" = 1'-0"

WATERPROOFING

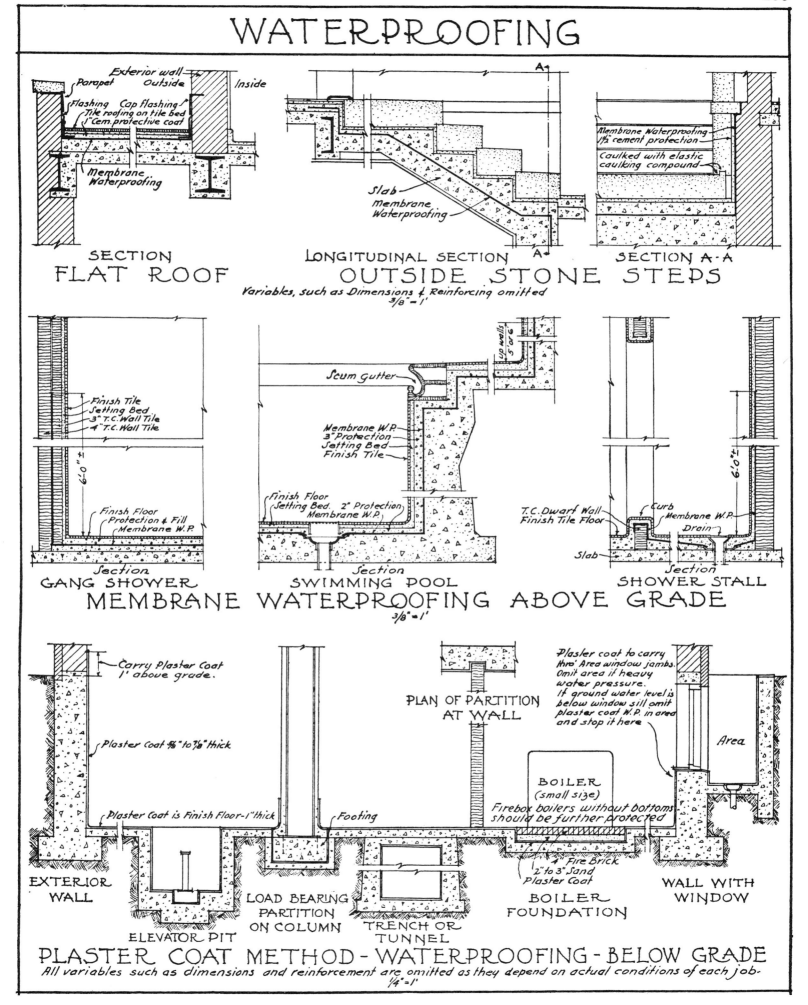

SECTION
FLAT ROOF

LONGITUDINAL SECTION
OUTSIDE STONE STEPS
Variables, such as Dimensions & Reinforcing omitted
3/8" = 1'

SECTION A-A

Section
GANG SHOWER

Section
SWIMMING POOL

Section
SHOWER STALL

MEMBRANE WATERPROOFING ABOVE GRADE
3/8" = 1'

PLAN OF PARTITION AT WALL

EXTERIOR WALL
LOAD BEARING PARTITION ON COLUMN
ELEVATOR PIT
TRENCH OR TUNNEL
BOILER FOUNDATION
WALL WITH WINDOW

PLASTER COAT METHOD — WATERPROOFING — BELOW GRADE
All variables such as dimensions and reinforcement are omitted as they depend on actual conditions of each job.
1/4" = 1'

WATERPROOFING - PLASTER COAT

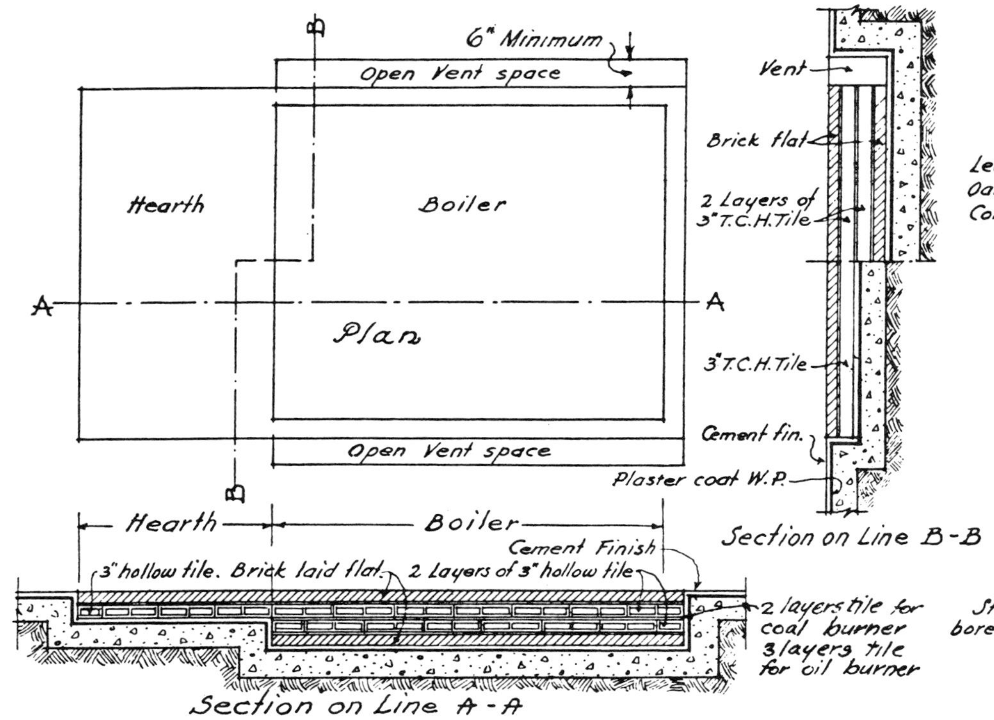

INSULATION TO PROTECT W.P. UNDER BOILERS
PLASTER COAT METHOD
Similar method may be used with Membrane Waterproofing.
Method developed by the Western Waterproofing Company..
1/4" = 1'

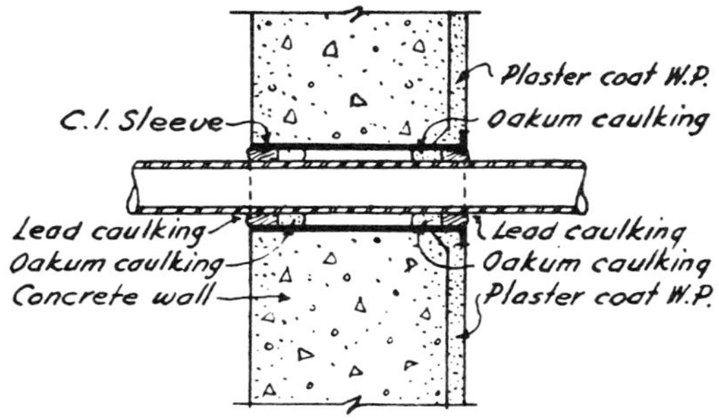

STEAM PIPE THRO WALL
3/4" = 1'

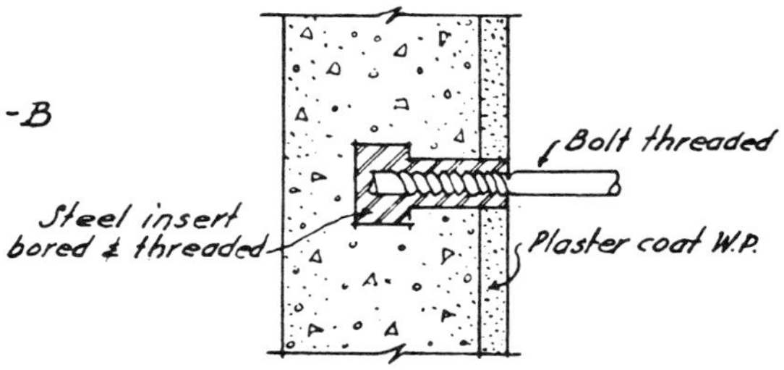

BOLT ANCHORAGE.
SECTION
1½" = 1'

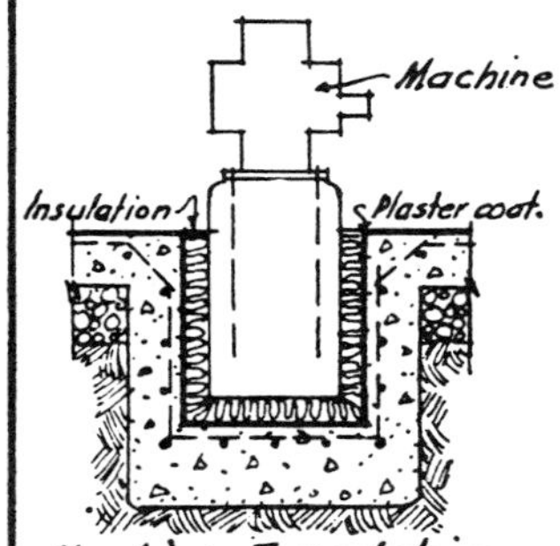

Machine Foundation with insulation under

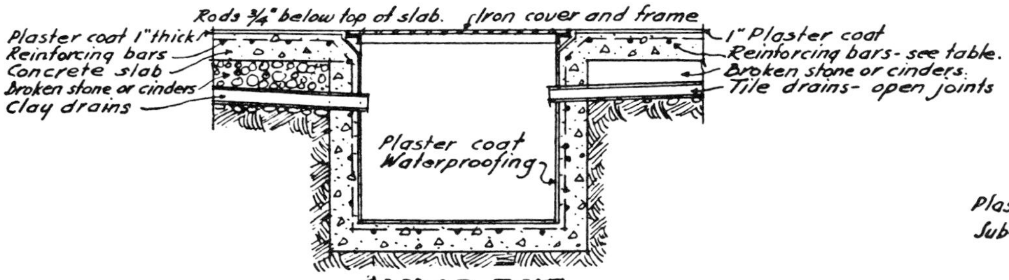

SUMP PIT

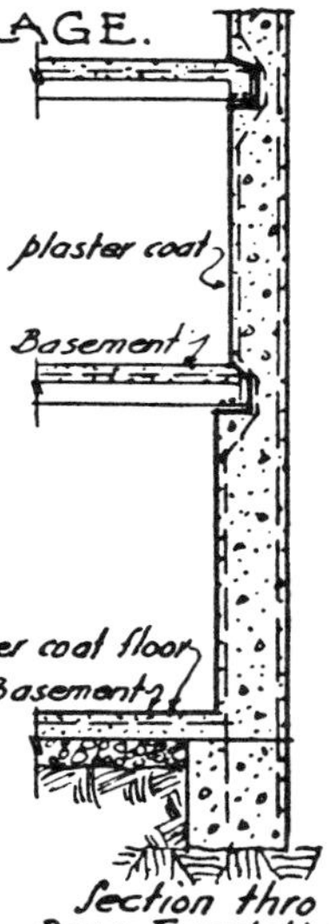

Section thro Deep Foundation.

HEAD OF WATER ABOVE BOTTOM OF SLAB	SPAN	6'-0"	8'-0"	10'-0"	12'-0"	14'-0"	16'-0"	18'-0"	20'-0"	22'-0"	24'-0"	LIFTING PRESSURE IN POUNDS PER SQ. FT.
1'	Slab	4"	4"	4"	4"							62½
	Steel	3/8φ-12"	3/8φ-12"	3/8φ-12"	3/8φ-12"							
2'	Slab	4"	4"	4"	4½"	5"	5½"	6"	6"	6½"	6½"	125
	Steel	3/8φ-12"	3/8φ-7½"	3/8φ-5"	1/2φ-7½"	1/2φ-7"	1/2φ-6½"	1/2φ-6½"	1/2φ-5½"	1/2φ-5½"	1/2φ-4½"	
3'	Slab	4"	4½"	5"	5½"	6"	7"	7½"	8"	8"	8½"	187½
	Steel	3/8φ-7½"	3/8φ-5"	1/2φ-7"	5/8φ-9"	5/8φ-8"	5/8φ-8"	5/8φ-7"	5/8φ-6½"	5/8φ-5½"	5/8φ-5½"	
4'	Slab	4"	5"	6"	6½"	7½"	8"	9"	9½"	10"	10½"	250
	Steel	3/8φ-5"	1/2φ-9"	1/2φ-6"	1/2φ-5"	5/8φ-7"	5/8φ-6"	5/8φ-6"	3/4φ-8"	3/4φ-7"	3/4φ-6½"	
6'	Slab	4¾"	6"	7"	8"	9"	10"	11"	11½"	12½"	13½"	375
	Steel	1/2φ-7"	1/2φ-5"	5/8φ-7"	5/8φ-6"	5/8φ-5"	5/8φ-4½"	5/8φ-4"	3/4φ-5½"	3/4φ-5"	3/4φ-5"	
8'	Slab	5½"	7"	8"	9½"	10½"	11½"	13"	14"	15"	15½"	500
	Steel	1/2φ-6"	5/8φ-7½"	3/4φ-8½"	3/4φ-7½"	7/8φ-8½"	7/8φ-7½"	7/8φ-7"	7/8φ-6½"	7/8φ-6"	7/8φ-6"	
10'	Slab	6"	7½"	9"	10½"	12"	13"	14½"	15½"	16½"	18"	625
	Steel	1/2φ-5"	3/4φ-9"	7/8φ-10"	7/8φ-8½"	7/8φ-7½"	7/8φ-6½"	7/8φ-6"	7/8φ-5½"	7/8φ-5"	7/8φ-5"	

Table based on simple span - Concrete stress 650 lbs per Sq." and steel 16000# Mix: 1-2-4. Provide distribution rods 3/8"φ - 12" o.c. for slabs 8" and less, and 1/2"φ 12" o.c. for thicker slabs running perpendicular to main reinforcing and wired thereto. Slabs are designed to resist upward pressure of heads indicated. Table redrawn by courtesy of the Western Waterproofing Company—

THICKNESS & REINFORCING of SLAB FOR WATERHEADS from 1 to 10 FEET - SPANS 6' to 24'

WATERPROOFING & DAMPPROOFING OF RESIDENTIAL BASEMENTS

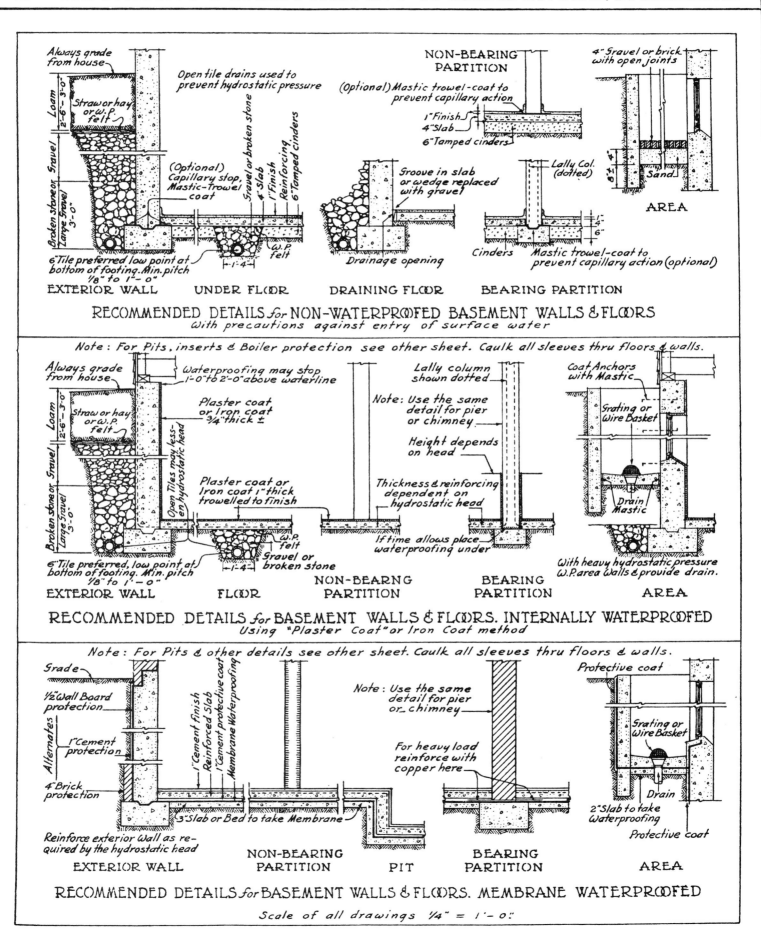

RECOMMENDED DETAILS for NON-WATERPROOFED BASEMENT WALLS & FLOORS
With precautions against entry of surface water

EXTERIOR WALL — UNDER FLOOR — DRAINING FLOOR — BEARING PARTITION

RECOMMENDED DETAILS for BASEMENT WALLS & FLOORS. INTERNALLY WATERPROOFED
Using "Plaster Coat" or Iron Coat method

EXTERIOR WALL — FLOOR — NON-BEARING PARTITION — BEARING PARTITION — AREA

RECOMMENDED DETAILS for BASEMENT WALLS & FLOORS. MEMBRANE WATERPROOFED

EXTERIOR WALL — NON-BEARING PARTITION — PIT — BEARING PARTITION — AREA

Scale of all drawings ¼" = 1'-0"

WIREWORK

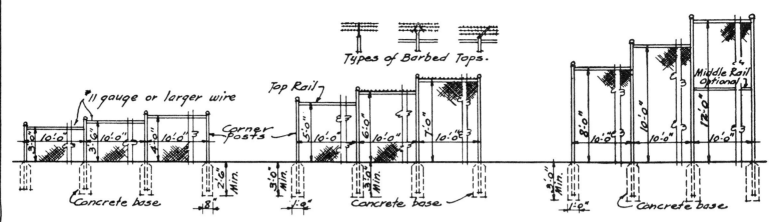

Types of Barbed Tops.

#11 gauge or larger wire

Top Rail

Corner posts

Middle Rail Optional

3'-0" 10'-0" 3'-0" 10'-0" 4'-0" 10'-0"

5'-0" 10'-0" 6'-0" 10'-0" 7'-0" 10'-0"

8'-0" 10'-0" 10'-0" 10'-0" 12'-0" 10'-0"

Concrete base

2'-6" Min. 8" 3'-0" Min. 1'-0" 3'-0" Min. Concrete base 2'-0" Min. 1'-0" Concrete base

FOR SMALL HOUSES, LAWNS, ETC.　**FOR LARGE ESTATES, INDUSTRIAL, SCHOOLS, INSTITUTIONS.**　**FOR TENNIS COURTS & SPECIAL HIGH PROTECTION.**

Barbed Tops are often used on these
Scale ⅛"=1'-0"

MATERIALS :

Wires-　Gauge- Usually #11 or #9 W.&M. for specially rugged fence use #6. For tennis courts usually #11
　　　　Mesh - Usually 2". For tennis courts usually 1⅝" or 1¾" of chain link steel hot dip galvanized
　　　　after weaving. Top and bottom selvage may be barbed or knuckled.
Corner & End Posts:　For Lawn fences usually 2" O.D.
　　　　For Estate fences 2" for low and 2½" for medium and 3" O.D. for heavy or high
　　　　for Tennis Courts 3"-O.D.
Line or Intermediate Posts　For Lawn　1⅝" or 2" O.D. round.
　　　　For Estate, etc. 2", 2¼", 2½" H or I sections.
　　　　For Tennis Courts 2½" round O.D. or 2¼" H or I sections
Gate Posts -　The same or next size larger than the corner posts. footings for gate posts 3'-6" deep.
Top Rails -　1⅝" O.D. except some lawn fence may be 1⅜" O.D.
Middle Rails-　on 12'-0" fence same as top rail.
Gates -　Single or double any width desired.
Post Spacing-　All posts 10'-0" O.C.
　　　　The above sizes are not standard but merely represent the average sizes used

O.D.= Outside Diameter

WIRE FENCES

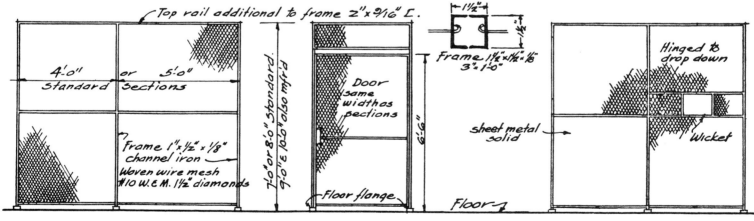

Top rail additional to frame 2" x 9/16" L.

1½"

Frame 1½" x 1½" x ⅛
3"= 1'-0"

4'-0" Standard　or　5'-0" Sections

7'-0" or 8'-0" Standard
9'-0", 10'-0" also mfr'd

Door same width as sections

6'-6"

Frame 1" x ½" x ⅛"
channel iron

Woven wire mesh
#10 W.&M. 1½" diamonds

Floor flange

Floor

Hinged to drop down

sheet metal solid

Wicket

STANDARD SECTIONS　　　　　　　**SPECIAL SECTIONS**

Standards of the National Assoc. of Orn'tal iron, bronze & wire Mfrs.

WIRE PARTITIONS

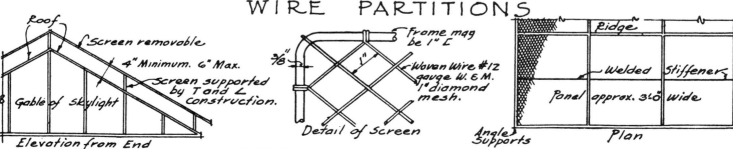

Roof

Screen removable

4" Minimum. 6" Max.

Screen supported
by T and L
Construction.

Gable of skylight

Elevation from End

Frame may
be 1" L

⅜"

1"

Woven Wire #12
gauge W.&M.
1" diamond
mesh.

Detail of Screen

Angle Supports

Ridge

Welded Stiffener

Panel approx. 3'-0 wide

Plan

SKYLIGHT GUARDS

MARBLE FLOORS, WALLS & WAINSCOTS

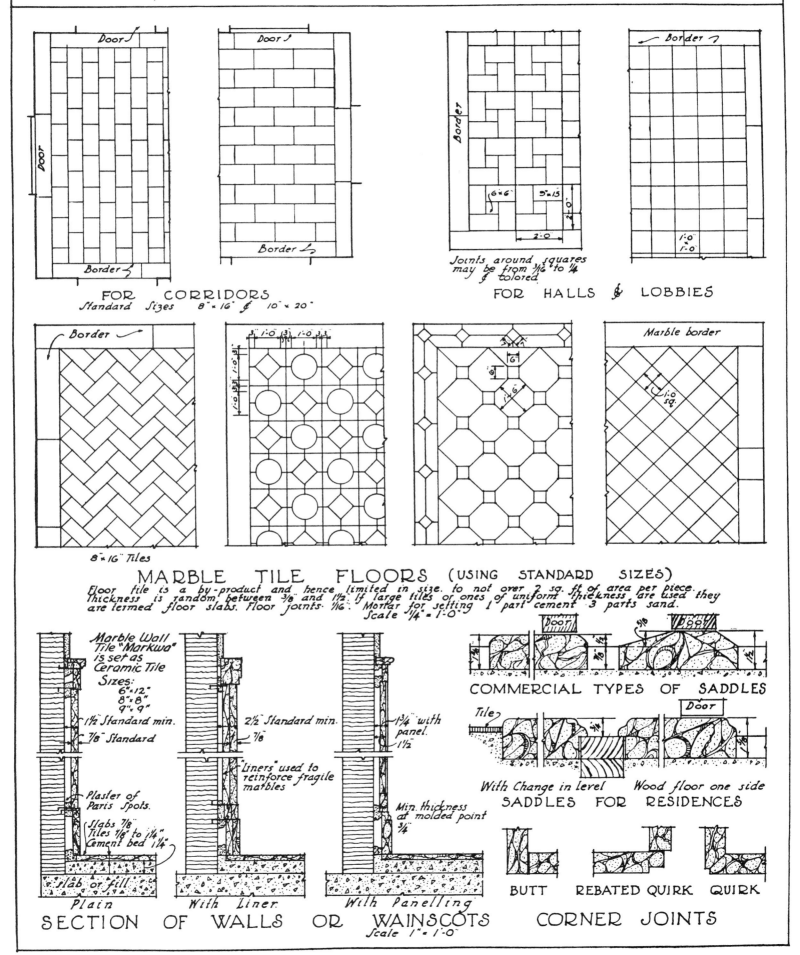

FOR CORRIDORS
Standard Sizes 8"×16" & 10"×20"

FOR HALLS & LOBBIES
Joints around squares may be from 1/16" to 1/4" & colored

8"×16" Tiles

MARBLE TILE FLOORS (USING STANDARD SIZES)

Floor tile is a by-product and hence limited in size to not over 2 sq. ft of area per piece.
Thickness is random between 3/8" and 1½". If large tiles or ones of uniform thickness are used they
are termed floor slabs. Floor joints 1/16". Mortar for setting 1 part cement 3 parts sand.
Scale 1/4" = 1'-0"

Marble Wall Tile "Markwa" is set as Ceramic Tile
Sizes:
6"×12"
8"×8"
9"×9"
1½" Standard min.
7/8" Standard
Plaster of Paris Spots.
Slabs 7/8"
Tiles 1/8" to 1¼"
Cement bed 1¼"
Slab or fill
Plain

2½" Standard min.
7/8"
"Liners" used to reinforce fragile marbles
With Liner

1¼" with panel.
1½"
Min. thickness at molded point 3/4"
With Panelling

SECTION OF WALLS OR WAINSCOTS
Scale 1" = 1'-0"

COMMERCIAL TYPES OF SADDLES

With Change in level   Wood floor one side
SADDLES FOR RESIDENCES

BUTT   REBATED QUIRK   QUIRK
CORNER JOINTS

SEWAGE DISPOSAL

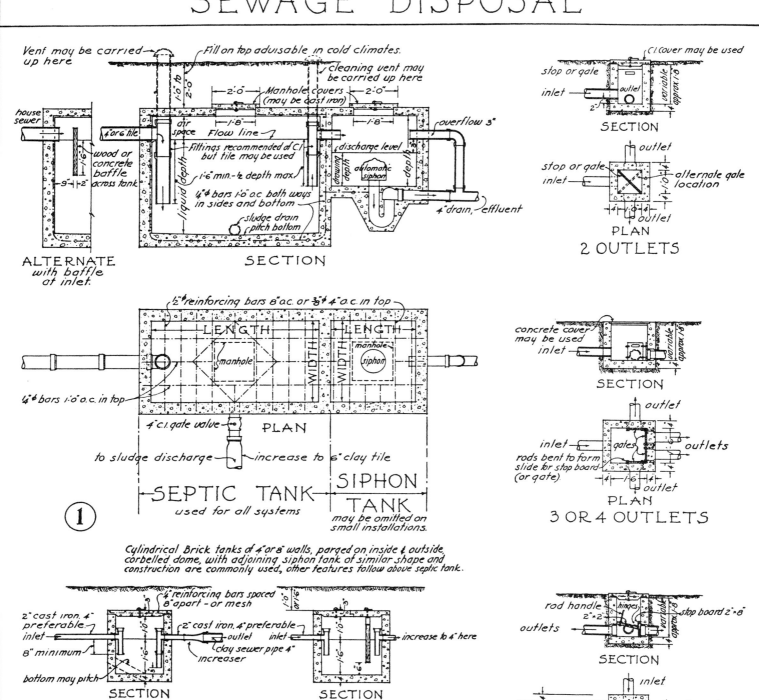

Vent may be carried up here

Fill on top advisable in cold climates.

cleaning vent may be carried up here

Manhole covers (may be cast iron)

house sewer

air space

Flow line

4"or 6" tile

wood or concrete baffle across tank

Fittings recommended of C.I. but tile may be used

1'-6" min. -½ depth max.

4"φ bars 1'-0" o.c. both ways in sides and bottom

sludge drain pitch bottom

liquid depth

overflow 3"

discharge level

drawing depth

depth

automatic siphon

4" drain, effluent

ALTERNATE with baffle at inlet.

SECTION

½"φ reinforcing bars 8" o.c. or ⅜"φ 4" o.c. in top

LENGTH   **LENGTH**

manhole   manhole siphon

WIDTH   **WIDTH**

4"φ bars 1'-0" o.c. in top

4" c.i. gate valve

PLAN

to sludge discharge   increase to 6" clay tile

SEPTIC TANK used for all systems

SIPHON TANK may be omitted on small installations.

①

Cylindrical Brick tanks of 4" or 8" walls, parged on inside & outside, corbelled dome, with adjoining siphon tank of similar shape and construction are commonly used, other features follow above septic tank.

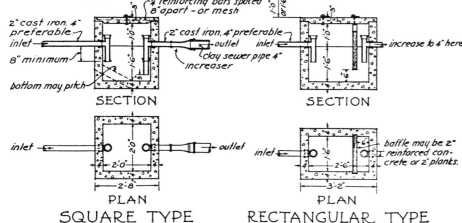

4"φ reinforcing bars spaced 8" apart - or mesh

2" cast iron, 4" preferable.
inlet
8" minimum
bottom may pitch

2" cast iron, 4" preferable.
outlet
clay sewer pipe 4"
increaser

SECTION

inlet   2'-0"   outlet
2'-0"

PLAN

SQUARE TYPE WITHOUT BAFFLE
Vol.= 6 cu.ft.

increase to 4" here

inlet   outlet

baffle may be 2" reinforced concrete or 2" planks.

2'-6"

SECTION

PLAN

RECTANGULAR TYPE WITH BAFFLE
Vol.= 5.625 cu.ft.

Cast Iron connections shown but these may be clay tile for economy.
May have 8" brick walls

②

Scale- ¼"=1 Foot

GREASE TRAPS
May be omitted in small systems

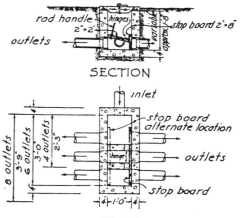

C.I. cover may be used

stop or gate
inlet   outlet
variable approx 1'-8"

SECTION

stop or gate
inlet   outlet
alternate gate location

PLAN
2 OUTLETS

concrete cover may be used
inlet

SECTION

outlet
inlet   outlets
gates
rods bent to form slide for stop board (or gate)
outlet

PLAN
3 OR 4 OUTLETS

rod handle   hinges
2"x2"   stop board 2"x8"
outlets
variable approx 1'-8"

SECTION

inlet
stop board alternate location
8 outlets
6 outlets
4 outlets
outlets
hinge
stop board

PLAN
4 OR MORE OUTLETS

③

DISTRIBUTING BOXES

All outlets must be set exactly level. Stop boards are used to provide a rest period for a part of the disposal field. Always used for filter beds and recommended for all but very small installations of all types.

Checked by Ralph Eberlin, C.E.

SEWAGE DISPOSAL

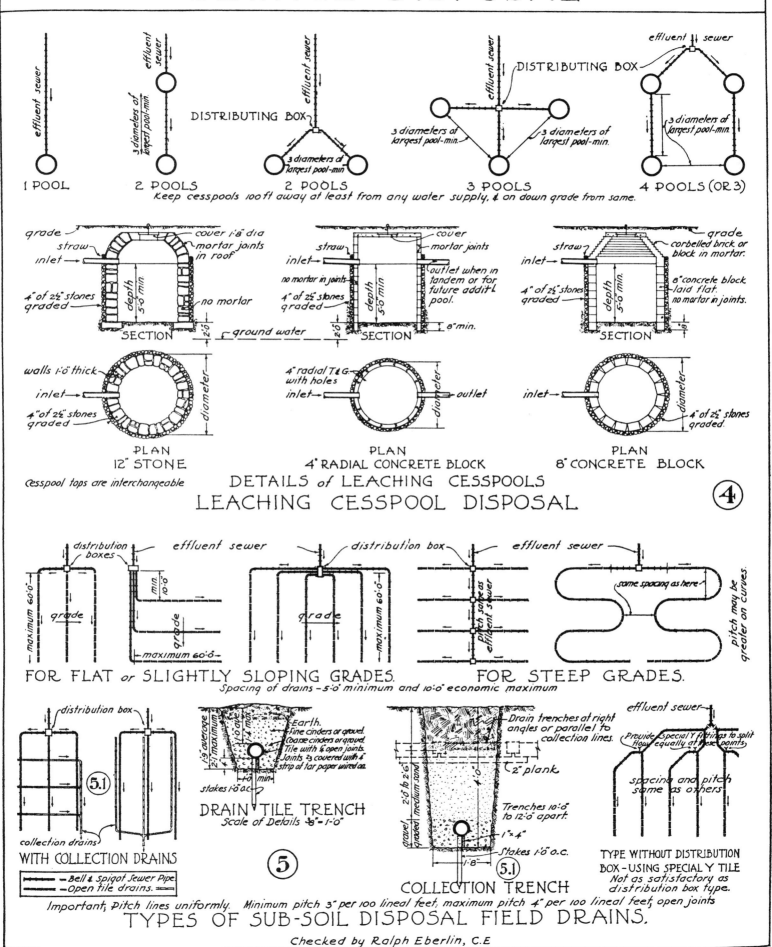

Keep cesspools 100 ft away at least from any water supply, & on down grade from same.

1 POOL

2 POOLS

2 POOLS

3 POOLS

4 POOLS (OR 3)

DETAILS of LEACHING CESSPOOLS

LEACHING CESSPOOL DISPOSAL

PLAN 12" STONE

PLAN 4" RADIAL CONCRETE BLOCK

PLAN 8" CONCRETE BLOCK

Cesspool tops are interchangeable

④

FOR FLAT or SLIGHTLY SLOPING GRADES.

FOR STEEP GRADES.

Spacing of drains - 5'-0" minimum and 10'-0" economic maximum

WITH COLLECTION DRAINS

⑤

DRAIN TILE TRENCH
Scale of Details ⅜" = 1'-0"

COLLECTION TRENCH

TYPE WITHOUT DISTRIBUTION BOX - USING SPECIAL Y TILE
Not as satisfactory as distribution box type.

━━━━━ = Bell & Spigot Sewer Pipe.
─────── = Open tile drains.

Important; Pitch lines uniformly. Minimum pitch 3" per 100 lineal feet; maximum pitch 4" per 100 lineal feet; open joints

TYPES OF SUB-SOIL DISPOSAL FIELD DRAINS.

Checked by Ralph Eberlin, C.E

SEWAGE DISPOSAL

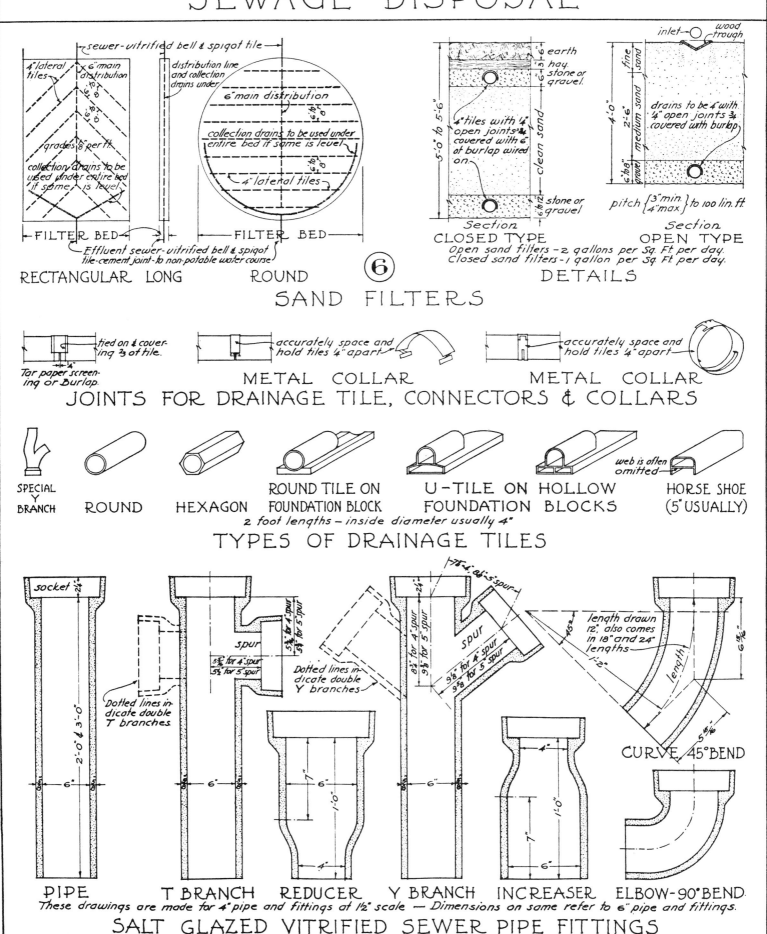

sewer-vitrified bell & spigot tile

4" lateral tiles | 6" main distribution

distribution line and collection drains under

grades 1/8" per ft.

collection drains to be used under entire bed if same is level

FILTER BED

6" main distribution

collection drains to be used under entire bed if same is level

4" lateral tiles

FILTER BED

Effluent sewer-vitrified bell & spigot tile-cement joint-to non-potable water course

⑥

RECTANGULAR LONG   ROUND

SAND FILTERS

earth
hay, stone or gravel.

4" tiles with 1/4" open joints 3/4 covered with 6" of burlap wired on.

clean sand

stone or gravel

5'-0" to 5'-6"

6" thz

Section
CLOSED TYPE

inlet — wood trough

fine sand

medium sand

gravel

drains to be 4" with 1/4" open joints 3/4 covered with burlap

4'-0"   2'-6"   6" to 8"

pitch { 3" min. / 4" max } to 100 lin. ft.

Section
OPEN TYPE

DETAILS

Open sand filters - 2 gallons per Sq. Ft. per day.
Closed sand filters - 1 gallon per Sq. Ft. per day.

tied on & covering 2/3 of tile.

Tar paper screening or Burlap.

accurately space and hold tiles 1/4" apart

METAL COLLAR

accurately space and hold tiles 1/4" apart

METAL COLLAR

JOINTS FOR DRAINAGE TILE, CONNECTORS & COLLARS

SPECIAL Y BRANCH   ROUND   HEXAGON   ROUND TILE ON FOUNDATION BLOCK   U-TILE ON HOLLOW FOUNDATION BLOCKS   web is often omitted   HORSE SHOE (5" USUALLY)

2 foot lengths - inside diameter usually 4"

TYPES OF DRAINAGE TILES

socket 2 1/4"

2'-0" & 3'-0"

6"

PIPE

spur

5 3/8" for 4" spur
5 5/8" for 5" spur

5 3/8" for 4" spur
5 5/8" for 5" spur

Dotted lines indicate double T branches

6"

T BRANCH

7"

1'-0"

4"

6"

REDUCER

7 5/8" for 4" spur
8 5/8" for 5" spur

8 5/8" for 4" spur
9 5/8" for 5" spur

9 5/8" for 4" spur
9 5/8" for 5" spur

Dotted lines indicate double Y branches

spur

6"

Y BRANCH

4"

7"

1'-0"

6"

INCREASER

length drawn 12", also comes in 18" and 24" lengths

45°

1'-2"

length

6 1/16"

5 1/16"

CURVE 45° BEND

ELBOW-90° BEND

PIPE   T BRANCH   REDUCER   Y BRANCH   INCREASER   ELBOW-90° BEND

These drawings are made for 4" pipe and fittings at 1/2" scale — Dimensions on same refer to 6" pipe and fittings.

SALT GLAZED VITRIFIED SEWER PIPE FITTINGS

Checked by Ralph Eberlin, C.E.

DRAINAGE ~ MANHOLES

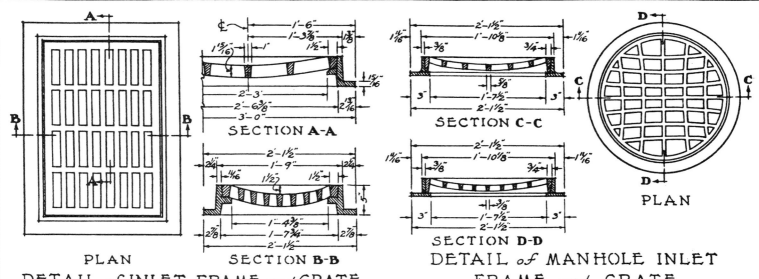

SECTION A-A

SECTION C-C

SECTION B-B

SECTION D-D

PLAN

PLAN
DETAIL of INLET FRAME and GRATE

DETAIL of MANHOLE INLET
FRAME and GRATE

Scale 3/4"=1'-0"

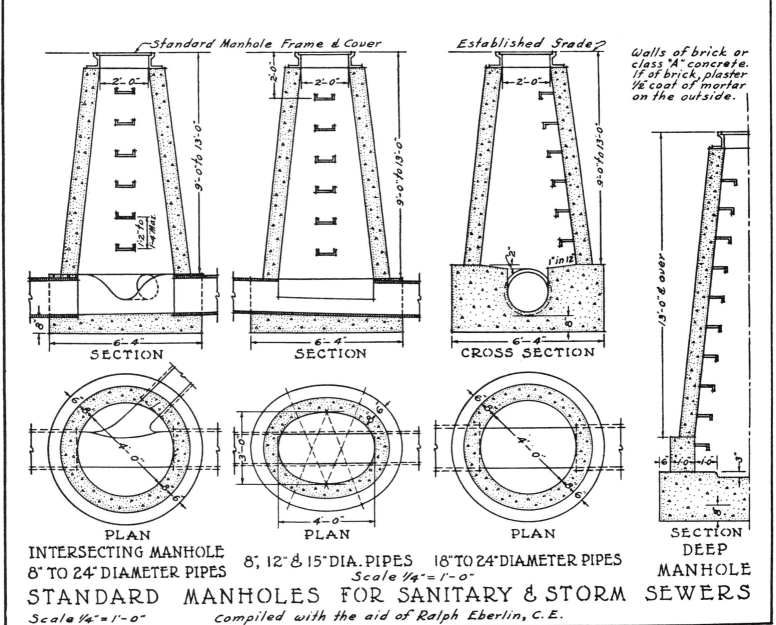

SECTION   SECTION   CROSS SECTION

Standard Manhole Frame & Cover

Established Grade

Walls of brick or class "A" concrete. If of brick, plaster 1/2" coat of mortar on the outside.

PLAN
INTERSECTING MANHOLE
8" TO 24" DIAMETER PIPES

PLAN
8", 12" & 15" DIA. PIPES

PLAN
18" TO 24" DIAMETER PIPES

Scale 1/4"=1'-0"

SECTION
DEEP
MANHOLE

STANDARD MANHOLES FOR SANITARY & STORM SEWERS

Scale 1/4"=1'-0"   Compiled with the aid of Ralph Eberlin, C.E.

DRAINAGE ~ EXTERIOR DETAILS

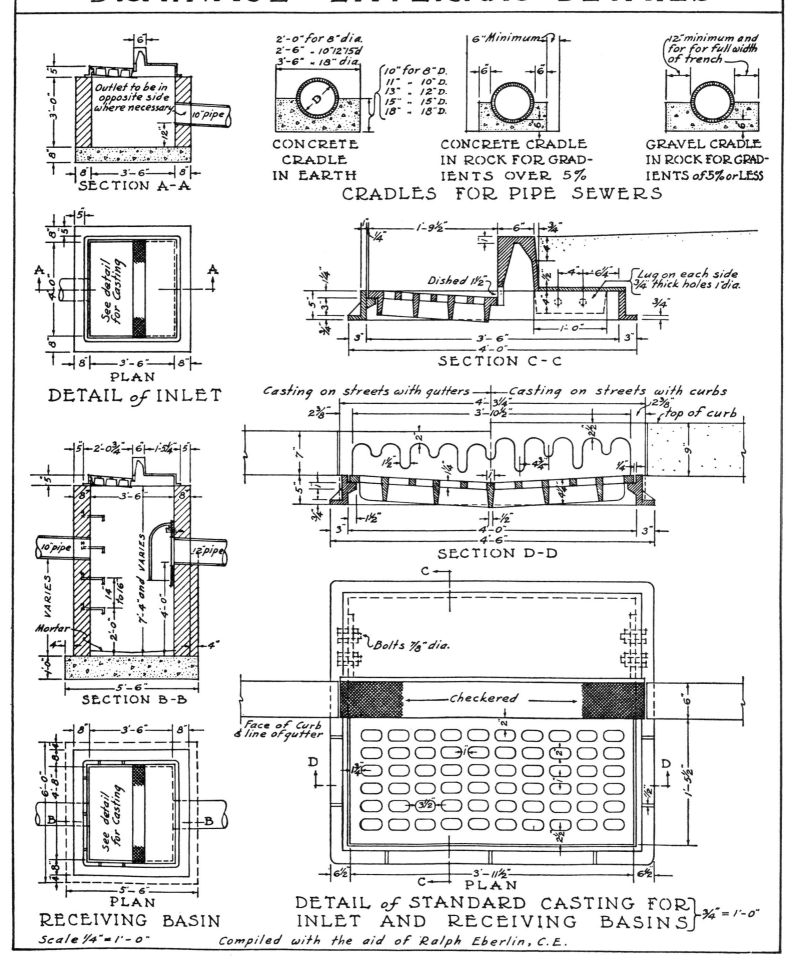

CRADLES FOR PIPE SEWERS

SECTION A-A

DETAIL of INLET

SECTION C-C

SECTION D-D

SECTION B-B

RECEIVING BASIN

PLAN

DETAIL of STANDARD CASTING FOR INLET AND RECEIVING BASINS

Scale ¼" = 1'-0"

Compiled with the aid of Ralph Eberlin, C.E.

DRAINAGE - EXTERIOR DETAILS

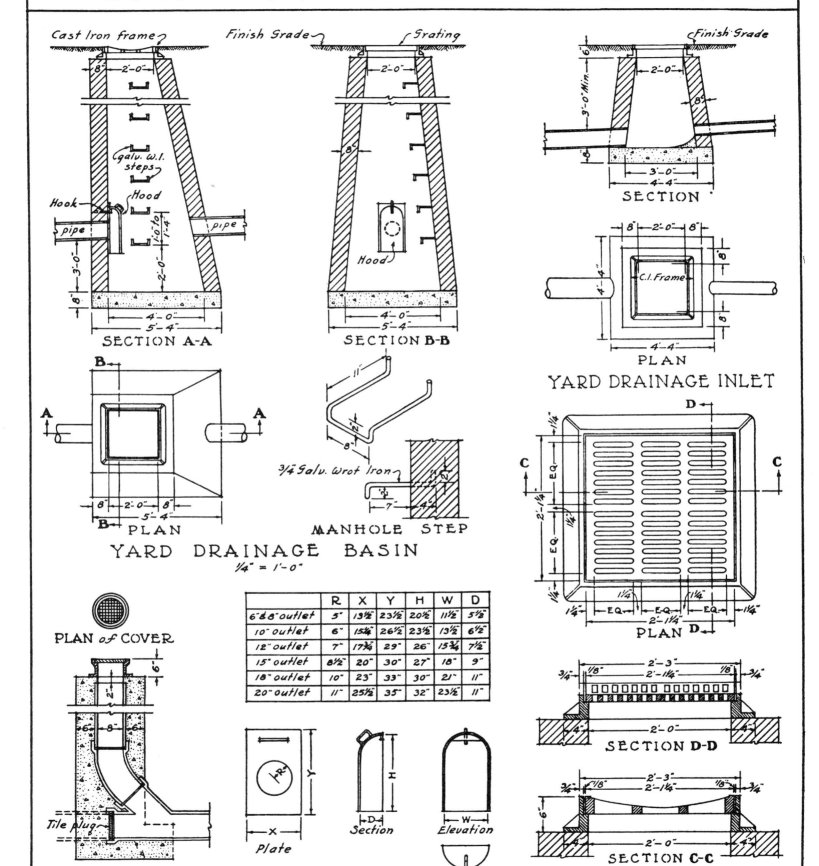

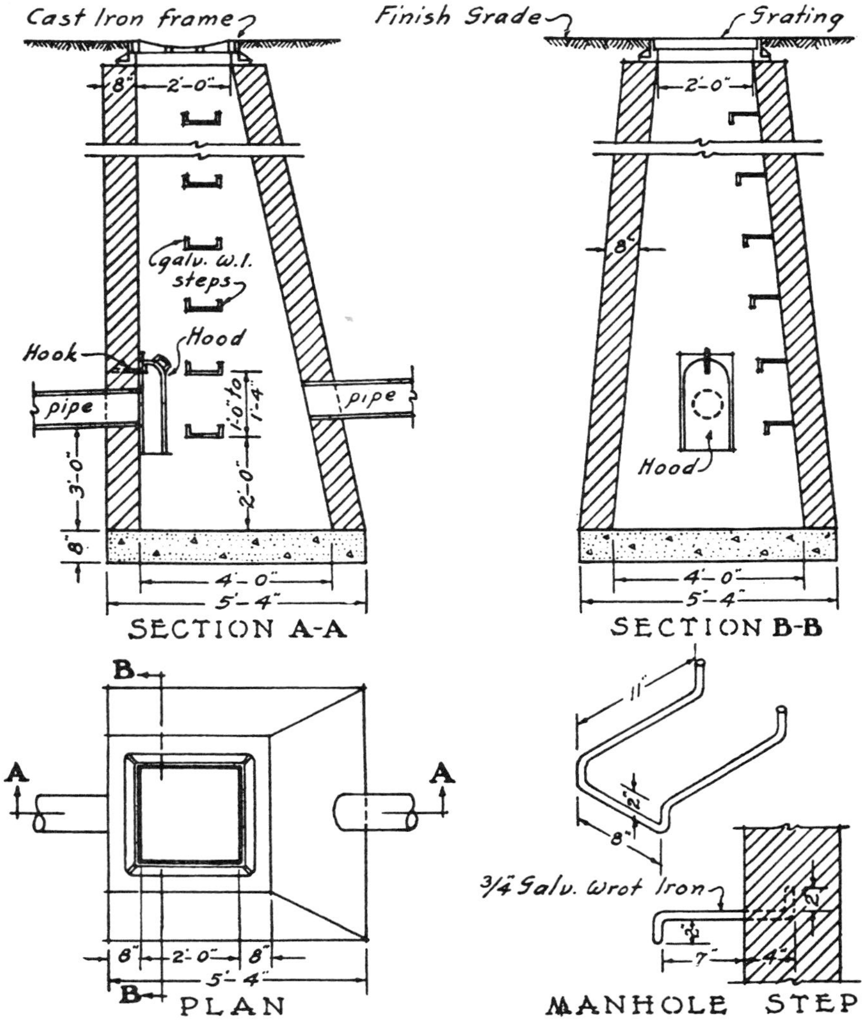
Cast Iron frame
Finish Grade
Grating
galv. w.I. steps
Hook
Hood
pipe
pipe
1'-0" to 1'-4"
3'-0"
2'-0"
8"
2'-0"
4'-0"
5'-4"
SECTION A-A
SECTION B-B
PLAN
A
B
MANHOLE STEP
3/4" Galv. Wrot Iron
11"
8"

YARD DRAINAGE BASIN

1/4" = 1'-0"

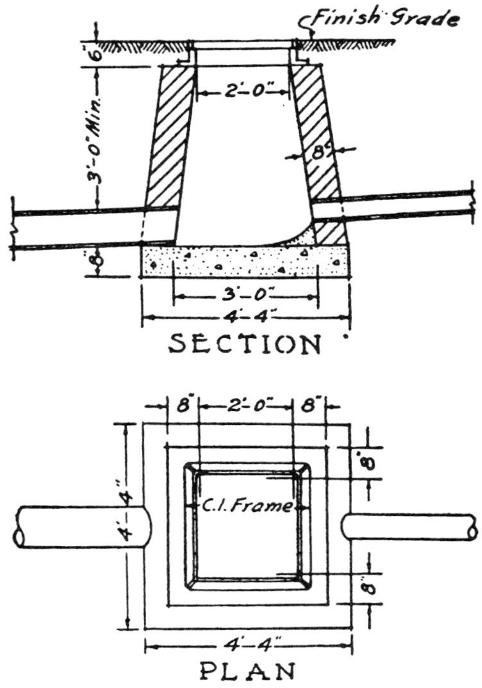
Finish Grade
3'-0" Min.
2'-0"
3'-0"
4'-4"
SECTION
C.I. Frame
PLAN

YARD DRAINAGE INLET

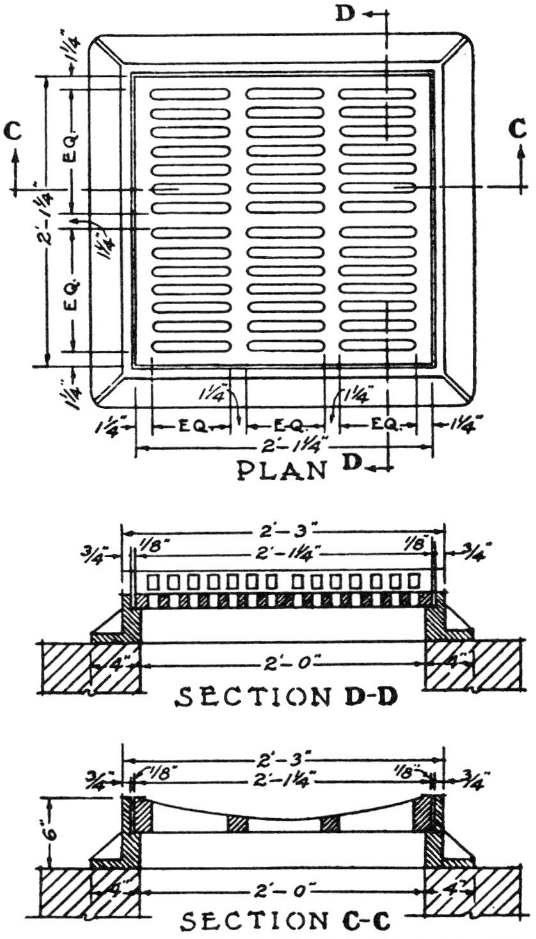
D
C
EQ.
2'-1¼"
PLAN
2'-3"
2'-0"
SECTION D-D
SECTION C-C

FRAME & GRATING FOR YARD DRAINAGE INLETS & BASINS

3/4" = 1'-0"

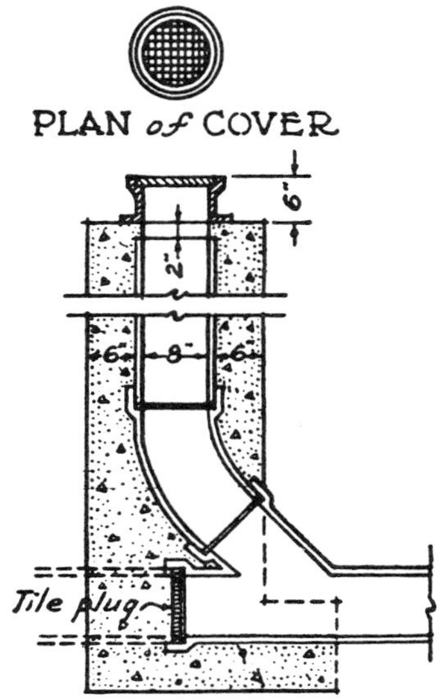
PLAN of COVER
Tile plug

DETAIL OF LAMP HOLE

3/8" = 1'-0"

	R	X	Y	H	W	D
6" & 8" outlet	5"	13½"	23½"	20½"	11½"	5⅛"
10" outlet	6"	15¼"	26½"	23½"	13½"	6½"
12" outlet	7"	17¾"	29"	26"	15¾"	7½"
15" outlet	8½"	20"	30"	27"	18"	9"
18" outlet	10"	23"	33"	30"	21"	11"
20" outlet	11"	25½"	35"	32"	23½"	11"

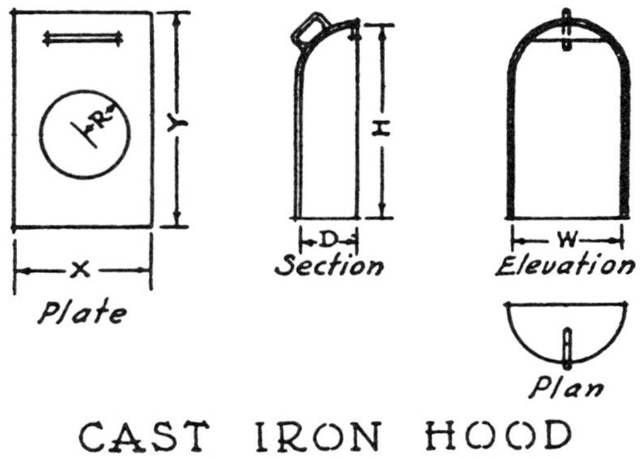
Plate
Section
Elevation
Plan

CAST IRON HOOD

Compiled with the aid of Ralph Eberlin, C.E.

BRICK PAVING

FLAT — ON EDGE
HERRING - BONE

ON EDGE — FLAT
BASKET WEAVE

PAVING PATTERNS-WALKS-TERRACES-PORCHES

Headers in border

RUNNING - FLAT — CROSS - FLAT — DIAGONAL - FLAT

PATTERNS USUALLY USED FOR WALKS

Joints grouted — Pitch ¼" — 1" Setting bed. — Sand in joints — Pitch ¼"

3" Foundation of 1 to 8 Cinder Concrete. If soil is clay use 4" bed of Cinders.
3" to 4" tamped sand or cinders. Sand in joints. This type is subject to Frost displacement. Ground must drain.
3" Foundation of 1 to 8 Cinder Concrete. If soil is clay use 4" bed of Cinders.

LAID ON CONCRETE SLAB — LAID ON SAND OR CINDERS — LAID ON CONCRETE

SECTIONS of TYPICAL WALKS or TERRACES.
¾"=1'-0"

Brick risers should always be flush; brick treads not projecting.
Treads bedded in cement mortar with mortar joints.
Brick cheeks may be omitted and earth warped to edge of steps.
Brick in front of tread should always be full headers.
This rise is not as easy as one on right of sheet.
Pitch steps ¼" but foundation to be level.
Brick in front of steps should always be full headers.
12" is minimum for all outside steps.
12" is minimum for all outside steps.
Concrete foundation 6" or 8"
6" or 8" Concrete
See Sections above for foundations of walks.
⅜"=1'-0"

WALKS - TERRACES - PORCHES - STEPS.
Recommendations of the Common Brick Manufacturers Association of America.

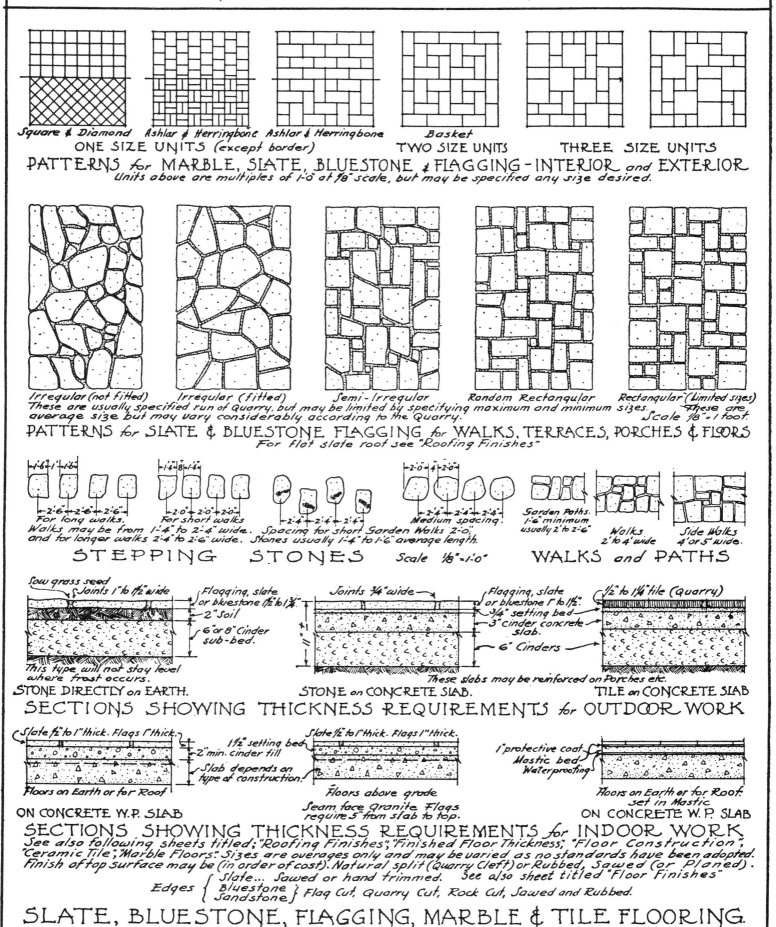

MASONRY FLOORING & PAVING

Square & Diamond — ONE SIZE UNITS (except border)
Ashlar & Herringbone · **Ashlar & Herringbone** · **Basket** TWO SIZE UNITS · THREE SIZE UNITS

PATTERNS for MARBLE, SLATE, BLUESTONE & FLAGGING – INTERIOR and EXTERIOR
Units above are multiples of 1'-0" at 1/8" scale, but may be specified any size desired.

Irregular (not fitted) · **Irregular (fitted)** · **Semi-Irregular** · **Random Rectangular** · **Rectangular (Limited sizes)**
These are usually specified run of Quarry, but may be limited by specifying maximum and minimum sizes. These are average size but may vary considerably according to the Quarry. Scale 1/8" = 1 foot.

PATTERNS for SLATE & BLUESTONE FLAGGING for WALKS, TERRACES, PORCHES & FLOORS
For flat slate roof see "Roofing Finishes"

For long walks. Walks may be from 1'-4" to 2'-4" wide and for longer walks 2'-4" to 2'-6" wide.
For short walks. Spacing for short Garden Walks 2'-0". Stones usually 1'-4" to 1'-6" average length.
Medium spacing.
Garden Paths. 1'-6" minimum usually 2' to 2'-6".
Walks 2' to 4' wide.
Side Walks 4' or 5' wide.

STEPPING STONES Scale 1/8"-1'-0" WALKS and PATHS

Sow grass seed. Joints 1" to 1½" wide. Flagging, slate or bluestone 1½" to 1¾". 2" Soil. 6" or 8" Cinder sub-bed. This type will not stay level where frost occurs.
STONE DIRECTLY on EARTH.

Joints ¾" wide. Flagging, slate or bluestone 1" to 1½". ¾" setting bed. 3" cinder concrete slab. 6" Cinders. These slabs may be reinforced on Porches etc.
STONE on CONCRETE SLAB.

½" to 1¼" tile (Quarry).
TILE on CONCRETE SLAB

SECTIONS SHOWING THICKNESS REQUIREMENTS for OUTDOOR WORK

Slate ½" to 1" thick. Flags 1" thick. 1½" setting bed. 2" min. cinder fill. Slab depends on type of construction.
Floors on Earth or for Roof — ON CONCRETE W.P. SLAB

Slate ½" to 1" thick. Flags 1" thick.
Floors above grade Seam face granite Flags require 5" from slab to top.

1" protective coat. Mastic bed. Waterproofing.
Floors on Earth or for Roof set in Mastic — ON CONCRETE W.P. SLAB

SECTIONS SHOWING THICKNESS REQUIREMENTS for INDOOR WORK
See also following sheets titled: "Roofing Finishes", "Finished Floor Thickness", "Floor Construction", "Ceramic Tile", "Marble Floors". Sizes are overages only and may be varied as no standards have been adopted. Finish of top surface may be (in order of cost): Natural split (Quarry Cleft) or Rubbed, Sawed (or Planed). See also sheet titled "Floor Finishes"
Edges { Slate... Sawed or hand trimmed. Bluestone Sandstone } Flag Cut, Quarry Cut, Rock Cut, Sawed and Rubbed.

SLATE, BLUESTONE, FLAGGING, MARBLE & TILE FLOORING.
Scale ¾"-1'-0"

ROADS and DRIVEWAYS etc.

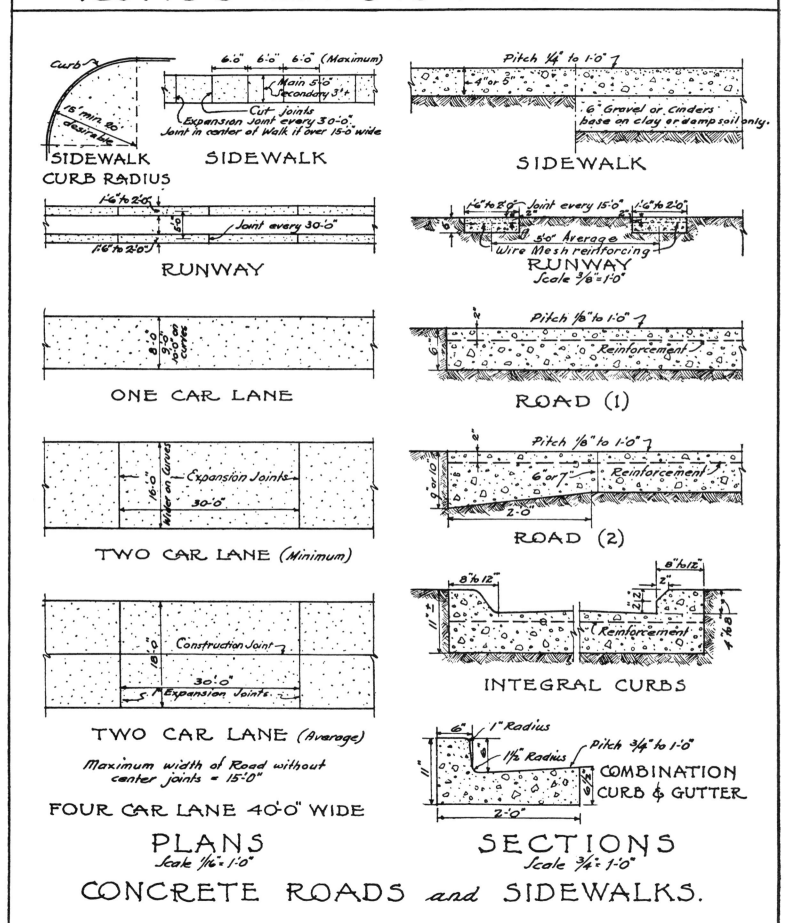

SIDEWALK CURB RADIUS

curb
15' min. 20 desirable

SIDEWALK

6.0" 6.0" 6.0" (Maximum)
Main 5'.0"
Secondary 3'±
Cut joints
Expansion Joint every 30'-0"
Joint in center of Walk if over 15'-0" wide

SIDEWALK

Pitch 1/4" to 1'-0"
4" or 5"
6" Gravel or Cinders base on clay or damp soil only.

RUNWAY

1'-6" to 2'-0"
5'-0"
Joint every 30'-0"
1'-6" to 2'-0"

RUNWAY
Scale 3/8"=1'-0"

1'-6" to 2'-0" Joint every 15'-0" 1'-6" to 2'-0"
6"
5'-0" Average
Wire Mesh reinforcing

ONE CAR LANE

8'-0"
9'-0"
10'-0" on curves

ROAD (1)

Pitch 1/8" to 1'-0"
2"
6"
Reinforcement

TWO CAR LANE (Minimum)

16'-0"
Wider on Curves
Expansion Joints
30'-0"

ROAD (2)

Pitch 1/8" to 1'-0"
2"
9 or 10"
6" or 7"
Reinforcement
2'-0"

TWO CAR LANE (Average)

18'-0"
Construction Joint
30'-0"
Expansion Joints

INTEGRAL CURBS

8" to 12"
8" to 12"
2"
11"
2" 2"
Reinforcement
4" to 8"

Maximum width of Road without center joints = 15'-0"

FOUR CAR LANE 40'-0" WIDE

PLANS
Scale 1/16" = 1'-0"

6" 1" Radius
1 1/2" Radius
Pitch 3/4" to 1'-0"
11"
6"
2'-0"

COMBINATION CURB & GUTTER

SECTIONS
Scale 3/4" = 1'-0"

CONCRETE ROADS and SIDEWALKS.

ROADS & PAVING

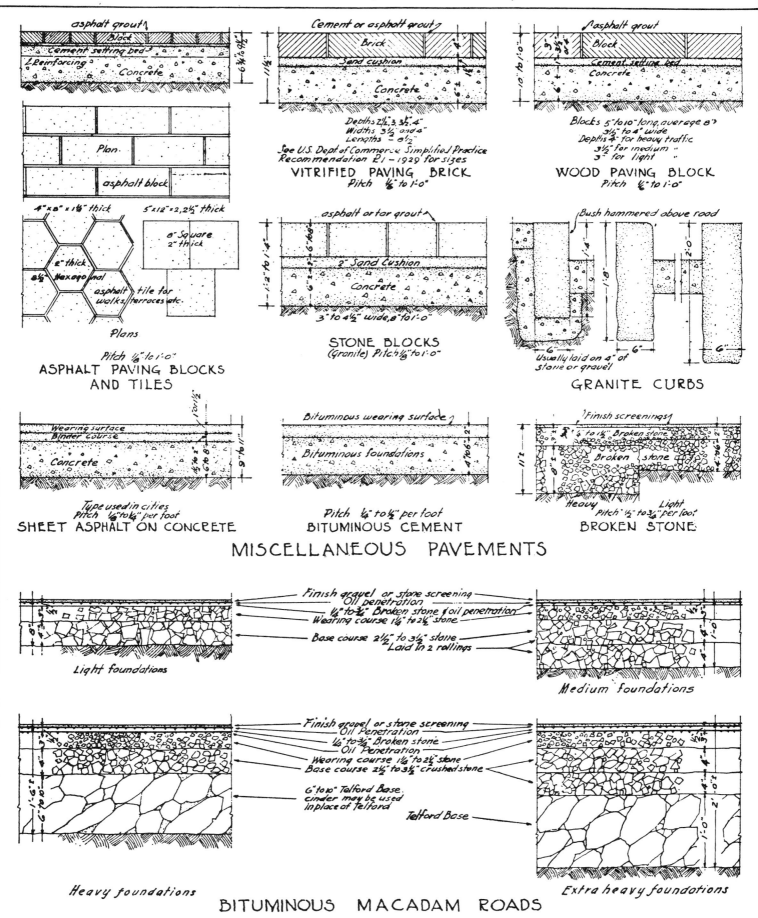

VITRIFIED PAVING BRICK
Pitch ⅛" to 1'-0"

asphalt grout
Block
Cement setting bed
Reinforcing
Concrete

Plan
asphalt block

4"x8"x1½" thick   5"x12"=2,2½" thick
6" Square 2" thick
6" thick
8½" Hexagonal
asphalt tile for walks, terraces etc.

Plans
Pitch ⅛" to 1'-0"
ASPHALT PAVING BLOCKS AND TILES

Cement or asphalt grout
Brick
Sand cushion
Concrete

Depths 2½, 3, 3½, 4"
Widths 3½ and 4"
Lengths = 8½"
See U.S. Dept. of Commerce Simplified Practice
Recommendation R1-1929 for sizes

asphalt or tar grout
2" Sand Cushion
Concrete
3" to 4½" wide, 8" to 1'-0"
STONE BLOCKS
(Granite) Pitch ⅛" to 1'-0"

asphalt grout
Block
Cement setting bed
Concrete

Blocks 5" to 10" long, average 8"
3½" to 4" wide
Depths 4" for heavy traffic
3½" for medium "
3" for light "
WOOD PAVING BLOCK
Pitch ⅛" to 1'-0"

Bush hammered above road
Usually laid on 4" of stone or gravel
GRANITE CURBS

Wearing surface
Binder course
Concrete
Type used in cities
Pitch ⅛" to ¼" per foot
SHEET ASPHALT ON CONCRETE

Bituminous wearing surface
Bituminous foundations
Pitch ¼" to ½" per foot
BITUMINOUS CEMENT

Finish screenings
¼ to 1½" Broken stone
Broken stone
Heavy   Light
Pitch ½" to ¾" per foot
BROKEN STONE

MISCELLANEOUS PAVEMENTS

Finish gravel or stone screening
Oil penetration
¼" to ¾" Broken stone, oil penetration
Wearing course 1¼ to 2½" stone
Base course 2½" to 3½" stone
Laid in 2 rollings

Light foundations

Medium foundations

Finish gravel or stone screening
Oil Penetration
¼" to ¾" Broken stone
Oil Penetration
Wearing course 1¼ to 2½" stone
Base course 2½" to 3½" crushed stone
6" to 10" Telford Base
cinder may be used in place of Telford

Telford Base

Heavy foundations

Extra heavy foundations

BITUMINOUS MACADAM ROADS

GARAGES & PARKING

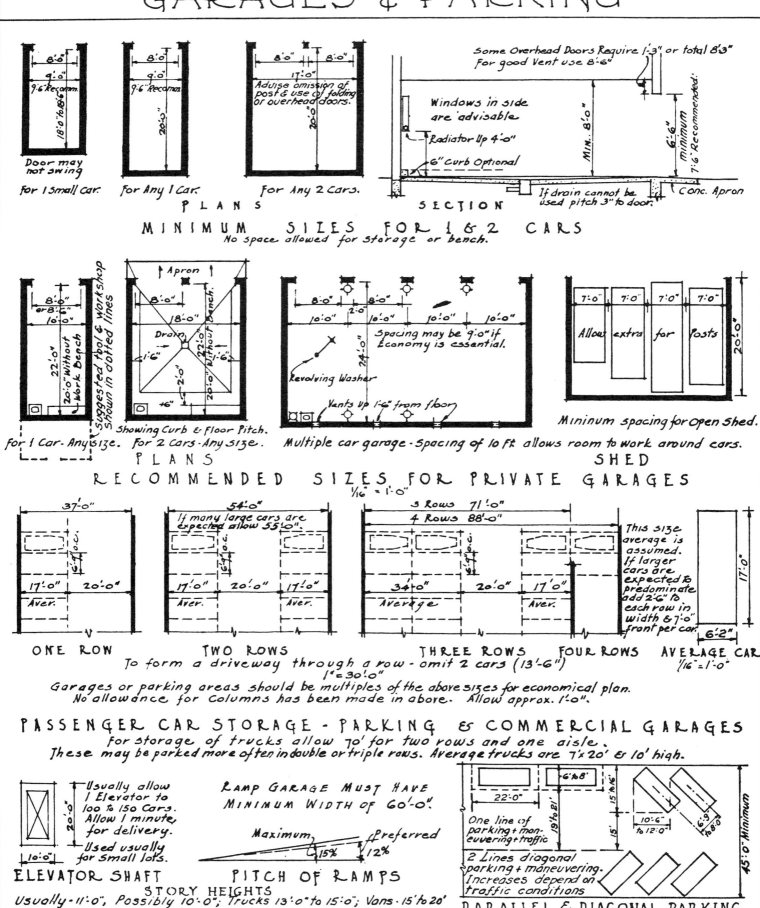

MINIMUM SIZES FOR 1 & 2 CARS
No space allowed for storage or bench.

RECOMMENDED SIZES FOR PRIVATE GARAGES
1/16" = 1'-0"

PASSENGER CAR STORAGE - PARKING & COMMERCIAL GARAGES
For storage of trucks allow 70' for two rows and one aisle.
These may be parked more often in double or triple rows. Average trucks are 7'x20' & 10' high.

ELEVATOR SHAFT   PITCH OF RAMPS
STORY HEIGHTS
Usually - 11'-0", Possibly 10'-0"; Trucks 13'-0" to 15'-0"; Vans - 15' to 20'

PARALLEL & DIAGONAL PARKING

GARAGES - PARKING & SPACE REQUIREMENTS FOR PRIVATE AUTOMOBILES

WOOD FENCES

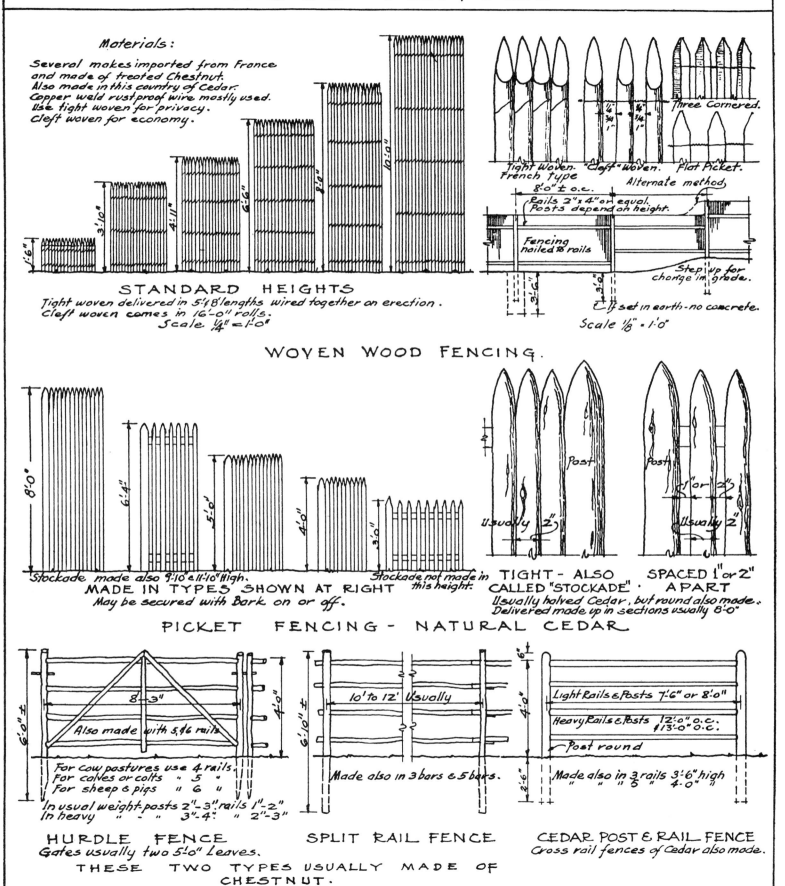

Materials:

Several makes imported from France
and made of treated Chestnut.
Also made in this country of Cedar.
Copper weld rustproof wire mostly used.
Use tight woven for privacy.
Cleft woven for economy.

Tight Woven. "Cleft" Woven. Flat Picket.
French type   Alternate method.

Three Cornered.

8'-0" ± o.c.
Rails 2"x 4" or equal.
Posts depend on height.

Fencing
nailed to rails

Step up for
change in grade.

If set in earth-no concrete.

Scale ⅛" = 1'-0"

STANDARD HEIGHTS
Tight woven delivered in 5'& 8'lengths wired together on erection.
Cleft woven comes in 16'-0" rolls.
Scale. ¼" = 1'-0"

WOVEN WOOD FENCING.

Stockade made also 9'-10" & 11'-10" High.

MADE IN TYPES SHOWN AT RIGHT
May be secured with Bark on or off.

Stockade not made in
this height.

Post

Usually 2"

TIGHT - ALSO
CALLED "STOCKADE".
Usually halved Cedar, but round also made.
Delivered made up in sections usually 8'-0"

Post

1" or 2"

Usually 2"

SPACED 1" or 2"
APART

PICKET FENCING - NATURAL CEDAR

8'-3"

Also made with 5,& 6 rails

For cow pastures use 4 rails.
For calves or colts " 5 "
For sheep & pigs " 6 "

In usual weight-posts 2"-3", rails 1"-2"
In heavy " - " 3"-4", " 2"-3"

HURDLE FENCE
Gates usually two 5'-0" Leaves.

10' to 12' Usually

Made also in 3 bars & 5 bars.

SPLIT RAIL FENCE

Light Rails & Posts 7'-6" or 8'-0"

Heavy Rails & Posts 12'-0" o.c.
& 13'-0" O.C.

Post round

Made also in 3 rails 3'-6" high
" " 5 " 4'-0" "

CEDAR POST & RAIL FENCE
Cross rail fences of Cedar also made.

THESE TWO TYPES USUALLY MADE OF
CHESTNUT.

282

PARK EQUIPMENT

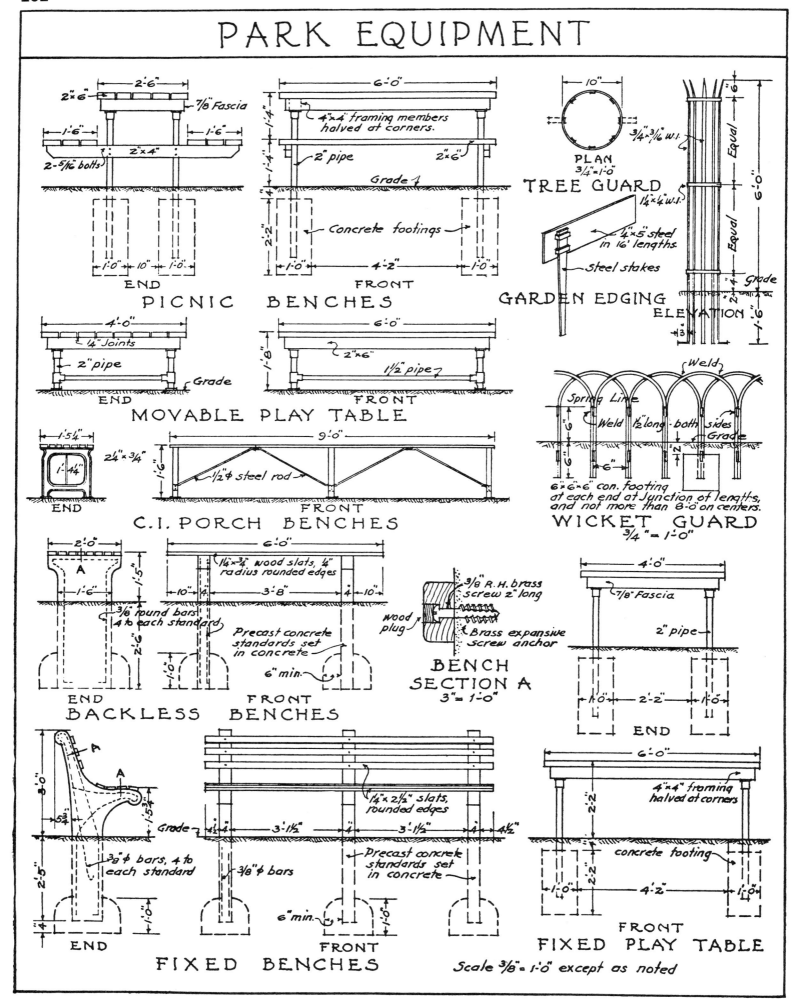

SWIMMING POOLS

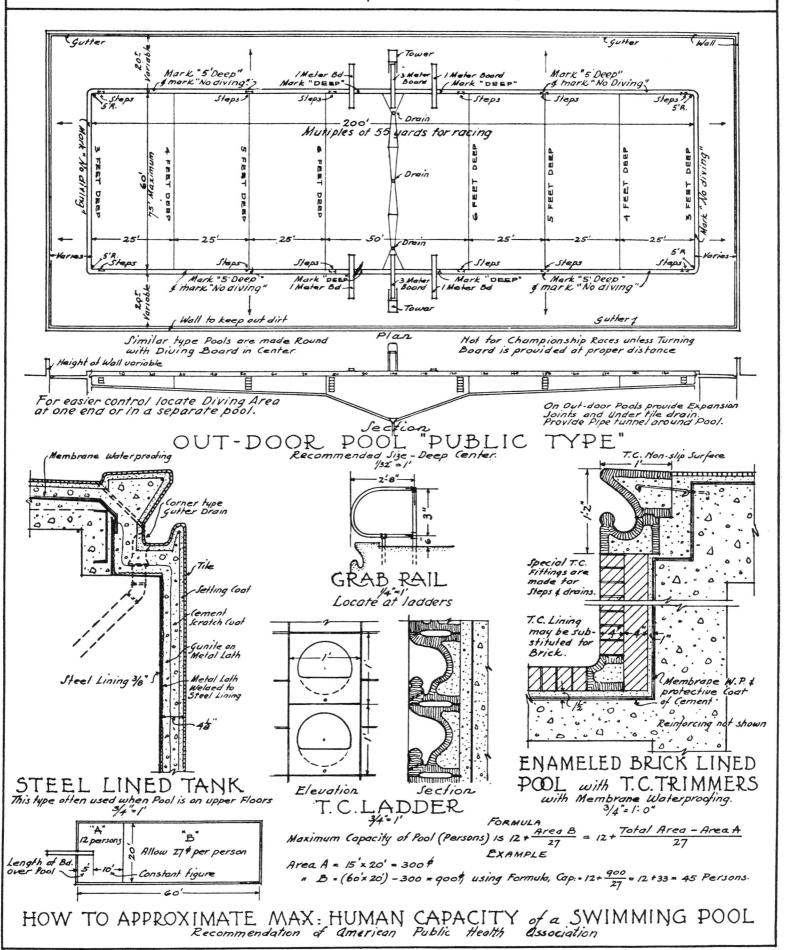

Plan

Similar type Pools are made Round with Diving Board in Center.

Not for Championship Races unless Turning Board is provided at proper distance

Height of Wall variable

Section

For easier control locate Diving Area at one end or in a separate pool.

On Out-door Pools provide Expansion Joints and Under tile drain. Provide Pipe tunnel around Pool.

OUT-DOOR POOL "PUBLIC TYPE"
Recommended Size - Deep Center.
1/32" = 1'

GRAB RAIL
1/4"=1'
Locate at ladders

STEEL LINED TANK
This type often used when Pool is on upper Floors
3/4"= 1'

T.C. LADDER
3/4"= 1'
Elevation   Section

ENAMELED BRICK LINED POOL with T.C. TRIMMERS
with Membrane Waterproofing.
3/4" = 1: 0"

FORMULA

Maximum Capacity of Pool (Persons) is $12 + \dfrac{Area\ B}{27} = 12 + \dfrac{Total\ Area - Area\ A}{27}$

EXAMPLE

Area A = 15' x 20' = 300 ◻

" B = (60'x20') - 300 = 900 ◻, using Formula, Cap.= $12 + \dfrac{900}{27} = 12 + 33 = 45$ Persons.

"A" 12 persons
Length of Bd. over Pool
"B" Allow 27◻ per person
Constant figure

HOW TO APPROXIMATE MAX: HUMAN CAPACITY of a SWIMMING POOL
Recommendation of American Public Health Association

SWIMMING POOLS

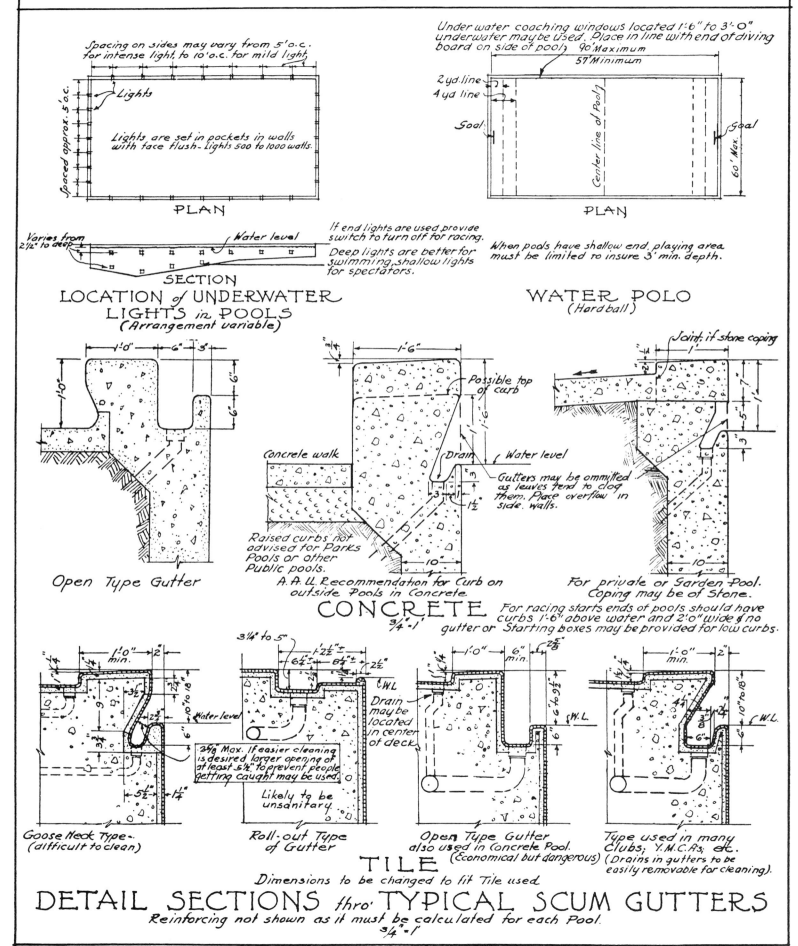

Spacing on sides may vary from 5'o.c. for intense light, to 10'o.c. for mild light.

Lights

Spaced approx. 5'o.c.

Lights are set in pockets in walls with face flush - lights 500 to 1000 watts.

PLAN

Varies from 2½" to deep

Water level

SECTION

If end lights are used provide switch to turn off for racing.

Deep lights are better for swimming, shallow lights for spectators.

LOCATION of UNDERWATER LIGHTS in POOLS
(Arrangement variable)

Under water coaching windows located 1'-6" to 3'-0" underwater may be used. Place in line with end of diving board on side of pool. 90' Maximum

57' Minimum

2 yd. line
4 yd. line
Goal
Center line of Pool
Goal
60' Max.

PLAN

When pools have shallow end, playing area must be limited to insure 3' min. depth.

WATER POLO
(Hard ball)

Open Type Gutter

Concrete walk

Raised curbs not advised for Parks Pools or other Public pools.

Possible top of curb

Drain

Water level

Gutters may be ommitted as leaves tend to clog them. Place overflow in side walls.

Joint if stone coping

A.A.U. Recommendation for Curb on outside Pools in Concrete

For private or Garden Pool. Coping may be of Stone.

CONCRETE
¾"-1'

For racing starts ends of pools should have curbs 1'-6" above water and 2'-0" wide & no gutter or Starting boxes may be provided for low curbs.

Water level

2⅞ Max. If easier cleaning is desired larger opening of at least 5½" to prevent people getting caught may be used.

C.W.L.

Drain may be located in center of deck

W.L.

W.L.

Goose Neck Type. (difficult to clean)

Roll-out Type of Gutter

Likely to be unsanitary.

Open Type Gutter also used in Concrete Pool. (Economical but dangerous)

Type used in many Clubs; Y.M.C.A's; etc. (Drains in gutters to be easily removable for cleaning).

TILE
Dimensions to be changed to fit Tile used.

DETAIL SECTIONS thro' TYPICAL SCUM GUTTERS
Reinforcing not shown as it must be calculated for each Pool.
¾"-1'

SWIMMING POOLS

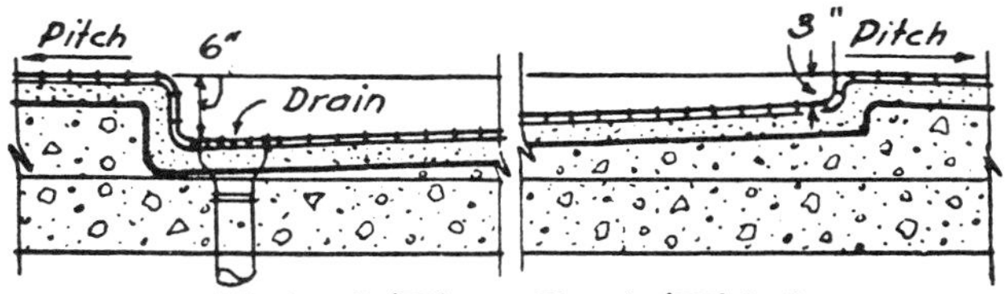

Pitch
6"
Drain
3"
Pitch

FOOT BATH
FOR SWIMMING POOL ENTRIES

Run Waterproofing to walls and up, and have curb at door. Non slip tile Starting grips for backstroke may be provided, in front face - 2 to each lane located 12" to 16" above water & 18" to 20" apart. Not used with gutter at ends.

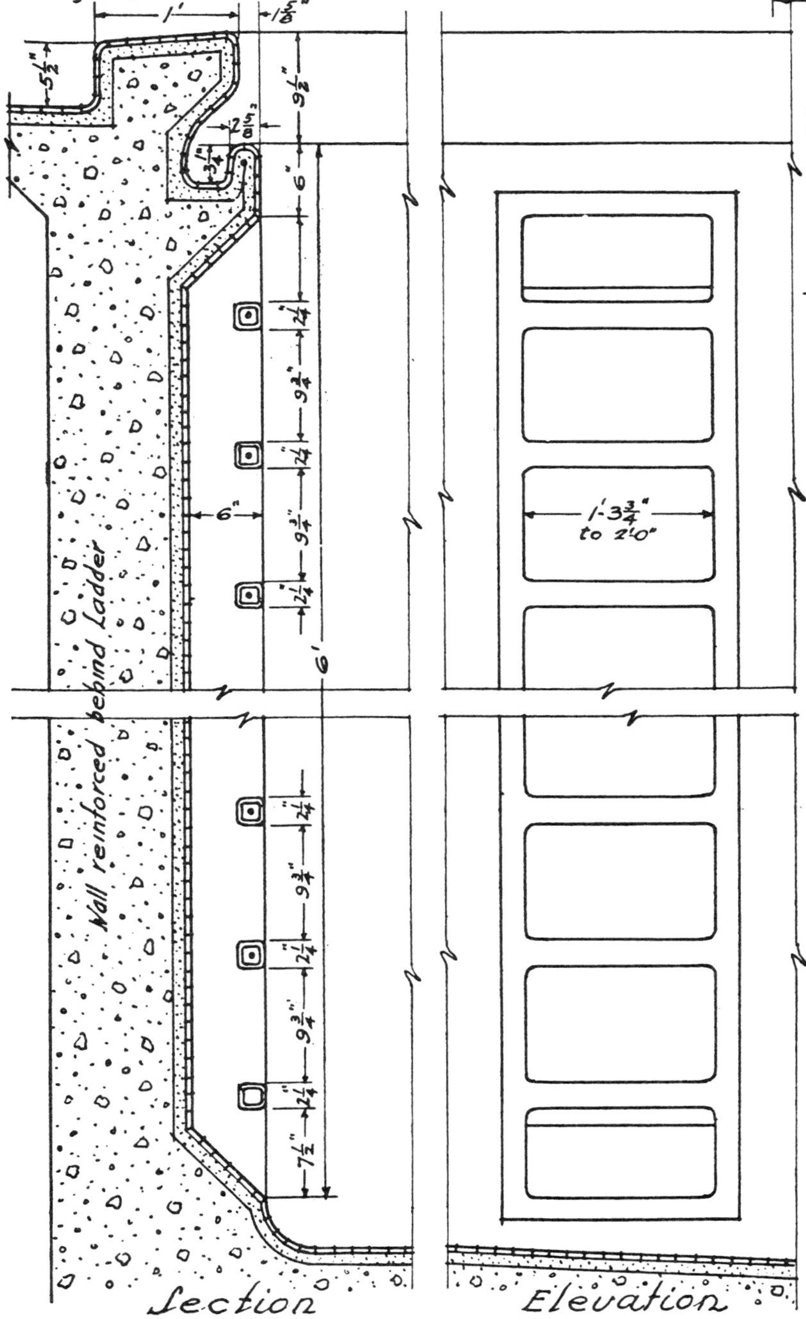

1'
1 5/8"
5 1/2"
9 1/2"
6"
6"
2 1/4"
9 3/4"
6'
Wall reinforced behind Ladder
7 1/2"
1'-3 3/4" to 2'-0"

Section Elevation

SWIMMING POOL STEPS
BUILT IN (Locate in Side wall)

3/4" = 1'

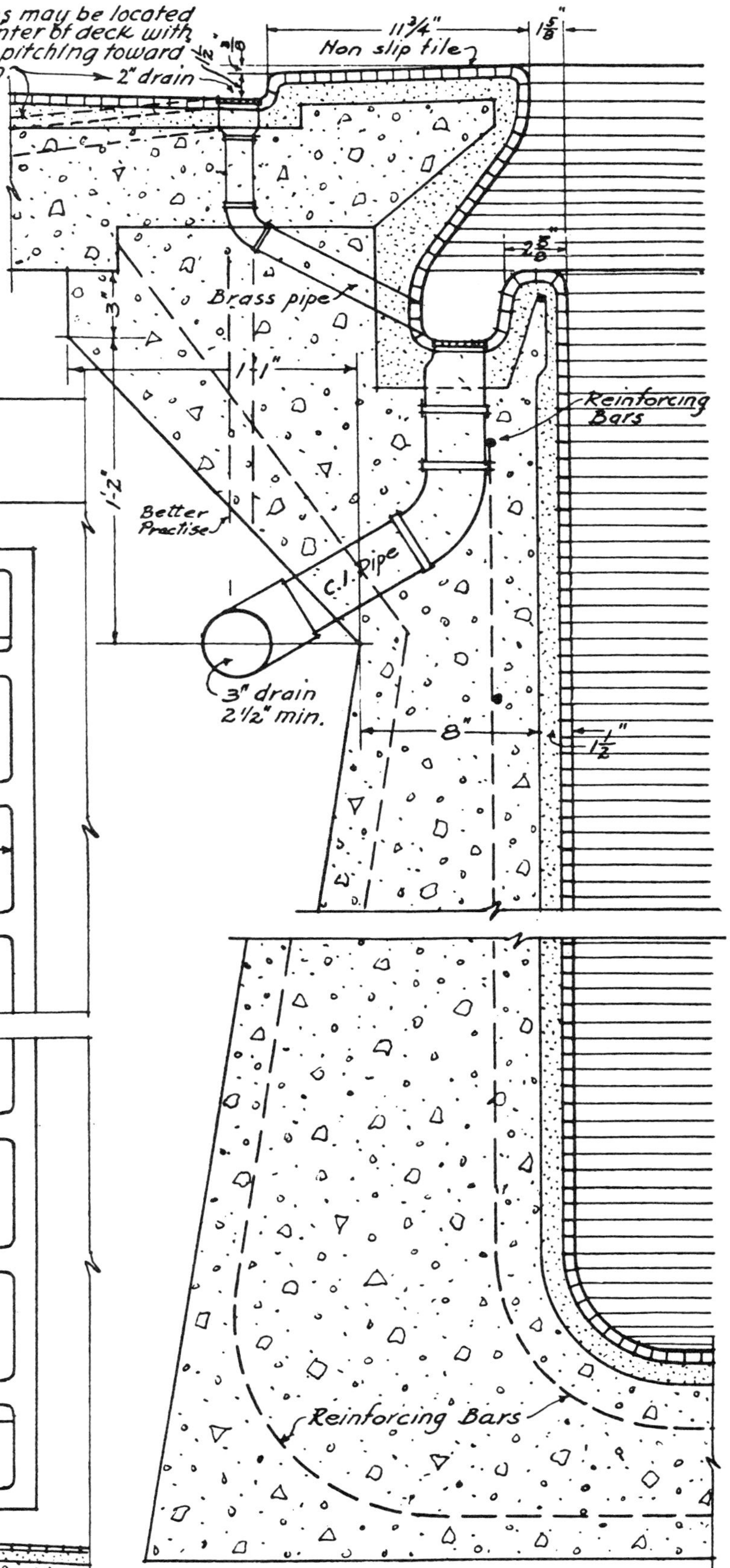

Drains may be located in center of deck with deck pitching toward drain
2" drain
11 3/4"
1 5/8"
Non slip tile
Brass pipe
2 5/8"
3"
1'-1"
1'-2"
Reinforcing Bars
Better Practise
C.I. Pipe
3" drain 2 1/2" min.
8"
1 1/2"
Reinforcing Bars

TYPICAL TILE POOL SECTION
Reinforcing Bars to be designed to meet conditions of each pool

1 1/2" = 1'

Pool shells, when on upper floors, are often of steel outside of Concrete

SPRING BOARDS

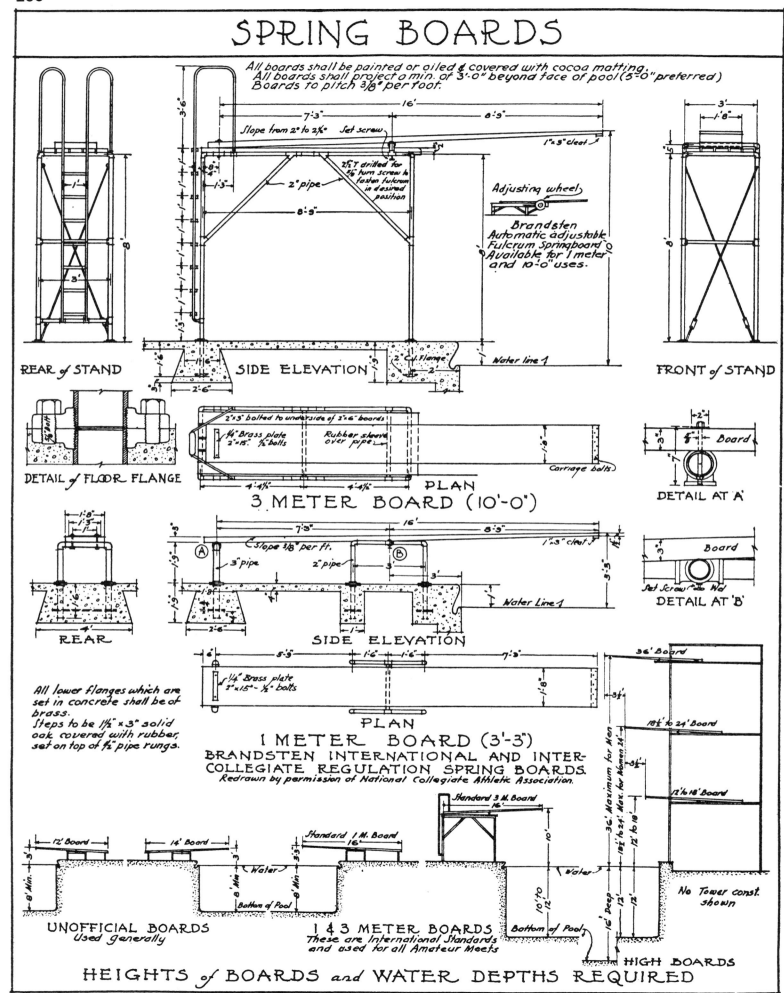

All boards shall be painted or oiled & covered with cocoa matting.
All boards shall project a min. of 3'-0" beyond face of pool (5'-0" preferred)
Boards to pitch 3/8" per foot.

REAR of STAND

SIDE ELEVATION

FRONT of STAND

Slope from 2° to 2½° Set screw

2½" T drilled for 5/16" turn screw to fasten fulcrum in desired position

2" pipe

8'-9"

Adjusting wheel

Brandsten Automatic adjustable Fulcrum Springboard Available for 1 meter and 10'-0" uses.

1"x3" cleat

Water line

DETAIL of FLOOR FLANGE

2"x5" bolted to underside of 2"x6" boards

¼" Brass plate 2"x15". ½" bolts

Rubber sheave over pipe

Carriage bolts

PLAN

3 METER BOARD (10'-0")

DETAIL AT 'A'

Board

REAR

SIDE ELEVATION

Slope 3/8 per ft.

3" pipe   2" pipe

Water Line

1"x3" cleat

Board

Set Screw to Wd.

DETAIL AT 'B'

All lower flanges which are set in concrete shall be of brass.
Steps to be 1½" x 3" solid oak covered with rubber, set on top of ½" pipe rungs.

¼" Brass plate 2"x15" - ½" bolts

PLAN

1 METER BOARD (3'-3")

BRANDSTEN INTERNATIONAL AND INTER-
COLLEGIATE REGULATION SPRING BOARDS
Redrawn by permission of National Collegiate Athletic Association.

12' Board   14' Board   Standard 1 M. Board
                              16'

Standard 3 M. Board
16'

36' Board

18½' to 24' Board

12' to 18' Board

(Water)

Bottom of Pool

No Tower const. shown

UNOFFICIAL BOARDS
Used generally

1 & 3 METER BOARDS
These are International Standards
and used for all Amateur Meets

HIGH BOARDS

HEIGHTS of BOARDS and WATER DEPTHS REQUIRED

ROADS—CLASSIFIED BY TRAFFIC LANES

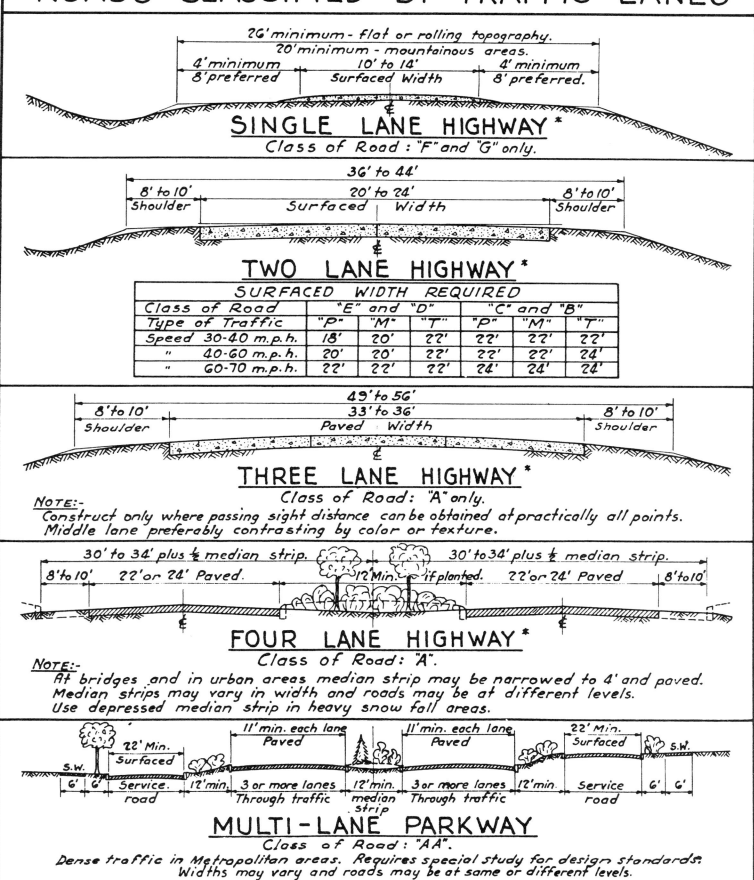

26' minimum - flat or rolling topography.
20' minimum - mountainous areas.

| 4' minimum | 10' to 14' | 4' minimum |
| 8' preferred | Surfaced Width | 8' preferred. |

SINGLE LANE HIGHWAY *
Class of Road: "F" and "G" only.

36' to 44'

| 8' to 10' | 20' to 24' | 8' to 10' |
| Shoulder | Surfaced Width | Shoulder |

TWO LANE HIGHWAY *

SURFACED WIDTH REQUIRED					
Class of Road	"E" and "D"			"C" and "B"	
Type of Traffic	"P"	"M"	"T"	"P"	"M"	"T"
Speed 30-40 m.p.h.	18'	20'	22'	22'	22'	22'
" 40-60 m.p.h.	20'	20'	22'	22'	22'	24'
" 60-70 m.p.h.	22'	22'	22'	24'	24'	24'

49' to 56'

| 8' to 10' | 33' to 36' | 8' to 10' |
| Shoulder | Paved Width | Shoulder |

THREE LANE HIGHWAY *
Class of Road: "A" only.

NOTE:-
Construct only where passing sight distance can be obtained at practically all points.
Middle lane preferably contrasting by color or texture.

30' to 34' plus ½ median strip.   30' to 34' plus ½ median strip.

| 8' to 10' | 22' or 24' Paved. | 12' Min. if planted. | 22' or 24' Paved | 8' to 10' |

FOUR LANE HIGHWAY *
Class of Road: "A".

NOTE:-
At bridges and in urban areas median strip may be narrowed to 4' and paved.
Median strips may vary in width and roads may be at different levels.
Use depressed median strip in heavy snow fall areas.

| S.W. | 22' Min. Surfaced | 11' min. each lane Paved | 11' min. each lane Paved | 22' Min. Surfaced | S.W. |
| 6' 6' | Service road | 12' min. 3 or more lanes Through traffic | 12' min. median strip | 12' min. 3 or more lanes Through traffic | 12' min. Service road | 6' 6' |

MULTI-LANE PARKWAY
Class of Road: "AA".

Dense traffic in Metropolitan areas. Requires special study for design standards.
Widths may vary and roads may be at same or different levels.

* Adapted from A Policy on Highway Types by A.A.S.H.O.

ROADS – TYPICAL SECTIONS –1

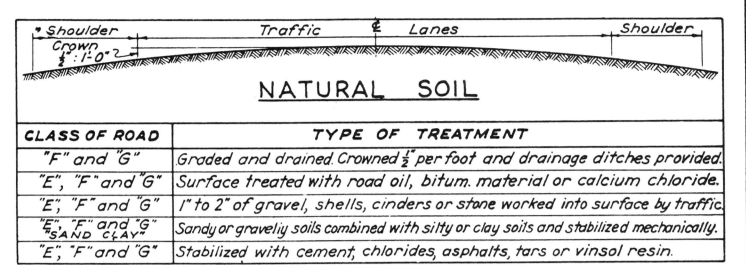

NATURAL SOIL

CLASS OF ROAD	TYPE OF TREATMENT
"F" and "G"	Graded and drained. Crowned ½" per foot and drainage ditches provided.
"E", "F" and "G"	Surface treated with road oil, bitum. material or calcium chloride.
"E", "F" and "G"	1" to 2" of gravel, shells, cinders or stone worked into surface by traffic.
"E", "F" and "G" "SAND CLAY"	Sandy or gravelly soils combined with silty or clay soils and stabilized mechanically.
"E", "F" and "G"	Stabilized with cement, chlorides, asphalts, tars or vinsol resin.

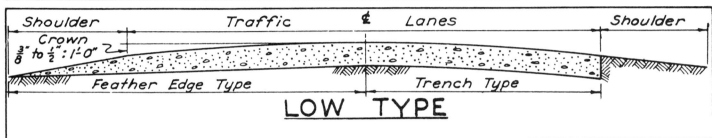

LOW TYPE

CLASS OF ROAD	SURFACE	SURFACE TREATMENT
"C", "D", "E" or "F"	6" of selected soil stabilized with Portland cement, bituminous material or calcium chloride.	Bituminous.
"C", "D", "E" or "F" "SAND CLAY"	6" to 10" of gravel, sand-clay, topsoil, lime-rock, caliche, scoria, shells, chert, shale, slag or cinders.	Road oil, calcium chloride or bituminous.
"C" or "D"	4" to 10" of traffic-bound macadam. 4" to 6" of water-bound macadam.	Bituminous.

INTERMEDIATE TYPE–BITUMINOUS

CLASS OF ROAD	SURFACE	BASE
"C", "D" and "E"	2½" mixed-in-place (Road-Mix).	6" or more of compacted gravel.
"C" and "D"	2½" low cost plant-mix or pre-mix.	6" crushed gravel or equal.
"B", "C" and "D"	4" to 6" of sand-asphalt.	6" sand-clay or equal.
"B" and "C"	3" bitum. penetration macadam.	3" to 6" crushed stone.
"C" and "D"	1½" bituminous pavement.	6" of stabilized selected soil.
"B" and "C"	1½" to 2½" bituminous pavement.	6" cement-treated base.
"B" and "C"	1½" natural rock asphalt.	6" to 8" water-bound macadam.
"B" and "C"	2½" bitum. penetration macadam.	8" Telford, broken stone, field stone.

References: Highway Design & Construction by A.G. Bruce.
American Highway Practice, Vol. I & II by L.I. Hewes.

ROADS — TYPICAL SECTIONS — 2

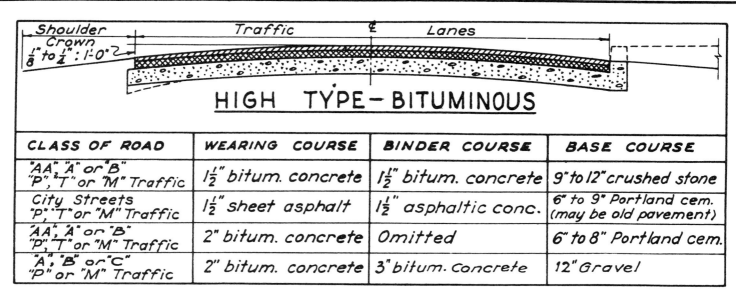

HIGH TYPE — BITUMINOUS

CLASS OF ROAD	WEARING COURSE	BINDER COURSE	BASE COURSE
"AA","A" or "B" "P","T" or "M" Traffic	1½" bitum. concrete	1½" bitum. concrete	9" to 12" crushed stone
City Streets "P","T" or "M" Traffic	1½" sheet asphalt	1½" asphaltic conc.	6" to 9" Portland cem. (may be old pavement)
"AA","A" or "B" "P","T" or "M" Traffic	2" bitum. concrete	Omitted	6" to 8" Portland cem.
"A","B" or "C" "P" or "M" Traffic	2" bitum. concrete	3" bitum. Concrete	12" Gravel

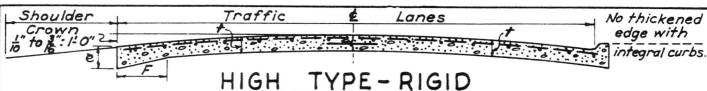

HIGH TYPE — RIGID
(PORTLAND CEMENT CONCRETE — PLAIN OR REINFORCED)

CLASS OF ROAD	t	e	F	TYPICAL DETAILS.
"AA","A" or "B" "T" or "M" Traffic	7" 8"	10" 8"	2'-6"	Key center joint with ½"⌀ x 2'-6" tie bars on 2'-6" centers. Dummy groove transverse joints spaced 15' to 25' with ¾"⌀ x 16" dowels on 12" centers. Transverse expansion joints spaced 60' to 120' with ¾"⌀ x 16" dowels on 12" ctrs. Typical mats are:- ⅜"⌀ steel on 12" to 24" centers; #6 wire mesh on 6" x 6" centers; #3 wire mesh on 6" x 12" centers.
"B" or "C" "T" or "M" Traffic	6" 7"	9" 7"	2'-0"	
"C" or "D" "P" or "M" Traffic	5½" 6"	8" 6"	2'-0"	

Based on average sub-grades with concrete of 700# P.S.I. flexural strength.

NOTE:- Equivalent sections of cement bound macadam may be used.

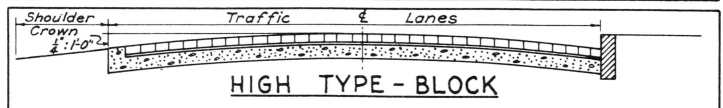

HIGH TYPE — BLOCK

MATERIAL	SIZE	FILLER	CUSHION	BASE	USAGE
Brick	3" x 4" x 8½"	Bituminous	¾" bitum. mastic	6" to 9" Concrete	City streets. Roads where economical.
Granite or stone	4" x 5" x 9"	Bituminous or grout	1" sand	6" to 9" Concrete	Heavy duty streets-dock & warehouse districts.
Asphalt	2" x 5" x 12"	Emulsified asphalt	½" mortar	6" reinf. Concrete	Bridge floors and approaches City streets.
Wood (creosoted)	3" x 4" x 8"	Bituminous or sand	½" bitum.	6" reinf. Concrete	Bridge floors. City streets.

Ref.: Asphalt Institute, Portland Cement Association (P.C.A.). Hard Pavements by A.G. Bruce.

ROADS – DESIGN OF CROSS-SECTION

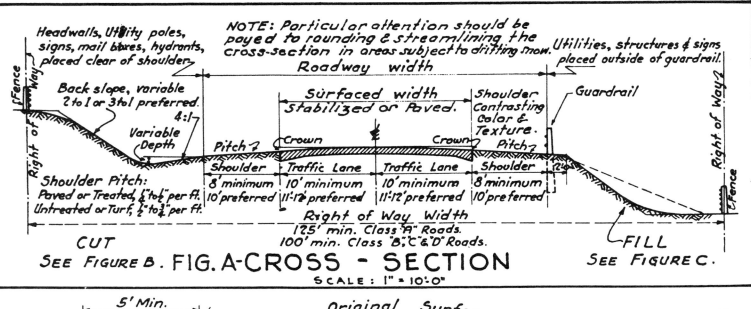

Headwalls, Utility poles, signs, mail boxes, hydrants, placed clear of shoulder.

NOTE: Particular attention should be payed to rounding & streamlining the cross-section in areas subject to drifting snow.

Utilities, structures & signs placed outside of guardrail.

Roadway width

Back slope, variable 2 to 1 or 3 to 1 preferred.

Surfaced width Stabilized or Paved.

Shoulder Contrasting Color & Texture.

Guardrail

Variable Depth

Pitch ↗ Crown — Crown Pitch ↗

Shoulder Pitch:
Paved or Treated, ⅛" to ½" per ft.
Untreated or Turf, ½" to ¾" per ft.

| Shoulder 8' minimum 10' preferred | Traffic Lane 10' minimum 11-12' preferred | Traffic Lane 10' minimum 11-12' preferred | Shoulder 8' minimum 10' preferred |

Right of Way Width
125' min. Class "A" Roads.
100' min. Class "B", "C" & "D" Roads.

CUT
SEE FIGURE B.

FILL
SEE FIGURE C.

FIG. A-CROSS-SECTION
SCALE: 1" = 10'-0"

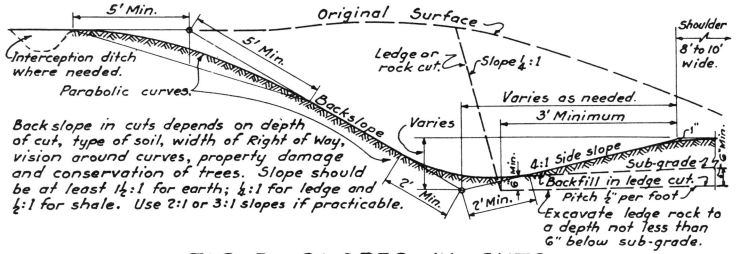

5' Min.

Original Surface

Shoulder 8' to 10' wide.

Interception ditch where needed.

Parabolic curves.

5' Min.

Ledge or rock cut.

Slope ¼:1

Backslope

Varies as needed.

3' Minimum

Back slope in cuts depends on depth of cut, type of soil, width of Right of Way, vision around curves, property damage and conservation of trees. Slope should be at least 1½:1 for earth; ¼:1 for ledge and ½:1 for shale. Use 2:1 or 3:1 slopes if practicable.

Varies

4:1 Side slope

Sub-grade

2' Min.

2' Min.

Backfill in ledge cut.
Pitch ½" per foot.

Excavate ledge rock to a depth not less than 6" below sub-grade.

FIG. B-SLOPES IN CUTS
SCALE: ⅜" = 1'-0"

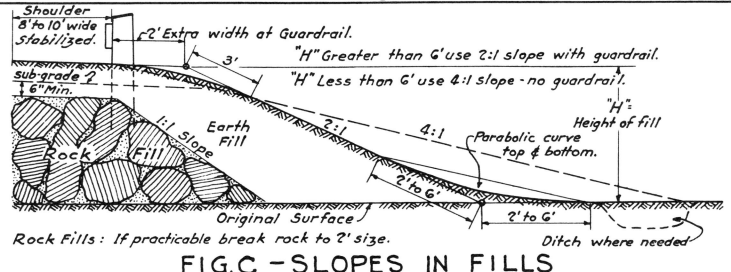

Shoulder 8' to 10' wide Stabilized.

2' Extra width at Guardrail.

3'

"H" Greater than 6' use 2:1 slope with guardrail.

"H" Less than 6' use 4:1 slope - no guardrail.

sub-grade
6" Min.

Rock Fill   1:1 Slope   Earth Fill

2:1   4:1   Parabolic curve top & bottom.

"H": Height of fill

2' to 6'

Original Surface

2' to 6'

Ditch where needed

Rock Fills: If practicable break rock to 2' size.

FIG. C -SLOPES IN FILLS
SCALE: ⅜" = 1'-0"

Ref.: Highway Design Policies by A.A.S.H.O.

ROADS – CURBS, GUTTERS & SIDEWALKS

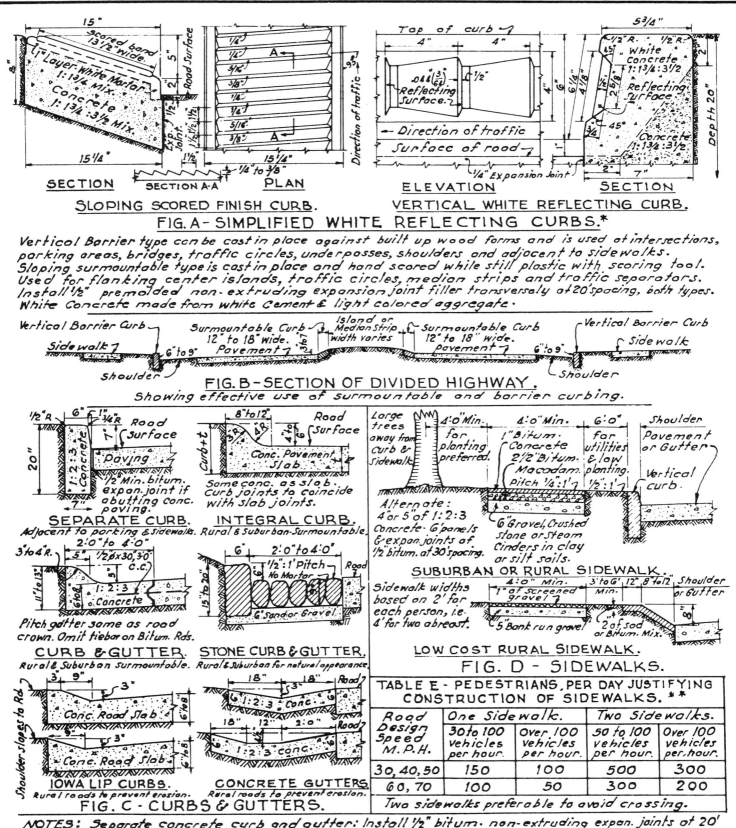

SECTION — **SECTION A-A** — **PLAN**

SLOPING SCORED FINISH CURB.

ELEVATION — **SECTION**

VERTICAL WHITE REFLECTING CURB.

FIG. A – SIMPLIFIED WHITE REFLECTING CURBS.*

Vertical Barrier type can be cast in place against built up wood forms and is used at intersections, parking areas, bridges, traffic circles, underpasses, shoulders and adjacent to sidewalks. Sloping surmountable type is cast in place and hand scored while still plastic with scoring tool. Used for flanking center islands, traffic circles, median strips and traffic separators. Install ½" premolded non-extruding expansion joint filler transversely at 20' spacing, both types. White Concrete made from white Cement & light colored aggregate.

FIG. B – SECTION OF DIVIDED HIGHWAY.
Showing effective use of surmountable and barrier curbing.

SEPARATE CURB. Adjacent to parking & sidewalks.

INTEGRAL CURB. Rural & Suburban-Surmountable.

SUBURBAN OR RURAL SIDEWALK.

CURB & GUTTER. Rural & Suburban surmountable.

STONE CURB & GUTTER. Rural & Suburban for natural appearance.

LOW COST RURAL SIDEWALK.

FIG. D – SIDEWALKS.

IOWA LIP CURBS. Rural roads to prevent erosion.

CONCRETE GUTTERS. Rural roads to prevent erosion.

FIG. C – CURBS & GUTTERS.

TABLE E – PEDESTRIANS, PER DAY JUSTIFYING CONSTRUCTION OF SIDEWALKS.**

Road Design Speed M.P.H.	One Sidewalk.		Two Sidewalks.	
	30 to 100 vehicles per hour.	Over 100 vehicles per hour.	50 to 100 vehicles per hour.	Over 100 vehicles per hour.
30, 40, 50	150	100	500	300
60, 70	100	50	300	200

Two sidewalks preferable to avoid crossing.

NOTES: Separate concrete curb and gutter: Install ½" bitum. non-extruding expan. joints at 20' transverse intervals, and longitudinally adjacent to any conc. slabs, sidewalks or structures. Precast units; length: 4' min. for closures, 5' min. for radials, 10' max. for straights; align with cast-in dowels or keys. Curb or gutter cast integral with or doweled to a pavement must have joints coincide with pavement joints. Vertical curbs are used adjacent to sidewalks. Rounded or sloping curbs may be crossed by vehicles.

* Adapted from Universal Atlas Cement Co. and N.J. State Highway Dept.
** From A.A.S.H.O.

ROADS – GUARD RAIL DETAILS

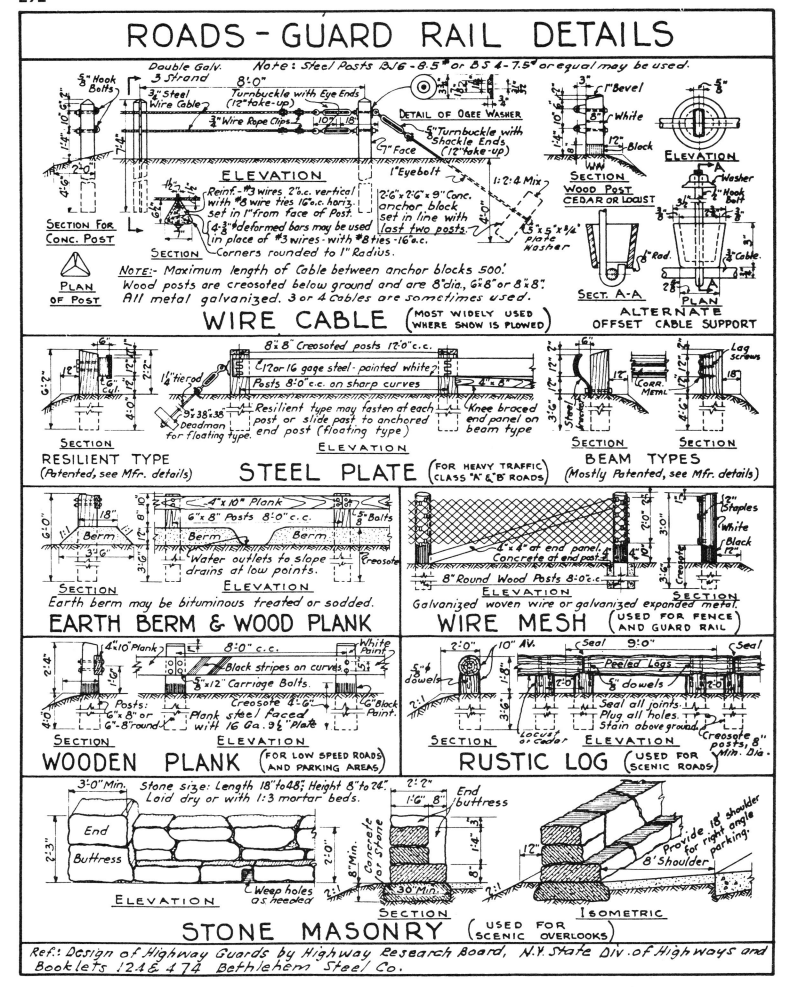

Note: Steel Posts BJ6-8.5# or BS 4-7.5# or equal may be used.

Double Galv. 3 Strand
⅝" Hook Bolts
8'-0"
¾" Steel Wire Cable
Turnbuckle with Eye Ends (12" take-up)
¾" Wire Rope Clips
DETAIL OF OGEE WASHER
5" Turnbuckle with Shackle Ends (12" take-up)
1" Face
1" Eyebolt
1:2:4 Mix
2'-6" x 2'-6" x 9" Conc. anchor block set in line with last two posts.
5"x 5"x ¾" plate Washer

ELEVATION

Reinf.- #3 wires 2"o.c. vertical with #8 wire ties 16 o.c. horiz. set in 1" from face of Post.
4-⅜" deformed bars may be used in place of #3 wires - with #8 ties - 16 o.c.
Corners rounded to 1" Radius.

SECTION FOR CONC. POST

SECTION

PLAN OF POST

NOTE:- Maximum length of Cable between anchor blocks 500'.
Wood posts are creosoted below ground and are 8" dia., 6"x8" or 8"x8".
All metal galvanized. 3 or 4 cables are sometimes used.

1" Bevel
White
12" Block

SECTION WOOD POST CEDAR OR LOCUST

SECT. A-A

ELEVATION

Washer
¾" Hook Bolt
1" Rad.
⅝" Cable

PLAN

WIRE CABLE (MOST WIDELY USED WHERE SNOW IS PLOWED)

ALTERNATE OFFSET CABLE SUPPORT

6" Cyl.
1¼" tie rod
8"x 8" Creosoted posts 12'-0" c.c.
12 or 16 gage steel - painted white
Posts 8'-0" c.c. on sharp curves
4" x 8"
9"x 38"x 38" Deadman for floating type
Resilient type may fasten at each post or slide past to anchored end post (floating type)
Knee braced end panel on beam type
Lag screws
CORR. METAL
Steel

SECTION

ELEVATION

SECTION **SECTION**

RESILIENT TYPE (Patented, see Mfr. details)

STEEL PLATE (FOR HEAVY TRAFFIC CLASS "A" & "B" ROADS)

BEAM TYPES (Mostly Patented, see Mfr. details)

18"
4" x 10" Plank
6" x 8" Posts 8'-0" c.c.
⅝" Bolts
Berm
Berm
Berm
Water outlets to slope drains at low points.
Creosote

SECTION

ELEVATION

Earth berm may be bituminous treated or sodded.

EARTH BERM & WOOD PLANK

4"x 4" at end panel.
Concrete at end post
8" Round Wood Posts 8'-0" c.c.
12" Staples
White
Black 12"

ELEVATION

SECTION

Galvanized woven wire or galvanized expanded metal.

WIRE MESH (USED FOR FENCE AND GUARD RAIL)

4"x10" Plank
8'-0" c.c.
White Paint
Black stripes on curves
⅝"x12" Carriage Bolts.
Posts: 6"x 8" or 6"-8" round
Creosote 4'-6"
Plank steel faced with 16 Ga. 9½" Plate
6" Block Paint.

SECTION

ELEVATION

WOODEN PLANK (FOR LOW SPEED ROADS AND PARKING AREAS)

2'-0"
10" Av.
Seal
9'-0"
Seal
⅝"ø dowels
Peeled Logs
⅝" dowels
Seal all joints.
Plug all holes.
Stain above ground.
Locust or Cedar
Creosote 8" posts, 8" Min. Dia.

SECTION

ELEVATION

RUSTIC LOG (USED FOR SCENIC ROADS)

3'-0" Min.
Stone size: Length 18" to 48"; Height 8" to 24".
Laid dry or with 1:3 mortar beds.
2'-2"
1'-6" 8"
End buttress
Provide 18' shoulder for right angle parking.
8' Shoulder

End Buttress
Concrete or Stone
8" Min.
12"
30" Min.
Weep holes as needed

ELEVATION

SECTION

Isometric

STONE MASONRY (USED FOR SCENIC OVERLOOKS)

Ref.: Design of Highway Guards by Highway Research Board, N.Y. State Div. of Highways and Booklets 124 & 474 Bethlehem Steel Co.

ROADS - STREET & HIGHWAY LIGHTING *

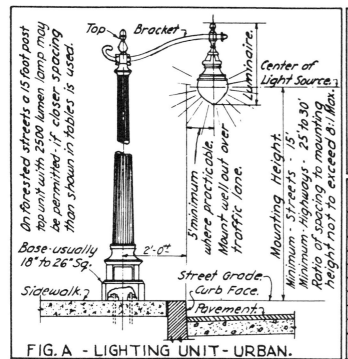

On forested streets a 15 foot post top unit with 2500 lumen lamp may be permitted - if closer spacing than shown in tables is used.

Top — Bracket

Center of Light Source.

Luminaire.

5' minimum where practicable. Mount well out over traffic lane.

Base - usually 18" to 26" Sq.

2'-0"±

Sidewalk.

Street Grade. Curb Face.

Pavement.

Mounting Height.

Minimum - Streets - 15' Minimum - Highways - 25' to 30' Ratio of spacing to mounting height not to exceed 8:1 Max.

FIG. A - LIGHTING UNIT - URBAN.

Roads: Ratio of spacing to mounting height not over 10:1.

½ Traffic Lane + Pole Clearance. Mount well out over traffic lane.

Guy.

Luminaire

Bracket & Light Source.

Mounting height 25' Min. to Pvmt.

Brace.

Light or Power Pole.

FIG. B - LIGHTING UNIT - RURAL or SUBURBAN.

TABLE C - MINIMUM MOUNTING HEIGHTS FOR VARIOUS LAMP SIZES.

LAMP SIZE LUMENS*	CONCENTRATED (a)	SEMI-CONCENTRATED (b)	DIFFUSING GLOBES (c)
1,000	15'	15'	15'
2,500	18'	18'	18'
4,000	20'	18'	18'
6,000	22'	18'	18'
10,000	25'	21'	18'
15,000	28'	24'	18'
25,000	33'	27'	20'

Approximate beam candlepower to lumen rating:
a = 9/10 ; b = 3/10 ; c = 1/10. *One lumen per Sq.Ft.= One footcandle

TABLE D - LIGHTING ARRANGEMENTS TO GIVE 0.2 to 0.5 LUMENS PER SQ.FT. ON LIGHT COLORED SURFACES FOR HIGHWAYS.**(Less than four intersections per mile - few pedestrians)

PAVEMENT WIDTH	LAMP LUMENS	MOUNTING HEIGHT - FT.	LUMINAIRE SPACING - FT.	PAVEMENT WIDTH	LAMP LUMENS	MOUNTING HEIGHT - FT.	LUMINAIRE SPACING - FT.
2 Lanes	6,000	25 - 30	240 - 250	4 Lanes (Illuminate both sides).	6,000-10,000	25 - 30	240 - 250
	6,000	25	200		6,000-10,000	25	200
	4,000	25	125		6,000	25	125
3 Lanes (Illuminate both sides).	6,000-10,000	25 - 30	240 - 250				
	6,000-10,000	25	200				
	4,000	25	125				

**Dark Surface - Provide 0.3 to 1.0 Lumen per Sq.Ft.
Dull Black Surface - Provide 1.0 to 2.0 Lumens per Sq.Ft.
On divided highways - light each roadway separately.
+ Install units on outside of curves & crests of hills.

TABLE E - LIGHTING ARRANGEMENTS TO GIVE APPROXIMATE ILLUMINATION VALUES of TABLE F FOR STREETS. (Trafficways other than highways.)

TRAFFIC - Nº OF VEHICLES MAX. NIGHT HOUR - BOTH DIRECTIONS	LAMP LUMENS	MOUNTING HEIGHT - FT.	LUMINAIRE SPACING - FT.	TRAFFIC - Nº OF VEHICLES MAX. NIGHT HOUR - BOTH DIRECTIONS	LAMP LUMENS	MOUNTING HEIGHT - FT.	LUMINAIRE SPACING - FT.
Very Light Traffic Under 150 Vehicles.	1,000	15	90-110 Stagger.	Medium Traffic 500-1200 Vehicles.	6,000	20 - 25	100-120 Stagger.
	2,500	20 - 22	130-170 "		10,000	22 - 27	130-170 "
	4,000	25 - 30	200-250 Center		15,000	25 - 30	130-170 "
Light Traffic 150 - 500 Vehicles.	2,500	16 - 18	100-120 Stagger.	Heavy Traffic 1200-2400 Vehicles.	10,000	24 - 28	100-150 Opposite.
	4,000	20 - 25	130-170 "		10,000	24 - 28	75-90 Stagger.
	6,000	22 - 25	130-170 "		15,000	24 - 28	150-180 Opposite.
				2400-4000 Vehicles.	15,000	25 - 30	100-150 Opposite.
				Over 4000 Vehicles.	15,000	25 - 30	100 Opposite.

Larger lamps or closer spacing are required on business streets. - See Table F.

TABLE F - AVERAGE FOOTCANDLES - MINIMUM FOR NIGHT TRAFFIC SAFETY.

	VERY LIGHT TRAFFIC		LIGHT TRAFFIC		MEDIUM TRAFFIC		HEAVY TRAFFIC		VERY HEAVY TRAFFIC	
	AVG.	MIN.	AVG.	MIN.	AVG.	MIN.	AVG.	MIN.	AVG.	MIN.
Principal Business Streets.			0.4	0.1	0.8	0.2	1.2	0.3	1.5	0.4
Secondary Business Streets.			0.3	0.07	0.6	0.15	1.0	0.25	1.3	0.3
Through High Speed Arteries (Other than business streets).			0.3	0.07	0.6	0.15	1.0	0.25	1.3	0.3
Express Freeways & Viaducts.					0.4	0.1	0.8	0.2	1.2	0.3
Residence Streets.	0.1	0.02	0.2	0.05	0.4	0.1				
Industrial Warehouse Streets.	0.1	0.02	0.2	0.05	0.4	0.1				

These recommendations apply where pavement reflection characteristics are favorable as in the case of light concrete or light finished asphaltum. Somewhat higher footcandle values should be employed where street surface reflections are less favorable.

* Recommended practice of Street Lighting 1940 And Code of Highway Lighting 1937. Illuminating Eng. Society.

ROADS - URBAN STREETS - 1

R/W or Bldg. Line. Clear Sidewalk Width ⌐ | Utilities and Planting 3' min. | Allow 2' extra when traffic lane is adjacent to curb. Parking Lane | Traffic Lanes | 2'-0" Traffic Lanes | ₵ | Trolley tracks, Median strip or Island. | Traffic Lanes | Pavement | Parking Lane | Right of Way or Bldg. Line. This distance commonly ⅙ to ¼ right of way width. | Pitch ¼" to ½" per foot

Frequently paved where curb parking is allowed. | Curb height 5" to 8" 6" or 7" preferred. | Crown ³⁄₁₆ to ¼" per ft. | Curb | Sidewalk Utilities and Planting. (Avoid large trees here.)

For this space allow:
10'-0" for each line of trolley tracks.
2'-0" to 4'-0" for flush or low type traffic separators.
4'-0" to 12'-0" for raised paved median strips.
12'-0" min. for planted median strips.
4'-0" min. for pedestrian refuge islands.

FIG. A - ELEMENTS OF STREET CROSS-SECTION.

TABLE B - CLASSIFICATION OF URBAN STREETS.

CLASS OF STREET	DESCRIPTION
Primary Business	Very heavy traffic - Commercial buildings of 4 or more stories.
Secondary Business	Heavy traffic - Commercial buildings of 4 or less stories.
Primary Residential	Medium traffic - Multi-family houses and apartment buildings.
Minor Residential	Light traffic - Single family houses.
Industrial	Heavy traffic - Dock, warehouse and factory districts.
Boulevards, Parkways	Restricted traffic - Divided roadways, landscaped or planted.
Viaducts	Usually heavy traffic - Street elevated over low area, R.R. yards, etc.
Express Highways	Heavy through traffic - May be at grade, elevated or depressed.

TABLE C - RECOMMENDED WIDTHS.

CLASS OF STREET	TRAFFIC LANES	SIDEWALK WIDTH	PARKING LANES	PAVEMENT TYPE	SIDEWALK TYPE	REFUGE ISLANDS
Primary Business	6 - 10' to 12' Lanes.	15' to 30'	Parallel parking 10'. Angle parking 15' to 18'.	Concrete, Sheet Asphalt, Bituminous Concrete, Brick or other high type block pavements. (e)	Concrete, Bituminous Concrete, Brick, Tile, Asphalt Mastic or Stone Setts.	4' min. width where pedestrians must cross 3 or more lanes of moving traffic. 4' min. width loading platforms where needed for busses and trolleys.
Secondary Business	4 - 10' to 12' Lanes.	10' to 20'				
Industrial	According to traffic.	6' to 15'				
Primary Residential	2 - 10' lanes minimum.	6' to 15'	2 - 8' lanes minimum.			
Minor Residential	(a) 2 - 10' lanes	(c) 4' to 6'	1 or 2 - 8' lanes. (a)	Concrete, Macadam, Bituminous or Brick.	Concrete, Bituminous, Cinders, Gravel, Flags or Brick.	
Boulevards, Parkways, Viaducts, Bridges, Tunnels	10' to 12' lanes for low speeds. 12' lanes for high speeds.	Provide 4' in width for each two persons abreast	8' to 10' for parallel parking where permitted. (b)	Concrete, High type Bitum. or High type Block. (e)	Concrete or High type bituminous.	

(a) For two-way streets allow for 2 traffic lanes and one parking lane, min. For one-way streets allow, one traffic lane and 2 parking lanes, min.
(b) Provide for disabled vehicles and scenic overlooks where continuous parking is prohibited.
(c) Suburban developments show tendency to eliminate walks along street to provide privacy; Service and access walks may be planned distinct from the street system.
(d) Sidewalks frequently omitted from express highways, viaducts and tunnels. (Safety walk of 2' min. with barrier curb is desirable)
(e) Block type pavements widely used for industrial streets, viaducts, bridges and tunnels.

TABLE D - TRAFFIC LANES FOR THROUGH TRAFFIC
FOR URBAN STREETS CARRYING OTHER THAN LOCAL TRAFFIC USE THESE WIDTHS.

DAILY TRAFFIC	TRAFFIC LANES	MINIMUM CURB TO CURB *	DAILY TRAFFIC	TRAFFIC LANES	MINIMUM CURB TO CURB *
Up to 750	2 - 10' Lanes Min.	24'	4,000 to 20,000	4 or 6 - 11' or 12' Lanes	48' **
750 to 4,000	2 - 11' or 12' Lanes	26'	Over 20,000	6 - 11' or 12' Lanes	70' **

* Bridges, Viaducts, Streets, etc. (without parking lanes). ** Plus median strips, islands or street R.R.s.

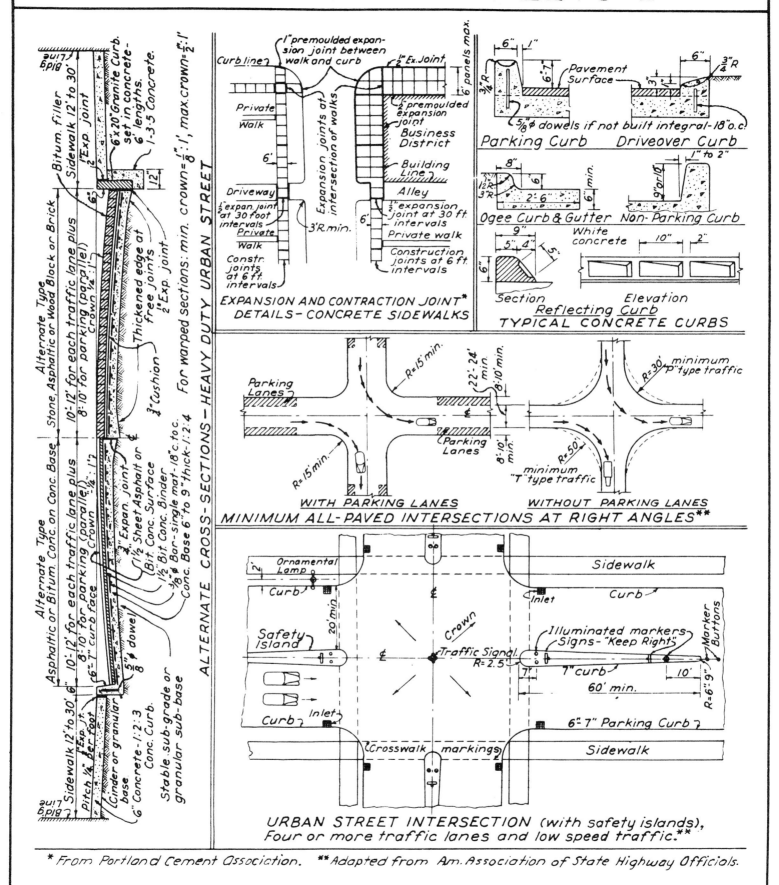

ALTERNATE CROSS-SECTIONS - HEAVY DUTY URBAN STREET

EXPANSION AND CONTRACTION JOINT*
DETAILS - CONCRETE SIDEWALKS

Parking Curb   Driveover Curb

Ogee Curb & Gutter   Non-Parking Curb

Reflecting Curb
TYPICAL CONCRETE CURBS

WITH PARKING LANES   WITHOUT PARKING LANES
MINIMUM ALL-PAVED INTERSECTIONS AT RIGHT ANGLES**

URBAN STREET INTERSECTION (with safety islands),
Four or more traffic lanes and low speed traffic.**

*From Portland Cement Association.   **Adapted from Am. Association of State Highway Officials.

ROADS – URBAN STREETS –3

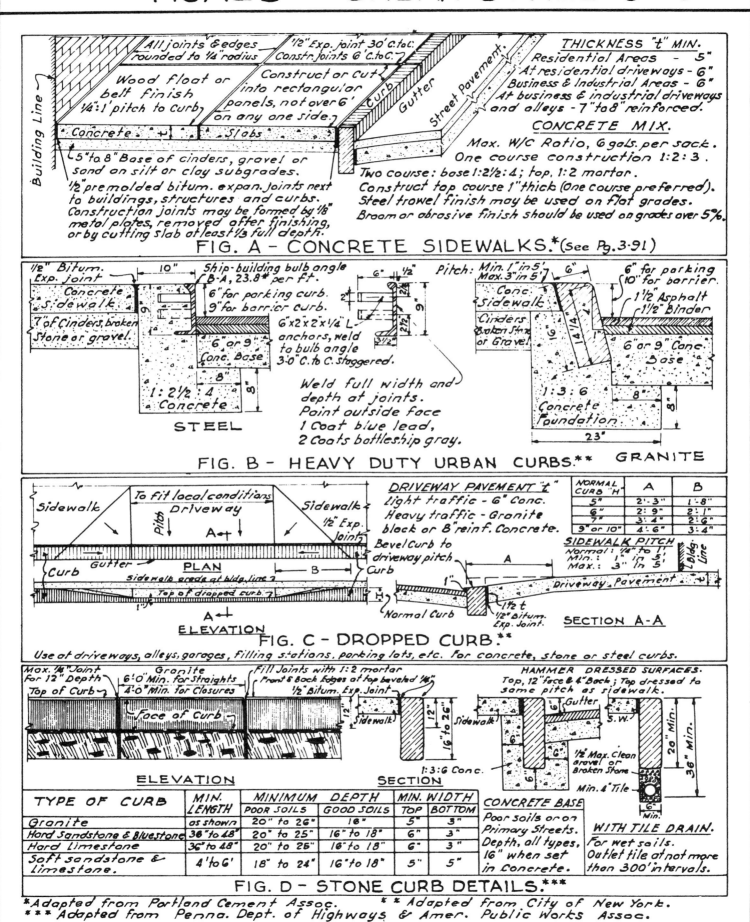

FIG. A – CONCRETE SIDEWALKS. *(See Pg. 3·91)

All joints & edges rounded to ¼"radius
½"Exp. joint 30' C. to C.
Constr. joints 6' C. to C.
Wood float or belt finish
¼:1'pitch to Curb
Construct or cut into rectangular panels, not over 6' on any one side.
Concrete · Slabs
Curb
Gutter
Street Pavement
Building Line
5"to 8"Base of cinders, gravel or sand on silt or clay subgrades.
½"premolded bitum. expan. joints next to buildings, structures and curbs.
Construction joints may be formed by ⅛" metal plates, removed after finishing, or by cutting slab at least ⅓ full depth.

THICKNESS "t" MIN.
Residential Areas – 5"
At residential driveways – 6"
Business & Industrial Areas – 6"
At business & industrial driveways and alleys – 7"to 8"reinforced.
CONCRETE MIX.
Max. W/C Ratio, 6 gals. per sack.
One course construction 1:2:3.
Two course: base 1:2½:4; top, 1:2 mortar.
Construct top course 1"thick (One course preferred).
Steel trowel finish may be used on flat grades.
Broom or abrasive finish should be used on grades over 5%.

FIG. B – HEAVY DUTY URBAN CURBS. **

½" Bitum. Exp. joint
10"
Concrete Sidewalk
7"of Cinders, broken Stone or gravel.
Ship-building bulb angle B-A, 23.8# per ft.
6" for parking curb.
9" for barrier curb.
6"x2"x2"x¼ L anchors, weld to bulb angle 3'-0" C. to C. staggered.
6"or 9" Conc. Base
8"
1:2½:4 Concrete
Weld full width and depth at joints.
Paint outside face 1 Coat blue lead, 2 Coats battleship gray.

STEEL

Pitch: Min. 1"in 5'
Max. 3"in 5'
6" for parking
10" for barrier.
Conc. Sidewalk
Cinders, Broken Stn. or Gravel.
1½" Asphalt
1½" Binder
6" or 9" Conc. Base
8"
1:3:6 Concrete Foundation
23"

GRANITE

FIG. C – DROPPED CURB. **

Sidewalk
To fit local conditions
Driveway
Sidewalk
½" Exp. Joint
Pitch
A
Curb
Gutter
PLAN
sidewalk grade at bldg. line
B
Curb
Top of dropped curb
1"
A
ELEVATION

DRIVEWAY PAVEMENT "t"
Light traffic – 6" Conc.
Heavy traffic – Granite block or 8"reinf. Concrete.
Bevel Curb to driveway pitch
1"
A
Normal Curb
1½ t
½"bitum. Exp. Joint
Driveway Pavement
SECTION A-A

NORMAL CURB "H"	A	B
5"	2'-3"	1'-8"
6"	2'-9"	2'-1"
7"	3'-4"	2'-6"
9" or 10"	4'-6"	3'-4"

SIDEWALK PITCH
Normal: ¼" to 1'
Min.: 1" in 5'
Max.: 3" in 5'
Bldg. Line

Use at driveways, alleys, garages, filling stations, parking lots, etc. For concrete, stone or steel curbs.

FIG. D – STONE CURB DETAILS. ***

Max. ¼"Joint For 12" Depth
Top of Curb
Granite
6'-0" Min. for Straights
4'-0" Min. for Closures
Fill Joints with 1:2 mortar
Front & Back Edges at top beveled ⅛"
½" Bitum. Exp. Joint
Face of Curb
ELEVATION

12"
Sidewalk
12"
16" to 26"
1:3:6 Conc.
SECTION

HAMMER DRESSED SURFACES.
Top, 12"face & 4"Back; Top dressed to same pitch as sidewalk.
Gutter
Sidewalk
S.W.
6"
6"
6"
½"Max. Clean gravel or Broken Stone
Min. 4"Tile
20" Min.
36" Min.
4"Min.

CONCRETE BASE
Poor soils or on Primary Streets.
Depth, all types, 16" when set in Concrete.

WITH TILE DRAIN.
For wet soils.
Outlet tile at not more than 300' intervals.

TYPE OF CURB	MIN. LENGTH	MINIMUM DEPTH		MIN. WIDTH	
		POOR SOILS	GOOD SOILS	TOP	BOTTOM
Granite	as shown	20" to 26"	16"	5"	3"
Hard Sandstone & Bluestone	36"to 48"	20" to 25"	16" to 18"	6"	3"
Hard Limestone	36"to 48"	20" to 25"	16" to 18"	6"	3"
Soft sandstone & Limestone.	4'to 6'	18" to 24"	16"to 18"	5"	5"

*Adapted from Portland Cement Assoc.   ** Adapted from City of New York.
*** Adapted from Penna. Dept. of Highways & Amer. Public Works Assoc.

DOCKS & PIERS · QUAYS · BULKHEADS

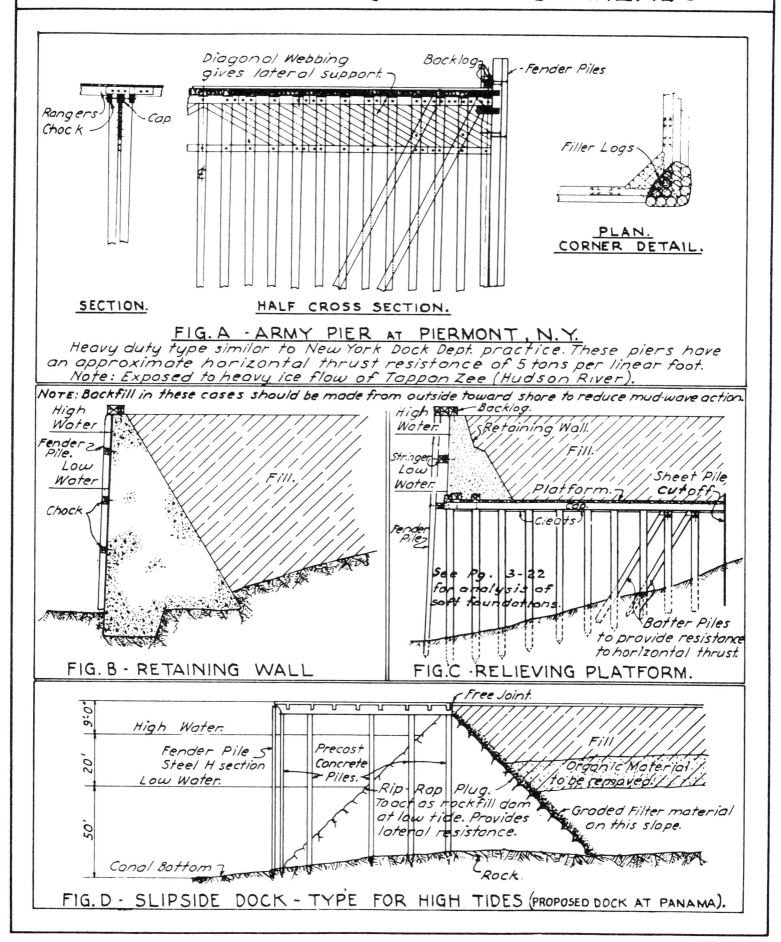

Diagonal Webbing gives lateral support.

Backlog. — Fender Piles

Rangers Choc k — Cap.

Filler Logs

PLAN.
CORNER DETAIL.

SECTION.   HALF CROSS SECTION.

FIG. A · ARMY PIER at PIERMONT, N.Y.

Heavy duty type similar to New York Dock Dept. practice. These piers have an approximate horizontal thrust resistance of 5 tons per linear foot.
Note: Exposed to heavy ice flow of Tappan Zee (Hudson River).

NOTE: Backfill in these cases should be made from outside toward shore to reduce mud-wave action.

High Water
Fender Pile.
Low Water
Chock
Fill.

FIG. B · RETAINING WALL

High Water
Backlog.
Retaining Wall.
Stringer
Low Water
Fender Pile.
Platform.
Cap.
Cleats
Fill.
Sheet Pile, cut off.
See Pg. 3-22 for analysis of soft foundations.
Batter Piles to provide resistance to horizontal thrust.

FIG. C · RELIEVING PLATFORM.

Free Joint.
9'-0"
High Water.
Fender Pile Steel H section
Low Water.
20'
Precast Concrete Piles.
Fill
Organic Material to be removed.
Rip-Rap Plug. To act as rockfill dam at low tide. Provides lateral resistance.
Graded Filter material on this slope.
50'
Canal Bottom
Rock.

FIG. D · SLIPSIDE DOCK · TYPE FOR HIGH TIDES (PROPOSED DOCK AT PANAMA).

DOCKS & PIERS - AUXILIARY STRUCTURES

DOLPHINS:

Are islands of piles tied together with bolts and wire cables to protect docks from ice and wearing of ships.

GROINS:

Are bulkheads built at angles to a beach and across it to prevent lateral scour, build up beach and to protect the foundation of sea walls from scour.

Spacing is a matter of study. A spacing equal to length has been recommended.

Depth is a matter of judgment. 10' below the beach has been recommended.

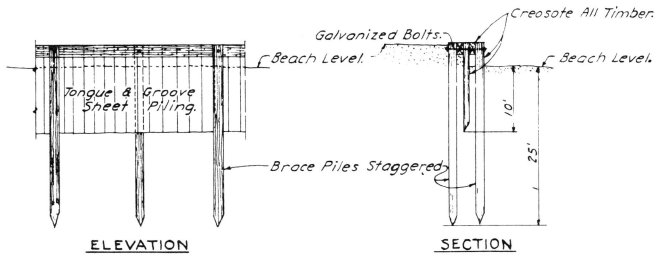

FIG. A - SUGGESTED SECTION FOR GROINS.

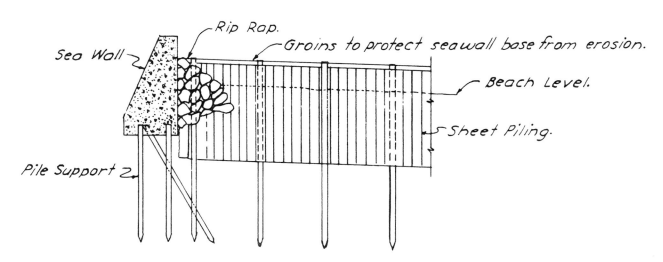

CROSS SECTION

Rock Fill for jetties or rip rap on structures subject to ocean wave action should be 1 to 6 tons in size.

FIG. B - ELEMENTS OF SEAWALLS BELOW HIGH WATER.

DRAINAGE-DITCHES-COMMON SECTIONS

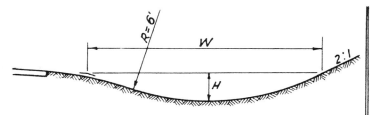

D-1 SEGMENTAL

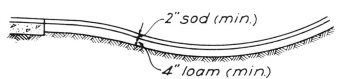

SODDED GUTTER

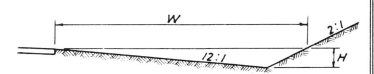

D-1A TRIANGULAR
Unequal side slopes

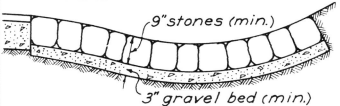

COBBLED GUTTER

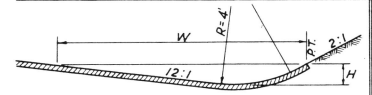

D-1B BITUMINOUS GUTTER

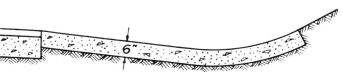

Base required same as for concrete pavement.

CONCRETE GUTTER

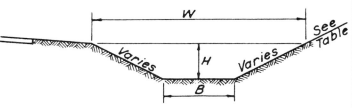

D-1C CURBED CROWNED STREET

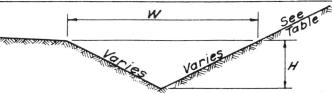

D-2, D-3, D-4, D-5 TRAPEZOIDAL

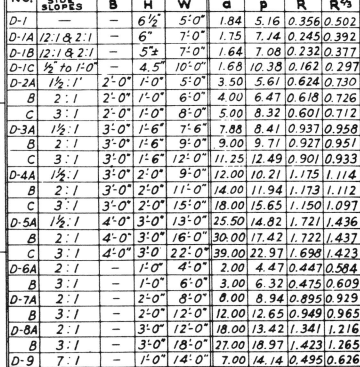

D-6, D-7, D-8, D-9, D-10, D-11
ISOSCELES TRIANGULAR
D-9, D-10 and D-11—Airport ditches

TABLE A — PROPERTIES OF DITCHES.

NO.	SIDE SLOPES	B	H	W	a	p	R	R^{2/3}
D-1	—	—	6½"	5'-0"	1.84	5.16	0.356	0.502
D-1A	12:1 & 2:1	—	6"	7'-0"	1.75	7.14	0.245	0.392
D-1B	12:1 & 2:1	—	5"±	7'-0"	1.64	7.08	0.232	0.377
D-1C	½" to 1'-0"	—	4.5"	10'-0"	1.68	10.38	0.162	0.297
D-2A	1½:1	2'-0"	1'-0"	5'-0"	3.50	5.61	0.624	0.730
B	2:1	2'-0"	1'-0"	6'-0"	4.00	6.47	0.618	0.726
C	3:1	2'-0"	1'-0"	8'-0"	5.00	8.32	0.601	0.712
D-3A	1½:1	3'-0"	1'-6"	7'-6"	7.88	8.41	0.937	0.958
B	2:1	3'-0"	1'-6"	9'-0"	9.00	9.71	0.927	0.951
C	3:1	3'-0"	1'-6"	12'-0"	11.25	12.49	0.901	0.933
D-4A	1½:1	3'-0"	2'-0"	9'-0"	12.00	10.21	1.175	1.114
B	2:1	3'-0"	2'-0"	11'-0"	14.00	11.94	1.173	1.112
C	3:1	3'-0"	2'-0"	15'-0"	18.00	15.65	1.150	1.097
D-5A	1½:1	4'-0"	3'-0"	13'-0"	25.50	14.82	1.721	1.436
B	2:1	4'-0"	3'-0"	16'-0"	30.00	17.42	1.722	1.437
C	3:1	4'-0"	3'-0"	22'-0"	39.00	22.97	1.698	1.423
D-6A	2:1	—	1'-0"	4'-0"	2.00	4.47	0.447	0.584
B	3:1	—	1'-0"	6'-0"	3.00	6.32	0.475	0.609
D-7A	2:1	—	2'-0"	8'-0"	8.00	8.94	0.895	0.929
B	3:1	—	2'-0"	12'-0"	12.00	12.65	0.949	0.965
D-8A	2:1	—	3'-0"	12'-0"	18.00	13.42	1.341	1.216
B	3:1	—	3'-0"	18'-0"	27.00	18.97	1.423	1.265
D-9	7:1	—	1'-0"	14'-0"	7.00	14.14	0.495	0.626
D-10	7:1	—	2'-0"	28'-0"	28.00	28.28	0.990	0.993
D-11	7:1	—	3'-0"	42'-0"	63.00	42.43	1.485	1.302

DRAINAGE - SUBDRAINAGE - 2

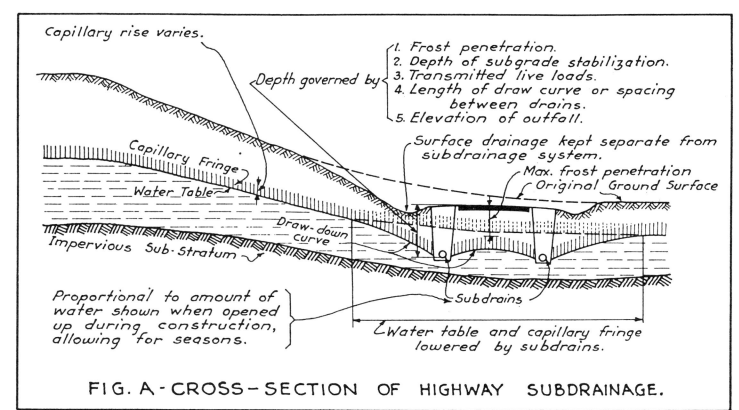

Capillary rise varies.

Depth governed by
1. Frost penetration.
2. Depth of subgrade stabilization.
3. Transmitted live loads.
4. Length of draw curve or spacing between drains.
5. Elevation of outfall.

Surface drainage kept separate from subdrainage system.

Max. frost penetration
Original Ground Surface

Capillary Fringe

Water Table

Draw-down curve

Impervious Sub-Stratum

Proportional to amount of water shown when opened up during construction, allowing for seasons.

Subdrains

Water table and capillary fringe lowered by subdrains.

FIG. A - CROSS-SECTION OF HIGHWAY SUBDRAINAGE.

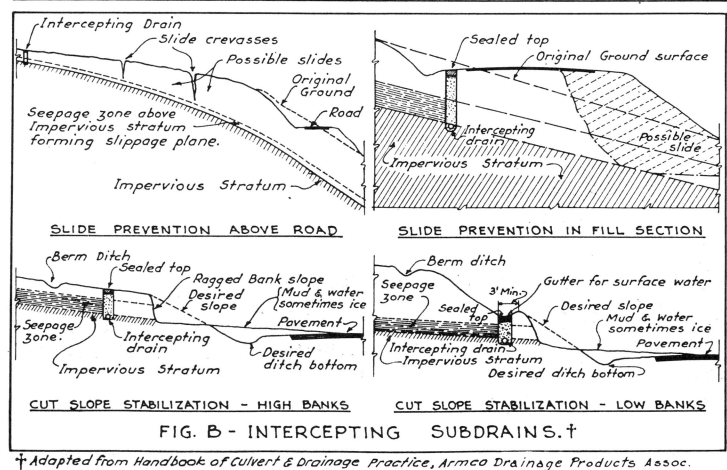

Intercepting Drain
Slide crevasses
Possible slides
Original Ground
Road

Seepage zone above Impervious stratum forming slippage plane.

Impervious Stratum

SLIDE PREVENTION ABOVE ROAD

Sealed top
Original Ground surface
Intercepting drain
Possible slide
Impervious Stratum

SLIDE PREVENTION IN FILL SECTION

Berm Ditch
Sealed top
Ragged Bank slope
Desired slope
Mud & water sometimes ice
Pavement
Seepage zone.
Intercepting drain
Desired ditch bottom
Impervious Stratum

CUT SLOPE STABILIZATION - HIGH BANKS

Berm ditch
Seepage zone
Sealed top
3' Min.
Gutter for surface water
Desired slope
Mud & water sometimes ice
Pavement
Intercepting drain
Impervious Stratum
Desired ditch bottom

CUT SLOPE STABILIZATION - LOW BANKS

FIG. B - INTERCEPTING SUBDRAINS.†

† Adapted from Handbook of Culvert & Drainage Practice, Armco Drainage Products Assoc.

DRAINAGE – HEADWALLS

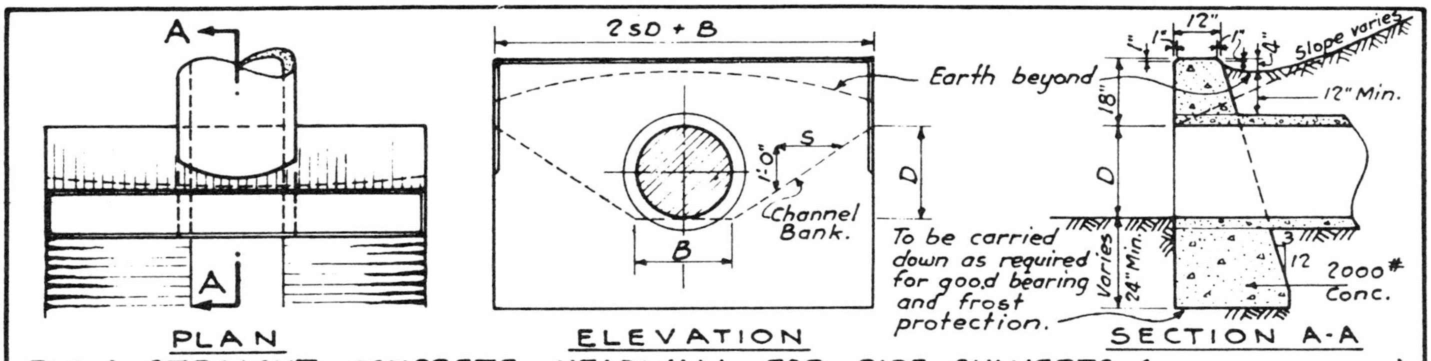

PLAN — ELEVATION — SECTION A-A

FIG. A-STRAIGHT CONCRETE HEADWALL FOR PIPE CULVERTS (INLET OR OUTLET).

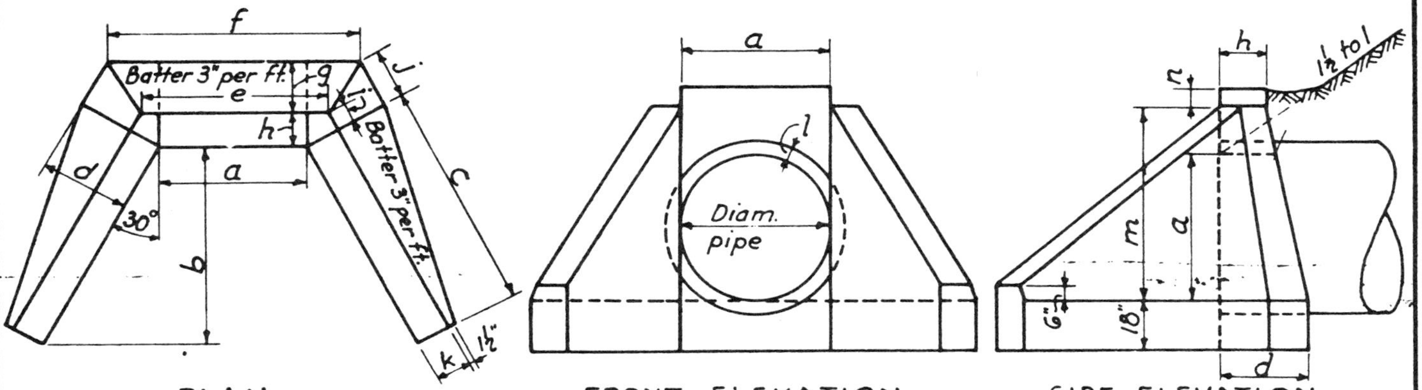

PLAN — FRONT ELEVATION — SIDE ELEVATION

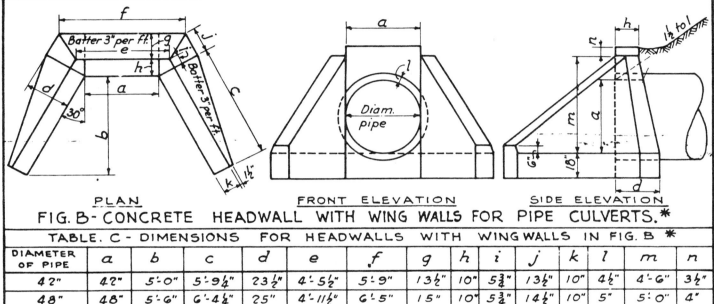

FIG. B-CONCRETE HEADWALL WITH WING WALLS FOR PIPE CULVERTS.*

TABLE. C - DIMENSIONS FOR HEADWALLS WITH WINGWALLS IN FIG. B *

DIAMETER OF PIPE	a	b	c	d	e	f	g	h	i	j	k	l	m	n
42"	42"	5'-0"	5'-9¼"	23½"	4'-5½"	5'-9"	13½"	10"	5¾"	13½"	10"	4½"	4'-6"	3½"
48"	48"	5'-6"	6'-4¼"	25"	4'-11½"	6'-5"	15"	10"	5¾"	14½"	10"	5"	5'-0"	4"
54"	54"	6'-0"	6'-11⅛"	27½"	5'-6¾"	7'-1¾"	16½"	11"	6⅜"	15⅞"	11"	5½"	5'-6"	4½"
60"	60"	6'-6"	7'-6"	30"	6'-2"	7'-10⅝"	18"	12"	7"	17⅜"	12"	6"	6'-0"	5"

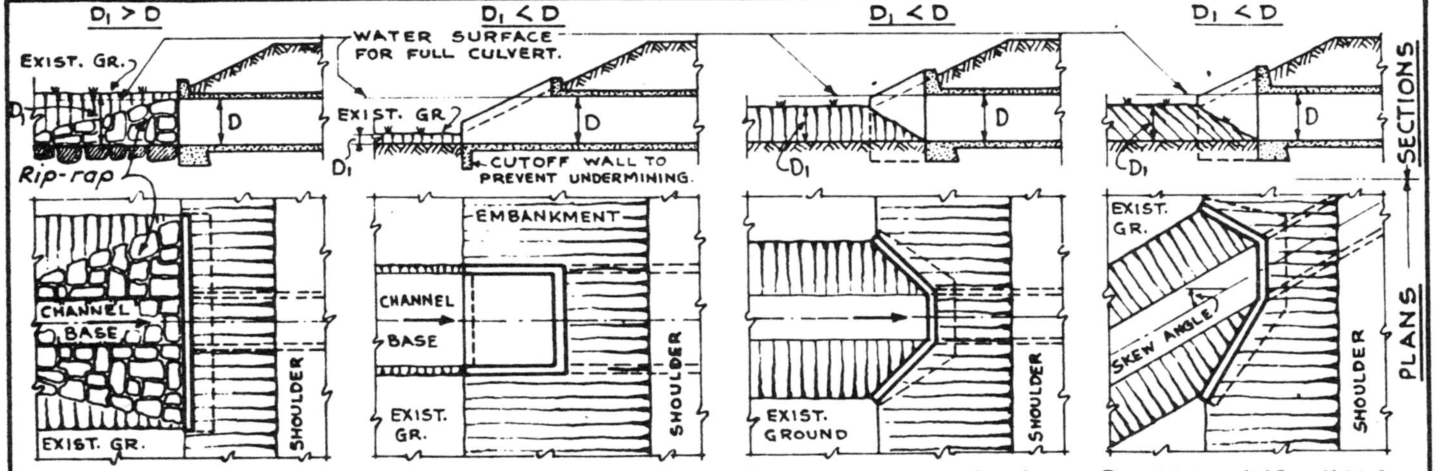

STRAIGHT HEADWALL PARALLEL TO ROAD — FOR CASE WHERE TOP OF DITCH SIDE IS ABOVE TOP OF CULVERT OR PIPE.

WING WALLS NORMAL TO ROAD — SHALLOW DITCHES OR UNDERPASS

FLARED WING WALLS SYMMETRICAL — FOR CASES WHERE TOP OF PIPE IS ABOVE TOP OF DITCH SIDES.

FLARED WING WALLS SKEWED CULVERT

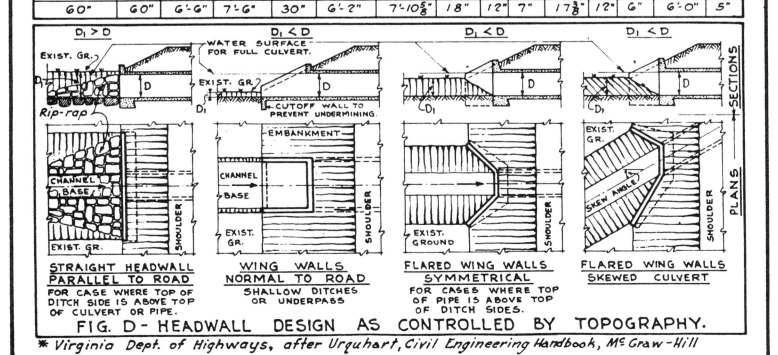

FIG. D - HEADWALL DESIGN AS CONTROLLED BY TOPOGRAPHY.

* *Virginia Dept. of Highways, after Urquhart, Civil Engineering Handbook, McGraw-Hill*

DRAINAGE - EROSION PROTECTION

TABLE A - MEAN VELOCITIES WHICH WILL NOT ERODE CHANNELS AFTER AGING.

MATERIAL OF CHANNEL BED	VELOCITY IN FEET PER SEC.	
	SHALLOW DITCH	DEEP CANAL *
Fine sand or silt, non-colloidal	0.50-1.50	1.50-2.50
Coarse sand or sandy loam, non-colloidal	1.00-1.50	1.75-2.50
Silty or sand loam " "	1.00-1.75	2.00-3.00
Clayey loam or sandy clay " "	1.50-2.00	2.25-3.50
Fine gravel	2.00-2.50	2.50-5.00
Colloidal clay or non-colloidal gravelly loam	2.00-3.00	3.00-5.00
Colloidal, well graded gravel	2.25-3.50	4.00-6.00
Pebbles, broken stone, shales or hardpan	2.50-4.00	5.00-6.50
Sodded gutters (See p.5-04)	3.00-5.00	—
Cobbled gutters, not grouted, or bituminous paving (See p.5-04)	5.00-7.50	—
Stone masonry	7.50-15.00	—
Solid rock or concrete	15.00-25.00	—

AGING OF CHANNELS increases resistance to erosion as density and stability of channel bed improve due to deposit of silt in interstices and as cohesion increases due to cementation of soil by colloids. New channels may be safely operated at less than maximum design velocities by use of temporary check structures.

VELOCITIES are to be reduced for depths of flow under 6 inches and for water which may transport abrasive materials.

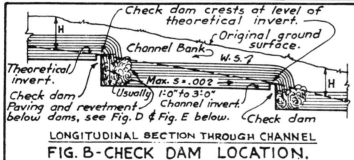

LONGITUDINAL SECTION THROUGH CHANNEL
FIG. B - CHECK DAM LOCATION.

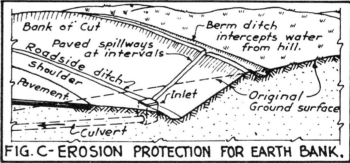

FIG. C - EROSION PROTECTION FOR EARTH BANK.

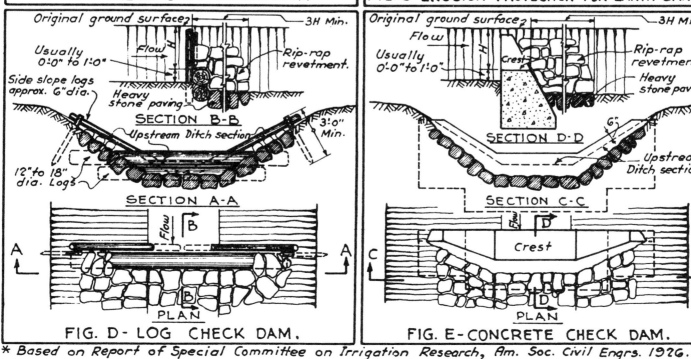

SECTION B-B

SECTION A-A

PLAN

FIG. D - LOG CHECK DAM.

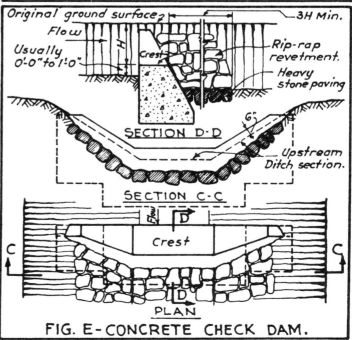

SECTION D-D

SECTION C-C

PLAN

FIG. E - CONCRETE CHECK DAM.

* Based on Report of Special Committee on Irrigation Research, Am. Soc. Civil Engrs. 1926.

DRAINAGE & SEWERAGE - MANHOLES

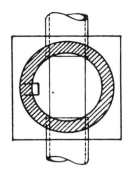 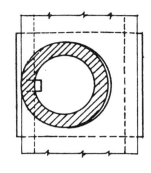 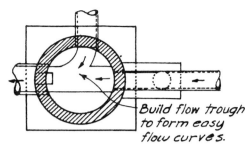 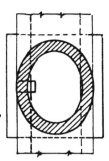

SECTION A-A   SECTION B-B   SECTION C-C   SECTION D-D

Build flow trough to form easy flow curves.

NOTE:- Walls to be 8 inches thick to 13 foot depth, walls to be increased to 12 inch thickness in section below 13 foot depth.

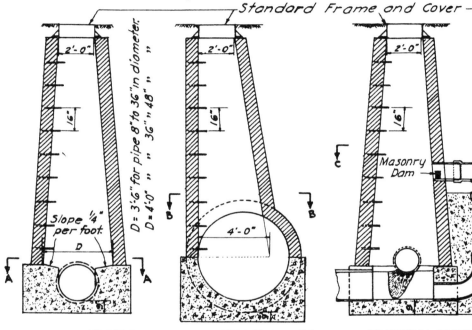 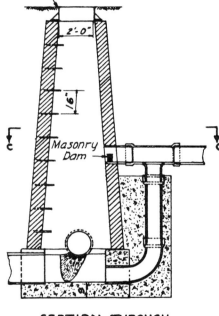 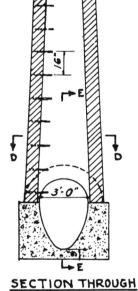

Standard Frame and Cover

D = 3'-6" for pipe 8" to 36" in diameter.
D = 4'-0" " " 36", 48" "

Slope 1/4" per foot.

Masonry Dam

SECTION THROUGH TYPICAL MANHOLE. FOR 8" TO 48" DIA. PIPE.

SECTION THROUGH MANHOLE FOR 54" & 60" DIA. PIPE.

SECTION THROUGH TYPICAL DROP MANHOLE.

SECTION THROUGH 4'-0"x 3'-0" MANHOLE ON 3'-6"x 2'-4" & 4'-0"x 2'-8" EGG SHAPED SEWER.

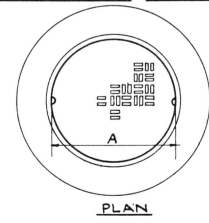

PLAN

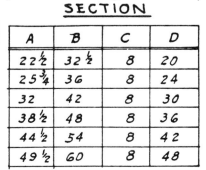

SECTION

A	B	C	D
22½	32½	8	20
25¾	36	8	24
32	42	8	30
38½	48	8	36
44½	54	8	42
49½	60	8	48

TYPICAL MANHOLE HEAD & COVER.

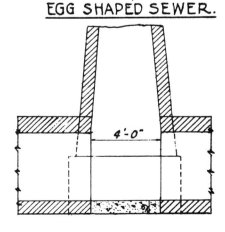

SECTION E-E

DRAINAGE & SEWERAGE-INLETS & CATCH BASINS

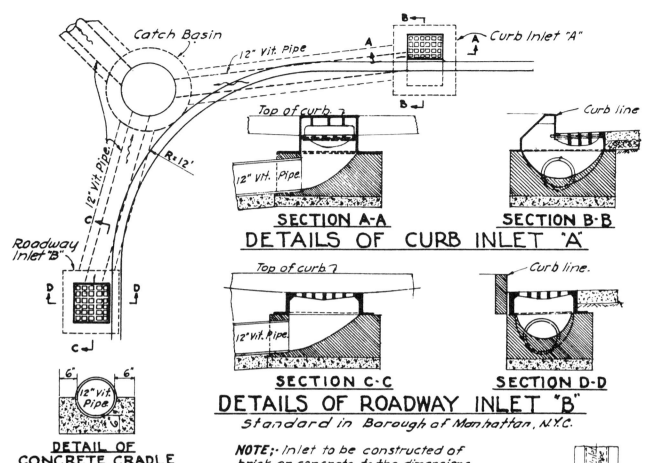

SECTION A-A

SECTION B-B

DETAILS OF CURB INLET "A"

SECTION C-C

SECTION D-D

DETAILS OF ROADWAY INLET "B"

Standard in Borough of Manhattan, N.Y.C.

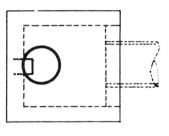

DETAIL OF CONCRETE CRADLE

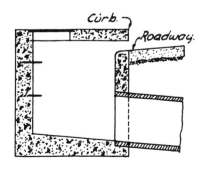

PLAN

SECTION E-E
INLET

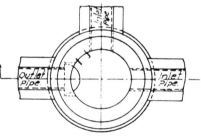

PLAN

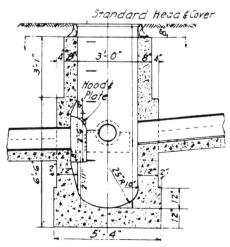

SECTION F-F
TYPICAL CATCH BASIN

Standard in Boro. of Manhattan, N.Y.C.

NOTE: Inlet to be constructed of brick or concrete to the dimensions and of the shape shown, and to be smoothly plastered both inside and outside with a layer of cement mortar ½ inch thick.

The interior of the inlet is to be sloped downwards from all sides towards the outlet.

Wherever possible culvert connection shall be laid in a 6 inch concrete cradle, and sufficient concrete placed under inlet to provide a maximum thickness of 6 inches.

Depth of inlet is dependent upon size of pipe and required cover over pipe.

For area of inlet openings use formula on page 5-17.

The required strength of casting to be determined from page 5-19.

Sump Type catch basins to be used only where labor is available for frequent cleaning and where stagnant water is not objectionable. They may be required where flat grades would cause silting up of drainage system.

DRAINAGE & SEWERAGE-MANHOLE & INLET COVERS

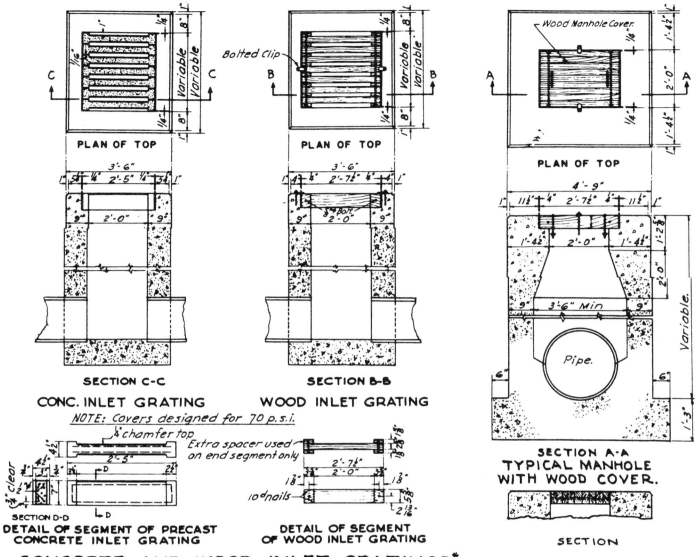

PLAN OF TOP

PLAN OF TOP

PLAN OF TOP

SECTION C-C
CONC. INLET GRATING

SECTION B-B
WOOD INLET GRATING

SECTION A-A
TYPICAL MANHOLE
WITH WOOD COVER.

SECTION

NOTE: Covers designed for 70 p.s.i.

SECTION D-D
DETAIL OF SEGMENT OF PRECAST
CONCRETE INLET GRATING

DETAIL OF SEGMENT
OF WOOD INLET GRATING

CONCRETE AND WOOD INLET GRATINGS.*

TABLE A — DESIGN DATA FOR CONCRETE & WOOD INLET GRATINGS.*

NUMBER OF BARS	CONCRETE			WOOD		
	WATERWAY OPENING (SQ.FT.)	DISCHARGE CU.FT./SEC.	LENGTH OF GRATE ASSEMBLY (IN INCHES)	WATERWAY OPENING (SQ.FT.)	DISCHARGE CU.FT./SEC.	LENGTH OF GRATE ASSEMBLY (IN INCHES)
5	1.38	2.0	19	1.63	2.3	23
10	2.68	3.9	42	2.98	4.3	44
15	3.98	5.7	64	4.36	6.3	65
20	5.28	7.6	87	5.68	8.2	87
25	6.58	9.5	110	7.04	10.1	108
30	7.88	11.3	133	8.40	12.1	129
35	9.18	13.2	156	9.75	14.0	150
40	10.48	15.1	178	11.10	16.0	171
45	11.79	17.0	201	12.46	17.9	193
50	13.09	18.8	224	13.82	19.9	214

Based on Formula, see pg.5-17, where c=0.6; g=32.2; h=0.2.
*From Engineering Manual- Chap. XXI, on Airfield Drainage.- War Dept., Corps of Engineers Mar.1943.

SEWAGE TREATMENT —SMALL SYSTEMS*—DETAILS

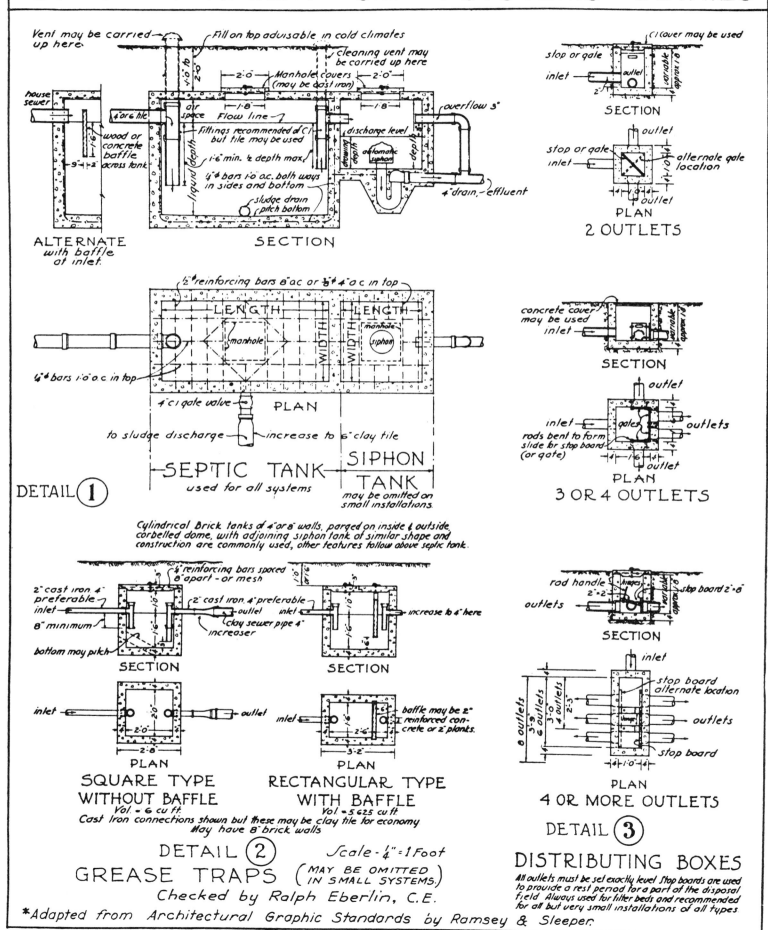

ALTERNATE
with baffle
at inlet.

SECTION

DETAIL (1)

SEPTIC TANK
used for all systems

SIPHON
TANK
may be omitted on
small installations.

Cylindrical Brick tanks of 4" or 8" walls, parged on inside & outside,
corbelled dome, with adjoining siphon tank of similar shape and
construction are commonly used, other features follow above septic tank.

SECTION   SECTION

PLAN   PLAN

SQUARE TYPE   RECTANGULAR TYPE
WITHOUT BAFFLE   WITH BAFFLE
Vol.= 6 cu.ft.   Vol.= 5.625 cu.ft.
Cast Iron connections shown but these may be clay tile for economy.
May have 8" brick walls

DETAIL (2)   Scale-¼"=1 Foot
GREASE TRAPS   (MAY BE OMITTED
                 IN SMALL SYSTEMS.)
Checked by Ralph Eberlin, C.E.
*Adapted from Architectural Graphic Standards by Ramsey & Sleeper.

SECTION

PLAN
2 OUTLETS

SECTION

PLAN
3 OR 4 OUTLETS

SECTION

PLAN
4 OR MORE OUTLETS

DETAIL (3)
DISTRIBUTING BOXES

All outlets must be set exactly level. Stop boards are used
to provide a rest period for a part of the disposal
field. Always used for filter beds and recommended
for all but very small installations of all types.

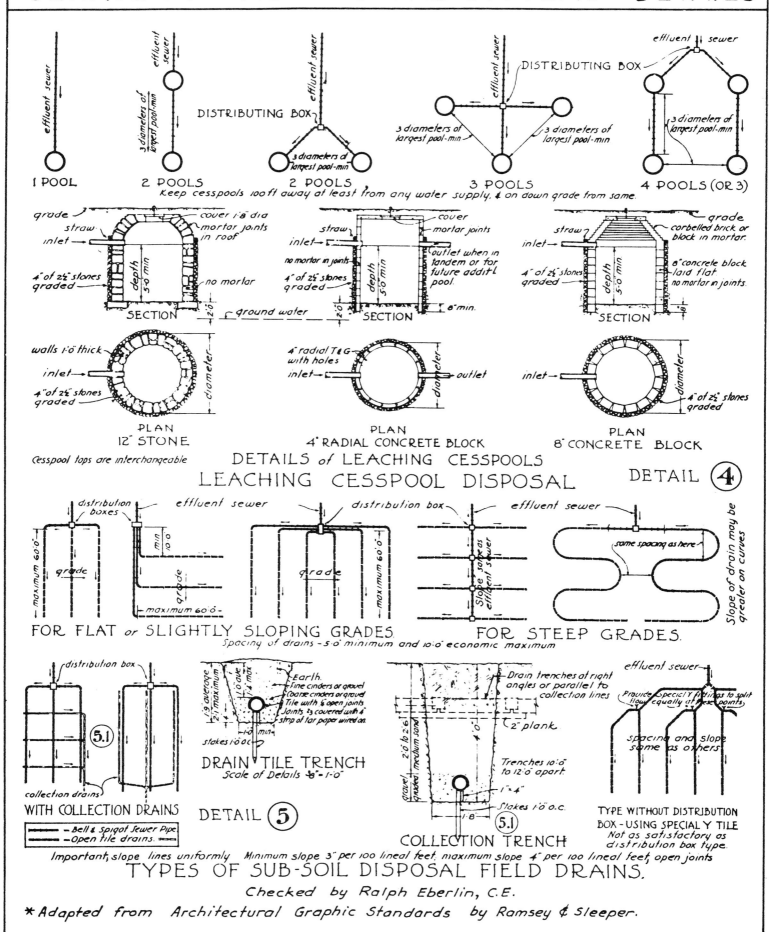

SEWAGE TREATMENT – SMALL SYSTEMS*–DETAILS

1 POOL

2 POOLS

DISTRIBUTING BOX

2 POOLS
3 diameters of largest pool-min

3 POOLS
DISTRIBUTING BOX
3 diameters of largest pool-min

4 POOLS (OR 3)
effluent sewer
3 diameters of largest pool-min

Keep cesspools 100 ft away at least from any water supply, & on down grade from same.

SECTION
PLAN
12" STONE

SECTION
PLAN
4" RADIAL CONCRETE BLOCK

SECTION
PLAN
8" CONCRETE BLOCK

Cesspool tops are interchangeable
DETAILS of LEACHING CESSPOOLS
LEACHING CESSPOOL DISPOSAL
DETAIL ④

FOR FLAT or SLIGHTLY SLOPING GRADES.
FOR STEEP GRADES.
Spacing of drains - 5'-0" minimum and 10'-0" economic maximum

WITH COLLECTION DRAINS
— Bell & Spigot Sewer Pipe
— Open tile drains

DRAIN TILE TRENCH
Scale of Details ⅛"=1'-0"
DETAIL ⑤

COLLECTION TRENCH 5.1

TYPE WITHOUT DISTRIBUTION BOX - USING SPECIAL Y TILE
Not as satisfactory as distribution box type.

Important; slope lines uniformly Minimum slope 3" per 100 lineal feet, maximum slope 4" per 100 lineal feet, open joints

TYPES OF SUB-SOIL DISPOSAL FIELD DRAINS.

Checked by Ralph Eberlin, C.E.

*Adapted from Architectural Graphic Standards by Ramsey & Sleeper.

SEWAGE TREATMENT – SMALL SYSTEMS*–DETAILS

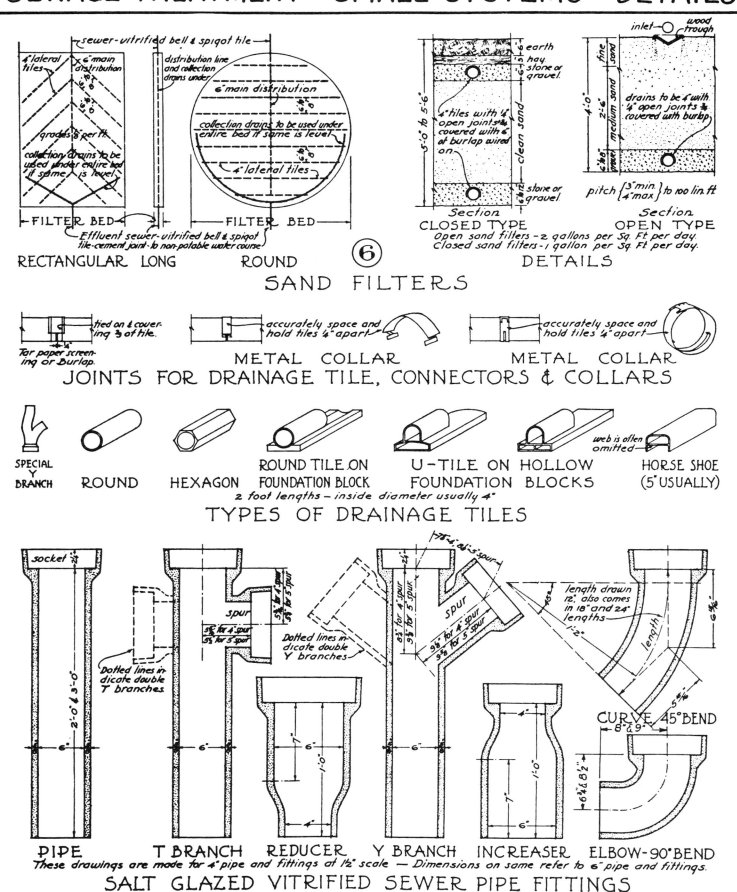

Open sand filters – 2 gallons per Sq. Ft. per day.
Closed sand filters – 1 gallon per Sq. Ft. per day.

SAND FILTERS

JOINTS FOR DRAINAGE TILE, CONNECTORS & COLLARS

2 foot lengths – inside diameter usually 4"

TYPES OF DRAINAGE TILES

These drawings are made for 4" pipe and fittings at ½" scale – Dimensions on same refer to 6" pipe and fittings.

SALT GLAZED VITRIFIED SEWER PIPE FITTINGS

Checked by Ralph Eberlin, C.E.

*Adapted from Architectural Graphic Standards by Ramsey & Sleeper.

WATER SUPPLY- DEEP WELLS

General Notes: 1. Well site should be 200 to 500 feet from possible source of pollution. Locate at elevated point if possible to prevent flooding. Fence in well site.
  2. Well building should be fireproof, ventilated and in cold climates insulate thoroughly and provide heat. Elevate above grade to provide drainage away from building.
  3. Pumping level is determined by continuous flow test at required well capacity, and the measurement of the resulting drawdown below the static water table.
  4. The top of screen should be 50 feet min. below grade to avoid surface pollution unless unusually impervious earth (10 feet of compact clay) occurs at the surface, or well is far removed from possible sources of pollution.

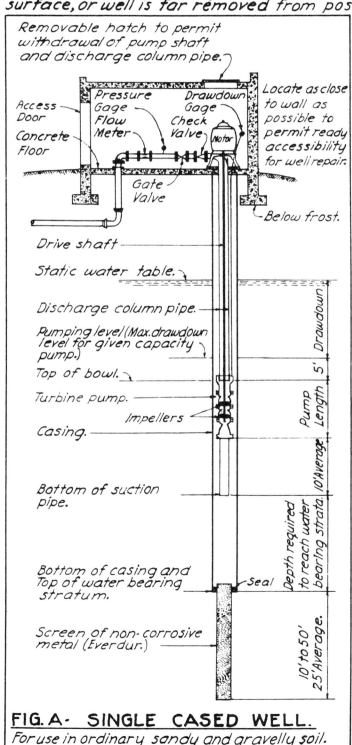

Removable hatch to permit withdrawal of pump shaft and discharge column pipe.
Locate as close to wall as possible to permit ready accessibility for well repair.
Access Door
Pressure Gage
Flow Meter
Drawdown Gage
Check Valve
Concrete Floor
Motor
Gate Valve
Below frost.
Drive shaft
Static water table.
Discharge column pipe.
Pumping level (Max. drawdown level for given capacity pump.)
Top of bowl.
Turbine pump.
Impellers
Casing.
Bottom of suction pipe.
Bottom of casing and Top of water bearing stratum.
Seal
Screen of non-corrosive metal (Everdur.)
5' Drawdown.
Pump Length 10' Average.
Depth required to reach water bearing strata.
10' to 50' 25' Average.

FIG. A - SINGLE CASED WELL.
For use in ordinary sandy and gravelly soil.

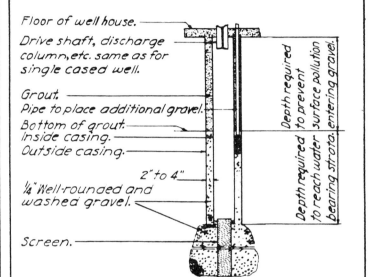

Floor of well house.
Drive shaft, discharge column, etc. same as for single cased well.
Grout.
Pipe to place additional gravel.
Bottom of grout.
Inside casing.
Outside casing.
2" to 4"
¼" Well-rounded and washed gravel.
Screen.
Depth required to prevent surface pollution.
Depth required to reach water bearing strata, entering gravel.

FIG. B - DOUBLE CASED GRAVEL WALL WELL.
For use where water bearing stratum is of uniform fine sand which is subject to flowing at the velocity the water enters the screen. The gravel provides a much larger area than the screen and the velocity of water at the outer line of gravel may be reduced to such velocity that the sand will not flow.

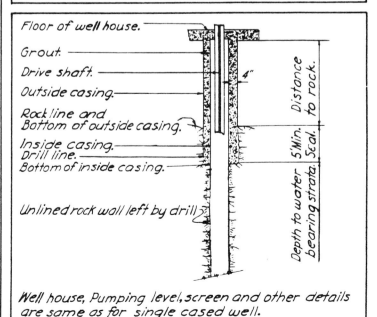

Floor of well house.
Grout.
Drive shaft.
Outside casing.
Rock line and Bottom of outside casing.
Inside casing.
Drill line.
Bottom of inside casing.
4"
Unlined rock wall left by drill.
Distance to rock.
Depth to water bearing strata. 5' Min. Seal.
Well house, Pumping level, screen and other details are same as for single cased well.

FIG. C - WELL IN ROCK.

WATER SUPPLY - INTAKES, DOMESTIC WELL, WINDMILLS

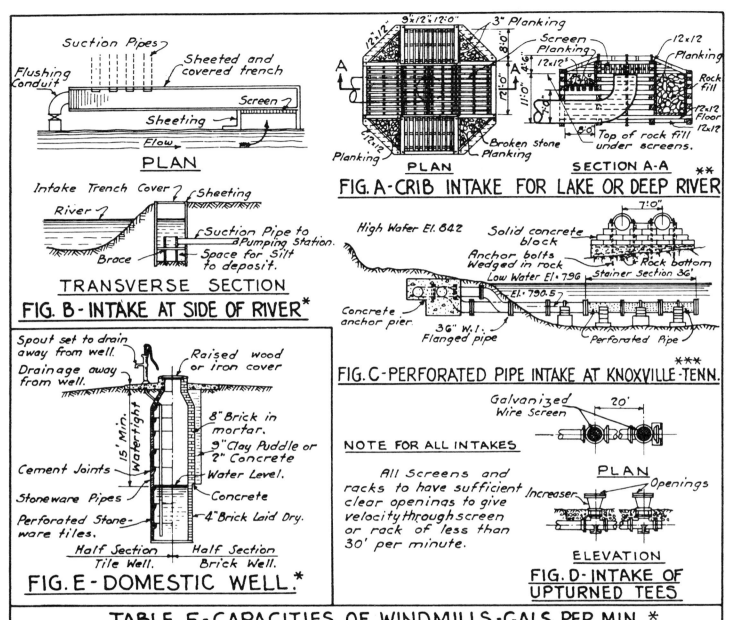

PLAN

Suction Pipes

Flushing Conduit

Sheeted and covered trench

Sheeting

Screen

Flow

TRANSVERSE SECTION

FIG. B - INTAKE AT SIDE OF RIVER*

Intake Trench Cover

River

Sheeting

Suction Pipe to Pumping Station.

Brace

Space for Silt to deposit.

PLAN

SECTION A-A ******

FIG. A - CRIB INTAKE FOR LAKE OR DEEP RIVER

9"x12"x12:0"   3" Planking

12"x12"   Screen Planking

12x12 Planking

12x12 Floor

Broken stone Planking

Rock fill

Top of rock fill under screens.

FIG. C - PERFORATED PIPE INTAKE AT KNOXVILLE - TENN. *******

High Water El. 842

Solid concrete block

Anchor bolts Wedged in rock

Low Water El. 796

Strainer Section 36'

Rock bottom

El. 790.5

Concrete anchor pier

36" W.I. Flanged pipe

Perforated Pipe

FIG. E - DOMESTIC WELL. *

Spout set to drain away from well.

Drainage away from well.

Raised wood or iron cover

15' Min. Watertight

8" Brick in mortar.

9" Clay Puddle or 2" Concrete

Cement Joints

Water Level.

Stoneware Pipes

Concrete

Perforated Stone-ware tiles.

4" Brick Laid Dry.

Half Section Tile Well.

Half Section Brick Well.

NOTE FOR ALL INTAKES

All Screens and racks to have sufficient clear openings to give velocity through screen or rack of less than 30' per minute.

Galvanized Wire Screen

20'

PLAN

Increaser

Openings

ELEVATION

FIG. D - INTAKE OF UPTURNED TEES

TABLE. F - CAPACITIES OF WINDMILLS - GALS. PER MIN. *

Diameter of blades in feet	Velocity of wind in miles per hour	Revolutions of wheel per minute	ELEVATION - FEET - RAISED						Equivalent actual useful h.p. developed
			25 ft.	50 ft.	75 ft.	100 ft.	150 ft.	200 ft.	
8½	16	70 to 75	6.19	3.02	------	------	------	-----	0.04
10	16	60 to 65	19.2	9.56	6.64	4.75	-----	-----	0.12
12	16	55 to 60	33.9	17.9	11.8	8.44	5.68	-----	0.21
14	16	50 to 55	45.1	22.6	15.3	11.2	7.81	5.00	0.28
16	16	45 to 50	64.6	31.6	19.5	16.2	9.77	8.08	0.41
18	16	40 to 45	97.7	52.2	32.5	24.4	17.5	12.2	0.61
20	16	35 to 40	125.0	63.7	40.8	31.2	19.3	15.9	0.78
25	16	30 to 35	212.0	107.0	71.6	49.7	37.3	26.7	1.34

*Adapted from Waterworks Handbook by Flinn, Weston & Bogert, McGraw-Hill
**Adapted from Babbitt & Doland, Water Supply Engineering, McGraw-Hill.
***Adapted from Engineering News Record.

GENERAL REFERENCES

References for the individual chapters of this book are given at the end of each chapter. Those lists include both general references for additional information and the sources for information used in developing the chapter contents.

The publications listed here consist of references that have information that spans over the topics of several chapters of this book.

SOURCES FOR GENERAL BUILDING AND SITE DESIGN

These are books of a general architectural topic scope that contain much information that is also applicable to site design and construction development.

Architectural Graphic Standards, 8th ed., 1988, Ramsey/Sleeper and the American Institute of Architects, John Ray Hoke Jr., Editor in Chief for the 8th edition, Wiley.
This book (the Site Detail Edition) consists of approximately one third of the 8th edition; as a result, the full copy of the 8th edition should be considered as a resource for additional information on many special topics.

Construction Principles, Materials, and Methods, 5th ed., 1983, Harold B. Olin, John L. Schmidt, and Walter H. Lewis, Van Nostrand Reinhold.
Although somewhat dated, this book represents a rich resource of information for the general topics of building and site construction.

Time-Saver Standards for Architectural Design Data, 6th ed., 1982, John Hancock Callendar, McGraw-Hill.
A general reference for data and details for building construction and planning.

Building Design and Construction Handbook, 4th ed., 1982, Frederick S. Merritt, McGraw-Hill.
A general technical reference on all aspects of the design of building construction and the various building subsystems.

Mechanical and Electric Equipment for Buildings, 7th ed., 1986, Benjamin Stein, John Reynolds, and William McGuinness, Wiley.
The most comprehensive reference on design of building subsystems for all topics other than structures and general building construction.

Building Structures, 1988, James Ambrose, Wiley.
The most comprehensive single volume on building structures, from basic concepts through systems design.

SOURCES FOR SITE DESIGN

These books deal specifically with the problems of site design and the development of site construction.

Site Planning, 3rd ed., 1988, Kevin Lynch and Gary Hack, MIT Press, Cambridge, MA.

A Guide to Site and Environmental Planning, 3rd ed., 1987, Harvey M. Rubenstein, Wiley.

Time-Saver Standards for Site Planning, 1984, Joseph DeChiara and Lee E. Koppleman, McGraw-Hill.

Simplified Site Design, 1992, James Ambrose and Peter Brandow, Wiley.

Time-Saver Standards for Landscape Architecture, 1988, Charles W. Harris and Nicholas T. Dines, McGraw-Hill.

Graphic Standards for Landscape Architecture, 1986, Richard L. Austin, Thomas R. Dunbar, J. Kip Hulvershorn, and Kim W. Todd, Van Nostrand Reinhold.

Site Details, 1989, Gregory W. Jameson and Michael A. Versen, Van Nostrand Reinhold.

Site Design and Construction Detailing, 2nd ed., 1986, Theodore D. Walker, PDA Publishers.

Simplified Design of Building Foundations, 2nd ed., 1988, James Ambrose, Wiley.

Standard Handbook for Civil Engineers, 1983, 3rd ed., Frederick S. Merritt, McGraw-Hill.

INDEX

AAU (Amateur Athletic Union) standards, basketball, 207
Abrasion resistance, 95
Abrasive tape nosings, 105
Absorption
  field, 271
  trench, sewage, 185
Access
  barrier-free, 3, 4, 21, 29, 56
  basins, 190
  controls, 59
  doors, 144, 159
  hatches, 159
  panels, 144
  roads, 38
ACI (American Concrete Institute), 79–82, 130
  concrete masonry standards, 130
Acid washing, elastomeric joint sealants, 110
Acoustics, effects of trees, 69
Acrylic, sealants, 108
Admixtures to cement, 80
Adobe
  brick sizes, 256
  construction, 140, 141, 256
Adult measurements, 3, 4
Aerobics training area, 231
Aggregates
  concrete mixes, 80
  concrete surfaces and finishes, 84
Agricultural tile, drains, 271, 272
Air-entrained concrete, 79
Air inflated structures, 174
Airports, 39–42
Air quality
  site development, 46
  trees, 69
Air sports, 230
Air-supported structures, 174
Air terminals, lightning, 191, 193

Aisle width, 6, 29, 209
  auditoriums, 6
  parking lots, 29
  stadium stairs, 209
Altitude of sun, 14–16
Aluminum
  alloy fasteners, 132
  coatings, 95
  flagpoles, 172
  grating, 104
  nails, 96–100
  nosings with concrete filler, 105
  sealants, 109
Ambulances, 24, 25, 28
  turning dimensions, 24, 28
Amenity considerations, subdivision layout, 52
Anchors and anchorages
  architectural terra cotta, 262, 263
  beam, 151, 152
  brick, 137
  manufactured homes, 36
  masonry, 90, 91
  reinforced masonry, 90
  self-drilling, 101
  shields for, 101
  stone, 93
  stone piers, 257
  stonework, 139
  terra cotta balustrades and copings, 262
Angles
  building layout, 143
  solar, 14–16
  stairs and ramps, 2
Angle support, cavity walls, 91
Anthropometric data, 3, 4
Apartment houses, mailboxes, 171
Aquatic sports, 215–225
Archeological considerations, site development, 46

Archery, ranges, 199
Arches
  anchorages, 151
  hinge anchorages, 151
  masonry, 138
  peak connections, 151
Architectural concrete, 83, 84, 135
Architectural drawings, 238, 239
Architectural symbols, 238
Architectural terra cotta, 262, 263
  anchors, clamps, clips, hangers, straps, 263
  balustrades and copings, 262
Area calculations, 240, 241
Area walls
  depths, 251
  design, 250, 251
Areaways, gratings, 104
Arterials, 53
Ashlar
  limestone strip, 260
  masonry, 259
  patterns, marble floor, 269
  stonework, 93
Ash trees, 64, 65
Asidbar impregnated wood, 107
Asphalt
  bound macadam roads, 279
  curbs, 120
  paving, 72, 120, 121
  paving block and tiles, 279
  sheet paving, 279
ASTM (American Society for Testing and Materials)
  CMU standards, 88
  concrete pavers standards, 72
  deformed bars and steel wire standards, 80, 81
  elastomeric joint sealants standards, 110
  masonry anchors standards, 91
  reinforcing steel, standards, 80, 81

ASTM (*Continued*)
  stone cladding standards, 92
  waterproofing standards, 154–156
Athletic field layouts, track and field events, 210, 211
Attached single-family development, 52
Auditoriums, 5, 6
  seating, 6
  sitelines, 5
Automatic siphon, 270
Automobiles
  driveways, 27
  parking and storage, 280
  private roads, 28
  sizes, 25
Awnings, 163
Azimuths, building layout, 143

Baby carriages, 24
Backboard, basketball, 196
Backfilling, retaining walls, 130
Backflow preventers, sprinkler systems, 179
Backing for squared stone granite, 261
Backless park benches, 282
Backstop, baseball, 202
Badminton
  field and equipment, 204
  net and post, 207
Baffle, septic tank, 270
Baggage claims, airports, 41
Balance beam, 197
Balcony rail, 145
Balloons and gliders, 230
Balls
  baseball, 201
  basketball, 196
  football, 203
  polo, 234
  racquetball, 198
  rugby, 213
  soccer, 212
  softball, 201
  tennis, 205
  volleyball, 204
Balusters, 145
Balustrades, terra cotta, 262
Banks, slope retaining, stone, 118
Barns, 232
Barrier-free design
  anthropometric data, 4
  parking lots, 56
  ramps, sidewalk, 21
Barriers
  site security, 59, 158
  tree protection, 70
Bars, reinforcing, 254
Baseball
  backstop, 207
  field and equipment, 201, 202
Base flashings, 157
Basements
  concrete steps, 252
  walls, 82, 153
  waterproofing, 153, 267
Baseplates, steel, 151
Bases
  major league baseball, 201
  terrazzo, 162
Basin, yard drainage, 275
Basketball courts, 196
  portable hydraulic goal, 196
  standard, construction, 207
Basket-weave
  floor pattern, masonry, 277
  pattern, brick wall, 276
Bath, foot, for swimming pool, detail, 285
Bathrooms, saunas, 168
Bats, baseball, 201
Batter parapet, pueblo style, 141

Bays
  loading docks, 34
  truck docks, 33
Beams
  anchor, 151
  bond, 130
  cable crash, 158
  concrete, steel reinforcing, 82
  concrete formwork, 86
  forming concrete, 86
  minimum thickness of concrete, 79
  reinforcement protection for concrete, 79
  upturned edge, 82
  wood, 147–149, 151, 152
Bearing capacities of soil, building codes, 251
Bearing walls, New York City Code, 253
Beech trees, 64
Beehive grate, 182
Bell pier foundation, 134
Bell and spigot sewer pipe, 270–272
Below-grade insulation, 20, 153
Below-grade waterproofing
  membrane, 264
  plaster coat, 265
Benches
  park, 282
  picnic, 282
  wood, 124
Benchmark, building layout, 143
Bicycles, 24
  facilities, 58
  parking, 58
  paths, 21, 58
  shelters, 58
Bikeways, classifications, 58
Billiards, 200
Binders in painting, 112
Birch trees, 65
Bituminous cement paving, 279
Bituminous coatings, 112
Bituminous membrane waterproofing, 156
Bituminous setting bed, 121
Bituminous surfaces, 120
Bleachers, 208
Blind rivets, 103
Block(s)
  backing for squared stone granite, 261
  stone granite, 279
  terra cotta, 262, 263
  and tiles, asphalt, 279
  wall heights, New York City Code, 253
  wood paving, 279
Bluestone
  flooring, 277
  steps, 252
Boating, boat shapes and sizes, 228, 229
Boat launching ramps, 116
Bocce, 213
Boiler protection on ground, 266
Bollards, 124, 158
Bolts, 101, 102
  stonework anchoring, 139
  wood construction, 146–152
Bond beams
  concrete masonry, 88, 90
  retaining walls, 130
Bond breakers
  membrane waterproofing, 154
  sealants, 108, 110
Braced excavations, 119
Brandsten International and Intercollegiate regulation spring board, 286
Brass, wire nails, 98
Brick
  adobe, 140
  anchorage, 91, 137
  arches, 138
  bonds, 89
  cavity walls, 255

dowels, terra cotta copings, 262
  joints, 89
  lined swimming pool, 283
  lintels, 136
  patterns for walks, 276
  paving, walks, terraces, steps and floors, 72, 121, 276
  positions, 89
  reinforced beams, columns, and pilasters, 137
  retaining walls, 137
  serpentine walls, 255
  sizes, 89, 256
  walls, 128, 129, 136, 137
  walls with stone quoins, 258
Broken range ashlar, limestone, 260
Broken range granite, 261
Broken stone road, 279
Building Code
  New York City, wall thickness, 253
  requirements for
    for bearing of soil, 251
    for footings, 251
Building orientation, solar, 12–19
Building permits, site planning, 47
Built-in swimming pool, steps or ladders, detail, 285
Bulkheads, 297
Bulletin boards, 11
Bullnose trim, tile, 111
Bumping posts, railways, 35
Bush-hammered concrete, 83
Butyl, joint fillers, 108

Cable crash beams, 158
Cadastral surveys, 143
CAD (Computer Aided Drafting), 48
Caissons, 134
Canoes, 228
Canopies, canvas, 163
Cantilever concrete stairs, 135
Cantilever retaining walls, 127, 130, 137, 250
Canvas, awnings, 163
Cap, pile, 134
Capacity of swimming pools, 283
Carborundum finish stone, 259
Card readers, garages, 27
Carpentry
  exterior decks, 146, 147
  exterior stairs, 146
  heavy timber, 148, 151, 152
  log construction, 150
  plank and beam framing, 148
  pole construction, 149
  timber retaining walls, 128
  wood fences, 132
Carports, 26, 27
Cars
  parking lots, 56, 57, 280
  sizes, 25
  turning dimensions, 28
Casement windows in cavity walls, 255
Cast concrete benches, 282
Cast-in-place anchors, railings, 145
Cast-in-place concrete, 81–87, 133–135
Cast iron
  hoods, yard drainage basin, 275
  manhole frames and cover, 273
  park benches, 282
  pipe, sewage disposal, 270
  receiving inlets and basins, sewers, 274
Cast metal, nosings, concrete steps, 105
Catboat rig, 229
Catch basins, 181, 183, 304
Catcher's box
  major league baseball, 201
  softball, 202
Catenary curves, 243
Catwalks, 3
  marine, 116

Cavity walls, 91, 93, 136, 253, 255
    angle support, 91
    brick, 255
    New York City Code, 253
Cedar, fences, 132, 281
Ceilings, access panels, 144
Cellar doors, steel, 159
Cellon treated wood, 107
Cement
    base primers, 113
    coated nails, 98–100
    mortar, tile-setting, 160, 161
    types, 80
Cement–water ratios
    concrete, 79
    slab strengths, 133
Centermatch lumber, 106
Ceramic tile, 111, 160, 161, 277
Cesspools, 307
Chain link fences, 131
    baseball backstop, 207
Chairs
    children's, early learning centers, 173
    wheelchairs, 4
Channels, surface drainage, 181, 304
Channel slots, masonry, 91
Check dams, 182, 302
Chemically treated wood, sitework, 128
Chemical resistance, coatings on metal, 95
Chestnut fences, 281
Children's furniture, 173
Chinking, 150
Chlorosulfonated polyethylene, 112
Chromium, 94
Cinder track, 206
Circles, properties of, 240
City tractors, 32
Clamps for architectural terra cotta, 263
Classrooms, early learning equipment, 173
Clay, tennis court surfaces, 205
Clay tile
    backing for squared stone granite, 261
    drainage, 196
    drainpipes, 180
    paving, 121
Clear coatings, 112
Cleft woven wood fences, 281
Clevis hangers, 103
Climate, site development, 46, 48
Climbers, playground, 122
Climbing
    gyms, 123
    rope, gymnastic, 197
Closed drainage systems, 181
Closed truck docks, 33
Cloverleaf highway, 38
Cluster development, 52
CMU (concrete masonry unit) construction, 88
Coatings, 112
    fasteners, 97
    on metal, 95
Cobblestone paving, 121
Code, New York City, wall thicknesses, 253
Cold weather, concrete construction and, 79
Collection drains, 271
Collector streets, 53
Columns
    angle guards for, 170
    bases, timber, 152
    caps, timber, 152
    concrete, 81, 82, 87
    concrete formwork, 87
    connections, 148, 151, 152
    corner guards, 170
    covers, 170
    footings, 82, 87
    guards, 170
    masonry anchors, 91
    pilaster

brick, 90, 137
CMU, 90
concrete, 85
reinforced brick, 137
reinforcing bars, 80–82
stone faced, 93
timber, 146–149, 151, 152
timber column, pole, 149
waterproofing membrane, 264
wood base anchorage, 146, 151
wood poles, 149
Combination foundation, 251
Commercial garages, 280
Common brick bonds, 89
Community design scale, 51
Community involvement in site planning, 47
Compass orientation, 13
Composite piles, 117
Computers, environmental site analysis, 48
Concealed drains, 182
Concept planning, 51
Concrete
    aggregates, 80
    architectural, 83–85, 135
    blocks, masonry, 88, 128–130, 136
    bollards, 158
    bricks, pressed, 72
    cast-in-place (sitecast), 79–87, 133–135
    collar, adobe parapets, 141
    columns, 82, 87
    curbs, 120, 278
    diving towers, 221
    drainpipes, 180
    drives, 278
    expansion and construction joints, 133
    finishes, 83, 84
    formwork, 83–87
    foundations, 134
    inserts, forming, 83
    isolation joints, 133
    joints, forming, 83, 133
    joints, slabs on grade, 133
    lightweight, weights, 246
    lintels, adobe construction, 141
    manhole, 273
    masonry construction, 88
    pavers, pressed, 72
    paving, 21, 120, 121
    planter, vehicle barriers, 158
    properties, 79
    proportion of structural elements, 79
    protection, 79
    reinforced columns, in masonry, 137
    reinforcement, 81, 82
    reinforcing bars, 254
    retaining wall mass and reinforced, 250
    road foundation, 279
    roads, 278
    runways, 278
        to garages, 278
    rustication, 85
    sealants, 109
    sidewalks, 278
    sitecast, 79–87, 133–135
    slab and beam forming, 86
    slabs, 252
    stairs, 135, 252
    stair treads, 105, 135
    surfaces, 83–85
    walks, surface treatment, 21
    walls, 82, 84, 85, 134, 153
        thicknesses, New York City Code, 253
    waterproofing, 153–157
    weather considerations in construction, 79
    weights, 80, 246
Concrete bases, anchorage of timber structures,
    146, 149, 151
Concrete-filled, masonry, 88, 90, 136, 137
Concrete masonry units (CMU), 88–91

garden walls, 129
lintels, 136
Connections
    glued laminated timber, 151, 152
    sign bases, 125
    timber beam, 151, 152
Connectors, tile drains, 272
Cosntruction joints
    concrete construction, 82, 84, 85
    concrete retaining wall, 250
    concrete slabs on grade, 133
    masonry, 89, 90
Control joints
    ceramic tile, 161
    concrete slabs, 133
    paving, 133
    retaining walls, 127, 130
    terrazzo, 162
Control posts, 145
Control systems, sprinkler systems, 179
Conventions of drafting, architectural, 238, 239
Conversion factors, metric, 247
Coping gutter for swimming pool, 284
Copings
    salt glazed tile, 262
    stone, 258
    terra cotta, 262
Copper, 94
    dovetail slots, 91
    nails, 98
Corner
    and column guards, metal, 170
    connection, wood framing, 148
    joints, marble, 269
Corridor floors, marble, 269
Corrosion, 94
Corrosion-resistant paint, 95
Corrosion-resistant wood, 107
Coursing
    of squared stone, granite and others, 261
    stone, 259
Courts
    basketball, 196
    bocce, 213
    handball, 198
    paddleball, 198
    racquetball, 198
    squash, 198
    surfaces, 205, 206
    tennis, 205
Covered walks, 163
Covers, manhole, 273
Cove trim, 111
Cradles for pipe sewers, 274
Crandalled stone, 259
Crawl spaces, 3
Creep, concrete, 79
Creosote preservatives, 107
Crib intake, water supply, 310
Crushed stone paving, 120
Culs-de-sac, 28, 52
Curb guards, 170
Curb gutters for swimming pools, 284
Curbs, 21, 196, 291
    concrete, 278
    granite, 279
    paving, 120, 121
    and walks, 21
Curling, 226
Curtain walls, New York City Code, 253
Curved surfaces, geometry of, 240, 244
Curves, drawing construction, 242, 243
Cut and fill computations, 241
Cut rock, channels, 181
Cut stone
    coursing, dressing, finishes and jointing, 259
    lintels, piers, sills, steps, 257
Cut stonework, 139
    paving, 121

Cutter, 229
Cylinder test for concrete, 80

Damp-proofing residential basements, 267
Dartboards, 200
Deciduous plants, 64–67
Decimal equivalents of feet and inches, 245
Decks, wood, 146–150
Declination of the earth, 12, 14, 15
Deep-ground temperature map, U. S., 20
Deep well, 309
Deflection, concrete, 79
Depth of water for spring boards, 286
Design
    area walls, 250, 251
    concrete steps and porch, 252
    reinforced concrete slabs, 252
    retaining walls, 127–130, 250
Diagonal floor pattern, masonry, 277
Diamond highways, intersections, 38
Differential leveling, 143
Dimensional lumber, 106
Dinghies, 228
Directional highways, intersections, 38
Disabilities, design data for, 4
Disposal
    drains, 271, 272
    field slope, 271, 272
    sewage, 270
    systems, sewage, 184–187
Distributing boxes, 270
Distribution
    box gate, 270
    field, 271, 272
    sewage effluent, 271, 272
Ditches, roadside, 299
Diverting box, sewage disposal, 270
Divider strips, terrazzo, 162
Diving boards, 215, 220–223
Docks
    marine, 116, 297, 298
    railway, 35
    truck, 33, 35
Door(s)
    access, 144, 159
    cellar, 159
    frames, adobe construction, 256
    garages, 26
    hatches, 144, 159
    jamb, adobe construction, 256
    sidewalk, 159
    sills, stone, 257
    steel plate, 159
    steel plate door and hardware, 159
Doorsill flashings, 157
Dosing chamber, sewage, 187
Dosing tank, sewage disposal, 270
Double curved surfaces, areas of, 240, 244
Double hung windows in cavity walls, 255
Double loaded wall, parking lots, 29
Dovetail, slots, 91
Dowels
    concrete, 81, 82
    foundation wall, 82
    masonry, 90
    slab, with control joints, 133
Drafting conventions and symbols, architectural, 238, 239
Drainage
    basins and inlets, 182, 183
    catch basins, 304
    cesspools, 307
    channels, 302
    check dams, 182
    details, exterior, 273–375
    ditches, roadside, 299
    field drains, sewage disposal, 307
    headwall, 182, 301
    inlets and catch basins, 183, 304
    manholes, 183, 273, 303

membranes, 153
parking lots, 57
playing field surface, 206
retaining walls, 127, 128, 130
and sewerage, 304
soil percolation test, 184
subsoil, 271–272
subsurface, 180, 206, 300
surface runoff, 181
tile, 272, 308
    types, 272
waterproofing, 154
yard, 275
Drain pipes, 180
Drains
    area, 121, 182, 183
    collection, 271
    connection to swimming pool gutter, 283
    disposal, 271, 272
    inlets, 182, 183
    footing, 153, 180
    in pavements, 121
    plaza, 155, 156
    residential basements, 267
    roof, flat, 121
    subsurface, 121, 180, 206
    terminations at, 155
    trench, 182, 183
    types, 182
    with unit pavers, 121
    waterproofing, 155, 156
Dressage, standard arena, 234
Dressed siding, 106
Dressed sizes of lumber, 106
Dressing
    asphalt for roads, 279
    for squared stone granite, 261
Drinking fountain, exterior, 124
Drive type screws, 103
Driveways, 27, 278
    paving, 279
Dry centrifugal pumps, 126
Dry-set cobblestone, 121
DuBois wood fences, 281

Early learning centers, equipment, 173
Earth anchors, excavations, 119
Earth channels, 181
Earth shelters, 20, 165, 166
Earthwork, 118, 119
Eberlin, Ralph, drainage details, 273–275
Edge beams, concrete, upturned, 82
Edging, paving, 120, 121
Educational equipment, 173
Effluent, sewage, 270, 271
Egress
    controls, 59
    spectator safety, 209
Elastomeric sealants, joint seals, 108, 109
Elbow, clay tile pipe, 272
Electrical equipment and accessories, lightning protection, 191–193
Electrical site utilities, 190
Electric heating, 189
Electronic timing deck boxes, swimming pools, 224
Elevators
    garages, 280
    handicapped provisions, 4
    shaft for cars, 280
Ellipses, 242
Embankment stabilization, 118, 119
End walls, 182
Energy conservation, site factors, 13, 17
Energy design
    compass orientation, 13
    earth shelters, 165, 166
    solar angles, 14, 15
    solar time, 12
    sun control, 12–19, 163, 164

Entasis, flagpoles, 172
Environmental considerations, 47
    road systems, 53
    site analysis, 48, 49
EPDM (ethylene-propylene-diene-monomer), single-ply roofing, joint fillers, 108
Epoxy
    adhesive, 160
    mortar, tile setting, 160, 161
    wood butt joints, 83
Epoxy resin, applied over previous coatings, 112
Equestrian stables, 232-234
Equipment
    athletic, 197, 208
    educational, 173
    park, 123, 124, 282
    playground, 122, 123
    site furnishings, 123, 124
Erosion protection, 302
Espaliers, 70
Evaporation, rate, plants, 70
Evergreens, 62, 63, 67
Excavations, 119
    layout for construction, 143
Exercise training equipment, 231
Expansion
    anchors, 101
    joints
        ceramic tile, 161
        concrete slabs, 133
        retaining walls, 127, 129
        waterproofing, plazas, 154–156
Exposed
    aggregate concrete, 83
    concrete rustication, 84, 85
Expressways, 38
Exterior coatings on metal, 95
Exterior drainage details, 273-275
Exterior primers, metal, 95
Exterior signs, 11
Exterior steps, 252
Exterior walls
    limestone ashlar, 260
    membrane, waterproofing, 264
    terra cotta copings, 262
Eye bolts, 102

Fabrication (on metals), 94
Face brick, 89
Face jointing, stone, 259
Facing, stone, 92
Fasteners
    anchor bolts, drilled in, 101
    expansion bolts, 101
    finishes and coatings, nails, 97
    nails, 97–100
    wood fences, 132
FEMA (Federal Emergency Management Agency), flood damage management, 44
Fences, 59, 127–132
    baseball backstop, 207
    chain link, 131
    steel and iron, wire, 268
    walls, 95, 129
    wood, 132, 281
    woven, picket, hurdle, split rail, stockade, post and rail, cedar, chestnut, 281
Fencing, 199
Fiber forms, concrete, 86, 87
Fiberglass, nuts and bolts, 102
Field drains, sewage disposal, 307
Field events, layouts, 210, 211
Field hockey, 213
Fieldstone, uncoursed, 93
Field tile drains, 271, 272
Filter(s)
    bed, 272
    fabric, in revetments riprap, 118
    mats, paving, 120, 121
    sand, 272

Filtration field, 271
Finished flooring thicknesses, 277
Finishes
    architectural concrete surfaces, 83, 84
    brickwork, 89
    concrete, 83, 84
    fasteners, 97
    metals, 95
    mortar joints, 89
    paints and coatings, 111–113
    paving, 72, 120, 121
    stonework, 259
    tile, 160–162
Finish lumber, 106
Fire, protection, site planning, 43
Fir trees, 62
Fixed park benches, 282
Fixed seating, theaters, 5, 6
Flagging, floors, 277
Flagpoles, 172
Flagstone
    installation, 121, 139
    steps, 252
Flashing, 157
    cavity walls, 255
    plaza membranes, 156
    stone copings, 258
    under stone copings, 258
    terra cotta coping, 262
    terra cotta copings and balustrades, 262
Flexible base paving, 121
Floating docks, 116
Flood damage control, 44, 45
Floor(s)
    exercise mat, 197
    finish, tile, 277
    hatches, 144, 159
    mounting, railings, 145
    patterns, marble, 269, 277
    thicknesses for exterior and interior flags,
        slate, tile, 277
    waterproofing residential basements, 267
Flooring
    brick, 276
    ceramic tile, 111, 160, 161
    flagging, 277
    lumber, 106
    marble, 277
    porches, terraces, walks, etc., exterior slate,
        tile, flags, marble, brick, 276, 277
    slate, flagging, marble, tile, stone, etc., 277
    stone, 139
    terrazzo, 162
Flowering shrubs, 63–66
Folding gates, 169
Football, 203
Foot bath for swimming pool, detail, 285
Footcandles, 178
Footings
    column, 82, 87
    concrete formwork, 87
    depth, 251
    drains, 134, 153
    earth shelters, 165
    flagpoles, 172
    formwork, 87
    pole construction, 149
    signs, 125
    spread, 134
    step, 134
    wall, 82, 153
    wood fences, 132
Form joints, concrete, 83
Form liners, concrete, 84
Forms
    architectural concrete, 83
    fountains, 126
Formwork, concrete, 83–87
Foundations
    basement, 153

concrete, 82, 87, 134
concrete walls, 82
drains, 134, 153
earth shelter, 166
formwork, 87
pole construction, 149
step, 134
wall, 82, 84, 85, 153, 166, 253
wall anchorages, masonry, 91
water-resistant, 153
wood decks, 146
Fountains, 126
Frame and cover, manholes, 273
Frame and grating, yard drains, 275
Frames, adobe construction, openings, 141
Framing
    anchors, 146–148, 151, 152
    decks, 146, 147
    heavy timber, 151, 152
    log construction, 150
    plank and beam, 148
    pole construction, 149
    wood, decks, 146, 147
Frearson screws, 103
Freestanding concrete stairs, 135
Freestanding garden walls, 129
Freeways, 38
French drains, 271, 272
French type wood fences, 281
Frost penetration map, 78
Furan resin grout, 161
Furniture
    auditorium seating, 5, 6
    coatings, 95
    playground and park, 122–124
    school desks and seating, 173

Gabions, 118
Galvanic action, 94
Galvanic corrosion, 94
Galvanic series, 94
Galvanized steel
    dovetail slots, 91
    pavement edging, 120
Garage doors, 26
Garages, 26, 27, 280
    driveways, 27
    floors, concrete slabs, 133
    parking, 29–31
    residential, 26
Garden edging, metal, 282
Garden equipment, 282
Garden tractors, 24
Garden walls, 127–129
Gates
    chain link, 131
    folding, 169
    sliding crash, 158
Geotextile
    filters, 120, 121, 153, 165, 180
    filter sleeves, 180
Girders
    concrete, 81, 82
    heavy timber connections, 151, 152
Glare, controlling with trees, 69
Glass
    shading devices, 19
    sun control devices, 19
Glazed, wall tile, 111
Glazing, swimming pool, 224
Glued laminated beams, connections, 151, 152
Gneiss, 92
Golf carts, 24
Gooseneck type curb for swimming pool, 284
Gothic copings, stone, 258
Grab rail, pipe for swimming pool, 283
Grades, reinforcing steel, 80
Gradients, slopes, bare soils, 118
Grading of highways, 38

Grandstands and bleachers, 208, 209
Granite
    curbs, 120, 279
    edging, 120
    floors on slabs, 277
    joint widths, 259
    paving, 72, 121, 139
    squared stone, 261
Graphic indications of materials, 238
Graphic methods, 240–244
Graphics, 9–11
    site graphics, 9
Graphic standards for drawings, 238, 239
Graphic symbols, 238, 239
    architectural drawings, 239
Grass, 68
    paving, 72, 121
    playing field construction, 202, 204
    surface drainage, 181
Grates, 182, 183
Gratings
    and frames, yard drains, 275
    manhole, 273
    and treads, 104
Gravel drains, retaining walls, 127, 128
Gravity retaining wall, 127
Grease trap, 270
Greenhouses, ventilation, 74
Grid systems, topographic survey, 143
Grillage foundations, 251
Grilles and louvers, 169
Gringo blocks, adobe construction, 141
Groins, 298
Ground covers, 67
Ground slope, disposal fields, 271, 272
Ground terminals, lightning, 191–193
Grout, retaining walls, 130
Grouted, hollow brick wall, 137
Guardrails, 143, 292
Guards
    fence, lawn, 282
    skylights, 268
    tree, 282
    wall and corner, 170
    wicket lawn, 282
Gusset plate, 149
Gutters
    concrete, 278
    curbside, 291
    inlet and receiving basin, 274
    road edge, 299
    steel lined tank, 283
    swimming pool, 217, 223, 224, 284, 285
Gymnasium equipment
    basketball, 196
    bleachers, 208
    gymnastic 197
    sports and games, 197
Gymnastic equipment, 197

Hall floors, marble, 269
Hammered stone, 259
Handicapped
    curb ramp, 21
    design data, 4
    parking, 29
    parking lots, 56
    signs, 11
    stairs
        slope, 2
        tread, 105
    swimming pool access, 215
Handrails, 145
    spectator circulation safety, 209
Hand tooled stone, 259
Hangers
    architectural terra cotta, 263
    beam, 151, 152
    glued laminated timber, 151, 152
    suspended concrete form, 86

Hang gliders, 230
Hatches, floor, 144
Hatchways, 159
Headwalls, 182, 301
Hearses, 24, 25
   turning dimensions, 28
Heaters, for saunas, 168
Heights
   for garage stories, 280
   springboards, 286
Helical inserts, stainless steel, 102
Helical ramps, 31
Helicoidal concrete stairs, 135
Helicopter landing facilities, 42
Heliports, 42
Herringbone
   brick pattern walks, 276
   floor pattern, masonry, 239
   patterns, marble floor, 269
Hexagon tile, drainage, 272
High jump
   construction, 211
   location, 210
High mast lighting, 178
High springboards, 286
High voltage distribution, 190
Highways, 38
   construction, 287
Hinge anchorage, wood arch, 151
Hollow cavity walls, 255
Hollow walls, New York City Code, 253
Honed finish, stone, 259
Hood for cast iron, yard drainage basin, 275
Hook, bolts, 102
Horizontal bar
   gymnastics, 197
   playgrounds, 123
Horizontal joints, reinforcement, 90
Horizontal masonry, 129
Horses
   clearances for, 232
   shows, 234
Horseshoe tile, 272
Hot-air balloons, 230
Hot tubs, 167
Hot weather construction, concrete, 79
House sewer, 272
Human body measurements, 3, 4
Hurdle fences, wood, 281
Hydrology, site development, 46
Hydrostatic uplift below slab, earth shelters, 166
Hyperbola, 243
Hyperbolic paraboloid, 244

Ice hockey equipment, 226
Igneous rock, 92
Illumination, interior landscaping, 73
Indoor soccer, 212
Indoor sports, 196–200
Industrial floor
   concrete, 133
   gratings and treads, 104
   wheel loads, 133
Industrial use, concrete slabs, 133
Industrial wire fences, 268
Inflated structures, 174
Inlets, 183, 304
   covers, 305
   frame and grate, 273
   street sewer, 274
   yard drainage, 275
Inserts, helical, 102
Insulated basements, 153
Insulated base paving, 121
Insulation
   adobe construction, 141
   basements, 153
   below-grade, 20, 153
   boiler on waterproofing, 266

earth shelters, 165
   plaza construction, 121, 154–156
Integrated play equipment, 122
Intensity standards, residential development, 50
Intercollegiate springboards, 286
Interior landscaping, 74–76
Interlocking, paving, 72
Intersecting runway, airports, 39
Intersections, bikeways, 58
Iowa concrete curb, 120
Iron
   coat waterproofing, residential basements, 267
   gates, garden walls, 129
   nosings, 105
   stair nosings, 105
Irrigation, lawn sprinkler systems, 179
Island parking layout, 30
Isogonic chart of the U. S., 13

Jet types, fountains, 126
Joint fillers, 108–110
Jointing
   limestone ashlar, 260
   stone, 259
   stone piers, 257
   terra cotta copings and balustrades, 262
Joints
   brick, 89
   in concrete, 83, 84
   concrete slabs on grade, 133
   concrete surfaces and finishes, 83, 84
   marble, 269
   masonry, 89
   retaining walls, 127
   sealants, elastomeric, 108–110
   stone walls, 93
   in stonework, 139
   waterproofing, 156
Joint sealants, elastomeric, 108–110

Kayaks, 228
Ketch, 229
Kindergarten equipment, 173

Ladders
   critical angle, 2
   swimming pool, 285
Lag bolts, shields for, 101
Lamp hole, drainage, 275
Land
   measurement, metric, 247
   planning, 44–55
Landing mats, 197
Landings, stairs, slip-resistant, 135
Landscaping
   earth shelters, 166
   grasses and ground covers, 67, 68
   interior, 74–76
   paving, 21, 120, 121, 133
   sprinkler systems, 179
   trees and shrubs, 62–65, 69
   walks, paths and terraces, 21
   walls and fences, 127–132
Lane striping, bikeways, 58
Lateen, 229
Lateral drains, 271
Latex, 112
   modified mortar, 121
   Portland cement mortar, 160
Lavas, 92
Lavatories, for handicapped, 4
Lawn
   benches, 282
   bowling, field and equipment, 204
   fences, wire, 268
   guard, 282
   irrigation systems, 179
Leaching
   cesspools, 271

pits, 186
Lead, 94
Ledgerock pattern, 93
Levelers, truck dock, 34
Leveling rods, 143
Life cycle costing, 7, 8
Lift chairs, 227
Lift crash gates, 158
Lighted handrails, 145
Lighting
   interior landscaping, 73
   pools under water, 284
   recommended levels, 178
   site, 178
   site security, 59
   streets, 293
Lightning protection, 191–193
Light wall footing, 251
Light wood framing, decks, 146, 147
Limestone, 92
   copings, 258
   door sills, 257
   joint widths, 259
   lintels, 257
   piers, 257
   quoins, brick walls, 258
   steps, 257
   strip ashlar, 260
Lintels, 136
   adobe construction, 141
   brick, 136
   concrete masonry, 88, 136
   design, 136
   stone, 257
Lips, fountains, 126
Liquid
   applied membranes, 155
   radiant heating, 189
Little League baseball, 202
Loading conditions, lintels, 136
Loading docks, 34
Lobby floors, marble, 269
Lockers
   bicycle parking devices, 58
   ski, 227
Locust trees, 65
Log construction, 150
London walks, 121
Long jump, 211
Long range ashlar limestone, 260
Long type random ashlar limestone, 260
Loose material paving, 120
Lots, subdivision layout, 52
Louvers and vents, for sun control, 164
Low level lighting, 178
Low wall railings, 145
L-type retaining walls, 130, 250

Macadam, roads, 279
Machine foundation
   waterproofing, plaster coat, 264
   waterproofing membrane, 264
Machine screws, 102
Machine tooled stone, 259
Mailboxes, 171
Mailrooms, apartments, 171
Major league baseball, 201
Malleable iron, 94
Mall lighting, 178
Manholes, 183, 273, 303
   covers, 305
   septic tank, 270
   steps, 275
Manufactured homes, 36, 37
Maple trees, 64, 65
Maps in environmental site analysis, 48
Maps of the U. S.
   deep-ground temperatures, 20
   frost penetration, 78

grasses, 68
isogonic chart, 13
plant hardiness, 62
sun time, 12
Marble, 92
  floors, 139, 269, 277
  mosaic floors, 269
  stairs, 139
  tile, standard, 269
Marine work, 116
Markings, outdoor swimming pools, 283
Masonry, 88–93, 136–142
  accessories, 90, 91
  adobe, 140, 141, 256
  anchors and ties, 91
  arches, 138
  brick
    cavity walls, 255
    sizes, 89
  cesspools, 271
  channel slots, 91
  CMU (concrete masonry units), 88
  concrete steps, porches, etc., 252
  cut stone coping, quoins, etc., 258
  flashings, 157
  flooring, flags, marble, slate, stepping stones,
    terraces, tile, walks, 277
  jointing finishes, and courses for stone, 259
  lintels, 136
  mortar joints, 89
  nails, 99
  references, 90
  reinforced brick, 137
  reinforcement precautions, 90
  rubble, 259
  sealants, 109
  squared stonework, 261
  stone, 92, 93, 138, 139
  stone piers, lintels, etc., 257
  walls, 89, 90, 93, 136, 137
    terra cotta coping, etc., 262
    thicknesses, New York City Code, 253
Mass concrete footing, 251
Mass concrete retaining walls, 250
Mastic grout, 161
Mathematical data, 242–245
Mechanical barriers, traffic control, 158
Mechanical finish, 95
Membranes
  basement, 153
  drainage, 153
  liquid-applied, 155
  waterproofing, 264
    above grade, 264
    below grade, 264
    plaza, 154–156
    residential basements, 267
  water resistant, 153
Mesh, wire fences, 268
Metal
  access doors, 144, 159
  bases, in primers, 113
  collar, tile pipe, 272
  connection devices
    heavy timber, 151, 152
    light wood framing, 146–149
  corner and column guards, 170
  detectors, 59
  edge paving, 120
  fasteners, 96–103
  gratings, 104
  guards and column covers, 170
  lath, adobe construction, 141
  louvers for sun control, 164
  pool liner with overflow, 217
  portable posts, 145
  railings, 145
  ties, masonry walls, 91, 136, 137
Metallic finish, 95

Metals, 94
Metamorphic rock, 92
Metric conversion factors, 247
Metric measurements, 247
Minitrap, 197
Mobile homes, 36, 37
Modular brickwork, 89
Moisture control
  basement walls, 153
  earth shelters, 165, 166
  logs, 10
  lumber, 106
  protection, 108–110, 153–157
  roof plaza, 154–156
Monel, 94
Monolithic terrazzo, 162
Mortar
  functions, 89
  joints, 89
  latex-modified, 121
  stone walls, 93
  tile-setting, 160, 161
Mortarless joints, 120, 121
Motorcycles, 24
Motor gliders, 230
Mountable concrete curb, 120
Mowers, 24
Mudslabs, 153
Multi-lane parkway, 287

Nailing
  table of uses, 96
  wood decking, 146, 147
Nails, 96–100
Natural light, 20, 163, 164
Natural stone, 92
Natural turf, 206
NBA (National Basketball Association)
  standards, 196
NCAA (National Collegiate Athletic Association)
  standards
  baseball, 201
  basketball, 196, 207
  football, 203
  high school court, 196
  public swimming pools, 218
  water polo, 225
NCX fire retardant treated wood, 107
Needle evergreens, 62
Neoprene
  coats, paving, 121
  gaskets, earth shelters, 165
  joint fillers, 108
  tack coat, paving, 121
Nested, nails, 97
Nets
  basketball, 196
  tennis, 205
New York City Building Code, wall thicknesses,
  253
NFIP (National Flood Insurance Program), 44, 45
NFL (National Football League) standards, 203
NFPA (National Fire Protection Association)
  standards
  aisle requirements, 209
  manufactured homes, 36
Nominal lumber dimensions, 106
Nonferrous metals, 94
Nonreinforced joints, waterproofing, 155, 156
Non-slip curb, swimming pool, 285
Nosings, stair
  metal, 105
  slip resistant, 135
  stone, 139
Nozzle patterns, sprinkler systems, 179

Oak trees, 65
Offices, concrete slabs, 133
Oil, in primers, 113

One-way joists, concrete, 82
One-way slabs, minimum thickness of concrete,
  79
Opaque solvent-based coatings, 112
Open excavation, 119
Open risers, 104
Open tile drains, 271, 272
  residential basements, 267
Open type gutter for swimming pool, 284
Organic adhesive, 160, 161
Ornamental metal, 144, 145
Outdoor brickwork, steps and walks, 276
Outdoor lighting systems, 178
Outdoor sports, 201–214
Outrigger poles, for flags, 172
Oval head screws, 103
Overflow gutters, swimming pools, 217, 284
Overhangs
  parking lot requirements, 56
  sun shading, 18, 19
Overhead flood lighting, swimming pools, 224
Overhead transformers, 190
Oversnow vehicles, 227
Overturning, retaining walls, 128

Paddles
  canoe, 228
  kayak, 228
  platform tennis, 204
Paddle tennis, 204
Pads, heliports, 42
Paints, 95, 112, 113
Parabola, 243
Parallel bars, 197
Parallel parking stalls, 29
Parallel runways, airports, 39
Parking
  diagonal and parallel, 280
  garages, 27
    ramp systems, 31
  lots, 29, 30, 56, 57
    dimensions, 29
    drainage, 181
    lighting, 178
  space, 280
Parks equipment, 122–124, 282
Parkways, suburban, 53
Partitions
  waterproofing residential basements, 267
  wire, 268
Passages and corridors, dimensions, 3
Passenger cars
  parking, 29–31
  size, 25, 280
  storage, 280
Passenger loading bridges, airports, 41
Passenger terminals, airports, 40
Passive solar design, building orientation, 13,
  17
Paths and walks, 21
  brick, 276
  masonry, 277
Patterns
  brick joints, 89
  for floors, masonry, 277
  paving, 72
  stonework, joints, 93
Pavements
  asphalt, 288, 289
  bituminous, 288, 289
  curbs, 291, 296
  curbside gutters, 291
  highways, 38
  surface drainage, 181
  typical sections, 287–290
  unpaved, 288
Pavers
  tile, 111
  unit, 72, 121, 139, 160, 161

Paving
  bikeways, 58
  blocks and tiles
    asphalt, 279
    wood, 279
  brick, 276
    roads, 279
    vitrified, 279
  curbs, 120, 121
  flashings, 157
  patterns, unit pavers, 72
  paving blocks, 72, 121, 139
  roof, 121, 154–156
  on suspended base, 121, 154–156
  types and sections, 279
Pedestals, pavers, 121
Pedestrians and bikeways, 58
Penetration roads, 279
Pentachlorophenol treated wood, 107
Perch, stone, 259
Percolation rate test, soils, 184, 185
Perforated drains, 180
Perimeter protection, security, 59
Personnel barriers, fences and walls, 59
Phenolic coatings, 112
Phillips screws, 103
Picket fences, cedar, 281
Pick-up trucks, 25
Picnic tables and benches, 124, 282
Pier foundations, 134
  manufactured homes, 37
Pier and panel garden walls, 129
Piers, 297, 298
  cut stone, 257
  stone jointing and anchoring, 257
Pigments in paint, 112
Pilasters
  brick masonry, reinforced, 137
  concrete, formwork for, 85
  garden walls, 129
  reinforced masonry, 90
Piles
  excavations, 119
  foundations, 251
  land capacity, 117
  pile-supported foundations, 134
  sheeting, 119
  sheetpile, 119
  soldier, 119
  types and characteristics, 117
Pile-supported foundations, 134
Pine trees, 62
Pipe
  sewage disposal, 270–272
  sewers, cradles, 274
Pipes, penetrations, 153, 155, 156
Piping, coatings, 95
Pitch
  of curbs, swimming pool, 285
  face stone, 259
  sewage disposal pipe, 271, 272
Pitcher's mound
  Little League baseball, 202
  major league baseball, 201
Planed or machine finished stone, 259
Plank and beam framing, 148
Planned unit development, 55
Planning and design data, 2–8, 24–43, 78
Planter drains, 180
Planters
  exterior, 70, 72
  interior, 74
Plant hardiness, map of U. S., 62, 68
Planting
  earth shelter, roof top, 165, 166
  interior, 74
  parking lots, 56, 57
  plant forms and sizes
    exterior, 75
    interior, 75

  rooftops, 70, 165, 166
  structures, 70, 165, 166
  trees and shrubs, 71
Plaster
  adobe construction, 141
  coat method waterproofing
    below grade, 265
    residential basements, 267
  coat waterproofing, 266
Plastic
  drain pipes, 180
  safety panels, post and railings, 145
  sealants, 109
Platforms, diving facilities, 220
Platform tennis, 204
Plats, 54
Play equipment, 122, 123, 173
  early learning, 173
  wading pools, 216
Playgrounds, 122
  equipment, 282
Playing field construction, 205–207
Playtable, 282
Plaza over occupied space, construction, 121, 154–156
Pleaching, trees, 70
Plumbing, sewage disposal, 184–187, 270, 271
Plummet, diving facilities, 220
Plywood
  butt joints, concrete forms, 83
  sheathing, 149
Pneumatic fasteners, 97
Pneumatic structures, 174
Pocket billiards, 200
Pointed stone finish, 259
Pole construction, 149
Poles, treated wood, 149
Pole vault layout, 210, 211
Polished finish stone, 259
Pollarding, trees, 70
Polo, outdoor field, 234
Polyester, 112
Polyethylene
  foundations, 153
  piping, 179
  sheets, 166
  watershed, 165
Polystyrene insulation, 121
Polysulfide sealants, 108
Polyurethane sealants, 108
Polyvinylchloride, 112
Pool(s)
  section, 1½″ = 1′0″, 285
  scum gutters and overflows, ¾″ = 1′0″, 284
  swimming
    outdoor type, plan and section, 283
    sections and step details, 285
Porch
  floor, reinforced concrete, 252
  flooring, flags, slating, tile, marble, stone, etc, 277
Portable bleachers, 208
Portable hydraulic goal, basketball, 196
Portable ring frame, 197
Portland cement
  based grouts, 161
  cement mortar, 111, 161
Postal facilities, apartments, 171
Postal specialties, 171
Post and rail fence, 281
Posts
  anchors, 146
  chain link fences, 131
  fence, 131, 132
  flagpoles, 172
  plank and beam framing, 148
  pole construction, 149
  railings, 145
  removable, 207
  sport facilities, 207

Poured in place concrete, formwork, 79–87, 133, 134
Precast concrete
  bicycle parking devices, 58
  bumpers, asphalt paving, 120
  lintels, 136
  masonry units, 88
  pressed concrete pavers, 72
  riprap, 118
Precast terrazzo, 162
Prefabricated drainage panels, 165
Prefabricated log structures, 150
Premolded control joints, 133
Premolded fillers, paving, 120
Preservatives, waterborne, 116
Pressed concrete pavers, 72
Pressure treated wood
  fences, 107, 132
  marine applications, 116
  paving, 120
Primers
  for cement bases, 113
  exterior, metal, 95
  paints and coatings, 112, 113
  sealants, 108-110
  for wood bases, 113
Private roads, 28
Protection
  for steel reinforcement, 81
  for trees, 70
Protection board
  foundations, 153
  paving, 121
  waterproofing, 154, 155
Public assembly seating, 6
  bleachers and grandstands, 208
  theater design, 5
Public review, site planning and, 47
Public roads intersecting private roads, 28
Public type swimming pool, 283
PUD (planned unit development), 50, 55
Pueblo style batter parapet, 141
Pumpable sand in revetments riprap, 118
Pumps
  fountains, 126
  for wells, 188
Purlin
  connections, 152
  hangers, concealed, 152

Quarry face
  squared stone, 259
  stone, 259
Quarry tile, 111
Quartzite, 92
Quays, 297
Quoins, stone, 258

Racks
  billiards, 200
  ski, 227
Racquetball, court and equipment, 198
Radiant heating, 189
Railings, 2, 145, 147
Railroad cars, types and sizes, 35
Railroad ties, retaining walls, 128
Railway clearances, 35
Rakers, excavations, 119
Rammed earth construction, 142
Ramps
  boat launching, 116
  critical angle, 2, 3
  driveways, 27
  garage, 27, 31
  pitch, 280
  wheelchair, 21
Random ashlar, limestone, 260
Random range ashlar, limestone, 260
Random range granite, 261
Range work, limestone ashlar, 260

Ready-set tile systems, 111
Receiving basin, street sewer, 274
Recessed doors, 144
Recessed handrails, 145
Red lead primers, 113
Reducer, clay tile pipe, 272
Redwood
  decks, 147
  paving, curbs, 120
  retaining walls, 128
Regional planning, 47
Reglets, cut stone, 258
Reinforced brick
  lintels, 136
  masonry, 137
Reinforced concrete
  formwork, 79–87
  porch floors, 252
  poured in place, 82–87, 133–135
  retaining walls, 250
  stairs, 135, 252
  surfaces, 83
Reinforced joints, waterproofing, 155
Reinforced masonry, 136, 137
Reinforcing
  applications, 82
  bars, spacing and splicing, 254
  grades, 88
  rods, 254
  steel
    brick masonry, 137
    concrete, 79–82
Residential
  development, intensity standards, 50
  land, surface drainage, 181
  site planning, roads and sidewalks, 21, 53
  streets, 53
  swimming pools, 215
  water supply, 188
Retaining walls
  brick masonry, 137
  concrete, 127
  concrete masonry, reinforced, 130
  garden, 128
  reinforced and mass, 250
  stone, 128
  structural design considerations, 128
  wood, 128
Retractable barriers, 158
Retractable bollards, 158
Retractable grilles, 169
Revetments riprap, 118
Rigid base paving, 121
Rigid plastic drain pipes, 180
Riprap, 118
Risers and treads
  concrete stairs, 135
  dimensions, 2
  nosings, 105
  open, 104
  stone, 139
  wood deck stairs, 146
River, side intake, water supply, 310
Riverine profiles, 44
Rivets, 103
Road drainage, sewer inlets, 274
Roads
  construction, 287–290, 295
  curbside gutters, 291
  ditches, 299
  driveways, 27, 278
  edge gutters, 299
  guard rails, 292
  highways, 38
  lighting, 293
  and paving, sections, types, 279
  private, 28
  site development layout, 52, 53
  typical sections, 287–290
Roadside ditches, 299

Roadside gutters, 297
Road tractors, 32
Rock
  anchors, excavations, 119
  face squared stone, 261
  face stone, 259
Rodeos, 234
Rods, reinforcing, 254
Rolling, shutters, 163
Roll-out swimming pool gutter, 284
Roof(s)
  adobe construction, 256
  lightning protection, 191–193
  paved, 121, 154–156, 165
  planting, 74, 166
  surface drainage, 181
Roots, capacity plants, 70
Rot damage, log construction, 150
Rough stone coursing, 259
Round columns, concrete forms, 87
Rowlock arch, 138
Rubbed finish stone, 259
Rubber form inserts, concrete form joints, 83
Rubberized asphalt surface, 206
Rubber nosings, stairs, 105
Rubble
  granite, 261
  masonry, 259
Rugby, 213
Running track layout, 210
Runoff
  calculations, 181
  control systems, 182, 183
  embankment stabilization, 181
  surface drainage systems, 181
Runways
  airports, 39
  concrete, 278
Rural highways, intersections, 38
Rusticated joints, stone, 259
Rustication, concrete wall joints, 83–85

Saddles, marble, 269
Safety areas, stadium seating, 208
Safety type gutter for swimming pool, 284
Sailplanes, 230
Salt glazed drain tile, 272
Salt glazed tile coping, 262
Sand
  cushion terrazzo, 162
  filters, sewage disposal, 186, 272, 308
Sandstone, 92
  flooring, 277
  joint widths, 259
Sanitary sewers manholes, 273
Santa Fe adobe details, 256
Satellite concept, airports, 40
Saunas, 168
Sawcut control joints, concrete slabs, 133
Sawed finish stone, 259
School(s)
  buses, 25
  turning dimensions, 28
  wire fences, 268
Schooners, 229
Screenings, road topping, 279
Screens
  CMU block, 88
  folding grilles and gates, 169
  wire mesh partitions, 169
  wood, 132
Screw and ring shank nails, 97
Screws, 101–103
Scum gutter
  details, swimming pools, 284
  pools, large scale, 285
Sealants, 108–110
  plaza waterproofing, 154
Seam faced squared stone, 261

Seating
  anthropometric data, 3, 4
  auditorium, 5, 6
  fixed, 5, 6
  grandstands and bleachers, 208
  handicapped, 4
  park benches, 124, 282
Seating capacities, bleachers, 208
Seawalls, 298
Security
  airport checkpoints, 41
  barriers, 158
  bicycle parking devices, 58
  guard booths, 59
  site, 58, 59
Sedimentary rock, 92
Sedimentation tanks, 270
Seepage pits and beds, 186
Seesaws (playgrounds), 123
Seismic design
  partially reinforced masonry, 90
  reinforced masonry, 90
Self-drilling fasteners, 101, 103
Self-locking nuts, 102
Semitrailers, 32
Semitransparent coatings, 112
Septic tanks, 184, 187, 270, 306
Serpentine garden walls, 129, 255
Set screws, 101, 103
Sewage disposal, 180–187, 270–272
  flow calculation, 184
Sewer(s), 272
  connection, manufactured homes, 37
  house, 272
  inlet and receiving basins, 274
  pipe cradles, 274
Sewerage, 180–187, 306
Shading devices, 18, 19, 163, 164
Shadow construction, 16
Sheared trees, 70
Sheet
  asphalt paving on concrete, 279
  membranes, elastomeric, 155
  metal
    flashing, 157
    form inserts, 83
    screws, 103
Sheeting
  steel, 119
  timber, 119
Sheetpile, steel, 119
Shelters
  for bicycles, 58
  civil defense, 20
Shields and anchors, 101
Shock free head, railways, 35
Shoring, excavations, 119
Shoulder (of highways), 38
Shower(s), waterproofing, 265
Shrinkage, foundation walls, 82
Shrubs, 66
  interior landscaping, 75
  planting details, 77
Shutters, rolling, 163
Side mounting, railings, 145
Sidewalk(s)
  concrete, 278, 291
  door, 159
  vault, waterproofing membrane, 264
Sightlines, theaters, 5
Signage, 10, 11
Signs
  site graphics, 9
  structural aspects, 125
Silicate, in primers, 113
Silicone
  rubber grout, 161
  sealant, 108
Sills, stone, doors, 257
SI metric, units, rules and conversion factors, 247

Single family clusters, 50, 51
Single family residential planning, 55
Single leaf floor hatches, 144
Single membrane roofing, 121
Siphon tanks, sewage disposal, 187, 270
Site
　access, 59
　analysis, 47, 51
　development
　　building solar orientation, 17
　　design considerations, 46
　　parking lots, 57
　　playing fields, 207
　　sewage disposal, 180–187
　　social impacts, 46
　drainage, 181
　graphics, 9
　improvements, 9, 56–59, 122–126, 178, 179
　security
　　barriers, 158
　　devices, 59
　　lighting, 59
　signs, 125
Sitecast concrete, 79–87, 133–135
Sitework
　decorative pools and fountains, 126
　excavation support systems, 119
　land planning and development, 44–55
　landscaping, 62–75
　marine work, 116
　paving and surfacing, 21, 72, 120, 121
　planting, 62–71
　playing fields, 210–213
　sewerage and drainage, 180–187
　sidewalks, 21
　site improvements, 9, 56–59, 122–126, 178, 179
　subsurface investigation, 78
　walls and fences, 127–132
Skate sailing, 226
Skeleton walls, New York City Code, 253
Ski equipment, 227
Skimmers, 217
Ski slalom, 227
Skylights, shades, 164
Slab hydrostatic uplift, earth shelters, 166
Slabs
　concrete, on grade, 82, 121, 133
　concrete formwork, 86
　concrete reinforcement, 81
　minimum strength concrete, 133
　for platforms, porches and steps, 252
　to receive floors, terraces, walks, 277
Slalom course
　skiing, 227
　water skiing, 225
Slate, paving, 139
Sleeves, geotextile, filter, 180
Slides, playground, 122, 123
Sliding crash gates, 158
Sliding gates, security, 59
Slip-resistance
　finish nosings, 105
　stair nosings, 105
　stair and steps, 135
Slips, marine, 116
Sloops, 229
Slope(s)
　bare soil, limits, 118
　of disposal fields, 271, 272
　runoff channels, 118
　stabilization, 118, 128
Slots, masonry anchors and ties, 91
Slotted screws, 103
Slump ranges, concrete slabs, 80, 133
Small lot, parking layout, 30
Snowmaking machines, 227
Snow melting systems, 189
Soaring, sailplanes, 230
Soccer, 212
Socketed pier foundations, 134

Softball
　backstop, 207
　plan of field, 202
Softwood lumber sizes, 106
Soil
　bare, slopes, 118
　bearing capacity, 78
　classes, subdrains, 180
　conditions, retaining walls, 127, 128, 130
　in environmental site analysis, 48
　fill for planting, 70
　mechanics, 78
　percolation, 184, 185
　properties, 78
　slope gradient ratio, 118
　surface drainage, 181
　types, 78
　weight, earth shelters, 166
　weights, 246
Solar control
　angles, 14–16
　awnings, 163
　building orientation, 17
　devices, 18, 19, 163, 164
　orientation, 13, 16–19
　path diagrams, 14–16
　time, 12
　use of trees, 69
Soldier piles, 119
Solvent-based coatings, 112
Spacing, reinforcement bars, 254
Span ratings, outdoor decks, 147
Spectator circulation safety, 209
Spiral, stairs, 135
Splicing, reinforcing bars, 254
Split face squared stone, 261
Split rail wood fences, 281
Sports
　air sports, 230
　aquatics, 215–224
　boating, 228, 229
　equestrian, 232–234
　field events, 210, 211
　gymnastics, 197
　indoor sports, 196–200
　outdoor sports, 201–214
　track and field events, 210, 211
　training rooms, 231
　winter sports, 226, 227
　wrestling mats, 197
Spread footings, 134, 251
Spring boards, 220
　details, heights, and sizes, 286
　height over 1 meter and 3 meter board, 286
　location, public type outdoor pool, 283
Sprinkler systems, lawn irrigation, 179
Squared stone
　granite, 261
　masonry, 259
Squash court and equipment, 198
Stables, 232, 233
Stadium seating, 208
Staggered floors, parking garages, 31
Stainless steel, 94
　dovetail slots, 91
　split-tail anchors, stone panel systems, 100
　stone wall anchors, 93
Stain resistance, finishes on metal, 95
Stairs
　angle, critical, 2
　concrete, 135
　design for physically handicapped, 105
　dimensions, 2
　nosings, 105
　　open metal treads, 104
　slip resistant treads, 105
　spiral, 135
　stone, 139
　treads and risers, 2, 104, 105
　U-type concrete, 135

　wood deck, 146
Staples, 97
Starting platforms for swimming, 223
Static water level, fountains, 126
Steel, 94
　access doors, 159
　baseplate, wood column anchorage, 151
　beam hangers, 151
　bicycle parking devices, 58
　columns
　　connections, heavy timber, 152
　　forms, 87
　connections
　　plank and beam framing, 148
　　timber framing, 148–152
　　wood decks, 146, 147
　doors, 159
　fasteners, 97–103
　fence posts, 268
　fences, skylight guards, partitions, 268
　flagpoles, 172
　form accessories, concrete, 84
　forms, concrete joist system, 86
　galvanizing, 95
　garding edging, 282
　gratings and treads, 104
　grillage foundation, 251
　hatches, 159
　lined swimming pool tank, 283
　lintels, 136
　masonry anchors and ties, 91
　piles, 117
　plate, doors and hatchways, 159
　reinforcement, 80–83, 90, 136, 137
　straps, square columns, 87
　tree guards, 282
　wire, sizes and guages, 81
Stepped foundation, 251
Stepping stones and walks, 277
Steps
　basement, of cement, 252
　bluestone, 252
　brick, 276
　concrete, 135, 252
　dimensions, 2
　exterior, 252
　flagstone, 252
　nosings, 105
　open metal, 105
　reinforced concrete, 252
　slip resistant, 105
　spiral, 135
　stone, 139, 257
　waterproofing, 265
　wood deck, 146
Stirrups
　concrete reinforcement, 82
　reinforced brick beam, 137
Stockade fence, wood, 281
Stone, 92
　arches, 138
　blocks, 279
　cesspools, 271
　copings, 258
　curbs, 120, 121
　door sills, 257
　dry stack, wall, 128
　flooring, 139
　floor on slabs, 277
　lintels, 257
　masonry, 93, 138, 139, 259
　paving, 72, 121, 139, 277
　perch, 259
　piers, jointing and anchoring, 257
　quoins in brick walls, 258
　retaining wall, 128
　riprap, 118
　roads, broken or crushed, 279
　saddles and sills, 139
　screenings for roads, 279

sealants, 109
squared, 261
stairs and flooring, 139
steps, 257
uses and finishes, 92
veneer, 93, 128, 261
walks, 277
wall, face patterns, 93
Stone work
coursing, dressing, finishes, jointing, 259
squared stone, granite and others, 261
strip limestone ashlar, 260
Stop boards, distribution box, 270
Storage for passenger cars, 280
Storefronts, awnings, 163
Storm drainage, inlets and catch basins, 182, 183
Storm sewers, manholes, 273
Story heights, garages, 280
Stove bolts, 102
Straps for architectural terra cotta, 263
Streets
construction, 287–290
curbs, 291, 296
curbside gutters, 291
intersections, 53, 295
layout, 295
lighting, 53, 293
paving, 54, 279
sections, 297
sewer inlet, 274
subdivision layout, 52
Strength, concrete, rate of gain, 79
Stretchers
brick, 89
concrete masonry, 88
Stringers, wood stairs, 146
Strips
rustication, concrete forming, 85
thin-set terrazzo, 162
Strollers, 24
Stucco, adobe construction, 141, 256
Studs, concrete wall forms, 85
Subdrains, soil classes, 180, 205, 206
Submersible pumps, fountains, 126
Subsoil
disposal drains, 271, 272
drainage, 180, 205, 206
Substrates, 154–156, 166
Subsurface drainage and filtration, 153, 180, 185–187, 205, 206, 300
Subsurface investigation, 78
Subtense bars, building layout, 143
Suburban site analysis, 49
Suburban townhouses, 50
Sun
altitude of, 14, 15
building orientation, 13, 17
and shadow patterns, urban site analysis, 49
Sun control, 12–19, 163, 164
awnings, 163
orientation, 13, 17
shading devices, 18, 19, 163, 164
solar angles, 14, 15
sun time and shadow construction, 12
Support gaskets, elastomeric, 155
Surfaces(s)
areas and volumes, 240, 241
brick wall fence, 89
concrete, 83–85
drainage systems, 181–183
stone wall face, 93
unit paving, 72
water runoff, 181–183
Survey data, site analysis, 49
Surveys, cadastral, 143
Suspended base paving, 121, 154–156
Suspended form hangers, 84
Swimming pools
coatings, 95
competitive, 50-meter, 216–219

diving facilities, 220–222
50 meter, 219
ladders, 223
lighting, window, float anchor, 224
outdoor types, 283
overflows, 217
public, 216–223
residential, 215
sections and steps, details, 285
shapes, 216
steps, ladders and targets, 223
trim, 111
25-yard, 218
wading, 216
waterproofing, 265
Swings (playground), 122, 123
Switch box, sewage disposal, 270
Switchgear, primary, 190
Symbols, graphic, 230, 238
Synthetic fabric filter, 118, 120, 121, 153, 165
Synthetic track, 206
Synthetic turf, 206
Systems, sewage disposal, 270, 271

Tables
billiards, 200
park and picnic, 124
for reinforced concrete slabs, 252
Table tennis, layout, 200
Tack rooms, 232, 233
Tanks
septic and siphon, 187, 270
swimming
scum gutters, 284
section and step details, 285
steel lined swimming pool, 283
Target shooting, 199
Team handball, 213
Telescopic bleachers, 208
Telford road foundation, 279
Temperature(s)
bars, 254
deep-ground, map, 20
reinforcement
concrete, 82
floor and roof slabs, 81
Tennis courts and equipment, 205, 207, 268
Terminals, airports, 40
Terracing, 118, 276
Terra cotta
anchors, clamps, hangers, 263
architectural, 262, 263
copings, and balustrades, 262
ladder for swimming pool, 283
lined swimming pool, 283
trimmers for swimming pools, 283
Terrazzo systems, 162
Theaters, design, 5, 6
Thermal breaks
retaining wing wall, 165, 339
Thermal insulation, basements, 153, 165
Thermal performance, earth shelters, 165
Thermal protection, 153–156, 165
Thick-bed mortar, 160
Thin-set
mortar, 160
terrazzo, 162
tile, 160
Three meter springboard details, 286
Throwing circle, construction, 211
Tiebacks, excavations 119
Tie-down
air structures, 174
manufactured homes, 37
Ties
cavity walls, 255
concrete formwork, 81, 84–86
masonry, 90, 91, 136, 137
reinforced brick masonry, 137
spacing, column reinforcing bars, 82

stone walls, 93
walls, concrete, 84, 85
Tie spacing, column reinforcing bars, 82
Tiles
ceramic, 111, 160
coping, salt glazed, 262
detail for foot bath, 285
drainage, 271, 272, 308
field drains, 307
floors for exterior and interior, 277
gutter for swimming pool, 284
installation of, 160, 161
marble floors and walls, 269
paving, 121
pool section, 285
resilient, 160
shower receptors, 161
steps, ladder and details for swimming pool, 285
swimming pool gutters and curbs, 284
Timber
curbs, 120
heavy, construction, 148–152
lagging, 119. 153
lintels, adobe construction, 141
log construction, 150
piles, 117
pole construction, 117
retaining walls, 128
sizes, 106
timber sheeting, 119
treatments, 107
Time zones of the U. S., 12
Toggle bolts, 103
Toilets, for handicapped, 4
Tongue and groove, concrete control joints, 133
Tooled mortar joint, 89
Tooling, nonsag sealants, 110
Tooth chiselled stone, 259
Topiaries, 70
Topographic survey-grid system, 143
Topsoil, 70
Torque tube connections, signs, 125
Touch and flag football, 203
Tower for springboards, 286
Townhouses, 50–52
Track and field, 210, 211
Traffic control, mechanical barriers, 158
Traffic generation, 53
Traffic controller, mechanical barriers, 158
Trailers, truck, 32
Training rooms, 231
Trampolines, 197
Transformers, 190
Transparent fences, wood, 132
Transportation, 24–42
site development, 46
Transporter concept, airports, 40
Trap shooting, 214
Trash trucks, 25
turning dimensions, 28
Treads, 105
coverings, 105
dimensions, 2
metal, 104
nosings, 105
open steel, 104
slip-resistant, 105
stone, 139
wood decks, 146
Treated wood, 107, 128, 149, 150
Trees
cutting and use, 70
deciduous, 64, 65
evergreen, 62, 63
guards, steel and iron, 282
hardiness map of U. S., 62
interior landscaping, 74
lightning protection, 192
over underground structures, 70

Trees (*Continued*)
  planting details, 71
  protection, 70
  regulatory effect, 69
  residential development, 50
  road systems and, 53
  site uses, 69
Trench
  covers, 144
  drains, 182
  drain tile, 271
Tricycles, 24
Trim, ceramic tile, 111
Triple jump, construction, 211
Troweled mortar joints, 89
Truck docks, 33, 34
Trucks, 32
Trumpet highways, 38
Tub, hot, 167
Tub enclosures, ceramic tile, 160
Tunnel, waterproof membrane, 264
Turbine pump, 126
Turf and subsoil drain, baseball field, 202
Turnbuckles, 103
Turning radius, vehicles, 24, 25, 27, 28, 32
Turnstiles, 59
Two-car garages, 26

U bolts, 102
U strap wood column anchorage, concrete base,
    146, 151
U tile, clay, 272
U type concrete stairs, 135
U value, concrete masonry units, 88
Uncoursed fieldstone, 259
Underbed, bonded terrazzo, 162
Underground
  buildings, 20, 154–156. 165, 166
  space, earth shelters, 20
  utilities, near existing trees, 70
  vaults, electrical, 190
Underwater lighting, swimming pools, 224, 284
Uneven bars for gymnastics, 197
Unit masonry, 88–91, 93, 136–141
Unit paving, 72, 121
Upturned edge beam, concrete, 82
Urban infill, 54
Urban site analysis, 49
Urban townhouses, 50–52
U. S. flag, proportions, 172
Utilities, subdivision layout, 46, 47, 52, 54, 70,
    190
Utility plans, 54

Valley grate, 182
Van delivery trucks, 25, 32
Vaulting buck short horse, 197
Vaults, underground, electrical, 190
Vegetation in environmental site analysis, 48
Vehicle(s)
  barriers, 59, 158
  capabilities of highways, 38
  dimensions, 24, 25, 32
  turning dimensions, 24, 25, 27, 28, 32
Vehicular traffic
  parking lots, 27, 29–33, 56
  paver types, 72
Veneers
  brick, 89, 91, 136, 137
  masonry, flashings, 91, 157
  masonry anchors, 91
  stone, 93, 128, 139
Venetian blinds, exterior, 163
Venetian terrazzo, 162
Vent pipes, 153
Vertical movement, pedestrian, 2
Vertical turbine pumps, 126
Vinyl, 112
  nosings, slip-resistant, 105

  in primers, 113
  rails, 145
Visibility
  signage, 10, 11
  stadium stairs, 209
  theater, sight line, 5
Vitrified clay sewer pipe, 184
Vitrified paving bricks, 279
Vitrified salt glazed coping, 262
Vitrified sewer pipe, 272
Volleyball
  equipment, 204, 207
  field, 204
  net and post, 207
Volumes of solids, 240, 241
Vomitories, *vs.* cross aisles, 209

Wading pools, 216
Wagons, 24
Wainscots, marble, 269
Walers
  concrete wall forms, 85
  embankment bracing, 119
  excavations, 119
Walks, 21, 291
  asphalt tile, 279
  brick, 27
  masonry, stepping stones, 277
Walk-up apartments, 50
Walkways, 21
  concrete slabs, 133
  lighting, 178
  paving, 120, 121, 124
  surfaces, parks, loose paving, 120, 124
Wall(s)
  adobe, 140, 141
  anchorages, foundations, 91
  barrier, 59
  basement, 82, 153
  brick cavity, 255
  concrete formwork, 83–85
  concrete masonry unit, 88
  flashings, 157
  footings, 82, 87, 251
  foundation, 82, 153
  garden, 127–129
  limestone ashlar, 260
  liquid-applied membranes, 155
  masonry, 88–91, 93, 136–141
  masonry, architectural terra cotta anchoring,
    269
  pilasters
    concrete, 85
    masonry, 88, 90, 137
  reinforced concrete, 81, 82, 153
    retaining walls, residential basement
      waterproofing, 267
  retaining, 127, 128, 130, 137
  stone, 93
  thickness of area walls, 250
  thicknesses, New York City Code, 253
  thin veneered, 93
  ties, concrete forms, 84, 85
  water-resistant membrane, 153–156, 165, 166
Washers, 102
Washes, stone copings, 258
Water
  absorption, stones, 92
  cement ratios, concrete, 133
  erosion, slope protection, 118
  fountains and pools, 126
  lawn irrigation, 179
  percolation test, 184
  polo, 225, 284
  pressure, fountains, 126
  pump capacities, wells, 188
  resistance
    foundations, 153
    under slabs, 153

  site analysis, 48
  ski jump, 225
  subsurface drainage, 180, 202, 205, 206
  supply
    crib intake, 310
    deep wells, 309
    domestic well, 310
    residential, 188, 310
    river, side intake, 310
    windmills, 310
  surface, runoff, 181
  surface drainage systems, 181–183
  windows, swimming pools, 224
Waterheads, slab thickness, 266
Waterproofing, 153–157
  adobe construction, 256
  basements, 153
  door sills, in opening doors, 256
  earth shelters, 20, 165, 166
  exterior walls, membrane, 264
  flat roof, 265
  foundations, 153
  interior and exterior columns, membrane, 264
  joint sealers, 108–110, 153
  machine foundations
    membrane, 264
    by plaster coat, 266
  membrane
    above grade, 265
    below grade, 264
  paving, 121
  plaster coat, 265, 266
  plaza liquid-applied elastomeric membrane,
    155
  plaza membrane over occupied space, 154–156
  plazas, 154–156
  of pools, 265, 283
  residential basements, 267
  seals and sealants, 108–110
  shower stalls, 265
  sidewalk vault, membrane, 264
  steps, 265
  stone walls, 93
  sump pit, plaster coat, 266
  swimming pool, 265, 283
Waterstops
  earth shelters, 166
  foundations, 153, 166
Wearing courses
  roads, 279
  waterproofing, 154
Weatherability, types of brick joints, 89
Weep holes, retaining walls, 127–130, 137
Weights of materials, 246
Weight training machines, 231
Welded wire fabric, 81
Wells and pumps
  deep, 309
  domestic, 310
  residential water supply, 188, 310
Wheel
  loads, industrial floors, 133
  stops
    asphalt paving, 120
    carports, 26
    parking lots, 56
Wheelchairs, 4
  ramp at curb, 21
Wicket guard, park equipment, 282
Wind
  loads
    flagpoles, 172
    signs, 125
  protection, trees, 69
  tolerance, plants, 70
Windmills, 310
Windows
  adobe construction, 141, 256
  in cavity walls, 255

Windsurfer, 228
Winter sports, 226, 227
Wire
  enclosures, tennis, 268
  fabric, welded, 81
  mesh
    baseball backstop, 207
    chain link fences, 131
    for fencing, 268
    gabions, 118
    partitions, 169, 268
  nails, 98
  steel, 81
  ties, masonry, 91
Wirework, fences, partitions, skylight guards,
  268
Wiring, adobe construction, 141
Wolmanized wood, 107
Wood
  beam connections, 151, 152
  benches, 124
  bicycle parking devices, 58
  butt joints, concrete formwork, 83
  columns, anchored with steel devices, 146,
    147, 151
  corrosion resistance, 107

curbs, paving edge, 120, 121
decay and insect resistance, 107
decks, exterior, 146, 147
edge, paving, 120, 121
exterior stairs, 146
fasteners, 98–100, 103
fences, 132, 281
fire retardant, 107
framing
  exterior stairs, 146
  plank floors, 148, 149
heavy timber construction, 148–152
log construction, 150
marine applications, 116
nails for, 98–100
paving, 72
  blocks, 279
plank and beam framing, 148
play equipment, 122
pole construction, 149
rails, 145
retaining walls, 128
screws, 103
timber
  framing, 148–152
  retaining walls, 128

treatment for preservation, 107
Workability of concrete, 80
Working drawings, graphic symbols, 238,
  239
Work stations for handicapped, 4
Woven wire fences, partitions and skylight
  guards, 268
Woven wood fences, 281
Wrestling equipment, 197
Wrought iron, 94

X-ray metal detector, 59

Yard drainage, 181–183
Yawl, 229
Y highway, intersection, 38

Zamboni ice resurfacer, 226
Zero-lot-line, 50, 54
Zinc, 94
Zinc, alloy, dovetail slots, 91
Zones
  of flood damage, 44
  of plant hardiness, 62
Zoning, 46, 47
Z-type anchors, masonry, 91